ANDREW ARSAN

Interlopers of Empire

The Lebanese Diaspora
in Colonial French West Africa

HURST & COMPANY, LONDON

First published in the United Kingdom in 2014 by
C. Hurst & Co. (Publishers) Ltd.,
41 Great Russell Street, London, WC1B 3PL
© Andrew Arsan 2014
All rights reserved.
Printed in India

The right of Andrew Arsan to be identified as the author of this publication is asserted
by him in accordance with the Copyright, Designs and Patents Act, 1988.

A Cataloguing-in-Publication data record for this book is available from the British Library.

ISBN: 978-1-84904-297-0

This book is printed using paper from registered sustainable
and managed sources.

www.hurstpublishers.com

To my parents

CONTENTS

ACKNOWLEDGEMENTS

I have accumulated countless debts in the—unfeasibly long—time it has taken me to bring this book to the presses (to say that it has been completed would be disingenuous; no book would ever really be complete if authors had their way). Fittingly enough for a work that moves through localities and across regions, these are scattered in a number of places. In Cambridge, I owe a great deal to Megan Vaughan, who agreed to supervise the doctoral dissertation that forms the basis for this book, accepted my gradual shift away from African history, stood up admirably in the face of missed deadlines and small panics, always shepherding and prodding me along with calm guidance, and provided me with a model of academic commitment and common sense. The same is true of Chris Bayly, who first took me under his wing when I was a helplessly disorganised and shiftless undergraduate, and has continued to inspire and encourage me ever since in ways both large and small. Tim Harper and Richard Drayton first gave me a taste for the histories of empire and displacement as a callow undergraduate, and it has been a pleasure to become their friend, and to continue to learn from them. Shruti Kapila continuously provokes, and has helped to jar me out of many of my easy assumptions, and to make me into the historian I am still becoming. Sylvana Tomaselli has been a wonderfully generous and considerate friend, and a source of continuous support since I first stepped into her office more years ago than either of us might care to remember—I only wish I'd listened to her advice more often. Sujit Sivasundaram, David Maxwell and Natasha Pairaudeau provided wonderful suggestions, and pointed to important questions, at a—very—late stage of the project. John Iliffe first taught me African history, and watched over the earliest stages of this undertaking. David Todd has shared, and stimulated, my interest in French imperialism. Jake Norris, John Slight and David Motadel have made Cambridge a better place to work on Middle Eastern history; long may it be that way. Marina Frasca-Spada, Andrew Spencer, Emma Spary, Stuart and Sibella Laing, and all the Fellows and staff of Corpus Christi have made me feel welcome, and have provided me with a congenial setting in which to finally put the last touches to this work.

Members of the World History Workshop crew and its tentacular extensions have been constant friends, drinking and dining companions, intellectual interlocutors, and sources of inspiration and encouragement since the very beginning. A massive shout-out (in strictly alphabetical order) to: Sunil Amrith, Rachel Berger, Matt Butler, Emile Chabal, Camille Cole, Mark Condos, Guillemette Crouzet, Leigh Denault, Derek Elliott, Stefanie Gänger, Carrie Gibson, John-Paul Ghobrial, Mike Golan, Clemens Häusler, Emma Hunter, Simon Layton, Elisabeth Leake, Rachel Leow, Su Lin Lewis, Andrew Jarvis, Justin Jones, Ali Khan, Daniel MacArthur-Seal, Andrew MacDonald, Alois Maderspacher, Joanna McGarry, Marc Michael, Chris Moffat, David Motadel, Eleanor Newbigin, Jake Norris, Sunil Purushotham, Nasreen Rehman, Anne-Isabelle Richard, Pernille Røge, Mike Rogers, James Roslington, Adrian Rüprecht, Taylor Sherman, Mishka Sinha, John Slight, Akhila Yechuri and Faridah Zaman.

In Princeton, Michael Cook, Şükrü Hanioğlu, Bernard Haykel, Michael Reynolds and Muhammad Qasim Zaman welcomed me into the Department of Near Eastern Studies. Michael Cook, in particular, was a constant benevolent presence, watching over my development and supplying cups of tea and wise advice; Michael Reynolds introduced me patiently to the intricacies and pleasures of American undergraduate teaching; and Şükrü Bey made something of an Ottomanist of me. The department's admirable language teachers also deserve thanks: Erika Gilson tolerated my presence in her Turkish classes, while Greg Bell and Nancy Coffin never asked me to be in theirs, and Amineh Mahallati ceded her sunny office space. Its staff—Bill Blair, Sarah Boyce, Tammy Bryant, Karen Chirik, Linda Kativa, Jim LaRegina, Christine Riley and Joyce Slack at the Transregional Institute—made me feel at home from the moment I stepped into Jones Hall, and answered my questions, however inane or ridiculous, with good grace and patience. Linda, in particular, put up with me sharing her office, and laughed at my English accent. My fellow post-docs Elvire Corboz, Nabil Mouline, İren Özgür, Thomas Pierret, Akın Ünver and Ben White reinforced my belief in intellectual community. Thomas and Mériam Sheikh were the most wonderful flatmates I could have wished for. Akın ferried me to the supermarket in his battered automobile, cast amused looks at the contents of my shopping trolley and indulged my pool addiction—all of which I'm grateful for. Cyrus Schayegh and Max Weiss both showed a keen, and unexpected, interest in my work and proved insightful and generous readers. My early morning coffees with Cyrus were an education in themselves, and I am glad that our conversations still go on, despite the time difference. Mike and Judy Laffan took me in, offered me lunches, laughs and advice—sorry about the bike; you surely didn't need another one lying around. Linda Colley and Phil Nord both allowed me to sit in on their classes, and taught me a great deal. The staff of Small World Coffee fuelled many hours of drafting and redrafting with a steady succession of espressos, brownies and discerning music.

Last, but by no means least, the following, in their different ways, made Princeton feel more of a home than I ever thought it could be, and made me sad to leave it behind: Catherine Abou-Nemeh, Loubna El-Amine, Usaama El-Azami, Alex Balistreri, Kevin Bell, Sara Bergamaschi, Edna Bonhomme, Vahid Brown, Alex Buckey, James Casey, Omar Cheta, Mehmet Darakcıoğlu, Rohit De, Catherine Evans, Zach Foster,

ACKNOWLEDGEMENTS

Alice Gissinger, Sam and Tally Helfont, Nate Hodson, Sarah El-Kazaz, Deniz Taner Kılıncoğlu and Sevil Çakır Kılıncoğlu, Eric Lob, Kate Manbachi, Jess Marglin, Kevin Mazur, Michalis Moutselos, Karam Nachar, Aaron Rock-Singer, Henry Shapiro, Padraic Scanlan, Kelly Schwartz, Faez Syed, David Weil, Dror Weil, Lev Ernst Weitz, Nur Fadzila Yahaya and Alden Young. Karam, in particular, has been an unexpected houseguest, a wonderful intellectual companion and an example of commitment in the face of great adversity; may his hopes for a better future be realised.

In Dakar, Nabil Milan and all the staff of the Hôtel Farid proved attentive hosts for the duration of my stay. Mara Leichtman was a patient tour guide, who showed me what Dakar had to offer, from Sunday mass to chocolate fondants. Eike Ohlendorf was a fantastic archive buddy, and very generously shared some of her vast cache of photographs after I had left Dakar. Ibra Sene very kindly took me for lunch and showed me the ropes of the archives. In Beirut, the Centre for Behavioural Research (CBR), American University of Beirut and the Lebanese Emigration Research Centre (LERC), Notre-Dame University Lebanon, provided institutional homes away from home. I am grateful to Samir Khalaf and all at the CBR, and to Guita Hourani, Liliane Haddad, Elie Nabhan and their colleagues at the LERC for the warmth and generosity with which they welcomed me, and for enabling me to complete the last stages of this research in such congenial and friendly surroundings.

In London, Olga Agueeva, Caline Aoun, Sehr Askari, Stef Beazley, Karim (and Abi) Coumine and Sarah Razvi, the Dahmash family, Will Davies and Emma Dillon, Daniel Faddoul, Shireen Farah, Yann Gelister and the rest of the clan, Mario González, Yinka Graves, Jimmy and all the Mouracadeh family, Olivier Pfanner, Patrick Sixsmith, Isabelle Stewart, Tic Zolleyn and a host of others kept me sane, and provided welcome distraction from the world of archives and seminars and overdue chapters. Nadim Shehadi was always on hand to impart titbits and chunks of his vast knowledge of all things Lebanon-related. Xerxes Malki provided encouragement in the early stages of this project on rambling walks through Oxford. The wonderful people at Albertini sustained me through long, dreary days and weeks at the British Library with their unremitting good cheer, the warmth of their welcome, world-class sandwiches and stellar coffee.

Further afield, Akram Khater in Raleigh, John Tofik Karam in Chicago, Sarah Gualtieri in Los Angeles, Maria del Mar Logroño Narbona in Miami and Amman, and Ilham Khuri-Makdisi and Stacy Fahrenthold in Boston have proved engaging interlocutors in the latter stages of this project; it is comforting to know that I have such wonderful travelling companions on my journeys through diaspora. I can only hope that we continue on our peregrinations together—as the proverb has it, *al-rafiq qabl al-tariq*.

A work like this would, quite literally, be nothing without the raw materials on which the historian depends. I'm therefore grateful to the staff of the following archives and research libraries for their tireless assistance in answering my endless demands for ever more files, microfilm reels rare books, and crumbling newspapers: the Centre d'Accueil et de Recherche des Archives Nationales de France and the

ACKNOWLEDGEMENTS

Ministère des Affaires Etrangères reading room in Paris; the Centre des Archives d'Outre-Mer in Aix-en-Provence; the Chambre de Commerce et d'Industrie Marseille-Provence and the Archives Départementales des Bouches-du-Rhône in Marseille; and the Archives Nationales du Sénégal in Dakar; the University Library in Cambridge, and particularly its Inter-Library Loan service; the British Library; the library of the School of Oriental and African Studies; the Bibliothèque Nationale de France; Firestone Library at Princeton University; the Jafet Library at the American University of Beirut, and in particular the staff of its microfilm reading room; and the library of the Institut Français du Proche-Orient in Beirut, and in particular Nada Chalabi. The Arts and Humanities Research Council funded the graduate work on which this book is based; without their support, it would have been impossible for me to embark on this career at all. I am also grateful to St John's College, the History Faculty, and Corpus Christi College in Cambridge, and the Department of Near Eastern Studies in Princeton, for their assistance with travel.

The following have been kind enough to read parts of the work, and have helped me enormously with their comments and suggestions: Michael Cook, Faisal Devji, Tim Harper, Simon Jackson, Eric Jennings, Akram Khater, Judy Laffan, Simon Layton, Elisabeth Leake, James McDougall, Thomas Pierret, Cyrus Schayegh, Robert Tombs, Max Weiss and Ben White. Megan Vaughan, Chris Bayly, Martin Evans and William Clarence-Smith deserve particular thanks for wading through the entire thing—in Megan's case, several times over. I'm also grateful to Chris, Faisal and James, Ben and Malika Rahal and Leila Fawaz for inviting me to share some of this material with seminar audiences in Cambridge, Oxford, Edinburgh and Boston. May Davie and the editorial committee of Chronos, Andrew Shryock and David Akin at Comparative Studies in Society and History and the teams of anonymous readers they assembled, suggested numerous improvements to the parts of this work that first appeared in their publications. Philip Stickler and David Watson turned my vague notions into wonderful maps. Michael Dwyer is as perspicacious a reader and shrewd a publisher as one could hope for as an author; he plucked me from obscurity, and has persevered in his support despite the endless delays and prevarication on my part—it's good to have him in my corner. Michael, Rob Pinney, Daisy Leitch and the entire Hurst team deserves my wholesome thanks for bringing this book to press, as do two anonymous readers for their insightful and helpful comments.

But my biggest debt is to my family—one and several. If ever proof was needed that kin and affection can survive the vagaries of time and distance, it can be found in my experience of the last few years. My aunt Mona, her much-missed husband Gaby, my cousin Marc, and Sabita; Zalfa, Dory and Dotty Chamoun and Priyanka (not to forget Mushu, Willow, Chloe, and Petunia); and Georges, Zeina, Marwan, Ghassan and Jalal Fallaha (and Lucy), all made me feel truly at home in Beirut, as did in Paris my uncle and aunt Amin and Gigi, and my cousins Youmna, Fayza and Joumana, the latter's husbands Fred and David, and their children Lucie and Emilie, and Quentin and Lena. My brother Jad provided vicarious support from his postings in Bayonne and Shanghai, and gave me the camera that I carried on my trips through

ACKNOWLEDGEMENTS

the archives; he and Joanne get extra brownie points for making the long trip from China for my graduation, and recording my embarrassing moments for posterity. Tic is like a brother from another mother. Sophie has kept me going and pushed me along through the last stages of this very long process, and has given me the most important things of all: love and happiness. Though she didn't live long enough to see the last stages of this project, my grandmother Helen first gave me my love for words, and encouraged my curiosity about the world. My father, Adel, has sustained me with conversation, advice, endless sandwiches, Portuguese pastries and cups of coffee through the various stages of this project; his fortitude is an inspiration. My mother, Jane, was my first reader, a ruthless editor, a wonderful cook and a great friend. I dedicate this book to my parents, who have encouraged my interest in the past, and given me faith in the future.

Versions of Chapters 2 and 4 have previously appeared in print. I am grateful to the editors and publishers for permission to reprint and revise them here:

Chapter 2, from *Chronos: Revue d'Histoire de l'Université de Balamand* 22 (2010), pp. 107–33

Chapter 4, from *Comparative Studies in Society and History* 53, 3 (2011), pp. 450–78.

ABBREVIATIONS

ADBR	Archives Départementales des Bouches-du-Rhône
ANS AOF NS	Archives Nationales du Sénégal, Dakar, Fonds AOF, Nouvelle Série
AOF	Afrique Occidentale Française
BAO	Banque de l'Afrique Occidentale
BCAF	*Bulletin du Comité de l'Afrique Française*
BMCCD	*Bulletin Mensuel de la Chambre de Commerce de Dakar*
CAOM MC FM AP	Centre des Archives d'Outremer, Aix-en-Provence, Ministère des Colonies, Fond Ministériel, Affaires Politiques
CAOM MC FM SG	Centre des Archives d'Outremer, Aix-en-Provence, Ministère des Colonies, Fond Ministériel, Série Géographique
CARAN AOF AS	Centre d'Accueil et de Recherche des Archives Nationales, Paris, Fonds AOF, Ancienne Série
CARAN AOF NS	Centre d'Accueil et de Recherche des Archives Nationales, Paris, Fonds AOF, Nouvelle Série
CCIMP	Chambre de Commerce et d'Industrie, Marseille-Provence
CFAO	Compagnie Française de l'Afrique Occidentale
CO	*Correspondance d'Orient*
EA	*Les Echos Africains—Satiriques—Humoristiques—Documentaires Libres*
EAN	*Les Echos d'Afrique Noire: Le Grand Hebdomadaire Colonial de Défense Française*
FAN	*France Afrique Noire*
IT	*Ifriqiya Tijariyya*
JA	*Jeune Afrique*
MAE NS T SL	Ministère des Affaires Étrangères, Paris, Nouvelle Série, Turquie, Syrie-Liban
OLJ	*L'Orient-Le Jour*
PA	*Périscope Africain*
QC	*Quinzaine Coloniale*
SCOA	Société Commerciale de l'Ouest Africain
SONOCO	Société Nouvelle Commerciale

OF NAMES AND WORDS

A NOTE ON TRANSLITERATION AND NOMENCLATURE

French functionaries employed a sometimes bewildering variety of terms to speak of Eastern Mediterranean migrants in the years encompassed by this study. In the years before the First World War, they were known simply as *Syriens*. However, as we shall see in the third chapter of this work, this was no neat marker of identity. Rather, it alternated between serving as a term denoting only Ottoman subjects, and a rather looser category, into which functionaries lumped not just Eastern Mediterranean migrants, but also Moroccan and Gibraltar Jews, Italians and Maltese. This administrative appellation denoted the geographical awareness of at least some of those who hailed from the Eastern Mediterranean, and would have spoken of their lands of origins as Suriya or Bilad al-Sham, the countries of Syria (or, more accurately, Damascus, the part standing here for the whole). But it also served, just as often, as a convenient shorthand for a host of indeterminate floating populations plying their wares through French West Africa, groups which all stood, in the eyes of administrators, on the margins of whiteness.

Such tricky matters of nomenclature were seemingly resolved in the interwar years by the coinage of a new hyphenated term, *Libano-Syriens*—an administrative construct which denoted only the citizens of the newly-created Mandatory states. But the old appellation proved resilient, and impervious to the novel facts of nationality—as it did among British officials and writers, who spoke of 'Syrians' or 'Levantines' well into the 1950s. It proved especially so when French administrators wrote of Muslims—who, in a telling indication of these functionaries' perceptions of the social and political make-up of the Mandate states, were often described as Syrian, regardless of their nominal nationality. This, in effect, served only to split off these seemingly restive, recalcitrant subjects from more quiescent, sympathetic 'Christian' Lebanese.

And while administrators continued to employ these various terms, each with its particular connotations and contexts well into the interwar years, migrants too drew on a shifting register of categories to speak of themselves in their letters, their petitions and speeches—as 'Libanais' or 'Syriens de la province du Mont-Liban', as *'amili* or *'arab*. Some of these names, like *'amili*, reflected an intensely local sense of belonging, some, like *'arab*, a broader notion of political identity. Others, like *Libanais*, may have been ways for migrants to define their political selves or, in the years before 1914, to remind colonial officials of the special status accorded to residents of the mutasarrifiyya, or autonomous district of Mount Lebanon, governed until the First World War by the terms of the Règlement Organique of 1864, a distinct administrative regime guaranteed by the Great Powers.

I have chosen, meanwhile, to speak of these men and women at times as Lebanese, at others as Eastern Mediterranean—save, of course, when I quote from the words of migrants themselves, or French writers, officials and settlers. The first of these semantic choices is not unproblematic, for it does not always match the political affiliations of migrants themselves. Nevertheless, it reflects—at the very least—the legal status of the majority of these men and women at any one time: inhabitants of the mutasarrifiyya, considered for administrative purposes as Lebanese did, after all, constitute the overwhelming majority of Eastern Mediterranean migrants to French West Africa before 1914, as did, after 1920, citizens of that new territorial construct, Greater Lebanon. The second, meanwhile, conveniently locates the geographical origins of these men and women in a manner less freighted with the heavy burdens of strategic thought and geopolitical calculation than more familiar terms like the 'Middle East'.

As for the names of people and places, I have relied here on a simplified version of the *International Journal of Middle East Studies* standard for transliteration—or, just as often, for re-transcription of the Arabic names I found in a variety of quixotic spellings in the French documents I have drawn on. While I have chosen to dispense with the various diacritic dots and dashes of convention, which might prove cumbersome to the non-specialist, I have kept the *'ayn* and the *hamza*, marked by an apostrophe. I have also followed the *International Journal of Middle East Studies* guidelines in transcribing most Lebanese place-names; however, the flattened *ta marbuta* has been marked with an *-eh*.

The names of African people and places have been transcribed in accordance with the standard spelling adopted in Francophone and Anglophone West Africa.

INTRODUCTION

MOVING PEOPLES, ENTANGLED HISTORIES

Let us begin with a story. One day in 1898, two rather unusual traders were noticed among the market-women of Conakry, the bustling, swelling capital of colonial French Guinea, with their dried fish and their spices. These 'Syrian hawkers'—as those who told the tale called them—set up their stall a little outside the morning market.[1] Throwing open the tattered cases they carried, they began selling their few baubles: coloured glass bracelets,[2] 'knives, mirrors and pearls',[3] and the like—gaudy wares which earned their compatriots the nickname of 'coral men' in neighbouring Sierra Leone. Before long, equipped only with a few rough cloth sacks and a set of scales, the pair began buying up balls of rubber from caravan porters who had carried their precious load from the hinterland to Conakry. These interlopers paid well, or at any rate better than the motley crowd of Frenchmen, Senegalese Wolof and Sierra Leone Creoles with whom the porters had previously dealt. And, what is more, they did so, not in swatches of cloth or bags of rice, but in coveted hard currency.[4] As more and more porters came to them with their rubber, and they secured the custom of the large European trading houses of the place, the business of these men rapidly expanded. Such was demand that they often sold on to the agents of these companies all the rubber acquired in the morning by the close of the day. Soon, others like them came to join them, pulled in by news of the money to be made in Conakry. Within a year—less even, according to some accounts—this swelling band of traders had effectively cornered the market.

Beginnings

All tales must start somewhere; I have chosen to begin here, with this, a vignette cobbled together from three variations upon a story repeated again and again, in the early decades of the twentieth century, by Frenchmen concerned with the fate of the federation of Afrique Occidentale Française, or AOF, as France's West African possessions came to be known.[5] It is, to be sure, but a provisional, arbitrary point of

1

departure. We have no means of knowing, in truth, when the first few travellers from the Eastern Mediterranean alighted in Dakar or Conakry, or when purposeful migration to West Africa began. Some among the Lebanese of Dakar still clung in the 1960s to tales of a man, known only by his first name—'Isa—who had landed in Senegal a century earlier.[6] Others told of a group of young men—Maronite Christians from the craggy escarpments of Mount Lebanon—who had found their way to West Africa some time between 1876 and 1880.[7] The Lebanese journalist 'Abdallah Hushaimah, travelling through the region in the 1930s, met in Lagos one Elias al-Khuri, who claimed to have first arrived in Nigeria in 1890.[8] The Dutch scholar Laurens van der Laan, combing in the late 1960s through old newspapers in the reading rooms of Freetown's Fourah Bay College, found the first mention of the Lebanese in the Creole press of Sierra Leone in 1895.[9]

And yet this snapshot can serve as a fitting introduction to the twin preoccupations of this work, the first comprehensive history of the largely overlooked Lebanese diasporic communities of French West Africa. I am concerned here, on the one hand, with reconstructing the social, economic and political lives of Eastern Mediterranean migrants to AOF, and with understanding the ways in which these might help us to reshape broader conceptions of diasporic existence. On the other, I wish to examine the fraught responses this unsettling presence prompted in French functionaries, publicists and *colons*, and the ways Lebanese men and women themselves came to echo, and to live through, these insistent tropes. I adopt, then, a contrapuntal approach, weaving together and shifting between these two complementary tales. In doing so, I seek to revise our understanding of both the tones and textures of diasporic life—of Janus-like existences lived in transit between different locales, and dependent on the constant to-and-fro of people, news and goods—and the elaboration and circulation of racial notions and narratives within the French imperial polity. For I look upon the lives of Lebanese migrants not just as beings in the world, but also as textual tropes, figures caught in the lines of colonial writing. Even as I attempt to tell the travelled stories of these men and women, I engage in a sustained examination of the texts through which we catch a fleeting glimpse of their existences, writings which both refracted and reflected the jagged details of daily life—and whose tropes had the power of reshaping, in turn, its conditions.

There is another tale, to be course, to be told about the Lebanese of West Africa, one that would focus not so much upon these migrants themselves as upon the legion African city-dwellers and rural cultivators, transporters and petty traders in whose midst they lived—and continue to live. This work does not neglect this entirely. Indeed, it would be difficult to do so, for Eastern Mediterranean migrants remained dependent for their very survival upon constant relations with their African neighbours, suppliers and clients, no matter how tense and equivocal these may have been at times. Nevertheless there is no doubt that this work has far more to say about Eastern Mediterranean men and women, their habits, strategies and stances, and the ambivalent attitudes the French commercial workers, administrators and publicists of West Africa harboured towards them.

INTRODUCTION

In part, this is a question of emphasis: to give proper consideration to the ways in which the autochthonous inhabitants of colonial Senegal, Guinea or Côte d'Ivoire apprehended these strangers among them would have required another work, quite different to that I have undertaken. But it is also a question of method. For telling this latter story would demand extensive oral work to compensate for the aporiae and absences of the colonial archive—broadly conceived to encompass printed as well as archival material—and the dismissive asides of migrants' own reminiscences. These are texts which stubbornly refuse to give up anything more than brief, tantalising, glimpses of the complexities and conflicts of the relations between Africans and Lebanese. And this text, in turn, deliberately sets out to understand the constraints imposed upon scholarly investigation, and commonplace thought, by the written record which has been handed down to us—the manner in which it frames our thoughts, favouring and occluding ways of looking upon, and living in, the world, and obstructing certain paths of inquiry while opening up others.

For the tale of shifty hawkers with which I began not only throws a chink of light on the daily practices of Eastern Mediterranean migrants, and the spaces they inhabited; it also reminds us of the power of such stories to shape the ways we view the past. With its tidy narrative arc of swift, inexorable commercial ascent, this particular vignette served as a convenient myth of origin for the French colonial administrators and writers who sought to account for the troubling presence of these canny figures, interlopers of empire whose mercantile proclivities threatened to upset the precarious balance of a colonial order of things premised on unquestioned European commercial supremacy. And, moreover, it continues to reverberate through accounts of the Lebanese of West Africa as perennial intermediaries, liminal figures fated to link up, and fall between, European and African, an awkward third term in the seemingly straightforward equation of colonial life. The symbolic and the material, the world and the word, I suggest here, cannot be disentangled; tightly bound together, they echoed and refracted each other in a constant feedback loop.

Drawing on sources in Arabic, French and English, ranging from the records of the Government-General of AOF, the French Ministry of Colonies and Ministry of Foreign Affairs, to colonial newspapers, magazines, monographs, gazetteers and journals, and the memoirs, account-books and travel accounts migrants themselves left behind, this work sets out to move beyond the exclusively economic approach which has tended to predominate in discussions of the Lebanese of West Africa. In its stead, I seek to craft a richer, 'affective' history—to borrow Dipesh Chakrabarty's term—attentive to the rhythms and registers of their daily lives, their patterns of dispersal and political thoughts and sentiments, as well as their commercial strategies and location in the colonial economy.[10] This is an account woven together from the intimate, individual tales of migrants, their peregrinations, progresses and failures. Such a choice is, in part, motivated by a 'desire to redeem', in Carlo Ginzburg's phrase, lives lost to historical inquiry—to rescue these men and women from the 'enormous condescension of posterity', to reiterate that well-worn sentiment.[11]

But stranding together these stories can also, I maintain, offer us another means of making sense of large-scale population movement and the workings of the imperial state and the colonial economy, processes which have all too often been peered down upon from an Olympian height, as by cartographers keen only to trace out their contours. It is not just a case of filling out these line-drawings with a mass of detail, patiently stitched together from archival scraps, the way a conservator might patiently piece together the shards of a shattered amphora. Rather, as Giovanni Levi has noted, we can comprehend 'social action' best if we look upon it as 'the result of an individual's constant negotiation, manipulation, choices and decisions in the face of a normative reality which, though pervasive, offers many possibilities for personal interpretations'.[12] Attending closely to the textures and trajectories of individual lives can illuminate what Polly Hill once called the '*basic* fabric of … economic life'—the 'style' and strategies of trade—in a colonial context still viewed by some in the schematic terms of dualist thought.[13] Furthermore, it can shine a light on the wider world of Eastern Mediterranean migration, enabling us to understand the ways migration altered irrevocably the lives of the many thousands of men and women who ebbed away from the region's shores from the 1880s onwards, scattering in places as far afield as New York and Buenos Aires, Manaus and Manila, Cape Town, Conakry, Lagos and Dakar.[14] For while some found their way back to the Eastern Mediterranean after a few years or decades, and others stayed away, all found that movement redrew their social relations and changed their sense of themselves.

I wish to examine much, then, which has received scant attention in past studies of Lebanese migrant life in colonial West Africa, works which have been overwhelmingly concerned with situating these migrants within the grand, ponderous structures of economic imperialism, and pegging their commercial progress to its juddering shifts in fortune,[15] to heap praise upon them as harbingers of the market,[16] or castigate them as compradors complicit in the development of underdevelopment.[17] Studies in stark chiaroscuro, these have shone an intense light upon a single aspect of this history, while leaving much else lingering in an ill-lit hinterland. In the following chapters, I will examine the particular concatenation of economic, social and demographic factors which made of migration an established strategy of social mobility throughout much of what is now Lebanon by the outbreak of the First World War; the strung-out networks of shipping agents, smugglers and hostel keepers who shepherded migrants from their home villages and towns to Beirut and Tripoli, and from there to New York and São Paulo, Dakar and Havana; the political sentiments of migrants, many of whom kept an ear cocked for news of the Eastern Mediterranean; the manner in which they sustained these commitments, and maintained their affective ties and working relationships with both the relatives and friends they left behind, and with others dispersed through the *mahjar*—or the lands of migration—in Brazil and Argentina, the United States and France; and the strains and adjustments of their everyday lives—or, to pun upon the language of home and hearth, the dislocations and accommodations of these existences played out in the *mahjar*, the continuation and transmutation of old practices, and the constant striving for social mobility and the comforts of home. And I will also trace the broader imperatives of imperial policy which prevented the Government-General of AOF from closing the gates of its colonies to Lebanese migration; the often—if not always—fraught relations with African peasants and townspeople and with the exiguous French communities of the Federation; and the virulent, venom-soaked discourses concocted by some in the ranks of settler society, who drew freely upon the anti-alien rhetoric of metropolitan French rightist propagandists to damn the Lebanese as feckless, dangerous cosmopolitans. All these are topics we must attend to, if we are to flesh out the rough thumbnail sketches others have supplied of the lives of the Eastern Mediterranean men and women of AOF—in the world, and in the text.

'Betwixt and between': colonial tropes and historiographical echoes

The Lebanese of West Africa, whose numbers currently range somewhere between 200,000 and 300,000, are the largest non-African migrant group of the region. From Senegal in the north to Gabon, the Democratic Republic of Congo and Angola in the south, these men and women play a conspicuous, and controversial, role in the economies of West and Equatorial Africa. Transnational citizens, who flit between West Africa and the Eastern Mediterranean, multiple passports in their shirt pockets, many belong to diasporic families: their parents, children, siblings and cousins are no longer concentrated in a single home place in Lebanon, but scattered through the *mahjar* from Michigan to London and Paris, Riyadh, Dubai and Abu Dhabi.[18] And yet they remain deeply invested in economic activities in West Africa, holding a stake in sectors as varied as diamond and cobalt mining, logging and timber exploitation, transportation, industrial production of consumer items ranging from rubber flip-flops to sweets and bread, and soap, detergents and beauty products, the restaurant and hotel trades, and real estate—with some estimating that a full 80 per cent of commercial properties in Abidjan are in Lebanese hands.

It is perhaps no surprise, then, that contemporary portrayals should centre upon the apparent 'tenacity, aptitude for business, and drive to succeed' of these migrants,[19] who remain defined by their seemingly indefatigable mercantile inclinations and 'indisputable economic success'.[20] Despite the very real disparities of wealth within their ranks, accounts of these communities are still woven around the 'impressive' tales of businessmen like the Paris-based Abbas Jaber ('Abbas Jabir), owner of the Senegalese groundnut-processing consortium SUNEOR and the Dakar-Bamako railway, and the 'prince' of Dakar real estate, Abdou Karim Bourgi ('Abd al-Karim Burji), or shadowy operators like Robert Bourgi, the Elysée's man in Africa turned whistleblower, awarded the Légion d'Honneur by Nicolas Sarkozy for his services to 'Françafrique', and Roland Daghir, Laurent Gbagbo's erstwhile *éminence grise*.[21]

Indeed, the Eastern Mediterranean migrants of West Africa have long been defined by their commercial inclinations. By the late 1930s, around 6,000 of these men and women—for the most part Maronite Christians from Mount Lebanon and Greek Catholics and Shi'a Muslims from Jabal 'Amil, in what had by then become southern

Lebanon—lived in AOF. While some became hairdressers, cabdrivers or bakers, providing services to the small European and Eastern Mediterranean populations of towns like Conakry and Dakar, most went into business as produce traders and shopkeepers. Whether they lived in the colonial capitals of the coast, inland trading centres like Thiès, Kaolack and Kankan, or smaller settlements scattered through their hinterlands, Lebanese migrants bought up produce from African producers: in Guinea rubber before 1914 and palm kernels thereafter, in Senegal and Soudan groundnuts, in Côte d'Ivoire kola nuts and then, towards the late 1930s, coffee and cocoa. And they supplied them, in turn, with consumer goods—textiles and clothes, canned foodstuffs, liquor, matches and the like. While women kept both home and shop, fulfilling the familiar duties of domesticity even as they lent a hand in supervising the family's commercial operations, men carried on the business of trade, bartering and pawning, lending and borrowing.

The exiguous band of scholars who have engaged in sustained study of the Lebanese communities of colonial West Africa have concentrated almost exclusively on these working lives. Wilfully neglecting other aspects of the stories and histories of these men and women, they have treated them as apparent 'prototypes of the economic man', as one British journalist put it in 1957—figures defined by their tireless pursuit of profit, whose existences might conveniently be treated as little more than commercial undertakings.[22] Moreover, they have often regarded them as quintessential middlemen, 'intermediar[ies] between the large European house and the native producer or consumer' who stood at the swinging doors of colonial trade, with its rudimentary logic of extraction, channelling to the coast the fruits of African agricultural labour which European steamers carried to the factories of the imperial heartlands, and disseminating far and wide through the hinterlands of Dakar, Freetown or Lagos manufactured goods imported from Europe.[23] It is true that most, though they set up on their own account rather than entering the employ of French or British firms, maintained symbiotic relations with companies like the Compagnie Française de l'Afrique Occidentale (CFAO), which supplied them with loans and merchandise, and eagerly purchased the produce they had collected.

However, the activities of these men and women far exceeded the narrow confines of colonial trade. Many engaged in buying and selling commodities like cattle, rice and kola nuts, long regarded by scholars as the preserves of a distinctly African trading order lying on the margins of the colonial economy. Furthermore, those who were able to do so rapidly diversified, combining their commercial activities with other mercantile undertakings: they emulated the business practices of the European firms, providing both credit and other financial services to those who were unable, or unwilling, to make use of conventional banking, and—for a few—importing and exporting goods directly; they bought up real estate both in Africa and in Lebanon, which might serve as a means not only of preserving their capital, but also of increasing their income through lettings; they began to purchase lorries, transporting goods both on their own account and, in return for a healthy commission, for others; they collected stocks in companies; and, in the case of but one or two wealthy entrepreneurs who set up small manufactures in Dakar or Bamako to produce goods for the local market, they engaged in industry. Eastern Mediterranean migrants, then, were constantly observing shifting patterns in trade, and looking out for new avenues to profit away from the simple two-way transactions of colonial trade.

But for all that, scholarly accounts of these men and women continue to regard them as eternal 'hyphen[s]' between European and African, white and black, formal and informal,[24] archetypal Simmelian strangers fated to fall forever 'betwixt and between' these clearly defined and curtained-off spheres.[25] As this suggests, the intensity with which popular and academic discussion has concentrated upon commerce is more than just a simple, straightforward reflection of the undeniable predilection of Lebanese migrants, both past and present, for business activities of one kind or another. Rather, colonial representations of Eastern Mediterranean migrants as an awkward third term in the seemingly simple equation of colonial life continue to haunt discussion of these men and women. This work, then, is not just a history of the Eastern Mediterranean men and women of colonial AOF. It is also a history of the ways in which Frenchmen, Lebanese and Africans have sought to make sense, and speak, of the unsettled and unsettling presence of these interlopers of empire. As such, it seeks to understand, and disentangle, the dogged binaries through which we view such pasts—notions of diasporic home and exile, of imperial centre and periphery, of coloniser and colonised, formal and informal—even as it strives, however haltingly, to transcend them.

We must find ways of making sense of the presence in colonial society of figures like the Eastern Mediterranean migrants of West Africa in terms which transcend the binary schemes of late colonial thought, and its anti-colonial obverse in the writings of Frantz Fanon and Albert Memmi. The texts of these men are hard-edged creations, which draw their singular oppositional power from the elemental starkness of their visions of colonial society as a 'world cut in two'—the terrain of a 'Manichean' confrontation between the thin white lines of the coloniser and the massed ranks of the colonised.[26] As Frederick Cooper has noted, these were echoes of the dichotomous categories of colonial thought itself, with its insistence on the divide between 'African backwardness and European modernity'—echoes which were, to be sure, distorted into a language of resistance, but whose origins in the lexicon of rule remain clear enough for us to trace.[27] Such appropriations are perhaps not surprising. After all, as Memmi himself insisted, none could escape the dialectic pull of colonialism, which 'traps both Coloniser and Colonised in the shackles of a merciless dependence, fashioning their personalities and dictating their behaviour'.[28] And yet, as Megan Vaughan has pointed out, Memmi—more equivocal and circuitous than the intransigent Fanon—could not help but acknowledge the presence in 'every colonial society, no matter how black and white in theory, … [of] liminal populations which haunted them from within', throwing into question seemingly clear questions of racial belonging.[29] In doing so, he also acknowledged his own ambivalent sense of self: a man who, though 'undeniably an *indigène* … by dint of my mother tongue … my sensibility and mores, my taste in music', 'knew him, the Coloniser, almost as well, and from within', having 'irrevocably chosen the French language, having dressed in Italian fashions, and even adopted with relish the tics of the Europeans'—familiar at once with coloniser and colonised, and yet awkwardly situated on the margins of both these groups.[30] Despite such slippages, Memmi's vision remained for the most part rigidly dyadic. Those populations which seemingly floated free of these binary categories—whether Jews like his own family, Italians or Maltese across French and British North Africa, South Asians in British East Africa or Greeks, Moroccans, Lebanese and Syrians in West Africa—could not escape the magnetic pull of colonialism and its Manichean ordering of the world. Though themselves 'neither coloniser nor colonised', they faced a stark binary choice: to lose themselves in the exiguous ranks of the coloniser, or to slip downwards into the colonised masses.[31]

I do not wish to dismiss such a vision of the world out of hand. It was one, after all, which Frenchmen, Africans and Eastern Mediterranean migrants alike resorted to in their efforts to make sense of the latter's presence in the colonial societies of AOF, or which they awkwardly attempted to steer around, finding no other means of conceiving of the predicament of these interlopers than as interstitial beings, slotted into the space between coloniser and colonised. However, even as we trace the insistent pull of this language, we must admit its analytical shortcomings. For Eastern Mediterranean migrants were not enclosed in a colonial context, their gaze perforce directed at their immediate surroundings, and turned enviously upwards at the French population of AOF. On the contrary, these men and women, while they attempted to find a berth in the colonial societies of West Africa, ceaselessly looked elsewhere for the material with which to fashion their lives—casting their gaze back to the Eastern Mediterranean, but also towards metropolitan France, its legal norms, fashions and domestic arrangements. Diasporic subjects, they lived in several contexts at once. Furthermore, they did not remain still, penned within the confines of their middling status as economic and racial intermediaries, but forever strove to better themselves, to move upwards through the ranks of commercial society—and, in doing so, to outstrip and belittle the European inhabitants of the colonies. For these men and women, physical restlessness and social mobility worked hand in hand. Indeed, one depended upon the other.

Moving tales

The Lebanese migrants of colonial West Africa were people on the move. They had journeyed far, of course, simply to reach the Federation. Most had taken the rough roads which wend their way down from the towns and hamlets of Mount Lebanon and Jabal 'Amil, distinct regions now agglomerated into the Lebanese nation-state, towards the coast, and the ports of Beirut and Tripoli; they had spent two or three weeks circumnavigating the Mediterranean, passing through Alexandria and Nicosia, Izmir and the Piraeus before reaching Marseille;[32] there, they had frittered away long, anxious weeks waiting for another ship which might take them onto Africa; and they had spent another three weeks aboard the *Banfora*, the *Augustus*[33] or the *Champol-*

lion,[34] sometimes sleeping on unsteady *chaises longues* out on the deck, under the stars and the rain, before finally reaching Dakar.[35]

But their displacements did not end there. Many flitted restlessly about in search of commercial opportunities, passing from one trading post to another, going up rail tracks, down waterways and across the flimsy demarcations between colonial territories. Others went regularly from Dakar or Conakry to Côte d'Ivoire and Sierra Leone to visit relatives, inspect the shops they had entrusted to agents or purchase from their compatriots kola nuts—for Eastern Mediterranean migrants rapidly seized upon the commercial potential of this precious quarry, channelling by sea or rail this bitter stimulant from the forest regions of the south, where it grew, to the savannah of the north, where it was much in demand. As the French administrator Jean-Gabriel Desbordes saw, 'the comings and going of this essentially mobile population, spreading out, regrouping, and dispersing again, with equal ease, across the different colonies of [AOF] constantly change its general aspect'.[36] Those who had the means to do so, meanwhile, travelled back and forth between West Africa and the Eastern Mediterranean. While some spent but the odd short summer sojourn in the place of their birth, others retired to the red-roofed homes they had built with the gains of long years of trading. And, in turn, those who departed for good were replaced by new arrivals. The Lebanese migrant communities of AOF, then, were inherently fluid, forever shifting shape and reconstituting themselves. They were not so much like billiard balls—hard, compact, units, travelling swiftly before coming to an abrupt rest—as like pools of population, irrigated and drained by streams of movement.

Furthermore, the movements and connections of migrant life were not limited to the 'constant two-way traffic' between West Africa and the Eastern Mediterranean.[37] These ramifications stretched further still, as these men and women plotted networks branching out to points across the *mahjar*. They did not just call on assistance from kin and compatriots who had stayed behind in the regions of their birth; they also maintained ties with those who had taken the paths of migration to Europe, the United States and Latin America, visiting relatives in Buenos Aires and Rio de Janeiro, and seeking out goods and credit in Marseille, Paris and Manchester. To be sure, not all these points were equal. Some, like Dakar or Marseille, became central nodes of entrepreneurial and affective life, thick knots of overlapping relations. Others, like Daloa in Côte d'Ivoire or Conakry in Guinea, were distinctly secondary, or became so as the centre of gravity of the colonial economy shifted away.

And yet, these various points existed in a complex web of symbiotic relations, bound together and sustained by their ties to each other. Traders in Côte d'Ivoire could not have purchased kola nuts without the credit of their wealthier kin in Dakar; but nor could the latter have derived such rich profits from the transit trade without the assistance of these distant agents. We cannot ignore these proliferating networks if we are to be alive to the constant movements, and the intricate linkages of kin and commerce between seemingly disparate groups, which supported Lebanese life in West Africa.[38] These men and women inhabited what Roger Rouse has aptly called a 'transnational circuit'; their lives intermeshed with those of family and friends elsewhere by the 'continuous circulation of people, money, goods, and information', they formed 'a single community spread across a variety of sites'.[39] Even those among them who remained still, drawing to a stop rather than moving on time and again, found their lives sustained by movement. Eastern Mediterranean migrants—to paraphrase James Clifford—dwelled in travel.[40] And this work, in turn, dwells upon their lives—both in the flesh, and on the page.

The tangled webs of diaspora

Doing so can provide us with a privileged vantage point upon the conditions of diasporic life. Commonly regarded as the 'first age of globalisation', the last decades of the nineteenth century and the first of the twentieth saw the transformation of the world into a single, vast, coal-streaked arena of movement, through which coursed in all directions men and women in their hundreds of thousands and millions, many simply seeking a better livelihood.[41] The First World War, it is true, slowed these tumultuous processes. But while the currents of movement would tarry in the 1920s and 1930s, as states adopted increasingly chary attitudes towards new arrivals at their gates, the consequences of these waves of migration would continue to play themselves out long afterwards.[42] From Sicilians and Calabrese heading for the canals and construction sites of the American North-East,[43] to the South Asians who worked on the railways of East Africa, the mines of Natal and the plantations of British Malaya,[44] the Chinese of Hawaii and San Francisco, Indochina and New South Wales[45] or, indeed, the Eastern Mediterranean pedlars and shopkeepers of the American Mid-West, the rubber metropolises of the Amazon and the peanut basin of colonial Senegal, diasporas were surely as much the 'exemplary communities' of these decades as of our own troubled 'transnational movement'.[46]

Their study, then, can yield much insight, helping us to look again upon two pervasive notions surrounding diasporic life. The first is the tendency to look upon it as a 'generalised condition of homelessness'—in the melancholy phrase of Edward Said, himself a figure dogged by a recurring sense of being sentimentally, intellectually and politically 'out of place' in the world.[47] The second, meanwhile, is the connected propensity to draw a stark contrast between the comforting core of the homelands and the disconsolate, peripheral status of life in the world beyond, regarding the relationship between one and the other simply 'in terms of origin to copy'. As Stuart Hall has observed, such a hierarchical distinction between 'primary source [and] pale reflection' simply will not do.[48] Anthropologists and theorists like Hall and James Clifford have certainly done much in recent years to dispel longstanding notions of culture as an organic unit born of a particular territory—a 'rooted body that grows, lives, and dies' in the soft soil of the homeland.[49] However, in treating diaspora as the paradigmatic predicament of a globalised world, in which all feel a little lost and without bearings, some have stressed a little too intently the dislocation and indeterminacy they see as the migrant's ineluctable lot—the fundamental 'unhomeliness', as Homi Bhabha put it, the uncanny sense of detachment, born of being a stranger in a strange land.[50] To be sure, Eastern Mediterranean migrants to West Africa were not entirely free of such nagging anxieties. Some went so far as to offload the heavy burdens of displacement in print, like 'Ali 'Abdallah Muruwwah, who warned those who contemplated following him to AOF that 'pain covers Africa from one end to another, and illness lies in wait for each and every migrant'.[51] This, though, was not so much an existential lament as a warning of the potential failures and travails that awaited those eagerly preparing to leave Lebanon.

For the most part, the existences of the Lebanese of West Africa were not isolated, disconsolate existences, painfully eked out a long way from home. It is telling, in this regard, that migrants came to christen certain localities in West Africa Qabb Elias or Bait Shabab after their birthplaces.[52] Such nicknames emphasised the extent to which their existences in these places, among familiar faces and recognisable names, could seem extensions of those they had left behind in the Eastern Mediterranean. For they did not just reflect the continuing intensity of the dispersed affective ties, business connections and political affiliations migrants kept up across the *mahjar*, but also something of the intimate arrangements of their day-to-day lives: the food they ate, their patterns of sociability and religious observance. As one French administrator perceptively noted in the mid-1940s, even those who remained for long spells in West Africa and 'had no intention of returning to settle' back in Lebanon retained a 'strong attachment' to the ways of home.[53]

That is not to say, to move on to our second point, that these practices were static, unchanging, entities 'transcending place [and] time'—salvaged mementoes migrants could pack into neat little bundles and carry along on their travels, safe in the knowledge that transit would leave them unscathed. On the contrary, as Hall has suggested, they were subject to the 'continuous play of history'.[54] While migrants did seek to pack away the fragile dispositions of daily life and arrange them, upon arrival, as they had once stood, this was not—to paraphrase Charles Tilly—a process of wholesale import, but one of selection and occlusion.[55] Some ways of living and doing were carried along, but others were readily jettisoned along the route—discarded because they were too impractical in new locales, or simply no longer desirable. Moreover, this was not a one-off process, neatly demarcated in time: the collections of practices and objects—of ways of living, and things to live with—the Lebanese of West Africa built up were constantly revised and refreshed, as they discarded some and added others.

It is clear, then, that Eastern Mediterranean migrants did not simply forge 'new cultures' from a narrow array of 'old materials', precious artefacts of a lost *patria*.[56] But nor did they constitute their own distinctive lives in relation to an 'invented' 'homeland', which existed 'only in the imagination' or,[57] alternatively, discard all vestiges of the past—throwing themselves into a dialectical engagement with their surroundings, from which were born ways of living tailored to the 'idiosyncrasies of their new locations'.[58] We are little helped by simply flipping the terms of the relation between 'home' and diaspora, and suggesting that the labours of culture were all carried out on the peripheries. These men and women were not so much *bricoleurs*—'handymen' making do with a restricted supply of raw materials, as Claude Lévi-Strauss suggested—as *braconniers*, to borrow Michel de Certeau's apposite image, 'poachers' who took elements from this place and that to constitute their daily lives.[59] For the constant revisions and alterations they brought to their everyday habits were the product of a three-way engagement with their immediate colonial environs, their native places in the Eastern Mediterranean and, increasingly, metropolitan France. It is to these three locales that they looked simultaneously for the stuff of their daily lives.

To misquote Paul McCartney, the Lebanese migrants of West Africa were at once here, there and elsewhere. It is certainly true, as Engseng Ho has suggested, that 'mobility leaves in its wake a trail of absences'—that, inevitably, 'to be present in one place is to be absent everywhere else'.[60] And yet I want to suggest that these men were, in some senses, simultaneously present and absent in West Africa and the Eastern Mediterranean. Though physically absent from their home towns and villages, they also maintained a palpable presence there. This was not simply because their 'lack', the void they left behind, was itself a continuing force in the affective lives of their kin and neighbours.[61] More importantly, their material presence was itself everywhere to be seen—in the wives, sons and daughters who stayed behind or came back, in the remittances they sent to their families, in the ostentatious houses they built and the land they purchased.

Their lives in West Africa, meanwhile, hung on a rather different kind of paradox. Though their livelihoods depended on their staying *in situ*, they also constantly sought to evade their surroundings, to elide their own conspicuous presence and escape the frequently scornful gazes of their African and French neighbours. And, as they retreated away from prying eyes into the privacy of their own homes, furnished with the fruits of their success, they also increasingly sought to slip away from Africa in their quotidian practices, devising ways of being in the world which owed the most to distant locales. That is not to say that these men and women took nothing from their immediate environment—far from it. However, there is no doubt that to move up in the world also meant, for them, to move away—figuratively, if not, at least immediately, literally. In their homespun hierarchies, West Africa was at once the place that was most important to them—the locale which allowed them to keep up their train of life—and the least important, striving as they did to live according to norms and rhythms which had little to do with their immediate environs.

This was as true of their everyday habits, and the spaces in which they lived, as of the notions of domesticity, respectability and race migrants increasingly adopted in the 1920s and 1930s, ways of thinking about life which suited newly improved circumstances. These owed much, on the one hand, to the new material culture of middle-class life which developed in the Eastern Mediterranean—itself patterned on French fashions and forms while retaining its own distinct bent.[62] On the other, they lent heavily upon the pendant of such domestic accoutrements—the discourses of masculinity, femininity and family which underwent such thoroughgoing revision in the region in the decades bookending the First World War.[63] And it was true, also, of their political thoughts and sentiments.

Both Christian and Muslim migrants attempted, in their own ways, to remain plugged into the political debates of the Eastern Mediterranean: they read newspapers and journals from home; they raised funds for cherished causes; and they carried on a constant chatter, commenting on the news which reached them, and stating their own adherences and opinions in speeches and late night conversations, petitions and telegrams. Piecing together the political cultures of these migrants is a task of great import. Not only does it go some way towards correcting past neglect of those who left the region among political historians of the Eastern Mediterranean.[64] It also shines a light on the shifting political thoughts and practices of men—and the sources speak only of male participation in the political realm—who were neither communal leaders nor military officers or party cadres, journalists or civil servants, in a field still dominated by accounts of such stock figures of nationalist politics.[65] Indeed, if anything, it disrupts understandings of the political history of the Eastern Mediterranean in the interwar period which continue to focus unremittingly on nationalism—showing the endurance of other means of imagining political space, and conceiving of political engagement, well into the 1930s.[66] And it does so in a way which shows the very ordinariness of these practices—the way in which they were woven into the habitual, the everyday business of trade and family life—in a field which still all too often privileges exceptional moments of popular insurrection, great conflagrations like the revolts which shook Mesopotamia in 1920–21, Syria in 1925–26 and Palestine in 1936–39.[67]

I attempt in this work, then, to disrupt the 'assumed isomorphism of space, place and culture' which lingers on in much study of the Eastern Mediterranean—its insistence upon retreating into the comforting embrace of the regional, and treating its people as intimately tied to territories scholars regard as 'hermetically sealed entities' rather than as 'part of a permeable interwoven' set of relationships.[68] Historians like James Gelvin and Keith Watenpaugh have sought in recent years to rework our understanding of the political senses of the region's people—taking up Prasenjit Duara's insight that nationalism is rarely an easy and consensual identity, but 'rather … the site where different representations of the nation contest and negotiate with each other'.[69] And in doing so, they have contributed to a sophisticated series of attempts to rethink the region's entanglement with the world beyond, the understandings of modernity its people and rulers crafted, and those others sought to impose upon them.[70] However, even as these works have redrawn our understanding of the region's cultures—doing away with any notions of a monolithic cultural identity rooted in regional soil, supinely absorbing or vociferously resisting the influences of the West—they have rarely strayed beyond its conventional territorial limits. I seek here, on the contrary, to rupture these boundaries. This is all too urgent a task, for too many of the region's scholars remain cantoned in self-made confines, leaving the lives of the many thousands of migrants who left its shores to other histories, and other historians.

Colonial lives and racial selves

This work also considers another diaspora of empire: the French settlers, commercial workers and administrators who left their scattered traces in the ample remnants of the colonial public sphere. I treat these reams of newspapers, magazines, monographs, gazetteers, journals and travel accounts as textual artefacts, moulded by the conventional requirements of their genres and the specific strategies of their authors. Their distinctive form; the circumstances of their composition; their authors' political persuasions, difficult as these may sometimes be to discern; the source materials they drew upon and made their own; the registers they used—whether the plain-speaking demotic of political journalism, or the sparse scholarly prose of the monograph, the dry language of trade or the clinical terminology of bacteriology; and perhaps most importantly, their ostensible intentions—what they sought to achieve by writing in a particular fashion, using particular terms, about this subject in particular: all of this matters a great deal.

As Natalie Zemon Davis has argued, we should consider these texts as fictions. That is not to say that we should regard them as mere assemblages of distortions and misrepresentations, structures 'of lies or of myths which'—as Edward Said observed some three decades ago—'were the truth about them to be told, would simply be blown away'.[71] Rather, we should take heed—as Davis enjoins us to—of the 'other, broader sense of the root word *fingere*', examining the 'forming, shaping and moulding elements' of these texts, 'the crafting of a narrative',[72] from the rough-hewn detail of life and the realm of the ideological. For these texts were not just representations. On the contrary, as Sander Gilman noted in his reading of the manner in which Jews were written of in *fin-de-siècle* physiological and psychiatric tomes, 'there are "realities" … which also become part of the social construction' of the subject of analysis.[73]

The fraught, anxious existences of small French commercial workers, forever worried by the fear they might be edged out by Lebanese competitors or bought up by the companies, and the sheer exiguity of the French communities of West Africa: these were refracted and reworked through these texts.[74] French colonial society always remained small in AOF, its numbers rising from 7,640 in 1921[75] to around 28,000 in the 1930s—military men, administrators, missionaries, company agents and independent traders, wives and children all counted.[76] Its commercial ranks were thinner still, and French traders were outnumbered, in many places across the Federation, by migrants from Mount Lebanon and Jabal 'Amil. Already in 1911, the minister of colonies counted in French Guinea 986 'Syrians' against 963 Frenchmen—of whom some 491 were administrators. This, as he put it, meant that 'in reality, only 472 of our traders find themselves grappling with around a thousand Asiatic traders'.[77] This elementary fact might account, in large part, for the sheer ferocity with which the French inhabitants of AOF responded to Eastern Mediterranean migration. The particular intensity, and inflection, of the exclusionary discourses crafted by these commercial workers—and the publicists, propagandists and administrators who shared their opinions—will form the last strand of this tangled history.

Their examination may shed light not just on the clammy anxieties of colonial life in Senegal and Guinea, but also on the vital role metropolitan tropes of race played in the constitution of Lebanese migrants as interlopers lying beyond the bounds of whiteness. This can, in turn, complicate our understanding of the traffic in notions of race between the French *métropole* and its colonies in the early twentieth century. Historians of France and French imperialism have done much over the last decade or so to enhance our sense of the ways in which—as Ann Laura Stoler and Frederick Cooper put it—'both colonies and metropoles shared in the dialectics of inclusion and exclusion'.[78] They have not, of course, been alone in seeking to set these two sites within a single analytical space, nor in wishing to show the ways in which colonialism helped to shape, and reshape, metropolitan cultures—reversing older assumptions which placed the weight of agency at one end of the scale, regarding imperialism as a force which fundamentally transformed the colonies but remained largely marginal to European history.[79] But scholars of France have had their own reasons for insisting that empire did—and does—matter. In part, they have sought to address the looming, monolithic presence of Britain in the field of imperial studies. However, a more important consideration has perhaps been their desire to correct what they regard—not without reason—as the continuing neglect of imperial history in France itself. This, they insist, is untenable. Not only was empire, they argue, a 'laboratory of modernity' in which notions of statecraft and social planning seen as inherently metropolitan were first elaborated.[80] Moreover, it might serve as a privileged site from which we can reflect on the inherent and longstanding tensions running beneath notions of republican universalism. This, in turn, can 'alter our core understanding of the republican nation', and refigure 'the meaning of French history' by pushing its borders back beyond those of the territorial nation-state itself.[81] Indeed, some have maintained that we must think of France in the years before 1960 not as a nation, but as an empire-state—an imperial polity perpetually attempting to reconcile the antinomian notions of universalism and particularism.[82]

There can be no doubting the value of much of this work. As Sue Peabody and Tyler Stovall have argued, we cannot understand the place racial thought has occupied in metropolitan French history without tracing its connections to the colonies.[83] However, in attempting to state so forcefully the transformative effects of colonialism upon the *métropole*, scholars have perhaps overlooked the manner in which metropolitan racial discourses continued to flow in the other direction and to inform, in some circumstances, ostensibly colonial discourses of exclusion.[84] In the years before 1914, both the commercial workers who protested in their petitions against the 'invasion' of Eastern Mediterranean migrants who threatened their livelihoods, and the administrators and writers who attempted to account for this presence built their arguments not just—in some instances—upon metropolitan legislative precedents, but also on notions of commercial probity and masculine respectability which drew in large measure upon the lexicon of metropolitan anti-Semitism, with its hard distinctions between upstanding, settled Frenchmen and feckless, errant cosmopolitans. In the 1930s and 1940s, their supporters drew increasingly explicit parallels between Lebanese and Syrian migration to AOF and the foreigners who, they felt, had infested the metropolitan body politic.

Of course, these various writers did not simply import metropolitan notions wholesale into their texts. Rather, they cut and customised these discourses, tailoring them to the particular exigencies of colonial political life. Still, there seems little doubt that they did depend upon the potent registers of metropolitan anti-Semitism. Furthermore, from the 1930s onwards, French *colons* increasingly showed concerns about France's tangled relationship with Lebanon and Syria, its costs to the *métropole* and its repercussions upon their own commercial lives in AOF. The Federation's French *colons* were—as much as its Lebanese and Syrian migrants—caught in a three-way relationship with the *métropole* and the Eastern Mediterranean. We should treat France's empire as a single political space through which ideas were in constant circulation. But we must also remain aware that they went in all directions, creating criss-crossing paths of intellectual exchange.

A concert of voices: migrants in the archives

The grammar of difference which courses through, and structures, the texts of publicists, functionaries, journalists and scholars also left its imprint upon the archival sources I lean upon here—documents drawn, for the most part, from the vast repositories of the Government-General of AOF in Dakar and Paris, the French Ministry of Colonies, preserved in Aix-en-Provence and the Ministry of Foreign Affairs, then still stored in its ornate building at the Quai d'Orsay. However, to treat these merely as expressions of the 'official mind', or products of the relentlessly reifying and distorting forces of colonial discourse, is not quite to tell the whole story. Among them, of course, are tersely worded administrative reports and hurriedly scribbled memoranda, composed by ministers and consuls, colonial governors and *commandants de cercle*, police commissioners and intelligence officers. But they also include the account books and bankruptcy statements some Eastern Mediterranean migrants deposited before the courts, documents which take stock, in minute—and sometimes excruciating—detail, of the goods these traders kept in their shops and warehouses, of the real estate they owned, the debts they owed and the money they lent. However, we should not treat the latter as preferable, privileged documents offering alongside the few memoirs and travel accounts left behind by Lebanese migrants and visitors a clearer vantage point on a past hidden from view in the remainder of the archives, with its bureaucratic preoccupations. Nor should we simply regard the dog-eared dispatches of functionaries as impersonal indices of convention, set in a cipher we must carefully unscramble to get at the details of daily life, always worried that we are simply imposing our own representations. It may sometimes seem that these memoranda and reports are texts whose authors' subjectivity resembled 'a face drawn in the sand at the edge of the sea' only to be washed away by the lapping waves, in

INTRODUCTION

Michel Foucault's haunting phrase.[85] This isn't just an effect of the tedious labour of the archives, as one squints to make out the recursive, hackneyed turns of administrative language from a crabbed, hurried hand, whose marks flicker faintly away on an antiquated microfilm reader.[86] Colonial administrators did themselves sometimes deliberately strive for the anonymous production of bureaucratic knowledge. Organising the ragged details of daily life into the predetermined 'grids' and boxes of bureaucratic priority and 'intelligibility', the monthly and yearly reports of French functionaries in Dakar and the *cercles* of Senegal through the 1920s and 1930s—broken down as they were into accounts of the running of this or that administrative department or endeavour—seem willing to include only that which might fall under such concerns: entry and exit statistics for the port of Dakar compiled by the immigration service, to cite an apposite example, or the amounts of money advanced by the providential societies to cultivators in the surrounding region, and the problems faced in attempting to collect their produce. They seem, then, attempts to 'represent and regulate a society' by efficient and 'socio-technical' means, as Paul Rabinow has put it.[87] This, at times, makes it difficult to draw much from such material; only now and then does a stray detail break out, like Barthes' *punctum*, shooting 'out like an arrow and [piercing]' the reader.[88]

It is important that we consider such attempts to implement these 'practices of reason'.[89] As Ann Laura Stoler has noted, we should attend to the 'texture and granularity' of the archives before attempting to read them—to consider their 'densities and distributions' of interest and information, the rationale governing omissions as well as inclusions in this documentary domain.[90] It is telling, in this respect, that much of the material on the Lebanese in the depositories of both the Ministry of Colonies and the Government-General of AOF should have been classified in files relating to *affaires politiques* or *affaires étrangères*. Even as the colonial state classified Lebanese migrants as commercial men, it deemed them worthy of sustained concern only when they seemed to pose a political threat. This, inevitably, affected the manner in which administrators at all levels approached this population—the sorts of questions they asked and the type of knowledge they sought to gather. Their fears of the political carryings-on of Shi'a migrants in particular—and their constant fretting that they did not know, or understand, enough about activities which might expose Muslim *indigènes*, otherwise insulated in their eyes from the wider currents of Islam, to subversive notions of pan-Islamic militancy—make it easier, in a sense, to reconstruct the political thoughts and sentiments of these men than their social or commercial arrangements.[91] But we must be aware of the way such epistemic dispositions changed over time.

Such shifts, and the possibilities they offer the historian, become clear when one peers over the reports compiled by administrators in French Soudan, Côte d'Ivoire, Guinea and Senegal in early 1945 on the social, political and economic conditions of Lebanese migrants in these territories. These, too, are clearly dictated by reasons of state—the desire to take stock of these communities in the wake of the Second World War, and the concern that the fraught process of Lebanese independence might have affected the disposition of these men towards France, pushing them into the embrace of the United States and Britain. But it is telling that the *commandants de cercle* and *administrateurs de circonscription* who put these together should have been given a broader set of questions than those which framed their inquiries in the 1920s and 1930s—on the lifestyles of Lebanese migrants, say, or their relations with local African populations—and that they chose to answer them in sometimes expansive detail. The authors of these documents show a concern for the lush complexities of life often lacking in their predecessors' reports—a product, perhaps, of the increasingly ethnographic training administrators received at the École Nationale de la France d'Outre-Mer under the direction of colonial paternalists like Robert Delavignette.[92] These reports, then, display both the growing anxieties of the late colonial state, and the changing casts of mind of its officials—and offer us, in the process, much that we might make our own.

Moreover, they reveal the essentially dialogic processes by which administrators sought out information on Lebanese migrants. These documents, and others like them, are not only formed from clumps of knowledge culled by functionaries from the archives of state, who reworked them into their own, essentially historical, narratives. They are also made up of strands and snatches of dialogue—a speech at a political meeting, jotted down by a Senegalese interpreter, titillating tattle on the amorous relations and animosities of Dakar businessmen, the reports of a Bamako bank manager on the financial arrangements of his Lebanese clients—'intercepted' and interpolated words roughly stitched into the fabric of these accounts.[93] Reading such documents, one sometimes senses the constant, tumultuous hubbub of colonial life finding its way into the dusty stillness of these texts—like the stray sounds, the car horns and raised voices from the streets outside which filter in to the reading rooms at Dakar through bay windows left ajar. Furthermore, such products of official concern jostle for space in the overflowing files of the Government-General of AOF and the Ministry of Colonies with the letters and petitions of Lebanese migrants, requests for visas for this or that relative or employee, to create or disband a committee or host a visiting dignitary—documents which allow us to track the trajectories of particular individuals, and to retrace the skein of family relations upon which they drew and the tangled webs of associational life they wove. When read in such a manner, the archives seem not so much a sepulchral mausoleum to the monolithic written remains of the state, in which one can hear only the uniform strains of colonial discourse, as a crowded arena filled with a teeming cacophony of voices and registers, of arguments and crossed purposes, borrowings and interpolations.

That is not to suggest, of course, that they are without their absences. Administrative reports and memoranda leave us with little sense of the way in which African townspeople and rural producers apprehended the Lebanese, or of what the latter made of their hosts, their landlords and clients. We are able to establish how much they owed each other in rent or interest on loans, how many bags of produce or swatches of cloth they purchased from each other—but not, in spite of some tantalising glimpses here and there, to draw from these sources a detailed picture of their relations. This is truer still of the lives of Eastern Mediterranean women. Their names are there on the census-rolls, along with their men. We can establish where they were born, and when; we can know the names of their parents, those of their husbands and children; we can even know that they did work as hawkers, sitting behind a tipped-over box on a street-corner, or handling the till in their family's store. We are able, then, to get a sense of the routines and practices of these women's daily lives from our combing of the sources. But we remain unable to retrace the individual paths of particular women as we can with male migrants. Indeed, it is telling that the memoranda and reports deposited in the archives focus upon the public matters of trade and politics, refusing to cross the threshold of domesticity. We must remain aware of the ways such a grammar of difference affects our own reading of these sources.

Travelling histories

This, then, is a tangled history of the webs of movement—of men and women, goods and credit, sentiments and ideas—between the Eastern Mediterranean, metropolitan France and West Africa. It is divided into three parts, or movements, each concerned with a particular aspect of this story. Part One, 'Roots and Routes', reconstructs the social and economic history which gave rise to the peregrinations of these men and women. While Chapter One attends to the circumstances which impelled the two central streams of Lebanese migration to AOF—one from Mount Lebanon, the other from Jabal 'Amil—Chapter Two pursues this path further, tracing the roots and routes of Eastern Mediterranean migrants, and looking again at the place of notions of kin, place and confession in their lives, and the complex mix of motives which drew them to West Africa.

Part Two, 'Words and Laws', examines the ways in which Frenchmen dealt with the disruptive presence of these men and women. Chapter Three homes in upon the ways in which commercial workers and company directors, administrators and colonial publicists wrote of these migrants in the years before 1914, attempting to unravel the different registers upon which the opponents, and advocates, of these interlopers drew. Chapter Four then looks in greater detail at the empire-wide legislative context for this migration, and the affective discourses and strategic imperatives, born of France's own entanglements in the Eastern Mediterranean, which prevented administrators in AOF from checking the movements of Lebanese migrants.

The third and final movement, 'Days, Thoughts, and Things', attends to the quotidian lives and prosaic strategies of Lebanese migrants. Chapter Five focuses on the trading lives of these men and women, in an effort to understand in greater detail their predilections and tactics, and to replace them within colonial circuits of trade. Chapter Six considers the changing living arrangements and aspirations of these men and women, the ways they set themselves off against the other components of colonial society, and drew on the registers of metropolitan and Eastern Mediterranean middle-class culture. Chapter Seven, finally, moves from the terrain of daily life to that of migrants' political thoughts and sentiments.

It is clear that we must, if we are to write the cultural, economic and political history of Lebanese migration to AOF, become mobile ourselves, travelling back and forth between continents, and tacking between disciplinary areas and seemingly disparate bodies of scholarship—on the exclusionary discourses of the French right and Eastern Mediterranean political culture, the global histories of migration or the economic ecologies of Mount Lebanon and Côte d'Ivoire, Senegal and Soudan. In looking upon these men and women with 'diasporic eyes',[94] we might not only understand something of their own fates, but also of the ways in which their displacements brought 'disparate points' of the French empire, and the world, into a tangled 'new relationship'.[95]

PART ONE

ROOTS AND ROUTES

1

A TALE OF TWO MOUNTAINS

Migrants, it is clear, came from across much of the Arabic-speaking Eastern Mediterranean to West Africa. The French administrator Jean-Gabriel Desbordes listed no fewer than 138 villages and towns within the then-new state of Lebanon alone, from Bainu 'Akkar in the northern marches of the country to Almat al-Sha'b, only a few miles from the borders of Mandatory Palestine. Significant clusters came from Beirut, with 556 migrants; the Biqa', with 476; the region of Jazzin, with 352; the Shuf, with 326; the Kisrwan, with 282; 'Akkar, with 258; the region of Batrun, with 168; the Syrian city of Homs, with 149; Tripoli and the adjoining villages, with 145; Damascus, with 100; and the villages of Rashayya, Hasbayya, and Marj 'Ayun, on the slopes of the Anti-Lebanon, with eighty-eight migrants. However, none of these various regions were more important than Bait Shabab and other Maronite localities of the Matn, overlooking Beirut from their position at the heart of Jabal Lubnan, or Mount Lebanon; and the low ranges of the largely Shi'a region of Jabal 'Amil, extending to the south of Mount Lebanon towards Galilee. By 1938, these accounted for, respectively, 1,432 and 1,546 of the Eastern Mediterranean migrants of AOF.[1] I will attempt in this chapter to disentangle these intertwined threads of movement, examining the quite different factors which led men and women from these regions down the paths of migration, and the manner in which these changed from 1898 to 1939.

Tales of misery

It was long a truth universally acknowledged that migration from the Syrian provinces of the Ottoman Empire was essentially a response to sectarian unrest and the depredations of a senescent and despotic administration. This view was held as much by scholars of the Middle East—who should perhaps have known better—as by scholars of migration, often all too content to account for departure in largely sche-

23

Figure 1: Lebanon and Syria.

matic terms. The sociologist Clark Knowlton could still insist, in 1992, that migration had been provoked by the effects of faltering rule—'banditry, economic decay, poverty and religious and social conflict'—and the propensity of the 'better armed Druze and Muslim' inhabitants of Mount Lebanon to perpetrate exactions upon their Christian 'neighbours' 'in times of religious strife'.[2] That same year, Charles

Table 1: Origins of migrants in AOF (1936) [list only includes localities with more than fifty migrants living in the Federation].

	Men	Women	Total
Bait Shabab (M)	598	378	976
Sur (JA)	470	201	671
Beirut	373	183	556
Qabb Elias (B)	251	74	325
Qana (JA)	186	57	243
Nabatiyya (JA)	194	43	237
Juwayya (JA)	144	48	192
Kfar Huna (JA)	140	25	165
Homs (Sy)	116	33	149
Bikfayya (M)	110	36	146
Bainu 'Akkar (A)	99	39	138
Tripoli	97	35	132
Zrariyya (JA)	85	24	109
Karm Sadde (S)	59	44	103
Damascus (Sy)	65	35	100
Saida (JA)	72	22	94
Alma al-Sha'b (JA)	49	33	82
Bisharre (S)	47	26	73
Mazra't al-Shuf (Sh)	58	14	72
Shwuifat (Al)	60	11	71
Shawiyya (M)	43	27	70
Qara'un (B)	59	9	68
Dair al-Qamar (Sh)	49	15	64
Zahle (B)	36	28	64
Jbail (K)	50	11	61
'Aqura (K)	51	9	60
Qurnat Shahwan (M)	39	15	54
Ras al-Matn (M)	42	12	54
'Ain Ibl (JA)	37	17	54
Miziara (S)	31	21	52
'Abbasiyya (JA)	48	3	51

Key: 'Akkar (A); 'Alay (Al); Biqa' (B); Jabal 'Amil (JA); Kisrawan (K); Matn (M); Shimal (S); Shuf (Sh); Syria (Sy).
Source: Desbordes, Jean-Gabriel, *L'Immigration Libano-Syrienne en Afrique Occidentale Française*, Poitiers: Renault & Cie, 1938, p. 28.

Issawi—an economic historian of the Middle East—maintained that 'the communal clashes and upheavals of the 1840s and 1850s provided the stimulus for large-scale emigration from Lebanon'.[3]

In their blithe acceptance of this bleak historiographical script, with its vision of life in the Arab provinces as mired in sectarian strife and 'Turkish' (mis-)rule, scholars overlooked its troublesome genealogy, running back to the writings of reformist Ottoman authors like Khalil Ghanim. A Maronite deputy for Beirut in the 1876 Ottoman parliament, Ghanim went into exile following its dissolution in 1878, attacking in a series of works the man he held responsible for the suspension of constitutional rule—Sultan Abdülhamit.[4] 'Despotism and fanaticism', he declared in 1901, 'are the paramount causes of the empire's decadence, and the decay, growing more marked by the day, of the dynasty'.[5] Indeed, he asserted, the Ottoman state was one of those in which 'man is considered no more than a slave'. He 'enjoys no individual liberties, and can rise above his fellows only through the favours of his master', for the sultans 'exercise an unchecked despotism, and nothing, from the summit to the very base of the hierarchy, may happen without their consent'.[6]

This powerful, corrosive vision of utterly unchecked Oriental despotism was, in turn, given a local inflection by Ghanim's younger brother Shukri in writings such as the *Mémoire sur la Question du Liban*—composed in 1912 with his acolyte Khairallah T. Khairallah. In this short pamphlet, the two men called for wholesale reform of the autonomous administration of Mount Lebanon, established in the wake of the civil war of 1860, declaring that the 'regime of Hamidian oppression, which bore down so heavily upon all Turkey, did not spare Lebanon. Its privileges were withdrawn one by one, unexpectedly or arbitrarily; its autonomy was dismembered, each governor picking off a strip to offer to his master in Constantinople, and it now exists in no more than name.'[7] These narratives were carried over by French writers into their own texts. There, woven into a wider web of preconceptions regarding the Ottoman polity, they were used to account at once for the rise of nationalism, and for the waves of migration ebbing away from the Eastern Mediterranean. Desbordes, drawing heavily upon the writings of Georges Samna—another of Ghanim's Parisian collaborators—asserted that migration, 'this exodus of traders and miserable agriculturalists, was provoked by the atrocities the Christians suffered, and the erosion of the autonomy guaranteed the Mountain' in the 1860s.[8]

Moreover, migrants invoked these tales of misery and oppression to justify their wrenching departure. These stories continue to circulate among their descendants, who proudly recount lachrymose narratives of hardship and perseverance, painting their forebears as heroic pioneers forced by 'oppression and heartless treatment' to flee their native lands.[9] 'For centuries', one Lebanese-American recalled, 'the Ottomans had taken great pleasure in oppressing and persecuting' the Christian inhabitants of Mount Lebanon, who built their churches with low doors, 'to combat the favorite Ottoman sport of desecrating Maronite churches after entering them on horseback'.[10] Migration was abstracted, in these accounts, from its historical circumstances, and remade into a weapon of the weak—a tool of resistance which the Lebanese used as a means of eluding the grasp of a callous, cruel imperial state whose servants were driven by a fanatical animus towards disbelievers.

These tales, however, circulated far beyond the confines of the Maronite communities of Mount Lebanon. Tellingly, Shiʻa writers contemplating growing migration from Jabal ʻAmil in the interwar years echoed many of their refrains. Nur al-Din ʻUsairan, for instance, complained in 1931 of the 'lack of effort' on the part of the 'Mandatory government' to 'reform matters and improve the situation' in Lebanon, which had led 'an ever-growing number of the sons of our beloved land' to migrate to 'foreign lands' where they were but a 'morsel in the mouth' of hostile governments which sought to 'stop' these 'movements'.[11] The target of this ire was now no longer the Ottoman, but the Mandatory state—reflecting both the slight lag in migration between Mount Lebanon and Jabal ʻAmil, and the frequent outward hostility of ʻAmili men of letters towards France's presence in the region. But the tropes remained essentially the same: dispossession, abuse and governmental inefficacy.

Ordinary ʻAmili migrants, too, told stories remarkably similar to those of their peers from Mount Lebanon. As the son of Mahmud Fakhri, who migrated to West Africa in the early twentieth century, recalls: 'my father did not feel at ease in his home village, Zrariyya. Lebanon was at that time under Turkish domination, and Shiites like my father didn't feel comfortable under the rule of the Turk.' To make matters worse, 'my father belonged to a family that dreamt of social ascension, but there was the oppression of the feudals, who had the support of the Turks'.[12] The local circumstances of the village, and the prosaic desire for social advancement, were recast in accounts like these into elements of a broader political struggle, as migrants and their descendents strove at once to give their journeyed lives a wider historical import, and to alleviate the guilt of leave-taking. This is not to suggest that these tales were entirely fictional, delusions pulled out of thin air. Rather, they were pragmatic adjustments of the past, useable histories that could serve as palliatives to the pains of displacement. Moving tales, in both senses of the word, they could offer both explanation and expiation.

The long peace

Such interpretations, which continue to offer comfort and relief to migrants' descendents, have also proved remarkably resilient in scholarly circles. Only in recent years have historians begun to redraw this bleak picture of late Ottoman rule, drawing upon the vast archival resources of the Porte to point to remarkably pliable and responsive patterns of provincial governance. Thus, Engin Akarlı has argued that the establishment of the autonomous district of Mount Lebanon, in the wake of the civil strife which tore through the mountain in the summer of 1860, ushered in a 'long peace' for the area—a period of unbroken tranquillity and relatively benign rule which lasted until the outbreak of war in 1914, and from which the Jabal emerged with an impressive administrative apparatus.[13] More recently, Akram Khater has striven to demolish what he regards as a pervasive 'myth' of persecution, peddled by previous generations of scholars and migrants concerned with crafting a distinctly Maronite sense of identity.[14] Migration, he suggests, was provoked by neither the exactions of the Ottoman government upon the Christian inhabitants of the Mountain, nor the abuses they suffered at the hands of their Druze and Muslim neighbours. Rather, it was the consequence of a concatenation of social and economic factors which began to come together in the 1880s—a full generation after the civil strife of 1860.

There is much to be said for this redrawn picture of life in the autonomous district of Mount Lebanon. While those who petitioned the Quai d'Orsay for reform of the Règlement Organique in 1912 drew a picture of a province crippled by an oppressive fiscal load, the inhabitants of the *mutasarrifiyya*, far from being taxed out of their homes, benefited from remarkable advantages. By 1910, when the male population had exceeded 200,000, personal tax was still being collected on the basis of the census of 1861, which had counted only 99,843 adult men. Moreover, the transport infrastructure—another source of frequent complaint—had in fact expanded considerably under the mountain's privileged regime. In 1861, there had been a mere 38 kilometres of road; by 1912, there were 1,104. The Russian consul in Beirut was not unjustified in pointing out in 1885 that, 'despite the many faults one can find in the Lebanese administration … one must admit that this administration has contributed in large degree to the improvement in the material and moral state of the population. … For the current administration has guaranteed for the Lebanese a greater measure of tranquillity and social security, and it has guaranteed individual rights.'[15] The lives of the young men and women who left behind the *mutasarrifiyya* in the 1890s and early 1900s were not, then, quite as bleak and desperate as scholars might once have argued.

Moreover, it seems the majority of these migrants were too young to have lived through the disorder of the middle decades of the nineteenth century—96 per cent of those who entered the United States from the 1880s onwards were forty or younger, and most did so from the late 1890s onwards.[16] Many—perhaps most—were born in the wake of the bitter, cruel, civil war of 1860.[17] They knew only the 'long peace' which prevailed in the wake of these clashes between Druze and Christian inhabitants of the Jabal, the culmination of a series of periodic outbreaks of violence which had troubled the Mountain since the early 1840s, and the end of the Shihabi order.[18]

It is clear these events could not have affected many migrants directly. However, we cannot discount entirely the part they played in leading Maronites from the Matn and the Shuf—or, for that matter, Greek Catholics from Zahleh and Greek Orthodox from Rashayya, where fighting was equally intense—to migrate. The young men and women who left the Jabal at the turn of the century were the children of the long peace. But, even so, they could not escape the shadow cast by the events of that year. The memories of their parents and neighbours, we could argue, were woven together into 'collective narratives of … loss', which were 'preserved', 'ritualised' and handed down.[19] In 1861, when the wounds of recent events were still raw, the ceremony of inauguration for Dawud Pasha, the *mutasarrif* of Mount Lebanon was 'more than once interrupted by the painful incident of a number of widows of Deir al-Kamar and other places where massacres were perpetrated making their appearance on the ground wailing and shrieking for their lost kindred and clamouring for vengeance on their murderers'. Others marked these events in quieter, but no less telling, ways. At the turn of century, some of those who had fled the Mountain and Damascus—where the Sunni population attacked the Christian quarters of the city—to settle in Beirut still dated events to 1860.[20] In 1889, the Ottoman consul in Barcelona, Yusuf Bey, complained of the Lebanese migrants 'wandering about in the streets of Marseille, Havre [sic], Barcelona and other French and Spanish cities begging for mercy and alms'. This 'crowd of men, women and children dressed in rags', he protested, were doing 'great harm … to our national image' with the 'ridiculous stories about the massacre of their wives and children' they told 'to increase the compassion' of their public.[21] Yusuf Bey was not entirely wrong. Lebanese migrants were not above drawing advantage of their own position as Eastern Christians to play upon the piety and pity of their clients. Many new arrivals to Mexico, claiming to be from the Holy Land, carried 'rosaries and crucifixes', religious trinkets they had purchased in the ports of Europe, and which they gradually replaced with 'pens, threads, knives and cloth', 'glass, hardware, … perfume and toys'.[22] However, these tales of violence might also be regarded as the distillation of enduring memories of the events of 1860—cast by Maronite historians as both an 'unusual event', a 'cataclysm' which disrupted ordinary 'communal coexistence', and a 'plot' instigated by those who 'sought to destroy Christianity in the Levant'.[23]

Moreover, the discombobulating disorder of the middle decades of the nineteenth century may have shaped the choices of those who migrated a generation later in another, significant, fashion. The unrest of these years provoked a growing flow of migrants towards Beirut, as those who could afford to do so—and, increasingly, those who could not—sought refuge from the uncertainty of mountain life. Beirut's population doubled between 1830 and 1850, before doing so again in the early 1860s. Some of the new arrivals were, to be sure, Muslim—merchants from 'Akka or Saida, or Egyptian soldiers and administrators who stayed behind after the departure of Ibrahim Pasha's occupying forces in 1840. Others were Greek Orthodox fleeing the massacres which ravaged the Christian quarters of Damascus in 1860. But many were Maronites from the mountain. In the 1830s they represented a mere 10 per cent of the town's inhabitants, but by 1860 this proportion had more than doubled to 21 per cent—a figure which remained constant until the 1920s.

Some chose to settle in Beirut for professional reasons, working as silk brokers or exporters. Many more, however, were compelled to leave the Mountain by successive outbreaks of violence. In 1840–41, and again in 1845, 'large numbers' of Maronites from the Shuf localities of Dair al-Qamar and 'Abay fled to Beirut in the wake of fighting with their Druze neighbours.[24] The Maronites of Mount Lebanon had long been a people on the move: as their numbers grew in the seventeenth and eighteenth centuries, they expanded ever further southwards from the regions around Qadisha and Jubail; called upon by Druze *mashayikh* to work their lands, some among them eventually settled in the Matn and the Shuf.[25] The displacements of the middle decades of the nineteenth century, in turn, helped to make migration—with all its disjunctures and adjustments—familiar again. They accustomed both migrants to Beirut, and those who remained in the villages of the mountain, to a life of remote contact—separated geographically from their kin, and yet bound by frequent visits, exchanges of commercial information, news and gossip, and resilient and often profound affective ties. Nevertheless, there remains a distinction between moving to Beirut—a city only a few hours away or days from even the most remote localities of the Mountain in the 1900s—and boarding a steamship in the hope of winding up, somehow, in the New World. Such a move entailed separation of a quite different order. What, then, compelled the inhabitants of the Jabal to migrate in such large numbers from the 1880s onwards? The answer lies, as Khater and others have argued, in the social and economic circumstances of the Mountain—and, most importantly, in the waxing and waning fortunes of silk.

Silken ties

This precious commodity had long been produced in Mount Lebanon. Since at least the seventeenth century, peasants had raised cocoons and cultivated the mulberry trees upon which silkworms fed on their lands, and weavers had unspooled the tightly woven coils of material in their workshops. But this sector was given a tremendous impetus by the growing number of European manufactures which opened in the Mountain from the late 1830s onwards. The French merchants Nicolas and Georges Portalis opened the first mechanised silk manufacture of the Mountain in 1838 in the Shuf village of Btatir. In 1841, the Englishman Scott founded a spinning factory in Shimlan, in the Gharb; around the same time, the Comte de la Ferté did the same at 'Ain Hamada in the Matn.[26]

By the early 1850s, there were some nine or ten spinning manufactures in foreign hands in these mountain districts.[27] Another four or five, meanwhile, belonged to local mercantile families like the Asfar and Sursuq.[28] The fortunes of these enterprises, regularly shaken by price fluctuations, were bolstered somewhat by the ravages the *pébrine* disease wrought among French suppliers of cocoons in the late 1840s and 1850s. The urgent need of the producers of Lyon, starved of their local sources, helped to inflate the price offered for cocoons in the silk market of Beirut. Spurred on by this sudden demand, the value of an *oka* shot up from an average of twelve Ottoman piastres in 1848—much the same as it had been twenty years earlier—to between twenty and twenty-four piastres in 1852; in 1857, it reached a high of forty-five piastres.[29]

Neither the recurrent disturbances of the 1850s nor the bloodletting of 1860 did much to arrest the expansion of silk manufacture. A British consular report written in 1861 noted the 'surprising progress in wealth, population, and general prosperity' of the Mountain. Indeed, if anything, the reconstruction of Christian-owned manufactures and spinning shops by soldiers of the French expeditionary force dispatched by Napoleon III, and the outlay of 'some £250,000' in charitable donations on 'new spinning and weaving equipment', helped in the infrastructural development of the silk industry.[30] The shortage of cotton provoked by the American Civil War, meanwhile, led to a marked increase in the value of silk during the 1860s. This, more than anything, favoured the rapid recovery, and considerable expansion, of the Mountain's silk production. Thus, the number of factories owned by local entrepreneurs rose from thirty-three in 1862 to forty-seven in 1867.[31] This expansion continued until the close of the century, relatively unaffected by regular fluctuations in local yields and prices on the international market. By 1893, there were 149 manufactures in local hands scattered through the *mutasarrifiyya* and the adjoining districts.[32]

The majority of these followed the lead set by French and British entrepreneurs like Portalis and Scott, opening their establishments in the Shuf and—especially—the Matn. The French consular official Gaston Ducousso estimated in 1913 that 113 of the 186 factories then in operation were situated in the latter region, and another thirty-one in the Shuf.[33] This choice was, in part, dictated by transport considerations—the Beirut-Damascus road and its offshoots, linking these mountain areas to the sea, had opened in the 1860s, making them more easily accessible than the regions of the Kisrwan, Batrun and Kura to the north of Beirut. However, while the populations of the Matn and Shuf were made up of Maronites, Greek Orthodox and Catholics, Druze and Sunni and Shi'a Muslims, all but a few of these factories—171, or nearly 92 per cent, of those in operation in 1913—were in Christian hands.[34] More significant still, the largely female workforce of the manufactures was overwhelmingly Maronite—8,500 of the 14,000 employed in 1913.[35] It is little surprise, then, that these factories were often clustered in largely or entirely Maronite localities like Mu'alaqa al-Damur in the Shuf, and Bait Shabab, Jurat al-Ballut, and Baskinta in the Matn.[36] The men of these villages, meanwhile, tended to their silkworm sheds and mulberry trees—seeking to satiate rising demand for cocoons both locally, among the swelling band of local manufacturers who set up shop in their villages, and in France. Ducousso estimated that annual production of cocoons throughout the Syrian provinces stood at 960 tonnes in 1861. Twenty years later, this had increased to 2,800 tonnes. In 1900, the agriculturalists of the *mutasarrifiyya* and the neighbouring *wilayat*, or provinces, produced 5,000 tonnes of cocoons.[37] That the Maronite *fallahin* of the Matn and the Shuf produced much of this explains in large part why members of this community were among the first to take the paths of migration.[38]

The sustained growth of these years made of silk in its various marketable forms—simple cocoons, raw textile or, more rarely, finished cloth—the single most important export product of the Mountain. Between 1836 and 1857, when the first manufactures were established, silk represented on average no more than 22 per cent of the total value of exports from Beirut. By 1873, 275 million of the 335 million Ottoman piastres of goods leaving the port came from silk—some 82.5 per cent of the total.[39]

The contrast could not be starker. On the eve of the First World War, when the silk economy had already begun to contract, the population of Mount Lebanon continued to draw from sericulture 80,000,000 piastres—or about 72 per cent of its total domestic revenues, according to the Ottoman administrator Ismail Haqqi Bey. This sum represented four times the amount brought in by other agricultural goods, and eight times that produced in artisan workshops and manufactures.[40] The importance of silk was only magnified in those areas of the Lebanese mountain where it was concentrated: in 1906, the inhabitants of the Maronite village of Dardurit earned 173,320 piastres from silk—fourteen times the 12,000 piastres they made from their olive oil.[41] By the later years of the nineteenth century, the peasants of the *mutasarrifiyya* were more caught up than ever in a silken web binding them to local producers—and, ultimately, to the manufactures and lending houses of Lyon, which supplied much of the capital swilling about the Lebanese mountain.[42] Around 165,000 people are estimated to have been involved in the care of mulberry trees and the raising of cocoons, while another 14,000 or so men, women and children were employed as spinners.[43] In 1913, it was thought that more than 40 per cent of the mountain's population earned its livelihood through silk.[44]

Such thoroughgoing engagement with the European economy brought apparent benefits to many cultivators, allowing them access to goods that had previously been the preserve of the wealthier *mashayikh*. Rice had long been considered a precious luxury—a 'king' among foods.[45] Its purchase was considered positively ruinous: as the proverb warned, 'better cover your arse than eat rice'.[46] Indeed, such was its scarcity that it was not even mentioned in French consular reports of the 1840s itemising imports to Beirut. This situation had changed drastically by 1888, when some 5 million kilograms passed through this port. Rice had been transformed, in the space of some fifty years, from a rare item whose consumption seemed the very height of profligacy into a foodstuff common enough for the French consul to remark in 1889 that 'the locals make daily use' of it.[47]

Moreover, this new affluence did more than simply allow those involved in the silk economy to satisfy old aspirations; it also reshaped expectations. The inhabitants of the Mountain had traditionally had little use for sugar, relying instead upon local sweeteners such as carob or grape molasses. Such was their reluctance to depart from these staples that it was mocked in proverbs—one claiming 'the fellah went down to the city and wanted nothing but *tahini* and molasses', preferring this rough rural dessert to the rich and sophisticated offerings of urban life. But the apparent prosperity of the second half of the nineteenth century created, it seems, a taste for conspicuous consumption of this hitherto insignificant item. As Akram Khater has noted, the quantity of sugar imported into Beirut more than tripled in the space of twenty years—jumping from 1.3 million kilograms in 1861, at the beginning of the silk boom, to 5 million in 1888, at its height. By then, per capita consumption of sugar stood at more than four kilograms each year.[48] This seems as much a matter of status as of taste: through their sweet tooth, mountain-dwellers sought to show off their improved station in the world.

32

Declining fortunes

However, this economic success rested upon rather flimsy foundations. The silk producers of Lyon began to import, from the mid-1870s onwards, growing quantities of silk from Japan and China—a trend which became increasingly marked in the 1890s.[49] This did not directly affect the quantity of silk they bought from the Eastern Mediterranean. Indeed, the share of Syrian silk used at Lyon only increased between the 1870s and 1914, from 3.9 per cent between 1873 and 1875 to 6.8 per cent between 1911 and 1915.[50] However, the growing importance of these new sources of supply in East Asia did dampen the price of silk on the world market. From a high of 105 francs per kilogram in 1872, the value of raw silk at Marseille collapsed to fifty-seven francs in 1875. After dipping to thirty-four francs in 1896, it rallied around the forty-franc mark for much of the 1900s.[51] This depression in prices affected, in turn, the markets of Beirut. There, silk had been traded at an average of thirty-nine piastres per *oka* in the years between 1866 and 1870. By 1911, this price had fallen by almost half to 20.2 piastres—lower than it had been in the early 1850s.[52]

The Lebanese silk sector was ill-equipped to deal with this steep fall in prices. Production was mired in inefficiency at every stage. Cocoons were still raised at the turn of the century in much the same fashion as they had been in the 1830s, by individual farmers in small sheds on their land.[53] Such methods made it extremely difficult to maintain stable conditions of production. As one observer noted in 1906, 'most … years the [silkworm] crop is not good because of the unsuitability of these [hatching] places that were generally very humid'.[54] Moreover, the conjunction in the late 1860s of swelling demand and silkworm disease which decimated local eggs led many to 'leave every year' for 'Egypt, Cyprus and Candi' in search of supplies. However, imported eggs—bred in quite different environmental conditions—could not provide yields similar to local sources. In 1854, 25 grams of local eggs produced nearly 54 kilograms of cocoons. In the 1880s, the same amount of Japanese eggs yielded a mere 29 kilograms. This figure had fallen further still to a slim average of 22.733 kilograms in the years between 1906 and 1911.[55] Such conditions conspired, as Ducousso observed bleakly, to produce one of the lowest silk yields anywhere in the world.[56]

The changing fortunes of Lebanese silk affected, in turn, the lifestyles of the *fallahin* who produced the bulk of local cocoons. It was not merely that falling prices at Beirut and Marseille trickled down to reduce their incomes. The affluence of the late nineteenth century was in large part fuelled by easily available credit. The brokers who coursed the Mountain, buying up silk from small producers, were 'inclined'—as Ducousso noted—'to advance peasants the little money that they might need at cxorbitant rates' of interest, which varied between 36 per cent and 60 per cent.[57] These men provided—at interest—a cash advance to agriculturalists at the beginning of the year, before buying up their crops at a fraction of their real value.[58] Peasants were little helped by their growing neglect of subsistence crops like wheat and lentils in favour of mulberry trees, which had little use other than as fodder for silkworms.

At the beginning of the nineteenth century, the number of these trees in Mount Lebanon stood at around 3.3 million. Some eighty years later, there were some twenty-eight million in the *mutasarrifiyya*, and a further nine million in the *wilaya* of Beirut.[59] By 1890s, mulberry trees occupied around half of the available land in the Mountain.[60]

Such choices pulled peasants deeper into the market, exacerbating the effect of the falling value of silk on local and French markets. Moreover, their reliance on credit meant that while they were able in good years to allow themselves expenses which had previously been beyond their reach, in bad years they fell only further into debt, struggling to hold on to their lands.[61] The collapse in prices from the mid-1870s onwards resulted, it seems, in a significant contraction of credit. Its effects were deeply felt in the latter half of that decade, as a series of poor silk crops in 1876, 1877 and 1879 coincided with a sharp fall in the value of the bonds in the Ottoman public debt held by many of the Beiruti bankers and merchants who supplied credit to the manufacturers and brokers of the Mountain—this brief commercial crisis forced some silk factories to close temporarily for lack of funds.[62] A drastic reduction in land prices, meanwhile, forced many who had purchased plots on borrowed money to sell these on at a loss.[63]

It is interesting that the first few hundred migrants to leave the Jabal did so in the late 1870s and early 1880s—perhaps spurred on by the worsening condition of the regional economy. However, these early migrants did not take the paths of the *mahjar* because of poverty and deprivation. Migration, it should be remembered, was an expensive undertaking. Akram Khater has estimated that nearly 2,500 piastres were needed to make it to Ellis Island or Santos—a sum equivalent to the annual salary of a policeman. As such, migration lay beyond the reach of the bankrupt and destitute; for the latter lacked not only the necessary wherewithal, but also the social capital needed to obtain sufficient credit from commercial brokers or fellow villagers willing to lend on interest. Those who left, as Khater has argued, were 'not seeking financial salvation, but rather financial amelioration'.[64] They searched not to escape ruin, but to maintain the credit-fuelled lifestyles to which the inhabitants of the Jabal had become accustomed, and to elude the growing economic insecurity of the 1880s and 1890s.

Indeed, it seems the regular fluctuations in the value of silk gradually wore down the patience of peasants. There thus appears to be a relationship between dips in the price of silk and hikes in the number of migrants. In 1885, the value of an *oka* of fresh cocoons fell from 26.5 piastres to 23.5 before rising sharply to thirty piastres in 1886, and slipping downwards again to twenty-four piastres in 1887. It is interesting that migration seems to have picked up sharply that year. We might speculate that while a hurtful fall in prices in 1885 encouraged silk cultivators to seek alternative livelihoods, the boon of a good harvest the following season gave them the means to do so. This seems to be borne out by an examination of patterns of migration in the 1890s and 1900s. The price of silk sank in the mid-1890s, stagnating at an average of eighteen piastres between 1892 and 1897, before rallying again to between twenty-four and twenty-eight piastres in 1898.[65] And, concomitantly, the rate of migration shot up: in 1896, it was estimated that 5,500 Lebanese had boarded steamships headed for the ports of Europe in Beirut; by 1899 this number had risen to 13,000.[66]

More generally, a moderate rally in silk prices in the 1900s, after the stagnation of the 1890s, was accompanied by a sharp rise in the number of those leaving the *mutasarrifiyya*. In 1899, 8,727 Ottoman subjects had entered Brazil, Argentina and the United States; 14,796 did so in 1907.[67] This change is reflected, too, in the statistics Desbordes assembled on Lebanese migration to AOF. He could find traces of only eighteen men in Guinea in 1897. Ten years later their numbers had swollen to 477.[68] If anything, these figures—though far smaller than those for the United States and Latin America—provide a clearer picture of the motives driving migration from the *mutasarrifiyya*. While the immigration departments of these states failed to distinguish between those entering from Jabal Lubnan and the neighbouring *wilayat*, most of those who found their way to Guinea in these years were from the Matn village of Bait Shabab. Situated at the very epicentre of the silk economy, this Maronite locality depended heavily upon sericulture: around it were clustered no fewer than five factories, ranging in size from the large concern of Shaykh As'ad Tubia, with its hundred basins, to that of 'Abduh Murad al-Fakhuri, with a mere ten.[69] Much the same conclusions can be drawn from observing migration from 'Akkar. Its Greek Orthodox and Maronite villages, like Bainu and Rahbe, produced some 80 per cent of the region's silk.[70] And only the inhabitants of these localities had both the urge, and the means, to migrate, beginning to head for West Africa just before the First World War.

Silk, then, was central to the decisions of many inhabitants of the Jabal and its surrounds to migrate. The French consul De Sercey asserted in 1903 that around 55,000 of the 80,000 who had left the *mutasarrifiyya* since 1888—some 69 per cent—were Maronite, 15 per cent or 12,000 were Orthodox, 11 per cent or 9,000 Greek Catholic and a mere 5 per cent or 4,000 Druze and Shi'a.[71] These numbers—rough though they are—fit neatly with the confessional distribution of employees in the silk factories of the Mountain: of these women, 60.72 per cent were Maronite, 17.85 per cent Greek Orthodox, 14.28 per cent Greek Catholic and 7.14 per cent Druze, figures which reflected the involvement of these various confessional communities as a whole in sericulture.[72]

Scarce land

However, it was not alone in determining their choices. Severe demographic pressures only exacerbated the effects of this downturn. The population of Mount Lebanon had increased from 120,000 to 200,000 between 1783 and 1860—growing by two-thirds in the space of seventy-seven years. In 1913, by contrast, around 414,800 individuals dwelt in the *mutasarrifiyya*, while another 155,600 or so of its inhabitants had left for the *mahjar*.[73] The years of the 'long peace', then, witnessed an increase in population of 185 per cent. This formidable demographic growth was not matched by any concomitant expansion in the availability of land, always a scarce commodity in the Jabal, with its narrow agricultural terraces carved into the mountainside. The Ottoman census of 1864 had found that 125,238 *dunum* of land were under cultivation—some 175,586 acres. In 1918, the figure stood at 140,000 *dunum*—an increase of barely 12 per cent.[74] As De Sercey put it in 1903, 'The era of calm and security which followed, from 1860 onwards, in the wake of almost uninterrupted agitations, has had two effects: first of all, the development of the entire country—there is not an inch capable of being planted which has not been claimed for cultivation—and, secondly, a constant augmentation of the population, which has gradually outgrown its narrow, unproductive territory.'[75] The effects of the demographic squeeze which affected Mount Lebanon in the years before 1914 were clear: there was, quite simply, not enough land to go round.

More than that, ownership was increasingly fragmented. Both Druze and Christians favoured inheritance practices which divided the land of the father equally among his children—or, in the case of Christians, his boys. As a consequence, individual shares grew smaller and smaller as population continued to grow. 'Abdallah Sa'id has found that in the Matn village of 'Ain Qinya, around eighteen *dunum* of private agricultural land were shared out between twenty-one family units.[76] This situation was little helped by the strong demand for silk, which led owners to turn increasingly to *mugharasa* and *musaqat*—contractual arrangements by which they handed a share of their land to labourers in return for their work in planting and maintaining mulberry trees.[77] These practices, we might speculate, disproportionately affected Maronite inhabitants of the Mountain. Not only were they involved to a far greater extent in the production of silk than their Druze neighbours; they also reproduced at a greater rate. Already, in 1847, the French consul had estimated that the average Maronite family had 6.2 children. By contrast, the norm among Druze was 4.6 children.[78] By the 1890s, land had become so scarce that 'it had got the point where what was divided among the heirs was no longer a piece of land but the thick branches of mulberry trees ... and the olive tree crop'.[79]

This alienation from the land was too much to stomach for many male *fallahin*. Honour, for these men, was understood to hang upon both the *'ard*—the good behaviour and unblemished reputation of their female relations—and the *ard*, the land they worked. Some—probably the poorest—were prepared to forsake the good standing of their wives and daughters, allowing them to work as spinners in the silk factories in order to retain their own ties to the land, upon which depended their 'immediate and individual honour'.[80] However, losing their land, and the sense of worth they derived from its cultivation, was—it might be argued—a step too far for many. While a few thousands chose to work as servants in the bourgeois homes of Beirut, or to find employment in the *mutasarrifiyya*'s *gendarmerie*, these options seem to have held no great attraction for the men of the Mountain, for they entailed a separation from their land—and, in the case of domestic service, a sense of debasement. By contrast, migration offered a means of gaining a livelihood without losing face. As one inhabitant of the Greek Catholic town of Zahleh who had migrated to the United States put it:

The Zahlehwi won't work at a job that he thinks is beneath him ... Over there [in the *mahjar*], he lost this pride in order to make money and because no one knew him. His pride came first. What mattered most was how he saw himself in the eyes of his townsmen. In America, he would shine shoes, but not here—not if he was starving.[81]

Migration to the United States, Latin America or West Africa not only carried less stigma than work as an agricultural labourer or domestic servant, it also made greater economic sense, offering far greater promise of holding on to—or reclaiming—one's status through purchasing property in the home village. As news of the riches to be made in the United States or Africa filtered back in letters sent by those few who had departed in the late 1870s and 1880s, more and more young men were drawn to take the ways of the *mahjar*. Michel Hadi remembered that in 1892—the year of his departure—'not many people were going to America' from his village of 'Ayn 'Arab on the foothills of Mount Hermon. Then, one day a family 'wrote back ... [to say] they made $1000 [in three years] ... When people ... saw that ... all of 'Ayn 'Arab rushed to come to America ... like a gold rush we left ..., there were 72 of us.'[82] More convincing still were the migrants who came back to the village with their 'western suits, leather shoes and gold watch fobs', and their homespun tales of fantastical wealth.[83] One woman who migrated to the United States remembered: 'well, I had no picture of America ... But my aunt had already been there and she made a lot of money peddling and she went back for a visit. Ho! She was dressed and fixed and what ... silk and ostrich feathers and diamonds and a watch pinned to her chest ... Oh she came back and she had the money.'[84] Many were those who returned for a short visit to their hometowns or villages and left again with brother, cousins or friends in tow—their ostentatious displays of wealth helping to make of migration an increasingly attractive proposition.

But such returning migrants were not the only ones to entice young villagers to take the ways of migration. A veritable 'emigration industry' had rapidly emerged to capitalise upon the desires of these men and women, as shipping agents and brokers, bondholders and moneylenders, muleteers and rowers and smugglers, hostel keepers and frippery merchants sought to cater to their needs and channel their movements.[85] As early as 1889, the Ottoman consul in Barcelona, Yusuf Bey, had uncovered the existence of a vast illicit people-carrying network. Based in Tripoli, its tentacles stretched both inwards to the Lebanese mountain, and abroad towards Marseille, Bordeaux and Le Havre. Its agents, touring the villages of Mount Lebanon and the province of Beirut, not only found steamship tickets for willing migrants, but also made all the arrangements needed to bypass Ottoman port officials and ship inspectors at a time when emigration remained illegal, often smuggling passengers crowded into small rowing boats to ships waiting off shore.[86]

The *simsar*—or migration agent—had, by the early 1900s, become a familiar sight throughout much of the *mutasarrifiyya* and the neighbouring *wilaya* of Beirut. As a crowd gathered round in the village square, these men would tell 'of the wonderful way to make money, where to go, what to do, in fact everything necessary for the emigrant to know'. Indeed, many had themselves sojourned for a spell in the United States or Latin America. They could claim to speak with authority of the *mahjar*, and show off the accoutrements bought with the wealth one might well acquire there—as other returnees could. Moreover, these brokers, who often in the employ of shipping lines like the Messageries Maritimes, also knew of the comings and goings of ships at Beirut and Tripoli, and of the constantly shifting conditions of migration to this or that destination—the epidemics which had broken out in port, the intro- duction of a new requirement or the increase in a deposit. Such talk was evidently persuasive: as a Presbyterian missionary noted in 1906, 'it is a poor day when [the agent] does not obtain a number of deposits for steamer tickets'.[87] Migration, by the early twentieth century, not only offered the promise of improving one's station for those who undertook the long journey to New York or Buenos Aires; it had also become big business.

Returns

As the 1900s wore on, and returning migrants pulled constantly growing numbers in their wake, the Mountain's economy came to rely ever more heavily upon these young men and women. Migration not only provided opportunities for enrichment and betterment for those who had themselves taken the paths of the *mahjar*, but also an increasingly important source of wherewithal for those who stayed behind. British consular reports of the early 1890s had put the money transfers sent to Mount Lebanon by migrants at between ten and twelve million piastres a year. By 1913, the amount entering the *mutasarrifiyya* had increased to between fifty and seventy-five million piastres. The German Zionist emissary Arthur Ruppin went further still, estimating that remittances supplied the inhabitants of the Mountain with ninety million piastres of their income on the eve of the First World War.[88]

Moreover, these flows of money were accompanied, in the years before 1914, by swelling numbers of migrants returning from the *mahjar* with thoughts of settling back into village life. Many—if not most—of those who left the Mountain in the 1890s and 1900s hoped to return after a few years, having amassed enough capital to buy some land and build upon it. Migration was not so much a means of making a new life elsewhere as a chance to improve one's station back at home in the Jabal. By no means all migrants were able—or willing—to return. Nevertheless, figures from the United States Immigration Commission put the rate of 'Syrian' migrants leaving America at 26 per cent between 1908 and 1910.[89] Ruppin, meanwhile, asserted that anywhere from a third to a half of those who had left the Mountain 'returned to their homeland as soon as they have saved enough money'—using the '10,000 to 20,000 francs' they had accumulated in 'five to ten years' in the *mahjar* to purchase a property.[90] As they fulfilled their ambitions, and others built houses with remittances or money their relatives had left before returning abroad, migration began to leave a perceptible mark upon the Mountain. In 1894, the Scottish missionary Dr Carslaw reported that 'houses were having the old clay roofs taken off, and new roofs of Marseilles tiles put on'—'eighteen years' earlier, when only a brace of migrants had left Jabal Lubnan, 'there was not a tiled roof in the whole district'. By 1903, 'a village in the most remote parts of the Lebanon … has … at least 2 or 3 new houses with tiled roofs and … even whole villages have been thus constructed'.[91] These 'American home[s]', as they came to be known, were a permanent reminder of the wealth to be made through migration. However, they also served to thicken the ranks of those leaving in another, more insidious, way. The land purchases made by migrants and their relatives, flush with wealth sent from the *mahjar*, only pushed up further already inflated land prices. In 1903, the French consul de Sercey reported that the appetite of returning migrants for property had led to its value increasing fivefold.[92] By 1916, a *fiddan* of *mutasarrifiyya* land planted with mulberry trees would cost 4,000 francs—twice its price in the environs of Tripoli, in the *wilaya* of Beirut.[93] Such high prices effectively narrowed the chances of acquiring land—and status—for those who had resisted the lure of the *mahjar*.

By 1914, there were signs that migration was taking on the role silk had once played as an avenue of social mobility. The latter still provided the bulk of the domestic earnings of the *mutasarrifiyya* in 1913. However, the sums remitted by migrants had, by this stage, come to rival in importance sericulture as a source of income. Moreover, growing numbers of the Mountain's inhabitants were beginning to abandon their cocoon sheds and spinning wheels. In 1907, an official at the French Ministry of Commerce estimated that only 115 of the 174 mills dotted about the Mountain were still in operation.[94] Then, in 1910, a British report observed that peasants in some areas had begun to uproot their mulberry trees, planting orange orchards in their stead.[95] By 1914, migration had become a thoroughly familiar economic strategy. More than this, it was probably the most tempting means of improving one's financial situation and standing for the inhabitants of the Mountain.

The war and its long wake

The outbreak of global conflict in late 1914 abruptly cut off this road to social mobility. While some 16,739 left through the port of Beirut in 1913–1914, this figure dropped by almost two-thirds to 6,109 in 1914–1915.[96] What is more, it seems likely most of these departures occurred in the early part of 1914, before the beginning of hostilities. Certainly, by 1915 the imposition of a seemingly impermeable blockade by the Entente powers had brought traffic through Beirut and other Eastern Mediterranean ports to an absolute standstill. Its effects upon Bilad al-Sham—and Mount Lebanon in particular—were to prove cataclysmic. Not only did the blockade curtail migration and disrupt the flow of remittances upon which so many in the Jabal had come to depend. Fatally, by severing the Eastern Mediterranean seaboard from external sources of grain, it served only to exacerbate growing shortages of food throughout the Syrian provinces provoked by poor harvests in 1915 and 1916, the diversion of available supplies towards the war effort, widespread profiteering and the decision of the provincial governor Jamal Pasha to ban all movement of grain to the coast and to collect in kind all taxes in the grain-producing regions of the Hawran and the Biqa' in 1915—a measure which led to further hoarding and price hikes.[97]

By 1916, this confluence of factors had led to widespread famine. Nowhere, it seems, were its effects more disastrous than in the *wilaya* of Beirut and, in particular, the *mutasarrifiyya*. Heavily dependent upon external supplies of grain—in part because land once used for growing cereals had long since been given over to silk and other cash crops—these areas were effectively starved of all sources of food. Even those smugglers who had brought grain from the Hawran were no longer able to do so in 1916, because of the heavy snowfall that year, which made their mountain tracks impassable.[98] The few able to escape to Cairo that year described scenes of utter desperation: people ate what they could, picking up 'orange and lemon peel' from the streets, or 'went out into the fields and picked weeds and other green stuff that sprouted up, in a desperate attempt to keep body and soul together'.[99] The Turkish feminist Halide Edib, then running orphanages in Lebanon, recalled the ghoulish cries for hunger she often heard echoing through the streets of Beirut that year, 'piercing and insistent and cutting the air like a knife'. The American consul, still taking his 'early evening walks' that summer, recorded the streets 'filled with starving women and children', the gutters strewn with dead bodies.[100] The situation was worse still in the *mutasarrifiyya*: in 1916, British secret agents stationed in the Mountain estimated that 80,000 had already died in Jubail and the Kisrwan; conditions in the Shuf, to the south of Beirut, were no better. The complete breakdown of food supplies in 1917–1918 only exacerbated an already dire situation. By the end of hostilities, some 500,000 had lost their lives across Bilad al-Sham—200,000 died in Mount Lebanon alone.[101]

The effects of the *safarbarlik* (as the famine came to be known after the Turkish term for 'travel by land', or internal exile, a semantic slippage which highlighted its connection in peoples' minds to the exactions of military administration) continued to reverberate through the interwar period. The immense privation of the war years led, as Elizabeth Thompson has argued, to a 'crisis of paternity'. During the famine, men whose sense of self rested upon their capacity to protect and provide for their families were unable to do so—their memories were not only of harrowing suffering, but also of a 'world gone awry' in which 'gender roles' were suddenly thrown into disarray.[102] Migration, it might be argued, presented one means of establishing themselves anew as patriarchs capable of feeding their families.

Moreover, the famine had 'shattered' 'family networks', making 'female-headed households'—already more common in Mount Lebanon than other places because of the high incidence of male migration in the pre-war years—all the more widespread.[103] This placed new pressure on both women and their children to find new means of earning a livelihood. Nadra Filfili, who migrated to Senegal in 1923, recalled the effect the death of his father in 1919 had upon his family. Filfili, still only sixteen and studying for a secondary diploma at a local missionary school, found himself forced to work as a waiter in the teachers' dining room to support himself. As the value of the crops harvested from his father's lands—a large holding of 125 hectares, which his family had once exploited in conjunction with sharecroppers—continued to wane, Nadra put aside thoughts of taking over this estate or continuing his studies to embark upon the 'adventure' of migration.[104]

How, Filfili asked some fifty years later, could he have done otherwise, finding a means of supporting his studies at a time when a 'single suit' cost the 'equivalent' of 'THIRTY FIVE sacks of barley'? Indeed, he recalled, he was not alone in facing such a predicament: all across Lebanon 'those who planted or exercised crafts worked, but they lacked a sense of control over their own lives and futures, while professionals turned around in circles, finding no way of expanding their clientele'.[105] Filfili was not wrong. It seems life for many—especially in rural areas like his native Kura, the Matn or Jabal 'Amil—remained difficult and devoid of opportunities throughout the interwar years.

This was, in part, a consequence of the process of economic disengagement between various parts of the world which began in the wake of the First World War. The terminal decline of the silk industry, once so central to the livelihoods of Mount Lebanon's inhabitants, was but one manifestation of this process of 'deglobalisation'.[106] It is a sad, but telling, irony that while the industrialists of Lyon had petitioned for French control of Lebanon because of their ties to its silk factories, Lebanese silk represented only 2.4 per cent of Lyonnais supply in 1924—less than half what it had been before 1914.[107] Production did pick up somewhat in the late 1920s and 1930s. In 1927–1928, the factories of the Mountain turned out some 330,000 kilograms of raw silk—around 75 per cent of their pre-war average.[108] But this revival was short-lived. By 1932, production of cocoons had collapsed again—hard-hit by the Depression and the growing protectionism it brought in its wake, but also by ever-growing competition from cheap Japanese and Chinese silk and the advent of synthetic rayon. Most factories closed their doors in the wake of renewed economic crisis—by the end of the decade, there remained only a handful in the Matn and the Shuf.[109] Moreover, silk was—as Filfili discerned—far from the only sector to be affected by the poor economic conditions of the 1920s and 1930s. Jacques Couland has estimated that the purchasing power of wages fell in Lebanon by a full 100 per cent between 1913 and 1937.[110]

Such circumstances may well have made many wish to migrate in search of more secure livelihoods. However, economic precariousness and falling standards of living, even as they created a desire for migration, made this enterprise—always expensive—all the more difficult. It is noticeable that—as in the 1890s and 1900s—periods of relative clemency, during which wages picked up and credit became more readily available, were accompanied by an upswing in migration, while the number of migrants fell away in difficult years. Between 1923 and 1926, an average of 7,779 people migrated each year from Greater Lebanon. By contrast, the deep depression of the early 1930s had a drastic effect upon this flow: a mere 1,171 left in 1932.[111] More telling still, the 'economic revival' of the late 1930s, brought on by better harvests and—significantly—by the devaluation of the French franc, was accompanied by a lurch upwards in the number of migrants towards AOF.[112] In the first ten months of 1937, 998 migrants from the Mandatory states disembarked in Dakar; November alone brought 301 more. This increase, commented one administrator, was not merely the consequence of 'the propaganda' conducted 'during their holidays by Lebanese and Syrian traders settled in Senegal, where the economic situation of the last few years has allowed them to make important profits'. Currency devaluation had also made migration more feasible: while 29 gold *livres* had once been needed to cover travel costs and the payment of a guarantee upon arrival, this amount had more than halved, by 1937, to 14 gold *livres*.[113] It seems, then, that more favourable economic conditions spurred migration, allowing people to embark on what had become a thoroughly familiar route to social mobility.

Indeed, the markedly lower rate of migration from Greater Lebanon over the entire interwar period can be explained not only—as it usually is—by decreasing opportunities and more stringent controls upon entry in the United States and Latin America, but also by the high cost of life in the Mandatory states of Lebanon and Syria, which put this undertaking beyond the reach of many. While 'young men without work, cultivators fearing hunger, [and] commercial workers fired because of the slump' may well have wished to go abroad, it is by no means clear all were able to do so.[114] Robert Widmer was not mistaken when he noted, in the mid-1930s, that 'a large proportion of emigration' from Lebanon was still 'motivated by a laudable ambition for more of the better things in life rather than by a lack of actual necessities'—if only because those suffering from real deprivation could ill afford such an onerous undertaking.[115] Those who went away, it is clear, were not compelled to do so; they chose 'the ways of flight'.[116] And, crucially, they were able to make this choice, possessing the capacity to cobble together savings or contributions from relatives, to sell land or to gain access to credit, but not the means or inclination to 'improve their mode of living' in Lebanon itself.[117]

Market towns and middling men

This was, perhaps, all the more true of the migrants of Jabal 'Amil. It is not that few migrated from this region. The census of 1921, despite systematic inconsistencies and under-counting, put the number of migrants from the *qada*, or district, of Sur at 6,254—15 per cent of a total population of 41,294.[118] This proportion was not much lower than that of those leaving Mount Lebanon: by de Sercey's 1903 estimate, some 80,000 had left since the early 1890s, a fifth of its estimated population of 400,000.[119] But, despite appearances, migration remained the purview of the few. It was restricted, to a far greater extent than in Mount Lebanon, to certain localities and social groups. Those who headed for West Africa thus hailed from a small number of places: most important of all, Sur, which accounted alone for 671 of the 'Amilis living in AOF in 1936; but also Qana, with 243; Nabatiyya, with 237; Juwayya, with 192; Kfar Huna, with 165; and Zrariyya, with 109.[120] To this list, we might add

Tibnin and Bint Jubail, whose migrants clustered in Sierra Leone. Perhaps most significantly, the inhabitants—or erstwhile inhabitants—of these places all had gained significant exposure to both movement and the market.

It is perhaps no coincidence that those who first migrated towards West Africa were those who had the greatest experience of these dislocating forces: the Greek Catholic and Maronite inhabitants of Sur. Not only had their forebears, like their coreligionists in other localities throughout the Syrian lands, begun to move towards Egypt in the eighteenth century, establishing commercial ties with Damietta, Alexandria, and Cairo which would endure long into the twentieth.[121] Furthermore, this was but another leg in a long series of journeys for these families, whose genealogies were reminders of their constant mobility. The Thabits, for instance, originally hailed from 'Aqura, in the northern marches of Mount Lebanon, before some members moved to Damascus and, some 'four and a half centuries ago', split into branches scattered through Beirut, Dair al-Qamar in the Shuf, Dair al-Ahmar in the Biqa', Bhamdun and Sur. The Salims, meanwhile, had arrived in Sur from Acre, though some claimed they originally hailed from Aleppo.[122] Through their 'noteworthy' involvement in trade, these families remained in 'constant interaction with their coreligionists in Beirut, Saida, and Mount Lebanon', contacts which would have made them aware of the swirling mass of movement enveloping the surrounding regions. Moreover, their activities allowed some to learn the 'foreign tongues' so useful in commercial interchange, and to lead the 'most sophisticated' of domestic lives. It may have been to protect these 'lifestyles', painstakingly acquired over generations of mobility,[123] that some sent their kin to West Africa, as their hometown sunk ever further into commercial insignificance, bypassed even by the few Ottoman and British schooners that still stopped at its northern neighbour Saida to collect oranges, olive oil and silk cocoons they carried on to Istanbul and the Ionian Islands, Egypt, Odessa and France.[124]

However, the Christian inhabitants of Sur were exceptional neither in their propensity for movement, nor in their taste for the profits of the market. Craftsmen like the shoemakers of Bint Jubail, renowned for their expertise, had long criss-crossed the Hawran, the Golan, Jordan and Galilee, plying their trade, sometimes settling in these regions for long stretches.[125] Even the cultivators of Zrariyya, in the 1920s one of the most important new sources of migration to West Africa, were not suddenly wrenched from the stagnation of rural life into trans-oceanic movement. On the contrary, movement had long marked their lives, in good years as in bad: when they had enough produce to sell, they travelled to Nabatiyya, Marj 'Ayun or the Galilee to do so; when the crops failed, they sought out labour in Palestine.[126] Towns like Bint Jubail, Nabatiyya and, to a lesser extent, Juwayya and Tibnin were all hosts to weekly markets which sold 'all kinds of goods, from various types of cloth, to seeds and animals and poultry and fowl, vegetables, salads, and fruits, and ploughs and buckets and jugs and tractors'. These drew in crowds from 'across Jabal 'Amil and its villages, and from the adjoining regions like the country of Safad and the coast of Acre, the Hula, the Golan, the Wadi al-Taim, and the Biqa', and others still'.[127]

Mustering together some 10,400 inhabitants in the years before the First World War,[128] the twin towns of Nabatiyya al-Fawqa and Nabatiyya al-Tahta—or upper and lower Nabatiyya—were not only the largest of these localities, but also the site of the most sizeable of such gatherings, which attracted in the last decades of Ottoman rule 'some five to six thousand' sellers and buyers every Monday, who travelled from 'twelve hours' distance'.[129]

As Mounzer Jaber and Souha Tarraf-Najib have argued, localities like these became 'nerve centres' for the new spatial organisation of Jabal 'Amil, in which the region was incorporated into Beirut's economic sphere of influence. Serving as points of transit, they were nodes for the diffusion of manufactured goods brought into the region by the *wukala'* and *makariyya*, the 'agents' and 'muleteers' who proliferated from the 1880s onwards, and the collection of its wheat and tobacco cash crops.[130] Even in the 1920s, when Nabatiyya had been 'hit by [a] recession … which particularly affected commerce, the only support of its inhabitants'—a situation only aggravated by the imposition of 'customs barriers between Lebanon and Palestine', which nullified the advantages it had gained from 'its location at the junction between southern Lebanon, Syria, and Palestine'—its annual trade was still worth 'no less than a million Syrian pounds'. These, again, were apposite conditions for migration: shrinking opportunities, which served as an incentive, and a measure of prosperity, which provided the means. It was no surprise that, by the interwar years, 'exile' had begun to 'deprive' the town of its 'active hands'.[131] Indeed, circulation through the regions of the Eastern Mediterranean seaboard, and migration 'beyond the seas' were tightly interconnected, 'steps' along the same path.[132] Mahmud Fakhri, who left Zrariyya in 1907, had abandoned agriculture when still a boy to give himself over to commerce. Carrying on the transit 'trade between the village and the town', he became a transporter with his own small drove of donkeys.[133] Though his departure from Jabal 'Amil was in one sense a sharp rupture, in another it marked an underlying continuity in his activities.

It is clear that many 'Amili migrants were a far cry from the simple peasant of popular imagination. To be sure, some cultivators did migrate, like those of Zrariyya. But even these often hailed from the wealthier portions of such villages. For life in at least some localities in Jabal 'Amil differed sharply from the plain picture contemporary observers like Jean Donon and Marxist historians like Farhan Salih painted of an undifferentiated peasantry of *'ujara'*, or hired hands, entirely in hock to the small band of large landowners whose 'latifundia' they worked.[134] There is no doubt that mercantile families like the Zain or Sulh, and *zu'ama'*, or rural powerholders, like the As'ad clan, were able to siphon off a sizeable portion of the gains of the cereal trade. However, the dominant position they held in the 1970s, when they controlled all available land in 36 per cent of 'Amili villages, was not the sign of a region mired in age-old feudalism—as some, like Salih, would argue—but the product of the fundamental redrawing of social and economic relations caused by the introduction of cash-crop cultivation, which allowed them to consolidate their existing holdings. A locality like Zrariyya was marked by sharp internal differentiation; on the one hand stood the landless, who survived on loans strung out from one harvest to the next, on the other their wealthier counterparts. Migration only accentuated such divisions, for it not only provided those who had left with the means to buy up significant quantities of land, capitalising on the need of the As'ad for ready cash to plough into their political undertakings in Beirut; it also induced them to accept bourgeois prescriptions which urged them to become *malakin*, or 'owners', in their own right.[135]

Other migrants, meanwhile, were of markedly different stock. Men like 'Ali As'ad, Hasan Shams al-Din or Husain 'Usairan, who migrated to AOF in the 1920s, belonged not to the *'amma*, the ordinary people, but to the *khassa*, families distinguished from the undifferentiated mass by religious charisma, temporal power or wealth. It seems likely the first of these men was a member of the As'ad clan—still in these years the most powerful political force in Jabal 'Amil, despite the challenge posed to its standing by the emergence in the second half of the nineteenth century of the *wujaha'*, urban merchants who used their wealth to secure positions in the Ottoman bureaucracy and political influence. Indeed, the third of these men, Husain 'Usairan was himself a *wajih*, belonging to a Shi'a family which had risen to prominence thanks to its commercial activities and hereditary possession of the Persian consulship in Saida. Hasan Shams al-Din, meanwhile, belonged to a *bait al-'ilm*—a 'house of learning', which derived influence from its long lineage and tradition of religious scholarship.[136] These men do not seem to have belonged to the main branches of these families. Nevertheless, it might be argued that their standing and associations made them more likely than their neighbours and acolytes in Dakar—men of the *'amma* like Haidar Taha—to have at their fingertips the funds or credit necessary for migration.

Conclusion

I have sought to account here for the two central streams of Lebanese migration to AOF in the years between 1898 and 1939. The Matni men and women who flocked to Conakry and its hinterland in the years before 1914—and who continued to dominate the Lebanese population of Guinea, French Soudan and Côte d'Ivoire well into the interwar period—were members of the great waves of migration from Mount Lebanon. As the fortunes of sericulture began to decline, they increasingly sought abroad means of holding on to their newfound material comforts or acquiring a measure of social mobility. 'Amili migrants, meanwhile, were drawn from different stock: many hailed from large market towns and ports, localities affected by shifting conditions in trade, but whose denizens retained sufficient capital or credit to undertake the onerous trip to Africa. Moreover, many hailed from families endowed with considerable wealth and social standing, attributes they hoped to reproduce through migration, while others found in such journeys a means of effecting dramatic social mobility. This, then, is a tale of two mountains—of their differences, but also their similarities.

·

2

ROOTS AND ROUTES

THE PATHS OF LEBANESE MIGRATION

It has long since become a commonplace of migration studies that ties of kin and place—those familiar 'structures of feeling'—helped to lay down networks and circuits of movement, of cyclical travel and return migration which drew men and women towards new locales. Driven by their desire to disrupt the Crèvecoeurian narratives of uprooting and assimilation propounded by scholars like Robert Park and Oscar Handlin,[1] who stressed the strenuous efforts of atomised individuals to melt into their host society, historians and sociologists like Donna Gabaccia, Rudolph Vecoli and Charles Tilly uncovered the ways in which migration was a collective undertaking—and one often directed towards the reconstitution of familiar surroundings through chain migration and marriage strategies.[2] This tendency has, in turn, manifested itself more strongly still in the work of scholars who have sought to uncover the history of Eastern Mediterranean migration towards the United States.[3] For the latter have been influenced not only by the enjoinments of historians of Italian-American life like Vecoli and Gabaccia, but also by the strong stress anthropologists and historians of the Eastern Mediterranean have long put on the importance of kin, locality and confession—the holy trinity of 'land, people and religion' binding the community together.[4]

However, these aspects of quotidian life were not universal prescriptions, understood and implemented in the same way by all—'neat little box-like arrangements of non-contradictory categories and unproblematic behaviours', as Marshall Sahlins has put it—but constantly open to interpretation, contestation and manipulation.[5] 'Family, village, and religion' did frequently provide 'the markings of [migrants'] communities', as Akram Khater has argued.[6] But they did not always do so in straightforward ways. While family relations and marriage alliances did help to draw migrants from Mount Lebanon towards West Africa, they did not simply serve as blueprints for the reconstruction of familiar communities. And nor were they the sole determinants of an individual's decision to migrate and choice of destination. Rather, as I will argue here, a complex concatenation of factors pulled growing numbers of people towards AOF and determined their settlement choices there.

Happenstance, hangovers and windfalls

Lebanese migrants continued well into the twentieth century to trade stories of the pioneers who had reached Senegal or Guinea before the 1890s, seeking with these tales to claim primacy for this or that village or region. In the late 1950s, local tradition in Dakar still claimed that the first Lebanese—young men from Hadath al-Jubbeh, far up in the northern reaches of Mount Lebanon, or the market town of Dair al-Qamar, in the Shuf—had arrived in the late 1870s. However, it is clear such precursors, shadowy figures lost to history, were few and far between.[7] Eastern Mediterranean migration to French West Africa only began to acquire any sense of purpose, coherence and continuity in the 1890s. As Kamil Muruwwah pointed out in 1938, 'we cannot with any precision know the date at which migration towards Africa began, though it is possible to estimate that it did so around 1880'. But 'the number of migrants remained truly minuscule in this period, and … migration only began' in earnest 'after 1897, when migrants began to head towards Africa in their tens and hundreds'.[8] Thus, some recalled that the first 'commercial establishment founded in Saint Louis and Dakar' was that of Najib Abi 'Akar, which opened in 1896. The 'first caravan, made up of a few dozen men', followed soon after, arriving in 1899 'or shortly before'.[9] These claims seem to be born out by the population estimates of Jean-Gabriel Desbordes. Senegal counted only ten migrants in 1897; by 1900 this figure had grown to ninety-nine, and by 1908 to 281. Guinea, the first pole of Eastern Mediterranean life in West Africa, experienced an even larger expansion: from eighteen in 1897 with the number of migrants in the colony increasing to 150 in 1898 and to 697 in 1909.[10]

But even as this flow slowly grew in amplitude, we cannot know how many of these *ruwwad*, or 'pioneers'—as they came to be called by later generations of migrants—had the intention of making Dakar or Conakry their final destination. Some early migrants to AOF seem to have made the relatively short crossing from the Canary Islands, having likely been dumped there by Spanish or Italian steamships headed from Barcelona or Cádiz to Latin America. In November 1905, the government of Guinea returned to Tenerife five 'Syrian subjects' who had disembarked in Conakry without proof of identity.[11] Others alighted in Dakar, which had served since the 1860s as a coaling station for French lines towards Latin America,[12] as they returned to the Eastern Mediterranean from sojourns in the New World. Unwilling or unable to go home just yet, they chose to remain in West Africa, like the man who, in 1892, disembarked from a ship coming from Argentina, before settling in Guinea.[13] One Lebanese migrant in Dakar told me of his grandfather who, returning to Beirut in 1912 after a spell in Venezuela, left ship for a night on the town in

Dakar. Stumbling back, rather the worse for wear, towards the port the next day, he realised the vessel had left without him; hungover and without a way to get home, he chose to stay on in Senegal. He cannot have been alone in doing so.[14] Indeed, migration, rather than flowing entirely freely, followed the routes devised by French, British and Italian shipping lines. Eastern Mediterranean migrants were directed down particular paths, and towards particular destinations, by the ways and byways these took. Had the Messageries Maritimes and the SGT frequented São Vicente and Tenerife rather than Dakar, it seems unlikely Lebanese migration to West Africa would have taken on the importance it did.

Happenstance played a part in other ways. 'Abdallah Hushaimah claimed that the first few men to discover the opportunities of Guinea had arrived from Sierra Leone, which the Lebanese 'had known before the other lands of the blacks', some 'thirty-eight years ago'—that is to say, in 1892 or 1893. In this account, the first migrant to arrive in Conakry—one Ya'qub Bitar from Bait Shabab—did so entirely by chance, when the 'ship' he was travelling on from Freetown to Gambia 'for the purpose of trade' 'was forced onto the shore by a storm'. Stranded in Conakry, Bitar 'was given shelter by some blacks, who bought [all] his goods', thus securing him a 'profit he could not have dreamed of'. Seeing this 'new … field of wealth' 'open' up before him, he returned to Freetown, where he 'prepared another trading trip', and 'pressed his friends and countrymen' to accompany him in haste. At first refusing to believe he had not reached Gambia, they eventually followed him to Conakry, 'where they [too] rapidly succeeded'. Emboldened by this first foray, 'they no longer hesitated', and 'established themselves permanently in Conakry', where 'the sons of Bait Shabab, in particular, … occupy the rank of royal operators'.[15]

Marseille, however, was probably the point at which most chose to head for West Africa—or found themselves compelled to do so. Many were the migrants who followed the counsel of shipping agents in Beirut who advised those leaving Beirut to wait in France a short while to take stock of the changing opportunities available in the lands of the *mahjar*, and the shifting regulations preventing access to this or that destination. Others lacked the money for the ticket to Santos or Buenos Aires, and hoped to make up the shortfall in France, or were duped into stopping at Marseille, having been led to believe they had purchased a full fare.[16] While some of those who headed from Marseille towards Africa did so unwittingly, having been 'sent' by unscrupulous shipping agents to 'Sierra Leone … Capetown' or Dakar still believing they would soon reach New York,[17] others illegally 'boarded a cargo ship in the hope it would allow them to reach America', only to find that it took them instead to Saint Louis. But the 'onerous price of travel from Marseille to the New World' was not the only cause for such a change of plans. For some discovered that 'their physical condition was not in accordance with the severe health regulations in America for new migrants'.[18] Mahmud Fakhri was one of those told by medical inspectors he could not continue towards the United States, wary of migrants—those dangerous vectors of disease, pathogenic beings travelling through the world. Leaving Jabal 'Amil in 1907 in the hope of reaching America, he failed his medical examination in Marseille because of trachoma. Wondering 'what to do', he remembered he 'had a cousin, a certain Mr Tarraf, who had left before him for Senegal. Not wanting, above all else, to return to Lebanon, he headed towards Senegal.'[19] He was not alone in having his choices thus disrupted by the physicians, officials, brokers and ship captains who swarmed around the port of Marseille. It would be wrong, however, to believe that only compulsion, trickery and the odd twists of fate led Eastern Mediterranean migrants to West Africa. On the contrary, many 'modified their routes, and headed for Africa' upon hearing in Marseille tales of the riches to be found there.[20]

There is, then, much contingency and happenstance in these stories, which reveal the somewhat haphazard nature Eastern Mediterranean migration to West Africa retained, in some instances, until the First World War. But they also point to the growing sense of Africa as a viable destination, one in which migrants could make rapid gains. These men and women were buoyed, in large part, by the expansion of the colonial economy in the last decades of the nineteenth century, as France sought to 'pacify' its West African possessions, and to capitalise upon the commodities they produced. Thus, Guinea became the 'principal centre' of Lebanese life in AOF in the 1890s and 1900s in large part due to the short-lived boom in rubber prices which jolted the colony into a commercial frenzy.[21] These rose from around three and a half francs a kilogram in 1896 to a high of fifteen to twenty francs in 1910, before falling sharply after 1911, as rubber from Brazil and the Dutch East Indies—both more plentiful and of better quality than Guinean rubber balls collected in the wild— dampened demand for Guinean stock.[22] But, just as this source of prosperity was drying up, the Senegalese groundnut economy was beginning to bear fruit. In 1840, Senegal had exported a single, meagre, metric ton of groundnuts.[23] By 1890, exports had risen to 27,221 metric tons. In 1914, they stood at 280,526 metric tons. The rapid expansion of these years was helped along by the relative steadiness of local prices, which rose gently from about fifteen francs per hundred kilograms in 1890 to between eighteen and twenty-four francs in 1914.[24] This expansion continued apace in the wake of the First World War and the brief slump in commodity prices it brought in its trail. Indeed, the interwar years were, despite the cruel interlude of the Depression and the regular sharp fluctuations in price, a period of sustained growth in production—the 'golden age of the groundnut'.[25] These broad economic transformations affected the decisions of migrants—helping them to make choices which were at once small in the larger scheme of things, and momentous in the run of their own lives.

Marseille: the gateway to the world

Moreover, these tales remind us of the significant role the various entrepreneurs who serviced the needs of migrants played in determining their destinations. Shipping agents, as we have seen, had not only become a conspicuous presence throughout Mount Lebanon and the adjoining areas by the turn of the century, but had also formed etiolated networks stretching far beyond the shores of the Eastern

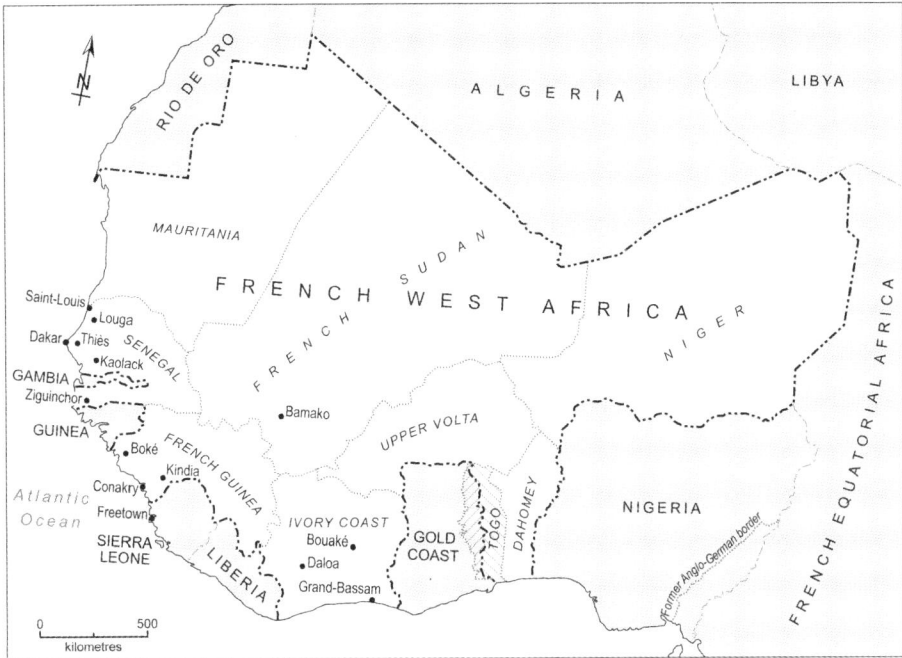

Figure 2: AOF.

Mediterranean. These chains of brokers and hostel-keepers, strung out along the paths of migration, concentrated in the main European hubs of steam transport—and, more particularly, in Marseille. For this 'animal with its four foot hostelries', as the Lebanese literary man Amin Rihani caustically put it, was the 'second station on the 'Via Dolorosa' of Eastern Mediterranean migration, a path studded with pain which would lead from Beirut to the 'Paradise' of the lands of migration. Migrants would often spend long days and weeks there, awaiting a ship that might carry them on to their desired destinations. Wandering the streets of a foreign place, often with only a smattering of French or English words and a little money to get by, they provided rich pickings for the coaxers who worked the docks of Marseille, those 'rapacious bats' that 'hover[ed] around the emigrant', 'who differ only from the boat-men of Beirut' in their propensity for 'pantaloons' and tendency to intersperse their Arabic with a few choice words of 'French slang'.[26] The police archives of Marseille are replete with tales of men like the enterprising Sursuq, who established a store to sell sundry goods to Eastern Mediterranean migrants—and who, even before acquiring his stock, had hired a team of agents; bedecked with a 'cap with Arabic characters', they were charged with descending on the port to 'recruit and bring to his establishment' any new arrivals.[27]

Indeed, so large were the numbers of Eastern Mediterranean migrants passing through Marseille—some six to seven hundred a week, by one count—that many agents and hostel owners came to target them specifically.[28] By 1902, eight of the eighteen establishments offering accommodation to migrants catered specifically to these men and women. While Greek hostel-keepers like Lefteris, Gianélos or Nimbis also had an understandable interest in this sizeable clientele, many of these entrepreneurs themselves hailed from Mount Lebanon.[29] The first of this constantly shifting cohort, Nicolas Faris, had settled in Marseille as far back as 1890.[30] He was joined by a rotating cast of coaxers and hostel-keepers, many of whom clustered together in the narrow alleyways of the Panier, the old neighbourhood above the port. There could be found the establishments of men like Faris Abu 'Arab, Milhim Skaff, Jirjis Antun, Wadi' and Nadra Shamiyya, and Ibrahim Samsur.[31]

These hostel-keepers did more than simply offer accommodation to migrants—who were, for all the promises proffered by dockside coaxers, piled by the dozen into each 'absolutely bare' room, and left to sleep on a hard floor.[32] They also provided these men and women with the means to exchange the 'Asiatic accoutrement' in which they had arrived for European garb,[33] swapping the 'fez and waistcoat' of the mountain villager for 'a suit of linsey-woolsey and a hat of hispid felt'.[34] And they supplied these travellers 'various objects like linens and utensils of all sorts ... which they take with them, ... for personal use or to sell them on to their coreligionists already established in America'—or, more likely, to peddle along the roads of Vermont or the streets of Freetown.[35]

Such goods came, of course, at a cost: in 1902, one informant put the cost of accommodation and food at twenty-five francs, and that of 'various purchases and clothes' at seventy-five francs; when added to the eighty francs migrants had spent on their ticket from Beirut to Marseille, and the 175 francs they would disburse for their passage to America, the total came to 355 francs.[36] Migrants were little helped by the rampant profiteering and fraud in which these entrepreneurs indulged. Jibran Elias reported in 1899 of how he had been accosted, while out walking one day, by one Bulus Khawam, who asked Elias and his three companions where they hoped to head. On being told they were awaiting a ship to Brazil, Khawam informed them that he 'knew the place well' and, as a 'trader', could help them to 'purchase some objects, watches, chains, razors, etc. at a very good price, and which we could sell on over there for five or six times the amount'. Only after having spent 180 francs on goods Khawam had picked out in a store of his choosing did Elias realise that the 'silver chains' whose merits the latter had vaunted were nothing of the sort.[37]

Nonetheless, these entrepreneurs fulfilled an essential function—not least because they possessed the capacity to make travel arrangements for migrants, supplying them with the means to move on from Marseille. It was not merely gain which encouraged shipping agents and brokers in Beirut to sell migrants only a ticket for Europe, or two tickets—the first for Marseille or Genoa, the second, exchangeable in their port of call, for their final destination. Rather all—migrants and entrepreneurs—were well aware of the rapidly shifting nature of the stock of information on which migrants depended to choose their destinations. The advice of self-interested operators, but also knowledge of changing economic conditions or entry requirements gleaned from conversations with fellow travellers, often led migrants to alter their plans during their stay in Marseille. As the *grand reporter* Albert Londres put it in the 1920s, the migrant 'would go where he could—his fate would be played out in Marseille'.[38]

However, hostel-keepers were not puppet-masters, pulling the strings drawing migrants towards particular destinations—far from it. They were engaged in a complex call-and-response with these men and women, tailoring their services to their changing predilections and desires. The name of Ibrahim Samsur's establishment, the Hôtel d'Afrique, was, on one level, an allusion to Marseille's vaunted status as the *porte de l'Afrique*—France's doorway to Africa.[39] But it may also have been an attempt to capture migrants headed for AOF. By the close of the First World War, some had certainly begun to cater specifically to those travelling to this particular destination, like the 'Amili Mahmud Burji, who opened a hotel near the port in 1917, which he ran alongside a trading house with interests in Senegal.[40] This was a sign of the growing importance of this particular stream of migration. While many of the men and women who passed through Marseille in the interwar years continued to favour Latin American destinations like Brazil, Argentina and Uruguay, two of the three remaining Eastern Mediterranean establishments catering to new arrivals—the Hôtel du Levant and the Hôtel du Mont-Liban—drew a significant share of their business from the constant stream of migrants travelling to and from West Africa.[41]

Kin, commerce and other considerations

The expansion of Eastern Mediterranean migration to AOF from the late 1890s onwards fit neatly, on the face of it, into the tidy explanatory frameworks of migration theory, with its stress upon chains of kin pulling men and women across the seas. Thus, the French administrator Jules Poulet found in 1911 that more than half of all those living in Guinea hailed from a single locality: the small Maronite town of Bait Shabab in the Matn. Migration from this locality had picked up after the return from West Africa of fifty-one men. Reporting that the thriving rubber trade allowed them to 'collect [in Guinea] the same sum as in America in a third of the time', they brought back some two million francs between them, which they used to buy land and build handsome, red-roofed, sandstone houses.[42] Many others were impelled to follow their lead, and within a few years some 800 of the town's 1,250 male inhabitants had migrated to Guinea and neighbouring Sierra Leone.[43] Such was the amplitude of this outflow that Bait Shabab—the home of the young—came to be rechristened, in a bittersweet acknowledgement of its changed demographic composition, as Bait al-'Ajaza—the home of old age.[44]

The inhabitants of Bait Shabab were not alone in regarding the trading posts of AOF as favoured destinations. By the mid-1900s, Greek Catholic, Shi'a, Maronite and Greek Orthodox migrants from the Jabal 'Amil port of Sur, and the villages in its hinterland like Juwayya, had begun to set up businesses in Dakar, Thiès and Conakry.[45] Alongside these two preponderant streams ran a third, smaller rivulet from the large Greek Orthodox village of Bainu, deep in the harsh recesses of the 'Akkar region—but, perhaps, near enough to the port of Tripoli to enable some to take the paths of migration.[46] Such migration was, moreover, not limited to AOF. Migrants from these three regions flowed into Sierra Leone, too, in the years before 1914: Greek Orthodox and Maronites from Rahbe and the Tilal villages of 'Akkar; Maronites from the Matn; and Shi'a from the localities of Tibnin, Bint Jubail and Nabatiyya, market towns lying inland from Sur.[47] Some among the latter group, too, seemed to regard West Africa as a place of easy profits, using the capital they accumulated there to sponsor others headed for the assembly lines of Ford in Detroit.[48] By 1914, then, migration from these localities towards Senegal, Sierra Leone and—especially—Guinea had become an organised, purposeful undertaking.

This was an enterprise driven by a keen sense of the economic opportunities to be found in West Africa, and directed by ties of family and friendship. At times, these movements conformed to the simple, familiar, patterns of chain migration—clusters of population forming in gradually extending concentric circles, as migrants called first upon their spouses, siblings and children, then upon their more distant kin.[49] Mustafa As'ad and his eldest son Musa arrived in Guinea from Sur in 1909, settling in Conakry; they were joined in 1911 by Musa's younger brother Darwish and then, in 1918, by the youngest of Mustafa's sons, 'Ali.[50] In 1917, 'Abdallah Hamid requested permission for his brother's son, Muhammad, to join him in Dakar from Mexico.[51] A year earlier, the Dakar merchant Joseph Ganamet—perhaps a Hispanic rendering of the Arabic Ghanma—had requested visas for his parents-in-law, Amin Hajj and his wife, 'currently resident in Buenos Aires', to settle in Senegal.[52] These moves seem entirely predictable strategies both for giving business operations strength in numbers, and for reconstructing the comforting ties of family. Indeed, migrants in both French and British West Africa continued to call upon family members and prospective employees in this fashion throughout the colonial period. The anthropologist Fuad Khuri, who spent some time among the Shi'a of the Sierra Leone town of Magburaka in the early 1960s, found that the first Lebanese man to arrive in the town, in 1921, was a member of the Shamil patriline of Bint Jubail. His brother followed in 1924. In 1938, these two men sent for their sister's son, and that of their paternal uncle. The sister's son was, through his father, a Qazzan, and he established that line in Sierra Leone. Then, in 1939, one of the Shamils married, on a visit to Lebanon, a Bazzi girl—and she, in turn, led other members of that family to Sierra Leone.[53]

Such a pattern of family reconstitution became increasingly common in the inter-war years. The rough headcounts carried out by French administrators in 1918, and again in 1924 and 1927, reveal that most who ventured without family ties to West Africa, both before and after the First World War, were young men or boys. Some were barely adolescents when they headed for AOF—like Hanna Qusayyir, who arrived in Cayor in 1900 at the age of eleven.[54] Few, however, were above the age of thirty—though there were exceptions to this general trend, like Georges Abu Rizq, who arrived in Senegal in 1907 a widowed forty-three year old, calling upon his thirteen-year old son Alexandre two years later.[55] But by the 1920s many of those who had arrived before 1914 had, as they grew older, acquired some measure of prosperity—which allowed them to return to Lebanon to find a wife or to call upon relatives.

This, in turn, changed the gender balance of these earlier streams of migration. Eastern Mediterranean migration to West Africa was never, it is clear, an entirely male phenomenon. Women—and children—were among the first few migrants who set up stall in the port-cities of Senegal and the trading posts of French Soudan at the turn of the century. Gabrielle (Abi) 'Akar, for instance, arrived on 10 June 1900 in Rufisque with her brothers, Habib and Najib, to join their youngest sibling, Philippe, there since 1897.[56] Jean 'Isa, who lived in Saint-Louis at the time of the yellow fever epidemic of 1900, was accompanied by his wife Mariam, 'the mother of two little girls'.[57] By no means all Lebanese migrants to AOF—even in this movement's earliest years—were 'men without women',[58] who had left their wives and children behind to wait or were still too young to be married before their departure.[59] Furthermore, there are tantalising hints that some women migrated—and worked—alone, complicating understandings of migration which have long viewed women only as the 'appendages of husbands, brothers, and fathers'.[60] Thus, one Mme Mukhaira—the *commandant de cercle* of Kayes noted in 1918—had lived in this Soudan trading town with her daughter Marie since 1893—two years before the arrival there of the first Eastern Mediterranean man, Antoine Ashqar. These women, described by the administrator as *commerçants*—note the masculine—seem to have worked independently.[61] For all that the scripts of bourgeois respectability to which migrants increasingly attempted to adhere strove to obscure these activities, these women cannot quite be erased from the archival record—or omitted from our consideration.

Nevertheless it is also clear, despite striking exceptions like Mme Mukhaira, that many women did follow in the wake of male relatives or husbands. While women represented nearly a quarter of migrants in Senegal in 1900, this ratio was abnormally high for these years. In 1907, there were only forty-two women for 424 men in Guinea; children, meanwhile, represented a mere 2 per cent of this population.[62] Women, then, were far fewer among Lebanese migrants to West Africa in the years before 1914 than among those heading for the United States—where women represented a full 32 per cent of entrants between 1899 and 1914.[63] It seems this had little to do with the perceived hardships of life in Africa. After all, there were four women among the ten migrants who had reached French Soudan by 1900, going far beyond the railway into the interior of AOF.[64] Rather, it might be accounted for by the relative novelty of this stream, and the aspirations of many of those who migrated in these years. These men, as they told Jules Poulet in 1911, hoped to put together a tidy sum as rapidly as possible before returning to the Eastern Mediterranean—and could, therefore, have had few thoughts of settling down in Conakry or Dakar, with or without their families.

Nevertheless, many *did* do so—remaining for long, unbroken spells or, at least, continuing to shuttle back and forth between West Africa and the Eastern

Mediterranean every few years. And, as they did, they began to regard their businesses as lasting undertakings rather than short-term adventures, and to yearn for the trappings of domesticity—and the respectability it brought. Those who had managed to accrue enough capital, and who envisaged staying on at least for the moment, returned to Lebanon to pick out their brides. Indeed, men 'who came from Africa or America looking for a marriage' themselves came to be sought-after commodities; prized 'because they were rich', they enjoyed all the trappings of their success. 'How many', asked 'Abdallah Hushaimah, were those 'who had returned to the homeland and married girls of the finest stock and noblest lineage, who would have seemed [inaccessible] ladies to them before they migrated'. Hushaimah also hinted at the darker costs of such practices, founded upon the desire of some for social status and of others for a 'wealth' whose 'extent' they could never quite know before embarking with their new spouses. 'Of every twenty brides who left these lands, only one finds the "happiness" she had dreamed of'; the fate of the others he failed to spell out, letting his sentence tail off in a discreet ellipsis.[65]

Others unable to return to Lebanon resorted to a practice that French administrators pruriently named 'marriage by proxy', and which migrants themselves called 'marriage by photo'; receiving images of prospective brides 'from their family and their village', young migrants 'chose a wife' from the remote fastness of Côte d'Ivoire or Senegal—a practice which became all the more common in the years after 1945.[66] By 1936, women represented some 36.7 per cent of migrants from Bait Shabab living in AOF, and 32.3 per cent of those from Sur. By contrast, men were almost four times more numerous among those who had left Qabb Elias, and nearly six times more numerous among those from Nabatiyya.[67] Those men who arrived from 'Amili towns like Nabatiyya or Zrariyya in the 1920s and 1930s only began to call, in turn, for their own women and children in the late 1940s and 1950s.[68]

These practices tell us something of the various roles women took on in the *mahjar*. On the one hand, they reveal the ways in which matrimony was used to consolidate the bonds of community and commerce, and to expand the ranks of migrant society by bringing into its fold new strands of kin which had previously not extended to West Africa. Marriage was not simply a private affair founded on companionate feeling, but a vector for a wider set of social relations: it helped both to strengthen family ties etiolated by distance, and to underwrite new partnerships and ventures. Women, then, served as crucial nodes in the networks of affect and profit stretching through West Africa, mediating relations between men. On the other hand, they were also more than just go-betweens and pawns in male transactions, or mere vessels of procreation. Mariam 'Isa, like Zarifa Maruni, and Farida and Sultana Nasif—the other women among the twenty-four migrants living in Saint-Louis in the first years of the twentieth century—was listed as a *colporteur*, or hawker. As students of Eastern Mediterranean migration to the United States have long since argued, such women clearly played an active part in Eastern Mediterranean commercial life.[69]

Moreover, wives were not the only kin to be called upon by male migrants; children, nephews, parents-in-law: all were beckoned to take up their place in the shop and the home. The proportion of children under the age of fifteen—while it tended to increase across the board as the 1920s and 1930s wore on, from nearly 30 per cent in Dakar in 1935 to a full 40 per cent two years later, from nearly 27 per cent in Guinea in 1931 to 34 per cent in 1936, and from 21 per cent in Senegal in 1935 to 25 per cent the following year—was noticeably higher in those places which had witnessed sustained migration since the years before 1914.[70] That it was not higher still across these various communities, it seems, was largely down to the fact that many women left their children with grandparents or uncles, or sent those born in AOF to relatives or—for those who could afford it—to boarding schools in Lebanon or France. Muhammad, the son of the Dakar kola merchant Haidar Taha, attended the Shi'a 'Amiliyya school in Beirut, dividing his holidays between their hometown of Nabatiyya and Senegal.[71] Sa'id Ghandur's son Georges, meanwhile, was schooled at the Maronite Sagesse boarding school in Beirut before returning to Dakar in 1941 on the completion of his studies.[72] In 1918, his namesake Georges Jabre joined his father Joseph in Guinea at the age of sixteen, after having been brought up in Marseille.[73] More telling still was the large number of those born in Guinea who lived in AOF in the late 1930s—some ninety-seven. By contrast, only fifty-five migrants present in the Federation at that point had been born in Senegal, and a mere twenty-four in Dakar.[74] This spoke both to the longer vintage of migration in this territory, but also to the desire of those—fathers and mothers—who had stayed behind in Conakry or Mamou while their children returned to Lebanon to call upon them to come and take their places, as they grew old and sought to retire in the old country.

Eastern Mediterranean men and women, then, were clearly concerned with mending, and holding together, ties of kin that might all too easily be torn and frayed by distance and displacement. Even when they were unable to return in person, they strove to maintain contact with the Eastern Mediterranean, using those imperial means of communication, the telegraph and the steamship. Farid Anthony, who grew up in the Sawpit district of Freetown, told in his memoirs of the way his father's ship had been met by the town's Lebanese inhabitants, who would customarily convene on the Government Wharf to 'enjoy the invigorating sea-breeze' and talk business, and to greet new arrivals 'from whom they obtained the latest news and perhaps an occasional letter or parcel of Lebanese fruits and foodstuffs'.[75] And they themselves sent word to relatives as often as they could—by passing a message with a returning friend, perhaps, or by telegram. In early 1942, the Vichy administration of AOF, in an attempt to counter the 'Anglo-Gaullist propaganda' reaching the *Libano-Syriens* of the Federation,[76] allowed some to send messages to relatives and friends in Lebanon by radio.[77] From Abidjan, Muhammad and Najib Yasin assured their family in Nabatiyya that they were in good health, and asked them to send news by letter. Mme Najib Harun asked for news of her mother, Mme Veuve Gabriel Cobti (Qubti) in Sur. The Haddad family asked Mr Salim to send his condolences to his aunt. From Dabou, Georges Haddad told his wife: 'write to me—thousand kisses for Tony', their son.[78] Na'man 'Assaf in Gagnoa asked Badi' Hashim, headmaster of the school at Kfar Shima, for news of his son Émile—and, he added, 'tend to his needs—will send any amount as soon as possible'.[79] These short messages hardly stray beyond the anodyne, their authors perhaps penned in by discretion and concern about the censor's prying eyes or the correct, conventional French turns of phrase they deployed. Despite their limitations, such seemingly bland expressions of sentimentality reveal the desire of migrants to keep abreast of lives unfolding far away, with all their petty turns and cataclysmic events.

These connections did not extend merely to Lebanon, a bilateral set of relations between given migrants or communities and the towns and villages of their birth. On the contrary, they stretched in all directions, forming a proliferating, sprawling network of linkages of affect and interest. In early 1919, Joseph Qustantin requested administrative permission for his brother 'Id, living in Mopti in Soudan, to join him in the Guinean town of Kankan.[80] That same year, Antoine 'Abduh asked that his brother George be allowed to spend a few months with him in Dakar on his way from Freetown to the Eastern Mediterranean.[81] That families like these should have been spread out across both French and British West Africa is unsurprising; as we will see, their commercial undertakings often depended upon such separation. However, these ties ran well beyond the confines of colonial West Africa. In early March 1917, Ibrahim Zughaib, who had lived in Senegal for some seven years, requested permission to leave the colony for New York. He had, he explained, been without work for a year and, seeing his health growing steadily worse, felt certain he could not spend an eighth winter in Senegal. In his broken French, he 'begged' 'your high personality' to 'grant me this permission to go to New York to be among my relatives and family'.[82] He was not alone in seeking to get away for a while. In August, Marie Qastun, who resided with her son Hanna in Dakar, requested permission to visit her brothers Michel and Elie in the Argentine province of Cordoba for 'a few months'. But these leaves of absence were not only occasioned by the desire for a 'change of climate',[83] or the pangs of family. That same year, Michel Salman—then working as an accountant for Ibrahim Hallaq in Thiès—requested permission to head for Marseille to see to the 'hotel for migrants' he had established there after a first spell working for Hallaq in M'Bour in 1913.[84]

As these letters reveal, the eyes of migrants were not fixated longingly upon the homeland. Rather, they turned their gaze this way and that, always keeping an eye on friends, relatives, and business partners dotted through the vast distances of the *mahjar*. Furthermore, these missives show the essentially cyclical, circuitous, nature of Lebanese migration in the early years of the twentieth century. While some certainly did settle for a single destination, which they left—if ever—only for a few short holidays in the Eastern Mediterranean, others came and went constantly. Some spent a spell in West Africa, or elsewhere in the *mahjar*, then returned to their families, immersing themselves in their old lives for a time, before heading off again as their money ran out or their patience grew thin. Ahmad al-Hajj Hasan was one such sojourner. Having migrated to the United States, he served in the American Expeditionary Force during the last months of the First World War, and was naturalised—taking the name of Frank Fayz—before returning to Qana, in Jabal ʿAmil. There he stayed till 1936, when he headed for AOF, settling first in Senegal then moving, in 1937, to Côte d'Ivoire, where he remained till 1944—when he returned to Lebanon, through Algiers, in the midst of war.[85] Hasan was, in a sense, a bird of flight coming home to roost. But while others showed similar restlessness, their peregrinations did not necessarily lead them back to the Eastern Mediterranean. Some saw no sense in returning, for their families were no longer there, but spread out, like that of the Ganamet, across the *mahjar*. Others, like Michel Salman, travelled where their interests called them.

We would do well, then, to think of the circuits of circulation Lebanese migrants plotted not merely as chains, which pulled one family member after another from the Eastern Mediterranean towards West Africa, but as routes. For this language allows us to conceive of migration, its motives and course in more flexible terms better able to fit the messy ways of life. On the one hand, it is clear that the crowded highways that joined up these two parts of the world sat amidst a broader network of well-travelled branch roads connecting Senegal, Guinea and Sierra Leone to places elsewhere in the *mahjar*—whether in the United States, Europe or Latin America. On the other hand, these routes opened up the possibility of travel towards West Africa without any of the directives and formal arrangements of migration—all those letters and telegrams and bundles of money to pay for the crossing.

There were, in 1918, nineteen adult members of the Ashqar family of Bait Shabab living in Guinea; eighteen of the Bijjani; fifteen of the Fakhuri; thirty-five of the Ghusub; twenty-two of the Hayik; twenty of the Qusayyir; and thirteen of the Mukarzil.[86] However, the internal relations between the various members of these extended patronymic groups—each of which traced its lineage back to a single putative ancestor—were at times blurred and complex, defying the simple schemata of chain migration theory. Some of these men and women were, it is clear, close kin. The Mukarzil, for instance, did include three sets of siblings—Joseph Mansur and Hanna Mansur, who had come together to Guinea in 1903, Nasri Joseph Ibrahim Stambuli and Milhim Ibrahim Stambuli, the first of whom arrived in 1906 and the second in 1908, and Nasif Elias Ayyub and Mme Faris Harb Mukarzil—characteristically, we do not know her name, though we do have that of her mother, Simone Nasif—who both arrived in 1905.[87] Mme Mukarzil was married, meanwhile, to her first cousin, Faris Harb Naja, who came to the Colony in 1911, six years after his wife. Michel Matar, who arrived in 1905, and Qais Naʿman Maʿushi, who arrived five years later, were also most likely first cousins. However, these two groups of cousins were not tied by any close link—patrilineal or matrilineal—either to each other, or to the other members of the extended Mukarzil family living in Guinea.[88] Thus, though these individuals all belonged to a single patronymic group, the ties of kin between them were not equally distributed. They proliferated in some directions, crossing back over each other like a set of pick-up sticks strewn on the ground, while in others they seemingly finished in dead ends, or stretched so far back in time that they defy our attempts at joining up these individuals, and seeing them as links in a single chain.[89]

These men and women clearly migrated towards Guinea safe in the knowledge they would find there others to whom they were bound by a common ancestry, however tenuous, and a shared name—links which created expectations of reciprocity and rendered the enterprise rather less daunting. The path leading from a locality like Bait Shabab towards Guinea was, by 1914, well-trodden and crowded with *awlad baladna*—'children of our country', as the people of the Lebanese mountain called their neighbours and kinfolk.[90] However, we must acknowledge the possibility that they moved not upon the entreaty of a relative or a friend, but precisely because this destination had become so well-known—because they had heard captivating tales of the riches of Africa, or had looked on enviously as a distant cousin built a new home with his rubber money. They were prompted to head for AOF as much by familiarity as by family ties. This pattern became more pronounced still in the interwar years. Indeed, chain migration alone can hardly account for the expansion in the Eastern Mediterranean population of AOF in the 1920s and 1930s. In 1909, there had been 1,110 'Syrians' living throughout the Federation. In 1923, this figure had grown to 2,152. By 1936, 5,792 citizens of the Mandatory states lived in the Federation.[91] This represented a demographic lurch upwards of 269 per cent, even as the flow of Eastern Mediterranean migration to other parts of the world was, on the whole, steadily decreasing.

Moreover, it would be wrong to regard the chains of migration as made up only of the sturdy stuff of kin. In 1917, the Mansur brothers took on a certain Grégoire Abu Hatab as an accountant for the business they had established in Grand-Bassam, in Côte d'Ivoire.[92] These men were bound neither, it seems, by parentage nor by shared origins: while the Mansur were most probably from Mount Lebanon, like their employees Spiro Sa'd and Habib Shuqair,[93] Abu Hatab was born in Damascus in 1886.[94] But he had going for him his status as a former Greek Orthodox priest, his string of appointments—first as an attaché to the Russian legation in Buenos Aires, then as an employee of the Forges et Chantiers de la Méditerranée in Marseille and finally as an interpreter at the Russian embassy in Paris—and his obvious erudition: as well as speaking Arabic and Russian, which he had perhaps picked up during his theological studies, he wrote French correctly, if rather clumsily.[95] For all his credentials, the relationship between Abu Hatab and the Mansurs rapidly fell apart, Abu Hatab leaving after only a few months to join the employ of César 'Abduh in Dakar.[96] Nevertheless, it is a sign that kin was not always all-important. Reputation and respectability—a man's learning and station in life—might equally serve as justifications for calling upon him.

Migrants showed similarly business-like dispositions in their missives and visits to Lebanon. At times, of course, it is difficult—not to say unproductive—to disentangle questions of kin and commerce. The imperial telegraph lines were used not just to transmit short, tender messages, but also to convey monies. Migrants from Bait Shabab remitted more than 200,000 francs in cheques and postal orders in 1910 alone.[97] On the eve of the Second World War, bank transfers from French Soudan averaged some two million francs a year—though this figure, deemed rather 'insignificant' by administrators, included only licit transactions.[98] Far more than mere monetary transactions, these were means for migrants to sustain the livelihoods of loved ones and kin, and to buttress their own social position in Mount Lebanon or Jabal 'Amil. These remittances were not just transfers of wealth, placements driven by economic calculations; they were also—and perhaps more importantly—investments of social capital and distributions of affective concern.

But these communications could also be put to more straightforwardly commercial ends. Thus, the telegraph and the steamship could serve to inform relatives of changing business opportunities. As a French administrator speculated in late 1935, the 'important increase' in the number of new arrivals from the Eastern Mediterranean that year had arisen largely because established migrants, already 'satisfied with the previous campaign, which they compared to the particularly brilliant years of 1927 and 1928', had predicted 'large profits' upon the opening of the trading season in December.[99] Return trips to Lebanon, meanwhile, could serve as much to recruit new apprentices and agents as to seek out a wife or visit a parent. Haidar Taha and his partner Hasan Shams reportedly returned in 1930 from their summer sojourn in Nabatiyya with 'eight men of that locality' in tow.[100] While French intelligence officers suspected that these were the agents of a 'methodically organised' 'secret political organisation', it is just as likely that they were prospective migrants Taha and Shams had recruited.[101]

It is clear, then, that the 'constant movement' of people and information 'to-and-fro' between West Africa and the Eastern Mediterranean 'fed' the growth of the Lebanese population of AOF 'by a sort of social capillarity'.[102] But it would be wrong to imagine that this movement was entirely familial, drawing in only 'wife, children, brothers, cousins, etc.', or that those attracted 'to West Africa by their wandering dispositions [were] few' and far between by the late 1930s.[103] Indeed, the torrential flow of new arrivals during the two crests of Eastern Mediterranean migration—first between 1923 and 1926, then between 1935 and 1937—took established migrants unawares. The latter had—as an administrator noted in 1924—at first welcomed the 'batches of 200 or 250' miserable souls disembarking from each new ship arriving at Dakar as 'useful' additions to their ranks. However, they had rapidly grown 'weary of this … disorganised movement'—and wary of the competition these interlopers might present. And while some in AOF called in the mid-1930s for reinforcements, sending news home of their profits, the 'considerable influx' of migrants which followed—'many of whom had set off with no assurance of finding employment'—surprised many.[104]

Some of those who headed 'off for adventure' in the Federation without kin or connection there may have heard of the opportunities on offer in West Africa in the old way, from migration agents in the village square, or on the docks of Beirut and Tripoli where, among the catcalls of porters and boatswains, brokers broadcast a constantly shifting stock of information.[105] Others were swayed by the conversations they had with fellow steamship passengers, or the talk of Marseille hostel-keepers.[106] Joseph Sahyun was a nineteen-year-old agronomy student in Marseille when he glimpsed, in 1925, a young man his age driving a luxury car through the streets of the city. Upon asking this dandyish figure what he did, he was told that his father worked in Africa. This was enough to make up his mind, and he left for AOF, where he first set up a small liquor store in the Senegalese hinterland and briefly played for a semi-professional football club in Dakar, before settling down in Côte d'Ivoire, where he made his wealth through the kola trade.[107]

Moreover, changing local circumstances played their part in 'pushing' and persuading Eastern Mediterranean men and women to take the paths of the *mahjar*. The two peaks of migration to AOF—the first lasting from 1923 to 1926, and the second from 1935 to 1937—coincided with relatively clement economic conditions in Lebanon and Syria, which might have encouraged some to leave while they could afford it. This desire to depart may have been reinforced by the onset of insurrectionary violence in southern Syria in 1925, and in Palestine in 1936. These revolts, which overlapped with uptakes in movement, probably did not force any migrants out. But they may well have heightened the longing of some to get away from home in search of steadier and more prosperous lives—especially as unrest spread from the Hawran and Galilee into Jabal 'Amil and the Shuf.

Just as important, though, was the 'propaganda' migrants conducted on their return to Lebanon, especially in the wake of good commodity harvests, which gave them thoughts of expanding their business and seeking out reinforcements.[108] After all, the groundswells of the mid-1920s and mid-1930s also corresponded with the largest booms in groundnut production of the interwar years. The amount of Senegalese groundnuts commercialised grew year-on-year from 273,000 tons during the 1922–23 *traite* to 486,000 tons in 1925–26. A similar lurch occurred in 1935 and 1936, when exports rapidly expanded again after the lean years of the slump, from 364,000 tons in 1934 to 466,000 tons in 1935 and 605,000 tons in 1936—the peak for interwar production.[109] Their pockets full from these windfalls, migrants were all too happy to spin alluring tales to attract new recruits. Shi'a migrants in Magburaka—some 78 per cent of whom had been sponsored to make the journey to Sierra Leone—told Fuad Khuri they had been told seductive stories of a place 'where money making is shovelling in sand, the fun of living is heightened by the easier availability of women, and where harmony and good will among the Lebanese community prevail'.[110] And these tales took on lives of their own; rapidly reaching beyond their intended audiences, they circulated far and wide, serving to make of Africa a seemingly accessible and attractive destination. Whether those who headed for AOF in the interwar years saw their costs covered by friends or kin, or whether they speculated on hearing of the profits to be found in West Africa, a newfound sense of opportunity drove them on.

An Africa of the mind: the imaginaries of migration

Whether consciously or inadvertently, the returning Eastern Mediterranean traders and shopkeepers of West Africa served as 'agents of migration' in their home localities and regions. Some of them, to be sure, deliberately showed off the 'substantial profits' to be made in Senegal, Guinea or Côte d'Ivoire, singing the praises of Africa to draw in potential employees. But all this talk also had unintended effects. Migrants who affected the trappings of 'comfort', putting on the appearances which had come to be expected of the returning migrant, helped to spread a perception of AOF as a 'land of riches'.[111] In the mid-1930s, some 'fifty wealthy migrants from the various colonies of Africa returned to spend a few months in the homeland' in the wake of 'gains ... the likes of which they had not seen for years'. Upon their return to Lebanon, they 'distributed money left and right'—driven, as Kamil Muruwwah charitably put it, by a desire to 'do some good with their profits and to allow their country to share in their benefits'. At the sight of this 'procession', many 'peasants', struggling in the grip of a 'suffocating economic crisis', were overcome with emotion and desire. The 'young', in particular, could only see the 'resplendent, plentiful gold in the hands of a small number of returning migrants', all too easily forgetting the 'straitened circumstances in which the overwhelming majority struggled in the deserts and forests of the Dark Continent'.[112] It is telling that many new arrivals in the 1920s came from villages and small towns like Bikfayya, Shawiyya, Qurnat Shahwan and Qurnat al-Hamra in the vicinity of Bait Shabab,[113] and Almat al-Sha'b, Naqqura, Qana and Nabatiyya, which lay along the roads which jutted out like spokes from Sur into its hinterland.[114] Knowledge of AOF as a plausible, and potentially profitable, destination spread out-wards from these localities, circulating along the networks of gossip and conversation which wound their way along the roads of the Matn and Jabal 'Amil.

Moreover, it reached further still, spilling out beyond the confines of these regions. The headcounts French administrators conducted in 1924 and 1927 pointed to new—or newly important—streams of migration. Men and women were now com-ing to West Africa in significant numbers from the port cities of Beirut and Tripoli; from smaller Lebanese localities like the town of Qabb Elias in the Biqa' plain, with its mixed population of Greek Orthodox, Greek Catholic and Sunni, or the small Maronite villages of Ras Kifa and Karm Saddeh in northern Lebanon; from the Syrian city of Homs; and from Haifa, in Mandatory Palestine.[115] We cannot be sure, now, of the ways in which news of West Africa filtered to migrants from these various localities. Here, too, communications probably played an important part: Qabb Elias lay along the road linking Beirut to Damascus, an artery along which information could easily travel; Ras Kifa and Karm Saddeh lay in the mountains overlooking Tripoli. But whatever the case, it seems clear that knowledge of West Africa was, by the 1930s, no longer confined to a few localities. Rather, it had become common currency throughout much of the new state of Lebanon—and beyond.

This knowledge consisted at times of little more than a rudimentary geography, a list of names gleaned from a geography textbook or map—'Guinea, Sahara, Gold

Coast, Sahel, Fouta … Ethiopia, Sudan, Senegal, Congo'.[116] Sometimes, it was even less than that. Charles Issawi, speaking in the 1940s to a Lebanese villager preparing to leave for Senegal, was told: 'I am emigrating to that part of Amerka that is under French rule; it is very hot there and the people are black.'[117] But such misconceptions must have been rare by this point—though they had once, of course, been common among Eastern Mediterranean migrants, like those who first arrived in Australia in the 1880s believing that they had landed at *al Na-Yurk*.[118] Fanciful 'rumours' certainly did spread in the early years of migration of Africa as a land where 'gold fell like rain from the sky upon migrants'.[119] However, most—even as they were taken in by the promise of riches—surely perceived their essentially metaphorical quality. Lebanese migrants had by the interwar years come to regard the lands of the *mahjar* not as 'a paradise of eternal bliss, but a world in which one's material condition could be improved through choice, work, and increased opportunities'.[120]

Table 2: *Estimated Lebanese and Syrian population in the territories of AOF 1897–1936.*

	Dakar	Senegal	Guinea	Soudan	Côte d'Ivoire	Dahomey	Niger	Mauritania
1897		10 (incl. Dakar)	18					
1898			150					
1900		99 (incl. Dakar)	163	14				
1904		101 (incl. Dakar)	260					
1907			477			8	1	
1908		281 (incl. Dakar)	554	16	3	10	1	2
1909	173	211	697	16	4	8		
1923	578	651	684	165	56	18		
1929		2,088	925		183			
1930	1,389	1,599	909	402	243	35		1
1931	1,130	2,002	1,011	315	148	45		2
1932	1,400	1,938	1,184	303	174	49		1
1933	1,836	2,064			250	18		
1935	1,272	2,714		417				
1936	1,269	2,560	1,367	305	254	33		4

Source: Desbordes, Jean-Gabriel, *L'Immigration Libano-Syrienne en Afrique Occidentale Française*, Poitiers: Renault & Cie, 1938, pp. 17–8.

Indeed, while the flow of information reaching back to the Eastern Mediterranean was highly filtered—and successful migrants remained rather likelier to send news or remittances than their less fortunate peers, struggling to make ends meet and too weighed down by shame to write home—those who stayed behind were not unaware of the difficulties and disappointments of the *mahjar*. As Nadra Filfili put it, they '[knew] the stories of failure; they [knew] the names of those who returned defeated, broken, … ill, they [knew] the names inscribed on coffins brought back on the cargo-ships, and all the names which were erased without coffins'.[121] They had been warned not 'to allow themselves to wander through the Dark Continent', where 'thousands of migrants long to return to Syria, but find it impossible to scrape together even the fare for the journey'.[122] But this was not enough to dissuade men and women from the Matn and Jabal 'Amil, 'Akkar and the Kisrwan from venturing towards Africa. The narratives of migration they heard were not for them unrealisable tall tales, which could serve only to escape for an instant the small, confined spaces of everyday existence. On the contrary, they were 'staging ground[s] for action', prisms through which men and women could begin to visualise new lives which lay firmly within their grasp.[123] As Filfili, who travelled towards Dakar in 1923, remembered: 'everything seemed to point to Senegal'.[124] We should be wary, then, of treating the men and women who migrated towards West Africa as naïve rustics, utterly unaware of the world that lay beyond their mountains. Rather, they were all too aware of the dangers and opportunities on offer, the changing contingencies of travel and the factors to weigh up in choosing this destination or that.

Among the latter, France's longstanding entanglement with the populations of the Eastern Mediterranean may well have helped to make up the minds of some to head for AOF. On the one hand, Eastern Mediterranean migrants were drawn to the Federation by awareness of the fact that its gates remained open to them at a time when states elsewhere were battening down the hatches. On the other, the mere fact that AOF was French seemingly influenced others. Historians of Eastern Mediterranean migration to the United States have long speculated on the role American missionaries dotted through the Lebanese mountain played in giving this flow its initial impetus.[125] Certainly, their conspicuous presence seems to have made some increasingly aware that 'there was a very great and active land outside of Mount Lebanon and that it might be possible to find something better to do than be a monk', like the migrant who recalled in 1903 staring longingly from his school bench at the 'great many pictures of American cities, streets and scenes' his teacher had pinned to the classroom wall.[126] Similarly, Ibrahim Rihbani remembered hearing much about the United States on the benches of his Protestant school. There, he 'studied its geography, heard of its great liberator Washington, and almost every Sunday listened to … preachers speak of the zeal of its people for missionary work among the heathen of the earth'—though, tellingly, he confessed that 'more exciting tales of America came to me through returning … emigrants', who 'spoke … of its wealth and how accessible it was' and, in a few cases, of its 'civilization', 'free schools, [and] free churches'.[127] Just as the presence of a few Baptist and Presbyterian missionaries seemingly spurred some to head towards *Amirka*, the networks of French Catholic schools scattered across present-day Lebanon played their part in drawing some to AOF. Thus, many of the Lebanese population of Soudan had attended in their younger years the Jesuit school or the Collège des Frères in Beirut, the Collège Saint-Joseph in 'Aintura, the École des Pères Saint-Sauveur in Saida or the mission school of Bikfayya.[128] This education taught these men French: it is striking how few of those who petitioned the governor-general of AOF with requests over the years resorted to public letter-writers, and how many wrote in an elegant, if somewhat convoluted, style befitting their ornate, flowery hand. But it also made them more familiar with French culture—and, possibly, French colonialism. And, moreover, it reinforced the sentimental ties some certainly felt for France.

In 1933, the government of Senegal sent out copies of a brochure prepared by the Mandatory High Commission in Beirut, which discussed the evolution of France's relations with Lebanon and Syria. It did so on the urging of the Ministry of Colonies, which sought to canvas the opinions of the colony's Mandatory citizens on the options discussed in this short text by High Commissioner Ponsot: the continuation of Mandatory rule or independence under a treaty establishing a French protectorate. The answers given reveal both the growing political cleavages around this question, and the attachment some felt for France. All thirty-five of the Syrian respondents in Thiès favoured independence; thirty-six of the thirty-eight Lebanese who provided answers, meanwhile, wished for the continuation of the Mandate—though their declaration that 'we unanimously recognise the generous efforts France has not ceased to make … to lead us towards independence, the ideal of every man who loves his country' was not unambiguous.[129] The migrants of Mekhe went further still. The Lebanese, they maintained, 'had, for years and centuries, seen in France a disinterested and sure protector'. Considering themselves 'the adopted sons of this country', these eleven men not only came down unanimously in favour of the Mandate; they also declared that, 'should [it] be contested, we would request the … attachment of Lebanon to France on the same basis as Algeria'.[130] This was strong stuff. Though some respondents clearly sought to safeguard their own claims to protection by showering praise upon France, such language cannot simply be dismissed as the product of a pragmatic obsequiousness. Rather, it reflected the very real affection some felt for France—the *umm al-hanuna*, or 'tender mother', which had come to the protection of the Christians. These feelings were, as the Lebanese of Mekhe acknowledged, both deep-rooted and profoundly contested.

However, the establishment of Mandatory rule may have played its part in pulling migrants towards AOF even in regions, like Jabal 'Amil, whose population remained restive and resentful of French occupation. Tawfiq Jabir, born in Nabatiyya in 1893, left Lebanon for Senegal in 1922. He had, until his departure, served as a *gendarme* for the French authorities in Beirut; his brother Muhammad, meanwhile, had enlisted in Gouraud's troops in 1920.[131] The Jabirs were among the many former Ottoman state employees the French administration recruited—and who acquired, in the course of their service, a familiarity with the French language and French institutions. We cannot know how many others were affected by such an influence. But we can be reasonably sure France's ambiguous, fraught relations with the Eastern Mediterranean was one of the factors that drew some in Jabal 'Amil towards AOF. Indeed, such a decision did not always entail loyalist sentiment. Quite the contrary: among the migrants who rose to petty political prominence in the mid-1930s was one Husain Wihbi, a former member of one of the *'isabat*, or armed bands, that had coursed the countryside of Jabal 'Amil in these years.[132] Wihbi, then, earned respect for his erstwhile resistance to French imperialism, even as he capitalised upon the circuits of communication which it had opened up to seek out a new livelihood in West Africa.

Dispersing—and gathering

The widespread dissemination of imaginaries of Africa in the 1920s and 1930s, and the manner in which they opened up new channels of movement between the Eastern Mediterranean and AOF, is a reminder of the difficulties entailed in writing a linear, unitary narrative of migration. There was, in a sense, no single starting point for Lebanese migration to Africa, but a multiplicity of beginnings. As Frank Thistlethwaite pointed out in a magisterial essay first published in 1960, the 'undifferentiated mass surface' of migration rapidly 'breaks down' when peered at 'through a magnifying glass', 'into a honeycomb of innumerable particular cells, districts, villages, towns'.[133] And each of these streams had not just its own chronology, but also its own particular patterns of movement.

Matni migrants continued in the interwar years to head for Guinea and Soudan—as they had done since the beginning of the century. Some 750 migrants from Bait Shabab lived across AOF in 1936. Of these, some 409 were in Guinea and another 153 in Soudan. By contrast, only 146 lived in Senegal, and a paltry eight in Dakar—despite the tempting opportunities presented by the Federation's capital, whose increasing importance as a nodal point for navigation and commerce drove a steep demographic climb in these years. By contrast, there were eighty-two migrants from Nabatiyya in Dakar, and seventy-five in Senegal—but none in French Soudan. The overwhelming majority of those from Qabb Elias, some 268 men and women, favoured the trading posts of the Senegalese interior.[134]

This propensity for demographic concentration went further still. Migrants with common origins did not just flock to particular colonial territories; they also clustered together in given regions. Those who lived in Mekhe and Kelle in the *cercle* of Cayor in Senegal were, with one exception, from the villages of Karm Saddeh, Miziara and Bqurqasha, which lay along the roads winding their way through the mountainous Maronite heartlands, high in the hinterland of Tripoli.[135] The few who lived in Casamance, meanwhile, hailed for the most part from Bait al-Sha'ar, Dbayyeh and 'Imarat Shalhub, coastal settlements just to the north of Beirut.[136] The subdivision of Foundiougne in the Sine-Saloum was peopled entirely by Matni migrants from Bait Shabab, Qurnat Shahwan, Qurnat al-Hamra, Shawiyya and Dair al-Qal'a.[137] Lebanese migrants appear not only to have sought to reconstitute families, but also to have recreated the social geographies of the regions they had left behind. As Kamil Muruwwah put it, Eastern Mediterranean men and women formed 'regional blocs' or coalitions—*takkatul iqlimi*—in West Africa: 'one saw, for instance, the migrants of Zrariyya in Dakar and Côte d'Ivoire, and those of Tripoli and Damascus in the Gold Coast, and those of Juwayya in Boké and Lagos, and those of Miziara in Nigeria, and those of Sur in Senegal and Sierra Leone'.[138]

What is more, such patterns seem roughly to have followed lines of religious belonging as well as regional origins. Thus, the migrant populations of Senegal, Guinea and—especially—French Soudan remained essentially Christian, despite the growing numbers of both Shi'a and Sunni flowing into AOF in the interwar years. In 1931, administrators estimated that some 854 Maronites, 472 Greek Catholics, eighty Greek Orthodox and nine Syrian Protestants lived in Senegal, but only 390 Muslims (tellingly, they did not care to distinguish between Sunni and Shi'a).[139] Such confessional clustering was not simply a by-product of the differing distribution of communities across Lebanon itself—the fact that while Jabal 'Amil was overwhelmingly Shi'a, the Matn and, especially, the Kisrwan were heavily Christian.

For it seems that in West Africa—just as in Lebanon—a certain religiosity fed, in some instances, the sense of place to which migrants clung long after leaving behind the Eastern Mediterranean. Thus, a French administrator noted in November 1944 that the Greek Orthodox of Soudan—all of them from Bainu 'Akkar—looked upon the far more substantial Maronite and Greek Catholic communities of the colony 'almost as foreigners', strangers who shared neither their ways of speaking nor their religion.[140] The migrants of Dahomey, who hailed for the most part from the Maronite town of Miziara, wished for Lebanon's independence largely because they 'dread being dominated by the Syrians'; 'separated' from the latter 'by a different civilisation and by Islam', they looked upon them with a mixture of 'contempt and fear'.[141] One might be tempted to dismiss such words as little more than the wilful efforts of a colonial administrator to fabricate difference. But they cannot be so easily treated this way, nor considered entirely as the manifestations of novel facts of identity, born with the Ottoman reforms of the mid-nineteenth century, which created the conditions for the 'deployment of religious heritage as a primary marker of modern political identity'.[142] The sentiments of these migrants—hard as they are to make out through the refractions of administrative writing—seem, rather, instances of the homespun 'ideologies of the mountain' Albert Hourani once wrote of, hanging upon the sense of 'a compact community' defined by both its dwelling place and its own particular rites.[143] While far from being the sole measure by which migrants defined themselves, religion seems to have fed into a deep-rooted sense of regional specificity which displacement could not do away with. Part of what it meant for these migrants to be from Bainu 'Akkar or Miziara—or, we might add, Jabal 'Amil or the Matn—was to be Greek Orthodox, Maronite, or Shi'a.

It is perhaps no surprise, then, that the comforting knowledge that neighbours shared their religion—their daily observances and small pious habits, as well as their festivals and moments of mourning—seem to have played as important a role as family ties or shared origins in migrants' decisions to alight in particular localities or regions. It would thus appear from the summary headcounts conducted by administrators that Dakar's Eastern Mediterranean population not only hailed in large part from Sur, but was also increasingly dominated by Shi'a. There were already thirty-nine Muslims among Dakar's eighty-seven male Eastern Mediterranean inhabitants in 1918—some 45 per cent. While Christians remained in a slight majority directly after the First World War, their demographic share was steadily eroded with each new wave of heavy migration to Dakar. It was estimated in 1931 that around 59 per cent of the city's *Libano-Syriens* were Muslim.[144] By the mid-1950s, they represented 75.5 per cent of Dakar's Eastern Mediterranean population.[145] All those originally from Sur and Qana who lived in Thiès, meanwhile, were of various Christian denominations.[146] These residential choices were seemingly born of a desire to isolate themselves from other Eastern Mediterranean migrants, recreating—or creating—confessional communities closed to outsiders. This was certainly the case in some instances. As Kamil Muruwwah put it of the Lebanese of Guinea, the 'relations between the various components'—or *anasir*, a term that by this stage was also being used to denote distinct races—'of the colony … suffered from the blight we complain of in the homeland': 'each group lived an independent, isolated life, in its own surrounds', unconcerned with others.[147]

This apparent self-segregation was even more apparent in the Senegalese hinterland. Those who lived in the Senegalese river port of Kaolack and its hinterland hailed from across Lebanon: from Zahleh and Qabb Elias in the Biqaʻ, Sur and Kfar Huna in Jabal ʻAmil, Antilias and al-Kharba in the Kisrwan, Dair al-Qamar in the Shuf, Bait Shabab and Bikfayya in the Matn, and Karm Saddeh in the north of the country. Each of these small bundles of population was made up of one or two families—at times no more than a husband and wife, or a couple of brothers, at others an extended group like the Hajjar and Shuwairi from Qabb Elias, or the Zakariyya from Shawiyya—which gave it an internal cohesion.[148] But little seemed to bind all these men and women together—save, that is, for religion. For all were, without exception, Uniate Christians, both Maronite and Greek Catholic. Religious belonging seems, on occasion, to have trumped place: 'what' one was mattered as much, if not more, than where one was from…

Sometimes—but not always… For Eastern Mediterranean men and women did not always remain cantoned in enclaves defined exclusively by religion. Christian and Muslim ʻAmilis alike were to be found in the Senegalese coastal town of Rufisque, where Greek Catholics and Shiʻa from Nabatiyya lived alongside each other. Much the same was true of the Gambetta neighbourhood of Dakar, despite the growing preponderance of Shiʻa migrants in the capital of AOF. There, the shops and homes of Christian and Muslim were dotted along the same streets—Rue Vincens and Rue Sandiniéry, Avenue Gambetta and Rue Victor Hugo—without any apparent residential segregation.[149] Such proximity could sometimes go further still. Mme Salomon thus recalled in the 1990s that she and her husband Georges, who had arrived in Grand-Bassam in 1920, had shared their marital home—a large, twelve-room dwelling Georges had bought from a departing Englishman—with ʻAbdallah Hijazi 'and his family', and with ʻAbd al-Latif Fakhri and his wife, who 'lived for three years in our home, while they built their house'. All would 'eat together at the dining table' at the end of a long day's trading. Such reminiscences must be placed against the backdrop of the events of the late 1970s and 1980s, when the migrant community of Côte d'Ivoire had been torn apart by the factional and sectarian divisions of the Lebanese civil war, disputes which gave force to Mme Salomon's lament for lost days of 'trust' and neighbourly assistance.[150] But they do tell of the ways in which Lebanese migrants could, sometimes quite literally, cohabit in the faraway spaces of the *mahjar*.

In this sense, their existences seem to have departed in significant ways from those led by the inhabitants of a mixed town like Sur, whose 7,500 or so pre-1914 inhabitants, divided equally between mostly Greek Catholic Christians and largely Shi'a Muslims,[151] apparently lived either side of an 'imaginary, but impossible to breach, barrier'.[152] Not only were its 'Christian quarters distinct from its Muslim quarters, the former living in the north and north-west of the town', the Sunni in their own, small, neighbourhood, and the Shi'a in the 'remaining parts'.[153] Moreover, the Shi'a cleric Sayyid Ja'far Sharaf al-Din insisted that these various populations, which had arrived in the town after it had been rebuilt by Shaikh 'Abbas al-Saghir in the late eighteenth century, held on to their distinctive accents, the Sunni speaking with a Saida lilt, while the Shi'a spoke with the distinctively 'Amili intonations of their home villages.[154]

We cannot know whether the lives of mingled communities in AOF were marked by the same awkward accommodations and ambiguities which characterised relations between Uniates and Shi'a in regions like Jabal 'Amil and Bilad Jubail. There, important dates in the Christian and Muslim ritual calendars—like the Assumption or the ceremonies of *'ashura'*, held to commemorate the martyrdom of Husain at the battle of Karbala—could in quieter times be occasions for shows of careful reciprocity.[155] However, the religious sentiments of each could rapidly be mobilised and reshaped into a hostile discourse of irreconcilable difference in moments of strife like the late 1850s or the early 1920s.[156] The awkward balance between harmony and conflict was palpable in the wartime reminiscences of the prominent 'Amili man of religion Shaikh Sulaiman al-Zahir. The 'presence of the Christians' in the region, he insisted, 'was no more than two centuries old'. Most were Maronites who had fled southwards from Mount Lebanon during the eventful years of 1859–60, and who had been welcomed by the Shi'a, who 'housed' them in villages and towns like Kfur and Zahrani. In Nabatiyya al-Fawqa, the local inhabitants had gone so far as to build a Maronite convent at the behest of the 'rulers of the region'. Thereafter, 'Christians and Shi'a' lived in 'perfect understanding' until the end of 'Turkish' rule. Only with the coming of the French 'invasion' did 'some' Christians 'renounce' their 'Shi'a brothers'—though this, Zahir insisted, was only the work of the 'ignorant', and the cause of much fear among the 'wise' of 'both factions'.[157] This was a narrative that stressed in turn the capacity of all for comity, and the fragility of such a way of life, exposing the limits of coexistence by casting the Christians as interlopers—ungrateful guests who had been tempted by the lures of French imperialism into spurning the generosity of their hosts.

But the decisions of Christian and Muslim men and women to live alongside each other is a reminder that migrants' lifestyles were not always exact replicas of those of the Eastern Mediterranean, and their communities careful miniature reproductions of those they had left behind. Nor, it might be argued, did they necessarily want them to be. But it is also a telling corrective—if one is still needed—to the notion that confession was an unchanging and all-pervasive prescription, a heavy tradition dominating the lives of migrants, determining choices both large and small. Rather, it was an inherently unstable discourse. Endlessly mutable and malleable, it could be muted at times, or used strategically at others. Thus, for all that they did sometimes matter, religious differences did little to prevent migrants from living together or engaging—as we shall see—in commerce across confessional lines.[158] And while the Eastern Mediterranean men and women of AOF drew upon notions of kin, place and confession in deciding where to settle, and among whom to live, they did so in ways which were complex and not always consistent, confounding attempts to ascribe to them a binding allegiance to the 'Aristotelian logic of "social structure"'.[159]

Moreover, migrants often followed more level-headed calculations in choosing where to settle, preferring locations where profits could be found. It is no coincidence, for instance, that the Eastern Mediterranean population of Dakar should have grown from 173 in 1909 to 1,269 in 1936,[160] making this 'colony' the 'largest' of 'any African city'.[161] The port had, by the interwar years, displaced its erstwhile competitors Saint-Louis and Rufisque as the most important coastal outlet for the groundnut trade; by the 1930s, 28 per cent of Senegal's yearly crop was loaded at Dakar—and only 10 per cent at Rufisque.[162] But Dakar was more than just the gate to Senegal's cash crop economy. Its role as the capital of AOF and as a point of transit for French and international maritime traffic—which made it 'France's fourth port' by the 1930s, on the same footing as Dunkirk—played a part, too, in the city's expansion, helping to create a variegated urban economy which, while dependent on the peanuts flowing in from the interior, had also a distinct life of its own. By the 1930s, Dakar truly was an 'imperial metropolis': in 1902, it had numbered 8,737 inhabitants; by 1935, its population stood at some 94,000.[163]

The residential choices of the Lebanese of Dakar only further reflected their mercantile bent: Gambetta, the neighbourhood in which they concentrated, was conveniently close to both the city's main market and the port. The same was true in Saint-Louis, where some 80 per cent of the town's dwindling community still lived in the 1960s in the old commercial neighbourhoods of Saint-Louis Nord and N'Dar Toute,[164] and in Conakry, whose market-place was 'lined with Lebanese and Syrian shops', which spread along its main artery, the Avenue Ballay.[165] This propensity was also evident at the territorial level: as groundnut production increasingly shifted in the interwar years from the Wolof heartlands of Cayor and Baol southwards and eastwards towards the regions of Sine and, especially, Saloum, Eastern Mediterranean migrants followed. In 1922, the *cercles* of Diourbel in Baol and Cayor-Sud produced, respectively, 85,000 and 74,000 tons—a level of output roughly comparable to that of Sine-Saloum, which commercialised 84,500 tons the same year. However, by 1930, Sine-Saloum had rapidly outstripped its former competitors, producing some 48.5 per cent of Senegal's groundnuts.[166] Furthermore, the commercial centre of these regions, Kaolack, benefited from its position as a river port to draw in produce from as far afield as eastern Senegal and Soudan, which travelled along the Dakar–Niger railway, finally completed in 1923; in 1933, 52 per cent of Senegal's groundnut exports were loaded on its wharves.[167]Accordingly, the adult Eastern Mediterranean population of the *cercles* of Sine-Saloum stood at 250 in 1924.[168] By contrast, there were 122 migrants living in the Baol[169] and sixty-six in the *cercle* of Cayor.[170] The lack of popularity of Casamance and Saint-Louis, which lay too far to the south and north of the 'peanut basin', reflected more starkly still their growing marginality to the groundnut economy: they only drew in twenty and forty-eight migrants respectively.[171] Furthermore, the popularity of the Sine-Saloum and, in particular, of Kaolack and its immediate hinterland only increased as the 1920s wore on—by 1927, there were some 127 adult *Libano-Syriens* in the subdivision of Kaolack, and 229 in the town itself.[172]

Constant motion

However, Eastern Mediterranean migrants did not simply settle upon a single locality and remain there. Their movements, as it were, did not end with migration. Some, especially in the late 1890s and early 1900s, travelled down the coast from Dakar aboard the small steam packets and schooners which serviced the ports of West Africa—gaunt, 'yellow-skinned' figures standing on the deck 'without even a sunhat to protect their heads' amidst the 'Ashantis', Hausas and 'Lagos boys'.[173] Joseph Hayik, who arrived in Guinea in 1900,[174] recalled alighting in Conakry with four or five companions when the ship they were on experienced mechanical difficulties.[175] Others followed the railways as they cut thin, straight paths into the interior in the early 1900s. In 1911, the administrator of Kaolack noted the arrival with the rail of 'ever-growing numbers' of Eastern Mediterranean migrants in Sine-Saloum, who were the 'first to trade' in the small settlements which grew up alongside the tracks.[176] In Guinea, too, migrants travelled into the interior along the railway threading its way from Conakry to Kankan. Though the *Syriens* concentrated at first in the trading post of Mamou, where some three to four hundred set up shop in 1909 as it enjoyed a short-lived commercial primacy at the head of the rail, they eventually broke up into small clusters scattered through the railway towns of the interior.[177] Members of the Mukarzil family, for instance, could be found not only in Conakry and Dubreka, in the nearby bay of Sangarea, but all along the railway, in Mamou, Kindia and Dabola.[178]

Such restlessness, however, cannot simply be read as a sign of the relentless search for profits that characterised the life of Eastern Mediterranean migrants in AOF. It is, at times, a reminder of the failures and disappointments that awaited many. Joseph Habib, expelled from Senegal in 1911 as a threat to public order after he attacked a French administrators, had, until this incident, drifted listlessly between various localities, attempting to peddle his borrowed goods first in Saint-Louis, then Podor, Thiès, Saint-Louis again and finally Dagana.[179] Habib was, in one sense, a rather exceptional figure. Apparently born in 1898, he had arrived—seemingly alone—in

Senegal in 1904, at the age of six. Still barely thirteen when he received his expulsion order, he had already quarrelled regularly with his African neighbours—and when these arguments degenerated into fist-fights, as they often did, he did not hesitate to draw his revolver. Indeed, it was one of these 'altercations' which led him to his confrontation with the *commandant de cercle*; accused of fleecing two local herdsmen he had taken on to lead some heads of cattle to Louga, he had refused to answer any of the administrator's questions, before flying into a rage and attacking him.[180] Upon his arrest, Habib was taken to the *hôpital civil* in Dakar, where the doctors who watched over him concluded that he suffered from 'fits of acute anger which render him irresponsible', and recommended his confinement in an asylum—or, failing that, his expulsion.[181] Habib was, in more ways than one, poor and lost—a child adrift in Africa. Nevertheless, he was far from alone in having to move on to escape a financially precarious situation. Many were those who, unable to get off the ground in one place, shifted about AOF in the vain hope of succeeding elsewhere.

Conclusion

I have sought here to unpack the bundle of motives that drove Eastern Mediterranean migrants to head for AOF in the early years of the twentieth century, and led them to settle in particular localities. The example and injunctions and monetary assistance of friends and relatives, with whom those who stayed behind remained in contact, and the desire to recreate—or create—family ties: these all certainly did matter in drawing Lebanese migrants to the Federation, as some sought to weave webs of relations around themselves. But just as important, perhaps, were the potent tales of profit which circulated through the villages and market towns of Mount Lebanon and Jabal 'Amil—stories that migrants told, but which were then propagated far beyond their immediate audiences, or which were spun by the migration agents and hostel-keepers strung out along the paths of migration. These helped to foster a certain vicarious familiarity with AOF, to make of it a plausible destination—one which was governed by France, and to which access remained relatively easy, despite the fraught attempts of colonial administrators to police their gates. And this same complex amalgam of factors—a desire for the familiar faces and accents of home, an inter-mingled sense of locality and confession, but also rumours of opportunity and new openings—pushed migrants to settle in particular places, or to keep moving restlessly about, coming and going within and without Africa. It makes sense, then, to think of Lebanese migrants in AOF not just as men and women bound to others by common roots, but also as fellow travellers moving along a series of routes. Kin, place and confession, while they did matter, did so in unstable, unpredictable ways. Like the text of a play, different actors read, and performed, these seemingly all-pervasive strictures in different ways—some choosing to stress certain aspects, others excising or passing over passages they found particularly troublesome.

PART TWO

WORDS AND LAWS

3

FEARS OF A 'SYRIAN GUINEA'

COMMERCE, CONTAGION AND RACE IN FRENCH WEST AFRICA, 1898–1914

On 29 December 1898, a group of small traders established in Conakry, the capital of French Guinea, dispatched a petition to the colony's governor. Claiming to speak in the name of the town's commercial community, they urged the administration to take action to circumvent 'the … danger which the ever-growing number of Syrian traders invading the principal locality of the colony present to local business'.[1] This was not to be the last time that Frenchmen in Guinea were to attempt action against the *Syriens*. In 1902 and 1904, European traders in Conakry, Boke, Dubreka and Coya sought to league together in an effort to shut these men out of the rubber trade—in imitation of the 1898 boycott whose failure had pushed a number of *négociants* to draft their petition to the governor of Guinea.[2] In 1907 commercial workers in the towns of Boke and Kindia in turn called for greater protection against this 'Asiatic invasion'.[3] The presence of the *Syriens* in Guinea, it is clear, stirred profound anxieties in the years before the First World War. *Colons*, administrators and metropolitan commentators saw Lebanese migrants as troublesome interlopers who threatened not only the effective monopoly of European houses over the rubber business, but—more worryingly still—the very prosperity and stability of the colony. Moreover, they sought ways to expurgate and exclude these men from Guinea—both materially, through boycotts and immigration ordinance, and figuratively, in discourses which marked the *Syriens* as not quite white.

We are, in a sense, on familiar ground here. Scholars have devoted much attention, in recent years, to the profound anxieties which stalked European society in the colonies—and to the ways in which various imperial actors sought to demarcate its boundaries, fashioning discourses which constituted difference and created distance between suitable members of the community, and those who lay beyond the pale.[4] A great deal of this work has homed in upon the constant preoccupation of authors and administrators with the intimacies of colonial life, examining their attempts to police the private domains of domesticity and desire.[5] As Ann Laura Stoler has observed, 'assessments of civility and the cultural distinctions on which racial membership relied were measured less by what people did in public than by how they conducted their private lives—with whom they cohabited, where they lived, what they ate, how they raised their children, what language they chose to speak to servants and family at home'.[6] Excessive physical or sentimental proximity to the colonised came to be construed as threatening to the cohesion of European society, and colonial authorities struggled to cope with the men and women hovering at its margins—those who had slipped the bounds of respectability because of their material circumstances or choice of lifestyle,[7] or whose accession to European status was questioned and contested.[8] What is more, even as they acknowledged that somatic and sexual contact with cooks and nannies, concubines and prostitutes was effectively unavoidable, Europeans sought to control the terms on which such bodily transactions were conducted, straining to secure the boundaries of community.

The writings on the 'Syrian question' produced by French commercial workers and administrators, company executives and colonial propagandists between 1898 and 1914—petitions and official correspondence, articles in Conakry newspapers and Parisian journals, chapters or passages in gazetteers and monographs—share with such domestic discourses a desire to define the borders of European identity. However, they seem different in one, significant, respect. Whether they urged the expulsion of *Syrien* traders, defended—as a few did—their actions, or simply provided ambivalent appraisals of their role, these texts concentrated upon the public matters of business, and were voiced in the terms of commercial work and economic policy. Some of these authors couched their calls for exclusion or accommodation within the discourses of preference and free trade. Many, meanwhile, invoked commercial honesty and industriousness, as the—public—standards by which the suitability of the *Syriens* for acceptance into Guinean society was to be determined.[9] While those favourably inclined towards these men stressed their propensity for hard work, those who called for their expulsion painted them as profoundly untrustworthy—finding their sharp practices sorely lacking in comparison with the integrity and sound methods of European traders. Such distinctions drew, I will argue, upon notions of middle-class male respectability then current in metropolitan France, which placed great importance upon professional diligence and honour, while giving them a distinctly mercantile inflection.[10] That is not to say that these authors showed no concern for intimate matters of the body. On the contrary, none spoke only the language of trade. Rather, they often drew upon the lexicons of hygiene and disease alongside those of economic equity and commercial probity. But while allegations of filth and infection could themselves be grounds for exclusion, they were essentially intended to buttress claims of commercial disreputability. In depicting the *Syriens* as both dirty and dishonest, their critics intimated that they were doubly deficient—not only morally unsound, but also physically lacking.

FEARS OF A 'SYRIAN GUINEA'

This preoccupation with matters of trade is not entirely unsurprising. After all, those who complained most vociferously of the presence of the *Syriens*—the traders of Conakry and Boke, and the newspaper editor Gabriel Ternaux, whose vituperative tirades I will examine below—were themselves engaged in commerce. So, too, was the most consistent advocate of the benefits of this migration, Frédéric Bohn, the president of the CFAO. Others, like the *conseiller du commerce extérieur* Aspe-Fleurimont, André Arcin, a former chief of staff to the governor of Guinea or Fernand Rouget—whose work was commissioned by the Government-General of Afrique Occidentale Française, or AOF, to accompany the Colonial Exhibition held in Marseille in 1906—wrote of the *Syriens* in rather more ambivalent terms. However, they too accorded trade a central place in their monographs on Guinea. In page after page detailing the commercial aptitudes of the colony's African populations, describing the development of Conakry wharf or the Niger railway, or listing shipping costs and tariff duties on sundry goods, they sought to present an image of a colony rich in natural resources and ripe for economic development—an 'Africa of exploitation', as William Schneider has put it. Guinea, these men argued, was particularly suited to the bold undertaking of *mise en valeur*—an enterprise underpinned, of course, by trade.[11] These various authors all regarded Guinea as essentially a commercial colony. They were not wrong to do so; after all, most of its European inhabitants were indeed engaged, in one way or another, in the daily truck of the rubber trade. In a trading society, it seems, what mattered most were the ways in which people went about their business—and where they stood in the commercial pecking order.

These notions of commerce and class intersected at numerous points with commonplace ideas of race, creating a construct of overlapping representations. Not only did authors like Arcin or Rouget seek to impose neat racial gradations upon the messy world of commercial relations, in their efforts to distinguish Frenchmen from Lebanese and African traders. What is more, the traits which made the *Syriens* such good traders—their talent for bargaining, say, or their unscrupulous ways—marked them not only as disreputable, but also as somehow less than European. In turn, the stigmata of their racial difference—such as their capacity to withstand the Guinean climate—facilitated their commercial ascent. These distinctions of class and race, I hope to make clear, were profoundly gendered: the *Syriens* were to be mistrusted, their critics suggested, because of their failure to meet the public and private standards of propriety expected of European men.[12] Such associations were only strengthened by a perception of migration as both errantcy and errantry—the flipside to the settled conventions of the mercantile middle-class. In much French hygienist and political writing of the time, migrants—like Jews—were conceived as aberrant, inherently degenerate beings. Indeed, it seems opponents of the *Syriens* drew consistently upon metropolitan anti-Semitic writing to create visions of these men as pathogenic, effeminate and rapacious—an immanent danger to the health and tranquillity of the colonial body politic and its members. These notions ran like a single weave through the writings I will consider in this chapter, tying together the seemingly disparate languages of commerce and contagion, class and race.

Controlling interests

Opposition to the presence of the *Syriens* in the years before 1914 was, it is clear, not an isolated phenomenon. Rather, it should be placed in the context of a more general desire to bypass African rubber brokers and hawkers, go-betweens who—it was argued—threatened the dominant position of French traders. Creating direct relations with the interior—through forbidding the *marchés de contact*, African centres of exchange, centralising trade in localities chosen by the administration as *points de traite* and opening new arteries of communication—was a matter of commercial considerations. As the administrator Cousturier baldly admitted in 1891, the 'necessity to create without delay' a road joining the commercial centres of the Futa Jalon to Dubreka, in the near hinterland of Conakry, was born of the need to circumvent the Susu traders who 'travelled to the great markets of the interior and formed caravans descending directly to the factories of the coast'. 'Commercial operations' with these convoys, Cousturier argued, were 'generally quite unrewarding because the Susu knows too well the value of both produce and merchandise and is therefore much more demanding in this respect than the Fula'.[13] Controlling and channelling the movements of intermediary traders—if not doing away with these groups—was necessary to protect the profits of European traders.[14] This was true as much of Lebanese migrants as of African itinerant brokers.

However, many deemed the methods the *Syriens* adopted particularly galling. These threatened not simply to upset an advantageous state of affairs, but effectively to put European traders out of business. Thus, complained Aspe-Fleurimont in 1900, the *Syriens* had begun upon their arrival to purchase rubber balls from African suppliers in cash, at a higher price than the European houses of Conakry. An effort to smother this threat by enforcing a boycott of their produce having foundered when one company continued to purchase from them, 'each began to receive their offers and, if need be, to provoke them: a new and considerable rise in prices ensued'. This sudden inflation, in turn, inflamed African caravan porters. 'Driven to distraction by the high rates' the *Syriens* offered, they 'began first to cheat on the quality' of their produce, then diverted 'a good part' of the rubber they had deposited in trading houses caravanserais to the *Syriens*. The European establishments of Conakry, 'having lodged and fed … caravans weighed down with rubber on their arrival, found themselves' out of pocket, and left with lots reduced by half.[15]

In dealing, then, with the headmen of caravans in the markets or in the public caravanserai constructed by the administration, the *Syriens* had already undone the old patterns of trade—in which caravans effectively remained the captive clienteles of the trading companies. Housed and fed, they effectively had little choice but to sell their freight to their hosts, and to purchase any goods they desired from their shops—or rather, to exchange the rubber balls they had carried for swatches of textile or bags of salt.[16] Indeed, the *Syriens*' insistence upon paying in cash—by contrast with French commercial establishments which 'wanted only to pay part in currency and part in kind, in order to make a profit on the purchase of the produce, and another on the sale of their goods'—[17] threatened to put an end to the bartering which remained at the close of the nineteenth century 'the oldest, still most significant and most rewarding' method of exchange for Europeans.[18] The abrogation of such time-honoured practices, Aspe-Fleurimont argued, would endanger even the 'great trading houses' which lay behind Conakry's 'swift rise to prosperity', whose 'vast installations' now lay redundant. The 'tolerance accorded to the *Syriens* and the construction of the public caravanserai', inveighed Aspe-Fleurimont, had 'destroyed, in less than a year, the legitimate hopes of those who, their past experiences having made them confident in the future, had laid out large expenses in order not to be overtaken by the growing demands of trade'.[19] Indeed, he insisted, 'if a commercial crisis should occur in Conakry, it could almost entirely' be attributed to this rubber market, where free exchange led only to inflation and price-fixing.[20] This deep-seated fear of the effects 'foreign competition' might have upon the French traders of Conakry led Aspe-Fleurimont to lend his support to the calls of Guinean traders for protective administrative action. Indeed, he consciously drew upon the proposals elaborated in the 1899 petition, which called for 'fiscal measures' to guard them against the 'Asiatic invasion' they faced.[21] These men had seemed sure, upon presenting their petition to the governor of Guinea, that their demands would be met. After all, they asked, had it not been enough in the past merely 'to signal' the existence of a 'veritable danger' for it to be dealt with in the 'appropriate' manner?[22]

Colonial differences

However, the requests of *colons* and their allies did not receive the expected reception from the colonial state. Thus, Governor-General Roume dismissed the Boke petition of 1907 with a contemptuous brush of the hand: it was an 'insignificant manifestation' of the discontent of a few 'turbulent traders', 'unhappy' at the competition they faced from the *Syriens*, 'against whom they wanted protective measures which the administration cannot take'.[23] Not only were administrators hampered by diplomatic imperatives which severely restricted their capacity to impose checks on the entry and activities of Lebanese migrants; they were themselves unwilling, until 1910, to take meaningful action against these traders. Indeed, while *commandants de cercle* were capable of quite virulent hostility towards the *Syriens*, higher-ranked functionaries—not least Roume—remained largely committed to commercial liberty, and a belief in the merits of competition and the need to stimulate exchange.[24] André Arcin—who had been chief-of-staff to the governor of Guinea, and presided over Conakry's *tribunal de première instance*—neatly summed up this way of thinking. Despite his profound ambivalence towards the *Syriens*, whom he regarded as—at best—a 'necessary evil', he acknowledged in 1907 that these men 'had their uses at the beginning', facilitating 'Conakry's development, and contributing to the distribution of large quantities of currency, whose circulation allowed transactions to multiply'.[25] The introduction of more stringent controls upon Lebanese migration after 1910 marked a shift away from such a stance—which may be attributed both to the beginnings of the rubber slump, which sharpened commercial tensions, and the appointments of William Ponty as governor-general and Camille Guy as governor of Guinea, both far less well-disposed towards the *Syriens* than their predecessors Roume and Frézouls.

Moreover, the repeated failure of the exclusionary schemes concocted by determined French traders should alert us to the divisions which ran through Guinean commercial society. We must remain attentive to such differences between larger concerns—and in particular the CFAO—and smaller brokers, and proponents of protection and free trade. Thus, the boycotts of 1898 and 1904—efforts to cut off Eastern Mediterranean migrants from their source of livelihood in the rubber trade—foundered upon the refusal of the CFAO and the German firm Colin to submit to this entreaty.[26] Proposals to enact similar measures in 1902, meanwhile, failed even to get off the ground, stalled by the commitment of some in the Permanent Commission for Commerce and Industry—the body representing local trade—to free exchange.[27]

The staunch opposition of the CFAO to exclusionary measures targeting the *Syriens* was born of its firm commitment to free movement of goods and people. It cannot be denied, of course, that the Compagnie's agents often came to favour Eastern Mediterranean brokers because they found them cheaper and more reliable than European employees. At the same time, however, its directors seemed convinced that the *Syriens'* practices would push the Guinean economy in the right direction—helping to create a fully monetised society with an appetite for consumer goods. In a memorandum circulated to its Guinean agents in 1904—at a time when others were attempting to enforce a boycott of the *Syriens*—the Compagnie reminded its employees that 'we absolutely cannot abandon the principle which has continually guided our actions until now: that of the widest possible commercial liberty, freedom of exchange and circulation'. Indeed, the note's author argued, the 'commercial freedom granted up till now to the *Syriens* and *assimilés*' had apparently had no ill effect upon the 'general prosperity of the colony and its inhabitants'. On the contrary, the rise in the price of rubber—despite the 'apparent damage' it had caused to traders—had 'provided a very real benefit to the mass of producers and had thus contributed to the development of the local market of Conakry and, by extension, those of the other buying points of the colony'. What is more, he suggested, the presence of the *Syriens* may well have spared the traders of Guinea from their own greed—wondering whether 'without this stimulus, [they] might not have inadvertently, in order to maintain a slightly larger profit margin, indirectly favoured ... neighbouring colonies' like Sierra Leone.[28]

This was a wide-ranging argument: the *Syriens*, far from harming the Guinean economy by provoking a precipitous increase in the price of rubber, as French *colons* had argued, had in fact contributed to its development. Their inflationary activities had helped some of the wealth accrued from the rubber trade, previously conserved by French traders, to leach down to producers; while desirable in itself, this greater prosperity could only benefit France's colonial trade, increasing the number of 'commercial transactions' conducted throughout Guinea.[29] Indeed, in pushing up prices, the *Syriens* had encouraged rubber porters to continue selling their wares in Conakry and other localities, rather than crossing over into Sierra Leone—and, in so doing, had protected the colony's position against British competition. The men of the CFAO effectively turned the arguments of *colons* on their head. Eastern Mediterranean traders not only provided a needed spur to Guinea's *mise en valeur*, creating the conditions for wider affluence; they also helped to protect France's influence against foreign depredations.

The arguments put forward in this memorandum were wholly in keeping with the company's general commercial policy. This hinged upon the nurturing of a fully monetised economy in West Africa, untrammelled by protectionist tariffs, which might provide not only a source of raw materials for France, but also a market for its consumer goods. The company's president, Frédéric Bohn, had thus stressed in 1899 the need to 'pay the black man the highest possible price for the products he offers, and reciprocally to sell him merchandise at the lowest possible price'. Only by doing so—he contended—could one create the conditions needed to transform the local population from 'people who do not possess anything' into 'consumers and clients'.[30] Bohn maintained, then, that free exchange would both create relatively prosperous African producers, capable of purchasing the goods they desired, and benefit the French and Lebanese traders who were their clients and suppliers.

Moreover, the Compagnie's repeated interventions in favour of the *Syriens* depicted free exchange and circulation not just as economically beneficial, but also as more equitable—a moral stance, as well as a mercantile position. Thus, the note circulated to company employees in 1904 reminded them that—while they remained bound by 'the limits of the law'—they should not 'distinguish between or exclude individuals because of their origins or nationality'. Bohn had made much the same point five years earlier, protesting that 'we cannot accept that people may be harried and mistreated, whatever their colour or race, only because their commercial competition displeases a few local tradesmen'. 'Unfortunately', he went on, 'you are not unaware of the fierce prejudice against all things foreign which exists among certain of our country's classes'—a charged allusion to the Dreyfus affair and its long aftermath, by which Bohn effectively equated opposition to the *Syriens'* presence and activities with the profound injustice of this case. In such circumstances, the Compagnie had little choice but to 'insist above all on the "material" advantages the presence of these elements who, while foreign, are hard-working and relatively intelligent, can bring to the colony, to ensure they are not bothered. For far too few are concerned with the "moral and humanitarian" point of view, despite the lessons of History, some of which are all too recent.'[31]

Bohn, then, was not only scornful on commercial grounds of the anxieties of Guinean *colons*, whose demands he dismissed as unjustified. Exclusively economic arguments, he intimated, were no more than concessions to those driven more by crass self-interest than moral consideration. The untrammelled circulation of goods and people was but one aspect of an essentially universalist vision of the French nation as a place of asylum, bound to principles of equity and freedom. Protection and national preference, meanwhile, were no more than manifestations of a blinkered particularism.[32] Bohn buttressed this claim by intimating that opposition to the *Syriens* was born of baleful sentiments similar to those unleashed in the wake of the Dreyfus affair. The demands of French commercial workers were not only petty obstacles to the beneficial forces of competition. They were also—and just as significantly—injurious to the principles of liberty and justice, signs of an inhumane disregard for the 'lessons of History'—no doubt another allusion to the Dreyfus affair, but also to the perceived persecution of the Lebanese at the hands of the Ottoman state.

But Bohn was not alone in presenting economic arguments as founded upon moral claims, nor in drawing upon metropolitan discourses of political economy and nationhood. Proponents of protection, too, resorted to such tactics. Thus, the traders of Conakry cited the measures regulating commercial activity in Parisian markets as a blueprint for their desiderata. These included increasing the commercial licence the *Syriens* paid to 600 francs, bringing them in line with other 'itinerant' traders; prohibiting trading in rubber on the public thoroughfare; making the keeping of a shop compulsory; imposing a heavy duty on all those who had fixed premises but wished to keep trading on the public highway; and implementing a residence tax of 500 francs for all 'foreign traffickers in possession of a first class commercial licence for less than a year'.[33] These measures, the authors of the petition maintained, would 'be of the upmost fairness' and—perhaps more importantly—'certainly effective'.[34]

In citing such instances of administrative intervention, the authors of this petition sought at once to lend greater credence to their proposals by reminding Guinean administrators of successful precedents, and to embarrass these functionaries by unflattering comparisons with their metropolitan counterparts. Thus, they reminded the colony's governor, European traders bore a variety of heavy charges—including not only the expenses of maintaining their establishments and keeping a 'costly European personnel', but also 'licences, taxes, and duties on alcohol, wine, tobacco, salt, etc.'. The *Syriens*, meanwhile, paid only a 'simple hawking licence' to carry on, 'from sunrise till sunset', their 'enormous traffic' of around 800 to 900 kilograms of rubber per day—worth some 5,000 francs. This inconsistency, the authors of the petition argued, was patently unfair. The administration simply had to take 'protective measures, without delay' to re-establish the 'equilibrium' between these two groups—following the example of 'public authorities' in France which had 'long been busy warding off' the dangers associated with itinerant trade 'by regulating, with … rigour and severity, trade in the *halles* and markets', in order to maintain a balance between 'regularly established' tradesmen and hawkers.[35] Refusal to do so, the authors of the petition intimated, would be irresponsible—and would serve only to demonstrate the administration's disregard both for its pastoral duties and for metropolitan models of good government.

The traders of Conakry sought also, in invoking this precedent, to underline the crucial difference between the established companies of Conakry and the *Syriens*. Much like the hawkers plying their wares in the *halles* of Paris, the *Syriens* of Conakry possessed 'nothing more than the spot they occupy on the public thoroughfare'.

Meanwhile, the French traders of the town were, like their metropolitan counterparts, 'serious and honest' men who had built up 'important installations, at great expense'.[36] They were *négociants*—merchants or wholesalers. Lebanese migrants, meanwhile, were no more than *trafiquants*, mere traffickers or pedlars. The qualitative difference between these terms could not be clearer: the first implied both success in business and stolid respectability, the second commercial insignificance and dishonesty. Aspersions upon the honesty of Lebanese traders, who had diverted—a word which does not quite capture the ambivalence of the French *détourner*, with its connotations of embezzlement and misappropriation—caravans away from European establishments shaded imperceptibly into assessments of their respectability. The *Syriens* were no more than hawkers practising a dishonourable trade; they lacked both means and morals. They could not, then, be admitted into the fold of European *commerce*—a word which, again, carries a double meaning, denoting at once the mercantile community and its activities. Both they and their trading methods were unacceptable.

The distinctions the traders of Conakry drew between the European commercial community and Lebanese migrants were carried over into other writings. Aspe-Fleurimont, drawing directly upon the 1899 petition, likewise couched these differences in the register of mercantile weight and respectability. European traders, with their impressive installations and heavy investments, were indubitably 'serious'. The *Syriens*, on the other hand, were simply 'not capitalists'—lacking substantial resources, their trade could not have survived 'had they not found, among the local traders, one or two counters willing to take from them, at a slight profit, the rubber they had bought from the *indigènes* on the market'. They were 'men of few means', whose circumstances—as much as their noxious actions—hardly entitled them to the 'benevolent apathy' of functionaries. Their European competitors, meanwhile, were '*worthy of interest*', rather than the 'incomprehensible' damage which the administration had done to their fortunes, threatening to 'reduce' them to the 'simple role of traffickers on the public thoroughfare'—no better, in other words, than the *Syriens*. Thus, Aspe-Fleurimont counterposed the bourgeois diligence and respectability of the French companies of Conakry against the *Syriens*. The former had 'contributed to Conakry's rapid prosperity' through the 'considerable' amounts they had expended.[37] While their positions were threatened by administrative incompetence and unfair competition, their past accomplishments remained proof of their standing and substance. The latter were no more than petty traders. They not only lacked wherewithal, but had also largely achieved their position through the complicity of others—rather than with graft and dedication. These men were, he intimated, of little worth—whether material or moral.[38]

Such a dichotomy was, I would argue, a fiction lending legitimacy to the claims of Guinean *colons*. Aspe-Fleurimont envisioned the commercial community of Conakry as made up only of '*grandes maisons de commerce*', or important trading houses.[39] However, as he must have known, the reality was rather different. In 1899 there were, to be sure, fifteen large factories worth more than 50,000 francs at Conakry. However, there were also seventy-five trading houses lacking such heavy infrastructure.[40] The majority of those who had agreed, in 'near unanimity', to the petition presented to the administration that year must have fallen within this latter category.[41] While some larger establishments certainly participated in efforts to exclude the *Syriens*, many of those who presented their complaints to the colonial administration were independent brokers or representatives of smaller companies, without the capacity to invest in spacious premises. Thus, the status of the signatories of the petition prepared in 1907 by 'a group of small traders' in Boke is revealing. Four of these men were representatives of trading houses: Colas (agent of the COFCA), Besse (the German firm Pelizaeus), François (Beynis) and Jacquinot (Chavanel). Of these companies, only the Bordelais house Chavanel, founded in 1879, possessed installations throughout Guinea, a measure of its commercial reach and strength. The remainder confined their operations to the coast. Moreover, they were relative newcomers to Guinea, and lacked the resources of larger concerns like the CFAO or Maurel et Prom. While Beynis Frères had begun trading only in 1905, the COFCA had been founded in 1898 with a capital of 250,000 francs—by contrast, that of the CFAO stood at nine million in 1907. As for the other signatories—Kah, Goertz, Grange and Duchez—all were independent traders, the last three on the verge of bankruptcy in 1907.[42]

Talk of middle-class ease and comfortable respectability could be no more than a consolation for such men, far closer in their living and trading conditions to the less prosperous *Syriens* than to the agent of one of the larger companies, who might have expected to earn some 12,000 francs a year—along with another 4,000 to 6,000 francs in bonuses.[43] Indeed, the rancour of French *colons* in Boke was aimed at larger concerns like the CFAO as much as at the *Syriens*. Thus, the journalist Boulland de l'Escale, travelling through Guinea on a fact-finding voyage, reported in 1909 that the 'small traders of Boke and its surroundings continue to insist that [the *Syriens*] are protected and supported by the big capitalists and ruin the smaller concerns'.[44] Deep cracks, then, ran through the monolithic facade Aspe-Fleurimont sought to present: beneath criticism of the *Syriens* there often lurked resentment of the large concerns which had facilitated their ascent. There is no doubt that the lives of these small traders were difficult and anxious—their livelihoods effectively contingent upon the fortunes on the international market of rubber, which made up, on average, 73 per cent of Guinea's exports between 1892 and 1913.[45] It is the precariousness of their existences, and their proximity to the *Syriens*—far greater than they would have cared to admit—which gave such sharp urgency to the entreaties of these *colons*.

Scruples and salaam*s*

These distinctions between the *Syriens* and their honest and honourable European competitors came to form the basis for representations of Lebanese migrants as inherently unscrupulous and lacking in commercial probity. Fernand Rouget stressed that the *Syriens* 'tricked the black man as best they could by using false weights and measures in their purchases or knowingly committing errors in their price calculations'.[46] For André Arcin, these men 'used any means available to deceive the black man: cajoleries, interminable discussions, false weights, Muslim *salaams* performed in public, when most of [these men] are Catholic or Jewish'. Furthermore, they were 'damned by the European, who resented their competition, which both their fraudulent operations and their precarious establishments, free from general expenses, rendered unfair'.[47] Arcin effectively envisioned the sharp practices of the *Syriens* and their lack of capital and substantial establishments as inextricably bound together—two sides of the same coin. He was not alone in doing so. The Permanent Commission for Commerce and Industry insisted in 1904 that entry to the territories of the Protectorate—the Guinean hinterland through which the Conakry–Niger railway cut—should be restricted to 'French merchants and those foreigners presenting sufficient guarantees of their reputation, solvency and morality'.[48]

Indeed, authors and *colons* saw evidence of the *Syriens*' moral unsoundness not just in their trading methods—proof of their disregard for the conventions of commercial propriety—but also in their insalubrious living conditions. As Georges Vigarello has observed, cleanliness was, from the mid-nineteenth century onwards, increasingly seen by metropolitan politicians, hygienists and urban planners as a badge of morality: while salubrity was associated with order, dirt could denote only 'vice and disorder'.[49] It is no coincidence, then, that critics of the *Syriens* 'reproached' them, all at once, 'their sordid existence, their rapacity, their lack of dignity, their tendency to elude administrative authority, but above all their bad faith, and the duplicity of their methods'.[50] The 'repulsive filthiness' of these men was a somatic mark of their immorality.[51]

The itinerant ways of the *Syriens*, meanwhile, were not simply unfair advantages and marks of their lesser social standing. Such habits were themselves threatening. Constant movement and instability were the defining features of their condition: 'passing traffickers, without attachments or homes in the town', they operated on the public thoroughfare, bereft of 'installations'.[52] Neither in their domestic or commercial lives were they settled—one of the meanings of *s'installer*—their flighty, fraudulent ways standing in sharp contrast to the fixity of the 'established' traders of Conakry, embodied in their expensive premises. Without 'ties' to the colony, the *Syriens* were always liable to move on. This was, in one sense, little more than the expression of a suspicion of movement common at the time in metropolitan France. Daniel Nordman's remarks on the errant men and women of early modern France remain true for these years: itinerant people of all kinds were seen as inherently suspicious, 'sedentary populations' regarding the vagabond as 'a thief and a brigand' because of his or her condition.[53] Indeed, the events of 1898 in Conakry coincided with the arrest in the *métropole* of an itinerant gang known as the '*vernisseurs*', a 'band of malefactors' which—one newspaper alleged—could be charged with 'nearly all the crimes that have ravaged the department of Eure in recent times'.[54] Floating populations of all kinds were commonly seen as troublesome, their movements and motives difficult to pin down. It is no surprise, then, that the *Syriens* were deemed 'vagrants worthy only of suspicion'.[55]

Moreover, the *Syriens* were no mere hawkers, but 'foreign traffickers', strangers to the body politic.[56] They were migrants—'individuals who, having abandoned their country of origin, finding themselves homeless and with no means of subsistence, go abroad in search of adventure'.[57] The 'vagabonds' of a people, they had breached the boundaries of settled life and broken with home—as such, their motives were all the more suspicious. They could be considered as no more than the 'refuse' of a population—its waste products, who had left behind their origins to wander without aim.[58] Migration itself was seen, then, as a transgressive, demeaning act. What is more, it was—as Paul Leroy-Beaulieu had argued in the preface to an influential treatise—'an instinctive fact, which belonged to all ages of society'. Colonisation, meanwhile, was something altogether 'grander': a 'considered' act, 'dependent upon rules, and which can only stem from advanced societies'. 'Savages and barbarians emigrate sometimes, often even ... only civilised peoples colonise.'[59]

The French commercial workers of Guinea were—in their own eyes, and those of their supporters—*colons*, committed to the bold task of *mise en valeur*. They had contributed, Aspe-Fleurimont insisted, to the 'prosperity' of Guinea,[60] and had made numerous 'sacrifices' for the colony—as they themselves argued vigorously. Not only had they invested significant funds in building up their trading houses; they had also borne unflinchingly the burden of 'heavy' taxes and charges, and were disposed to continue doing so 'to facilitate the construction by the local Government of the railway from Conakry to the Niger'—attempting to play upon the fiscal worries of administrators, and their regard for railroads as the embodiment of progress, capable of 'open[ing] up to civilisation the immense regions' of French West Africa.[61]

Eastern Mediterranean migrants, meanwhile, were essentially unproductive. The *Syrien*, wrote the *colon* Gabriel Ternaux in 1913, lives in a 'shack which isn't his, as [he] does not build'; there, his 'clientele grows bit by bit', and his 'merchandise becomes more varied'. 'Not far away', 'the European trader, solidly set up to live in the country, who often cultivates a plantation in the surroundings, sees his business collapse'.[62] The distinction could not have been clearer: Frenchmen held a permanent bond to the land, worked upon it, watched over its products. The *Syriens* did not so much as lay a brick—always poised to move on, they simply accumulated profit in their flimsy, impermanent premises, their commercial ways putting paid to the aspirations and efforts of French traders. They contributed nothing to the development of the colony. Quite the opposite, in fact—they 'withdr[ew] considerable sums from the Colony each year', 'taking to their country the fruits of their skill'.[63] As one journalist put it, they were resented for 'living in Afrique Occidentale Française without contributing to its living. They go there to carry on their petty trade, send all their profits to Syria, do not consume, produce nothing and leave as soon as they have built up a little capital.' Such visions of the *Syriens* effectively complemented representations of these men as 'rapacious' and dishonest traders.[64] They not only duped African producers, and played European trading houses off one another in an effort to increase their profits, but were also profoundly unproductive;[65] the 'archetype of the parasite', they lived off the toil of others, whose energies they slowly sapped.[66]

An infection of the body politic

A term like 'parasite' carried not only a clear economic charge, but also powerful biomedical connotations. Lebanese migrants came to be envisioned—because of their supposed disregard for hygiene and proximity to Africans, their propensity for movement and, significantly, their racial origins—as a pathogenic population, each newcomer a potential harbinger of disease. Such talk was, at one level, the expression of a tangible fear of contamination, based upon the fragile sciences of climatology and bacteriology.[67] Powerful new perceptions of disease and its causes informed 'sanitary measures' like those implemented by the governor of Guinea, who ordered in 1901 the 'disinfection' of Eastern Mediterranean migrants. '[T]he arrival of these extremely dirty individuals covered with parasites who land at Conakry after having passed through places we have no knowledge of, and where they might have picked up germs and contagious illnesses', he anxiously insisted, 'poses a very real danger for Guinea'.[68]

However, this novel sense of the potency of pathogens did not obliterate older notions of disease and immunity. As Bruno Latour put it, 'the social context of a science is … most of the time made up of a *previous* science'.[69] Bacteriological explanations of illness were often simply stirred into hygienist explanations which saw racial constitution and physical environment as determinant factors, helping to foster illness or keep it at bay. The explanations for the outbreak of yellow fever in Senegal in 1901 provided by administrators and physicians hung upon such admixture—and heavily implicated the *Syriens* in the spread of this epidemic, helping to create a certain perception of this population. The disease—according to the authors of an administrative report into the causes of this epidemic—had 'begun on the periphery of the European town, or upon contact with the indigenous inhabitations'. Indeed, 'numerous cases' had been noted amidst the 'floating population' of '*Syrien*, Moroccan and Portuguese Jewish traders' who lived in the area around Rue de la Prison and Rue Vincens. These were the 'exterior boulevards' of the European town—the boundary beyond which lay the 'heaped mass of houses and shacks in which the blacks lived'. The high incidence of cases in this area was 'of the greatest importance' for any prophylactic efforts, drawing attention to the 'facility with which [Africans] introduced or disseminated this illness'. Equally significant, however, was the 'relatively low' rate of mortality in the 'Syrian (Maronite) group'. This seemed to signal that they too, unlike the Moroccans of the town, were affected primarily by 'abortive and incomplete' manifestations of the fever, which occurred 'almost exclusively' among 'the indigenous races or those close to them'. Such 'attenuated' cases were of particular concern, for these individuals, who 'eluded … all surveillance', were often 'the direct or indirect agents of importation or dissemination'. Moreover, the inherent tendency of this group for movement only increased the danger they posed. Thus, the temporary lifting of quarantine measures led to the 'exodus' of a 'great part of this floating population, disseminating through the trading posts and reaching as far as Saint-Louis'—and carrying the epidemic with them.[70]

Such epidemiological understandings were never entirely innocent. Hygienism and climatology, depending as they did on rigid racial and social gradations, easily lent themselves in turn to justification for the policing of these lines of demarcation. Bacteriology, meanwhile, provided a ready set of metaphors to speak of subversion and political disorder. It is perhaps unsurprising that these concepts were harnessed to buttress the exclusionary discourses of administrators and settlers.[71] Thus, Arcin's remark that the *Syriens* 'lived far more miserably than many blacks in huts … where not a single European could resist the climate' served to mark these men as off-white, lying beyond the pale of European society.[72] Their lack of concern for their surroundings, living '*à l'indigène*',[73] was a sure sign of their difference from Europeans. White men were not supposed to live in such conditions in the colonies. They should dwell, according to one guide to life in West Africa, in well-lit, ventilated apartments, neither too hot nor too humid. If they found himself 'obliged' to 'settle' for a while in a 'indigenous' village, they should ensure that this habitation should be more 'spacious' than those of the Africans, and 'a little isolated' to prevent the spread of disease and dirt.[74] Resistance to the depredations of the climate, meanwhile, only served to confirm this distinction between Frenchmen and *Syriens*. On this, climatologists were clear. As Alfred Virchow had put in 1885, those peoples most capable of acclimatising to the tropics were Mediterranean populations, like the Jews and Maltese, who were the 'least Aryan', and whose stock was of 'Semitic origins'.[75] The languages of contagion and hygiene, climatic and racial determinism, then, often performed essentially political tasks.

Indeed, ostensible attempts to contain contagion could sometimes disguise crude political motives. Governor-General Ponty—in a memorandum to local administrators spelling out the implications of the 1911 immigration ordinance—insisted that physicians carrying out medical examinations on new arrivals from the Eastern Mediterranean 'should not lose sight of the great powers they have been given to protect the colony against … individuals whose deplorable habits' could not but attract the suspicion of 'those charged with safeguarding public health'. Ponty, then, intimated that functionaries should not hesitate to step beyond the letter of the law in their efforts to stem migration—turning individuals free of disease away arbitrarily in order to limit the number of Ottoman migrants entering AOF. Such was the dirtiness and propensity for disease of *Syriens* that they constituted—whether fit of body or not—an inherent danger to the 'public health and order' of the colony.[76] The use of this couplet—health and order, presented as a natural pairing—meanwhile, should alert us to the constant cross-pollination between the languages of disease and politics. The *Syriens* were construed as dangerous not only because they carried illness, but because they themselves were pathogens of a kind—foreign entities entering the body politic and disrupting its orderly functioning.

FEARS OF A 'SYRIAN GUINEA'

Metropolitan traces

While these exclusionary discourses were ostensibly colonial in their focus—casting the *Syriens* as 'undesirable' because they threatened both French commerce and *mise en valeur*, *colons* and colonisation—they drew to a significant extent upon metropolitan political expression.[77] In speaking of an 'invasion'—a word first used in the petition of 1898, and which recurred insistently in following years—administrators and commercial workers sought to underscore the urgency of their entreaties. But they also belied the profound imprint the preoccupations of metropolitan France—a political culture defined, in many ways, by fear—had left upon their ways of thought.[78] 'Invasion' was a loaded term, which conjured up visions of the humiliating defeat of 1870, and of incurable demographic weakness in the face of the danger posed by stronger, more prolific foreigners.[79] This particular strand of metropolitan thought bled into anxieties, born of the sheer exiguity of colonial society, that Frenchmen might be outdone, and outnumbered, by *Syriens* in Guinea—for, as the minister of colonies nervously observed in 1911, 'a mere 472 of our traders are facing down some thousand Asiatic[s]', who threatened not only France's economic 'interests', but also her 'very influence' in Guinea.[80]

Most significantly, however, the term directly invoked fears of a creeping Jewish 'invasion' of France, a 'conquest' which would reduce an entire nation to tillers of the soil—as the 'prophet' of anti-Semitism, the journalist Édouard Drumont, had ominously put it.[81] It should not be forgotten that the first attempts to shut the *Syriens* out of Guinean commercial society coincided with the marked upsurge in anti-Semitic sentiment which followed the outbreak in autumn 1897 of renewed controversy over the conviction of Alfred Dreyfus. Moreover, these *colons* had much in common with the shopkeepers and commercial workers who participated in the anti-Semitic riots which broke out across France in the early months of 1898.[82] The traders of Conakry shared with others in Paris, Bordeaux or Marseille not only a seething resentment of 'foreign' competitors—whether these were *Syrien* or Jewish—but also more specific recriminations and demands. As the socialist Paul Lafargue tartly remarked, anti-Semitism was, in many ways, an 'issue for shopkeepers'.[83]

Such similarities were sometimes striking. Thus, the president of the Union Commerciale de Roubaix et de ses Cantons wrote in 1898: 'You have worked for forty years to create a little business that will feed your small family; you pay your taxes, you contribute to the prosperity and well-being of the town; … then, suddenly, on the prompting of doctrinaires, capitalists from every country under the sun set up cooperatives that are privileged in various ways and pay no taxes, and you are completely ruined; the business you were so proud of is worth nothing.'[84] Much like the petition drafted in Conakry the same year, this text regarded small French traders as epigones of hard work and dutiful domesticity deserving of recognition, citizens who had given a great deal to both state and community. Moreover, it drew upon a shared resentment of free trade, the misguided 'doctrinaires' who imposed it and the rapacious, irresponsible foreigners who exploited it. The police commissioner of

Nantes, meanwhile, reported in January of the same year that the *négociants* of the town, arguing that 'they could not hold out against Jewish competition because of the lowness of the taxes' these shopkeepers paid, and which 'they claim are not in keeping with the multiplicity of goods and merchandise they sell', sought to create an association capable of defending 'their interests against the Jews and [presenting] their desiderata to the public authorities'. While the actions of the traders of Guinea were born of the quite particular circumstances they faced, we would be wrong to regard them in isolation. We must, it is clear, set them against the context of anti-Semitic agitation and commercial resentment which ran through French towns and cities in 1898. These men were not alone in drawing lines separating 'upright' traders from the 'dishonest' competitors who undercut them, threatening their livelihoods—and marking these distinctions in a language which conflated the registers of race and business.[85]

Indeed, the discourses administrators and traders spun sometimes seem tracings of the vituperative tirades of prominent anti-Semitic publicists like Drumont, whose *La France Juive*—which had sold anything between 65,000 and 150,000 copies within a year of its publication in 1886—enjoyed renewed popularity in these years.[86] Such borrowings were most patent in the writings of Gabriel Ternaux, who had established a newspaper, *L'AOF—Écho de la Côte Occidentale Française*, in the late 1900s to 'defend the interests' of *colons*. While Ternaux maintained that his slim publication was intended as a 'free tribune' for all settlers to voice their opinions, it was largely given over in practice to his own attacks upon Eastern Mediterranean migrants—and the administrators who had done little to stop the inroads of these interlopers.

In an article entitled 'L'Invasion', he presented the contest between Frenchmen and the *Syriens*—those 'barbarian cohorts', intent upon the 'conquest' of West Africa—in stark, martial terms. This confrontation was a 'struggle of the new ages, more violent and cruel even than that of earliest times'—an inevitable by-product of modernity, which brought with it untrammelled exchange and movement of people. The consequences of such disruptions and displacements were 'inexorable': they could not but result in a 'war, ferocious and pitiless' for commercial supremacy fought out on the 'vast economic battlefields' of West Africa. A contest with unprecedented consequences, it would reduce its 'innumerable' victims to the status of mere 'slaves', and make 'masters' of its victors. Moreover, it would undo the efforts of *colons* to make something of Africa; the 'superb remains' of France's possessions would 'expire, convulsing, under the burning sun'. Ternaux's seething resentment of the *Syriens*, then, belied a belief in the regenerative potential of the colonies—ruined by the depredations of these foreign aggressors—and a profound unease with the changes consuming both France and its overseas possessions in the first years of the twentieth century.

It is no accident that he should have chosen to sign this article with the classical 'Xanthos'. In so naming himself, he sought to mark his own position, standing against the tides of modernity. However, he also alluded by this act to the city of

Xanthos, whose men had, according to Herodotus, destroyed their acropolis and killed their dependents before engaging in a suicidal sortie against their Persian besiegers. This pseudonym stood as the handy signifier for a vision of an embattled French people, engaged in a doomed confrontation with foreign elements, in which each protagonist deploys the 'genius of [his] race'. While France, the inheritor of Hellenic virtue, stood for civilisation and manly order, its 'barbarian' aggressors represented only destruction and Oriental cruelty, taking on the role of the effeminate Persians. Indeed, his anger found expression in a language which drew in equal measure upon the registers of race and gender.

Thus, 'they'—these invaders, enemies whom Ternaux refuses to name, reducing them to anonymous alterity—had arrived neither 'clad with iron', nor 'even heroically naked, the axe or pike in hand, ready for the fair combat'. Instead, they came 'vile, creeping, treachery in their hearts, ruse in their eyes, lies upon their lips; imposture guide[d] them, hate move[d] them'. Here were the militaristic undertones of talk of honour and loyalty laid bare. The *Syriens* were lesser men because of their innate cowardice, their despicable dishonesty—fairness was beyond them. These men, whose 'furious cavalcade' through Guinea threatened to destroy the colony, were but an 'ill-fed horde'—the assonance between *famélique* and *féminin*, underscoring the association between weakness and effeminacy, lost in translation. Ternaux, by speaking of these aggressors only in the plural as a 'horde', a nameless multitude, drew upon perceptions of the crowd common in the early years of the Third Republic.[87] To be subsumed into the masses involved 'a regression to a primitive state'—men, in entering this space of contagion and suggestibility, surrendered their individuality, and became capable of 'savagery'. Moreover, the crowd was explicitly feminine—uncontrolled, and difficult to control.[88] Indeed, the 'dusky minds' of the *Syriens* were 'feverishly haunted' by visions of 'perverse fortune'. They 'dream[t] of returning' to the 'hearth', 'arrogant and proud, to lay out … their conquered riches'.[89] Giving themselves over—like women—to the 'bewildering play of feeling', they were 'incapable of being guided by fear of shame', and were ruled by their basest emotions, by cupidity and cruel desire.[90]

Moreover, Ternaux argued elsewhere, the disordered psyches of these men manifested themselves in disorderly acts.[91] Recounting the shoot-out between Christian and Muslim 'Orientals' in Mamou, he intimated that such violence was a product of their 'turbulent' natures, an essential part of their being—after all, 'every self-respecting *Syrien* owns at least one' Browning. Furthermore, such outbreaks of brutality were unavoidable in a society riven by confessional difference. These men were simply behaving 'as [they would] in Syria',[92] 'that harsh fatherland tyrannised by hatreds and wild massacres'.[93] Ternaux, then, assembled an exclusionary discourse of exceptional virulence from notions of the Orient as a space of disorder, despotic violence and feminine unreason—turning upon their head appeals for benevolence to Eastern Mediterranean migrants as victims of brutal sectarian oppression. In doing so, he seemingly borrowed from the anti-Semitism of Drumont and others. 'Imposture', slyness, an innate mental weakness, arrogance and cupidity, pride without honour, all these were traits which recurred again and again in contemporary accounts of the Jew's nature. Moreover, these texts came to view the confrontation between Frenchman and Jew in terms of a secular confrontation between Aryans and Semites, a 'war of the races' which snaked its way through history. The Trojan wars, the Arab 'invasion of Spain and the Midi', the 'heroic revolution of the Crusades whose superior effects lasted three centuries' all were instances, for Drumont, of this conflict which pitted Christendom against an indistinct Orient—at once 'Saracen' and Semitic, Jewish and Muslim.[94]

Jews and others

While no other critic of the *Syriens* wrote in terms quite as virulent as those of Ternaux, he was not alone in drawing upon such notions. For Rouget, Eastern Mediterranean migrants showed a 'special aptitude for commerce', and a gift for duplicity.[95] The Jewish race, too, had a 'special aptitude for acquiring capital', insisted Goncourt in 1897.[96] Indeed, argued Drumont, 'the Semite possesses a vocation for traffic, a genius for everything that is exchange, for everything which might constitute an opportunity to do over his neighbour'.[97] This was no more than a cruder statement of the views expressed by Proudhon—upon whom Drumont had explicitly drawn: '[h]e is an intermediary, always fraudulent and parasitic, who operates, in trade as in philosophy, by means of falsification, counterfeiting [and] horse-dealing'.[98] The *Syriens*, wrote Arcin, were '"soft and treacherous", bearing without complaint the insults heaped upon them, [and] the measures taken against them' while carrying on their trade—their failure to take offence another sign of the lack of honour they belied in their commercial dealings.[99] 'The Jew', opined Léon Daudet in 1896, 'has no pride, no tact, no sense of honour, no pity, no capacity for honour. He is thus able to insinuate himself into the confidence of Christians and set them against each other.'[100] The Semite, a figure 'so hermetically sealed to our conception of honour' that he could only hope to play the pretence of masculinity,[101] had 'replaced violence with ruse'. His tactics had 'nothing brutal' about them; he had about him 'an insinuating way of chasing the indigenous inhabitants from their houses'.[102] Indeed, Semites were always ready to seize the fruits of others' labour. While the 'Aryan undertakes the voyages of exploration and discovers America', the 'Semite', who has 'no capacity for creation', 'waits until the land has been 'explored and cleared to enrich himself at the expense of others'.[103] The *Syriens*, likewise, were unproductive, profiting from the colonising efforts of Frenchmen who had sacrificed their capital for the development of Guinea. The Jews' essential distaste for production and order, suggested Drumont, was born of their errant state: 'the Jewish race can live in no organised society. It is a race of nomads and Bedouins. When it has set up camp somewhere, it destroys everything all around.'[104] As Jacques Bainville put it in 1905, 'the Jew does not plant, because he has no roots'.[105] Both *Syriens* and Jews, then, were associated with vagabondage, with suspicious opportunism and a flight from responsibility.

This implicit analogy between Jew and *Syrien* manifested itself even in the act of naming this latter population. As contemporary commentators readily acknowledged, *Syrien* was a capacious term in early-twentieth century French West Africa, used to denote not only people from the Eastern Mediterranean, but also a motley population of 'Italians, Moroccan and Gibraltar Jews, Maltese, Egyptians'—though not, it seems, Muslim Moroccans, established in the localities of the Sahel since at least the mid-nineteenth century.[106] This practice was, in one sense, a matter of administrative convenience—of subsuming quite different groups into a simple, more legible, category.[107] However, it was more than that. Shoving these various populations into a single bracket was a means of denying them a stable past, of tainting them with the blemish of diversity and rootlessness. Thus, André Arcin insisted that *Syriens* 'came not only from Asia Minor … but from all the Mediterranean ports of Asia and Africa'.[108] The members of this conglomerate sprang not from one single place, but from points scattered around the rim of the Mediterranean; they had no fixed point of origin. Indeed, Famechon, the head of the Guinean customs service, had explicitly argued as much, labelling this amorphous, shifting population as 'cosmopolitan' in 1900.[109] This was no innocent, handy epithet, but a word weighted with a quite specific meaning—for, as contemporaries well knew, it carried clear associations with anti-Semitism. Both well-known propagandists, and ordinary members of the anti-Dreyfusard demonstrations of 1898, frequently used the term to distinguish themselves—'good Frenchmen, children of our old soil', as one journalist put it—from their opponents, the 'dregs of cosmopolitan gangs'.[110] Jews were, for Drumont, 'atrocious cosmopolitans, stinking and scabies-ridden, who peddled their oranges on the port of Tunis or Alexandria'—a virulent description which shares with Arcin's account of the diasporic origins of the *Syriens* a vision of the Mediterranean and its port cities as a space of constant displacement.[111] Fernand Rouget, meanwhile, recounted the appearance, 'one day on the marketplace' of 'a Levantine, come from we know not where'.[112] Such a striking image resonated closely with Drumont's description of Jews as men who 'arrive from who knows where', and 'live in a mystery'.[113]

I am not arguing that authors like Arcin and Rouget drew directly upon such passages in putting together their visions of the *Syriens*—we have no way of knowing that for certain. Nonetheless, it seems clear enough that they called upon a shared stock of anti-Semitic imagery to cast doubt upon the origins of the *Syriens*, using its commonplace images to make of them men of no nation comparable to the Jews of metropolitan exclusionary thought.[114] Indeed, this process of appropriation was facilitated by the gradual displacement, in the last years of the nineteenth century, of a specific anti-Judaism by a more diffuse anti-Semitism, which lent such discourses both a categorical edge and a wider currency.[115] Administrators, journalists and *colons* drew a multitude of unspoken analogies between *Syriens* and Jews. The former, much like the latter, were irrefutably different from Europeans. They showed an innate propensity for truck; free from scruples, they excelled at exchange, and yet were incapable of production. Shifting from place to place, they belonged to no nation;

they were fated to remain vagabonds wandering the world, sowing destruction in their path. Shifty and devoid of morality, sly and soft, where Europeans were settled, straightforward and upright, they were somehow not quite men. Their behaviour, but also their dirty, disease-prone bodies, betrayed a certain deficiency. The writings of Drumont and other anti-Semitic publicists provided ready material for such comparisons—cloth that was cut and fitted to their particular exigencies by writers concerned with the 'Syrian question'. While metropolitan writers warned ominously of the coming of a 'Jewish France', the latter feared the outcome of an 'invasion' 'so strong that one of these Syrian traders had had cards made giving his name and address in 'Syrian Guinea'.[116]

Moreover, analogies between *Syriens* and Jews also shaded into the comparisons these authors consistently made between Eastern Mediterranean migrants and the African traders of Guinea. Such pairings were sometimes arrived at through rhetorical slights and slippages, but also the ways in which these authors organised their texts, synoptic accounts in which they described in turn each of the populations of the colony. For Arcin, the *Syriens* came from 'Asia *and* Africa': they were at once foreign to Guinea and yet, somehow, also of the place—in a way in which Frenchmen were not, and could not be.[117] What is more, he described the Sarakhole as 'the Jews of West Africa'—a group that shared with the *Syriens*, that 'mainly Catholic and Jewish' floating population, both wandering ways and a gift for trade. Guébhard, meanwhile, argued that the Dyula villages of Futa Jalon had their origins in the settlement of 'Mandingo or Sarakhole merchants' who lived 'near the sovereigns, *almamys* or province chieftains', 'paying the protection' these rulers afforded them by providing 'loans in kind or specie'. These traders were 'in a sense … individuals of the same type as those Jews, Levantines and Lombards who set up their ghettoes in our towns under our kings and feudal lords'.[118] In making such a comparison, Guébhard drew a connection between contemporary migrants to Guinea—'Syrians', North African Jews and Italians—and the Dyula and Sarakhole populations of Futa Jalon.[119] Such links, as I have suggested, did not simply seep through the language of these texts; they were also incorporated in their very structure. Guébhard considered both African and Eastern Mediterranean traders in a single section entitled, simply, 'The Dyula. Their commercial methods. The Syrians'.[120] Arcin, meanwhile, dealt with commercial 'races' like the Dyula and Sierra Leone Creoles and the *Syriens* in one sweep, before moving on to speak of 'European commerce'—marking the break between non-white and white with an emphatic '*Enfin*'.[121]

These layers of comparison, overlapping like Venn diagrams, served not only to mark both African itinerant traders and *Syriens* as somehow Semitic, and therefore inherently suspicious, but also to draw Eastern Mediterranean migrants into the world of African commerce, thereby casting them as all the more different from their European competitors. Thus, Arcin maintained that the Sarakhole, Dyula and Sierra Leone Creoles formed, alongside the *Syriens*, the 'transition between indigenous and European commerce'.[122] Rouget, meanwhile, painted a rather more sharply defined picture of the commercial world of Guinea. The large trading houses, which sat at its apex, were followed by 'second class merchants' who lacked the 'resources needed to establish' a substantial operation; after these came 'Syrian traders', then the Sierra Leonean, Susu and Wolof with their 'small shops' in the towns and coastal villages, and finally 'indigenous' hawkers, 'the last intermediaries through whose hands goods pass before arriving to the consumer'.[123] In this hierarchy, commercial capacity and racial status were intermeshed.

Indeed, distinctions between Frenchmen and strangers in the colonies depended, for Aspe-Fleurimont, not only upon metropolitan notions of class and standing, but also upon local notions of racial difference. The *Syriens* had set up stall, he maintained, 'on the market where had been sold, until then, the small goods used by the blacks in their cooking, peppers, dry fish, fruits', and such like. There, they 'trafficked their bazaar objects by the side of the indigenous women' who traded these products.[124] Eastern Mediterranean migrants, rather than setting up shop in the fashion of European traders, operated on the market. This was at once an explicitly African space, where mere foodstuffs—relatively insignificant goods—were bought and sold, and an arena for female activity. The *Syriens* remained closer, in this representation, to Africans than to Frenchmen; their association with the market-women of Conakry, meanwhile, underlined their babbling, unmanly trading methods. Finally, the goods these men offered had little value when set alongside the textiles European traders offered in their premises: they were no more than shoddy *pacotille*,[125] 'trifling bazaar goods'.[126] This was a pregnant choice of words, evoking Oriental difference. There ran through such descriptions, I would argue, a determination to draw clear lines of demarcation between European commerce—with its formal infrastructure and rational underpinnings, its account-books and upstanding managers—and non-European trade conducted in informal conditions on the market. These are categories which are still with us, framing our understanding of economies in Africa and elsewhere. We must remain alert, then, to the conditions in which such distinctions were constituted.

Conclusion

Warwick Anderson has written that colour was the 'least' significant aspect of the complex 'racial calculus' early-twentieth century Europeans grew used to carrying out. Whiteness was not defined by skin tone, but any number of physical and psychological criteria—'a typical bodily constitution or temperament; a cultural legacy or thought style; a virility or femininity; … a predisposition or resistance to certain disease', and so on.[127] I have sought in this chapter to draw out the manifold ways in which Frenchmen in Guinea worked out such reckonings of difference, and to sort Europeans from *Syriens*. Administrators, colonial propagandists and commercial workers drew upon commonplace metropolitan notions of commercial morality and equity, of hygiene and disease, and of social and racial difference in their efforts to discriminate and demarcate. Splicing here and stitching there, they fashioned new discourses from old, fitted to the task of marking off these men as strangers in the colonies.

4

FAILING TO STEM THE TIDE

LEBANESE MIGRATION AND THE COMPETING PREROGATIVES OF THE IMPERIAL STATE

The functionaries of AOF consistently failed to introduce effective legislative controls upon Eastern Mediterranean migration to the territories under their purview in the years before 1939. That they did so was not for lack of trying. Administrators both in the territorial government of Guinea and in the Government-General of the Federation in Dakar repeatedly attempted, from 1905 onwards, to close its gates to these interlopers of empire. However, despite their attempts to channel and stem this flow, the administrators of AOF remained unable to impose effective legislative checks upon the movements of these men and women.

Their failure to do so seems all the more striking when one remembers these years were marked by sustained efforts to bolster bulwarks against human movement across the world.[1] Such initiatives, it has recently been recognised, began in many cases well before the outbreak of global conflict in 1914. As early in some places as the 1880s and 1890s, decades long regarded by scholars as the heyday of untrammelled migration, administrators and politicians in the United States and France, Australia and South Africa sought to regulate the movements of itinerant peoples and migrants deemed 'undesirable' on racial grounds.[2] And they did so not only by imposing restrictions upon entry, but also by making use of powers of expulsion.[3] These measures grew increasingly rigid during the First World War, when passport controls were widely reintroduced, before being cemented in its wake by legislation like the American Reed-Johnson Acts of 1921 and 1924, which introduced a series of quotas upon migration from various parts of the world.[4] The second of these measures was particularly significant, making of 'remote control', as Aristide Zolberg and others have named the screening of migrants at their point of departure, a central feature of migration control.[5] This regulation, rapidly replicated by governments elsewhere, required passengers to present a visa, granted by the appropriate consular authorities, before boarding ship.[6]

The early years of the twentieth century, then, did not just see a gradual erosion of the liberty of movement. They also witnessed both the growing sophistication of administrative initiatives—which shifted, as John Torpey has argued, from efforts to supervise migrants on the territory, to checking their entry at the border and finally towards remote control—and their proliferation, as innovations in one country were rapidly emulated, and augmented, by others keen to strengthen their defences against human movement. In the words of Adam McKeown, this period witnessed the universalisation of 'the basic principles of border control', which came to serve increasingly as the 'foundation of sovereignty for all states within the [international] system'.[7] By the Second World War, many states had come to resemble—at least on paper—'the wall-enclosed towns of the medieval period'.[8]

But while governments everywhere strove to fasten their bolts, the administrators of AOF kept their doors reluctantly open. This chapter examines the causes of this failure. The latter was, in essence, a consequence not of its own lack of administrative wherewithal, but rather of external pressures which significantly constrained its capacity to act. Particularly significant was the unyielding position of the French Ministry of Foreign Affairs, whose functionaries insisted that Lebanese and Syrian migrants be accorded particularly lenient treatment both on grounds of diplomatic reciprocity and, more significantly, in order to protect France's cherished interests in the Eastern Mediterranean.

The inconsistencies of empire

We may learn much from a sustained examination of the frustrated legislative schemes of the administrators of AOF; their fraught exchanges with the Quai d'Orsay—always quick to protect aggressively its own prerogatives; and dealings with migrants who sought to capitalise upon France's political and sentimental commitments in the Eastern Mediterranean to obtain clemency in the face of unfavourable rulings. This exercise can help us to understand better the ways in which the imperatives of governance and diplomatic reciprocity could—and did—prove impediments to the seemingly impermeable controls upon human movement erected in the first half of the twentieth century. I am concerned here not so much with telling again the familiar tales of inconsistency, evasion and fraud—with underlining the eternal disjuncture between the neatness of paper schemes and the messy reality of practical inefficacy. Rather, I wish to shed light upon an often neglected aspect of this story, stressing the ways in which administrative endeavour was stymied by prevailing reasons of state.

Furthermore, I wish to flesh out our understanding of the ways in which colonial states operated—or failed to operate. I intend to do so in several, closely interlinked, ways. I hope, first, to throw light upon the far-flung webs of interest in which administrators in any single colonial territory were regularly enmeshed, and which left their own powers severely curtailed by priorities well beyond their purview.[9] For it is easily overlooked by scholars of colonial statecraft that territorial administrations, and those who staffed them, did not dwell in glorious isolation. Rather, they were but part of an overarching 'imperial system'—if one which was markedly unsystematic in its composition, remaining to the end a patchwork quilt of varying administrative arrangements and contested prerogatives.[10] Indeed—and this is my second point—relations between the numerous departments which made up the French empire-state, that sprawling congeries of agencies and administrations, were marked by clear and deep asymmetries of power, which allowed some to assert their own priorities of rule above those of others.

Moreover, this unevenness in the power of departments and the status of territories was a structural feature of France's empire. The density of the Quai d'Orsay's strategic and affective investment in the Eastern Mediterranean, as much as its superior position to the Ministry of Colonies, determined the fate of the legal endeavours of functionaries in AOF in the years before the First World War. The Mandate states of Lebanon and Syria, meanwhile, were no simple colonial territories.[11] Rather, they were annexes of empire—at once inside, and outside, its formal realm. The relations of French functionaries to the constituents of these novel constructs were marked by a profound ambiguity. On the one hand, they retained a distinctly imperial attachment to the territories of the Eastern Mediterranean—often considering them, in what could perhaps never have been more than wishful thinking, as zones of uncontested French sovereignty. On the other, they sought to craft these polities in the image of 'the universal ideal of the sovereign state'. In their willingness to treat Lebanon and Syria as entities which stood apart from the main body of the French empire, and their citizens as that most paradoxical of creatures—colonial citizens—they participated in efforts to 'rework the Westphalian system … on a global, extra-European basis'.[12]

While the citizens of Lebanon and Syria undoubtedly bore the brunt of the postwar settlement in many regards, they were, in one important respect, its beneficiaries. For France's Mandatory commitments enshrined their right to free movement within both metropolitan France and its empire. The tale I recount here of the frustrated endeavour of functionaries in AOF might equally be told of the administrators of Guadeloupe and Martinique, who encountered much the same difficulties in their efforts to erect boundaries against Eastern Mediterranean migration.[13] Crucially, this right was accorded to them not as imperial subjects, but as citizens of 'most favoured nations'. Lebanon and Syria were considered in this regard—if not in other, perhaps more significant, domains of sovereignty—independent entities bound to France by treaties of reciprocity. This is a pertinent reminder of the inconsistent, incoherent legal basis upon which rested the new migration regime brought into being, in the interwar years, by the French government's ratification of a raft of bilateral agreements with countries such as Italy, Poland, Spain and Czechoslovakia.[14] It is no doubt true that, as Mary Dewhurst Lewis has argued, these created 'new inequalities among migrants' which 'reflected the uneven power relations … between nations in Europe and … European countries and their colonies', granting 'foreign nationals from treaty countries' 'more substantive rights' than were accorded to 'migrants from within the French empire'. But equally striking is the fact that Lebanese and Syrian migrants did not fall prey to such prejudicial measures, as did the Moroccans and Tunisians who nominally benefited from the protection of France. Rather, Mandatory citizens were granted a privileged position within the complex 'system of stratifications' by which various mobile populations were accorded social rights within the French body politic.[15] The stance of the French functionaries of the Quai d'Orsay and the Mandatory High Commission towards their Lebanese and Syrian charges was, then, Janus-faced. Eastern Mediterranean migrants were granted freedom of movement as the citizens of nominally sovereign polities. But they were accorded such a right only because French officials believed them to be bound to their own nation by the ties of imperial benevolence and appreciation.[16]

For France's imperial entanglement with the Eastern Mediterranean—though undoubtedly 'coded in languages and practices of dominance and possession'—remained 'amorously defined'. Its investment in the region, always as much sentimental as strategic, was 'bounded by and invested in demonstrations of love', its contours 'discursively shaped' by an amorous lexicon of reciprocal feeling, and a marked insistence on the familial ties which ruled the relations between the Christian communities of the Eastern Mediterranean, in particular, and France—their 'tender mother' and secular protector.[17] As Ann Laura Stoler has contended, such harping upon the affective was more than a 'smokescreen of rule, … a ruse masking the dispassionate calculations that preoccupy states'. Rather, imperial reason of state rested upon a 'visceral register'—on the constant deployment, and management, of notions of honour, charity and reciprocity, on contemptuous anger or kindly concern.[18]

The duty of care and protection enshrined in the Mandate was one functionaries at the Quai d'Orsay and the High Commission in Beirut seem to have taken seriously—if only because it permitted the management of affective states, the cultivation of feeling. As Elizabeth Thompson has argued, Mandatory rule over the states the French constructed from the smouldering remains of the Ottoman empire was marked by the emergence of a 'colonial civic order'. While administrative practice shifted perceptibly in the mid-1930s, with the creation of a 'colonial welfare state' providing 'social benefits' directly, in place of the rather more 'paternalistic' treatment previously meted out by French administrators through their local intermediaries, these bureaucrats remained committed—in some form or another—to the wellbeing of their charges throughout the interwar years.[19]

However, this was by no means a unilateral process. Lebanese and Syrian citizens participated in this new order, negotiating and defining their entitlements and rights through regular interactions with functionaries, routine transactions conducted across the 'desks and tables' of government offices.[20] As I will argue, migrants faced with orders of expulsion—and the Lebanese dignitaries and French functionaries whose assistance they enlisted—adroitly played the game of juridical politics, nagging at small tears in the legal fabric of empire until they succeeded in overturning the decisions of administrators in AOF.[21] Despite the existence of a clear legal framework, the latter found it difficult to frame their work within the 'fixed' 'rules' of 'laws or administrative regulations'.[22]

There was, as Gérard Noiriel has observed, little Weberian about a process in which administrators remained compelled by circumstance, continuing—as they had long done—to consider 'individual', 'particular' cases rather than reaching decisions based upon 'abstract criteria, identical' in all circumstances. Moreover, transactions between officials and migrants and their intercessors remained profoundly 'personal' throughout this period, lacking the anonymous detachment of bureaucratic practice. Not only were these exchanges often conducted directly between migrants or those lending them assistance, and high functionaries like the governor-general or the minister of colonies; they also drew upon 'Christian norms of charity far more than upon administrative principles', retaining many of the features of private correspondence in place of the form-filling and standardised language of bureaucratic process.[23] Retracing the often protracted tractations around migration controls and their application may allow us, then, to allow the uneven workings of a messy imperial order, riven with inconsistency and imbalances of power. But it can also enable us to understand the ways in which Eastern Mediterranean migrants exploited this convoluted web of legal obligations and pragmatic considerations.

'Creaking, jerking, jostling'

Scholars like Frederick Cooper and Peter Zinoman have, in recent years, come to query conceptions of colonial states as purposeful, monolithic institutions capable not only of performing the essential functions of sovereignty—retaining the monopoly over violence, enumerating people, gathering taxes and, of course, securing the integrity of the territories under their supervision—but also of modifying and moulding the behaviour of their subjects.[24] They have, instead, insisted that they were messy congeries of competing agencies and agendas, constantly frustrated by material circumstances and incapable of broadcasting—to borrow Jeffrey Herbst's term—their authority beyond a few scattered points.[25] Thus, Zinoman has argued that French Indochina's 'decentralised and heterogeneous' penal system, with its 'brutality, squalor and corruption', 'embodied the chaotic and unsystematic workings of the colonial state'.[26] Cooper, meanwhile, has maintained that 'power in colonial societies was more arterial than capillary'; far from diffusing through society, insidiously working away at the site of the individual, it was 'concentrated spatially and socially, not very nourishing beyond such domains, and in need of a pump to push it from moment to moment and place to place'.[27] In this perspective, colonial administrations were not so much antiseptic laboratories of modernity in which administrators could escape the constraints of metropolitan governance,[28] as faltering, belaboured enterprises—'creaking, jerking, jostling, gasping' declensions of the forms of state-craft elaborated in Europe during this time.[29]

Such visions of colonial governance have come to hold increasing sway in recent years. But they illuminate only what we might call the inner story of colonial power, its intimate failures and intrinsic weaknesses. The power—the capacity to act—of colonial functionaries was undermined not only by their administrations' impecuniousness or by their lack of numbers, but also by external exigencies which affected what they could, and could not, do—considerably narrowing, in some cases, the range of options available to them. As John Torpey has pointed out, a state's sovereignty does not rest simply upon its capacity to exercise authority within its realm. Affirmations of sovereign power can acquire meaning only with the assent of a wider society of states, and are governed by a 'set of norms and prescriptions to which individual [polities] must respond'.[30] This, of course, is all the truer of colonial administrations like those of AOF: the Federation's territories were not islands of authority, self-contained entities cut off from wider currents, but rather elements of a far more extensive imperial polity. As but one part of this overarching entity, their interests, and the ability of their administrators to reach decisions independent of the metropolitan state, could be—and, indeed, were—dismissed in particular instances.

It may well be, of course, that French *commandants de cercle* scattered through the administrative districts of AOF were, before 1939, the 'almost undisputed masters' of this empire in most matters. These men gleefully seized upon the Government-General's inability to broadcast its own directives to assert their own will, paying little heed to the 'growing pile of official journals and explanatory circulars' that Maurice Delafosse—an administrator in pre-First World War Côte d'Ivoire before he became an influential ethnographer—recalled stashing beneath his head as he fell to peaceful sleep at night.[31] However, *commandants de cercle* had no control over entry to the Federation, nor did they possess the power to expel undesirable migrants. They could only pass to their superiors their recommendations, which would then travel up the administrative hierarchy before being decided upon by the governor-general himself in Dakar. In this area of policy, at least, decision-making remained highly centralised.

More significantly still, the governor-general themselves, though nominally designated as 'depositor[ies] of the powers of the Republic', were never in practice proconsuls possessing plenipotentiary authority over the territories in their trusteeship. The deep-seated fears of both the governors of individual West African territories, and functionaries at the Ministry of Colonies, that the creation of a powerful central executive in Dakar would wear down their own prerogatives led to the 'slow construction, often through jurisprudence' of a set of constraints upon the autonomy of the governor-general. These administrators, while they certainly did retain a degree of latitude, were ultimately bound in matters of legislation—and, particularly, those which might impact upon France's foreign relations—to the metropolitan government.[32]

In turn, the lowly position of the Ministry of the Colonies within the 'ministerial pecking order' left it at a distinct disadvantage in its dealings with other departments of state—and militated against the imposition of a special regime regulating the entry of Eastern Mediterranean migrants to AOF. Formed only in 1894—until which point France's overseas possessions had been administered, with a few exceptions, by the Ministry of the Navy—the fledgling colonial administration established at the Rue Oudinot was still regarded some twenty years later as the 'Cinderella Ministry'. It not only consistently faced the considerable hostility of the Ministry of Foreign Affairs and that of the Interior, disdainful of this poor and somewhat embarrassing relation, and wary of any attack upon their prerogatives in North Africa. Further-more, it was hampered by its chaotic organisation—a 'muddled assemblage of small bureaucratic contrivances', as an internal report put it in 1911—and chronic internal discord, 'the inability of all its officials to arrive at general views or to coordinate their efforts' becoming infamous in Parisian administrative circles.[33] Functionaries at the Rue Oudinot could hardly hope, in such circumstances, to provide any tangible opposition to the desires of their counterparts at the Quai d'Orsay.

There can be no doubt, then, that formidable institutional impediments stood in the way of any attempts by administrators in AOF to develop a migration policy away from the scrutiny and strictures of their superiors at the Ministry of Colonies—and, crucially, the Quai d'Orsay. If, as John Torpey has maintained, the monopoly to authorise and restrict movement must be considered an essential attribute of the state, it was one which was never held solely by administrators in French West Africa, who effectively lacked the capacity to decide alone on the legal status of Lebanese migrants.[34] Rather, they had to pay heed to the will of metropolitan agencies of state.

'The friendship of souls'

The opposition of the Quai d'Orsay to the introduction in AOF of prohibitive measures targeting Eastern Mediterranean migrants in the years before the establish-ment of the Mandate was born of a deep-seated, and growing, concern for the safeguard of French political, commercial, educational and religious interests in the Eastern Mediterranean. In particular, France's vaunted moral protectorate over the Maronite and Greek Catholic populations of Greater Syria—long a cornerstone of her policy in the region—took on greater significance as her position in the Ottoman empire came under increasing pressure from foreign competition.[35] While Wilhelmine Germany secured economic concessions like the Baghdad railway, Italian and Anglo-American missionary establishments threatened the spiritual monopoly of French education. As Maurice Pernot, the editor of the *Journal des Débats*, declared in 1913, 'in certain parts of Lebanon, where we assume our influ-ence to be preponderant, English is certainly better known than French; Italian is making rapid progress at certain points along the coast. Elsewhere, we are holding our own, but nowhere are we gaining ground.'[36]

This was all the more worrying for, as John Spagnolo has noted, French diplomats saw their nation's presence in the Eastern Mediterranean as inextricably 'linked to favourable relations with their political clients in Lebanon'.[37] France's economic interests—her considerable stake in the Ottoman public debt, but also in financial institutions such as the Imperial Ottoman Bank, which controlled the state tobacco monopoly and a number of public utilities and railway companies; in port concessions at Beirut, Tripoli, Haifa and Jaffa; and in mines, road construction and various other operations—were dispersed widely throughout what remained of the empire.[38] However, the Ottoman empire was, for many of those most intimately involved in furthering French interests in the Eastern Mediterranean, 'not merely a field of economic activity for France. It [was] also, and above all, a territory for the radiation of her intellect and the expansion of her culture.'[39]

And, as French colonial propagandists and Catholic missionaries never ceased to reiterate, 'none of the Catholic communities of the Orient calling upon France's protection since the Crusades has shown greater gratitude and devotion than the Maronites'.[40] In a series of articles, pamphlets and books, historians and journalists elaborated, in florid terms, a narrative of an enduring and secular reciprocal friendship—stressing equally the 'love for France' with which the towns of Mount Lebanon 'humm[ed] and vibrat[ed]' and France's own obligations towards their Uniate inhabitants.[41] As Gabriel Hanotaux put it, the Maronites 'who saved their liberty, their religion, their race, simply by *holding out*, when others elsewhere richer and more powerful bowed their heads', were indissolubly bound to France. Indeed, he insisted, she simply could not relinquish her longstanding obligations towards them, for 'these peasants—whose friendship for France has been handed down from father to son for twelve centuries—… lived, from afar, the lives of our own fathers … they are, all in all, ours; they possess a part of our thoughts, our will, our heart. France has never abandoned them; and she will not abandon them.'[42]

These words were more than just fig leaves pruriently disguising the cruder designs of power. Rather, both a set of deeply-rooted conceptions of the Orient as an inherently spiritual place and an idealist understanding of the world led statesmen and thinkers to insist that France's position in the Eastern Mediterranean rested upon her sentimental ties to its Christian populations. It is not that strategic considerations did not figure in such a political calculus. As Georges Leygues, one of the architects of France's Syrian policy during the First World War, declared: 'It is in the Mediterranean that can be found the axis of French [strategy]. One of its poles passes, to the West, through Algeria, Tunisia and Morocco. The other must be to the east, through Syria, Lebanon and Palestine.'[43] However, mere power alone could not suffice. For— as Jules Cambon put it—'religion and nationality' were 'indistinguishable' 'in the Orient', making of the 'religious protectorate a considerable force which benefited France's moral influence and, *hence*, her political authority'.[44]

For figures like Maurice Barrès, who travelled to the Eastern Mediterranean on the eve of global conflict, France's entanglement with the world was quite distinct from that of other states. 'To others, sometimes', she conceded the 'primacy of force and business'; 'but to us, always and in spite of everything [falls] the friendship of souls'. Jaurès' supposed insistence that 'it is both right and inevitable that intellectual preponderance should belong to those who are economically dominant' was, to Barrès, both wrong-headed and dangerous. After all, the 'belief in a material law of the world, according to which only economic ascendancy, and the prestige of the trader and the engineer, could generate spiritual actions', was not simply difficult to square with the sight 'in Canada, in the Philippines, of an intensive commerce with the United States [which] has hardly affected moral dispositions'. It also threatened to undermine the edifice of France's 'spiritual power' in the world.[45]

Such an expansive sense of sentimental commitment informed policy-making at the highest level—for, as Ann Laura Stoler has suggested, '"political rationalit[y]" …—that strategically reasoned, administrative common sense' was 'grounded in' the 'affective' and its cultivation.[46] The majority of those involved in formulating the Quai d'Orsay's line on the Middle East were members of the Comité de l'Asie Française, dedicated to furthering France's interests from Asia Minor to Japan.[47] Their numbers included prominent figures like François Georges-Picot and Robert de Caix, whose vision of a constellation of statelets under French tutelage was implemented in the years after 1920.[48] Stephen Pichon, meanwhile, 'a staunch supporter of imperial expansion in the Middle East' as minister of foreign affairs between 1917 and 1920, served in the pre-war years as president of the Comité d'Orient, and was one of the founders of the Comité de Défense des Intérêts Français au Levant.[49] Actively committed to protecting France's interests in the Middle East, these men were keen to stress her reciprocal ties to the region's Uniate communities, and to cajole and placate their representatives—men like the émigré journalists Shukri Ghanim and Georges Samna, who regarded themselves as the spokesmen of the peoples of Lebanon and Syria, lobbying the Quai d'Orsay on their behalf. Furthermore, figures like Flandin and Leygues, so prominent in the war years, had not only campaigned actively before 1914 for the reform of the Algerian *indigénat*, but had also grown convinced that Syria should have a far more liberal regime than that in place in French North Africa—standing, in other words, apart from France's other possessions, basking in the gentle light of a particularly benevolent mode of rule. These ties and convictions—together with France's diplomatic obligations to the Ottoman empire—led the Ministry's functionaries in Paris, Istanbul, Beirut and Damascus to obfuscate as best they could the efforts of their counterparts in Dakar and Conakry to erect boundaries against Eastern Mediterranean migration.

Reciprocity and protection

The position of the Quai d'Orsay on Lebanese migration to AOF in the years before the First World War did not just reflect the Middle Eastern commitments of its senior functionaries. It was also consistent with the stance the Ministry had adopted throughout the 1880s and 1890s in the face of proposals to implement a discriminatory tax on foreigners working on French territory. This measure, while enormously popular with parliamentarians, was repeatedly vetoed by the Ministry's officials, who argued it would contravene the clauses guaranteeing free circulation included in agreements with a number of other states. Introducing such a piece of legislation, maintained one legal scholar, would be tantamount to a self-imposed exile from the community of nations.[50]

The need to respect the binds of diplomatic reciprocity was repeatedly cited in the years before 1914 by both the Quai d'Orsay and administrators in West Africa as a significant impediment to any exclusionary measures targeting Eastern Mediterranean migrants. As early as 1904, the Ministry of Colonies advised Governor-General Roume that the French government had 'undertaken, by conventions agreed with most of the Powers, including Turkey, to assimilate to its own workers citizens of the signatory states [residing] in its overseas possessions'.[51] These obligations effectively prevented the creation of a special tax on Ottoman subjects in AOF, a measure Roume had sought to implement in order to stem the growing influx of Eastern Mediterranean migrants.[52] For, as France's consul in Damascus, Couget understood 'the protests of ... Syrian migrants, who will not fail' to complain of measures which, 'if too rigorous, may be contrary to the clauses of our treaties with foreign powers', severely curtailed the 'choice' of means available to 'our colonial administration'.[53]

Furthermore, the stringent measures colonial administrators continued to press for may well have seemed, to the Quai d'Orsay, not merely undesirable on grounds of diplomatic reciprocity, but also inconsistent with its own regular interventions on behalf of Lebanese migrants elsewhere in the world. This duty, it is true, seems—far from being a deliberate policy choice—to have been forced upon French agents in Latin America, pressed into playing the role of protectors by the repeated entreaties of Eastern Mediterranean migrants themselves. Such requests had become so frequent by the beginning of the twentieth century that the minister of foreign affairs, Delcassé, thought it necessary in 1902 to clarify that France could not 'officially and regularly' consider 'the Syrians or other Ottoman subjects, whatever their religion' as 'French protégés'. The French 'protectorate' over the Maronites 'in the Levant', he insisted, was simply a 'religious protectorate, which has no purpose beyond this region': 'in another country, a Maronite is no more than an ordinary Ottoman subject; our agents have no rights to act on his behalf, and he himself has no right whatsoever to request their official protection'.

However, Delcassé went on to fudge this seemingly unequivocal line quite significantly. In practice, he acknowledged, French representatives had 'often ... intervened to protect these Orientals'. While such a course of action could only be considered a 'favour', it fitted too well into France's 'traditions of humanity' to be 'discarded entirely'. Moreover, Delcassé continued—in rather more pragmatic terms—'the traditions binding us to Syria's populations are too precious for us to run the risk of seeing them broken, or even weakened, by our refusal to grant our unofficial protection to these Orientals when this duty is in keeping with our obligations towards the Ottoman government'.[54] The informal assistance in which Delcassé acquiesced was, for all his evasions, little more than a thinly disguised attempt to spread the blanket of French protection over those Christian Ottoman citizens living far beyond the confines of their Eastern Mediterranean homelands.

This directive served only to rubber stamp prevailing practice among French plenipotentiaries, which often went far beyond the bounds of appropriate behaviour dictated by the Quai d'Orsay. In 1903, France's envoy in Port-au-Prince, Paul

Desprez, citing 'the instructions of the Department [of Political Affairs] regarding the officious protection granted by the French government to the Syrian populations established in the Americas', sought to ensure the repeal of an act imposing upon 'all Syrians' resident in Haiti the liquidation and closure of their wholesale and retail businesses, and allowing them to trade only on consignment'.[55] However, Desprez's ultimately unsuccessful attempts to safeguard the commercial interests of Eastern Mediterranean migrants arose, not in response to the instructions of the Quai d'Orsay, but out of a longstanding engagement with Haiti's Eastern Mediterranean population. He had not only kept a register of Ottoman subjects who had presented themselves to the French legation, but had gone so far as to issue to some passes to the 'interior of the country' and, more rarely, travel documents to France and Beirut. In doing so, he effectively treated these migrants not as nationals of another power, but as his own consular charges. Desprez seems to have been particularly keen to indulge the 'conviction', which all new arrivals from the Eastern Mediterranean seemed to share, that 'they will find in Haiti' a 'degree of protection at the very least equal to that which they receive in their country of origin'.[56]

But for other plenipotentiaries like Boulard-Ponqueville, France's ambassador to Colombia, the 'unofficial protection of Syrian Ottoman subjects' offered 'real political interest' not simply in the Ottoman empire, but also in their own fields of operation in Latin America. While Boulard-Ponqueville acknowledged that Eastern Mediterranean migrants, with their constant petty requests for assistance, could easily be seen as little more than as pesky irritants, he maintained that these men and women—with their commercial links to compatriots in France and preference for French manufactured goods—could lend the Republic invaluable assistance, helping to carry her reputation to the furthest reaches of countries where her prestige 'tends unfortunately to slip away a little further by the day'. Their commercial activities could serve as a 'powerful means of propaganda and influence which others, should we abandon it, would be quick to seize upon'.[57] For some among the Quai d'Orsay's agents, then, Eastern Mediterranean migrants were not just the passive pupils of French civilisation and recipients of republican benevolence, bound to France by secular ties of sympathy; they could also serve as the agents of her civilising mission in other parts of the world, working to buttress what diplomats regarded as her once-uncontested commercial reputation.[58] It is little surprise, then, that the Quai d'Orsay should have acted to overturn measures in France's own West African possessions when these seemed injurious both to the Ministry's 'obligations' to the Porte, and to its 'duty' to its Eastern Mediterranean protégés.

Diplomatic reason of state compelled Governor-General Roume to act again in 1906, repealing two decrees instituted by Frézouls, the lieutenant-governor of Guinea, regulating the landing and residence of foreigners in the colony. The first of these required all migrants to present a passport upon entry, and to register within twenty-four hours of arrival with the local police or *commandant de cercle*—only upon fulfilment of this obligation would individuals be granted a residence permit. The second, meanwhile, forbade all ship captains to allow passengers to disembark without the explicit authorisation of the local authorities.[59] Roume did not 'dispute the utility' of 'safeguard[s]' against the entry of undesirable migrants. However, he argued that these measures constituted a breach of federal legislative arrangements. These required all decisions affecting foreign relations to receive the assent of the governor-general, and stipulated that the provision of punishments for offences beyond the ordinary purview of criminal law needed 'the approbation of metropolitan authorities'. Moreover, he felt that these two acts, 'because they target all foreigners without any distinction of origin or situation', were both incapable of effectively regulating immigration, and 'likely to give rise to the objections, not only of individuals, but also of governments whose citizens are subject to the ordinary regulations of international law, or with which we have trade or shipping treaties'.[60] As Jean-Gabriel Desbordes was to point out, these measures 'constituted, more than a simple check, a veritable regulation of foreign immigration', which threatened to affect France's 'foreign relations'.[61] Diplomatic imperatives dictated their abrogation.

Such failures did not prevent administrators in AOF from presenting a new scheme for the imposition of a special tax on Ottoman subjects to their superiors at the Rue Oudinot in 1909.[62] However, this was also turned away by an intransigent Quai d'Orsay, which reiterated the stance it had relayed to the Ministry of Colonies in 1904, insisting that Ottoman subjects 'enjoying the treatment [accorded to nationals of] a most favoured nation, should be assimilated to our own nationals in our overseas possessions, and that no consideration could allow at the present time any modification to the obligations incumbent upon the French government by dint of our treaties with foreign powers'.[63] This was a quite unequivocal statement, effectively placing diplomatic reason of state ahead of the concerns of colonial administrators.

The obduracy of the Quai d'Orsay could not prevent Camille Guy, the new lieutenant-governor of Guinea, from finding a means of circumventing the obligations of international convention in late 1910. With the support of Roume's successor, William Ponty, Guy—profoundly hostile to the Lebanese and Syrians, whom he was later to deem the 'Chinamen of West Africa'—implemented a decree, applied at the federal level some six months later, imposing a series of stringent checks upon new migrants to Guinea.[64] Under the terms of this legislation, only those capable of providing a birth certificate and an *extrait de casier judiciaire* confirming their unblemished criminal record, translated into French, certified and accompanied by a photograph, were to be granted residency. Passengers wishing to disembark were now also to be subjected to a compulsory medical examination, designed to check they were free of 'epidemic and contagious diseases'. Moreover, they were required to deposit the costs of their repatriation with immigration officials upon their arrival.[65]

These measures, as Desbordes observed, could be seen as doing no more than establishing 'general administrative and sanitary control[s]'. They therefore could not be charged with singling out 'Syrian' migrants upon entry, nor accused of violating international obligations.[66] However, as Ponty made clear, their apparently general character was no more than an administrative ruse, disguising a tightly circumscribed exclusionary measure. In a circular in which he sought to elucidate 'the exact scope of the new regulations', he informed the lieutenant-governors of the Federation that the principal objective of the legislation was 'to check Syrian immigration'. Officials, he insisted, should not 'burden' with quite unnecessary procedures passengers whose 'identity and morality' they had little reason to doubt. Rather, they should take 'particular care' to apply these measures 'without pause' to Eastern Mediterranean migrants, calling upon police commissioners to 'verify minutiously' the required documents. Moreover, he intimated, functionaries should not hesitate to exceed the letter of the law in their efforts to stem this particular stream of migration. Thus, he called upon administrators to remind physicians charged with carrying out medical examinations that they 'should not lose sight of the great powers entrusted in them to protect the colony' against the deleterious consequences of migration—and, in doing so, to dismiss cases arbitrarily in order to check the number of Ottoman subjects entering the Federation.[67]

The strains of war

Despite its stringent requirements, this legislation failed to stem the constant stream of new arrivals, who rapidly found means of supplying proof of their identity and probity, calling upon friends and relatives to vouch for them and provide the costs of repatriation. Nevertheless, it remained in place until 1921. It was augmented, in May 1918, by a set of restrictions upon the circulation of 'Syrians and Ottoman subjects' prompted—rather belatedly—by the war. Noting that the 'frequent' journeys these individuals undertook 'for extremely diverse and trivial causes' were intolerable in wartime, Governor-General Angoulvant urged territorial administrators to turn away all requests for travel—save in cases of dire medical need or departure from the colonies.[68] This ban was an essential element of a raft of prohibitive measures introduced in the spring and summer of that year in order to trammel the activities of these 'undesirable Lebanese'—'Asiatics' whose 'mercantile ways' posed a grave threat to the growth of 'French and indigenous trade'.[69] Under these measures, Ottoman subjects were forbidden from acquiring land for the duration of the hostilities, while their movements and correspondence were to be closely controlled.[70] Furthermore, Angoulvant pressed the Ministry of Colonies to accede to his plans to prevent Eastern Mediterranean traders from participating in the annual *traite* in Senegalese groundnuts, now conducted, under wartime provisioning regulations, with a single purchaser—the colonial state itself. Indeed, Angoulvant seems to have wished to achieve nothing less by this than the 'elimination of Syrian business'.[71]

'Small vexatious measures', he argued, would do no longer in the face of a population who 'oppose our hygiene and public health regulations … with an inertia equalled only by their esteem for dirt', whose 'noisy', 'sometimes bloody' 'quarrels' disturbed the 'public peace', and whose fraudulent ways were an 'insolent and permanent challenge to public morality and commercial probity'. In doing so, Angoulvant echoed the complaints of those *colons* and propagandists who had campaigned in the years before 1914 for prohibitive measures against Eastern Mediterranean migrants.

The latter's presence, he insisted, was to be feared all the more in wartime. Not only did their constant rumour-mongering, and the suspicions of spying which hung over some of them, mark them as a threat to the 'security' of the colony. Transforming their shops into 'veritable desertion agencies', they 'had trafficked in personal effects, sold disguises, and hidden absentee conscripts'. Perhaps most significantly, the 'boundless' 'arrogance' and 'insolent luxury' of the Syrians, their 'noisome opulence', so profoundly at odds with the 'contemplative dignity of the European and indigenous population, its apprehensions and hopes', and 'the vulgar fanfare of their pleasures'—an insult to 'our mourning'—could no longer be tolerated.[72]

The governor-general called for the imposition of conscription upon all migrants resident in AOF for over a year. This, he maintained, was the sole adequate response to the constant abuses by which men who, before the war, had 'scraped by in their miserable shops', had accumulated vast sums and acquired 'sumptuous establishments'. Moreover, it might well prove fitting punishment for the disdain with which migrants had greeted the call to arms issued by the Légion d'Orient, created in 1916 to incorporate young Lebanese and Syrian men willing to fight under the French flag. Thus, while Frenchmen were struggling to secure the 'liberty' of Lebanon and Syria, and to free these lands from the 'yoke of Turkish tyranny', migrants in AOF had profited from the absence of competitors gone to the front to accumulate vast sums by means fair and—more often than not—foul.[73]

Such behaviour, it might be argued, seemed utterly beyond the pale to Angoulvant. Not only had migrants reneged upon their obligation towards France by their stubborn refusal to take up arms in the Légion d'Orient, their ingratitude belying the myth of an enduring and reciprocal friendship between the peoples of the Eastern Mediterranean and their secular protector, they had also, in doing so, made a show of their deep-rooted opportunism, dishonesty and cowardice. These complaints were informed by a keen sense of the respective merits of France's civilising mission in the Eastern Mediterranean and West Africa, itself founded upon an essentially affective assessment of these two undertakings. For Angoulvant, there could be no doubt that African *indigènes* were 'appropriate carriers and recipients' of the sentiments of patriarchal benevolence which framed the *mission civilisatrice*.[74] *Syriens*, for their part, were worthy only of contempt for the insolent indifference with which they treated the French authorities.

But, for all the wounded eloquence of his repeated entreaties to the Rue Oudinot, functionaries there refused to acquiesce to his demands for the introduction of conscription and the wholesale exclusion of Eastern Mediterranean migrants from the produce trade. While particular cases were open to consideration, 'general principles affecting all Syrians' were inadmissible so long as 'allied aliens' remained untouched by similar measures.[75] The rather ambivalent legal status of Lebanese and Syrian migrants in particular—considered as neither allies nor enemies by the Ministries of Foreign Affairs and the Interior, but rather as 'special protégés' enjoying a certain degree of latitude—prevented the imposition of such severe impediments upon their commercial operations.[76] Angoulvant found himself, then, compelled to implement a far less substantial set of strictures than he had initially desired—and one in which the prohibition of movement took on a central importance.

However, the Ministry of Foreign Affairs did not hesitate to issue a severe rebuke to Angoulvant for even these attenuated measures. In a memorandum drafted in November 1918, it reminded its counterparts at the Rue Oudinot that the Ministry had decided, upon the end of diplomatic relations with the Ottoman state, not to extend the status of enemy subjects to the 'numerous Ottoman[s] …, for the most part not Muslims, who resided on French territory, and whose respectability, morality, and Francophile sentiments were well known'. The decision to maintain the special protection these individuals had been accorded in the past had been vindicated, over the course of hostilities, 'by political necessities of an imperious kind'. Indeed, 'It seemed consistent', insisted this missive, that 'any measure intended to abrogate or even to restrict our benevolent measures towards our traditional clients would not only be discordant with our traditions of generosity but also, and most importantly, constitute a grave political fault. The Syrian colonies of French West Africa therefore have a right, as in the past, to benefit from our kindness.'

Furthermore, the memorandum brushed away Angoulvant's request for conscription, insisting that French functionaries could not 'begrudge the Syrians of Dakar and other towns [in West Africa] their failure to enlist'. Not only had the 'Government of the Republic' not adopted 'at any moment' this 'attitude towards the Syrians, Armenians and other non-Muslim Ottoman subjects resident in the *métropole*'. It was prevented from doing so by the international agreements of The Hague, which forbade the executive 'to corral, even by indirect means, nationals of an enemy state into serving under our flag'. Such an argument was, it could be said, not mere bluster, but a means of—quite literally—putting Angoulvant in his place. Its author both intimated that the course of action the governor-general had contemplated was driven by little more than resentment against a 'state of affairs created by conflict and not by the Syrians',[77] who could not be blamed for their immunity, and stated quite unequivocally that Angoulvant could have no grounds for considering the implementation of measures rejected by the metropolitan government, and contrary to international law. These, the memorandum made clear, held an authority far superior to that of a simple colonial governor, who was in no position to adopt a divergent course of action.

In a letter to Angoulvant bundled together with this reprimand, the minister of colonies, while acknowledging that criticism of the *Syriens* could be 'justified by their lack of hygiene … and their often disloyal competition', stressed that 'the Syrian question in French West Africa cannot be divorced from France's policy in the Orient generally, and more particularly in Syria. The attitude of local authorities in our West African possessions can indeed not fail to have repercussions on this question, and threatens to hinder the actions of the Government of the Republic at a time when it is striving to attach the populations of Syria' to France by a 'definitive settlement'. Though careful not to disavow completely the measures Angoulvant had sought to implement—insisting that the Department of Political Affairs had 'long since' been aware of the problems created by the 'introduction' of Eastern Mediterranean migrants to AOF—the minister of colonies was compelled to recognise the paramount importance of the exigencies of Middle Eastern policy.[78] It is clear, then, that both the Ministry of Colonies and the Government-General of AOF had little choice but to bow to the diplomatic imperatives which the Quai d'Orsay defended so vigorously.

Mandatory commitments

France's precarious position in the Eastern Mediterranean was foremost in the minds of functionaries in 1918, its claims to control over Bilad al-Sham threatened both by the rival claims of Sharif Faisal, and by the recalcitrance of the local population. However, the establishment of its Mandate in the early 1920s was to consecrate the Quai d'Orsay's commitment to a migration policy of the utmost tolerance in both the metropole and the colonies. Furthermore, intervention on behalf of Lebanese and Syrians in the lands of the *mahjar* was no longer seen in the interwar years as a 'favour' to be granted at the discretion of France's plenipotentiaries, but rather as an obligation dictated by the terms of Article 3 of the League of Nations Mandate, which considered 'nationals of Syria and the Lebanon living outside the limits of the territory' as being 'under the diplomatic and consular protection of the Mandatory'.[79]

This situation contrasted starkly with the status of other non-European migrants who sought to move between the various parts of the French imperial body politic in the 1920s and 1930s. The war years had witnessed a sharp increase in the number of North African, Indochinese and Chinese labourers in metropolitan France, as these men were recruited to compensate for the constant loss of Frenchmen to the front. In particular, the number of Algerians, freed in 1914 of the need to present permits for travel to the *métropole*, had risen dramatically. However, the French state hastily sought upon the close of hostilities not just to repatriate these workers—who, their usefulness exhausted, were viewed as an insidious danger to the body politic—but also to erect a 'series of administrative hurdles that significantly limited freedoms guaranteed' to North African migrants, in particular, by 'existing legislation'. By 1921 only 200 of the wartime labourers recruited from Morocco, Tunisia and Algeria, and 1,400 of those from Indochina and China, remained.[80] Migration did not, of course, cease—picking up again with the 'shift from repatriation to improved surveillance' on the soil of the metropole.[81] The number of Algerians resident in France had risen, by 1928, to more than 60,000.[82] However, both Algerians—who remained under the care of the Ministry of the Interior—and Moroccans and Tunisians—who, as subjects of nominal protectorates, depended on the Quai d'Orsay—had to surmount a raft of measures designed to serve as obstacles to free movement, from obtaining nationality certificates and identity cards to securing contracts approved by the Ministry of Labour and medical certificates.[83]

Furthermore, Eastern Mediterranean migrants were able to secure far more substantive entitlements from the French state than, say, Moroccans. The ambiguous status of Morocco certainly matched that of Lebanon and Syria—considered at once French possessions and foreign states. This, however, rarely afforded its constituents any privileges in metropolitan France. Quite the opposite—as one Moroccan migrant who appealed for compensation for a workplace injury was told, 'as a Moroccan you are a foreign worker; returning to Morocco which is not a colony but a protectorate, you cease to live in French territory'. While reciprocity in Franco-Moroccan relations would have seemed intolerable to French administrators, Lebanese and Syrian citizens were entitled to a share of 'social citizenship'—which gave them not only freedom of movement between their own states and metropolitan France and its colonies, but also afforded them French protection elsewhere in the world.[84]

This commitment—enshrined in the terms of the Mandate—was pressed into service by French administrators in their efforts to manage the sentiments of Lebanese and Syrian citizens, and to maintain at least a measure of acquiescence to the Mandatory presence. As oft-repeated pieties about the longstanding attachment of these populations to France came to ring hollow in the face of the wearying realities of rule, the Quai d'Orsay faced calls from officials in Beirut to assist Eastern Mediterranean migrants facing difficulties in the lands of the *mahjar*, in the hope that such intercession might bolster their own embattled position. As the High Commissioner pointed out in 1929, intervention on behalf of migrants in Portuguese Guinea could have only 'beneficial results' in the Mandatory territories themselves, for 'relations between Syrian and Lebanese migrants and their families remaining in the country of their birth are close and sustained, and the services the Mandatory Power might be able to provide the former can only serve to bring the latter to appreciate the utility of the Mandate'.[85] He was not alone in doing so. As Simon Jackson has recently argued, the Syrian and Lebanese diaspora had come to be seen, by the close of the First World War, 'as a powerful, and potentially unified, political and economic force'. It is no surprise, then, that the High Commission should have regarded these men and women as 'essential' to the *mise en valeur* of their homeland—potential 'collaborators in our economic and moral expansion' who might serve 'the double interest of France and the countries under French mandate'.[86] Such pragmatic concerns were compelling enough motives for officials both in Paris and Beirut to ensure that Lebanese and Syrian migrants were treated as nationals of most favoured states both in France's own colonial possessions and in other territories.

The Quai d'Orsay was drawn in 1928 into a protracted dispute with the Liberian government by the latter's decision to ban all trade by foreign citizens of countries with which it had not agreed a commercial treaty—a measure which affected, in the main, Lebanese and Syrian traders. Upon being informed of this threat by the French consul in Monrovia, Peytaud, officials at the Ministry of Foreign Affairs urged him to 'intervene firmly', 'in order to obtain at the very least a stay of execution' until League of Nations arbitration had reached its course.[87] Indeed, they sought to resort to the terms of the Mandate in order to safeguard the interests of their Levantine protégés, pointing out that Article 11 prohibited any 'discrimination in Syria or the Lebanon' 'against the nationals of any member-state of the League of Nations',[88] and suggesting that reciprocal treatment for Lebanese citizens in Liberia might be expected.[89] It is clear that the Quai d'Orsay, rather than merely affirming the principle of protection, sought to safeguard the commercial position of Lebanese and Syrian citizens abroad, and to ensure—if need be through recourse to lengthy arbitration before the League of Nations—the upholding of their rights.

Interwar migration controls in AOF, meanwhile, both steered clear of any measures of exception which might contravene international convention, and submitted AOF to metropolitan law. The 1911 *arrêté*—seen as failing 'to correspond to the principles regulating the settlement of foreigners in France', and deemed 'vexatious' to passengers—was abrogated in 1921, in an attempt to bring AOF into line with metropolitan practices. Crucially, the decrees of 1921 and 1923 were—unlike prewar measures—intended to regulate the activities of foreign nationals upon the territory of AOF rather than policing its borders. While they forbade foreigners from practising certain professions without administrative authorisation, they failed to impose restrictions upon entry. Thus, the 1921 regulations demanded—in stark contrast with those of 1911—nothing more of migrants than a simple declaration of identity to their landlords. While the decree of 28 April 1923 did stipulate that identity cards could be granted only to migrants who had paid a guarantee equivalent to the costs of repatriation, new arrivals were allowed to provide a guarantee given by a 'solvent licensed trader, already established in the colony' in place of this sum—a concession which quite deliberately did away with a significant impediment to migration. The only recourse available, in such circumstances, to administrators wishing to channel or stem the inflow of people from the Eastern Mediterranean was to refuse identity cards to migrants already on the soil of the Federation.[90] These skeletal controls upon migration were, it is true, supplemented by subsequent decrees in 1925, 1927 and 1932, which required travellers wishing to disembark in AOF to provide proof of identity, a criminal record and a medical certificate, along with a monetary guarantee set in 1927 at 4,800 francs for Lebanese and Syrian citizens.[91]

While these measures went some way towards re-establishing the legal *status quo ante* on paper, they failed in practice to provide effective checks upon migration from the Eastern Mediterranean. It might even be argued that they were not intended to do so. Thus, the payment by migrants of a guarantee seems to have acted as an essentially budgetary measure, intended to shift the costly burden of repatriating indigent aliens away from the administration, rather than a means of barring those unable to meet this requirement from entry. Had functionaries regarded this consignment as an exclusionary measure, they perhaps would not have been so willing to accept the guarantees of migrants already established in AOF, nor the payment by commercial companies, shipping lines[92] and the Mandatory authorities in Beirut,[93] on behalf of their employees, travellers and administrative charges. Moreover, officials scrupulously avoided any suggestion of prejudice against migrants. Governor-General Carde went so far as to stress in 1925 that even criminal offences did not disbar new arrivals from being granted residence. The stipulation that passengers present a criminal record for visa, he made clear, did not grant local authorities the capacity to 'oppose the disembarkation of convicts'. This procedure was no more than a means of gathering 'information' to be used 'in the enquiry which precedes the issue of a definitive identity card'. Under no circumstances could the evidence thus acquired 'justify a refusal' to grant the right to land. This was contingent only upon providing the appropriate documents, rather than their content.[94]

Frustrated by the inefficacy of such local measures, which offered no real means of 'selection' among the hundreds and thousands of migrants who disembarked in AOF each year, Governor-General de Coppet suggested in 1936 the creation of what amounted, in effect, to a system of 'remote control'. Under this scheme, the issue of visas to prospective migrants before their departure would be conditional upon the personal authorisation of the governor-general in person, who would base his decision upon the advice of both the Mandatory authorities and the territorial lieutenant-governors, better able to assess the situation in their own colonies.[95] However, as the head of the Federation's Sûreté Générale complained bitterly in an internal memorandum, the Department of Political Affairs at the Rue Oudinot had still not responded to this proposal almost a year later. What is more, a request to 'strengthen the existing regulatory measures'—formulated in response to both a sudden hike in the numbers of new migrants over 1936 and 1937, and the mounting tension between *colons* and *Libano-Syriens*—which the Ministry of Colonies had passed on to the Quai d'Orsay had 'to this day' received no answer. He could not but conclude, then, that 'the local Administration can count only upon itself to face down, using the legislation already in place, the dangers associated with the growth of Lebanese and Syrian migration to AOF'.[96]

Lebanese and Syrian migrants could be neither selected before their departure from Beirut or Tripoli, nor turned away at the borders of AOF. They could only be subjected to a screening process while already resident in the Federation. However, while identity documents, which doubled as residence permits, could be refused to new arrivals awaiting permission to remain in AOF, such rejections were 'unfortunately … rare', as the director of the Federation's Sûreté Générale conceded in 1937, castigating local authorities for failing to make use of an administrative tool enabling them 'to select immigrants to their territories'.[97] Furthermore, though the colonial state could, by the letter of the law, withdraw identity documents from foreigners who failed to observe residence requirements or were found in breach of public health regulations, such provisions were rarely—if ever—used to expel *Libano-Syriens* from AOF. As the Department of Political Affairs took pains to point out in 1936, expulsion orders would only be accepted in cases where migrants had committed criminal offences, as Lebanese and Syrian citizens were 'not to be treated with the same rigour as other foreigners'.[98]

Indeed, they were entitled, 'by dint of the Mandate', 'to our protection, which is accorded them in France and the colonies on the same terms as to our own citizens and subjects, in keeping with the directives of the Ministry of Foreign Affairs'.[99] This was no more than an extension to the colonies of regulations already implemented in the *métropole* in early 1935, and which accorded Lebanese and Syrian residents in France the status of 'citizens of a most favoured nation', in reciprocal recognition of the preferential treatment accorded French nationals in Lebanon and Syria. While this measure did not alter existing regulations upon the registration of foreigners and delivery of identity papers, Lebanese and Syrians were to be treated with benevolence in matters of 'settlement, residence, the exercise of trade, occupations and professions, the purchase, ownership, and occupation of all mobile and immobile goods and, generally, the right to dispose of them, conscription and state benefits', and were to remain free of any special taxes, aside from residency taxes.[100] Moreover, while the signing of independence treaties with 'the states of the Levant' in 1936—never, in the event, ratified—put an end to the status of Lebanese and Syrian citizens as formal protégés, they were to continue benefiting from the same exceptional treatment as 'nationals of a most favoured' state.[101] Such clemency sometimes extended even to expulsion orders issued for criminal offences or breach of residency requirements.[102]

Interlopers and intercessors

Migrants often enlisted the assistance of both Lebanese dignitaries and French administrators in their individual and collective appeals to the Ministry of Colonies and the Government-General of AOF. Recourse to such intercession had its origins in the years before the First World War. Already, in 1910, the migrants of the commercial centre of Kayes expressed their dissatisfaction with the treatment meted out by the colonial administration in a letter to Sulaiman al-Bustani, the Maronite deputy for Beirut in the Ottoman assembly.[103] It is clear, then, that—as Simon Jackson has argued—efforts to draw benefit from the 'culture of legality' in which Mandatory rule was embedded had their origins in the lobbying and jurisdictional politics of the late Ottoman period.[104] However, it became increasingly common in the interwar years, when Eastern Mediterranean migrants in AOF regularly sought out—and received—the assistance of Lebanese dignitaries.

Of these, Monsignor Fighali, the Maronite vicar patriarchal in Paris, was perhaps the most frequent intercessor—intervening regularly on behalf of Lebanese citizens, both Christian and Muslim, against whom expulsion orders had been issued throughout the 1930s. While not always successful, Fighali seems to have been confident enough of his capabilities to ensure the repeal of such decisions to continue dispatching entreaties to the Ministry of Colonies, appealing for clemency for his compatriots. Thus, he did not shy away from ending a letter acknowledging the expulsions of Zabat 'Abd al-Jabir, Salim Sahli and Bishara al-Rayyis from Côte d'Ivoire with a further request for clemency in the case of Ahmad 'Isa Khudr. Already expelled from AOF, Khudr hoped to 'be authorised to return to his family'—and, in particular, his pregnant wife—and Fighali called upon Marius Moutet, the minister of colonies, to consider again his case and 'to see whether it would not be possible, with a little kindness, to allow him to return home'. Moreover, the vicar patriarchal assured Moutet, 'I am certain that this Lebanese national will become, like his compatriots who have already seen their identity cards returned, a most devoted friend to a benevolent and generous France'. This was a carefully-worded appeal, ably moving between the overlapping lexicons of Christian charity for a man 'with eight people at his charge' and nationalist sentiment—a delicate game of praise and gentle persuasion, in which Fighali attempted to pull a concession from Moutet by pricking his conscience while simultaneously flattering his patriotic sensibilities.[105] It is a mark of the Monsignor's self-assurance that he should have attempted it despite his failure to prevent the expulsions of 'Abd al-Jabir, Sahli and al-Rayyis.

Indeed, he was able to secure some striking successes. In 1936, he obtained stays of execution in the cases of Ibrahim Tsham, Husain Wihbi, Muhammad Hilal and Elias Abu Rizq, whose identity papers had been confiscated for their political activities, appealing on their behalf as 'the representative of the Maronite Patriarch to the French government, as a Frenchman, and as Professor of Oriental Languages at the Sorbonne and the Faculty of Letters of the University of Bordeaux'. In a pair of letters to the governor-general, Fighali asked him to reverse his decision, maintaining that 'an act of clemency towards [these men] would be welcomed by … their Lebanese compatriots, at a time when they are amicably discussing with France the terms of a treaty of friendship'.[106] What is more, he explained, he addressed himself to the governor-general on the suggestion of functionaries at the Quai d'Orsay, who had advised him, when he had 'brought up this matter the other day', to 'write to you directly, asking you to examine carefully the case of these unfortunate Lebanese, currently France's protégés, and soon to be her friends and allies'. Benevolence towards these men would be 'most opportune', coinciding with the French government's decision 'to reward the fidelity, the unshakeable commitment of the Lebanese towards France, their protector and friend for more than ten centuries', with independence.[107]

Fighali, then, was prepared to deploy all the rhetorical means at his disposal in pursuit of a favourable decision. Capable of humbly presenting himself as an ordinary French citizen, hinting at his influence as a Lebanese plenipotentiary who could—his turn of phrase suggested—casually drop by the Quai d'Orsay to discuss the position of his compatriots, and underlining his authority as a religious emissary and accomplished scholar, he stressed the advantages of a favourable decision in terms which conflated immediate political exigency and longstanding commitments. Such wiliness was not without effect for, while Hilal and Abu Rizq had already left the Federation, Governor-General Brévié did postpone the expulsions of Tsham and Wihbi, assuring Fighali he was 're-examining with the utmost benevolence the situation of these citizens under French Mandate'. Moreover, he reminded the Monsignor that 'the withdrawal of a foreigner's identity booklet is not in itself an expulsion order', and that requests for readmission to AOF at a later date may well be welcomed—attempting to gloss over his decision to expel Abu Rizq and Hilal by presenting the possibility of their return.[108]

Cases like these are profoundly revealing. They shine a light on the workings of the paternalistic civic order created by the French in Lebanon and Syria, within which religious representatives like Monsignor Fighali were treated as favoured interlocutors, entrenching an enduring form of bureaucratic confessionalism. But they also reveal the intimate language of 'friendship', 'fidelity' and 'benevolence' which shot through such exchanges. Furthermore, they allow us to trace the distant reverberations of such a policy in AOF, whose administrators found their own capacity to act constrained by the sentimental imperatives of the Mandatory state. Significantly, these functionaries remained unable—even after the introduction of the 1932 decree, intended to centralise and rationalise all migration procedures—to deal with the cases of Lebanese migrants according to the inflexible procedures of Weberian bureaucracy. Rather, they found themselves enmeshed in the webs of empire—laboriously moving through a tangled weave of personal commitments and sentimental ties.

Conclusion

This chapter has traced the attempts of administrators across AOF to devise and implement measures that might check Eastern Mediterranean migration. Such endeavours were repeatedly stymied by the interventions of metropolitan departments of state, and by the entreaties of migrants themselves. This tale of frustration and half-measures, then, underlines the fact that no colonial territory was an island unto itself whose administrators—safely marooned upon the periphery, away from the intrusive politicking of the imperial capital—were entirely free to make law as they saw fit; in important areas of sovereignty—such as matters of international law and foreign relations—French possessions remained clearly subordinated to directives issued from Rue Oudinot. That the Ministry of Colonies was itself, in turn, forced to bow before the directives of the Quai d'Orsay is a telling reminder both that we cannot truly speak of *a* colonial state in the singular, but rather of an imperial system, whose constituent parts were administered by a congeries of departments of state, each with its own priorities and imperatives—and that there existed stark asymmetries of power between these various agencies which might allow one to protect its own interests at the expense of others around it.

But this account also shows the ways in which this empire-state retained essentially personal, affective forms and norms of governance, even as it dealt in matters of international law which showed little concern for the circumstances of particular individuals. Governors and ministers of state were not only pulled into protracted personal correspondence with migrants and their advocates; they also often found themselves forced to respond to such entreaties, and to frame their own arguments, in emotive registers which bore scarce relation to the abstract language of jurisprudence. Imperial reason of state, then, rested upon the intimate registers of sentimental commitment.

PART THREE

DAYS, THOUGHTS AND THINGS

5

MERCHANTS AND MAGPIES

THE TRADING LIVES OF EASTERN MEDITERRANEAN MIGRANTS

Historians of Eastern Mediterranean migration to West Africa have focused unremittingly on the economic lives of these communities. Many, in doing so, have treated historiography as moral reckoning. They have thus written of these men and women only, or largely, to heap praise or pin blame upon them for the role they have played in Africa's long history of extraversion, which they regard variously as beneficent involvement in the flows of the global economy or as pernicious entrapment in the manacles of economic imperialism.[1] Some, like Michael Crowder and Neil Leighton, have lauded the part Lebanese traders played in 'opening up West Africa to increased international trade',[2] by 'linking urban and rural, advanced and lagging, modern and traditional, through a complex nexus of finance, trade, kinship and the provision of "political capital"'.[3] Such assessments shared much with the pragmatic optimism of developmentalist economists like P.T. Bauer, who insisted 'Levantines' had an 'important part to play in the development' of West Africa by encouraging the multiplication of external linkages and the spirit of free enterprise.[4] But even as Leighton and Crowder clung to the hopeful refrains of late colonialism, others like Martin Kaniki, Samir Amin and Jean Suret-Canale, driven by their increasingly sombre assessments of Africa's seemingly cursed entanglement with the world beyond, damned Eastern Mediterranean migrants as a 'rising gentry'.[5] Eastern Mediterranean migrants not only profited, they argued, from the 'development of underdevelopment', the 'brutal curtailment of the potential for growth of a colonial [trading] bourgeoisie';[6] they participated in this corrosive process, their usurious practices compelling—as Suret-Canale put it, quoting Marx—'reproduction to proceed under even more disheartening conditions'.[7]

Scholars like Laurens van der Laan and Saïd Boumedouha, meanwhile, have taken a rather more agnostic tack upon the affairs of Eastern Mediterranean hawkers and shopkeepers. They have been largely concerned with tracing the conspicuous success of these communities to the structural architecture of the colonial economy, and its jerking twists and turns of fortune, as commodity prices rose vertiginously or plummeted suddenly on the world market. Thus, Boumedouha noted that sociological theories ascribing the success of mercantile minorities like the South Asians of East Africa, or the Chinese of South-East Asia,[8] to the niche they occupied in the economic structures of colonialism left little room for their 'personal qualities'. But, even as he did so, he saw the 'evolution' of this 'community' largely in terms of the external circumstances 'responsible for the expansion and contraction of its trade': the First and Second World Wars, the Depression, the Korean War, and the shifting attitudes of the colonial state and the large trading companies.[9] Laurens van der Laan, too, adopted a self-consciously 'external approach', seeking 'an explanation for [the] activities' of Lebanese migrants in Sierra Leone in the 'opportunities … available' in the colony's economic 'environment'. While maintaining that Eastern Mediterranean migrants deserved 'credit for [their] optimism and tenacity which enabled [them] to make full use of the economic opportunities which arose', he ultimately concluded that these men and women 'succeeded because of the rapid economic development which took place during the colonial period'.[10]

No matter their perspective, all have essentially sought to situate Eastern Mediterranean traders amidst the structural dispositions of the colonial economy, and the wider webs of global exchange in which it was enclosed. There is something to be said for this. The arrivals and departures of Lebanese migrants, their successes and bankruptcies must be situated against the backdrop of the colonial economies of French and British West Africa if they are to be understood at all. The prevailing prices of commodities on the world market; the changing economic policies of colonial administrations; and the commercial outlooks of companies like the CFAO and the SCOA all, clearly, played an important part in the history of Lebanese migration to AOF. But in concentrating only on these broader structural factors, scholars have paid scant attention to the practices of trade.

These, to scholars like Crowder, are only so much trivial matter, which can scarcely account for the success of these men and women. Crowder, it is true, attempted to sketch—in rather broad strokes—a picture of the commercial habits which made these men and women 'more competitive' than their African rivals: their capacity to open up 'new markets' beyond the reach of the railway line and the feeder road, where timorous European firms feared to tread; their willingness to engage in endless palavers with their African clients and to extend credit; their ability to live off scraps, keeping overheads low and recycling every penny of profit back into their businesses; and, finally, their ability to thrive on the 'collective support' lent by kinsmen, rather than be dragged down by parasitical extended families. But, he concluded, such methods were not sufficient to 'secure' their 'position … as intermediaries between the European import-export houses and the African producer'. The success of the Lebanese would have been impossible without access to the credit which trading houses and banks supplied, even as they refused to extend it to Africans.[11]

Most have followed this line. Drawing sharp distinctions between a 'traditional' African commercial world mired down in familial obligations and hampered by structural disadvantages, and the voraciously enterprising Lebanese, they have regarded the latter as commercial—and cultural—intermediaries, Simmelian strangers who remained 'betwixt and between',[12] occupying the interstices of colonial society and linking up European and African, coloniser and colonised. Some have, it is true, expressed doubts about the viability of such categories. Van der Laan, for one, argued that regarding these men and women as occupying a 'culturally and economically intermediate position' is to misapprehend their manifold engagements in different, if complementary, economic activities.[13] But others have resolutely clung to the view that these operators possessed, as Crowder put it, the monopoly of the 'middleman trade'.[14]

Such scholarly insistence, however, hinders our understanding of the complexities of their commercial lives. The term is, of course, an apt enough description of the activities many did take on as retail or wholesale dealers in manufactured merchandise, and as brokers in commodities—trading in groundnuts in Senegal and Soudan, in rubber then palm kernels in Guinea, and in kola nuts, coffee and cocoa in Côte d'Ivoire. After all, most traders are intermediaries of one kind or another, links in the often long supply chains stretching from the production to the market. But, perhaps precisely for this reason, that term remains deeply unsatisfactory, failing to capture the highly differentiated, and constantly shifting, nature of this commercial society. Even those who have frowned upon its use have insisted that portraying 'the Lebanese as a homogeneous group … is both possible and useful, as far as economic analysis is concerned'.[15] However, glossing over the internal stratifications of Eastern Mediterranean commercial society threatens to obfuscate, not to assist, understanding. For in doing so we fail to appreciate the distributions of capital and credit—of commercial power—which allowed it to operate. What is more, to regard the Lebanese as mere brokers is to overlook the range of economic activities, some legal, others not so licit, that these men and women carried out.

Just as importantly, the term remains bogged down in the tired dualism of modernisation theory, with its distinctions between the modern, capitalist economy of the European firms, tilted towards external trade, and the 'traditional', inward-looking, trade in cattle, kola nuts and dried fish—a framework which was only slightly altered by some to account for the 'semi-western firms' of the 'Levantines and Indians' of Nigeria.[16] These dualistic notions still linger on, decades after the works of Boeke,[17] van der Leur[18] or Geertz,[19] in much writing on the commercial life of colonial AOF. Scholars are correct, of course, to point to the profound asymmetries of power between European and African economic operators: the uneven distribution of credit and trust, and the spatial and material marginalisation of the latter, pushed down the commercial scale to positions as agents, and out into less profitable regions.[20] More tenuous are claims that the different circuits of trade through the Federation in the early twentieth century—some carrying commodities like groundnuts or palm kernels destined for export towards Europe, others goods like kola nuts or rice destined for internal consumption—represented nothing less than the expression of two distinct economic systems and ways of thought, the one 'capitalist', the other 'lineage-based'. For these understate not only the complementary nature of these networks, but also the common ground between their operators.[21] As Jean-Loup Amselle has pointed out, there is a need to make non-Western trading activities banal, to free them from culturalist assumptions.[22]

Rajat Kanta Ray, then, is no doubt right to argue that one cannot simply see in colonial situations like these the confrontation of a European *Gesellschaft* and an Asiatic (or African) *Gemeinschaft*—a way of trading founded on the primordial ties of community, which was both more organic and simpler, and immeasurably more fragmented and weaker, than its Western counterpart. However, Ray's insistence that there emerged instead a face-off between two competing *Gesellschaften*, 'one European and the other Eastern'—or, we might say here, Eastern Mediterranean—rather obscures the extent to which Lebanese entrepreneurs, at least, were emulators as much as innovators, magpies who poached commercial ideas and seized upon opportunities.[23] In contrast to the exiguous bunch who have examined Lebanese trading practices in West Africa, scholars of trade diasporas—those networks of enterprise extended across long distances—have often looked for the key to their success in the particular 'institutions, practices, values and way of thinking' of these mercantile societies.[24] In keeping with such a tendency, scholars have often argued that what qualities the Lebanese did possess were both distinctive and intrinsic. However, Eastern Mediterranean migrants are perhaps interesting for their very unoriginality. I am not suggesting, of course, that they were 'economic men'—rational creatures of classical economic theory, operating in abstract circumstances. But though these entrepreneurs—both large and small—retained much that was their own, carrying practices over from the Eastern Mediterranean, their working methods were also emulative when they needed to be, a strategy which allowed them to remain afloat in the harsh world of colonial trade, with its small gains and perilous fluctuations, or to rise above it. It is the commercial methods and logics of both large and small Eastern Mediterranean traders that I will examine here—their sources of credit and investment strategies, their patterns of spatial dispersion and hierarchical arrangements.

Mobile hierarchies

On his arrival in Senegal in 1923, Salim Salqa worked for Jean Thabit in M'Bour for five months, before opening his own shop, which he managed to keep afloat for three years. He then became a lorry driver for Mansur Tu'ma in Joal, and a shop hand for Joseph Halawi in M'Bour and—after a brief, seemingly unsuccessful, venture as an independent transporter—for Mitri Halabi in Tattaguine. With the small capital he had built up during these stints—some 2,500 francs—he again tried his luck alone, opening a shop in M'Bour in 1929, just as the depression was setting in. Unable to recover the loans he had handed out to clients, he left the interior for Dakar, where he rented a locale on Rue de Thiès. When it became clear he could not afford this, he moved into a smaller shop on Rue de Raffenel—but even the rent for this proved beyond his scanty means. He declared bankruptcy in late May 1930, only two weeks after this final move.[25]

Salqa's tale is yet another reminder of the constant mobility of Lebanese migrants. This, in itself, was a commercial strategy of sorts. But his drifts in and out of various localities and jobs are also evidence of another important feature of migrant commercial life: the willingness of those who were more successful to take on others—whether bound to them by kin or not—either, at first, as apprentices serving time on the shop floor as they learned the tricks of the trade, or as seasoned employees. In late 1923, an administrator reported that the 'Syrians' 'now arriving in AOF ... off their own back', without 'anyone calling upon them', were 'taken in' by the established migrants of Dakar.[26] The latter either found them work in the capital of the Federation or the 'interior' of Senegal—or, if unsuccessful in their search, paid for the new arrivals to move on to Conakry or Bassam, where they might be more fortunate. As Kamil Muruwwah put it, 'new arrivals from the homeland or the American *mahjar*', though they came 'practically empty-handed, their only weapons their good spirits and hope', could count 'upon a relative or countryman': 'few were those who ventured into work without assistance'.[27]

Just as often, however, traders held on to these new arrivals. They took them on as apprentices, forcing upon them an arduous training: the first year new arrivals worked without wages, 'learning his trade and the local idiom'; in the second, though they were entitled to five thousand francs 'if no commercial upset' occurred, they were often 'rewarded only' by the lachrymose 'lamentations' of their employer, who berated 'a negative, if imaginary, balance' to evade his obligations. The administrator who reported these practices insisted that fed up apprentices 'generally' 'stole ... from their bosses' in their 'third or fourth year of employment', and 'obtained credit from a complicit compatriot, who benefits from a prebend or gifts in kind'.[28] However, it is clear such relationships often ended rather less acrimoniously, with the trainee setting out to a 'region of his choice' with a few goods borrowed on credit from his patron, for whom he remained an 'agent', buying up commodities on his behalf.[29] Muruwwah thus reported that while many, 'when they felt they had acquired the skill to trade alone, left service and opened a small shop with the minute capital and know-how' they had accumulated, others received 'significant assistance' from established traders, who paid for the costs of their establishments, and 'provided guarantees to the [European] trading companies which lent them goods on credit'.[30] These practices, it seems, were implemented with little variation throughout West Africa—and they changed little over time. Thus, Fuad Khuri found much the same pattern of sponsorship in the Sierra Leonean town of Magburaka in the early 1960s—recording the ambivalent relations between trainees, who resented the trials they had endured, and sponsors who feared seeing their achievements eclipsed by new arrivals, and tried to hold on to this cheap labour as long as they could before ultimately relenting and providing 'capital in trust, without formal transactions, and ... in commodities'.[31]

Despite the rifts they could sometimes occasion, practices such as these could offer clear advantages to both parties. They might allow the apprentice to find his feet and gave the bankrupt a lifeline. But they also gave more successful traders a source, at first, of cheap, ready labour—and, later, a means of subcontracting activities like produce collecting, which they found too inefficient or tiresome to carry out themselves, to individuals with whom they had incrementally built up a measure of commercial trust.[32] After all, the 'produce traders of the villages' were the 'fundamental component of Lebanese and Syrian trade'. Without these figures, and their willingness to traipse from locality to locality 'in the days of the harvest', buying up 'groundnuts and the like', the whole edifice of Eastern Mediterranean trade would topple.[33] Such apprenticeships are a reminder of the ways in which Eastern Mediterranean migrants could play upon the formal expectations of reciprocity, manipulating them to business-like ends—and of the strains and ambivalences that always lay slightly beneath the surface of solidarity. Mobility, then, could be a tool in the individual's kit of commercial strategies. But it was also a reminder of his place within a highly stratified trading hierarchy.

As Emmanuel Grégoire and Pascal Labazée have noted, the tendency of scholars to seek out and stress instances of solidarity between members of a particular trading network has tended to obscure the extent to which these 'mercantile organisations … show a pyramidal structure resting on a body of dependences built and sustained' by dominant entrepreneurs.[34] The Lebanese traders of AOF, as much as any other commercial network, were thus divided into three distinct if intimately interconnected groups: 'wholesale merchants'; 'semi-wholesale and retail merchants'; and the 'produce traders of the villages'—*tujjar al-qura wa al-mahsulat*.[35] The exiguous number of 'operators' at the apex of this structure were those who 'define[d] the professional possibilities' of each participant.[36] They did so not only through despatching apprentices or employees to particular localities, but also—and perhaps most importantly—through the distribution of credit. This was as true of the European trading companies which sat at the apex of the colonial commercial order as it was, increasingly, of well-to-do Lebanese merchants who came to play the role of bankers and creditors to their less prosperous compatriots.

Creditable operations

The few scholars who have examined the place of Lebanese entrepreneurs in AOF have argued that they essentially served as the agents of the Federation's European trading houses. This was certainly the way in which some migrants—and their visiting compatriots—saw it. Thus, Kamil Muruwwah insisted that the companies exerted a hegemonic hold over the colonial economy, 'behaving as [they] wished, and imposing [their] will on the markets'. The Lebanese, meanwhile, served as the 'principal link between the companies and their black clients': 'buying goods' from the former 'wholesale or semi-wholesale, they sold them after much effort at a meagre profit, and bought in turn produce from the black which they sold to the companies for equally small gains'.[37] In doing so, they rapidly rose in the companies' esteem, providing 'services' which were 'indispensable' in a 'market situation where there is a low level of capital in circulation and a poor state of transport and communication requiring a multiplicity of small merchant-creditors'.[38] There is, of course, much truth in this. The CFAO, in particular, had from the early years of the twentieth century come to favour semi-wholesale activities to the daily exigencies of retail trade; this policy led it to build agencies in only the most strategic locations, such as regional marketing centres where it could easily buy up commodities, while supplying merchandise to smaller Lebanese, Wolof and *Soudanais* traders who could then distribute them among their clients.[39] Profoundly conservative in its management methods, the Compagnie still, it seems, attempted wherever possible to avoid extending credit to its clients. In place of this 'abominable system',[40] it sought to maintain into the interwar years the practice, which had briefly held sway at the beginning of the century among its competitors, of taking on *traitants à gages* or commissioned brokers.[41] Thus, it was reported in 1937 that its Dakar offices were a million francs in the red, because the Paris headquarters had taken to covering the deposits of Eastern Mediterranean migrants boarding ship for AOF in Marseille; its expenses were then defrayed by its subsidiary in the Federation's capital, to which these new arrivals were in turn bound by their debts.[42] However, for all its caution, the CFAO increasingly began to follow its competitors' practice of handing out generous credit to Lebanese traders in advance of the Senegalese *traite*. In 1935, the Kaolack branch of the SONOCO had alone distributed 850,000 francs to Eastern Mediterranean brokers in Sine-Saloum; though figures were lacking for the other large trading companies—the CFAO, Chavanel, Maurel et Prom, Maurel Frères and Vézia—it was reported that they had exceeded this amount, in their attempts to beat down the competition presented by the providential societies sponsored by the administration.[43] As historians have long known, the Eastern Mediterranean traders of AOF clearly depended heavily on the credit facilities provided by large commercial outfits such as these. The Lebanese were thus 'undoubtedly'—at least in part—'indebted to the companies for their success, just as the companies were indebted to them for their part in securing such consistent gains'.[44]

Less well understood is the manner in which this credit was distributed. European trading companies did sometimes prove willing to grant rather insignificant loans to smaller Lebanese traders; Jamil Haddad, who declared bankruptcy in 1931 with a mere 2,000 or so francs of merchandise to his name, had contracted debts with both Lecomte and the Tivaouane branch of Vézia.[45] More typical, however, of the impecunious multitude of shopkeepers and small-time brokers sustained only by the largesse of their creditors was Farid Ja'fari. On his bankruptcy the same year, he owed money to some fourteen creditors. Only two of these, Lecomte and Vincent Goux, were French traders, who had lent him the relatively trifling sums of 4,857.85 francs and 2,025 francs. The remainder were all Lebanese compatriots, ranging from his relatives As'ad and Jamil, to whom he owed, respectively, 35,000 and 10,000 francs—sums which demonstrate the lengths to which some went to fulfil the obligations of kin—to prominent and prosperous traders like Sa'id Nujaim and the Sayigh and 'Abduh brothers.[46] It was with men like these—or, at the very least, merchants of the middling sort like Michel 'Abdallah—that the French trading houses of Senegal, Guinea and Soudan preferred to do business. 'Abdallah—whose merchandise was worth in the region of 107,000 francs when he bankrupted—owed some 72,000 francs to trading firms like Delmas and Lecomte, along with another 60,000 or so to Lebanese traders like 'Abbas 'Abbud and Mustafa Hudruj.[47] For his part, 'Abbud had outstanding debts of more than four million francs,[48] while the Risha brothers, with their *comptoirs* in Dakar, M'Bour and Fatick, their bakery in Thiès and their transportation business, owed some 2,700,000 francs.[49]

Men like these not only depended on constant flows of credit to purchase stock and pay the rent on their locales, keeping little in their tills and bank accounts. They also extended these lines of credit to others lower down the commercial pecking order. Thus, 'Abdallah was owed more than 60,000 francs by various debtors.[50] 'Abbud, meanwhile, had distributed the rather more considerable sum of 1,456,014 francs in loans and merchandise to various clients.[51] Such arrangements were, it seems, often made without any of the fuss of legal formalities. Ahmad Zayyat, for example, owed some 619,543.37 francs in bills of lading and 50,188.85 francs to 'various creditors'. While the former sum was, we might intimate, for merchandise he had purchased from European trading firms, the latter was probably what he owed to other Lebanese traders.[52] The merchandise they informally supplied, and the cash loans they handed out, did certainly insulate some from the worst of the depression—as French administrators noted, Lebanese habitually advanced sums to those who had fallen behind in their repayments to suppliers. However, the willingness of more prosperous traders to provide credit, and to nurse their debtors back to financial health when they fell on hard times, had as much to do with a keen sense of commercial opportunity—and a desire to protect their own reputations, bound up to the fortunes of their clients—as with any sense of 'solidarity' or fellow-feeling for those lower down the commercial pecking order.[53] The Conakry merchant Butrus Rizq, for instance, not only supplied loans at high rates of interest to his compatriots for their commercial undertakings, but he also demanded a share of any profits they might make. While Rizq had no bank account, other prosperous Lebanese traders used their good relations with financial institutions like the BAO to turn themselves into merchant bankers of sorts, repackaging the loans they received and passing them on to others.[54] Thus, while the majority of Bamako's Lebanese entrepreneurs had bank accounts by the late 1940s, most used them only to deposit what was left in their tills, and to wire transfers to their trading partners in Dakar and Kaolack. A few, however, used the banks not just for such rudimentary operations, but also for 'all sorts of credit operations … advances … mortgages … letters of credit for their external suppliers'.[55] Muruwwah reported that some merchants had, before the crash of 1931, credit lines 'of half a million francs with every bank without guarantees'.[56] These 'notables' were not only 'advisors' to their compatriots, but also 'intermediaries' who offered them 'their own credit on variable terms'.[57]

Such wealthy operators were not, of course, legion. Nevertheless, they were rather more numerous than one might expect from conventional portrayals of the Lebanese of AOF as a relatively homogeneous group of commercial intermediaries. They included in Dakar Sa'id Nujaim, who owned two buildings, worth five million francs, and had some 775,000 francs in his bank accounts; Mahmud Fakhri, who owned five buildings worth six million francs in total; Mahmud Burji, who owned seven buildings worth five million; and Emile Ashqar, who had deposits of some 1,800,000 francs.[58] The latter had his main business interests in Bamako, whose Lebanese traders seemed particularly affluent: eighteen among them possessed working capital of over a million francs, and four firms—those of the Naja brothers, Milhim Nassar, Mas'ad and sons, and the Watshi Hayik family—had more than eight million at their fingertips.[59] The Naja—whose total worth was estimated at some fifty million francs in 1945—also had sizeable interests in Guinea, where only Paterson Zochonis and the CFAO had more working capital at their disposal. These assets included fifteen million francs in bank accounts, a commercial building in Conakry worth some three million francs and a plantation on the city's outskirts.[60] Though none of Guinea's other Eastern Mediterranean traders could quite challenge this affluence, the Naja were not alone in possessing substantial means—'Abdallah Ja'far, whose annual turnover ran to 1,400,000 francs, owned total assets of around fifteen million francs,[61] while the Fakhuri had some five to six million francs in liquid assets besides their real estate holdings. In Côte d'Ivoire, meanwhile, the Nassar brothers possessed between ten and fifteen million francs of assets between them, while the capital of 'Abd al-Latif Fakhri amounted to anywhere between five and twenty million francs.[62] It is difficult, of course, to know what to make of these figures. They were but a snapshot of rapidly fluctuating fortunes, which shot up or down with the stock of commodities. As Lebanese traders in Dakar told Kamil Muruwwah in the late 1930s, 'it is impossible to know' the precise extent of any 'fortune', for trade necessitated the constant exchange of monies and contracting of debts, so that individuals traders' holdings were forever in flux.[63] Furthermore, as administrators freely admitted, they could be but estimates, such was the tendency of even wealthy operators to use the services of financial institutions sparingly, and to disseminate their capital through a variety of investments, placing some in the businesses of former associates and apprentices, and investing some in interests and real estate in or AOF, or—less amenable to scrutiny—the Eastern Mediterranean. 'Abbas 'Abbud, for instance, had 426,200 francs of stocks in the Société Electrique Cadicha, in northern Lebanon.[64]

Nonetheless, they do tell us something of their investment strategies. These men seem to have regarded real estate as an essentially speculative activity—a means of swelling their capital, rather than one of keeping it immobile. Kamil Muruwwah reported that Eastern Mediterranean migrants owned 10 per cent of the buildings of Dakar—and 30 per cent to 40 per cent of those owned by 'whites'. However, these were used not just for their own dwellings or commercial premises. After all, there were only 1,629 *Libano-Syriens* in the city in 1936, a number incommensurably smaller than their investments. Rather, they were a fruitful investment opportunity. While yearly profits from real estate could not exceed 10 per cent in Lebanon and Syria, they reached 30 per cent in 'some parts of Africa', providing a welcome source of profit, 'not least in Dakar, Côte d'Ivoire, and Nigeria'.[65] Moreover, it was one they seem to have cautiously regarded as safer than financial products like stocks and bonds. The Risha brothers, for instance, had only 100,000 francs in shares in the Société Électrique de Casamance, and more than 6,600,000 francs in real estate. But such caution could backfire. The Rishas, when they sought liquidation in 1931, explained to their notaries that the cause of their trouble was not just the loss of 'very large sums'—some 3,200,000 francs—during the dire groundnut trading seasons of 1929 and 1930. Despite these losses, they were able to keep trading for a while using their rents to pay off their mortgages and face their trading debts. It was only when these dried up as tenants whose own fortunes were hit by the depression vacated their premises, leaving their buildings in Thiès, M'Bour and Fatick laying empty, that the Risha faced a liquidity crisis which threatened the collapse of their interests.[66]

Entrepreneurs like these, when they did not—as we will see—engage in the import and export business themselves, dealt at the very least in semi-wholesale activities, buying produce in bulk from their compatriots, supplying them with the manufactured goods they sold in their shops and often serving as their landlords. The activities of these men, as much as those of European trading companies like the CFAO, propped up the edifice of Eastern Mediterranean enterprise, for it was through their hands that trickled much of the credit and goods on which its middling and lower ranks depended.

The lower orders: of middling men and wandering souls

These smaller traders and shopkeepers were by the late 1930s an increasingly varied lot. There were many, to be sure, who still corresponded to the conventional portrait of the impoverished and ill-looking migrant, 'living in little shacks or native huts and displaying a stock of bright cloths, salt, tobacco, gin … and cheap wares generally known as trade-goods'.[67] Some, like Tawfiq Wahid, clearly lived in abject conditions, seemingly unable to find success in any venture. Wahid, after living for a time at his father's in Grand-Bassam, had struck out on his own in 1939, trying his luck—without much success—as a photographer in the region of Daloa, before finishing up in 1943 at Seguela, further inland still. Setting up home on the outskirts of the town, he eked out a 'miserable' existence, relying upon handouts from his neighbours Tawfiq and Muhammad Jabir to supplement the meagre income he scraped together selling coal to Africans from the surrounding villages.[68] Others saw their hopes succumb to the sharp, periodic jolts of the colonial economy, like Bashir Suniaz, who saw—as the Depression hit—his goods linger on the shelf and his loans disappear along with his customers,[69] or simply proved incompetent spendthrifts. This was the case of Ibrahim Faituni, who had been reduced by his improvidence to living in a 'wooden shack' on Avenue Jauréguiberry in Dakar. Having exhausted the patience of a succession of partners—including his own brother, Salim—with his laziness and habit of selling goods beneath their asking price 'with the sole purpose of acquiring money for his personal expenses', he had given up on trading entirely, spending most of his days wandering Dakar or sitting in the shops of one acquaintance or another.[70] The Lebanese communities of AOF had, it is clear, their fair share of drifters and hucksters.

But it would seem many others—more fortunate, or capable, than such hapless characters—were able to acquire a measure of commercial security and material comfort in the interwar years. Fifty-two of the 250 or so migrants in Côte d'Ivoire owned assets of more than 600,000 francs in the mid-1940s.[71] This was an unusually high proportion of well-to-do traders—a product, perhaps, both of the highly specialised nature of commerce in this colony, which had brought in well-established migrants from Guinea and Senegal, and of the development of a wartime economy of smuggling and subterfuge. Some thrived in such conditions, while others were caught out by a conflict for which they were unprepared, and by practices for which they had perhaps little taste. Thus, the Nassar brothers, who had trouble transacting business of a few thousand francs before the imposition of import controls, apparently profited from the war; As'ad Mansur, meanwhile, whose working capital had been outdone only by that of the European companies, saw his business decline sharply.[72] But the Lebanese communities of Senegal, Guinea and Soudan, too, were marked by rising prosperity. While the wealthiest man in Senegal, according to Kamil Muruwwah's informants, was worth between five and seven million francs, another two hundred had fortunes of between half a million and two million francs each. The largest fortune in Guinea, meanwhile, was in the order of four of five million francs; fifty Lebanese residents of the colony were worth half a million francs, and another hundred half a million francs.[73] Of the 254 traders dotted through Soudan in the mid-1940s, some 108 had between 100,000 and 500,000 francs in capital, and seventy-seven between 500,000 and three million francs; only thirty-one had less than 50,000 francs.[74] Lebanese traders, meanwhile, owned some 200 buildings in Dakar in the 1940s.[75] Of course, many of these may only have housed the 'one-door family businesses, christened "general stores"' that Nadra Filfili saw on his arrival in the colony in the mid-1920s.[76]

The increasing commercial heft of Eastern Mediterranean traders, then, hid continuing disparities of income within the seemingly undifferentiated middling orders of this community. But, despite their differences of income, all but the members of a relatively exiguous mercantile elite engaged in essentially similar pursuits. They were those who ran the general retail stores of the coastal cities and trading posts of AOF. In 1935, Dakar alone counted some 455 such establishments.[77] Even if we account for the tendency of these traders to 'establish several branches in the larger cities to facilitate the sale of stocks', this speaks to the considerable expansion in their numbers in the interwar years. By the late 1930s, they were 'the largest component' of Eastern Mediterranean society. One sign of their growing sense of themselves as a cut above was their gradual withdrawal from direct participation in the purchase of produce: many no longer coursed through the hinterland themselves in lorries loaded with hemp bags heaving with groudnuts, but left it to their employees or subcontractors—men recently arrived from the Eastern Mediterranean, or who had just completed their apprenticeships and were now arduously earning their spurs in the interior—to whom they 'despatched goods and monies shortly before the season'.[78]

The tactics of trade

Eastern Mediterranean migrants were—it should be stressed—traders before they became brokers. Furthermore, this transition did not always occur at the same pace as in Guinea, where those who arrived at the turn of the century seized rapidly on the rich pickings of the rubber boom. Nor did it follow the same progression—from hawker to small-time broker to shopkeeper, renting a locale with the profits of their marketplace speculation. In Saint-Louis and Dakar, pedlars were rapidly transformed into shopkeepers by administrative diktat, when an interdict on street-vending passed in 1903 pushed them into shops where they began to sell 'canned goods, candles, sugar, and cloth' alongside the glass baubles and beads they had once hawked. While most sold cheap goods targeting their largely African clientele, a few 'stocked their shops so well that they attracted, at least in Dakar, a few Europeans'. By 1912, two of these men—perhaps Joseph Ganamet and César 'Abduh—had begun work on 'impressive buildings whose grocery stores will provide serious competition to those of our compatriots'. But while some were showing signs of growing prosperity, D'Anfreville de la Salle noted that these migrants—unlike those in Guinea—remained retailers, who played no part in the 'great commercial activity of this country, the groundnut trade'. He was, perhaps, not entirely correct in this estimation—some had already begun buying up peanuts in small quantities in Casamance, Sine and Saloum when he wrote this account; nonetheless, his testimony provides telling evidence of the different commercial trajectories Eastern Mediterranean migrants took across AOF.[79]

Whatever the case, these two activities—retail and brokerage—largely relied on the same repertoire of commercial strategies. This was especially true in the railway towns and small trading posts of the interior of Senegal, Guinea or Côte d'Ivoire, where they were essentially complementary. These relations relied, at the most basic of levels, upon the capacity to attract customers and suppliers. The cheap everyday wares and baubles Lebanese shopkeepers sold in Saint-Louis in the years before 1914 contrasted sharply with the 'Arabic costumes of fine cloth, silk mantles ... and Korans printed in Egypt' stocked in Moroccan shops, where a 'rich' African 'clientele' 'dressed in the fashions of Fez, just as our snobs follow the trends of London'.[80] However, by the interwar years, Eastern Mediterranean traders had increasingly diversified their wares, seeking to draw in a broader custom. Michel 'Abdallah thus kept in his shop at Mekhe in the Saloum, besides 'sundry goods' such as canned and bagged foodstuffs—silver bracelets, gold earrings, 'amulets', 'Syria cloths', 'Damascus shawls' and horse-saddles.[81] The stock of Na'im Risha's shop in Fatick, meanwhile, included goods ranging from tins of sardines, matches and 'Sudanese tobacco' to bottles of rosewater perfume and brilliantine, purses, harmonicas, toy guns and pianos, and—for the most part—a wide selection of cloth and clothes, from 'Indian vests' and *boubous* at five francs, to 'European trousers' at ten francs, and cuttings of percale and Japanese cloth.[82]

But they also depended on rather more interventionist—shall we say—tactics to draw in their African suppliers and customers. This, like the other methods used by Eastern Mediterranean produce buyers and shopkeepers, can best be understood by examining in closer detail the highly seasonal peanut economy of Senegal—whose commercial year was divided between the four or five months of the *traite*, the groundnut trading season with its frenzied round of negotiations, and the *hivernage*, when peasants busied themselves in planting and tending to their crops or seeking work.[83] Eastern Mediterranean traders began, some time before the official opening of the trading season, to tour the countryside, buying up groundnuts from producers eager to refresh their supplies of cash after the lean times of planting.[84] At times traders conducted these rounds themselves—setting out under cover of night to avoid unwelcome administrative attention, and touring the villages of the countryside in their lorries;[85] at others they hired local Wolof or Serer, who served as factotums and muleteers—earning a little cash to supplement their own agricultural income—and could, conveniently, claim to be transporting their own crops if intercepted by an administrator.[86]

We know little without the collection of further oral evidence about the attitudes these men—and, indeed, other Senegalese traders—took towards their Lebanese employers and competitors. Some small, occasional traders seemed to work 'almost exclusively with the Lebanese' who provided them with goods in exchange for salt—though we do not know their reasons for doing so.[87] Others, meanwhile, bitterly resented these commercial interlopers. In 1944, the Bloc Africain de Kaolack—the market town at the very heart of the peanut economy—called for the 'commercial sphere' to be 'reserved for the native son and the importer-exporter, whatever his nationality'. This, they maintained, was the sole means of providing work to the 'indigenous trading masses' who languished without employment because of the 'multiple anti-Senegalese manoeuvres' of the *Libano-Syrien*, that 'noxious element of penetration'.[88]

The advance buying Lebanese relied upon had an element of rudimentary speculation about it—of betting on the sharp rise in prices which, traders hoped, would come, especially in the last months of the *traite*. Indeed, it was not without its dangers. In some ways, as Kamil Muruwwah correctly surmised, it resembled a 'stock market', in which the trader bet upon the forthcoming harvest, exposing himself to the vagaries of local supply and global demand.[89] But there was also something cautious about this strategy—an attempt, perhaps, to guarantee a share of the market, and to insure themselves against the costs of the inflation to come. Credit, too, served as both a lubricant of exchange and as a commercial guarantee—at least for the trader, who could pull suppliers and clients into a continued relationship, which would ensure him a share of the market in an environment of frantic competition. The credit Eastern Mediterranean shopkeepers and brokers provided their clients ranged from small cash loans to pawning—of 'loincloths, *boubous*, and jewels',[90] and millet, bought in the early 1950s at fifteen to eighteen francs the kilogram in October, when the producers' cash reserves were exhausted, and sold again in May or June at twenty-five to thirty francs when peasants were still flush with the gains of the *traite*, but short of foodstuffs.[91] In 1935, the administrator of Thiès reported that twelve Eastern Mediterranean traders had handed out 375,000 francs between them in sums of around a hundred francs to each customer.[92] Nicolas 'Isa, meanwhile, forwarded in July 1937 some 12,095 francs to twenty-six debtors from his shop in Guinguineo in the Sine-Saloum. While a few—whom he perhaps perceived as less credit-worthy or important—received one or two hundred francs, most were granted loans of four hundred francs. Two, perhaps *sous-traitants*, or commercial agents, received 950 francs, while one, Khassim Mbacke—a *marabout* of the Murid Sufi brotherhood—received some 3,700 francs.[93] We do not know whether it was his mere status which afforded him such a sum, or his control over a network of producers, but this is a telling indication of the hierarchies of worthiness and trust Lebanese traders relied upon. These traders often depended, in villages with a large population of producers, on a single figure—often an old client—to collect and distribute credit, and always kept 'the same producers' to whom they disbursed loans year after year. This allowed them both to gauge the reliability of their debtors, and to bind customers into a continued relationship, which guaranteed them a market share in an environment of frantic competition.[94] These, of course, came at a high cost to the African customer. For not only did clients have to reimburse their creditors in cash and kind at rates of interest hovering between 50 per cent and 100 per cent, in hard currency, jewellery or bags of groundnuts,[95] they were also bound by their monetary obligations, or simply by their desire to regain the goods they had pawned, to these traders.

It is no surprise, then, that while a few Senegalese political activists had come by the 1940s to argue that the 'Senegalese manages to produce the quantity of groundnuts necessary to maintain his economy' only thanks to the 'assistance and collaboration of these traders, settled in the train towns and trading posts',[96] some Senegalese peasants should have remembered with resentment the *naar*—the Arabs, as they called Eastern Mediterranean traders—criticising them for the abusive rates of interest they charged.[97] But while these loans tied producers into the cash market, they also had their advantages, allowing 'consumption to be spread more evenly throughout the year'—by keeping cash and foodstuffs flowing in dribs and drabs through the lean winter months. The old Wolof peasants James Searing questioned in the 1990s remembered, to be sure, the '"cheating", "theft", "usury", and "chicanery" of colonial chiefs and merchants'. But they clung, nonetheless, to the sense that the days of colonial cash-crop production had witnessed the growth of a *koom-koom*, a 'real economy'. This contrasted starkly with the declining opportunities of the post-colonial years.[98] Selling peanuts, it seems, offered both Wolof and Serer peasants the means not only of engaging in the 'hedonistic pragmatism' of immediate consumption,[99] as French administrators, with all their petty prejudices about African tastes, so often accused them of doing, but also of consolidating and reproducing household structures. Older men were able to maintain their patriarchal role by purchasing livestock, recycling their cash earnings into cattle wealth—a practice particularly common among the Serer of Sine—while the young were able to accumulate some money to found their own families. These changes allowed these men to transform themselves from *badolo*, mere peasants, into *beykat*—a term with connotations closer to the English 'farmer'.[100]

These, it is clear, were not simply monetary transactions. It is not just that both parties invested in such exchanges a range of meanings and interests.[101] They were also performances, dependent on a whole economy of phrases and bodily gestures, as both sides haggled away, each attempting to wear down the other. Bargaining, as Clifford Geertz has argued, was fundamentally about the control of information—about the quality and quantity of the good in play, its desirability and its price.[102] These exchanges hung on the ability of one side or another to conceal, reveal or falsify valuable information. Eastern Mediterranean traders picked up the groundnuts, passing them through their fingers to feel their worth, and reached to the bottom of the bag to check on those kernels of lesser quality hidden beneath the cream of the crop.[103] They sought not just to gain such knowledge, but also to withhold information of their own, not least by the tricks of obfuscation and distraction. Women, it seems, played a significant part in such noisy, riotous performances. Fuad Khuri recalled witnessing the manner in which the wife of a shopkeeper, when hearing the price he proffered to a customer for a particular good, would jump in—offering in a lower, and therefore more correct, estimation of her own. Man and woman would then engage in mutual retribution, husband scolding wife for her improvidence and wife taking man to task for his cupidity, leaving the client unsteady and unsure of where he stood.[104] This is a reminder of the integral role women played in Lebanese business operations. Some, indeed, seem to have gone beyond such supporting roles—though they were perhaps allowed to do so only out of exigency, like Mme 'Id Dahir, who ran his affairs 'in a satisfactory fashion' while he remained in Lebanon during the Second World War, or Mme Veuve Mussi, who owned a few buildings in Conakry and ran an outfit buying palm kernels with her deceased husband's partner, As'ad Ghantus.[105]

Other procedures were used, too, to gain the upper hand. Lebanese traders commonly bought produce by the bag. This practice, of course, made their life easier, for it obviated the need to bag the produce—just as in turn, both European and larger Lebanese trading firms found advantages in 'buying a proportion of their produce' from individual brokers, 'which saved dealing' with proliferating networks of clients 'and worrying over bags … one at a time, all of which requires staff', as one commentator noted in Sierra Leone.[106] This reminds us that commerce consisted of a constellation of small transactions, each conducted with different partners on different terms. But buying by the bag also allowed Lebanese traders to use rough approximations—fixing, for example, a donkey's load at 110 or 120 kilograms.[107] These, of course, could be conveniently manipulated for small gain by either side—as could weights and measures. While some peasants resorted to attenuating their produce with sediment or sand to increase bulk,[108] some Eastern Mediterranean traders turned the tipping of the scales in their favour into a fine art. In 1910, the magistrate of Ziguinchor, in Casamance, reported on the continued misdemeanours of one Jamil Sarduq. Despite two previous convictions for commercial fraud, Sarduq had 'not renounced his fruitful way of weighing the produce which he buys at prices defying all competition'; he had simply improved his illicit operation by installing a 'network of watchers and beaters' to avoid detection, and surrounding himself with acolytes like Bashir, for whom 'card games and knife tricks hold no secrets'.[109]

Some migrants, it is clear, did not simply live in ignorance of commercial codes and regulations, operating in a legal penumbra because of their inability to draw up contracts or keep rational accounting. After all, it seems even impecunious scrabblers like Ahmad Haidar kept inventories of goods or debtors sufficient for their purposes, while others maintained a careful watch on their affairs, recording and breaking down their takings, losses and exposures.[110] Rather, they consciously sought to benefit from marginality, both in the small-scale matters of individual transactions, and on a larger scale through smuggling operations. These were on one level simply efforts to evade border controls. Such was the case of Sufian Darwish, who tried to smuggle gold dust from Sierra Leone into Guinea in a double-bottomed suitcase in the hope of exporting it to France. But these practices also represented attempts to capitalise upon such controls—and the price differentials and conditions of scarce supply they could create. Elias Rubaiz, for instance, was caught in 1935 trying to smuggle a consignment of cigarettes he had unloaded at Port Étienne in Mauritania by lorry to Saint-Louis—maximising his profits by evading tax.[111] This, it seems, was quite the family business: administrators reported that the Rubaiz were well known for the illegal trade they carried on along the Petite Côte, to the south of Dakar.[112] Lebanese traders like these sought out not only licit profits, but also marginal gains.[113]

However, bargaining was not just about deception and concealment, but also about courtesy. Transactions between Lebanese traders and their Wolof or Serer commercial interlocutors involved the granting of gifts, like meals of fish and rice or millet, presents of perfume, sweets or small swatches of cloth, or seeds or small cash sums to stave off the efforts of the colonial administration to store producers' grain in the locales of its *Sociétés de prévoyance*, and its demands for taxes.[114] These, of course, were not simple acts of giving, but profit operations—small transactions which created expectations of reciprocity, an expense which could then be recouped in produce or interest. Moreover, Eastern Mediterranean traders worked to make their clients and interlocutors at ease in their commercial premises. It was not just that the Lebanese were 'closer' to Africans than European traders, who 'clung to their high social status'; it was also that they seemed more 'willing to deal with them'. They engaged with them with 'equanimity and respect'—in Muruwwah's kind estimate— allowing them, for instance, to browse 'for a quarter of an hour' or more, or to linger at the doorway to the shop—practices Europeans could never countenance.[115] And they also used a repository of formulas of courtesy and stock phrases from which buyer and seller could extemporise. Boulland de l'Escale noted that the 'Catholic' migrants of Boke in Guinea 'do not hesitate, despite their religion, to do *salam*' with the *indigène*.[116] The '*Syrien*, who is often Muslim, or pretends to be, [and] who speaks Arabic',[117] played upon a common vocabulary of piety and greeting—much of which cut across confessional lines—to establish affinities with African customers. Most did not stop there. Nadra Filfili remembered how, when he had first arrived in the village of Tielmakha, he had kept a notebook, in which he jotted down all the Wolof words he could learn, and their phonetic pronunciation, having 'quickly learned that the only way to communicate on a friendly footing with my neighbours would be to learn their language', and realised that 'my trips over syllables and sounds, which they corrected with laughter, created a bridge between us'.[118]

The ways of home

Such practices have often been treated as somehow characteristic of the particularly mercantile mindset of the Lebanese, of a form of social organisation especially conducive to profit. Eastern Mediterranean migrants, it is true, showed a marked propensity to enter into trade wherever they went—working as pack pedlars and shopkeepers in Australia and the United States, Argentina and Brazil, the Caribbean, Mexico and Colombia. In Mexico, for instance, 55.35 per cent of Eastern Mediterranean migrants occupied trading positions in the 1920s.[119] However, this seems as much a matter of opportunity as of inclination. Though far, far more work needs to be done to flesh out such comparisons, Eastern Mediterranean migrants seem to have profited in Vermont and Alabama as much as in Haiti and Rio Grande do Sul, or Guinea and Senegal from relatively undeveloped marketing networks for manufactured goods.[120]

However, it should have helped that many of these men and women were hardly greenhorns in matters of trade. Rather, their lives before migration had been shaped by their constant entanglement with the market as Mount Lebanon and Jabal 'Amil were pulled, in quite different ways, into the networks of the world economy. The first migrants to come to AOF brought with them an experience of market transactions similar, in many ways, to those in which they would engage in West Africa. Turbulent flows of credit swilled about the economy of Mount Lebanon in these years, just as in Senegal or Guinea. The myriad intermediaries who sprung from the ground to service the needs of the trading houses of Beirut, most of whom remained free agents rather than *bi-l-amana*—brokers 'in the trust', or employ, of the firms—borrowed their working capital, and they in turn used this money to advance sums to silk producers at inflated rates of interest or to purchase their precious quarry at advantageous prices 'in anticipation'. In 1851, for instance, the advance price of the *oke* had been nine to twelve piastres; this almost doubled at harvest time to around eighteen piastres.[121] Both brokers and producers, then, depended on a constant flow of loans to carry on their business—and, indeed, to purchase the commodities they thirsted after.

Furthermore, traders and producers alike depended on forms of ensuring trust and enforcing contracts essentially similar to those prevalent in Mount Lebanon in the nineteenth century. There, written contracts remained relatively scarce until late in the century, and, when drawn up, served as little more than *aides-mémoire*. Verbal arrangements—sometimes passed in Christian areas in church, 'under the eyes of the Virgin'—were regarded as binding and guaranteed by the mutual expectations created by ties of family, by the need for neighbourly concord or by the hierarchical relations between a patron and his client. The honour, not just of a single individual, but of the *jumhur*—the 'general mass' of his family—depended upon such an agreement. This was an economy, then, which—even as it was thoroughly monetised, dependent on cash and credit—still clung to a definition of personhood as a weave of broader relations. Indeed, even the asymmetric exchanges between landowner and producer—known, tellingly, as a *sharik* or partner—were built upon such expectations in areas like the Kisrwan, where the harvest was divided up according to a fixed formula each year, and the arrangement renewed, on a rolling basis, and without recourse to written documents.[122] Early migrants to West Africa were the sons of this verbal economy of trust. It is no surprise, then, that they used familiar expectations of reciprocity and forms of hierarchical partnership to give sense and strength to their own trading organisations.

Similarly, the oft-remarked facility of migrants to speak new tongues was no product of their particular genius, but rather—it could be argued—of the 'constant switching of codes and styles' in which they engaged in the market towns and port cities of the Eastern Mediterranean. This, as Tim Harper has argued, was essentially born of the interactions and negotiations between local idioms and identities and the 'homogenising forces' of commerce, empire and faith.[123] Thus, villagers and town-dwellers tried as best they could to bridge the gap between their own demotic Arabic and the ornate language of the Gospels or the Qur'an, pulling words together from these different registers in their rhymes and songs. Some also knew a smattering of Ottoman Turkish—itself a *lingua franca* composed in significant part of loan words—and of Italian, or French, or English, or Russian, acquired variously in mission schools or marketplaces. While access to these various languages and registers depended on where one was born, how well one was educated and what one did in life, the vernacular Arabic Eastern Mediterranean migrants spoke was a cosmopolitan composite, borrowing from here and there, and bearing the traces of these various influences. The manner in which they incorporated sundry elements into their everyday language foreshadowed the little loans and appropriations that characterised their commercial lives in West Africa.

Magpies of trade

For practices like coaxing or lending on credit had nothing particularly Lebanese about them. As James Searing has noted, 'the entire edifice of the trade economy was based on the extensive use of credit'.[124] All the brokers—Mauritanian and French,

Wolof and Lebanese—who engaged in the groundnut trade gave out credit on different terms to Senegalese cultivators. The French traders of Thiès, for instance, provided their clients in the early years of the twentieth century with loans at rates of between 25 per cent and 30 per cent, if provided in merchandise, and 40 per cent and 60 per cent, if handed out in cash—taking as collateral what jewellery or tools producers could spare.[125] Such rates of interest only got steeper with time. In 1935, the *négociants* of Thiès—or their shop assistants—had handed out around 110,000 francs in credit. Carrying on 'the same traffic' as the Eastern Mediterranean traders of the place they, too, charged between 50 per cent and 100 per cent.[126] In the countryside around Louga, meanwhile, the African *sous-traiteurs*—or agents—of Devès et Chaumet, Peyrissac, and Maurel et Prom extended that same year credit both in cash and in sugar, tobacco, biscuits and percale.[127] French companies across AOF had long used African agents like these as coaxers: in the Guinean market of Kindia, they were dispatched in the years before 1914 to greet the incoming caravans, and to 'deal with them, if not strip them';[128] in 1937, cultivators in the Saloum remained at the mercy of these agents, who doubled as muleteers, carrying the peasants' bags of groundnuts to the shop of their employer.[129] But while these transporters and agents were still known by the old, nineteenth-century, term as *maîtres de langue*, many independent European traders—like the Alsatian Hartman, who had arrived in Thiès in 1904—spoke Wolof fluently by the mid-twentieth century.[130] The proceedings of the town council of Prades, in the south-western region of Ariège—from which so many of the small brokers who lived in places like Thiès and Louga hailed—were sometimes, it was said, held in Wolof, 'so that the retired *Sénégalais* (as they called themselves) could keep their adopted language alive'.[131] This vignette may well have been apocryphal. But, true or not, it is a telling indication of the extent to which some Frenchmen bent to their surroundings.

Indeed, there was often little to distinguish French shops from those of *indigènes* or *Libano-Syriens*. No matter the origins of their tenants, and regardless of whether they were '"independent" or in the service of a trading firm, one found almost everywhere the same arrangement'—sometimes a construction built of solid materials, or more often a flimsy 'shack covered of corrugated iron or tiles', but 'always made up of two parts: the shop and the lodgings'.[132] All those who participated directly in the frenzied transactions of the groundnut *traite*—an entire economic year collapsed into four short months—used much the same tactics—and lived in largely similar conditions, loath as Europeans were to admit it. Whether French, Senegalese or Eastern Mediterranean, their desperation to take a share of the spoils pushed them to the margins of colonial law, as they tried to guarantee their profits amidst sharply fluctuating prices by engaging in advance buying, and to maximise their gains by steep rates of interest.

The Senegalese trading season, in a sense, does remind one of the distinct type of economic organisation Clifford Geertz thought to have discerned in the markets of Indonesia and Morocco, one in which trade was broken up into a myriad small transactions, conducted in unstable price conditions.[133] But, it might be argued, there was little dualistic about the peanut basin—no sharp contrast could be found, at this level of direct involvement in the 'micro-dynamics' of trade, between the approaches of European, African or Eastern Mediterranean participants.[134] Moreover, it mattered little if these participants were employees of the trading companies or small, independent traders. This, too, complicates distinctions between a 'modern', 'rationalised' economic domain, built around firms which employed 'organised' labour on a permanent basis, and an informal sector, in which a multitude of small-scale operators swam about, often engaging in illegitimate activities.[135] Indeed, analysis of colonial trade in AOF has perhaps been hindered by a tendency to regard firms as monolithic units of marketing, rather than as 'value chains'—to borrow the jargon of the management theorist—'collection[s] of independent although interrelated activities'.[136] Such activities could at times be performed by employees of companies like the CFAO or Maurel et Prom, just as they could at others be outsourced, for the purposes of efficiency, to a variety of independent operators.

Big men

Large Lebanese merchants—keenly aware of their own dependence on these trading firms, and eager to increase their profits—increasingly sought ways of escaping such subsidiary tasks, and of circumventing colonial credits of credit and trade. By the late 1930s some in Senegal had taken to ordering goods—in the main, it would seem, textiles—directly from 'the large producers of France, England, America and even Japan'.[137] This wholesale activity had 'gradually grown more organised', so that by this period some had 'permanent agents in foreign supply centres like Paris, Marseille, Manchester, Liverpool, etc.'. Some had gone so far as to split their activities 'into two parts, one branch in Europe for sourcing, and another in Africa for distribution'.[138] Indeed, this trade had apparently reached such amplitude that 'one saw' on the eve of the Second World War 'entire French or foreign ships unloading at Dakar goods for a single [Lebanese] trading house'.[139] The most prosperous Lebanese traders in Bamako, too, engaged in such traffic by this time. While the Mas'ad and Watshi imported sundry manufactured goods, the Naja brothers specialised more particularly in 'French cotton goods' like the percale and the 'special type of head-wrap' they had created, and which they had made for them by a factory in the Vosges, as well as producing kapok locally themselves. Others like Emile Ashqar, Milhim Nassar, the Ghusub and the Daghir imported, meanwhile, wholesale consignments of manufactured wares from Dakar.[140] One might be tempted to regard such increasingly ambitious and diverse activities as the acts of a mature commercial elite, which had patiently increased its capacities over the decades.

However, it seems that Eastern Mediterranean migrants had, from the very earliest years of their presence in AOF, been able to rely on alternative sources of supplies and credit. In 1912, the colonial writer D'Anfreville de la Salle remembered hearing 'once, a while ago, that Mr X, the best known of the Syrians of Senegal received funding' directly 'from an Anglo-Egyptian bank'; distributing in turn loans and goods to 'most of his compatriots' in Saint-Louis, he now dealt only in wholesale.[141] We have no way of knowing who this mysterious Mr X might have been. As far back as 1906, Arcin reported—in an aside tucked away in a footnote—that the traders of Guinea were financed 'by several clearing houses and, especially, by one of their compatriots, a banker in Paris'.[142] More light was shed on these early operations by Kamil Muruwwah's Lebanese informants, who told him that those who had settled in the colony in the early 1900s depended on 'a Lebanese merchant resident in Paris, who would come to them bringing goods, and take from them their monies, which he would send to their kin through the intermediary of a Syrian banker' in the French capital.[143] By the close of the First World War, traders established in Guinea received loans from the Armenian bank of Manouk Frères, and merchandise from the firms of Guépara, Mukarzil and Bijjani.[144] The latter were among the small group of companies established in Paris in the late nineteenth century to supply 'French manufactured goods' to Eastern Mediterranean migrants like Juan (Hanna) Turbay, who stopped in the French capital on his way to Bucamaranga in Colombia to purchase 'precious merchandise to bring to that distant town',[145] or Mr G.H. who obtained a credit line of 20,000 gold *livres* from a Lebanese trader there before heading, too, to Colombia.[146] This was a trade, one 1901 report estimated, worth 'several millions' a year.[147]

While several of these houses were in the hands of Bethlehemite merchant families like the Diqrit, Hirmas, Jasir and Murqus, who traded with their countrymen in Latin America,[148] some of the most sizeable were controlled by Lebanese traders with active ties to the lands of migration. The firm of Fayyad was thus a joint undertaking between Ghantus Fayyad, who lived on Rue Fénelon, a few short, convenient steps from the Gare du Nord,[149] and his relative Darius, one of the most important traders in Cartagena, who travelled every year to France to acquire merchandise.[150] The firms of Mukarzil and Bijjani, meanwhile, belonged to kinsfolk of two of the most sizeable Lebanese families in Guinea at this time.[151] That the commercial ties of 'Abbas Bijjani—a Christian, despite his first name—extended further still is clear from the fact he represented the migrants of Mexico at the 'First Arab Conference', a gathering of Eastern Mediterranean reformists held in the French capital in April 1913.[152] Others, too, had personal relations in the French capital. César 'Abduh, who had set up shop in Dakar in 1910, spent some eighteen months of the First World War in Paris with one Nasrallah 'Abbud,[153] before heading back to Senegal in late 1916.[154] Upon his return, he quickly altered his letterhead, which now proudly announced the sale of 'Paris goods'.[155] Others seem to have extended their interests from Marseille. The port city was itself becoming—as we have seen—a central node of Eastern Mediterranean trading activity; its Lebanese, Syrian and Armenian migrants, who occupied the shops and offices of the Rue des Chapeliers, could be found 'at all levels of the commercial hierarchy, from the merchant and the broker to the miserable retailer'.[156] While Mahmud Burji first ran a hostel in Marseille before setting up a trading company and investing in real estate in Dakar, the family firm run by six of the Jabre—or Jabr—brothers, Michel, Najib, Hatem, César and Shukri,[157] began its operations in Marseille, before extending its interests to Conakry, where Najib opened a branch in 1903, and from there into other parts of AOF.[158] Indeed, its headquarters remained in France well into the 1940s.[159]

When such links did not exist, migrants sought to manufacture them, creating small-scale familial networks of their own to compensate for their lack of contacts. In 1919, Petros Na'um sought permission for him, his wife, his son and two daughters, his sister and cousin to leave Porto-Novo in Dahomey, where he had been established for some twenty years, for Bordeaux, where he wished to set up an export business. Tellingly, he left behind his two brothers, Antonio and Salomon, who had been convicted of illegally exporting currency.[160] This gambit—and their continued reliance on murky dealings, smuggling goods at night back and forth to Lagos—seems to have paid off, for by the 1940s the aggregate fortune of the Na'um was estimated at some seventy million francs.[161] These ties not only provide further proof of the ways in which the bonds of kin were stretched out across long distances in the name of profit, but also suggest another tantalising connection between the Eastern Mediterranean, metropolitan France, AOF and the wider world of the *mahjar*.

Moreover, wealthier Lebanese traders did not simply attempt to do away with their dependence on the importing facilities of the French trading companies. They also tried to break into the export business themselves. In 1916, Joseph Ganamet asked to be allowed to travel urgently to Marseille to 'settle a consignment of groundnuts'.[162] This was only an extension, of course, of the semi-wholesale activities in which he was already engaged; in 1917, he travelled, in the company of his accountant Antoine Hanaini, to Ziguinchor in Casamance to supervise in person the loading of groundnut shipments he had purchased.[163] Others followed similar trajectories. Antoine 'Assaf, who arrived in Ziguinchor in 1907,[164] moved from peddling to shop-keeping, and from shop-keeping to produce trading, before freighting himself shipments of groundnuts on board schooners headed for Dakar, and eventually exporting directly to France.[165] We cannot know how many more engaged in such direct exports in the years before 1939, but it is clear they remained the preserve of a relatively small mercantile elite. Its members, however, could not carry on such transactions unaided.

They relied instead on increasingly sophisticated commercial organisations, patterned—in some ways—upon French trading houses, with their networks of subsidiaries and clerks. Men like Joseph Ganamet or the Mansur brothers hired, as their businesses expanded, accountants and commercial agents to transact their affairs, even as they continued to rely on family ties. Georges Hadifa sought in 1918 to leave Kouroussa, in the company of his secretary Joseph Tiyan, to conduct an inventory of the shop he owned there, whose manager, Jamil Sha'ya, had recently died.[166] The six Jabre brothers, meanwhile, not only depended on their own strength in numbers to run the branches of their business in Marseille, Conakry, Kayes, Bamako and Dakar. They also employed their cousin, Kalim—charged, in a neat reminder of the hierarchies of kin, with taking care of their furthest outpost in Kayes—[167] and an accountant, Fu'ad Khuri, who worked under Najib Jabre's supervision in Conakry, but was seemingly well enough trusted to collect credit on his behalf from the firm's clients in Dakar.[168] Family enterprises like these had began to transform themselves by the early 1920s into firms with a swelling staff—selected, it would seem, not simply because of their belonging to the same kin group, but also because of their expertise—and proliferating networks of trading connections and interests. As one French administrator put it in 1945, those 'who succeed' 'multiply' their 'subsidiaries' and 'operations', and 'create companies'.[169]

And they used these sliding networks of hierarchies to collect not just products for export like groundnuts and palm kernels, but also commodities like cattle, rice or kola nuts conventionally seen as the preserve of African trading networks lying on the margins of the colonial commercial order. Such engagements have too often been seen as ancillary activities, which Lebanese traders were pushed towards when still newly-established and impecunious, as in Côte d'Ivoire in the early 1920s, where they traded in 'salt, smoke-dried fish and sheep',[170] or when blocked off from participating in the produce economy, as in Guinea, where wartime controls forced them, with much resentment, to broker local products like 'chillies, honey, wax, indigo cloth, and orange essence'.[171] However, not all who traded in such products were poor, peripheral sorts like Joseph Habib with his twenty cows. Michael (Mikhail) Elias dispatched some 15,000 heads of cattle every year from Kano to Lagos.[172]

Bitter profits

Lebanese involvement in the kola trade was deeper still. By the last years of the First World War, this made up a significant share of the commercial activities of Eastern Mediterranean migrants, and only grew in importance in the interwar years. Kamil Muruwwah could thus, by 1938, boast that 'the kola trade in all the colonies of West Africa, whether buying or selling, is 100 per cent in our hands'.[173] So proud were the Lebanese traders of Côte d'Ivoire of their dominance that they nicknamed themselves the 'kings of kola'.[174] However, such self-aggrandising talk disguises the extent to which Eastern Mediterranean migrants emulated the longstanding practice of conveying this bitter commodity from the forest zones of the southern coast of West Africa to the savannah of the north. African traders dealing with the western parts of the *sahel*—present-day Mali and Senegal—had long moved their goods along two distinct routes, one leading along the seaboard, and the other moving up inland, through a series of relays, from the forests of Côte d'Ivoire and Sierra Leone. While *juula* traders favoured the first of these routes, the Lebanese merchants of Senegal seem initially to have purchased their kola in the main from Sierra Leone, where many had family or relations who could act as brokers on their behalf, and from whence this quarry could be dispatched by sail or steam up the coast, at a time when railway networks remained piecemeal. This, of course, obviated the need to travel oneself to purchase or sell kolas—a time-consuming exercise for men like the Thiès trader Georges Sulaiman, who sought to spend six months in Grand-Bassam buying kolas in 1917,[175] or Musa As'ad, who wished to spend three months in Dakar offloading the kola he had bought in Conakry.[176] Thus, traders like Joseph Ganamet, whose brothers-in-law and cousins, Lutfallah and Sa'dallah Hajj, lived in Freetown,[177] Sharaf Sharaf, whose brother held a shop there,[178] or Antoine, César and Salim 'Abduh had all established connections with Sierra Leone by the First World War. Freely using the steamboat and the telegraph to keep in touch and transact their affairs rapidly, these men built up wholesale businesses, importing kola nuts in bulk to Dakar.[179] While existing family relations seem to have drawn some of these traders into the kola business, others seem instead to have sought out partnerships in their efforts to capitalise upon this opening. The 'Abduh brothers first opened a general merchandise store in Dakar in 1911, before setting up in business with Shibli in Freetown in 1914.[180]

Others without ties in Sierra Leone sought out sources of kola untapped by their compatriots. This search for new supplies pushed migrants like 'Abd al-Latif Fakhri, whose father Mahmud had arrived in Dakar before the First World War,[181] east towards Côte d'Ivoire in the late 1910s and early 1920s. 'Abd al-Latif, who arrived in Côte d'Ivoire in 1927, owned properties in Grand-Bassam to the tune of 240,000 francs. More significantly, he regularly kept in his store consignments of kola nuts worth some 200,000 francs, which he dispatched to his father. Such was the volume of his trade that administrators estimated that 200,000 francs were transferred between the two houses each month. This was, to be sure, a difficult business, not without risks. Georgette Haddad thus remembered that 'one could not be scared to go into the bush, or to take risks, as one had to trust the small [*juula*] vendors with money', remaining dependent upon the trust of traders from beyond the community.[182] Furthermore, prices fluctuated considerably, gravitating between a franc and ten francs per kilogram in the 1930s.[183] But it was also a profitable one. One could 'grow rich very quickly'. This explains the attraction of the trade for men like Georgette's father Wadi', who sought to make a fortune and establish themselves. Others, like 'Abd al-Latif Fakhri, went to Côte d'Ivoire to prove themselves and to expand their family businesses. This was also the case of Mahmud Smaish, who was sent by his father to Côte d'Ivoire in 1938 as a sixteen-year-old strapling. As Smaish confessed, he hardly knew on his arrival 'what to do, or how to work'. He thus recalled 'losing seven or eight kilos in weight when I came from Senegal. There, I ate at my mother's house. Here I had to make do with whatever I could find, sometimes just a box of sardines.' But, despite such travails, he was fortunate enough to have a cheque of 20,000 francs on the Banque Commerciale de l'Afrique. Seeing his compatriots 'who went into the bush to buy kola, coffee, and cocoa', he bought a second-hand lorry and began to do the same; spending four or five days at a time in the village of Yakassémé, not far from Abidjan, he would buy up his produce before returning to town, from where he would send the produce to his father in Senegal.[184] Côte d'Ivoire, then, fast became a place of potential—a colony in which the young men of established trading families could learn the tricks of the trade and prove their worth, while helping their fathers to branch out into profitable new lines of business, or in which greenhorns fresh off the boat could make their way.

By the 1940s, the Lebanese of Daloa, in the southwestern forests of the colony, traded between 800 and 1,000 tons of kola nuts per year.[185] While some, like Fakhri, sent their kola by sea towards Dakar, extending this older maritime route eastwards into Côte d'Ivoire,[186] others began transporting their goods in lorries up the well-worn routes northwards to French Soudan and Bamako, where they were bought up by large brokers like the Watshi or Emile Ashqar. From Bamako—the 'central point' of both Lebanese and African kola networks—their loads would be scattered by lorry or rail through Soudan and Senegal along distribution networks which, like those which ran between Freetown, Grand-Bassam and Dakar, were founded on ties of kin: Ashqar, for instance, traded with his brother Joseph in Kaolack.[187]

These two trading routes seem, on the face of it, to have been founded upon reciprocal relations of kin, trust and credit, which remained effectively closed to outsiders. This was certainly the charge some migrants levelled at their competitors in times of crisis. The interruption of maritime traffic between the colonies of AOF during the Second World War forced a number of kola traders to relocate from Senegal and Bamako. Attempting to adapt to their new circumstances, around twenty-five of these new arrivals carried on transport operations, driving down to Côte d'Ivoire and back in their lorries, while fifteen busied themselves distributing supplies with commercial relations in the Senegalese peanut basin. However, they complained bitterly to administrators of the difficulties they faced in transplanting their operations, because of the 'commercial trust' the established traders of Bamako had set up.[188]

But, however hermetic these two networks may have been, they were not exclusive cabals of consanguinity. The first of these networks, based in Dakar and operating along the maritime routes along the coast of West Africa, was made up for the most part of the 'Amili Greek Catholic, Shi'a and Greek Orthodox who had settled in the capital of AOF. The second, which worked the transport routes and railways of the interior, was largely in the hands of Maronite migrants from the Matn who had spread outwards from Guinea in the early years of the twentieth century, first heading north towards Soudan, then east towards Côte d'Ivoire. The comfort of common origins—rather than the ties of kin and confession—seems to have determined the composition of these two networks. But even this was no hard-and-fast rule, and these two trails mingled at certain points as migrants moved freely about through the territories of colonial West Africa. To cite one instance, the firm of Jumayyil and Ayyub—respectively from Bikfayya and Bait Shabab—founded its operations in Grand-Bassam, trading kola nuts up-coast to Dakar, like its 'Amili neighbours and competitors.[189] This, then, is a further reminder that the commercial strategies and living arrangements of Lebanese migrants were never entirely determined by the monolithic forces of kin, confession and locality; the more serendipitous, less predictable forces of contingency, circumstance and initiative also played their part.

Furthermore, the participation of Lebanese entrepreneurs in the kola trade reveals the tenuous basis for any division between a 'modern' sector, exporting commodities overseas, and a 'traditional' sector which remained cantoned in inter-regional transfers, from zones of production to areas of demand. It is not just that these operations were, in any case, founded upon the same, rudimentary, principles of supply and demand. Moreover, Lebanese traders—much like Hausa or Mande kola traders— were quick to capitalise upon the potential of technology to ease the speedy communication of goods and vital commercial information.[190] And, finally, the trades in kolas and export commodities like groundnuts in Senegal or cocoa in the Gold Coast were effectively complementary. On the one hand, some Lebanese traders—like the Hausa Agalawa and Tokarawa kola traders of northern Nigeria—participated simultaneously in both, recycling their profits from one sector into the other.[191] The 'Abduh brothers built up a prosperous business in Dakar and Freetown as 'general merchants and dealers in cola-nuts, ground-nuts, rice, palm-kernels, palm-oil, hides, rubber, egusi, dry pepper, benneseed, and other produce', trading in a mixed inventory of goods.[192] On the other, the growth of the Senegalese groundnut economy transformed kolas from a luxury good, given in bridewealth or at funerals, into an item of essential consumption—and, indeed, one poorer rural and inhabitants not only appreciated for its stimulating qualities, but also relied upon to quell their hunger in leaner times—chewing a nut after their meal instead of a cigarette, or consuming one instead of breakfast.[193] Thus, the expansion of the kola market was very much contingent on the fortunes of the colonial economy and the small consumer demands it created.

Lebanese traders, then, emulated the practices of *Soudanais* kola traders—as French administrators interchangeably called the long established *juula* traders who had moved further and further south through the colony as pacification gathered pace, and those, of more recent vintage, who had come to lay down its railways and build its trading towns, and had stayed behind, setting up shop.[194] But they also depended upon them to collect kola, and provided them in return with merchandise, passed down through chains of credit from larger European or Eastern Mediterranean firms, and with transportation in their lorries, stopping off wherever the *juula* wished, and loading or unloading his merchandise without asking too many questions.[195] Conflicts could, of course, arise. In 1932, an argument that broke out in the fish market of Bouake, in Côte d'Ivoire, between *juula* sellers and their Lebanese customers, degenerated into an unseemly scuffle. After four Lebanese and eight *juula* were prosecuted, Eastern Mediterranean migrants agreed to leave Bouake.[196] But these relations seem—difficult as these things are to make out from fragmentary written evidence—to have been marked on the whole by a certain commercial confidence, fostered by the 'almost complete interpenetration' between Lebanese and *Soudanais* traders all along the kola routes leading through Côte d'Ivoire to Bamako.[197] There, *kooroko* kola traders told Jean-Loup Amselle that they had tended, in the 1940s, to trust the Lebanese more than they did each other.[198] Such a situation was perhaps exceptional. But it underlines the difficulties involved in attempting to generalise about relations between African and Lebanese traders across AOF—whose various territories, integrated at different times into the broader colonial economy, still followed quite distinct rhythms in the late 1930s, even as they were brought together by overlapping, intermingling networks of Eastern Mediterranean, African and European traders.

Conclusion

The Eastern Mediterranean traders of AOF were not, it should by now be clear, a homogeneous bunch occupying the middle ground of colonial commercial society. By the late 1930s they were a highly differentiated lot. The seemingly swelling middling ranks of shopkeepers and small-time produce brokers and transporters were hemmed in from below by impecunious drifters like Salim Salqa or Ibrahim Faituni, whom they took on as apprentices and shop hands, and from above by a few wealthy import-export merchants with subsidiaries, interests and contacts across the Federation—and beyond, in Sierra Leone, Marseille, Paris or Beirut. Furthermore, this was a highly stratified commercial order. Far from a network of solidarities, it was a set of hierarchies, through which capital and goods flowed downwards from larger Lebanese entrepreneurs, and the French trading firms and banks of AOF, until it finally trickled down to the producers whose cash-crops smaller Lebanese traders purchased each year.

Such brokers *were*, in a sense, intermediaries, dependent on credit from semi-wholesale or wholesale buyers, which they then redistributed. There is no getting away from that. But these men—and women—were more than that, too; their activities spilled beyond, or bypassed, the narrow channels of colonial commerce—into the kola and rice trades, and out to the margins of the law, into real estate investment, informal banking activities or import-export activities, all the while using an eclectic repertoire of strategies and logics, cobbled together from here and there. Finally, this order was far from static. Fortunes could be made, or lost, with equal rapidity; all it took was a sudden dip in commodity prices, or the introduction of trade controls, which encouraged some to dive enthusiastically into the black market, while others dipped their toes half-heartedly. The chance of swelling their profits and improving their lot, but also a certain caution, a desire to hold on to gains already acquired—these were equally powerful motives for Lebanese entrepreneurs.

6

HERE, THERE AND EVERYWHERE

THE LIVES OF LEBANESE MIGRANTS IN AOF

The Lebanese of AOF were people on the move. They were so not just because of their ceaseless physical displacements, but also because of their restless search for social mobility. Migration was for them a 'journey' into a 'middle-class of their own making', as Akram Khater has put it—a means of maintaining the precarious life-styles they had left behind in the Eastern Mediterranean, or of securing gains which were no longer available in their home towns and villages.[1] And yet, I will argue in this chapter, we cannot treat their lives merely as a relentless pursuit of middling status. On the one hand, they did not regard the Lebanese *jaliyyat*, or 'colonies', of West Africa—as they came to call their own communities—as undifferentiated units. Migrant society was not in their eyes a horizontal plane, but a highly hierarchical structure. It was shaped, of course, by considerations of commercial prosperity and seniority: it had its 'big men' (its *grands*) or *misyurun*, as Kamil Muruwwah put it in an admixture of French and Arabic; its 'men of the middling sort', who formed the 'overwhelming majority'; and its 'small', destitute, scroungers. And it had its 'elders', its 'pioneers' and its greenhorns, newly arrived from the Eastern Mediterranean.[2] But this was not simply a system of economic gradations. Differences of confession, of education, of social distinction, sartorial measures and material dispositions—all played their part in the constitution of migrant society.

On the other hand, they refused to be considered as another group of imperial brokers, like the 'Greeks' or the 'Hindus' of Madagascar, whose 'standard of life' remained frozen, just above that of the native, but forever beneath that of the French-man.[3] To be sure, Eastern Mediterranean migrants were all too willing at one level to don the 'garb of intermediates'.[4] They took on the mantle of the 'indispensable intermediary between the large European house and the native producer or con-sumer' which the more sympathetic administrators of AOF bestowed upon them.[5]

151

Speaking in the terms of this colonial rhetoric, these trading men and women presented themselves to the world as 'hyphen[s]' between European and African,[6] and as the 'connecting link' between inland markets and littoral cities, small producers and large firms.[7] The Lebanese, those interlopers of empire, harped on the 'utility' of their interstitial economic role, in the hope that it might assure them of a place in a colonial society seemingly ordered along the neat binaries of the ruler and the ruled, the coloniser and the colonised. They presented themselves—as Joseph Ashqar put it, echoing the phrases of colonial discourse—as 'irreplaceable intermediaries of commerce', in order to justify their presence in the face of enduring suspicion and hostility.[8] But they also bridled against its sociological corollary, refusing 'to fit in between the indigenous African population and the European colonials'—a single, homogeneous, stratum which might neatly be slotted into the colonial order, like a bookmark between two pages.[9] To be in-between was also, for these men and women, to be in 'excess' of the 'parts' of difference—to exceed, to go beyond, the terms and confines of colonial society, to outdo those closest to them, to make more money, and to live better and more ostentatiously.[10] This was the enduring paradox of migrant life: even as they remained dependent upon the context of the colonial societies of West Africa for their material survival, and prosperity, they sought to insulate and distinguish themselves from their surroundings.

As migrants prospered, and bettered their material circumstances, they increasingly strove to create distance between themselves and the African populations of AOF, and to acquire the accoutrements—dwellings and furnishings, foodstuffs, cars and clothes—that would allow them to live, as administrators put it, *à l'européenne*. This phrase was both closer to the truth, and further away from it, than the functionaries who employed it could have known. For their sense of European comforts was certainly not one gleaned from their observation of the Federation's exiguous population of French settlers. They did not so much seek to emulate the latter's living practices as scorn them, reserving particular contempt for the diminished circumstances of the *mange-mils*, the small-time traders who scrabbled away in the trading towns of the hinterland. In this respect, Albert Memmi was right: these interstitial figures of colonial life, 'neither coloniser nor colonised', sought not only to mark themselves off from the Africans among whom they lived by a language of racial gradations and cultural distinctions, but also to 'distance' and differentiate themselves from the Frenchmen of AOF.[11] The Eastern Mediterranean men and women of West Africa looked beyond the Federation's borders for political intercession and material inspiration; regarding colonial life as precarious and undignified, they turned towards metropolitan France, its powerful ministries and fashionable outlets. The increasingly 'European' bent of their everyday practices, then, was not an outright imitation of those directly about them. Rather, it had the effect of 'mimicry': looking 'almost the same' as their French counterparts, with their short-sleeved shirts, their slicked-back hair and pith helmets, they remained resolutely distinct from them—if in ways that were sometimes small and barely perceptible.[12] And, in doing so, they sought to state difference on their own terms, and to make a mockery of the exclusionary discourses of the French. The latter, they suggested in an ironic riposte, were the ones who found prosperity tantalisingly out of reach, who lagged behind, unable to close the gap with their Lebanese competitors.

But, on another level, this phrase obscures the extent to which these men and women sought to tailor the everyday practices of the Eastern Mediterranean—recipes and quotidian routines, interior decors and habits of sociability—to their new circumstances. In a sense, Lebanese migrants did not attempt to live in a European way at all. The blueprints upon which they built their lives—schemes they subtly redrew to fit changing terrain—were borrowed from the regions of their birth. However, we should not simply replace one centre—the imperial *métropole*—with another—Lebanon—and treat the latter as the true heartlands of the Eastern Mediterranean diaspora. For it was not just a centre of production—a core from which ways of living were exported to the peripheries of migrant life—but also a site of synthesis and circulation, a transit point at which particular practices were refitted and repackaged before being sent out again into the world.

By the interwar years, Keith Watenpaugh has recently argued, the attainment of 'undisputed middle-class status' in cities like Aleppo or Beirut 'had become contingent on being *seamlessly* European'.[13] Watenpaugh is certainly correct to stress the universality of this register of living. For those who stayed in the Eastern Mediterranean as for those who migrated away from the region—and many others like them across the globe—being middle-class rested on 'multilayered, translocal repertoires of … economic interest, gendered discourses, … and racial categorizations' that helped to define 'historical subjects and experiences'.[14] However, I would argue that we should conceive of these repertoires less in diffusionist than in dialogical terms. They were not so much transported from central places in Europe or North America in which modernity existed in an 'original … unfractured' condition, as built up in conversations carried on in many points across the globe.[15] To take but one instance, the conceptions of gender to which Lebanese migrants in West Africa adhered were neither imported wholesale from the West, nor homegrown notions which developed along the Eastern Mediterranean seaboard; rather, they were elaborated by other migrants elsewhere in the *mahjar*, in the rural backwaters of the United States and the throbbing cities of British Egypt, in a series of sometimes fraught exchanges with the changing understandings of domesticity and companionship, labour and love they encountered there.[16] Modernity, then, was in its very nature uncentred—it was itself diasporic, a scattered set of processes playing themselves out through the world.[17]

There is no doubt that the Lebanese migrants of AOF borrowed ways of living, of thinking and of speaking that—much like their food or the consumer goods with which they furnished their homes—were imported from elsewhere. Theirs, then, was a derivative modernity. But it was not straightforward in its borrowings. These men and women depended on idioms of life which could be immediately intelligible elsewhere—which, indeed, drew much of their charm from their fluidity, their capacity to be deployed anywhere, in any context. To be middle-class was, for them, to be modern; and to dwell in modernity was to live in the world, feeding upon, and finding inspiration in, wider connections.[18] Modernity was, in a sense, a universal condition, even as it now seems to contemporary scholars to be striated with difference, inconsistency and unevenness.[19]

This constant tendency to look elsewhere was not just the product of a familiar pining on the part of Lebanese migrants for the comforts of home, or an awareness that the trappings of prosperity, with which they might make a show of their success, could only be brought in from outside. It was also another manifestation of their ambivalent, anxious, relation to their immediate surroundings. These various concerns all led these men and women, I argue, to withdraw into their 'newly comfortable domestic interiors, to the electric kitchens, to the enclosure of private automobiles, to the interior of a new vision of conjugality and an ideology of happiness built around the new unit of middle-class consumption, the couple'.[20] Only rarely did they stray into the public sphere—and when they did, it was most often to stress their detachment from politics, making a fussy display of the bourgeois values of charitable concern they were so keen to exhibit. Unlike the self-conscious intellectuals of colonial northern India or Mandatory Syria, whose middling status was acquired through the pen, they shirked overt engagements.[21] For these might only expose them to the criticism of Frenchmen and Africans alike.

I will seek to trace in this chapter the ways in which these other groups looked upon the Lebanese, tracing the tensions of neighbourhood life, the contests over public space and the press campaigns they waged—and the ways in which the Lebanese, in turn, looked upon themselves and the society around them, and lived their lives. These migrants were, in a sense, caught in a double bind. They had no choice but to engage, even on mitigated terms, with the society around them, for they were well aware that the prosperity migration had brought hung on the businesses they owned and maintained; it depended, other words, on staying on in Africa. And yet they constantly looked elsewhere—for discourses, and material goods, befitting their new, improved, circumstances, but also for the intercessors who might allow them to hold on to their precarious livelihoods. This was the enduring paradox of migrant life: even as they sought to insulate themselves from their surroundings, they remained dependent upon them.

Trading people

Colonial administrators, when they did, on the rare occasion, write of the relations between Africans and Lebanese, tended to describe them as awkwardly utilitarian. The *commandant de cercle* of Daloa in Côte d'Ivoire noted in 1945 that while Eastern Mediterranean men and women looked on Africans with 'no goodwill', 'caring only for what will attract the customer', Africans 'reciprocated this distant attitude, showing no respect or consideration towards them'. Theirs, he insisted, was nothing more than a '*modus vivendi* based on the material services they render each other'.[22] There might be something in this. Eastern Mediterranean traders—it could be argued—were treated, and their presence understood, on terms essentially similar to other 'stranger-trader' groups who came into contact with the populations of West Africa in the region's long history of extraversion.[23]

These terms, however, were not static, undergoing significant revision in the early years of the twentieth century. This, I think, might be seen more clearly by focusing on Senegal. As Philip Curtin has remarked, Senegambian populations like the Wolof, Serer and Malinke had no 'strong commercial tradition' prior to the fifteenth century, when they first entered into contact with Portuguese navigators.[24] These societies not only lay away from the trading routes which crossed the savannah and the *sahel*—the vast 'coast' of the Sahara—running north towards present-day Mauritania and Morocco. They also seemed to present few opportunities to long-distance merchants: relatively self-sufficient in salt, a valuable commodity in more eastern areas of the savannah, polities like Kajoor produced no gold and offered few slaves for external consumption.[25] Moreover, these states accorded trade no special place in the highly stratified system of castes upon which they were founded, with their strict distinctions between freemen, themselves further divided into an aristocratic order and a free peasantry; endogamous professional orders like blacksmiths, leatherworkers or *griots*, liminal figures often accorded foreign origins,[26] and whose occupations remained prohibited to those not born to them; and slaves.[27] These 'quintessentially non-egalitarian' societies were effectively organised for self-subsistence.[28] And, accordingly, they left what little external trade they carried on to mercantile diasporas like the Zawaya Berbers or the *juula* and the *jakhanke*—Malinke groups which connected the savannah to the forest zones to the south.[29] The growing importance of the Atlantic slave trade from the sixteenth century onwards brought Wolof and Serer polities into uneasy contact with a growing variety of outsiders—French and British slavers, Afro-Portuguese *signères* and *métis* or Wolof traders from Saint-Louis-du-Sénégal.[30] But, for all the far-reaching changes Atlantic commerce brought on, it seemingly did little to upturn attitudes. Trade remained an activity for outsiders.[31]

This was reflected, in the forest regions of present-day Côte d'Ivoire and Guinea, in the way in which the Malinke term *juula* went through a process of lexical conversion and enrichment, passing through—as Jean-Loup Amselle has put it—a 'system of transformations'.[32] It had initially, it seems, meant no more than trader. But, as Malinke-speaking people migrated south from the fourteenth century onwards, it came to serve as a way of distinguishing these strangers from the people among whom they lived.[33] However, so strong was the association of these men with the long-distance trade in kola nuts, metal, salt and leather—both in their own sense of themselves and among their neighbours—that their collective designation returned to its original meaning, becoming by the early twentieth century virtually 'synonymous with trade'.[34] It was this meaning French administrators picked up on, using the term *dioula* to speak indiscriminately of all itinerant trading groups.

There are tantalising hints that the manner in which Africans spoke—and thought—of the Lebanese followed such semantic feedback loops. Towards the end of his life, the anthropologist Fuad Khuri recalled being stopped by an immigration official at Kumasi airport in Ghana. On being asked his nationality, he answered, without a thought, "Lebanese". The officer then, Khuri recounted, 'tilted his head forward and repeated slowly: "Na-tio-na-li-ty?". When again being told "Yes! Le-ba-nese," he took a deep breath and said, with a touch of anger, "Sir, I am not asking about your profession!"' Khuri jokingly presented this tale as an instance of just the sort of cross-cultural confusion he had set out to clear up in his professional life. But this does not seem so much a story of mutual incomprehension as one of translation. The 'intimate' 'association' between the Lebanese and trade Khuri remarked on shaded at times into metonymy.[35] The Creoles of Freetown, in the early twentieth century, christened the Eastern Mediterranean migrants in their midst 'coral-men'—a contemptuous put-down which identified them all too closely with the cheap glass beads they peddled. Around the same time, the Wolof and Serer peasants of Sine and Saloum referred to these men and women both as *naar*—as 'Arabs'—and as 'shoulder shopkeepers' because of the packs of goods they carried through the countryside, always ready to peddle.[36] The Wolof inhabitants of Saint-Louis, meanwhile, knew them as *yaouts*—a corruption of the Arabic *yahud*, or Jew. This appellation might well have served to mark the city's largely Christian Eastern Mediterranean population as 'infidels', 'traitors to the Prophet Muhammad', as Camille Camara speculated.[37] But it may just as well have referred, rather disdainfully, to their mercantile bent—and in particular, their way with credit. Senegalese townspeople and peasants—we might speculate—defined Lebanese traders by their occupation as much as by their extraneity. What they did, and what they sold, as much as where they came from, defined who they were. Attitudes to the Lebanese, then, perhaps bore something of the old ambivalence with which the societies of Senegambia had looked upon strangers and traders. Often one and the same, they were awkwardly incorporated into the body social—accepted on tenuous terms, but regarded with contempt for engaging in the demeaning domain of commerce.

And yet it is clear we cannot simply regard the Wolof and Serer peasantries of the peanut basin of Cayor, Baol, Sine and Saloum as rooted, essentially introspective social entities, bound to the land by secular ties and wary of interlopers. The early twentieth century was not only a time of rapid social change in these regions, but also of considerable physical movement, as the groundnut economy pulled in migrants from across AOF towards the heartlands of peanut production. Many of these were *navétanes*—'those who spend the rainy season', as Senegalese peasants called the labourers who came each year to lend a hand in planting and tending to the peanuts, working four days of the week for their hosts in return for food, housing and a plot of land on which they might grow some groundnuts of their own.[38] Only a few among this motley crowd—Soninke from the Senegal valley, Bambara from Soudan, Futanke from French Guinea and Diola from Portuguese Guinea—chose to stay for good in Senegal. However, the sheer intensity, and diversity, of this annual migratory flow—which reached some 76,000 in 1936—inevitably redrew social relations, as Wolof and Serer households sought to accommodate these useful strangers by treating them much as they would *surga*, young unmarried men. Many of these men bypassed the regions of Cayor and Baol, heading instead for the thriving Sine and

Saloum. These regions rapidly became the focus of labour migration, receiving some 37,222 of the 45,503 *navétanes* enumerated in 1937.[39]

They were not alone in moving to this 'strategic quadrilateral' on which the Senegalese economy increasingly depended.[40] Some of the Wolof peasants of Cayor and Baol, densely populated regions whose role in the peanut economy steadily decreased in the interwar years, chose to migrate south and east towards Sine and, especially, towards the 'new lands' of Saloum—which, far less heavily peopled than its almost exclusively Serer neighbour, seemed to present more promising opportunities. Though by no means made up entirely of members of the Murid brotherhood, this movement was largely orchestrated by this Sufi *tariqa*, whose leaders founded a series of new settlements as it grew in strength and numbers. First pushing before 1914 into the eastern desert fringes of Baol, they turned southwards, as the 1920s and 1930s wore on, towards the Saloum—whose economy was, as Paul Pélissier noted, 'given life' in these years 'by the rise in peanut prices, the growth of the port of Kaolack and the massive influx of *Libano-Syriens* traders'.[41]

Pélissier was not wrong. Murid and Eastern Mediterranean migrants moved, it seems, in tandem. In the years before 1914, these two streams had already proceeded in parallel along the rail tracks unfurling into the backcountries east of Louga, Diourbel and Kaolack. The Lebanese 'followed the rail' spreading eastwards from Kaolack in 1911, setting up stall in the 'nascent trading posts of Kaffrine and Sagna', and racing ahead of the track to open their 'small shops' in Malem.[42] The Murid, meanwhile, 'intelligently perceived their interest in the advance of the Thiès-Kayes railway across Baol and Eastern Saloum; they staked out ... compounds at the stations of the line. Khombole, Bambey, Diourbel, Goussas, Guinginéo, Kaffrine, Malème and the small intermediary villages became gathering points for the brothers'.[43] This pattern continued after the First World War. The Murid village of Daru Musti, founded in 1912—at first a scratch settlement peopled by a few *talibé*, or followers, of Ahmadu Bamba—acquired a more permanent feel with the arrival of women and the digging of a well in 1919. Unsurprisingly, the first Lebanese trader soon followed, in 1920.[44] It seems, from such fragmentary evidence, that these two moving populations developed a sort of symbiotic relationship: while Eastern Mediterranean migrants found new markets for their wares in the localities which sprung up from the sandy soil of the Saloum, the Murid depended on them to buy up the groundnuts on which their livelihoods depended.

Such useful reciprocal relations developed at other points, too, where Eastern Mediterranean migrants participated in the frenzied colonisation of the peanut basin. Nadra Filfili found, upon his arrival in the Sine village of Guinguineo in the early 1930s, only three wells—two of which gave only brackish water, sold on at a healthy profit by the individuals on whose land they lay. Deciding to dig his own, he 'providentially' hit upon a 'perfectly potable' water table, before announcing—in keeping with his mother's advice 'to favour your close neighbour over your distant brother'—that this would be free for all to use. 'My name entered into songs,' Filfili remembered, 'but more important than this small token of traditional gratitude, my family and I were integrated and accepted'—and, moreover, profited from this endeavour, finding that the owners of the camels and mules which stopped to drink at the well became customers in his shop. A few years later, he heard of two Lebanese 'pioneers' who had settled in the village of M'Boss, in the dense woods of the Sine. While admiring their 'courage' he doubted their ability to survive long in this locality, for though it lay beyond the reach of the road, its inhabitants preferred walking thirty kilometres through forest paths to buying from these men, with their steep prices and harsh haggling. Seeing the opportunity this presented, Filfili undertook the clearing of a road through the forest, taking on to do the work the peasants of M'Boss, who christened this new way 'Nadra's road'. However, events thereafter exceeded even Filfili's expectations. Not only did new trading counters emerge at M'Boss, as he had hoped; new settlements began to mushroom, some drawing migrants from as far afield as Thiès. One of these, he remembered, was called 'Beyroutha'.[45]

We must, I think, approach such a tale with caution. It is not just coated with the sentimental gloss of old age and self-regard—though Filfili was perhaps not being disingenuous in stressing the Eastern Mediterranean norms of conviviality he claimed had informed his decisions—but also coloured by his comfortable relationship with Léopold Sédar Senghor. This link, which first developed in the 1950s when Filfili—whose fortune had, by then, blossomed fully—provided financial backing to Senghor, then the leader of the Bloc Démocratique Sénégalais, led him to stress instances of happy collaboration between Lebanese and Senegalese.

Nevertheless, it is clear some of the Lebanese migrants who concentrated in the 'peanut basin' of the Sine and Saloum were more than passive bystanders, keeping—and kept—warily on the margins of the economic changes redrawing the landscape of these regions, and recasting the social relations of their inhabitants. We cannot, then, simply try to piece together African attitudes towards Eastern Mediterranean migrants from what knowledge we have of pre-colonial Wolof and Serer attitudes towards strangers. The growth of the groundnut economy, and the displacements it provoked, made of the peanut basin a world in permanent motion—'where everyone seemed to be coming and going … where languages and cultures ran together in a cryptic hodgepodge'. And, just as on the Zambian Copperbelt, these constant movements threw into doubt 'who is an insider and who an outsider, who is local and who is not'.[46] In these zones of transformation, the Lebanese became just one more moving group. Just as their conspicuous participation in the colonisation of the 'new lands' of the peanut basin left its mark on the lie of the land and found acknowledgement in the names of its places, it seems some Eastern Mediterranean migrants were incorporated into bounds of reciprocity in which a sense of mutual profit mingled with recognition and trust. The same was apparently true in other places in movement, like the forest regions of Côte d'Ivoire, where Lebanese 'tutors' provided for the clothes, school fees and medical expenses of African children. We must be just as wary of these tales, kept up in the 'collective memory' of Lebanese and Africans alike, as of those Filfili told in his dotage, for they too are coloured by the stress put upon comity in the official pronouncements of the Ivoirian state under Houphouët

Boigny's presidency.[47] Nevertheless, they do speak of the ways in which Lebanese wove their way—and were welcomed—into local relations of kin and obligation.

The distinctions of race

However, Eastern Mediterranean migrants retained profound ambivalences and prejudices about Africa and African life. Both migrants themselves and the travel writers who set out for AOF to raise funds for their philanthropic schemes, or to gather information on the Federation and its Lebanese communities, often adopted deeply jaundiced attitudes towards Africa. These were plainly apparent in articles like that of 'Ali Muruwwah, published in the 'Amili religious, scientific, literary and political journal al-'Irfan in 1932. Muruwwah began by noting that 'the habits, customs and traditions of the blacks of Ivory Coast are as strange as can be'. Though 'the colonialism of the whites had been in place for some fifty years, they had remained savage to the upmost degree, despite the vigilant efforts of the government to put them on the path to progress and the presence of Jesuit missionaries'. The rest of his account, interspersed with full-page photographic plates of bare-breasted women and hunters in extravagantly-plumed headdresses, detailed the exotic and abhorrent ways of the inhabitants of Côte d'Ivoire, from the 'bushmen', for whom it was ordinary for a son to inherit the possessions of his maternal uncle, to the 'tribe of the Jakuba', among whom 'some still seized any opportunity to obtain human meat'. The ways of these people, who 'ate the flesh of wild animals, dressed in their skins, and lived in recesses and caves', were reminiscent of nothing more than the 'disposition' of 'early man'.[48] Indeed, this comparison was only compounded by its juxtaposition with an article on evolution, which drew a sharp distinction between 'white man' and other 'human species', ending with a diagram which showed that, though all descended from Java Man and Peking Man, the tree of evolution had split into two branches, one leading to the 'white race', the other to 'Mongolian man'.[49] This rhetoric of progress and refractoriness fitted well into the pages of al-'Irfan, with its constant emphasis on the compatibility of science and reformed religion. As Muruwwah put it, 'religion was, and still is, the means of progress for man, and the first stone laid on the path of civilisation'.[50] Moreover, it was, as Max Weiss has argued, a means of facilitating a 'sort of cultural "upward mobility"' for Lebanese Shi'a by integrating a debased image of Africa 'into Lebanese cultural hierarchies'.[51] Insisting in such categorical fashion on their own whiteness and capacity for progress was not so much for Shi'a migrants, and their literary supporters, a means of address-ing the contempt of colonial administrators. Rather, their writings, published for consumption in a Lebanese—and largely Shi'a—public sphere, sought to refute the denigrating talk of men like Georges Thabit.

The son of a wealthy Christian family and the brother of a prominent magistrate, Thabit had been working as a pharmacist in Dakar for some seven years when he sought, in mid-1944, to give a French official in Beirut his own highly partial vision of the different Lebanese communities of AOF. The Shi'a, he explained, were not only guilty of 'making money by illegal means', commonly using 'reprehensible' practices Christians and Sunni only sometimes relied upon. They also 'lived in the same condition as the blacks, even marrying Negro women'.[52] In Thabit's words, the interlocking languages of class and confession—which cast the Shi'a as the lowest riffraff, whose poverty and casual criminality was compounded by their religious obscurantism—was folded into racial thought. That Thabit sought to bring together these disparate registers of exclusion was not only a sign that some Lebanese sought to buttress their own confessional prejudices and petty snobbery by drawing on the language of race, but also of the ways in which they sought to translate their own sentiments for French consumption.

As such talk suggests, both Christian and Muslim writers shared, at times, highly derogatory notions of African inferiority. Writers like Michel Hayik, 'Abdallah Hushaimah and Kamil Muruwwah—the first two Christians, the third a Shi'a—spoke of Africa in the same terms. The 'dark' or 'black' continent—al-qara al-muthalima or al-sawda—a place inherently opposed to progress, was inhabited by zunuj or 'abid. These terms held long and disparaging associations with slavery and bondage: while zanji or zunuj could—and did—refer simply to Africans, it also carried reminders of the zanj slave revolts of the ninth century, in which the men who worked the plantations of the Tigris-Euphrates delta rose up against their Abbasid masters; 'abd, for its part, was rather less ambiguous a term—denoting a servant, bondsman or slave, it was all too often used as a metonym for any African. These writers, then, folded the scientific racism they had lifted from their European readings into older tenets of Arab racial thought.[53]

Indeed, the vernacular prejudices of Eastern Mediterranean migrants increasingly led them to differentiate themselves from Africans in the interwar years. As the administrator of Daloa noted in the mid-1940s, they carefully 'maintain their distance'; considering 'themselves superior', they could 'conceive of no other relations' with their African neighbours than 'those between a trader and his client or a master and his servant'.[54] This functionary was mistaken, in a sense, to regard the relations between Eastern Mediterranean and African as 'exclusively commercial', for it seems many lone male migrants not only sought to accommodate their neighbours, but also established intimate ties with local women. This was perhaps most common in the more isolated areas of Senegal, Soudan and—especially—Côte d'Ivoire, where Eastern Mediterranean women remained few, and where strayed more impecunious migrants, unable to afford a return home, let alone the expensive undertaking of marriage. One, albeit rather extreme, example of this general tendency was the case of one trader, known only as Ahmad, who lived in the Bornu region of southern Niger in 1918. The only Eastern Mediterranean man in this territory, still under military administration, he had taken two local women as wives, 'living completely like the native and working as a dioula at Goure, where he carried on a very small trade'.[55]

The stances migrants adopted were, of course, never uniform. And it would seem—though it is difficult to speculate on the subject, not least because we depend largely on the rather fragmentary evidence Fuad Khuri recorded in the early 1960s—

the manner in which Lebanese men dealt with their relations with African women varied as much because of differing religious prescriptions as individual inclination. Though both Christians and Muslims apparently referred to these relationships with a singularly deprecating phrase—*bihatta 'andi*, 'I'm putting her at mine', words devoid of any sense of affective attachment, which cast these relations as casual material acts—Shi'a men often insisted upon formalising their relations through marriage and found few problems in recognising the children born of these unions.[56] Tawfiq and Muhammad Jabir, for instance, shared their home in Seguela with their local wives and the children they had borne them—both apparently 'good father[s]', in the approving words of the administrator who reported on these conjoined families, they 'took the greatest care of their offspring'. Arrangements like this one were facilitated by the relative ease with which marriage proceedings, which needed only a witness, could be carried out, and the acceptance of polygamy, and of the practice of contracting temporary *mut'a*, or 'pleasure', marriages. Both the Jabirs had, alongside their local families, wives and children in Lebanon, to whom they sent 'the necessary subsidies'.[57] But while some Shi'a men went a way towards formally recognising their intimate relations—though in a manner which often tended towards treating them as casual unions, contracted only for a fixed time—their Christian counterparts stubbornly resisted any such acknowledgement. Moreover, they increasingly looked upon these relations as illegitimate. The manner in which one migrant recounted to Fuad Khuri the manner in which his young help had brought him an undesired child is profoundly revealing in this respect:

I ask one of my African customers to find for me a young girl who can come to my home every day, clean the house, wash dishes, cook, and perform other domestic duties. May God curse our carnal desires! How a lonely man is easily tempted! Three months later, she became pregnant because she does not know how to take care of herself.

These words were not simply an attempt at absolution, Khuri's informant presenting himself as the passive victim of the arduous solitude of migrant life and the irresistible, cruel, forces of temptation. This man, one senses, regarded it as almost inevitable that such a misfortune should have befallen him. For if he blamed himself for anything, it was seemingly for relying upon his African customer—who proved incapable of finding him suitable, and less enticing, help—and for succumbing to his lustful urges for his African help—who did 'not know how to take care of herself'. This outburst, then, was both dripping with self-regard and laced with vernacular notions of race—casting Africans only as incompetent, shiftless subordinates orbiting around the teller's proud person.[58]

This tale shines a light not just on the racial casts of mind of Lebanese migrants, but also on their desire for the conventions of domesticity, and a measure of respectability. Their sense of themselves as men was bound up with the behaviour of the women around them—their *'ard*, or literally, what exposed their honour. They could maintain their honour only by ensuring that the latter did not cast opprobrium upon them by behaving inappropriately—as this man implied his servant girl had by dar-ing to fall pregnant… This may in large part account for the callousness with which many Lebanese men treated the children their African concubines bore them. The latter were 'one of the most important familial problems' facing Lebanese migrants in the interwar years. In the late 1930s, Kamil Muruwwah estimated that there were 'at least a thousand children' born of such transgressive unions, many of whom had been left with their mothers, and 'knew nothing of their fathers', and urged male migrants to show 'greater concern for the fate' of their offspring, those awkward reminders of the ways in which their untoward behaviour had breached their conceptions of race.[59]

But these migrants' sense of masculine achievement also hung upon their ability to better themselves—to have something to show for all their work, and to provide comfortably for themselves and their families. Social mobility and a desire for the good things were, after all, compelling motivations for many, if not most, migrants. This relentless pursuit of respectability—folded as it often was into the feelings of racial superiority many undoubtedly harboured—led Eastern Mediterranean men to take wives from home in growing numbers, and to disavow in the process the relations they had with African women. For we cannot disentangle the language of social advancement from that of race: to seek the comforts of bourgeois life was also to abandon practices and social spaces shared with Africans, just as living 'like an African' denoted the poverty migrants wished to move up and away from. This imbrication was apparent in the memories Muhammad 'Ali Safi al-Din retained of the difficult days of the Second World War. The fuel shortages created by the war having forced him to abandon his lorry, he had to 'make the sixty-kilometre round trip to fetch merchandise by bicycle once a month, travelling by night to avoid the heat of the day'. But just as telling a sign of these hardships was his food; he found himself having to 'eat the African way [à l'africaine]: rice, peanut sauce, aubergines, potatoes, and tropical fruit'.[60] But this shift was not demeaning simply because it connoted a proximity Eastern Mediterranean migrants wished to deny, but also because it returned them to a life they thought they had left behind. By the late 1930s, the Lebanese of West Africa, and the travellers who moved among them, had come to mythologise the early days of migration, when the migrant lived a 'life of misery and poverty', and 'slept on the ground or atop his counter, belittling himself with the food of the black, and exposing himself to insects and sickness'. However, they remained uncomfortably aware that this was what life was still like for 'a large part of our migrants, especially in the interior … for in some of the villages and distant corners, entire weeks pass by without migrants tasting bread and fruit, satisfying their stomachs with the food of the blacks and the fruits of the forests'. This was, in the eyes of the more fortunate, a 'blighted way of life'—ma'isha mardiyya; poverty was, for the Lebanese, a veritable malady.[61]

Thus, if some in Côte d'Ivoire had abandoned by the 1940s the 'food of the natives' on which they had subsisted upon their arrival 'twenty-five years ago', it was not just because of their contempt for local ways, but also because this was a reminder of their humble beginnings.[62] 'Yams, rice, bad oil, a bit of meat here and there': this

162

was still, after all, the daily stuff of the 'needy' migrant at this time. The more fortunate, meanwhile, 'wanted for nothing, neither butter, nor olive oil, nor canned foods of all kinds', despite the privations of wartime.[63] The governor-general of Guinea, meanwhile, reported with contempt that some, 'while they affected to spend a great deal on food' lived in conditions and wore clothes 'below average, and often hardly superior to those of the *indigènes*'.[64] Access to such foodstuffs, it is clear, did not just provide comfort and sustenance in often trying conditions. It also signified wealth— or, at the very least, a certain easy prosperity. This was not just because of their cost, but also because they suggested access to the world beyond Africa—if not to the Eastern Mediterranean itself—which was beyond poorer migrants. The more affluent, then, positioned themselves in relation both to their memories of their early difficulties, a past of which they were constantly reminded by their less fortunate compatriots, and to the Africans whose lifestyles they had once shared. This was a complex process—social mobility, for these men and women, was about both moving on from their own former circumstances, and creating distance and distinctions between themselves and those who represented poverty and lack of progress.

Similarly, if Lebanese migrants strove to settle in growing numbers in the towns and cities of AOF, it was not—or not simply—because they hoped to flee the intolerable proximity with Africans which life in the small localities of the hinterland brought. Rather, such a displacement was an attempt to move up in the world, a sign that one had achieved social mobility. As we have seen, new arrivals commonly headed for the hinterland—often upon the orders of a more successful compatriot already ensconced in the comfortable surroundings of Dakar or Conakry. While some drifted around before returning to Dakar in the vain hope of finding ampler commercial opportunities there, others 'little by little expanded [their] businesses and concentrated [their] undertakings', before settling 'in an urban centre where [they] employed [their] compatriots'. This was the route Nadra Filfili took to success, passing through illness and a series of inconclusive partnerships in the 1920s, before laboriously building up his resources in the 1930s and finally moving to Dakar in the 1940s.[65] Serving time in the hinterland was, for a man like Filfili, a means of getting on in the world—an essential staging point on the migrant's progress. Moving to the city, meanwhile, was often a hopeful gesture, an attempt to signal that one had arrived—or that success would not be long in coming.

But if a desire to escape the close contacts of the hinterland did play a part in the decisions of some in Senegal to relocate, city life, with its teeming, jarring diversity, hardly allowed them to get away from such promiscuity. Material comfort brought proximity of another order, with the domestic servants who were called upon to share private spaces, and intimate practices, with Lebanese families, even as they remained liminal beings, awkwardly on the fringes of the home. By the 1930s, few Lebanese homes were without 'one or two African servants, or more, depending on the needs of the master of the house and the size of his family'. These men and women were both essential accoutrements of comfort, signs of ease and respectability, and causes of concern for migrants who felt these figures had to be kept under 'constant observation', lest they stray from their duties. Perhaps most intimately tied to the family, and most sensitive, were the nurses who cared for Lebanese children. As Muruwwah put it, 'Africans raise at least around half of our migrants' sons and daughters', carrying these toddlers on their backs as they went about their business.[66] Thus, Tamir Fakhri remembered that his 'milk mother was an African, a Senegalese woman and I've known it since I was eight years old, I knew it, Maman always told me. So, I knew I had a link to Africa no one could take away from me. A real link, a lived link….'[67] Fakhri treated this as a sign of the inseverable ties binding him, and his compatriots, to Africa—a riposte to those who accused them of being strangers without attachments, foreign interlopers in the postcolonial state. This was a tale which suggested that the Lebanese were part of a national community held together by the exchange of maternal tenderness and bodily matter. However, it is also a reminder of the uncomfortable accommodations that all—African cooks and gardeners and nurses, and Lebanese men and women alike—were forced to undertake, and the blurred proximity which none could ever quite escape.[68] For even as Lebanese mothers and fathers were not prepared to forsake the comfort afforded by hiring African nurses, they remained concerned that their children 'played with the children of Africans, and learned African habits and African languages'.[69]

Furthermore scholars have argued that Dakar was not the 'world cut in two' of Fanon's powerful vision,[70] but a 'triple city',[71] whose population was divided into 'three distinct yet interacting circles of activity'.[72] Dakar's Europeans remained, in this scheme, in the administrative neighbourhood of the Plateau, at the thin end of the Cap Vert peninsula jutting out into the Atlantic—their barracks, hospitals, offices and villas lining the spacious boulevards around the governor-general's grand palace. Its African population, meanwhile, was penned back into the Médina—the planned village administrators expanded in the wake of the plague epidemic of 1914. This was a place where the indigènes could be kept at a healthy distance. But between these two quarters lay a third—variously called Gambetta, after its main artery, or Kermel, after the market upon which it was centred. This was where the Lebanese and Moroccans lived, an interstitial zone which seemingly reflected, in all too neat a fashion, their status as commercial brokers and cultural intermediates.[73]

But the reality was messier than these neat topographies of difference might suggest. Gambetta remained, well into the 1950s, a 'strange mixed neighbourhood',[74] in which 'Europeans and indigènes'—and, we might add, Eastern Mediterranean and Moroccans—'mingled'.[75] While the colonial administration had succeeded in forcibly removing most of Dakar's Bambara and Tukulor migrants to the Médina after 1914, it had fared less well in its attempts to relocate the city's Lebu. After a campaign orchestrated by Blaise Diagne, the Dakar originaire elected to the French Chamber of Deputies in 1914, the Government-General was forced to revise its ambitious plans for the creation of a segregated city.[76] In a declaration to the customary chief of the Lebu, Governor-General William Ponty assured him that 'lands belonging to the natives will be scrupulously maintained by them; these lands will remain their property and they may, after decontamination, return to construct in brick or stone, healthy houses'.[77] By the late 1920s, the population of the Médina was only 8,000, while some 20,000 *indigènes* remained in Gambetta and the adjoining districts of Maginot and Tound,[78] where many lived in the square compounds portioned out by the administration in 1926.[79] Alongside this largely Lebu population lived French, Lebanese and Moroccan company agents and independent traders. These men and their families were drawn to the area not just by its proximity to the port and Kermel market, but also by its relative affordability, in a city where rents and real estate prices remained inordinately high throughout the early twentieth century.[80] Indeed, the appeal of the neighbourhood was only heightened by the laxity with which the administration enforced building regulations there. This allowed its inhabitants to build wooden shacks and mud compounds, bungalows and storeyed houses—creating a diversity which contrasted sharply with the polished sheen of the Plateau's expensive whitewashed houses.[81]

Such a level of residential promiscuity resulted, it would seem, in an awkward accommodation—an uneasy situation sometimes flaring up into open shows of resentment, when one party or another felt the rules of neighbourhood life had been breached. This can be seen, I think, by looking at two incidents involving the Lebanese trader Muhammad Qaʿuq, who lived at the turn of the 1940s at 123 Avenue Gambetta, in the heart of this quarter. Qaʿuq was the sort of man who always seemed caught up in some incident or another. His naturalisation files are filled with complaints he made about the theft of a box of brilliantine, or a car fender dented by an inattentive lorry-driver manoeuvring through the crowded streets.[82] But Qaʿuq also seems to have brought trouble on himself—and others. In June 1950, he received permission to demolish a compound he owned, 66 Rue de Grammont, occupied by Lebu tenants. However, arriving at the site on the morning of 21 June in the company of a police inspector charged with ensuring that the destruction of this 'foul slum housing'—as the latter put it—went smoothly, Qaʿuq found that his tenants' French lawyer, Maître Crespin, had obtained a stay of execution, referring the affair to the appeal court. Returning again the next day after the presiding magistrate, Maître Senghor, ordered the demolition to go ahead, Barrère, the police officer, found a crowd of around a hundred onlookers gathered. Upon his arrival, he reported, the 'partisans of Assane Niang', the tenant, 'stepped onto the plot in a symbolic fashion, wishing to show the Lebanese trader as a matter of principle that they were, as Lebu, at home there'. Only on Barrère's intervention did Qaʿuq see reason, postponing the demolition—which was referred again to another, French, magistrate, Judge Rau. The latter, pronouncing that the landlord's scheme represented a 'grave breach of the inviolability of the private dwelling and ... individual liberty, as well as a mark of disrespect for the right to property', ruled in favour of his tenants.[83] The precarious equilibrium of quarter life, then, could sometimes tip over into open conflict, as one side or another pulled a little too hard at the tense ties of neighbourly life.

For while these neighbours were tied together in the tightly circumscribed neighbourhood of Gambetta, with its grid streets and low-lying houses, as they were elsewhere, their relations do seem marked by an underlying tension, a constant wariness. I am uncertain, in truth, quite what to make of the fragmentary written evidence on these relations. On one level, it is true that, for the most part, only moments of fracture and conflict found their way into the colonial archive, as police officers like Barrère punctiliously recorded the outrage of the injured parties, and reworked them according to their own prejudices. Cohabitation, getting along—these did not call for administrative intervention and inscription. But I am not so sure that is all there is to it, for it is striking how often Eastern Mediterranean men brought up in their own writings, or their conversations with journalists and administrators, the subject of theft and burglary—or worse still, of looting and dispossession, of being shunted out of Africa entirely by the concerted pressure of Creoles in Sierra Leone or *indigènes* in AOF. Farid Anthony—for all that he seemed to revel in his own complex Freetown *créolité*—told a mixed tale. He spoke, in the course of his rambling, disordered narrative, not just of the ease of life in the mixed neighbourhood of Sawpit, of his friendship with the Creole boy Teddy Wyndham, who taught him to swim down by the wharf, or of the happy childhood games played in Krio, but also of the first burglary his father faced, and of the stoic reaction of the community to the press campaigns and disparaging speeches of Creole dignitaries who inveighed against the 'Syrians'.[84]

Such sentiments were only accentuated in times of crisis. The decision in 1940 of the colonial administration to conduct a census of the Eastern Mediterranean of AOF, with a view to conscription, provoked deep ripples of discontent through the Lebanese communities of Senegal. Many simply protested against enrolment in the French army—some arguing that as 'foreigners benefiting from the right of asylum' they were not subject to the draft,[85] others complaining that the decision represented a 'breach of trust'. For, they insisted:

It had always been promised to the *Libano-Syriens*, notably by General Gouraud and President Alexandre Millerand, recognised protectors of the Lebanese, that the Mandate held by France over Lebanon and Syria, would never lead to conscription and compulsory military service, [and] that France had sufficient men and monies to ensure the protection of the countries under Mandatory rule and, more pertinently, her own protection, without calling upon their autochthonous inhabitants.[86]

We might be tempted to trace such recalcitrance to a deep-seated wariness of official authority, a sense of estrangement from the state. This was, perhaps, a hangover from the old fears of Ottoman conscription which had led Christians, exempt from military service in the imperial army until 1913, to flee its Arab provinces in droves in the years before the First World War—the *New York Sun*'s correspondent reporting that 'every steamer bound for North or South America has been crowded, mostly with Christian anxious to escape the … draft'.[87] Indeed, such fears—which predated the official introduction of conscription—seemingly found their way to AOF. In 1910, the Federation's governor-general turned down a request from the Ottoman consul in Dakar for the expulsion of Antoine Rustum, who had 'sought to make use of his influence upon his compatriots to convince them not to be recorded on the consulate's registers'—which he feared, we might surmise, might be used as a means of monitoring men of conscription age.[88] Moreover, the claims migrants made in 1940 were not simply an act of blustery rhetoric—but also, in part, the product of a genuine sense of expectation on the part of the Christian migrants who expressed them. These men seem to have believed that they were entitled to a degree of protection from military demands, both by the sentimental ties binding them to France, and—paradoxically—by their exemption from the French body politic. And, crucially, they saw themselves as bound to metropolitan politicians and Mandatory administrators, not to the administration of AOF, which had reneged on the promises made by these higher authorities and heroes. This is a reminder both of the ambiguity which continued to surround the Mandatory states—those peninsulas of empire at once attached to the imperial polity and yet somehow independent of this larger construct—and of the scorn of migrants for their immediate surroundings.

For beneath such high-flown claims lay a turbulent undertow of fears, rooted in the anxieties of quotidian life. The Eastern Mediterranean inhabitants of Sine-Saloum, reported an administrator, were 'truly panic-stricken', 'meeting and engaging in interminable discussions' over their fate. For, as one of them explained:

[I]f we are mobilised, our merchandise will stay in our shops. As the police in AOF isn't made of the same stuff as that in France, there's a fair chance that we won't find anything of what we left behind, as our shops will be looted in our absence. Even if we left our wives in our homes, it wouldn't stop them being burgled, as our wives are scared and the natives know it.

There was no point, he reiterated, in hoping to rely on the police 'to preserve our shops from looting'—it was simply 'inexistent' in most upcountry towns. Nor could the Lebanese put much faith, in his eyes, in 'local guards, as they'll be often the first to rob us'.[89] A lack of trust in the colonial state—that absent administration—mingled together in these words with profound suspicion of the Africans upon whom Lebanese traders were forced, despite themselves, to rely. Such fears were perhaps related to lingering memories of the 'Syrian riots' which erupted in Freetown in 1919, which broke out in the midst of severe rice shortages which many blamed, in the words of the 'leading members of the Creole community', on the 'inordinate hoarding of … the principal foodstuff of the community … by the Syrian merchants and traders for profiteering purposes'.[90] Some of the Lebanese of Dakar witnessed the riots first-hand, and were shepherded, along with the entirety of Freetown's Eastern Mediterranean population, to Wilberforce Memorial Hall. And they, along with others who had kin or friends in Dakar, sent panicked accounts of events unfolding in Sierra Leone to Dakar. Sharaf Sharaf reported, in a crabbed, tense telegram, an 'anti-Syrian native movement all night Friday all day night Saturday all shops dwellings ransacked looted three Syrians murdered'.[91]

But even as the fears of 1940 were, in part, the product of this prior knowledge—which bred an awareness of how rapidly things could go awry, resentment and recrimination slipping into violence—they were located in the midst of more immediate concerns. The words of this migrant thus revealed a host of anxieties not only about the constant, awkward, contiguity of Eastern Mediterranean and African, and the former's uneasy reliance on the labour of the latter, but also about the fragility of femininity and family. These were felt as much by Lebanese women themselves as by men. In 1943, in the wake of a renewed conscription drive by the new Free French administration, Madame Antoine Char—Sha'ar—sent a telegram to the Maronite patriarch of Lebanon, the Mufti of the Republic—the representative of its Sunni community—and Sayyid 'Abd al-Husain Sharaf al-Din, as head of the Ja'fari tribunal of Sur the highest Shi'a authority in the land, pleading for their intervention 'in the name of Lebanese women very affected by decision Government General ... in favour women and children left to their sad fate African bush and deprived of their support and means of existence'.[92] Sha'ar—who, tellingly, made herself known by her husband's name—exhibited not only revealing preconceptions about the 'bush'—the hinterland, with all its dangers—but also a distinctly modern sense of domesticity, of a family built around male endeavour and protection. Her words echoed those of another anonymous 'Lebanese trader' who provided his opinion on conscription in 1940. The 'little traders', he insisted, 'in the large centres as in the small, on the coast and in the bush, fear for their homes, their children, their wives, selling off at dirt cheap prices their stocks of goods, to obtain funds they will leave to their families' should they be called to the front, for 'only the head of the family is the support' propping up most 'Lebanese and Syrian families'.[93] This was a vision of the division of labour quite at odds with the reality of many female migrants' lives—but one which spoke of the aspirations of Eastern Mediterranean men and women alike to an ideal of middle-class domesticity.

What is more, the words of both this 'trader', who explained that many of his compatriots 'saw themselves all of a sudden oppressed, destitute, ruined and soldiers on the Maginot line',[94] and of the anonymous, worried migrant who fretted that 'most of us', in the event of mobilisation, 'will be reduced to indigence', spoke also of the precariousness of migrant life.[95] These men and women not only bore a memory of their own beginnings, an awareness of their social ascent—their 'homes and businesses for which they worked so hard their whole lives', as our 'trader' put it lachrymosely—which made them fearful of returning to the humble conditions they had striven to leave behind.[96] They also seem acutely sensitive to the ways in which their presence and prosperity was contingent not only upon the vagaries of the colonial economy, but also the sentiments of African *indigènes* and French *colons*, and—despite their 'favoured' status as citizens of the Mandate states—upon the goodwill of the colonial state. This man's remark that the local police was just not 'made of the same stuff' as that in France wasn't simply a racial judgement—though it certainly was that too—but also an assessment of the weakness of colonial power, the inability of the Government-General in Dakar to 'broadcast' its power far into the hinterland, which contrasted starkly in his mind with the solidity of metropolitan institutions.[97] In this, as in their ways of life, Eastern Mediterranean migrants seem to have been keenly aware of the differences between *métropole* and colony. But migrants were fearful not just of the state's ineffectuality, but also of its perceived biases against the Lebanese, and its desire to placate French *colons*, their exclusionary sentiments and dissatisfaction at the dominance of the large trading firms. As our trader put it opaquely, they worried 'that these measures' should be motivated by a desire to quell 'certain disagreements between large and small commerce'.[98] Another intelligence note was rather clearer: 'Lebanese and Syrian society is decidedly unwilling to trust any longer in the local authorities of AOF which they accuse of having been influenced by the group of French traders who founded *L'Afrique Noire*, [their] bitter enemies.'[99]

The Depression and its discontents

France Afrique Noire (*FAN*), to give this monthly magazine its proper title, was established in mid-1935 in an attempt to counter Eastern Mediterranean migration—that 'seemingly limitless foreign incursion' which posed a profound 'threat' to the 'French population, both white and black' of the Federation, as its founder Jean Paillard inveighed. Already, he wrote in his opening salvo, its *colons* had begun boarding 'ships' bound for France, 'never to return'; soon, its *indigènes* would be 'reduced … to idleness' in the 'tens of thousands' by the 'lethal affliction' of this 'commercial invasion'.[100] Paillard, the magazine's editor and its chief contributor was—though he belonged to a 'family of traders established in Senegal for more than sixty years', as Jean-Louis Turbé, the pugnacious president of the Dakar Chamber of Commerce, pointed out—no *colon*.[101]

Born in Bordeaux in 1904, Paillard began his journalistic career in 1928, when he joined the staff of *La Production Française*, the newspaper edited by George Valois, the founder of the virulently rightist *Faisceau* movement. By the mid-1930s, he had established himself as a successful 'publicist', carving out a distinctive niche as a specialist in colonial matters. Besides contributing occasional pieces to the short-lived *L'Insurgé*, established by two of Maurras' former pupils during the latter's imprisonment, in 1936–37,[102] Paillard contributed a dozen pieces to the colonial column of *Je Suis Partout*, the popular periodical run by Maurras' former secretary, Pierre Gaxotte. These included a long article on France's Middle Eastern mandates, 'La Syrie Déchirée', which appeared in mid-1937,[103] and an extended essay, 'L'Algérie, dominion?'.[104] But by far the most significant of these assignments was his editorship of the imperial pages of the *Action Française*—a position he took on in June 1935, only two months before launching *France Afrique Noire*. In the 'Lettre de France à nos Amis d'Outre-Mer', as this column was called, Paillard developed a 'truly nationalist' 'colonial programme' in perfect harmony with the corporative, xenophobic views of the *Action Française*. His regular contributions to the *Action Française* and its 'satellite publications', then, effectively 'structured the colonial thought of the *ultra* right' into the 1940s—as well as, we might conjecture, influencing the *Action Française*'s broad audience which, even at its financial doldrums in the mid-1930s, still averaged over 70,000 readers.[105]

These affiliations placed Paillard—a dedicated cadre of the Action Française who pronounced Bainville's funeral eulogy—firmly within the sprawling family of thought which developed around Maurras, scribbling endlessly away in his Paris apartment.[106] Indeed, Paillard—for all that he had spent a short, youthful stint working in trade in Senegal,[107] and had travelled widely through Western and Northern Africa—was himself a profoundly Parisian creature.[108] He sought, to be sure, to establish an institutional base in AOF through the Syndicat Corporatif et Economique du Sénégal, initially set up in early 1935 to 'combat the difficulties occasioned by the economic crisis and the speculation on Senegalese groundnuts by the Unilever trust'—threats he proposed to counter by the establishment of protective tariffs for the colonies. In May 1935, he announced it would henceforth serve largely as the vehicle for his campaign against the effects of Eastern Mediterranean competition on 'Senegalese trade and the Frenchmen of Senegal'.[109] Despite its bold aims, this remained in practice a rather flimsy conceit—and one whose day-to-day running Paillard delegated to his Senegal-based acolyte Louis Guiraud. He himself continued to live in Paris throughout *FAN*'s brief existence—at one point putting together the magazine from the plush environs of Avenue Foch, in the sixteenth *arrondissement*.[110]

Paillard, then, saw Eastern Mediterranean migration from an essentially Parisian perspective—both literally and figuratively. He did not just fear its immediate impact on the livelihoods of the *mange-mils*—as the *petits blancs* of AOF were known, not without a note of condescension, for their impecunious reliance on millet as a culinary staple. More importantly, he was concerned with its effects on the great, if gangrenous, construct of the French empire-state. For, as he put it, 'the fate of France is, more and more, bound to that of its colonies': 'everything' seemed to indicate that 'our Black Empire' would serve as 'one of the primordial factors of our destiny'.[111] It was essential that France's relations with her colonies remain intact; her very survival rested upon the ties between *métropole* and Black Africa, and *indigène* and *mange-mil*. And these were precisely the ties Lebanese migrants, those interlopers of empire, threatened to sunder. Like a 'fox in the chicken coop', they had entered the French empire, steadily corroding its structures from within.[112] 'Before long', he warned, 'you will find among them colonial administrators, police commissioners, *gendarmes*, customs officers, and perhaps even governors. And then we will have our colonies commanded by the *Libano-Syriens*.' This was not, for Paillard, beyond the realm of possibility. After all, were they not already a veritable 'state within the state'?[113] Moreover, Lebanese migration was but one symptom of a wider ill, just another 'blight' afflicting the imperial body politic, like the dominance of foreign 'trust[s]' like Unilever, that 'Anglo-German-Dutch' behemoth,[114] or the 'internationalist' convictions of the Popular Front, whose metropolitan and colonial representatives were 'in the service of communism and the foreigner'.[115]

However, Paillard knew what he was doing in focusing his caustic attention on Eastern Mediterranean migration. Typical of the 'new breed of free-lance' writers who populated the extreme-right circles of Paris in the 1930s, a 'marketer' concerned primarily with 'selling' his own brand of politics, he sought to play—albeit with somewhat limited success—on the resentment many small French traders undoubtedly harboured for the *Libano-Syriens*.[116] There seems no question that this only grew in intensity with the depression in commodity prices which began in 1927—and particularly affected Senegal's groundnut economy. By 1932, a mere 135,000 tons of groundnuts were exported from Senegal—a quarter of the colony's sales in 1927. And falling sales were accompanied, quite naturally, by falling profits: Senegalese revenues from the groundnut trade stood at 165 million francs.[117]

Many *mange-mils* found themselves cut off by the banks and trading companies of the colony—themselves short of reserves and unable to accept deferment of repayments. Short of the credit essential for their operations, independent French traders were left without the wherewithal to purchase produce and honour their obligations, or even to pay taxes.[118] While several medium and small establishments disappeared completely, others were bought up by the larger trading companies, or by their more solvent French and Lebanese competitors.[119] Eastern Mediterranean migrants offered a ready, and particularly conspicuous, target for the ire of his intended readership of disaffected *colons* reeling from the effects of the depression. Indeed, three members of the board of *France Afrique Noire*—Carrière and Lacombe father and son—had been reduced to selling off their Thiès businesses in the early 1930s. While Carrière's company was bought by the CFAO, that of the Lacombe family was most likely taken over by 'Levantine' competitors.[120] The younger Lacombe's anguished call, 'not more *Libano-Syriens* than Frenchmen', let out during Paillard's May 1935 speech at the Dakar Chamber of Commerce, seems no mere slogan, but a sentiment born of bitter personal experience.[121] For all the anger *petits blancs* threw at the 'frivolous administration which thinks only of pleasures' and the 'MAGNATES of local business … rendered lethargic by the millions they easily earned in the wake of the war', the *Libano-Syriens* presented to their eyes an altogether more immediate and less nebulous threat to their livelihoods.[122] It is no surprise that the Dakar Chamber of Commerce itself—a body which excluded even the most 'serious [and] esteemable' *Libano-Syriens* from its ranks—should have warned of the way in which these foreigners were 'little by little, replacing French enterprises in France'.[123] Citing the rising number of migrants entering AOF, the Chamber's president, Jean-Louis Turbé, compared them to the number of French electors in the chambers of commerce of Rufisque, Kaolack, Ziguinchor and Saint-Louis, which had decreased by 61 per cent between 1921 and 1935. The number of Lebanese holding commercial licences, he pointed out, exceeded that of metropolitan Frenchmen by 123 per cent. 'One has to admit', he concluded, 'that it is no exaggeration to use the term "commercial invasion".'[124]

By the close of the Second World War this resentment had taken on an increasingly bitter political edge as the French inhabitants of AOF watched the escalating crisis between the Lebanese and Syrian governments-in-waiting and de Gaulle. The expulsion of French citizens from Syria led the settlers of Agboville in Côte d'Ivoire to demand in early June 1945 that 'measures taken against our compatriots Syria be immediately imposed on all Syrians colony',[125] and the Comité France Combattante of Bobo-Dioulasso, in Haute-Volta, to try to broadcast on Radio-Brazzaville an appeal for 'expulsion all Syrian citizens' and 'confiscation all their goods' in 'French Empire'.[126] This seething tension found its expression not only in protests to the Government-General and carefully worded appeals but also in the streets and spaces of the city. Already on 24 May, hecklers in the crowd watching the newsreels at the Cinéma Palace in Dakar cried out 'here come the monkeys' when the Arab delegates to the San Francisco conference appeared on screen. Around the same time, graffiti appeared on a wall on Avenue Ponty, in the heart of the Gambetta neighbourhood, calling on the town's inhabitants to throw 'Les Druses [sic] à la mer'. This, in itself, was perhaps revealing of French attitudes, for this might be read not as a mistaken allusion to the confessional cast of the Lebanese migrants of Dakar, but as a reworked memory of the Syrian Great Revolt of 1925—demonstrating just how deeply the French military men and *colons* of the city associated Eastern Mediterranean men with recalcitrance and revolt. A 'procession' of migrants apparently filed by to read this scrawl, making shows of a 'muted indignation'—muted, perhaps, because rumours had begun to circulate they would be 'interned' should the conflict continue.[127]

Ambivalent responses

This sense that theirs was a community under threat provoked a set of essentially paradoxical responses on the part of the Lebanese. Many of the men whose opinions found their way into the colonial archive seem constantly caught in two minds, undecided between staying put and moving on. Many reacted to the rumours of mobilisation in 1940 in essentially contradictory ways: even as they deplored being forced to abandon the businesses they had built up, they attempted to leave AOF to elude mobilisation, cancelling their orders with wholesale suppliers and trying to liquidate their stock as rapidly as possible.[128] Though some seemingly hoped to enlist in Lebanon and Syria, or to lie low until the end of hostilities, when they would return to their businesses, few seem to have perceived the contradictory nature of their impulses: they were fearful of losing everything, and yet willing to let go.[129]

But by 1943, when the administration of AOF tried a second time to introduce conscription, some had apparently become more resolute in their desire to hold on to their gains in the face of obdurate opposition from Senegal's *colons* and Africans. In April of that year, an intelligence note reported that the Lebanese of Dakar—and 'a certain proportion of those in the interior'—had decided to purchase 'some or, if possible, all the buildings which will go on sale until the end of 1944'. This sudden buying frenzy was driven both by their desire to 'place their capital' in immobile investments, in the belief 'French money will [soon] be without value', and to outdo their competitors. As some supposedly said: 'the more ... properties we will have in Dakar and AOF, the more we will have an advantage over the blacks and even the Europeans'. The sums involved 'mattered little'—what was needed was for 'one or two Lebanese to be at the head of the greatest number of trading houses in [Dakar] and the interior'; that way 'they will be obliged to respect us'. All this may seem fanciful, an illustration of the extent to which the colonial archive was filled with distorted noises, with rumours and delusions. Nonetheless, it could be argued this report seemingly refracted the very real concerns of the wealthier Lebanese of Dakar, some of whom apparently 'declared they will only be satisfied the day they will have bought a house for each of their children, so that they will not have to go back to Lebanon, where it is impossible to make any money'.[130] This, then, was the central paradox of migrant life. Even as they remained in constant contact with the Eastern Mediterranean—as a part of their life remained invested there, in affective ties as much as in real estate or business holdings—they were aware of the advantages life in Africa, with all its ambivalences and anxieties, had brought them. They saw little choice but to stay put, and to perpetuate their families in Senegal or Guinea.

This same ambivalence shot through their public life, which remained hung in the balance between AOF and the Eastern Mediterranean—and permeated, more particularly, their attempts to find intercessors who might compensate for their own lack of local political representation. Fighting conscription tooth-and-claw through the Second World War, the Lebanese sought out assistance both near and far. In 1942, it was reported that a Lebanese delegation had offered Lamine Guèye—then a lawyer, newspaper editor and the prospective mayor of Dakar, and later a deputy in the Assemblée Constituante of 1946—'recognition' should he prove willing to 'intervene effectively on their behalf' with the administration—the quotation marks carefully placed around the word in the original text leaving little doubt as to what such recognition might have been.[131]

Furthermore, the Eastern Mediterranean communities of Dakar were willing to provide rather more public gifts in their efforts to ensure the assistance of political figures such as Guèye. In July 1945, an African informant reported that a number of Lebanese had convened at the home of Nadra Filfili on Avenue Gambetta before visiting Guèye to 'discuss their situation in the wake of the events of Syria' and to 'offer him their congratulations on his election' as mayor of Dakar. On this occasion, they apparently suggested to Guèye the gift of either a clocktower or a school to the city of Dakar, following the precedent of their compatriots in Lagos, who had already given a clocktower to its municipality.[132] Guèye preferring a school, they agreed to its construction. After protracted discussions, which stretched on for the best part of two years, building began on the school—open to all, 'European, African, Lebanese or Syrian', it would teach the public curriculum, while providing classes in classical Arabic to those who wished.[133] The school would be sited on the corner of Bel Air and Faidherbe, 'close to the neighbourhood more specially inhabited by the Lebanese and Syrians', where it still stands.[134] This seemed for the Lebanese community a way of inscribing their presence on the city, which fitted neatly with the new registers of colonial humanism and 'union'—marking its permanence and contribution to Senegalese life in a way which accorded well both with an administration espousing reformist talk, and the desires of évolués who might wish for their children to retain something of their Islamicate culture while receiving a French education. A clocktower or a school—these were, in their different ways, equally potent representations of linear progress. Indeed, stating the utility of the Lebanese community to Senegal, its adherence to progress, and loyalty to France, had become by 1945 a familiar tactic for the migrants of Dakar.

All these elements had already been present in the responses its representatives Habib Rizq and Sa'id Nujaim, the co-presidents of the city's Lebanese Committee, had penned to Paillard and his acolytes in the Dakar newspaper *Périscope Africain* in 1935. Rizq, in particular, sought explicitly to refute the claims Paillard and Guiraud had made. Insisting that their description of the strikes that had broken out in Lebanon and Syria in 1936 in protest at the renewal of the state tobacco monopoly as a 'revolt' was a deliberate 'error', designed to 'create an impression of hostility on our behalf towards the French authorities', he stressed the essentially cordial relationship between Lebanon and France. '[O]ne can disagree', he asserted, 'and even allow discussion to get a little heated, without there being any animosity.' But more than this, he took them to task for their depiction of the Lebanese and Syrians as 'backward'. 'Can one', he asked, 'use this word to speak of a people with its own civilisation—one which is certainly not comparable to yours, but which exists—and has its poets, its scientists, its historians, its doctors in medicine and law.' This acknowledgement of France's superiority in the cultural realm was more than a mere rhetorical feint. Rather, it belied the ambiguity of the Lebanese towards the French.

On the one hand, migrants did not just resent the condescension and contempt of colonial administrators and settlers—they also worried these might, in some way, be justified. Kamil Muruwwah thus noted of his conversations with Lebanese migrants that, though they 'acknowledged' that they did not face, 'in truth', the 'terror and enmity' to which they sometimes claimed they were subjected, they nevertheless 'feel something of a constraint, a pressure' pushing down on them, in the form of a 'moral' sanction, which 'hurt their interests, and caused them harm'. From the 'words [he] had heard from migrants, regardless of their class, wealth, or background … [he] had gathered that the source of their complaints was the lack of respect of the Europeans for some of them'. While there was no doubt that 'there were some amongst our migrants who occupy high social positions in the eyes of all, just as there are Europeans prepared to acknowledge the worth of the Lebanese', this lack of respect was an inescapable fact. For all the 'professional qualities' of Eastern Mediterranean migrants, to which could be added 'the moral attributes common to the peoples of the East, and the Arabs in particular, such as their generosity, refinement, moderation and hospitality, their willingess to help the needy, to help the weak and to offer assistance to the stranger', there remained an unbridgeable 'barricade, which separated the European and the Lebanese or Syrian migrant, and prevents the latter from attaining the high consideration he deserves from his white brothers'. The cause of this, for Muruwwah, was plain to see: 'the backward social life of a part of our migrants, morally lacking and soaked in niggardliness, ignorance, and obsolete tradition'. This was nothing particular to migrant society, he insisted: it was present 'in the homeland, in Europe and America, in all the countries of the world'. But, this notwithstanding, migrants needed to reform their ways if they were ever to earn the consideration so many deserved.[135] It is not clear how far Eastern Mediterranean men and women would have agreed with such harsh words. But they clearly reflected a sense of unease and fear at their enduring exclusion from European society. One senses this pain and disappointment in the letter Antoine Jummayil sent to the Grand-Bassam Chamber of Commerce in July 1935, on learning 'of a reception held … to introducers the traders of the town to the governor of Côte d'Ivoire'; 'I much regret,' he wrote, 'not having been invited to this reception, as I am a trader like any other, and I therefore have the right to be invited.'[136] Regarding themselves as 'white', and as equal partners in colonial society, Eastern Mediterranean migrants found it difficult to comprehend the slights and sanctions that came their way.

On the other hand, the *Libano-Syriens* were increasingly intolerant of such claims of inferiority. Turning the tropes of colonial rhetoric on their head, they insisted vehemently on their own worth and capacity for progress, arguing that in many ways they had surpassed the French of the colonies. Thus, Habib Rizq argued in 1935 that:

The Syrians are not the cause of your travails. Take to task, instead, your superannuated methods. Agree with me that the black has evolved in the last fifty years. He knows now the scale and the weights and asks about the prices. His needs have increased and he has become more demanding. As a consequence, one can no longer make a fortune in a few years. The ineluctable law of demand and supply is in play.[137]

This was an unequivocal statement. In the hard-headed domain of commerce and economic reason, the Eastern Mediterranean migrant held the upper hand. His methods were more in keeping with the times than those of the French, who remained stuck in the crude tactics of the first years of formal rule. And, just as importantly, he kept track of the needs and desires of the African consumer, of his own economic progress—he not only knew the African better than the Frenchman could, but also participated in the task of development.[138]

These claims were not simply for external consumption. On the contrary, they reflected these migrants' perception of themselves as a trading community, a group defined primarily by its involvement in commerce. This is apparent from the pages of *Ifriqiya al-Tijariyya-L'Afrique Commerciale*, the only Lebanese newspaper to appear in AOF until the 1950s. True to its name, it reflected its readers' mercantile outlook and preoccupations, and was peppered with articles on local economic circumstances;[139] the global economic 'crisis', which sought to discern its causes, and to provide 'analysis of what is needed from merchants' to escape the prevailing morass;[140] the commercial history of the Arab lands;[141] the moral underpinnings of trade;[142] and on the colonial state's local initiatives which depicted the Lebanese as partners in the fledgling project of imperial development.[143]

This latter notion was taken up by the Lebanese journalist 'Abdallah Hushaimah who, in his travelogue of the early 1930s, depicted Eastern Mediterranean migrants as agents of progress. Their presence, he noted, dated back to the 'time when these lands were still in the grip of rapid about-turns and developments, or to put it more clearly, to the period when they passed from the hands of their backward sons to those of the advanced nations which now control their resources'. Hushaimah recounted the tales 'our brothers there' in Africa had told him, of how 'some accompanied the invading armies in their campaigns in the interior of the country, and others moved ahead of these armies, opening the gates of the interior': 'before the European traders even knew of these wilds, they carried their goods [there], and intensified their travels, moving about and trading' under the benevolent gaze of 'the Merciful'. In this vision, the Lebanese were the veritable avant-garde of colonialism. More than simply handmaidens of imperialism, passive agents who had followed in its wake, profiting from the establishment of the colonial economy, they were its veritable creators. This was an unambiguous endorsement of imperial ventures, but one that strongly refuted the notion that these were exclusively European endeavours, carried out by French or British traders. On the contrary, they were the work of the Lebanese. Indeed, more than simply assisting European colonialism, the Lebanese had also benefited Africa, bringing progress to this benighted continent. Thus, 'many African towns and villages are indebted today for their infrastructural and commercial development to our migrant brothers'. The latter were consistently 'energetic in their labours'; helping to 'build up in which they live', they did not 'stint any effort or expenditure to this end'. And colonial 'governments … were aware' of this 'benevolence' (*husna*) and 'encouraged them to increase their good works'.[144] The role of the Lebanese of West Africa as architects of the colonial economy and the agents of beneficent development, Hushaimah suggested—repeating and reflecting the words of his migrant interlocutors—had to be acknowledged. Their presence on African soil could not be questioned for, without them, the continent and its colonies would simply not be the same.

But there is no denying that this language proved useful in refuting the attacks of French publicists like Paillard. It was in this context that Sa'id Nujaim put down any notion that 'the Syrian' remained reluctant to employ 'anybody but the members of his own family'. On the contrary, he wrote, 'we know of one house in Ziguinchor which employs alone more than 150 natives, between shopkeepers, agents, sailors, etc.'. 'If', he went on, 'there are unemployed Africans, it is not down to the Syrian' but 'in part to the slump and partly to the famous "blacklist" drawn up a few years ago which put a large number out of business'. The banks, which had abruptly cut off credit to these men, were the 'cause of their misery'. The 'Syrians', meanwhile, played an active part in the development of African commerce; far from curling up on themselves, they engaged with the society around them to a far greater extent than the French institutions of colonialism were prepared to do. This claim to engagement, to permanence, was central to both Nujaim's argument and that of Rizq, with his notion that quick fortunes could no longer be made—a reality the 'Syrian' knew only too well, while feckless, fly-by-night Frenchmen could still sweep into Senegal expecting easy gains. Rizq and Nujaim thus cannily turned the tables on their French adversaries: accusing them of being self-interested sojourners who refused to invest their lives and resources in West Africa, they levelled at them the charges they had long grown used to throwing at the Lebanese. The latter, they insisted, were part and parcel of West African life. Indeed, Rizq began his article by denouncing Guiraud's attempts 'to transport to other places' a 'discussion which should remain on commercial ground'. Frenchmen, he insisted, could not refer to the Mandatory states of the Eastern Mediterranean, and their political troubles, in an attempt to denigrate the migrants of AOF. Their lives were firmly located in the Federation, and they could only be judged on local grounds, rather than on the actions of their faraway compatriots. However, Rizq's speech was not—and perhaps could not be—entirely consistent, for he felt compelled to look both ways in his attempts to address Guiraud's slanderous claims, defending his compatriots both in AOF and the Eastern Mediterranean. Even as they sought to mark their presence in West Africa, Lebanese migrants remained ambiguously tied to the lands of their birth.

Club life

The associational life of the Lebanese, in which Rizq was such an active participant, reflected this duality. The Lebanese committee of Saint-Louis sought to 'defend the interests of the Lebanese, to come to the assistance of those who are in need, [and] to participate in all munificent actions, French and African'.[145] Rizq's own Lebanese Cooperative Committee, which he created after breaking off from Nujaim, aimed to 'come to the assistance of all those destitute', to 'provide for the repatriation of all indigent compatriots who are the victims of circumstances' and 'contribute to the moral and intellectual education of the youth';[146] the Comité d'Adhésion et de Bienfaisance *Libano-Syrien*, under the presidence of Mustafa Hudruj, strove to use 'its moral and pecuniary resources to improve the lot of those of its associates who would find themselves resourceless', and 'to organise a fund for the development of education … to publicise the education of girls; to publicise education in Arabic and French, in short to encourage education in all its forms'.[147]

   Such remits reflected the local exigencies and aspirations of their founders: they stressed their willingness to contribute something to colonial society and the ties binding them to France, and they used the familiar tropes of benevolence, improvement and education in order to distinguish themselves as respectable men worthy of distributing such attainments. Indeed, the Club Libanais of Kankan made clear such concerns in its own statutes—it would only admit men of 'good morality', whose reputability had been vouched for by two patrons.[148] The undertow of such attempts at self-fashioning, of course, was a persistent concern for securing the bounds of the community itself—by defending it not only from assailants like Paillard, but also from the blemishes of destitution and disreputability, which might throw the claims of these founding fathers into question. While Nujaim was careful to defend the sober striving of the less successful Lebanese from the attacks of Paillard, asserting—in an essentially Christian register—that 'poverty has never been a vice', he warily insisted that 'we unanimously condemn the bad eggs [*les mauvais*]' who might diminish the community's standing.[149]

However, the outlines of these committees were drawn in the image of the distant body politic—or, rather, were involved from afar in the contested definition of a polity just coming into being. While the Club Libanais of Kankan made clear in its statutes that 'all political or religious discussions are forbidden'—tellingly, this was the only clause in bold face—it traced its own boundaries upon those of the nation. Only Lebanese citizens could be members. Furthermore, these divergent definitions of nationality broke down along confessional lines, for while the associations headed by the Christian Nujaim and Rizq defined themselves as Lebanese, that founded by Hudruj, Muhammad Hilal and Ibrahim Tsham took as its first remit to 'group the Lebanese and Syrians and create between them ties of solidarity'.[150] Such cleavages reflected the quite different understandings of political space to which Christian and Muslim subscribed by the late 1930s—the former endorsing enthusiastically the idea of an independent Lebanon, while the latter held on to a vision of an integral Syria. Moreover, they showed the ways in which religiosity and regional differences could be reshaped into a more explicitly political sectarianism in the *mahjar* as in Lebanon—and the ways in which these political discourses could be used to further personal ends. These were the flaws for which visiting Lebanese journalists took their migrant compatriots to task in the 1930s. Thus, 'Abdallah Hushaimah noted with 'regret, … we are still, in our migrations, above all else Lebanese and Syrian. Wherever we are, we still hold on to our social weakness: there is no trust amongst ourselves, and each one of us wishes to keep the entire world in his clasp.'[151] Vainglory and mutual suspicion: these were in his eyes, the sad characteristics of the new polities of the Eastern Mediterranean. And migrants, far from escaping their grasp, carried these blights with them on their peregrinations.

If anything, Kamil Muruwwah argued, the 'social problems' of the migrant communities of West Africa were worse still than those the inhabitants of Lebanon and Syria faced. 'Here', as 'there', there was 'no general bond uniting their ranks'. The 'causes of this fragmentation' were plain to see: 'the … discord which reigns in the homeland, where each region lives a selfish life, separated from others by inequalities in the level of learning and culture and productivity, and differences in habits and traditions, and the diversity of confessions'. But while 'we have begun to feel some improvement in our situation in Lebanon, where the catastrophe which has befallen us has affected us all, and brought us together, and led us to feel something of the truths of national life, our migrants have remained isolated from these developments, living in a purely commercial environment, free of the social, political, and patriotic currents which are influencing society and its transformation'. Politics, that eternal corruptor, was partly to blame, for 'the same tendencies and principles that caused conflict amongst the sons of our country could also be found in the *mahjar*': 'in every colony [of West Africa], one found disagreement surrounding the independence of Lebanon, Syrian unity, or Arab unity, the Constitutional Bloc and the Unionists in Beirut, or the [National] Bloc and the opposition in Damascus, or the leadership of this person or that in one region or another'. But much of the responsibility could be laid at the migrants' own door. Committees and associations were 'an essential component' of their lives, the 'only support on which they could lean in their efforts to raise the status of the community, to ward off dangers, and to keep at bay oppression'. But they had been, in practice, nothing if not a source of 'fatigue and headaches'. Too many men had sought the 'presidency' of these bodies to ingratiate themselves with the colonial administration, or because 'the position gave its holder' valuable 'trust' with the 'companies and banks' of AOF, and too many had 'run towards [these associations] in a spirit of jealousy and competition'. Muruwwah's verdict was stark. 'When', he asked, 'had trade [ever] led to national or moral unity?'[152] Commerce may have been the source of the community's livelihood, and of its sense of itself as a coherent body, but it was also the root—in his eyes—of the evils that plagued it. For all the harshness of such a judgement, it provides an insight into the cleavages and disputes which ravaged the ranks of migrant society. And, moreover, it gives us a sense of the lineaments of these diasporic communities, whose members sought to define themselves on two quite different planes: as traders, imbricated in the colonial economies of West Africa, and as Eastern Mediterranean men and women—as Lebanese or Syrian citizens, Matni or 'Amili, Maronite, Greek Orthodox or Shi'a, followers of this or that faction or party.

In the balance of days

In other senses, too, the lives of migrants seemed poised between here and there, old and new—between staying still and constant motion. 'Abdallah Hushaimah described, in evocative, richly poetic terms, the effect of entering Rue Vincens in Dakar. There, he wrote, one found 'Lebanese and Syrian society in its most splendid aspects, … its nature, habits, and morals, [and] its ways of life.' Indeed, the lives of migrants faithfully followed, in his eyes, not just the 'ethical and social precepts' of their homelands, but also their small, everyday practices. For in the kitchens of this 'Lebanese and Syrian neighbourhood' could be found 'the sesame paste press, and the pestle in which one prepared *kibbeh*'—that quintessentially Eastern Mediterranean dish of cracked wheat, minced meat and pine nuts—and on its tables were laid out dishes like *ful mudammas*, or fava beans in oil, *hummus bi-tahina* and *baba ghanuj*.[153] As I have argued, getting hold of ingredients like olive oil and butter was a particularly significant concern for migrants. This was not just because these goods were expensive items of conspicuous consumption obtained from outside AOF, but also—and perhaps most importantly—because they allowed Eastern Mediterranean men and women to maintain 'habits … imported from the home country'.[154] By the late 1930s, if not earlier, 'there was not a single large town' without a 'few shops specialised' in selling *bada'i baladiyya*, or the 'produce of the homeland', like 'clarified butter, oil, lentils, beans, chickpeas, and bulgur wheat, sesame paste and *tahina*, molasses, roast nuts, sweets and pastries'. Most of these were 'imported' directly 'from the homeland', while a few others were brought from 'Italy, France, Spain, Portugal and North Africa'. Together, these were the 'ingredients necessary to prepare the Oriental dishes' so 'dear' to the migrant—and 'first and foremost the *kibbeh*'.[155] For

Lebanese men and women attempted as best they could to reproduce the dishes of home, and the context in which to make them. Umm Muhammad, who lived in Abidjan in the 1930s, thus remembered 'making everything', from *mujaddara*, a dish of lentils and rice, to *kibbeh t'ileh*—or *thaqila*, in formal Arabic. While 'Abu Muhammad helped me to make the salad, … I pounded the meat' to prepare *frakeh*, that distinctively 'Amili dish of heavily seasoned raw meatballs, hitting it against a marble surface to pulverise it in the absence of any mechanical help. To deal with the ever-present threat of insects, she 'put together, with the help of the boy', a makeshift *namliyyeh*, or larder: filling a barrel with water, she piled food into it, before covering it with a plastic sheet to prevent 'ants and insects from getting in'.[156]

Moreover, migrants were sometimes able to make do with goods they found locally, which could easily be substituted for those they had used in their cooking before their departure. The Lebanese physician Michael John Blell, born in Freetown around 1910, remembered that the Eastern Mediterranean migrants of that city used not just onions, tomatoes, potatoes, olives and olive oil 'imported by the French businesses from Europe and the Canary Islands', but also the already familiar foodstuffs the women found in the local markets, like okra and aubergines, runner beans and radishes, oranges and limes. A similar capacity for accommodation and improvisation was evident in other ways. The women still made the breads they had prepared back home, the flat *khubz* and *marquq*, though a few bakers set up trade, who perhaps also cooked meals for those without ovens in their homes, as they did in the Eastern Mediterranean. Backstreet butchers, meanwhile, kept the goats and sheep whose meat migrants used for their stews and pasties. Many planted in their yards fruit-trees or the climbers on which grew the luffas with which they scrubbed their bodies clean—along, maybe, with a small patch of parsley, mint and other herbs.[157] This, in particular, was a widespread practice: across West Africa, migrants apparently kept 'small gardens alongside their homes, where they grew the vegetables and herbs known in our countries, like parsley, mint, and onions, aubergines, tomatoes, peppers, lettuce, etc.', thus obviating the need to pay over the odds for these products.[158]

But while Lebanese migrants sought to recreate and reproduce the quotidian practices of the Eastern Mediterranean, few seem to have proved as resilient to adaptation, or as rapid to disavow their earlier accommodations, as those of Côte d'Ivoire—perhaps still keen in the 1940s to draw a line under their relatively recent success. The food of the Lebanese inhabitants of Freetown, for instance, carried in it not just the traces of home, but also the ineradicable marks of movement. They clung, to be sure, to old recipes. But they also, as time went on, worked into their meals new ingredients like snapper, cassava, mango and sop, groundnut or palm oil. Preparing and eating food, then, was at once a matter of making do—of adapting to new circumstances and the commodities they offered—and of keeping up old habits, sustaining the memories of home and passing them down to children at the evening meal—by enforcing, say, the interdict placed upon preparing fish with *laban*, or yoghurt, because of the common belief that the mixture was a poisonous one.[159] If 'each culinary habit' is a 'tiny cross-roads of histories', if into each meal is 'piled' the sediment of change, then the eating habits of Eastern Mediterranean men and women spoke of the accommodations as well as the strains of migrant life.[160]

The social and domestic lives of migrants were made up of the same admixture of old habits and interpolations, of changing desires and aspirations. The first few men and women who arrived at the turn of the nineteenth century in Saint-Louis, Dakar and Conakry used the scrimping, simple ways they had learned in the highlands of the Eastern Mediterranean to make do and put aside a little capital. One Moroccan migrant who had long lived alongside the Lebanese of Saint-Louis recalled being told that in the early days of this community its men and women had subsisted on nothing more than tomatoes and onions.[161] Though he did not know it, this was the frugal staple of the mountain-dweller. Furthermore, while early migrants were often damned for living *à l'indigène*, and blurring the lines of race by accepting conditions intolerably low for the European, their capacity to inhabit ramshackle shacks where they 'piled, numerous, in airless rooms'[162] or to 'retire to their 'beds' on the counters of their ... shops' may have had something to do with the simplicity of the dwellings they left behind.[163] Some had, perhaps, inhabited airy houses of sandstone and Provençal tile—which became, of course, all the more widespread with the growth of migration, and the wealth it brought back. But well into the twentieth century in some places, home remained for many a construct of rough-hewn stone, whose central—or only—room served at once as 'storeroom, workshop, [and] stable'. Tools and food reserves crowded its floor, and furnishings remained sparse and Spartan—a few cushions and rugs, and a heavy wooden chest.[164]

I am not suggesting, of course, that migrants preserved these conditions in Africa out of any residual affection; rather their choice, if they had any, was one born of exigency and pragmatism, a decision to invest what few resources they had into their businesses. Enduring such hardship remained an obligatory stop on the way to the prosperity they had pursued all the way to Africa—though whether they ever found it is, of course, another question. It came, in time, to be seen as a rite of passage—a mark of achievement migrants reminisced about into old age, telling their children of their difficulties. Thus, Tamir Fakhri remembered that his father had told him of 'his beginnings' in Dakar, 'where he had a small place where he traded and slept. A small shop or a small shack ... A shack, that's the word, in which he lived and worked,' and which he would leave only to travel to a market on the outskirts of the city; there, he would lay out his wares on a table, 'under which he would sleep' at night.[165] Well into the interwar period, new arrivals, impecunious drifters or those serving their stint 'in the interior' had to make do with a 'hut of wood or reeds'; their shop doubled up as a home, and their counter was 'transformed into a table at meal times and a bed when it came to sleep'.[166] But such conditions were, as I have suggested, often nothing new for these traders; on the contrary, there was a certain continuity to their experiences. They were not living in diminished circumstances. Rather, their knowledge of austerity in the Eastern Mediterranean helped to make the hardships of African life more palatable.

Indeed, the memories of Mount Lebanon and Jabal 'Amil allowed them to accept such conditions in another way. As Kamil Muruwwah pointed out, 'the home of the migrant' was often just that: 'the home of a migrant, of a man who had come to gather up wealth and return to his homeland, and not to settle in a strange land forever'; it was 'natural', therefore, that it should be a 'small, temporary home, furnished and arranged' in a makepiece way. On welcoming Muruwwah, that distinguished visitor from Lebanon, into their dwellings, migrants often apologised for their size, by exclaiming: 'I don't want to expand here in the hope of expanding in the homeland.'[167] Migrants, then, played for time and held out, made do and put up with what they had, while they waited for return.

But as the years passed and they remained in Africa, many allowed themselves a growing measure of comfort, spending some of the money they had accumulated on more capacious, comfortable dwellings. Even before 1914, a few in Guinea, Senegal and Sierra Leone had begun to 'move out' of their poky premises 'to a two-storied building and occupy the top floor as living quarters'.[168] This trend continued apace into the interwar years, as migrants put aside a little capital and built up a family. Indeed, the living conditions of migrants reflected both the vast disparities of wealth within their ranks and the growing number of traders of the middling sort. While one came across dwellings which 'range[d] from wretched huts to beautiful houses and elegant villas', most had come by these years to inhabit 'moderate' or modest homes—*manazil mu'tadila*, as Muruwwah put it. Often, this meant little more than a 'room or two behind or above the shop, or not far from it', which served as living quarters.[169] Thus, even as some were able to offer themselves a little more space or to accommodate a family and the expectations of comfort and domesticity that came with it, the 'shop and the dwelling' often remained conjoined.[170] This was especially true in the 'small towns' of the 'hinterland', where 'the shop was a single building, with one side giving onto the street for buying and selling, and another interior side for sleep and living'.[171] There was no true separation between the public world of work, and the private realm of the home. Rather, the two were intimately connected, overlapping and eliding any distinction between trade and family life.

What is more, the shop long remained a hub of male sociability, a place in which gatherings both pious and profane could be held. John Michael Blell remembered that in his youth men would call upon each other both in the daytime, when they would talk business over a cup of Arabic coffee, and for long evenings of poker and backgammon in backrooms filled with the smoke of rizla roll-ups.[172] Yusuf 'Ayyad, too, remembered that 'each morning, when I was small, the Lebanese men would gather in my father's shop. There was a whole ceremonial to it. They would have their coffee and talk, of their worries and hopes, of their fantasies, of their dreams.'[173] Shi'a migrants also used their shops for rather more chaste purposes in the interwar years. The establishment of Muhammad Taha and Haidar Shams on Avenue Ponty, and those of Mustafa 'Ayyad, 'Ali As'ad, 'Ali Basum, Husain Hajj 'Ali and Hasan Zahir on Avenue Gambetta served, by the early 1930s, as venues for 'meetings, which last long into the night, of some ten to twenty people'. These congregations were, it would seem, 'chiefly of a religious character', occasions for prayer and exegesis, for 'reading the Qur'an and other Arabic works' and—perhaps, as we shall see—for talk of politics.[174] The decision of these men to convert their premises into *ad hoc* gathering places was not simply born of the efforts of the colonial administration to prevent these migrants praying together with Muslim *indigènes*.[175] Rather, their conspicuous absence from the mosques of Dakar might also be explained by their disdain for the Africans who frequented them and their reluctance to pray in these Sunni places of worship. Furthermore, it can also be put down to their longstanding insistence on praying in public 'only if one of their *mujtahidin*', or religious authorities, 'is present',[176] and their belief that Friday prayers were at best unnecessary, and at worst sacrilegious, in the absence of the occulted *imam*.[177] Moreover, several centuries of rural life had led many to deem it permissible to 'collect together' their prayers, stringing them together at the end of the working day.[178] These convictions meant that the religious observances of 'Amili Shi'a were perforce 'less visible' than those of their Sunni counterparts, and 'often circumscribed to the domestic sphere'.[179] The shop became for Eastern Mediterranean men a space in which could be carried on the old patterns of social and ritual life—a place in which both Christians and Muslims could hold the *subhiyyat*, or morning gatherings, and where the latter could convene *majalis*, or religious sittings.

Male sociability also found other expressions. Farid Anthony recorded his father's memories of his early days in the Sierra Leone Protectorate, before 1914, when men broke the monotony of trading life with 'visits to each other's homes' during which they played cards, drank 'their inevitable whisky or brandy and sometimes [sang] Arabic songs, when the mood so took them'.[180] 'Abdallah Hushaimah, meanwhile, found the 'quiet and silence of the night' ruptured in Dakar by the songs which rang out of migrants' homes and shops, 'the refrains of … fatigue, and the *mawali* that stirred up secret sorrows, and brought memories to the sleeper'.[181] So strong were such predilections for whiling away the evening hours in talk and play, song and drink that some attempted—apparently with success—to turn them to profit. Najib Abi 'Akar, after fleeing Dakar—and the second of his bankruptcies—for Guinea in 1907, ended up in Sougueta where 'instead of trading, he spent his time gambling; drawing all his kind to his establishment, which remained open to them day and night, he transformed it into a veritable gambling den'.[182]

Moreover, men and boys came to venture out on 'the occasional hunting trip',[183] like that 'Abdallah Hushaimah was taken on in the bush surrounding Kaolack, recounting a tale of idealised homosocial companionship: 'five men in a car, their hearts open to the light of the dawn … and the breath of the breeze, and their breasts filled with all the strength and energy and hope of youth'. This was a day marked with the spirit of 'friendship', and interspersed with 'the shot of a rifle now and then', and the playful banter that accompanied hunting.[184] These were apt expressions of the bluff, calloused masculinity Eastern Mediterranean migrants came to develop—'self-made men' who spoke proudly of the hardships they had enduring, and crafting myths of heroic commercial endeavour. But they also hinted at the fast friendships forged in diaspora. As Tamir Fakhri put it: 'when I speak about Papa, I can't speak without thinking of the others, because when he talked, he always talked about a sort of group that was already there [in Côte d'Ivoire]. They had the same life. They all did the same thing. They were all in commerce. They formed a sort of little fraternity because they were all foreigners, and they all hailed from the same country.'[185] Trade, then, helped not just to define the contours of migrant community, but also to make and mark the friendships that ran through it. While commerce was founded on kin and companionship, companionship could also be born of commerce.

Women, for their part, were closed off from such activities, carrying on their talk in the sanctum of the living quarters: 'looking after the house and the shop, teaching their daughters domestic duties … telling the children about Lebanon and their family tree, and, of course … gossiping', they were assigned—at least in discourse—an essentially reproductive role.[186] On the one hand, they were to make children and raise them; on the other, they were to foster in them a sense of the Eastern Mediterranean homes they had never known, manufacturing memories that might make these boys and girls born in diaspora belong. But this gendered distribution of space and duties was no hangover of what life might have been like in Mount Lebanon or Jabal 'Amil for those early arrivals who came in the late 1890s and early 1900s, an old habit that distance froze in place by movement. Daily life was, for those without the means to build a more sophisticated dwelling, a mixed affair, in which all—men, women, children—jumbled and jostled together. Rather, the vision of coy female domesticity Blell depicted was the product of the relative affluence of the interwar years, which allowed some migrants to refurbish their living spaces, and which reshuffled their expectations of gender.

These were apparent in the admonitions of visiting travellers like Kamil Muruwwah. While he warned that women could sometimes be ruinous, spending all their husbands' earnings in lavish outlays upon the home, he insisted that 'a woman is essential for the migrant in Africa, if he is able to provide for her expenditures, for he needs someone to care for him and keep his home tidy, to prepare his food and provide distraction upon his weary return from work'. Here again, the discourses of race and class flowed into one another. Not only, Muruwwah insisted, could 'one … not trust the black' to fulfil such domestic tasks. Furthermore, Lebanese women policed the bounds of migrant society, and helped those who had strayed to reintegrate the fold. While it was permissible for *shabab*, 'young men' who could not marry for 'material reasons', to 'frequent black women', rather less acceptable, in Muruwwah's eyes, was long-term concubinage, and the birth of children from these mixed unions.[187] Here, as in other instances, one finds the writings of these Lebanese journalists and men of letters haunted by the spectres of colonial discourse, with its enduring normative concern for the disruptive effects of sexual unions across the seemingly clear lines of race. But just as the presence of women from home compelled Eastern Mediterranean men to sever awkward somatic ties to the Africans among whom they lived, it allowed these migrants to stake a claim to whiteness in other ways. In July 1933 appeared notice in *Ifriqiya al-Tijariyya* of a 'children's [beauty] contest', organised by the Frenchwomen of Dakar in the city's grand Chamber of Commerce. Alongside photographs of Lebanese women in their best dresses and elegant hats posing with their white-gloved children, the article reported with pride that Emile Sallum and Madeleine Shallah had both won prizes in the competition.[188] In this case, it was both about taking part and winning: the participation of these Lebanese women and their children signalled the aspirations of the people of the Eastern Mediterranean to take their place in colonial society, and to mark their ascent over the Frenchmen of AOF. But this is telling in other ways besides, showing the ways in which the women of the community—strenuously excluded, as we shall see, from political activity—were allowed into the public sphere of associational life only as paragons of domestic duty and achievement.

But there remained a sharp disjuncture between these discourses of domesticity and the lives of many women in AOF. For the latter, of course, did far more than simply clean the shop or busy themselves with 'cooking and sewing'—though these were, no doubt, part of their obligations. They also engaged in the running of the shop alongside their men—and continued to do so into the 1950s and 1960s. Far from being secluded in the private sphere as homemakers, they found their tasks doubled up. As Umm Muhammad remembered, she would 'take her child in its buggy to the shop', in the morning, 'leaving the boy instructions for the house', 'and help my husband' until lunchtime, 'when we would come back upstairs and I would prepare the meal, and we would eat'. Though women like this clearly did not 'do everything', receiving assistance from domestic workers, they were at once house-keepers and shopkeepers, playing an active part in the commercial life of their families.[189] This, too, in its own way reflected the changes wrought in the Eastern Mediterranean by the tilt of working economies towards commodity production. Just as the silk boom had drawn the women and young girls who worked in the weaving workshops of the mountain into the cash economy,[190] the tobacco production of Jabal 'Amil increasingly relied on the female labour of the workshops.[191] But the place of women in working life had become, perhaps, harder to admit for migrants who increasingly strove for the comforts of middle-class life.

However, these readjustments also had their effects upon men. While they undoubtedly retained greater control over their leisure time, their own social habits underwent a shift as they sought to tie themselves into family life, and live according to new ideals of domesticity and loving companionship. Sunday afternoons, Blell remembered, were a 'special' occasion, when the 'whole family went out together', the 'fathers, mothers, and kids, all in their Sunday best' going for walks along the Government wharf at Freetown, idling up and down the jetties. These were the familiar lineaments of middle-class domesticity, man and woman giving time together to the private realm of the couple and the family.

By the Second World War, the Eastern Mediterranean migrants of AOF, much like those of neighbouring Sierra Leone, spoke in the registers of middle-class respectability—of family life and domesticity, of charity and civility and petty prejudices. But here confessional differences crept in. While Shi'a migrants sought to mark their own ascendance within 'Amili society by sending their children to schools like the

'Amiliyya in Beirut, and to engage in the improvement of their community through the educational endeavours that men like Hudruj placed such emphasis upon, the Christian migrants of AOF spoke these languages of class with an increasingly French lilt. They looked, on the one hand, to the *métropole*, whose ways of life were far richer and sturdier in their eyes than those of the colony. French fashions were increasingly sought after in the interwar years, with traders like Antoine Jummayil proudly advertising his 'modern' 'haberdashery, hosiery, and lingerie' shop in Abidjan, which sold all the newest 'European' trends.[192] On the other hand, their engagement with 'the idiom of French cultural practice' was refracted through the prism of the Eastern Mediterranean's own entanglement with French culture.[193] Though many in AOF wished their children to have a French education, they wanted them to receive it in Lebanon. This was driven not only by a diasporic longing for home, but also by the perceived superiority of these establishments, and a desire for their children to acquire at once a sense of life in Lebanon and an acquaintance with French culture. And if they called their children Albert, Antoine, Michel, Hélène and Latifa, as Faris al-Miyya did, or Alfred, Adèle, Emilia and Joseph, as Shehadi Ghubayin chose to, it was only to keep up with the fashions of the Eastern Mediterranean, and to mark their accession to its Francophone middle classes while—at the same time—passing down the names of their fathers and mothers.[194]

However, theirs was a sense of modernity premised as much upon material goods as upon casts of mind. It shouldn't be forgotten that these men and women were also traders and wholesale merchants, shopkeepers and produce brokers. They inhabited a world of goods, in which they were constantly surrounded by commodities and confronted with the consuming desires of others. This, I think, gave their lives a particular materiality. Indeed, the transition from seller to consumer was often a seamless one—as Farid Anthony remembered it, if his parents 'needed something for the house which was used quite often they would buy it in quantities so they got it slightly cheaper, and would then sell from it whilst they were using that commodity'.[195] But their thirst for goods was also born of the particular conditions of their lives. These were men and women who, for the most part, had worked towards their prosperity—who had undertaken migration in search of social mobility. They remained, then, both acutely aware of the extent to which their comforts remained contingent upon continued profit, and forever keen to exhibit the gains they had made.

This was evident in their outward appearances. Kamil Muruwwah bemoaned in the late 1930s the tendency of the Shiʻa women of Dakar to wear the veil. But this, he noted, was no simple holdover of the traditions of the homeland: while those who already wore the *hijab* kept it in their travels, the 'village girls who travelled here put on the veil on their arrival'. While Muruwwah regarded this as a retrograde move, a 'narrowing' of feminine options, it seems that for these women and their husbands, this sartorial gesture was a sign of aspiration and respectability which marked their arrival in the *mahjar*, and the hopes of social ascendancy which came with it. Moreover, veiling was by no means the norm elsewhere—the Gold Coast and Sierra

Leone, 'our migrants had adapted with much wisdom to their surroundings', adopting modes of appearance which were at once less conspicuous and more in keeping with their desire for a way of life which transcended the confines of colonial society.[196] For many, this meant 'excellent dresses and European shoes of the latest fashion', like those advertised by Marcelle Zayyat[197] or the 'best' and 'most recent' 'Parisian fashions', which the dressmaker Liza Mukarzil copied in her shop at 57, Rue Vincens.[198] The stress here was both on the novelty of these wares, on the constant shifting patterns and trends of modernity, and on their foreign nature, their origins in fashionable Europe.

These inclinations were also visible in the appearance of men. Muruwwah noted with distaste the lack of concern of some for their 'clothes and cleanliness'; this, he noted 'with regret', was not 'confined to the poor, for some rich' migrants were just as dirty and dishevelled, to the scorn of Frenchmen and Africans alike. For Muruwwah, the reform of Eastern Mediterrean migrant society began from the outside in, with the eradication of such unkempt appearances and the adoption of the sartorial codes of middle-class respectability.[199] Many migrants would have agreed. The photographs that adorn the journalist Michel Hayik's account of his travels through Africa in the 1930s provide an unexpected visual archive of their sartorial inclinations. The short-sleeved, broad-collared shirts slightly open to the chest, the espadrilles and wide khakis they wore on casual occasions, the white summer suits they put on for more formal affairs and the neat partings into which they forced their hair, slicked and swept to the side with pomade—these were all markers of middle-class comfort, of a certain bourgeois ease attained through migration. But there is something else going on here. Looking through these images, one gets little sense of the places in which they were taken. This, I think, is their point—that they could have been taken anywhere in the world on a sunny day, in Beirut or Marseille, São Paulo or Dakar. They are records at once of the globalisation of vestimentary norms and forms, and of the desire of Eastern Mediterranean migrants to AOF to elide the particularities of their existence, to live lives shorn of context.

By the 1940s, some in Senegal had long since acquired American cars, fridges and transistors, goods which served as 'proof of their comfort' and allowed them to live *à l'européenne*.[200] Indeed, in 1918 Governor-General Angoulvant had already reported with distaste that the wealthy Lebanese traders of Guinea had purchased 'luxury cabs, and even automobiles'.[201] These were apt signifiers of the pleasures spatial and social mobility had afforded them. And, moreover, they signalled the integration of West Africa, and its Lebanese migrant communities, into a wider world of goods. This is apparent from the advertisements that appeared in in the early 1930s in *Ifriqiya al-Tijariyya* for Chrysler and Chevrolet cars and trucks. The latter vaunted, in utilitarian fashion, the suitability of Chevrolet lorries for 'hot regions and sandy soil'. However, 'Abbud Nasrallah, the Lebanese agent for Chrysler in AOF, described his products as 'the most splendid, beautiful, and sturdiest of cars'—epithets born out by the image which accompanied this copy, of a large, ostentatious vehicle parked before the Moorish gates to a verdant park. Its message was clear: acquiring a Chrysler signalled entry to an exclusive world of material joys.[202] Imported from beyond the confines of the Federation, these accoutrements symbolised the capacity of Eastern Mediterranean migrants to transcend its petty conditions of life, and to outdo in every sense their competitors, by obtaining a 'comfort many of the Federation's Frenchmen are far from knowing'.[203] These men and women sought to move at the pace of life in France and Lebanon, those distant metropoles to which they constantly looked, and which witnessed in the years after 1945 the 'almost cargo-cult-like, sudden descent of large appliances' into their kitchens, and the 'abrupt' appearance of new cars in their streets.[204] In some ways, they even sought to outstrip and outdo these distant poles of attraction. Finding sources of material supplies scattered through the world, they were bent upon showing just how far migration could take one. Already, in the late 1930s, 'one could see no difference whatsoever between the dwellings of our brothers in Dakar and Ziguinchor, and homes in other developed towns' across the world. For there was 'electricity, and running water, and electric fans, and all the comforts' one could wish for.[205] This was a way of life that was, by definition, extraverted. On the one hand, it depended on imports from elsewhere, and on the travelling prescriptions of bourgeois comfort and respectability, those universal designs for life. On the other hand, it sought to erase all the niggling specificities of life in Africa, to brush away the heat and insects and diseases that had blighted migrants' early days in AOF, and to create ways of living that could unfold anywhere in the world. And yet, paradoxically, the 'voluminous radio[s]' and 'no less enormous fridge[s]' with which Eastern Mediterranean migrants adorned their homes served also as reminders of their own installation in Africa, where they made increasingly 'comfortable' homes—homes whose distinctive arrangements it would be difficult to transport.[206]

Conclusion

The Eastern Mediterranean migrants of AOF defined themselves, then, in relation to the Federation's Frenchmen and Africans. They had no choice but to do so, for they were well aware that the prosperity migration had brought them hung on the businesses they owned and maintained—that it remained contingent, in other words, on staying on in Africa. And while Africans seem to have treated these commercial interlopers with a wary indifference, and the exiguous French populations of AOF sank into bitter resentment of their competition which was marked by the tropes of the rightist politics of the *métropole*, Lebanese migrants—in turn apprehensive of these other components of colonial society, and aware of the precarious foundations of their material success—sought to defend their privileges and preserve their positions. But they did so, paradoxically, both by brokering local accommodations and by looking elsewhere for support. This constant tacking to-and-fro was reflected, too, in their constant cobbling together of material goods and ways of living, in the way they adopted and adapted commodities, everyday practices, and notions of domesticity, of race and respectability brought in equal measure from France, the Eastern

Mediterranean and other places besides, both near and far. These men and women, then, lived here, there and everywhere. Remaining on African soil but keeping an eye always turned elsewhere, their seemingly still lives were shaped out of movement.

7

THE TIES THAT BIND

DIASPORIC POLITICAL CULTURE IN AOF

We must—to misquote Prasenjit Duara—rescue the history of political culture from the region.[1] Scholars have long sought to trace the movement of political notions through the Eastern Mediterranean, examining the ways ideas were transported and transformed by journalists, clerics and administrators.[2] However, they have largely remained hidebound by regional confines, failing to consider the political thoughts of the migrants who flowed out of the ports of Beirut, Jaffa or Tripoli in their hundreds of thousands from the 1880s onwards.[3] Like those who stayed behind, migrants had political allegiances and ideas of their own, often inflected by the experiences of diasporic life. Their affinities cannot simply be laid to one side, as though extraneous to the history of a neatly defined Middle East; we must stitch them back into the 'torn fabric of [a] past' in which regional lines were not so clearly drawn.[4]

I will attempt in this chapter to reconstruct the affiliations, desires and aspirations of the Lebanese shopkeepers and traders of interwar Senegal. The archival remains of the colonial state are fragmentary and episodic in nature—briefly alighting upon an issue, or interrupting a story mid-stream, before moving on, they repeatedly leave loose ends behind. Furthermore, they appear 'incomplete' in other ways. Pieced together from the claims and counter-claims of informants, inconclusive and riddled with errors, 'gossip and fantasy', they seem fragile foundations upon which to build an account of political life.[5] French intelligence agents and police officers remained in the grip of phantasmagorical fears of anti-colonial conspiracies, grand, well-laid plans facilitated by the 'nightly passage of seditious agents masquerading as priests and holy men'.[6] These were only compounded by the difficulties they faced in eavesdropping upon the hushed exchanges of Shi'a migrants in particular—'most of whom', one colonial official bemoaned, 'have only a passing acquaintance with the French language, and refuse to give any detail relating to their religion'.[7] Moreover, these administrators' attempts to solicit assistance from the High Commission in Beirut were frustrated by both the dilatory ways of imperial administration and the reluctance of their Mandatory counterparts, eager to protect their own local prerogatives, to accede to requests from AOF for information and clarification.

Nevertheless, much can be made of the reports of police agents and informants, individual intelligence files, records of banned publications intercepted at customs and correspondence between administrators in Dakar and Beirut. We cannot regard this as an extractive enterprise, through which we might excavate fully formed narratives from the files. Rather, we should engage in detective work of our own, seeking all the while to consider the ways colonial functionaries misapprehended and scrambled the information they strove to collect. Tracing the 'lines that converge upon, and diverge from' particular figures and locales cited in the archives,[8] I will search for the clues, the 'telltale detail' that might reveal to us something of the lineaments of migrant political thought and practice.[9] Just as valuable as these scattered but dense thickets of material are, the articles which appeared in *Ifriqiya al-Tijariyya*, the only Arabic-language newspaper printed in AOF in the period, published sporadically between 1931 and 1935. Taken together, they enable us to piece together the political culture of these men—the 'discourses and symbolic practices' through which they manifested and 'sustain[ed]' their political engagements.[10] I will first examine the scattered traces of Christian political activity in AOF, before homing in on the convictions and actions of Shi'a shopkeepers and traders in 1930s Dakar. This analytical partition is not one I am comfortable with. Nevertheless, it often follows closely the contours of political community that migrants themselves traced out—sectarianism serving as a prism which coloured their understanding of the world as a set of distinct communities defined by religion, and as a gateway through which they acceded to various versions of *patria* and *polis*.[11] However, there is no denying that while their definitions of political community diverged, sometimes significantly, their practices were often largely indistinguishable. I will consider here the newspapers, journals and books migrants received and read, the views they expressed in public and private meetings, conversations, petitions and telegrams, the causes to which they contributed funds, and the relations they cultivated with political figures, writers and religious scholars elsewhere—whether in Lebanon itself or further afield still, in Iraq and Egypt, France and the United States. I hope to uncover, by doing so, the inflections commonplace political thought took in the *mahjar*.

The political thoughts of both Christian and Muslim migrants to AOF were constructs built up of many overlapping layers of allegiances. Their political sense of the world resembled multistoried edifices, through which they moved up and down as circumstances and inclination dictated.[12] They were shaped not only by a close and constant attachment to the localities and regions of their birth, and a resilient sense of the bounds of sectarian community, but also increasingly by competing narratives of the nation and a strong appreciation of the more diffuse connections forged in diaspora. Indeed, they remained dependent upon dispersed networks of political exchange; spooling out through the various nodes of the Lebanese diaspora, and the publishing centres of an increasingly prolific and interconnected transregional Arabic-speaking public sphere, these often followed—even as they sought to undercut—imperial lines of communication. For all that historians of the Eastern Mediterranean continue to focus on discourses of national belonging, the affiliations of these figures consistently shrank away from, and spilled over, the borders of the nation.

The political history of the region is still dominated by discussions of Arab nationalism, its modular declensions and particularistic counterparts.[13] The historiography of Lebanon—to cite but the most germane instance—thus remains caught up in debates on the origins, development, prominence and social bases of Arabism, Syrianism and a distinctly Lebanese nationalism, sometimes glossed over as Phoenicianism for its appeal to the ancient past.[14] This is no surprise; after all, competing conceptions of the nation continue to cast their long shadow over the region. Indeed, Lebanese historians themselves have resolutely attempted to tailor the political senses of religious scholars, lay notables, and ordinary men and women alike to their divergent narratives of national community. The Christian writers of Mount Lebanon and Beirut, on the one hand, constructed neat teleological accounts of the emergence of the Lebanese nation.[15] On the other, their peers in Jabal 'Amil like the 'alim, or religious scholar, Muhammad Jabir al-Safa, stressed the unremitting Arabism of the region's inhabitants, and their unyielding opposition to Ottoman and French imperialism. As Safa put it, the 'Amilis' commitment to the 'salvation of the Arab countries' from the 'heavy yoke' of Ottoman rule was an 'old' one; despite their small numbers, they had long 'vehemently resisted the Turks, strenuously defending their identity'. As war and the assertion of Mandatory rule took their toll, such sentiments only grew stronger: 'there was not a Syrian conference or Arab nationalist meeting held at which ['Amilis] were not present in the vanguard, protesting the situation of their … region, and demanding union with Syria'.[16] These narratives have endured, finding their way into the works of contemporary scholars like Mustafa Bazzi, and helping to buttress the new discourses of resistance which have emerged with the latter-day rise of political Shi'ism.[17] Only recently have historians like Tamara Chalabi and Max Weiss begun to revise these irredentist scripts, persuasively arguing that parts of the region's political and religious notability rapidly forged a *modus vivendi* with the newly created Lebanese state. While they accommodated the latter's still precarious presence, it acceded—at least sometimes—to their demands, and afforded the Shi'a recognition as a sect, whose members were accorded their own, officially sanctioned, institutions.[18]

This enduring concern with nationalism threatens to obscure other ideologies and forms of political expression, and to obfuscate our understanding of the political culture of the Eastern Mediterranean in the first half of the twentieth century.[19] This tendency is visible, as it is elsewhere, in recent works which have sough to broaden the cast of Middle Eastern history, incorporating peasants, ordinary city-dwellers and the like alongside the stock figures of nationalist politics—journalists and schoolteachers, clerics, clerks and lawyers, soldiers, landowners and urban notables.[20] Such efforts are laudable. For too long, these seemingly minor characters passed through scholarly accounts of political life as mere shadows, ghosts fluttering meekly in the background, or automatons moved this way and that at the bidding of great men. This tendency was only reinforced by a scholarly tendency to view society as a set of sharply demarcated strata through which political knowledge trickled down, passing from the circumscribed circles of the intellectual elite, through a 'large number of second- and third-tier writers, journalists [and] thinkers', until it finally reached a wider reading public.[21] Again, only those at the very apex of this pyramid were seen to have played any active role in this process, while those beneath them served as transmitter-receivers, who communicated ideas rather than crafting them, or as passive recipients, empty vessels into which to pour particular convictions.

However, their obstinate search for traces of nationalist sentiment has often led these scholars to focus on those instances of insurrectionary violence in which they feel they might discern the traces of distinctive subaltern political sentiment. Examining afresh the course of events like the Great Syrian Revolt of 1925–27, they hope to reveal the 'ragged' contours of a 'vital and uncompromising' 'popular consciousness'.[22] But, as Keith Watenpaugh has recently argued, this approach seems at once profoundly 'one-dimensional ... and vaguely romantic'.[23] In their attempts to trace to events like the Syrian revolt the roots of a 'shared sense of destiny',[24] a 'common' national identity capable of 'eras[ing] and subordinat[ing] the varying allegiances and motives of participants',[25] scholars threaten to enclose their subjects in an ideological straitjacket—blotting out the constellation of different 'ideologies, worldviews and textures of identity' they might have called upon, even as they invoke the variegated nature of subaltern thought.[26] This approach, then, can all too easily reduce the past to a series of momentous conflagrations, and its denizens to mere combatants and collaborators, defined only by their stances—hostile or accommodating, violent or mollifying—towards foreign encroachment upon their native lands.[27]

However, those scholars bent upon salvaging a long-neglected political consciousness, like submarine foragers rescuing encrusted fragments of the past from a sunken wreck, are not alone in attempting to make out the thoughts and sentiments of past actors from their actions alone, as in a game of historical charades. At times, of course, we have simply lacked the resources to do otherwise, remaining dependent upon the hearsay of others who watched these men and women act out their political convictions. But this approach is also born of a desire to correct and counter earlier histories of political thought in the region. While earlier scholars like H.A.R. Gibb privileged the ideas of an exiguous set of educated thinkers, and treated them as free-floating entities unmoored from their socio-economic surroundings, more recent work has sought to treat nationalism as a social phenomenon, firmly anchored in the particular context from which it emerged.[28] Such an approach has undoubtedly yielded much fine work.[29] However, in attempting to understand the appeal and spread of these ideologies, historians have often adopted a form of stern social determinism, which regards ideas as mere epiphenomena of baser material considerations.[30] What is more, some have privileged the study of social practices of distribution and consumption over that of the political talk and writing of the time, losing sight of texts in their restless search for context.

The political order of things, though, was not so simple. I will move between examining the political activities of migrants—their reading and fundraising—and scanning their political talk in speeches, conversations and telegrams. While many were in contact with Lebanese politicians and religious dignitaries, none were bound to these men by dutiful allegiance. Neither were they simply passive recipients of political ideas. Rather, migrants had their own motives for political engagement, and their own understandings of place and political community. These definitions defy easy categorisation as one type or another of nationalist allegiance, as I argue in this chapter. In its first part, I scrutinise the acclamations and editorials of the Christian traders and journalists of AOF—words which, despite their superficial stress upon ties to the homeland, also hinted at a more diffused, complex vision of diasporic political community unbound from territory. In its second part, I move on to piece together the political outlooks of Shi'a migrants in Dakar—traders and shopkeepers like Haidar Taha and 'Abd al-Hasan al-Rida, Husain 'Usairan, Muhammad Hilal and Ibrahim Tsham. Though these men were neighbours in the streets of Gambetta—the neighbourhood in which so many of the Lebanese of Dakar clustered—and often shared common origins in the towns and villages of Jabal 'Amil, they were a heterogeneous lot. Some belonged to families of standing—lines of 'ulama', or religious scholars, as in the case of al-Rida, or wealthy urban families, like 'Usairan. Others, like Taha, could claim no such antecedents and had grown prosperous in Senegal, finding in migration a means of social mobility. These differences of social position did matter, as we will see. And yet they did not prevent all from engaging, and collaborating, in political undertakings—as the case of the impecunious bookseller Ibrahim Tsham demonstrates. There was in Dakar no obvious relation between social rank and political enthusiasm. And nor was politics merely an exceptional activity, reserved for special occasions, and standing outside the realm of the everyday. On the contrary, it permeated—saturated, even—the lives of Eastern Mediterranean migrants.

I wish to draw our attention to the more prosaic ways in which the Lebanese shopkeepers, traders, and petty editorialists and committee presidents of West Africa engaged in politics, diverting us from the outbursts of insurrectionary violence on which historical writing has so often focused—those momentous events so well suited to grand narratives of the inexorable rise of nationalism. But I also want to cast a light on exceptional moments of another, more intimate, order, less often examined by scholars—moments of grief which punctuated the political lives of migrants, bringing them together to commemorate significant figures like the diasporic editorialist Na'um Mukarzil or King Faisal of Iraq. As Judith Butler has noted, though many think of grieving as an essentially private, solitary gesture—a 'depoliticizing' act if ever there was one—it is on the contrary a highly charged political performance, capable of 'furnish[ing] a sense of … community of a complex order'.[31] We might speak, then, of a necrological politics. Funeral gatherings were occasions to enforce normative injunctions of social togetherness, and to mark—and extend—the limits of political community. But they also served to stress faraway ties, finding in loss a means of invoking a sense of belonging capable of surviving the vagaries of distance.[32]

These allegiances, however, did not always conform to the neat theoretical schemes put together by scholars of 'long-distance nationalism'.[33] For the latter have tended to stress migrants' enduring attachments to an 'ethnic homeland'.[34] While these vicarious attachments might entail, to some extent, the redefinition of 'the concept of the state, so that both the nation and the authority of the government it represents extend beyond the state's territorial boundaries', political identities remain founded upon the 'concept of a territorial homeland governed by a state that represents the nation'.[35] Despite dispersion, the territorial nation-state retains for these scholars its centrality in migrants' political imaginations, a sun-like orb from which radiated the rays of belonging. But Eastern Mediterranean migrants to West Africa lived 'scattered' political 'existences'.[36] While the territories of their birth remained, for many, profoundly important, they also formulated, or adhered to, distinctly diasporic modes of belonging which treated places like New York, Paris or Cairo—those capitals of the *mahjar*—as alternate poles of political and intellectual life. As historians of science have long since understood, 'each locality has the capacity to become central, to act as the node of a circuit of information'.[37] We cannot think of the lands of migration, then, as points on a wheel whose hub is the homeland, but rather as a 'polycentric communications network'.[38] These diasporic formulations, too, disrupt and complicate our understanding of Eastern Mediterranean political culture in the first half of the twentieth century.

Webs of information, ties of loyalty

As Juan Cole has pointed out, European dominance over the 'global information ecumene'—the web of telegram cables and shipping lines which spread over the world's surface through the nineteenth century—was continually 'challenged by the ways in which peoples of the global south appropriated the new technologies for their own purposes'. Thus, by the early twentieth century, the towns of the Eastern Mediterranean were 'gathered into a web of information and intelligence' which, while by no means new, was altogether more 'lush and rapid' than its antecedents.[39] Migrants, in turn, helped to spin this web far and wide beyond the confines of the region. This much is clear from even the most cursory examination of the lives of the Lebanese men and women who settled in AOF. Those who could afford to do so travelled regularly to the Eastern Mediterranean, returning with the talk of the town on their minds, while a steady stream of new arrivals carrying messages and gossip spilled off the steamships at Dakar wharf. What is more, many used the imperial communications system linking Dakar to Beirut—among other points—to convey telegrams and letters. These were used not only to maintain intimate ties with family and friends, or to carry on the dry talk of trade, but also to keep abreast of political events and debates. Indeed, it would seem many were keen and curious consumers of daily and weekly newspapers, journals, books and pamphlets, 'receiving newspapers in large amounts from the homeland' either directly through the imperial posts, or by the intermediary of the three Arabic bookshops of Dakar.[40]

Among the documents intercepted by French customs officials was a copy of a play entitled *Batl Lubnan Yusuf Bek Karam*—or 'Yusuf Bey Karam, Hero of Lebanon'. The work of the Bait Shabab editorialist Michel Hayik, this cast Karam, the leader of a rebellion against the notables of Mount Lebanon in the 1860s, as a nationalist hero who had struggled to secure the freedom of the Lebanese people. Published in a bilingual French and Arabic edition in Beirut in 1922, it opened with a florid dedication:

> To the sons of the great Mardaites,
> To the heirs to the eternal cedars,
> To those who broke the columns with Louis IX,
> To those who reinforced the structures of the emirate of Fakhr al-Din,
> To those who strengthened the majesty of the Amir Bashir,
> To the staffholders of Yusuf Bek Karam,
> To the children of Lebanon who have strayed to the ends of the earth [*abna' lubnan al-dariyyin fi mashariq al-ard wa magharibiha*]
> For the sake of precious Lebanon, and the high cedar.[41]

In Hayik's florid words, the conventional tropes of Lebanese nationalism dovetailed with a dutiful acknowledgement of the Maronites' enduring friendship with France—a strain of loyalism common among some partisans of Greater Lebanon in the early years of the Mandate. Into the genealogy of the Lebanese nation, whose unbroken history stretched from the late antique Mardaites—purported forebears of the Maronites—to the courtly circles of Fakhr al-Din al-Ma'ni and Bashir al-Shihab, whose periods of dominance over the Lebanese mountain were treated by nationalist historiographers and hagiographers as laying the foundations of a modern, independent state, Hayik wove an evocation of the Crusade of Saint Louis. France, this implied, had long been part of the history of Lebanon, and Lebanon part of that of France.

Rather less accommodating to this linear narrative of the nation were Lebanon's migrants, whose wrenching decision to leave the comforts of the homeland Hayik struggled to incorporate into his script. Hayik was all too aware of the importance of migrants to the nation-state he was so eager to shepherd into being. Still based in his native town of Bait Shabab, from whence he edited his newspaper *al-ʿAlam*—'the Flag'—he could hardly fail to appreciate the role migration had played in reshaping the social landscape of the Lebanese mountain. Indeed, diaspora remained important to his own personal and professional life. In the late 1930s, he embarked on a journey through the Lebanese communities of Africa, which took him as far as South Africa. Strewn with photographs of the author alongside local Lebanese notables and colonial officials, his account of his travels was clearly aimed at a migrant readership; its chapter headings usefully translated into French and English, it came with an appendix containing articles from the colonial press detailing his progress for those unable to wade through his prolix Arabic. By the time this account was published in the early 1950s, Hayik had seemingly reconciled himself to migration. Offering his work to Lebanon's president, Kamil Sham'un, and his 'migrant brothers, who have raised high the name of Lebanon throughout the world', 'in appreciation of [their] patriotism, heroism, and efforts', he treated—perhaps unsurprisingly—those who lived in the diaspora as an integral part of the national community. However, he could not altogether disguise his disquiet at the discomfiting fact of departure, evoking in the book's opening passages the 'white handkerchiefs … heartache and tearful eyes' of 'leave-taking'.[42] For all that migrants themselves were indisputably Lebanese, migration remained a rupture, which tore the nation's children from their native soil. Hayik's writings, then, remained wedded to a conventionally ambivalent understanding of the place of migrants in the Lebanese polity—liminal figures at once within the political community of the nation, and outside its territorial bounds.

That Hayik's work should have found its way to West Africa, meanwhile, suggests that the political allegiances and interests of Lebanese migrants to AOF can easily be fitted to extant understandings of long-distance political attachments. For its lachrymose patriotism fits all too well with simple understandings of these ties as a set of bilateral relations, underwritten by the pining affection and enduring loyalty of migrants for the homeland they have left behind. This is seemingly borne out, too, by the bulk of the newspapers to which Eastern Mediterranean readers in Dakar and Bamako, Louga and Conakry subscribed. Among the most popular in the early 1920s were Beirut periodicals like *Lisan al-Hal*, *al-Hurriya*, *al-Watan* and *al-Ahwal*, and the Cairo dailies *al-Muqattam* and *al-Ahram*—both edited by émigrés from Beirut and the Lebanese mountain. It is difficult, of course, to know what drew migrants to these newspapers, or how they might have read them—what articles and sections they cast their eyes upon first, and what they made of the news and editorials they found within. Nonetheless, this reading matter seems to suggest not just a sustained interest in the details of political, economic and intellectual life in Lebanon and what was then beginning to be called *al-sharq al-adna*—the 'Near East'—but also a desire to see the wider world through Eastern Mediterranean eyes. More than simple relays to migrants' homelands, these publications also served a periscope-like function, allowing their readers to look upon the world from a 'Near Eastern' vantage point, and to forget for a moment their presence in West Africa.[43]

But the police reports and press digests of the interwar years also included local periodicals such as *Dair al-Qamar* and *Zahla al-Fatat*, *al-Wadi*—also published in Zahleh—Michel Hayik's *al-'Alam* and *Sadda al-Shimal*, which appeared in the northern locality of Zghurta.[44] Christian migrants to AOF, it is clear, retained a strong attachment to the localities of their birth. For these more or less ephemeral news-sheets served several purposes: they allowed migrants to remain plugged into the political, social and ethical debates of the Eastern Mediterranean, given a pleasingly parochial inflection by these publications' editors; to glean news of their birthplaces, their inhabitants and particular concerns; and to make a show of the local ties that served as markers of identity in diasporic communities still all too concerned with origins. This was an intensely personal mode of politics, predicated upon the ties of locality and kin that undergirded much else in migrant life, from trading arrangements to settlement patterns.

However, these men did more than simply keep an ear cocked for the political chatter of home; they also strove to shape the political future of the states coming into being in the post-Ottoman Eastern Mediterranean. The end of the First World War ushered in a period of intense activity and feverish speculation among migrants scattered across Latin America, the Caribbean, the United States and Africa, who discussed the fate of the homeland, arguing over the shape of things to come. That such dissensions did exist in AOF is apparent from the first shows of support which filtered through from West Africa for the Comité Central Syrien, created in 1918 by the Parisian journalists Shukri Ghanim and Georges Samna—themselves Uniate émigrés long since settled in the French capital, where they had embarked on successful careers as editorialists and political entrepreneurs—to combat the claims of Sharif Faisal to tutelage over Syria.[45] Though the 'Syrian colony' of AOF contributed 3,500 francs—gratefully acknowledged by Ghanim—its spokesmen asked to be excused for the small size of this sum. While these men had 'tried to establish a committee' on the model of those set up elsewhere, they explained, they 'did not succeed' because of the lack of understanding among the migrants of the colony. These men, it seems, could agree 'only on the content, but not on the form'—a hint that some favoured the creation of a state centred upon the existing administrative entity of Mount Lebanon, rather than the plans for a broader Syrian federation put forward by Ghanim and Samna. Despite—or perhaps because of—such discord, all welcomed the 'decision taken by the Allies to place us under the aegis of France', whose 'guiding' presence, steering 'our unsure steps', seemed 'absolutely necessary' both in West Africa and the Eastern Mediterranean.[46]

The telegrams of support sent from Dakar, Kouroussa or Kankan to the Comité in Paris were not simply expressions of migrants' wishes for a homeland whose political life they lived only vicariously, but also of more immediate concerns. The thanks they extended to France for the role she had played in 'the liberation of the oppressed peoples' of Syria were perhaps evidence of a genuine sense of 'profound gratitude', another manifestation of the stubborn strain of loyalism that ran through the thought of some Eastern Mediterranean Christians in the post-war period.[47] However, these men also had other motives in taking up the notion—increasingly common, as we have seen, among French writers pressing their government to establish a formal hold in the Eastern Mediterranean—that France had long been the 'Protector' of the 'Syrians, who keep in their hearts from generation to generation feelings of gratitude' towards her.[48] Such lavish shows of loyalty were, in part, an attempt to secure the abrogation of the harsh measures Governor-General Angoulvant had imposed upon the Eastern Mediterranean population of AOF. Migrants, it seems, sensed that reiterating their affection for France might just help their own cause, playing upon the fears of functionaries at the Ministry of Foreign Affairs that the Christian populations of the post-Ottoman Eastern Mediterranean were slipping beyond their reach. They were perhaps not wrong, for Angoulvant was forced only a few months later to 'let it be known', under fierce pressure from the Quai d'Orsay, 'that he is prepared to look generously upon all Syrian requests compatible with the public interest'.[49] We should always be aware of what migrants sought to achieve through their political engagements. Their acclamations and declarations were also a means of pressing claims upon the various administrations to which they appealed in these decades. It would be wrong, of course, to regard—whether in Namierite or Marxian fashion, or in the vulgar materialism of Ernest Dawn or Elie Kedourie—their political sentiments as the bitter blooms of mere self-interest. But there is no denying that such speech acts could serve more than their declared purpose, playing their part in what Lauren Benton has called a 'jurisdictional politics', through which migrants lay claim to particular rights and exemptions.[50]

Nonetheless, there can be no doubt that the dissolution of the Ottoman empire, and the prospective parcelling up of its Arab provinces, prompted very real interest among the migrants of AOF. By 1919, when prominent members of the trading communities of Thiès, Dakar and Conakry recognised Ghanim as the Syrian representative at the Peace Congress, these migrants seem to have overcome earlier cleavages.[51] They now fell in step behind Ghanim and Samna, proponents of the notion of a 'federal' Syria, stretching from 'the Taurus to the Sinai, and the Mediterranean to the Desert'.[52] Furthermore, all asked—perhaps answering in their clipped, telegraphic tones a request for a show of unity from the leaders of the Comité—that France 'be handed responsibility reconstitution integral Syria as independent federal nation'.[53] Just as striking as migrants' concern for the regions of their birth, however, is the unmistakable fact that Paris was now—if only for a brief time—the centre of their political world. Though never home to more than a smattering of Ottoman migrants, this city—by dint of its status as an imperial capital—had by the post-war years become a hub of diasporic politics. Since the early 1900s, if not earlier, its Syrian denizens had taken it upon themselves to act as intercessors for their scattered compatriots—accruing, in doing so, significant amounts of social and political capital.

It is no surprise, then, that the Christian businessmen Naja, Jabre and Rizq should have turned to Ghanim to fulfil their political wishes—nor that they should have taken up, in the process, the latter's claims to representativeness, and declared themselves to be acting on behalf of the 'Syrian colon[ies]' of Senegal and Guinea. On the one hand, this is a further reminder of their desire to claim a comfortable spot within imperial structures of rule still underwritten by sentimental registers and personal intercession. On the other, it is a sign of the growing dispersion of political attention and interest among the denizens of the early twentieth-century Eastern Mediterranean diaspora, whose political poles of attraction included not just Beirut, Damascus and Istanbul, but also Cairo and Alexandria, Paris, New York, São Paulo and Buenos Aires.[54] There are also stray traces of this scattered interest in the archives of the colonial censor's office, which kept occasional copies of newspapers like *Mir'at al-Gharb*, published in New York by Najib Diyab, and *al-Fitra*, edited by Mahmud Muhammad Sallum in Buenos Aires.[55]

This dispersion was more apparent still in the pages of *Ifriqiya al-Tijariyya*, the periodical established in Dakar by the Matni migrant Najib Mukarzil in 1931. At first glance, this had all the hallmarks of a migrant news-sheet, bound by bilateral ties to the homeland. The Lebanese nation-state—treated as a stable, clearly defined territorial unit—seemed to act as the centre of its political universe. While the newspaper never abandoned the ambition on display in its opening issue, with its efforts to report on events both 'local'—or colonial—and 'global', carrying 'general telegrams', or agency despatches, showcasing its instantaneous connection to a world of news, it also tacked rather closer to home.[56] Throughout its short life, it published regular updates on the 'news of the homeland'—*anba' al-watan*. At first concentrating exclusively on Greater Lebanon under the editorship of the convinced Lebanese nationalist Mukarzil, it expanded its ambit somewhat after its takeover by Shukri Daghir and Ibrahim Tsham, who pined for the creation of an extensive Syrian polity. Alongside the latest 'airmail from Lebanon and Syria' were 'letters' from Lebanon and Palestine, juxtaposed to suggest the continuing interconnection of these political spaces, which Tsham, paying little heed to the borders between them, treated as a single concern. The political geography of the Eastern Mediterranean was replicated, under Tsham's direction, on the page.[57] But if this was an effort to participate in the homogeneous, empty time of the nation—to cite Walter Benjamin's oft-quoted formulation—then it was one doomed to fail.[58] Those living in the *mahjar* were quite literally fated to read yesterday's news, always running to keep track of the homeland and lagging one step behind.

However, another conception of political belonging and diasporic existence also emerges from a reading of *Ifriqiya al-Tijariyya*. The complexities of this vision were apparent in a November 1931 article, with the pregnant title 'the potential of migrants'. Detailing the contribution by the 'Lebanese migrant' Elias al-'Abd, the 'owner of large marble factories in Mexico', of a 'sizeable amount' to the striking tramway workers of Beirut, the newspaper noted the 'significant number of our migrants who wish to present gifts to the homeland which might benefit its backward elements [*al-mutakhalifin fiha*]', before bemoaning the 'absence' of 'a body supervising the distribution of these contributions'.[59] This language was telling. There was, on the face of it, seemingly little by which to distinguish Mukarzil's words from those of contemporaries like Hayik. The new Lebanese nation-state itself remained a stable territorial entity, whose confines—though contested by some—were clear. The diaspora, meanwhile, was its natural pendant. The Lebanese political community, then, was a composite one, made up on the one hand of 'residents'—*al-muqimin*—and on the other of 'migrants'—*al-muhajirin*.[60] The latter remained integral constituents of this community; they were 'Lebanese', no matter in which 'place' they lived. In this vision, diaspora and homeland came to resemble the panels of a diptych: while the two were quite distinct, neither could stand entirely alone, devoid of its complement.

But Mukarzil's choice of words to describe his fellow migrants—those 'people of potential'—is revealing. In his rendering, the relationship between homeland and diaspora—between the *watan* and the *mahjar*—was reversed. Migrants, far from attempting to hold on to the ways of home, to keep up and seek guidance, became the agents of its development, capable of bringing it up from backwardness by contributing to 'national education' and the attendant 'ethical, moral and literary projects' which the inhabitants of Lebanon itself undertook. Al-'Abd was exemplary in this respect, too, having recently donated two paintings to Beirut's municipality, to be hung in Martyrs' Square, in the centre of the city. One, significantly, was of the Eiffel Tower—that symbol of steely, unalloyed, modernity.[61]

This stance could sometimes lead to stark criticism of the deleterious habits of the Lebanese state. The latter, Mukarzil bemoaned in June 1931, had found only 'slow, unproductive' remedies to the 'economic crisis' blighting the country. There was 'no denying that the government was working to improve the state of agriculture and to increase the extent of cultivable lands and the yield of olives and mulberries', those mainstays of the Lebanese rural economy. Its policies, however, had failed to 'free' Lebanon from its 'dearth', eliciting only 'cries of complaint from every corner'. To make matters worse, its 'budget' was far too 'onerous' for a 'small, poor country' like Lebanon, whose state was unjustifiably swollen by 'needless [public] employees and offices'. 'Patriotic circles' could see no other solution than the 'pruning' of this overgrown civil service and the 'lightening of taxes'. For the country could 'hope for nothing from its migrants'; dissatisfied with the lacklustre 'hospitality' of their compatriots, they would no longer 'attempt to assist their kin, who had once turned to them in the face of similar adversity'. This was a stinging rebuke to the land Mukarzil and his diasporic readership had left behind: observing from afar the economic stasis and political incompetence afflicting Lebanon, they now threatened to turn their backs upon a country to which they could no longer trust their newfound 'wealth'.[62] While Beirut-based peers like Kamil Muruwwah described migration as a 'malady', which had severed a 'precious part' of the body politics from its territorial torso,[63] Mukarzil regarded diaspora as the remedy to Lebanon's ills—if one that a churlish patient, stuck in its bad ways, was unlikely to accept. If the homeland was a centre, then it was a distinctly hollow one—a wayward relative one still cared for, but whose misdemeanours had finally eroded all reserves of goodwill and patience.

It is no surprise, then, that Mukarzil's editorial gaze, rather than lingering longingly over Lebanon, consistently looked further afield. Read against his broader diasporic commitments, his mention of the continuing commitments of the Mexico-based 'Abd was not so much a report of happenings in the homeland as an attempt to remind his readers of the scattered diasporic polity of which they were constituents. Indeed, this desire to broaden the political and ethical horizons of his subscribers was palpable throughout the newspaper's short life. Among its most regular features were the 'letters from the Egyptian land' of the radical intellectual and reformer Felix Faris, who expounded in his columns upon the 'virtue of society', setting out normative conceptions of the well-led life which he hoped would bring about the *nahda*, or 'awakening' of his native society.[64] There is no mistaking the pedagogical intent undergirding Mukarzil's editorial choices. Nor is there any possibility of glossing over the hierarchy of locales to which he so clearly subscribed. According pride of place to Faris' attempts to inculcate moral precepts in his scattered readership, Mukarzil regarded Egypt as a central locus of Arabic learning, from which the Lebanese of West Africa, isolated on Atlantic shores, might glean instruction and guidance.

The United States, too, was elevated, like Paris and Cairo, to the status of a focal place, upon which diasporic attention should be trained. Mukarzil thus devoted the front page of several issues to the republication of a speech given by his namesake Na'um Mukarzil to the 'second Lebanese festival' held in Bridgeport, Connecticut in July 1931. Such attention is understandable. Na'um Mukarzil was perhaps the best known of the diasporic editorialists who had risen to prominence in the Eastern Mediterranean communities of the Americas in the early twentieth century. The editor of *al-Huda*, which he had founded in New York in 1902, he had also established in the years after the Young Turk revolution of July 1908 the Jam'iyya al-Nahda al-Lubnaniyya, or 'Lebanese awakening society'. He had used this association to protect the position of Lebanese migrants in the United States, and to press, first for reform of the statute of the autonomous Ottoman province of Mount Lebanon, then for the establishment of an independent Lebanese state in the wake of the First World War.

However, it was not simply Mukarzil's renown or political prestige that gave his words such currency. Rather, they carried a clear ethical charge which—Najib Mukarzil perhaps hoped—might course through the ranks of migrant society in West Africa, invigorating and reforming its ways. For this speech laid the stress upon the 'ethics', 'love and compassion' that should underpin migrants' relations with each other. Such 'compassion', Mukarzil insisted, was 'amongst the most blessed rights of reasoning beings'; upon it rested 'the glory of religion and majesty of the *patria*, the honour of the individual, virtue of man, and grace of woman'. A 'life without love', he continued, 'is like a loaf of dry bread amongst the most succulent of dishes'.[65] This message of mutuality and affection, with its roots in a distinctly Christian language of charity and harmony, resonated all too well with the concerns of migrants in West Africa, increasingly preoccupied with healing the bitter political and personal rifts which ripped through their ranks in the 1930s.

Najib Mukarzil's undertaking, it is clear, was firmly diasporic. It was so not just because of its seemingly excentric location, an offshore outpost lying beyond Lebanese territories, but also because of its conception of political belonging. Even as it was an essentially derivative project, which looked elsewhere for guidance, it took its cues not from Lebanon itself, but from the *mahjar* and its dispersed denizens, borrowing words and precepts from the United States or Egypt. This sense of the lands of migration as a distinct political and social space, with a life of its own which was as significant as that of the territorial home state—if not more so—was also apparent in Faris' own writings, such as the 'greeting' he extended to *Ifriqiya al-Tijariyya*, that 'new publication, a brilliant lighthouse to stand alongside the many built by our leading writers in the tumultuous lands of migration, through which our striving, energetic people has spread'. This passage, with its possessive pronouns and patriotic pride, was inflected with a deep sense of political community: the Lebanese,

whether in Egypt, West Africa or, indeed, Lebanon itself, belonged to the same col-
lectivity. However, this was not a single mass, a body politic lying comfortably upon
the well-made bed of the nation-state. Rather, it was a more diffuse, amorphous
entity, whose various constituents were dispersed through the diaspora—that map of
scattered but luminescent points Faris evoked so vividly. This was a vision of the
patria uncoupled from territory; political cohesion and community, in this understanding, were not contingent upon proximity, but upon the fellow feelings, 'economic, moral', and political, holding together this community.[66] The seemingly
natural pairing of land and people Michel Foucault once identified as the defining
feature of modern 'reason of state' fell apart in such passages.[67] Political community
did not map onto a single, self-contained space so much as unspool through the
world, a sturdy yarn stretched out through the networks and nodes of diaspora.[68]

If I have leant to such an extent on the editorial policies and concerns of *Ifriqiya
al-Tijariyya*, it is in part because the words of Mukarzil and his faraway peers allow
us to gain a sense of the diasporic political imaginaries still current among Christian
migrants in the interwar years. But it is also because there are so very few traces of
the political thoughts and sentiments of Maronite, Greek Catholic or Greek Orthodox
migrants in the archives of the French colonial state. This relative dearth of material
is—it is clear—a consequence of the stark dichotomies drawn by administrators, who
repeatedly distinguished between restive Muslim migrants, their heads filled with
subversive plots and schemes, and their essentially docile, Francophile Christian
counterparts. The latter, who repeatedly reiterated their sympathy for France's imperial undertakings in the Middle East and West Africa, seemingly posed no threat to
the stability of AOF. Accordingly, administrators rarely took pains to record their
affinities. By contrast, police officers and intelligence agents anxiously attempted to
keep tabs upon the activities of Shi'a migrants, beset by worries that these men might
disseminate ideas of insurrection among the *indigènes* of Senegal.

Echoes and fears

French scholars and functionaries had by the 1920s come to regard the faith pro-
fessed by their Senegalese subjects as a syncretic assemblage of animist beliefs and
garbled Islamic practices. Heterodox and parochial, this *Islam noir* bore but little
resemblance, in the eyes of administrators, to the legalistic piety of Middle Eastern
Muslims.[69] However, repeated insistences that West Africans remained—to paraphrase Jules Brévié, the governor-general of AOF in the early 1930s—essentially
impermeable to thoroughgoing conversion could not dispel deep-seated fears of the
political potential of Islam, with its capacity for mobilising networks cutting across
borders and providing a ready language of insurrection. Thus, the ethnographer and
erstwhile administrator Maurice Delafosse insisted in 1924 that AOF had become
the terrain of a challenge by the 'Arab civilisation' to France 'for moral conquest of
some twelve million' Africans. This confrontation, he argued, was the unavoidable
consequence of the 'new situation throughout the Muslim world created as a result

of European, but above all English policy in the Orient which has encouraged amongst Mahometans of all races and nationalities a complex sentiment in which nationalism … predominates over the purely religious idea'.[70] Administrators remained profoundly wary throughout the interwar period of the apparent threat to the security and stability of France's West African possessions posed by pan-Islamism—that powerful ferment, as they saw it, of ideology and religion with solid linkages to anti-colonial movements, Bolshevism and Fascism.[71]

Indeed, fears that Eastern Mediterranean migrants might indoctrinate colonial subjects into the inflammatory creed of pan-Islam, and school them in the arts of conspiracy and insurrection, surfaced at regular intervals in these years. As early as July 1922, Governor-General Carde urged territorial lieutenant-governors to maintain a 'discreet but vigilant' watch over the Eastern Mediterranean populations of their colonies. This surveillance was justified, he stressed, by reports that the 'Syrian nationalist movement'—with its close associations to 'Pan-Islamism' and 'revolutionary Bolshevik propaganda'—was 'growing stronger and more organised'.[72] In 1933, Brévié noted in a stern letter to the administrator of Dakar the dangerous precedent set by a meeting held in October of that year to mark the end of mourning for King Faisal of Iraq. Such an event, he remarked, was nothing less than the first 'manifestation of pan-Arabist sentiment, the tinder of pan-Islamism' to have taken place in AOF. While confident that such dangerous notions had not yet 'reach[ed] the indigenous masses',[73] the presence of 'fifteen or so *indigènes* who applauded confidently the praise showered upon the memory of a ruler whose policies and aspirations were notably Francophobe' was enough to raise concern. Indeed, he felt that this was evidence of wider trends of profound import: 'since 1930, oriental nationalists and extremists have come to conjugate their efforts in the Islamised world so that, if we are not careful, the Near East, North Africa, and even AOF could soon be compared to a great resonance drum, which will spread the echo of each incident' occurring in these far-flung regions—news of which would travel along the 'pan-Islamic network' to which the 'caravan routes connecting the Islamic centres of West Africa' were joined. Administrators in AOF should, he counselled, remain on their guard, exercising a 'constant and skilful surveillance' whose principal concern should be 'detecting the "foreign infiltrations" capable of introducing into autochthonous circles an inclination towards insubordination'.[74]

In the name of Jabal 'Amil: education and uplift in the mahjar

Directeur-Adjoint Verges reported a rather troubling find in late June 1930. During an inspection of postal deliveries newly arrived from the Middle East, customs workers had discovered three bags containing a number of banned publications. Among these were copies of *al-'Irfan*, a Shi'a publication to which many of the 'educated *Syriens* originating in Saida and Tyre' apparently subscribed. These were addressed to six 'Amili inhabitants of Dakar—'Ali As'ad, Mustafa 'Ayyad, 'Abd al-Hasan al-Rida, Muhammad Shams al-Din, and the business associates Haidar Taha and Hasan

Shams. These two, moreover, had apparently acted as distributors and agents for this publication in Senegal, 'subscribing those among their compatriots who wished to receive it'—a suspicion seemingly confirmed by the fact they were to receive the largest consignment. Shams al-Din, meanwhile, freely distributed his copy of the journal to those who wished to look over it.[75] While we do not know how many copies of al-'Irfan were found, hidden away in postal bags, it seems likely the circle of its readership extended—as Verges had surmised—beyond these men. After all, Kamil Muruwwah identified three types of man in West Africa—one 'group' that neither subscribed to nor read Arabic newspapers, and 'cared not for the news'; another that 'subscribed to the newspapers, some satisfied to glance at them, others gleaning them passionately'; and a third 'that did not subscribe to them, but which read them nonetheless, using that method so widespread in the homeland and borrowing them'.[76]

This is not entirely unsurprising. Branding itself a 'literary and scientific monthly illustrated journal', al-'Irfan had been established in 1909 by the 'alim, or religious scholar, Shaikh Ahmad 'Arif al-Zain in the 'Amili fishing port of Saida. As its pregnant name suggested, the journal hoped to bring 'knowledge', both divine and material, to its largely Shi'a readership.[77] Driven by an omnivorous, encyclopaedic ambition typical of the publications of the period, with their devotion to the task of nahda, or awakening, it covered topics as varied as religious debate among the Shi'a mujtahidin and hujjat al-islam of Karbala, Najaf or Shiraz; racial thought and evolutionary theory; and political news of the Arab world, North America and Europe. Such was its reach and reputation among the inhabitants of Jabal 'Amil that contemporaries recall calling all publications al-'Irfan, as though the very name stood for the printed word, and the enlightenment it brought in its trail.[78] While not entirely free of hyperbole, this is telling indication of the journal's broad influence, and its renown and esteem even among those who may not have been able to read it. Supported by the wealth his family had accumulated through commerce and the acquisition of large swathes of land in Saida's hinterland, Zain maintained through the interwar years a forum in which contributors like the 'Nabatiyya three'—the 'udaba', or men of letters, Muhammad Jabir al-Safa, Ahmad al-Rida and Sulaiman al-Zahir, who all hailed from the 'Amili market-town of Nabatiyya—wrote of history and poetry, politics and folklore, science and religion. The journal, as an editorial proclaimed in 1935, remained committed to serving the 'Arab cause', and the 'people of the East in general and Muslims in particular', to diffuse 'culture ... science and learning', and to support 'literati, poets and writers'. However, it focused 'particularly on Shi'i questions', and sought to encourage the people of Jabal 'Amil to 'compete with other nations'.[79]

This agenda was an apt reflection of the outlook of Zain and the Nabatiyya three. All had supported Sharif Faisal's efforts to establish an Arab kingdom centred upon Damascus at the close of the First World War. Sulaiman Zahir had gone so far as to serve as a judge in the fledgling Sharifian administration, and continued in his propaganda efforts on its behalf despite being removed from his position by the French in February 1919. At the conference of Wadi Hujair, held on 24 April 1920 in an effort to end the *fawda wataniyya* or 'national disorder' which had reigned in Jabal 'Amil for some two years, the clerics and notables of the region agreed to pledge their allegiance to Faisal, and to support his efforts to establish an independent Syria, undivided and free of foreign occupation. However, they also, according to Rida and Zahir, agreed to seek the administrative autonomy of Jabal 'Amil within this entity—what Rida called *istiqlal dakhili*, or 'internal autonomy' or independence.[80] The support of these men for Faisal was essentially contingent upon the place of Jabal 'Amil within the polity he sought to create. Their Arabism, staunch as it was, could not supersede their profound attachment to Jabal 'Amil.

Rida, Zahir, Safa and Zain pursued this double course—committed, at once, to a broad Arabism, and to the regeneration of the people of Jabal 'Amil—for much of the interwar period. They showed, to be sure, 'unshakeable idealism' in their commitment to Syrian unity and their opposition to the French Mandate throughout these years, and did not cease demanding the attachment of Jabal 'Amil to Syria until the Franco-Lebanese treaty of 1936; they attended the unionist conferences of 1933 and 1936, and the pan-Islamic conference held in Jerusalem in 1931.[81] Furthermore, they considered themselves men of the *nahda*, committed to the project of intellectual and cultural renewal. Historians have tended to consider this term a chronological marker denoting a particular phase in Arabic thought or an ideological label attached to a particular school of thought. However, contemporaries treated it in a rather more flexible, pragmatic fashion, a convenient umbrella term, which they might pick up and use to provide cover for their own reformist undertakings. Zahir and Rida, in particular, were deeply proud of their membership of the Arab Academy established by Faisal in Damascus, for which Rida prepared an Arabic lexicon in 1930. The Nabatiyya three, then, regarded the people of Jabal 'Amil as intrinsically Arab, and their commitment to Arab unity as beyond question. The writings they published in the pages of *al-'Irfan*—reminiscences and chronicles of the Jabal, the history of its villages and the lives of its notables—served to stress '"Amili participation" in [the] predominantly Sunni narrative[s]' of Islamic history and Arab nationalism. However, they also sought to underline the distinct identity of the region—to provide its inhabitants with a history that might, as it were, tell them apart.[82] The writings of these men retained the intensity of the local, with their evocations of the low-lying hills of their native *terroir*, and of the villages, market towns and families scattered through it; they spoke to a close-knit community of readers, familiar with the patronyms of scholars and the names of hamlets and springs, hills and pilgrimage sites. They remained committed, above all, to Jabal 'Amil and its political and social reform.[83] Such concerns resonated deeply with the Shi'a shopkeepers and traders of Senegal.

Men like Haidar Taha and 'Abd al-Hasan al-Rida were no mere detached readers of *al-'Irfan*. Rather, they sought to participate in the reformist undertakings of its writers. Alongside copies of the journal, customs officials had found stub-books, envelopes and papers addressed to Rida's grocery store on Avenue de la Liberté. Rida had already come to the attention of police officers for distributing around town a 'large number' of tracts in Arabic calling for donations to an association called the Committee for Mutual Uplift. This, he insisted, would be dedicated to the 'moral uplift of the Syrian colony'—though none of the latter's members seemed to know the least thing about this organisation and its aims. Now, however, this discovery shed new light upon his activities. The funds Rida sought to raise, it transpired, were not at all for the benefit of the Shi'a of Dakar, as he himself had claimed. Rather, they were intended for a committee based in Nabatiyya, and dedicated to collecting monies for the 'Librairie de Djabal Amel', which had been established there the previous year. It had not—Verges noted—been 'possible to discover the aims pursued by the founders of this Bookshop, nor their tendencies'. However, there could be no doubt that both the clandestine publications and the paraphernalia dispatched to Rida had been 'sent in the same fashion and by the same individuals'.[84]

Verges, for all the mistakes strewn through his reports, was not wrong to stress the link between *al-'Irfan* and the 'Librairie de Djabal Amel'. This library—not a bookshop as Verges had assumed—had been set up in 1929 by Ahmad Sulaiman al-Zahir, Muhammad Haidar Taha and 'Abd al-Husain Qadih. Housed in a 'modest room, in which were placed a table, a few chairs, and an old cupboard', it offered its thirty or so members 'newspapers and magazines',[85] along with some 150 to 200 tomes—for the most part 'works of religion or moral and popular novels translated into Arabic, donated by notables of Jabal 'Amil or purchased with funds provided by donations and subscriptions'. Zahir, Taha and Qadih were all three students at the same Beirut school. Returning to Nabatiyya only for the holidays, they left the running of the library in their absence to one Ra'if al-Hurr—'a young man of their age, but of a lesser education'. Indeed, the author of this memorandum insisted, the library had all the hallmarks of a schoolboy scheme: its 'existence … scarcely noticed' even by the inhabitants of the town, it seemed to have been created only 'to serve the pecuniary interests of its founders and flatter their literary pretensions'.[86] 'The nature of the works [the library] distributed, the insignificance of its managers and its poor reach' led the secretary general of the Mandatory High Commission in Beirut, Hoppenot, to conclude that it possessed no importance whatsoever.[87]

We ourselves cannot be so sure. The library was—according to intelligence agents in both Beirut and Dakar—under the patronage of Sulaiman al-Zahir, the father of one of its founders. Moreover, it benefited from the active support of Yusuf al-Zain, who intervened to ensure it received 'official permission' at the behest of its founders, who had learned of 'rumours it held books and publications hostile to the government'.[88] As Sabrina Mervin has pointed out, French intelligence officers had little understanding of the ambitions and influence of men of letters like Zahir, whom they dismissed as mere 'unionist agitators': 'an entire side of 'Amili political life' effectively 'eluded' the Mandatory administration, caught up in its tractations with powerful landowners like Kamil al-As'ad.[89] It may be, then, that the library had rather more influence than the intelligence note dispatched by the High Commission to Dakar had presumptuously accorded it.

After all, its collection—deemed by administrators too small to be of any significance—was not particularly exiguous by the standards of Eastern Mediterranean libraries of the day. The Khalidiyya, a library of some 2,000 volumes opened in 1900 by the Khalidi family of Jerusalem for public use, was still 'exceptional in its richness and variety' some thirty years later. Outside of large cities like Beirut, Damascus or Jerusalem, small collections of manuscripts and printed matter held by religious dignitaries, local schoolteachers or learned people seem to have been the norm. Moreover, the founders of the Maktaba hoped both to expand their collection and to found an Arabic school alongside their fledgling library.[90] In doing so, they sought to follow the precedent set by Sulaiman al-Zahir and Ahmad 'Arif al-Zain in encouraging the dissemination of knowledge. Their apparent admixture of philanthropic endeavour and commercial enterprise, meanwhile, was not uncommon. The Maktabat al-Andalus, founded in Jerusalem by the journalist Fawzi Yusuf, operated as a bindery, sold stationery and books in a number of joint ventures with schools and literary clubs, and included a lending library from which members could borrow tomes for the relatively modest sum of 8 qurush a month.[91]

We cannot, then, dismiss the Maktabat Jabal 'Amil as the money-raising scheme of a few enterprising schoolboys supported by their indulgent parents. In doing so, French intelligence officers failed to appreciate the ways in which the Maktaba fitted into the broader reforming ambitions of Zahir and his circle. Though its founders deliberately shirked overtly political commitments, they remained 'driven' by both a desire to educate their countrymen and by 'religious sentiment'—whether their wish to thwart the influence of the Protestant missionaries who had established a library of their own in Nabatiyya,[92] or their desire to escape the stinging condescension of their Christian and Sunni compatriots. A year after this affair, French officers happened upon another 'appeal' doing the rounds which, they surmised, came from the same source as the tracts they had found in Rida's Dakar shop. Calling for the establishment of a 'University of Jabal 'Amil' in Nabatiyya,[93] this short missive opened in provocative fashion:

It is incontestable that the Shi'a are miserable and regarded with contempt, and all this is due only to their intellectual inferiority. The only effective remedy to this inferiority is the creation, in Jabal 'Amil, of educational establishments which would provide free instruction to all our children, regardless of their social rank or the financial situation of the pupil. This charitable undertaking will enable them to live a more stable existence, and will provide them with the means to claim their rights before the other sects.

Only one association was in a position to carry out this onerous work: the 'Shi'a society of Jabal 'Amil'. Possessing a starting capital of at least '10,000 gold louis', it already had two locales capable of hosting 1,600 pupils, whose direction it would entrust to the 'most capable men of the sect'. In embarking upon this enterprise, the society's organisers had entrusted themselves 'first to the goodness of God, and then to you'—the tract's readers in the *mahjar*. The society could simply not continue its work without annual contributions of 1,000 pounds sterling. What was needed, then, was the support of 'energetic, devoted', and 'capable' men, willing to donate monies to the society's head, Ahmad Rida.[94]

The language of this tract was scored with paradoxes. On the one hand, it treated Jabal 'Amil as an essentially Shi'a land, and the Shi'a as irrevocably bound to Jabal 'Amil. The uplift of the community, it suggested, could only be achieved upon the soil of its home region. On the other, it turned to migrants—to those who had left the region's confines, if not their attachments, behind—for assistance in this task. Indeed, it could be read as an encomium to the enterprising ways of the latter. Far from bemoaning their departure as a breach of the organic ties between people and land, it heaped praise upon their energy and initiative; elevating them to close proximity with God, it promised them recognition in this world, undertaking to list the names of contributors as 'founders of the society' and to publish a note of 'gratitude' for their efforts in the regional press. This was an astute move, which resonated with the pride of these self-made men, at once happy with the success mobility had brought them, and eager for recognition from their fellow 'Amilis. But this, in turn, raised another contradiction. For the tract attempted to assuage donors' discomfort at the enduring hierarchies of life in Jabal 'Amil by assuring them that the schools founded would be open to children of any 'social rank'. And yet it also sought to mollify them by ensuring them access to the hallowed likes of Ahmad Rida.[95] This message, then, held up a mirror to the precarious sense of self of 'Amili migrants in West Africa, with their uneasy mix of assertiveness and uncertainty about their newly acquired status in society.

However, Rida's appeal also underscored the broader anxieties of the Shi'a community about its place in the changing political configurations of the Mandatory Eastern Mediterranean. It began by echoing longstanding evocations of the Shi'a as the *mahrumin*, or 'deprived', rendered wretched by the loss of the rightful claim to the caliphate, and bound together by their enduring grief at the deaths of Husain and his family at the Battle of Karbala, evoked each year in the ceremonies of *'ashura'*.[96] But far from treating the 'miserable' circumstances of the Shi'a of Jabal 'Amil as an immutable predicament, it considered them in historicist fashion as a condition of contemporary political and social circumstances—and ones it was therefore possible to remedy through the language and practices of progress. The 'contempt' of other 'sects', both Christian and Muslim, was no longer a transhistorical burden to be carried through the ages, but a changeable fact of social life—something the community could do something about through concerted efforts at reform. This revealed the equivocal response of Shi'a religious dignitaries like Rida to the alluring, confounding language of confession which assumed such prominence within the new Lebanese state. On the one hand, they remained resistant to such ascriptions, which could be all too easily reminiscent of Sunni heresiological literature painting the Shi'a as refractory sectaries who had departed from the true path of Islam. Underpinning such assertions of sectarian difference, they feared, were condescension and disregard on the part of Sunnis and Christians alike. This accounted, in large part, for the appeal of an Arab nationalism seemingly free of such religious markers. On the other hand, the Mandatory state's recognition of the Shi'a as a *secte* or *ta'ifa*, a religious confession, offered them a novel sense of potential. For official sanction afforded the Shi'a the means to establish in the open light of day the institutional building blocks of community, from law courts to schools. Against the narratives of obdurate resistance to the incorporation of Jabal 'Amil into Lebanon which men like Rida told, and which have been adopted by latter-day historians, we must counterpose this ambivalent acknowledgement of their place as one of the constellation of communities making up the new Lebanese polity, and of the potential as well as the pitfalls of sectarian talk. Refractoriness and accommodation, rather than remaining pitted in opposition, were bound together in a dialectical relationship. Moreover, both were ultimately subjugated to the needs of amelioration: the reform of Jabal 'Amil came first.

And, as this tract acknowledged, migrants were called upon to play an increasingly important part in this undertaking. A succession of visiting dignitaries thus descended upon West Africa from the 1930s onwards, eager to collect donations from its Eastern Mediterranean inhabitants. The first of these, of course, had been Shaikh Muhammad Muruwwah, the Shi'a *'alim* who spent some five weeks in Dakar in July and early August 1930, entrusted with collecting monies for the Maktabat Jabal 'Amil. Muruwwah carried home with him the fruits of the fundraising drive carried out by 'Abd al-Hasan al-Rida, Haidar Taha, and the latter's son Muhammad—one of the founders of the Maktaba, who collected 5,000 francs in Kaolack and its hinterland during a holiday visit to his father in June 1930.[97]

Then, in February 1936, came Muhammad 'Ali Humani. Educated, like Sulaiman al-Zahir and Ahmad Rida, at the Hamidiyya school of Nabatiyya, this poet and journalist had cut his teeth with *al-'Irfan* before setting up his own journal, *al-'Uruba*, in 1931.[98] This title referred at once to the political creed of Arabism and to a sense of belonging to an Arabic *ethnos*—his *arabité*, or 'Arab-ness', as the French would put it. There could, on the face of it, be no clearer manifestation of Humani's political stances. Indeed, he had declared in 1929 that he had 'no religion except the Arab emblem and no sect except love of the country'.[99] However, this seemingly unconditional attachment to Arabism allowed Humani, much like older figures like Rida and Zahir, to assert the political claims of the Shi'a of Jabal 'Amil, rather than to fold them into a broader political community shorn of regional and religious attachments. For Humani's espousal of *nahda* stemmed from a distinctly Shi'a sense of 'disinheritance', which had been only compounded by the feelings of 'neglect' and dislocation some had felt at the Jabal's incorporation into Greater Lebanon. As the poet 'Abd al-Husain Sadiq put it, 'one mountain [Mount Lebanon] had swallowed another [Jabal 'Amil]'. This was coupled with a deep sense of dissatisfaction as the social conditions of Jabal 'Amil itself. Humani had become associated with a group of angry young clerics—among them 'Ali al-Zain and Musa Sharara—who had established the *'Usbat al-Adab al-'Amili*, or 'Amili literary league, in the mid-1930s. Like them, he believed that literature could serve as a vehicle for opposition to both French Mandatory rule and the obscurantist *'ulama* and 'reactionary' *zu'ama'*, or feudatories, of the region.[100] Undergirding Humani's commitment to Syrian unity, then, was a staunch belief in the need for reform of 'Amili society, and the increase of its members' standing among their neighbours.

In order to achieve these aims, Humani sought to 'establish' under the auspices of *al-'Uruba* 'effective ties between the homeland and those of its children who now find themselves abroad'—as a circular letter accompanying a 1931 issue of *al-'Irfan* made clear.[101] His understanding of these ties, it would appear, was founded upon a conventional picture of the relations between homeland and diaspora. The latter, in his eyes, served as a dependency of the territorial nation, a faraway annex whose constituents were bound to share in the opinions of those who had stayed in the land of their birth. As he declared in a meeting with the 'most influential members of the Syrian Muslim community' of Freetown, the 'views and activities' of those 'living abroad' should 'remain' in perfect harmony with those of their compatriots in the Eastern Mediterranean.[102] Migrants, he seemed to suggest, should have no political thoughts or sentiments of their own, but only share vicariously in those of their distant kin. More than this, they were dependents in another sense. As he put it in a speech to the Lebanese migrants of Conakry:

You know that to free yourselves of the yoke of the Europeans, it is indispensable for you to gather behind those capable of defending you. You are far from your homeland here. If you want to be protected and defended, come to me. On my return to Lebanon, I will visit the President of the Republic who I will brief on your situation. You will thus have an organism connecting you to the Lebanese authorities.[103]

Humani clearly sought to draw a link between the continuing occupation of Lebanon and Syria and the campaigns waged against Eastern Mediterranean traders by Jean Paillard and his supporters in the Chambers of Commerce of Senegal, Guinea and Côte d'Ivoire. These, he suggested, were but two sides of the same coin: wherever they might be in the world, 'Amilis confronted the same issues and shared in the same struggle. But only those fortunate enough to have stayed at home could redress these inequalities, surrounded as they were with the strong structures of the territorial nation-state. Their compatriots in the harsh wastelands of the *mahjar*, isolated and without resources, had no choice but to turn gratefully towards them for assistance. Humani's declaration highlights, once again, the ways in which 'Amili men of letters ambivalently embraced the Lebanese state even as they continued to denounce its illegitimacy. However, its message of patriarchal benevolence towards Jabal 'Amil's prodigal sons, bound by ties of fealty and gratitude to the fatherland, is difficult to square with the purpose of his visit.

For Humani had embarked for West Africa on behalf of the Jam'iyya al-Khairiyya al-Islamiyya al-'Amiliyya, or 'Amili Benevolent Islamic Association, founded in 1923 in Beirut by the Shi'a notable Rashid Baidun. In 1929, this organisation had established the 'Amiliyya elementary school in the poor Beirut quarter of Ras al-Naba', to which growing numbers of Shi'a had begun to flock.[104] The school's curriculum, taught in Arabic and French, combined 'religious and scientific studies', and sought to instil in its students a 'patriotic spirit'.[105] Its directors sought to fund its continued expansion, and the creation of the 'higher establishment for education in Arabic in the modern sciences' that Humani had described to his audience in Senegal, largely through appeals to migrants in West Africa.[106] Humani was followed in 1938 by a 'delegation' dispatched by Baidun and the 'Amili Benevolent Association—by then shorn of any mention of Islam—to the 'lands of migration' to facilitate 'contact with migrants, and cooperation in the realisation of [the association's] educational projects'. Leaving Beirut on 19 April, this reached Dakar on 2 May, spending some four months touring Senegal, Guinea, Côte d'Ivoire, Sierra Leone, Nigeria and the Gold Coast before returning to Lebanon on 10 October.[107] Rashid Baidun himself made another visit to AOF in 1948, to fund further expansion to the school—though a wary governor-general warned the minister of Overseas France that this was most likely a 'pretext' for efforts to collect monies for the 'Arab League'.[108] He was not disappointed, raising 15 million francs CFA from the Shi'a migrants of Senegal, Guinea and Côte d'Ivoire.[109]

Indeed, it is clear that many 'Amili migrants shared the concerns of notables like Humani and Baidun, and gladly participated in their educational projects. The 'Syrians' of Freetown alone had given Humani 120,000 francs on his visit, according to their compatriots in Senegal.[110] Some went further, helping to coordinate these efforts on the ground. Muhammad Hilal, a trader of some 'influence' among his compatriots—not least because he supplied merchandise to so many of them on generous terms of credit—seems to have played an important part in fundraising efforts in Senegal. Described by Governor-General Brévié as the 'delegate' of the 'Amiliyya Association in AOF, he employed Elias Abu Rizq and Husain Wihbi—one of the leaders of the delegation, some hundred strong, which had welcomed Humani at the docks of Dakar on his arrival—to collect funds on behalf of Baidun's organisation.[111] The first of these campaigns, in June 1935, had raised 10,000 francs; the second, in September of the same year, had gleaned the more modest sum of 2,886 francs. A third, planned for early 1936, had apparently been postponed when Hilal heard of Humani's impending visit.[112] Hilal continued these activities under the auspices of the Comité d'Adhésion et de Bienfaisance, which he founded in 1938 with Mustafa Hudruj and Ibrahim Tsham. The creation of this organisation coincided with the visit of the 'Amili Association's 'delegation'. By February 1939, Hilal's organisation had apparently raised some 160,000 francs.[113]

Strong bonds of kin and sociability—and an enduring concern with social rank—helped to facilitate such exchanges of ideas and monies between West Africa and Jabal 'Amil. We should not forget that 'Abd al-Hasan al-Rida, entrusted with raising funds for the Maktabat Jabal 'Amil, was most likely a relative of Ahmad al-Rida, Sulaiman al-Zahir's longstanding acolyte. Nor is it insignificant that the sons of Zahir and the Dakar kola merchant Haidar Taha should have collaborated in founding the Maktabat Jabal 'Amil. Figures like Zahir were always ready to craft new alliances in their pursuit of political ends, rapidly reaching out to migrants in West Africa, whose attachments and financial resources they sought to capitalise upon. Both Taha and his son Muhammad, meanwhile, may have found prestige in their association with the illustrious Shaikh Zahir. That Muhammad and Ahmad Zahir attended the same school—most likely the 'Amiliyya—was a clear sign, meanwhile, that migration had begun to break down the social differences between the clerical class and the *'amma*, or general people. Migrants to West Africa sought not just to maintain their ties— political, social and affective—to Jabal 'Amil, but also to move through its social ranks, using their newfound prosperity as a means of propelling themselves upwards, as Ahmad al-Rida knew all too well, appealing to the vanity of the self-made man in his appeal for donations.

Ties of place also facilitated these connections. Haidar Taha, 'Abd al-Hasan al-Rida and Hasan Shams all hailed from Nabatiyya, the hometown of Sulaiman al-Zahir and Ahmad al-Rida, concentrating their philanthropic efforts on this locality. Common origins, it goes without saying, strengthened ties among migrants in AOF— Taha and Shams, we shouldn't forget, were business partners. But they also cemented the relations of migrants with 'Amili men of letters like Zahir and Rida. Migrants felt safe in the knowledge that the latter hailed from their places of birth and shared their own parochial attachments. Just as the civilising notions of the *nahda* were remoulded into a discourse with regional 'Amili resonances by Ahmad 'Arif al-Zain and other contributors to *al-'Irfan*, attempts to implement this reformist programme resonated most deeply at the level of the locality.

However, we should not think that migrants to AOF lent their support to such causes simply because they felt in thrall to the authority of men of letters like Rida and Humani or political notables like Baidun. Some undoubtedly held a figure like Humani in some esteem: Hasan Zahir, apparently a former pupil of the erstwhile schoolmaster, declared him a 'great speaker' and '*savant*'—a probable translation of *'alim*, a word which might connote at once religious authority and secular learning. Not all, though, were quite as forthcoming in their praise. Another migrant described Humani as an 'an intelligent if perhaps slightly pretentious' man, who only 'possessed an average culture in Arabic'—his words perhaps a reflection of the importance many Shi'a still attached to the long and arduous education which bestowed authority upon men of religion, and which Humani had not completed. Nevertheless, he admitted grudgingly, Humani was a 'very active [figure] who wants to work for his *patrie*'. Humani 'would like all Shi'a to be educated so that they might understand the utility of working in unison to arrive at something', and be better able to combat the 'contempt' in which they were held by 'Sunni and Christians'. Despite his reservations, he insisted that as Humani wanted 'to instruct our children, it is our duty to support him'.[114]

These fragments of conversation, scraps of opinion casually thrown out, are profoundly revealing of the ways in which Shi'a migrants in Senegal made sense of the pronouncements of 'Amili men of religion and letters. While these shopkeepers and traders regarded the learning of men like Humani with some admiration, they were not entirely uncritical of these *udaba*, or literati, and their pretensions. Moreover, the requests for financial assistance issued by Humani and others were—it seems—

greeted with enthusiasm not merely because of the ties of kin and place which often facilitated such exchanges, but also because the rhetoric of reform and regeneration consistently deployed by men like Humani struck a resonant chord with the concerns of migrants themselves. These men did not simply feel a personal obligation towards this or that man of religion or letters, but a deeper duty towards the 'Amili *watan*, a compulsion to assist the homeland—and a desire to stake out their place in its political and social life.

The deep attachment to Jabal 'Amil that courses through these exchanges, meanwhile, should caution us against regarding these activities as signs of a broader Syrian or Arab nationalism. These parochial reform schemes were not necessarily staging posts along the way to the establishment of a more territorially extensive nation-state, perceived as the paramount goal of political activity. Rather they were valid ends in themselves. And yet—and this is not as paradoxical as it might seem—we run the risk of misconstruing the meaning of these undertakings by describing them merely as local or regional in nature. All were conceived as service to the *watan*. This polysemic term is often treated as a cognate of the French *patrie* but, while helpful, this glosses over some of the layers of meaning the word contains—referring to one's place of origin or residence, it could stand for a neighbourhood or village, a town or region. Service to the *watan*, then, could denote activity within a quite circumscribed sphere of activity, rather than nationalist activism as we would understand it. While not unconcerned with the shape of the state, this was a form of political thought more concerned with the *polis*—the lush, overlapping networks of horizontal and vertical ties between the members of a political community bound together by a common affection for the land of their birth. Shi'a migrants to AOF, and their Lebanon-based partners, did not so much strive to build a Syrian state, as to reform 'Amili society.

Homespun Arabism

These loyalties did not preclude more far-reaching attachments. On 18 October 1933, some 700 people crowded into the Cinéma Sandaga, in the central district of Dakar, for a ceremony to mark the end of mourning for King Faisal of Iraq. The audience included 'a few Catholic Lebanese', and some fifteen local *indigènes*, among them the secretary of the town's Muslim court of law. However, it was made up for the greater part of 'the totality of the Lebanese-Syrian Muslims of Dakar', who listened as twenty-seven speakers sang the praises of the deceased monarch.[115] While most of the speeches had apparently been drafted by one Elias al-Khuri Abu Rizq—a Greek Orthodox who had once been in the service of Faisal—they reflected a distinctly 'Amili sense of affection for the Sharif. Indeed, assemblies were held to mark the fortieth day of mourning for Faisal in Bint Jubail and Saida, as they had been—under the auspices of Ahmad al-Rida and Sulaiman Zahir—in Nabatiyya for the death of Faisal's father Husain in 1931.[116] The Shi'a of Jabal 'Amil venerated these men as guardians of the holy sites of Mecca and Medina, and as *ahl al-bait*, or descendants of Muhammad. It is unsurprising, then, that some of the speeches pronounced that day in the crowded hall of the Cinéma Sandaga were bathed in a profound religiosity. After all, the principal purpose of the meeting was—as its chair, Husain 'Usairan, reminded his audience—the 'recitation' of the *fatiha*, the opening verse of the Qur'an, 'to send blessings upon King Faisal, the inhabitant of Paradise, forty days after his death'.

However, many of the speakers chose to depart from purely religious sentiment to laud the political actions of Faisal. Indeed, 'Usairan went so far as to reject traditional ties of allegiance founded upon the genealogy of the Sharif. He insisted in his opening address that 'we, the Arabs, do not honour this man because he is the son of the envoy of God' but as a '"isami man", or one who had himself acquired a claim to eminence. In claiming that Faisal was esteemed as much for having 'served all the Arabs' than for belonging to the 'tree of the Prophet'—if not more—'Usairan sought to give clear primacy to his political role.[117] Others followed suit. Ahmad Jawwad Taj al-Din lamented the loss of the Iraqi ruler—a man who 'we, and all other Arabs, desperately need to wake us from our slumber, lift our heads and lead us together upon the path of independence and glory'.[118] Hasan 'Arab, too, bemoaned the death of 'he who saved us from the tyranny of the Turks, he who sacrificed his life and efforts for the good of the nation, he upon whom all hopes were founded … who instilled in us [a] national spirit at a time when people rose up to safeguard [their rights] … who was the founder of our homeland', and established once again 'our glory, our name, and independence among nations'.[119] The words of Taj al-Din were at once a celebration of Faisal's past deeds and an angry appraisal of the current condition of the Arabs, who remained far away—for all the efforts of the Sharif—from attaining veritable independence. This was a profoundly conventional expression of nationalist sentiment, which used the well-worn images of slumber and submission to evoke the plight of the Arab peoples. 'Arab, too, drew upon the common narrative of the Arab nation, evoking its liberation from the Ottoman yoke. However, his words were less lofty than those of Taj al-Din. He sought not to present a mythical awakening, but to stress the rightful place of the Arabs in a community of nations—evoking at once the Arab revolt and the pervasive, powerful notion of self-determination in his talk of a 'time when people rose up to safeguard their rights'.

These were expressions, to be sure, of undiluted Arabism. But we cannot simply attribute to these Shi'a speakers a sense of identification with this ideology and classify them as nationalists before moving on. Taxonomy of this sort is not enough. Why did Taj al-Din and 'Arab return so insistently to the very notion of the Arab nation, occluding all religious elements from their speeches? Why did Husain 'Usairan explicitly dismiss such grounds for allegiance? Why, also, did he speak of Faisal as a man who 'served all the Arabs, the Arabic language, and all who pronounce the *dad*—the hard D which, as the Senegalese interpreter present helpfully explained for his French superiors, 'can only be pronounced by veritable Arabs'? What did he seek to achieve by repeated allusions to Arabic lore—to the honourable 'Isam, the loquacious Sha'ban and the incoherent Bakhil?[120] We must attempt to get at the elocutionary force of such acts of oratory—to understand what these men were doing in speaking in this manner.[121]

The references which peppered 'Usairan's speech were more than mere literary embellishments or shows of erudition designed to impress his audience. It is not for nothing that he spoke collectively of 'we, the Arabs'. His membership—and that of his 'Amili listeners—to the fold could not be assumed or taken for granted; it had to be affirmed and defended. By taking the unconventional step of dismissing religious grounds for revering Faisal, but also by stressing the linguistic foundations of Arab identity, 'Usairan sought to stress that the 'Amilis—for all their differences of rite from the Sunni majority—were incontestably Arab. His self-conscious comparisons to Shahban and Bakhil were, then, a means of placing himself—and other 'Amilis— in the slipstream of an illustrious tradition. Moreover, he sought to demonstrate not merely that the Shi'a of Jabal 'Amil were Arabs, but also that Faisal himself had considered them as such—after all, had he not 'served all the Arabs' equally, irrespective of their religion or origins? Taj al-Din and 'Arab, in turn, took much the same tack. By elevating Faisal to the rank of a national hero, they attempted to avoid any discussion of sectarian difference.

Indeed, this discomfiting fact was discreetly passed over by most speakers. Only one, 'Abd al-Rida Jabir, mentioned the issue in almost explicit terms—and then only to issue a call to 'reject fanaticism, hatred, and all that can harm our generous colony'.[122] The meeting's organiser, Muhammad Hilal, sought—it seems—to convey a sense of unity and ecumenism to proceedings. The speakers were mostly 'Amili Shi'a, but they also included the Christians Abu Rizq and Shukri Daghir, along with four Senegalese men and one Moroccan, Sidi Lahbib Ben Amur.[123] A simple market butcher—Jabir—took the floor alongside a man—Abu Rizq—who claimed to have been an 'intimate' of Faisal.[124]

In an act perhaps as loaded with symbolism, Husain 'Usairan presided over proceedings assisted by 'Ali As'ad. The former belonged to a wealthy family of merchants and 'ulama'. Rising to prominence in the nineteenth century as Persian consuls in Saida, they had bought up landholdings and secured positions in the Ottoman administration, establishing themselves as a force to be reckoned with through sheer financial clout.[125] The latter, meanwhile, was most likely a member of the As'ad clan. Though still powerful, its influence had steadily been eroded by the rise of families like the Zain and 'Usairan—towards which the al-As'ad often harboured a profound animus. This, then, may well have been an attempt to present a picture of a community brought together by exile—and joined in their adherence to the Arab cause.

Nonetheless, we might regard as significant the fact that Hilal, whose influence depended—as we have seen—upon his relative wealth and commercial weight, should have asked As'ad and 'Usairan to chair the assembly. Those vested with the most social and political weight in Jabal 'Amil—one a member of a chiefly family of zu'ama', the other a wajih, an urban notable of the coast—were called upon to assume positions of authority in Dakar. Hilal turned to these men to enhance the prestige of his meeting—and, in doing so, belied his own attempts to present a gathering untroubled by hierarchical or sectional differences. However, he also sought to heighten his own standing. Much the same could be said of his attempts to enlist Elias Abu Rizq and Husain Wihbi to raise funds on behalf of Rashid Baidun's 'Amiliyya college in Beirut. Abu Rizq—though never the 'private secretary' of Faisal, as some in Dakar claimed—[126] was probably the Iliya Khuri who had served as his intermediary in Jabal 'Amil in 1919 and 1920.[127] Wihbi, meanwhile, had belonged to one of the armed gangs that had roamed the region in these years, raiding Christian villages and sowing what some called *fawda wataniyya*—or national chaos.[128] As such, the nationalist credentials of these men were unimpeachable. Hilal could only stand to gain in influence by associating with them.

The alliances and friendships Hilal contracted were—like those of Haidar Taha, say—underpinned by a shared sense of place. Two of his closest collaborators— Ibrahim Tsham and Elias Abu Rizq—were, like him, from the coastal 'Amili town of Sur.[129] But while Taha or 'Abd al-Hasan al-Rida engaged in actions focused upon their own place of birth, Hilal and his acolytes sought to reach out to the wider world of Arab nationalism. Not only did they seek to mark their place within the main-stream of Arabism in their speeches that October day at the Cinéma Sandaga—Hilal calling for his listeners to transport themselves 'in spirit' to 'Baghdad and Mecca', central places of Islam richly evocative of Arab history,[130] they also fostered links with the Middle East. Hilal, as well as despatching a notice of the meeting he had organ-ised to *al-'Irfan*, sent a telegram of condolences to Faisal's son Ghazi.[131] He was also apparently in contact with an organisation called the 'Islamic committee of Jerusa-lem', which had attempted to send him a number of tracts calling for a 'plebiscite of the Arabs from the Taurus to the Suez Canal' in 1935.[132]

This growing inclination to seek political contacts further afield was, one might argue, the product of a generational shift. Haidar Taha had been born 'around 1880'. Slightly younger than the Nabatiyya three, all born in the early 1870s, he was much the same age as their close collaborator Ahmad 'Arif al-Zain, born in 1883.[133] As Sabrina Mervin has noted, '[t]hese men, educated in traditional 'Amili religious schools', lacked in a sense the means to adapt to the rapidly shifting political climate of the interwar period.[134] They clung throughout to their hopes of a Greater Syria, but also to their parochial affection for Jabal 'Amil. Taha, it seems, shared but this latter attachment. Hilal and Mustafa Hudruj—who, together, established the Comité d'Adhésion et de Bienfaisance in October 1938—were both born in 1900. Ibrahim Tsham, the committee's secretary, was born in 1907. These men, then, might be seen as belonging to the 'young generation of Arab nationalists' who emerged in the 1930s. Tsham, Hudruj and Hilal failed to achieve 'a coherent political organisation and a tightly defined political agenda'—and perhaps did not attempt to do so.[135] Nonetheless, their sense of belonging to a wider world of Arab nationalism can be glimpsed in their efforts to reach out in various directions.

This growing extraversion was most evident in the outlook of Tsham. The young-est of these men, he was still a teenager when he arrived in Dakar in 1924. There he scraped together a living as a tailor before establishing a bookshop in 1931. Still only twenty-four, he seems to have harboured ambitions to be rather more than a bookseller. As well as repeatedly petitioning the Government-General between 1932 and 1936 for permission to set up a publication of his own, he acted as the Dakar correspondent of the Beirut newspaper *al-Jadid*—provoking a furore in Lebanese circles in 1934 when he penned, with Elias Abu Rizq, a number of articles attacking the prominent Christian businessmen Saʿid Nujaim and Habib Rizq.[136] Like other Eastern Mediterranean men in the interwar period, he seems to have drawn no real distinction between writing, publishing and distributing.

However, it is Tsham's work as a bookseller which reveals most about his diffuse political inclinations—but also, it could be argued, those of his clients. As Robert Darnton has argued, booksellers were 'cultural middlemen'. By uncovering their 'social and intellectual world[s]', their 'values and tastes', we might learn a little more, too, about their clients.[137] Tsham still 'irregularly' placed orders for *al-ʿIrfan*. However, he also received in November 1936 five copies of *al-ʿUrwa al-Wuthqa*, the collection of articles written in the 1880s by the pan-Islamist Sayyid Jamal al-Din al-Afghani and his pupil Muhammad ʿAbduh. Moreover, he sold the periodicals *al-Sharq al-ʿArabi*—the Arab East—and, in 1938, *Tunis*. The former, published in Paris, was apparently 'inspired by the League against Imperialism and Colonial Oppression, but also by the leaders' of the Etoile Nord-Africaine, the Algerian nationalist organisation.[138] The latter, the organ of the Tunisian 'Old Destur' party, was edited by Tahar al-Safi, the 'political director for Africa of the Arab Office for Information and the Press' in Damascus. By receiving such publications, Tsham sought to join the increasingly cross-pollinating networks of Arabist activism spread across Europe, North Africa and the Eastern Mediterranean. However, we cannot discount entirely more prosaic issues of availability which might have conditioned Tsham's choices. A new edition of *al-ʿUrwa al-Wuthqa* had been published in Beirut in the mid-1930s.[139] A periodical like *al-Sharq al-ʿArabi*, meanwhile, circulated freely along imperial lines of communication. As such, it posed fewer problems of distribution than banned publications such as *al-ʿIrfan*, which needed to be secreted away inside bundles of newspapers before being smuggled into AOF. In a sense, Tsham was an intellectual *bricoleur*, cobbling together a repertoire of reading matter from these diffuse sources. Its 'heterogeneous' composition—at once 'extended' and 'limited'—was not the product of 'any particular [political] project', but was simply the sum of 'all the occasions which presented themselves to renew and enrich [his] stock'.[140]

Nonetheless, it is clear that Tsham and his clients increasingly sought purposefully to look further afield—even as they remained drawn to traditional ʿAmili fare. The 'wide-angled, unfocused' search for reading matter by Shiʿa migrants in the late 1930s did not displace entirely the 'single-minded, narrowly focused' tastes they had shown at the beginning of the decade.[141] Their growing interest in the wider currents of Arab nationalism and pan-Islamism both stemmed from and fed back into their attachment to Jabal ʿAmil. This can clearly be seen, I think, in their stance on the Palestinian question. The members of the Comité d'Adhésion et de Bienfaisance—

which numbered by this point some three hundred adherents—agreed on 9 December 1938, in a meeting chaired by Tsham, to raise funds from the 'Muslim Lebanese-Syrian element[s]' of Senegal for the 'Arabs of Palestine'. In order to avert suspicion, the 'open subscription list would bear the explanation, in Arabic "for a poor destitute without the means to return home"'—words which mingled compassion and bitter sarcasm. By 26 December, the Committee had raised some 40,000 francs.[142]

The Shi'a of Dakar were not alone in showing their concern for Palestine. Already in December 1933, the local administrator of Daloa, in the interior of Côte d'Ivoire, had intercepted a short, angry, message of protest from the 'Syrian colony' of the place. Addressed to 'HIS MAJESTY KING OF ENGLAND, LONDON', it read:

14 years experience should suffice demonstrate impossibility fulfilling utopia Jewish homeland Palestine—your Government obstinacy follow harmful policy sacrifice unfortunate Arab population will shake foundations your empire—Justice will avenge sooner or later blood our martyrs.[143]

These few words—whose authors were most likely Muslim, from the manner in which they spoke of themselves as Syrian, and their evocation of martyrdom, with its deep shades of meaning—serve as a reminder that concern for Palestine existed among Lebanese migrants in West Africa, even in a place as isolated as Daloa, before the Palestinian Great Revolt of the late 1930s. Indeed, the sympathy of 'Amilis for Palestine was born in part of old currents of mercantile exchange and migration between the Jabal and the region of Galilee to the south. As the sociologist Ahmad Baydoun has remarked, both 'commerce, and … labour' from southern Lebanon 'naturally turned towards Palestine', itself 'so close' to Jabal 'Amil; the older inhabitants of Baydoun's home town, Bint Jubail, still 'evoked nostalgically' in the 1980s 'the memory of those traders from Gaza or 'Arish' who regularly visited its bustling market before 1948.[144] Palestine was not—it seems—regarded by many 'Amilis as an abstract concern, but as a familiar place of exchange and travel. This sense of proximity fed into their political feelings.

However, there can be no question that the late 1930s was a time of growing mobilisation for Palestine. Across the Middle East and North Africa, students and professionals, scholars and journalists were spurred into action by the outbreak of the Palestinian Great Revolt in 1936. They formed committees, raised funds, and sent arms and fighters. As Basheer Nafi has noted, the Palestinian and Arabist movements 'converge[d] and interact[ed] as never before'.[145] Indeed, the flurry of activity in areas as far flung as Tunisia and Kuwait was in sharp contrast to the introversion and lack of interest in the Palestinian question of earlier years. Nowhere was this sea change more apparent than in Egypt. Press coverage of the 1920s—the 'heyday' of a purely Egyptian nationalism which discarded all outward attachments as unnecessary ballast—was painstakingly balanced in its appraisal of events in Mandatory Palestine. Fundraising, meanwhile, was practically non-existent; only an appeal for the renovation of the al-Aqsa mosque drew any response. From the mid-1930s onwards, organisations like the Young Mens' Muslim Association began to speak of Palestine as 'the cause of the Islamic world'. In an emotional outcry, the *'alim* Hasan al-Banna called out: 'oh brothers—your homeland does not end at the borders of Egypt, but extends to wherever a Muslim says, "There is no God but God"'. Even the language used by secular Egyptian journalists became markedly more 'emotional', mingling 'admiration for and identification with the Arabs of Palestine' in their struggle against British imperialism and foreign encroachment.[146] The growing commitment of many Arabists to the Palestinian cause in the late 1930s was both a sign of their lingering anxieties over the predicaments of their own homelands and of their sympathy for the Palestinians—increasingly thought of as fellow Arabs or Muslims. It is telling, then, that the appeal launched by the Comité d'Adhésion et de Bienfaisance in Dakar should have asked for funds for the 'Arabs of Palestine'—a hint that migrants like Tsham spoke, too, the language of nationalism.

A diasporic Syrianism

On 2 December 1935, Tsham received by airmail from Beirut a letter requesting his assistance in collecting funds for a 'Secret Popular Association', which sought to topple the governments of the Mandatory states. This organisation, which possessed branches in many of the major cities of Lebanon and Syria—Beirut and Tripoli, Damascus and Aleppo, Homs and Hama—was led, it was alleged, by a committee of twelve men including one 'Antoine SAMMANS or SAADI'.[147] A series of articles from the Beirut newspapers *Sawt al-Ahrar* and *al-Nahar*, sent by the Government-General to the Ministry of Colonies in support of these allegations, shed further light upon the identity of this secret organisation. This was none other than the Hizb al-Suri al-Qawmi—the Syrian National or Nationalist Party. Founded by Antun Sa'ada, an instructor at the American University of Beirut, in 1932, the party had grown over the summer of 1934 from a small group of about thirty students to a party with some one thousand members in Beirut, Damascus and northern Lebanon. This swift, sudden expansion left the party—whose cadres had sought to operate in conditions of strict secrecy—exposed to detection, and on 16 November 1935, Sa'ada and several others were arrested on charges of plotting against the internal security of the state.[148] Sa'ada, who considered himself the absolute leader of the organisation, regarded the territory stretching from the Taurus Mountains in the north to the Suez Isthmus in the south, and from the Euphrates in the east to the Mediterranean in the west, as falling within the bounds of the Syrian homeland.[149] These lands were, he insisted, a 'single indivisible unit'.[150] Sentenced in January 1936 to six months in prison, Sa'ada wrote in his cell *Nushu' al-Umam*—the Origins of Nations—a tract in which he spelled out his vision of the Syrian nation as a 'natural society',[151] whose distinctive shape had been born of long interaction with a particular 'physical environment'.[152] Its people, he argued, had shared a 'common life',[153] 'united in interest, [and] destiny',[154] 'within a well-defined territory'[155] and 'have acquired as a result of their interaction with that land, in the course of evolution, certain characteristics and qualities which distinguish them from other groups'.[156] They were bound together, then, not by race or language, but by 'national love and toleration'. There could be no place in this 'complete nation' for 'conflict of loyalties' or 'religious bigotries'.[157]

Such Syrianist notions appealed to many Shiʻa in the late 1930s and 1940s. Saʻadaʼs claim that the Syrian people were a composite held together by cultural affinity, and his relative indifference towards religious heterogeneity, resonated with educated ʻAmili, who considered themselves a distinct, and yet intrinsic, part of a wider entity, and had long been troubled by the disparaging attitudes of Sunni Arabists. Moreover, his partyʼs insistence upon the integrity of the Syrian nation provided solace in the wake of the Franco-Syrian and Franco-Lebanese treaties of 1936, by which France recognised the separate claims to independence of Lebanon and Syria. The ratification of the Franco-Syrian treaty, in particular, put paid to any lingering hopes of unification between the two Mandatory states among supporters of Syrian unity—both Sunni and Shiʻa—in Lebanon. As Khair al-Din al-Ahdab, the Sunni prime minister of Lebanon, bitterly put it in 1937, the leaders of the National Bloc in Damascus had treated their erstwhile allies in Beirut as no more than a 'pawn', dropping their claim to Lebanon in return for the independence of Syria.[158] Even those political and intellectual figures—like Ahmad Rida and Sulaiman Zahir—who had resolutely clung to the dream of Syrian unity abandoned these aspirations in the years of 1936. In 1939, the two men of letters attempted to set up a political party which would seek greater recognition of the rights of the Shiʻa within the framework of the Lebanese state. It is perhaps no coincidence, then, that the Hizb al-Qawmi established its first office in the ʻAmili port of Sur in 1936.[159]

Despite its deep-seated attachment to the Syrian land, Saʻadaʼs party did not restrict its activities to the Eastern Mediterranean. Himself a profoundly diasporic character who had spent much of his early life in Egypt, the United States and Brazil before returning to Lebanon in 1929 at the age of twenty-five, Saʻada placed great importance upon 'organis[ing] the Syrian Mahjar', embarking for this purpose on a trip through North and South America in 1938.[160] However, the request Ibrahim Tsham received in late 1935 suggests that efforts to enlist migrants began around the time of Saʻadaʼs arrest, running alongside the expansion of the Hizb al-Qawmi in Lebanon itself. Indeed, it may well be these processes were associated; Tsham, after all, was from Sur, the ʻAmili town in which support for the party was strongest. He had perhaps, then, learned himself of its activities in conversation or correspondence, or been sought out by party cadres—because of both his pronounced nationalist leanings and his position as a bookseller capable of reaching a network of clients sharing his inclinations.

Whatever the case, it would seem Tsham began to gather support for the Hizb al-Qawmi soon after receiving this request. He embarked in the spring of 1936 on a 'professional trip' through Senegal in the company of Shukri Daghir, a 'business agent and public writer who lived only on his wits'. While in the towns of the interior, the two men had made a number of 'tendentious remarks' on the political situ-

222

ation in the Middle East, which 'provoked some emotion among their compatriots; visiting their homes, they asked them, among other things, to support their brothers who had remained in their country and were [now] fighting for freedom and independence'.[161] We cannot, of course, be certain that the support Tsham requested was indeed monies for the Hizb al-Qawmi. This, though, seems most likely. What is more, it is clear that he remained in contact with the party throughout the late 1930s, helping to propagate its brand of Syrian nationalism among the Shi'a migrants of AOF. In June 1939, Sa'ada—passing through Dakar on his way to Brazil by steamship—met with Tsham, to whom he gave a number of small leaflets containing the statutes of the Hizb al-Qawmi. Tsham did not wait long before visiting his friend 'Ali Baidun in Kaolack. Together, the two men had distributed these pamphlets throughout the *cercles* of Kael, Coliban and N'Doulo collecting 'quite important sums' on their way for 'the Syrian nationalists'.[162] Even as older political figures like Sulaiman Zahir abandoned their dreams of Syrian unification, younger Shi'a migrants like Tsham, reluctant to relinquish such hopes, cast out in search of new allegiances.

Conclusion

I have sought in this chapter to reconstruct the political sentiments and activities of Eastern Mediterranean migrants to AOF in the interwar period. Many Christians maintained a lively interest in the news of the Middle East which reached them through imperial lines of communication. Their reading matter gives us a sense of their overlapping sense of belonging—showing at once their attachment to their places of birth and their interest in the high politics of the new state of Lebanon. However, they did not remain passive recipients of such information. They sought to contribute in their own ways—voicing in telegrams their opinions on the shape of political things to come. Moreover, they did not remain patiently wedded to Lebanon, faithful junior partners in a long-distance union. On the contrary, they came to regard themselves as moving ahead of a homeland which remained mired in maladministration and petty discord, an avant-garde capable of bringing prosperity and development to the lands they had left behind. And they looked further afield, casting themselves as members of an essentially diasporic political community, which reached through the vast expanses of the *mahjar*, even as they clung to their more conventional attachments. Their political culture was a tightly wound skein of loyalties; nationalism was but one strand among others.

We know far more, meanwhile, of the political culture of Shi'a migrants, monitored for much of the 1930s by colonial functionaries disturbed by their potentially subversive presence. The records of such surveillance—for all their inconsistencies and mistakes—allow us to reconstruct the multiple attachments of the Shi'a shopkeepers and traders of Dakar. These men, like their Christian counterparts, retained a strong attachment to the villages and towns they had left behind for West Africa. These parochial loyalties were sometimes buttressed by their ties to prominent 'Amili men of letters and religion who sought to call upon the generosity of migrants to fund their own schemes. At times, however, migrants regarded their fundraising efforts, not in the light of such relations, but as the manifestation of their 'Amili patriotism and commitment to the reform of the region. Indeed, younger migrants seem to have discarded their ties to *'ulama'* like Sulaiman Zahir by the late 1930s. They sought, instead, to assert the place of Jabal 'Amil within the wider world of nationalist politics—whether in embracing a thoroughgoing Arabism or, as in the case of Ibrahim Tsham, the distinctive Syrianism of Antun Sa'ada. Though they did not give up their attachment to Jabal 'Amil, continuing to be driven by their affection and concern for the homeland, they increasingly sought to claim an active role in its political life. Such demands and desires came into growing tension with the insistence of 'Amili notables and scholars that migrants should play an essentially passive role, following the homeland's lead and answering its calls for monies while muting their own concerns. These tensions between the diasporic and the territorial, between those who leave and those who stay behind, remain unresolved.

8

CODA

THE MAKING OF POSTCOLONIAL SELVES

'Moving brings revelations and leaves mysteries.'

Milton Hatoum[1]

'Being out of place is the only place to be.'

Stuart Hall, Edward Said Memorial Lecture, London, 17 May 2010

Ethiopian Airlines Flight ET409 bound for Addis Ababa crashed in the stormy early hours of 25 January 2010, only a few minutes after its departure from Beirut. There were no survivors. Of the ninety who lost their lives that night, twenty-two were Ethiopians—many of them domestic workers returning home for a brief break.[2] The majority, however, were Lebanese nationals. Most of these fifty-six travellers were heading not for Ethiopia itself, but onwards on connecting flights bound for Dakar, Abidjan, Lagos and Freetown. This disaster was the first that many in the wider world had heard of the seemingly incongruous presence of Lebanese migrants in West Africa. For others—not least members of these communities—it was a reminder of their continuing attempts to evade the quandaries of their existence in the world, and of the enduring ambiguities surrounding their travelling lives.

The story I have sought to tell is one without clear beginnings. Its first protagonists have taken on the feel of mythical figures. Apparitions who burst into the reports of bewildered administrators in Conakry and Freetown, Saint-Louis and Dakar as though from nowhere, they have long since passed on into memory. Their names are echoes, repeated and argued over down the years by the successive generations of migrants who have followed in their footsteps. But their movements were but the first of many, just as the lives of the men and women who made it to West Africa were marked by a series of displacements. Forever concerned with bettering their lot—a preoccupation which led them to undertake the long journeys from the shores of the Eastern Mediterranean, and the villages and market towns of Mount Lebanon, 'Akkar, or Jabal 'Amil, to the port cities and trading posts of colonial West Africa—they continued upon their arrival to move between locales and territories as exigency and opportunity dictated. Moreover, they contracted commercial ties which did not so much disregard distance and political demarcations as capitalise upon them, finding in the dispersion of their kin and countrymen through the lands of Eastern Mediterranean migration a potent source of profit.

And yet such displacements, I have argued, were not accompanied by dislocation, and plagued by the disconsolate pangs of nostalgia—that ache to return. On the contrary, these men and women showed a magpie-like propensity for poaching ways of living in the world from here, there and everywhere, stitching together homespun scripts of kin, gender and confession, place and political community, repertoires of commercial strategies, and registers of domesticity and respectability. The lives of these men and women were never quite settled, never defined by attachment to a single place: they did not remain irretrievably wedded to the ways of home, but nor did they meld unreservedly into their new milieu, like swimmers hurriedly casting off their clothes to throw themselves into the sea. These migrants, then, were beings in the world. Striving to lead existences spread and scattered over multiple locales, they made lives for themselves that were at once intensely material in their dependence upon commercial endeavour, their attachment to particular commodities, and intrinsic ties to particular places, and oddly immaterial in their desire to break these mundane physical bonds, to do away with distance and live in several points of the globe at once. For their particular wish was to have their presence felt in the Eastern Mediterranean even as they were in Africa, and to maintain a foothold in Africa even when they returned to Lebanon.

The tales of these men and women, then—of their travels through the world, their successes and their travails—can serve to dispel two, quite different, understandings of diaspora, each in its own way prevalent and laden with problems. The first is the enduring tendency to understand diasporic life in melancholy, binary terms, as a form of leave-taking, a sharp break with the familiar. As the Egyptian Jewish essayist André Aciman put it, 'an exile is not just someone who has lost his home; he is someone who can't find another, who can't think of another'; so total is this sense of 'transience', of dislocation, that he comes to read 'change the way he reads time, memory, self, love, fear, beauty: in the key of loss'.[3] This all-consuming grief for a lost life—a life which it is impossible to regain—is seen by essayists and anthropologists, literary theorists and sociologists as somehow paradigmatic of that 'generalised condition of homelessness' born of living in a late modern world, in which our very subjectivities seem so very uncertain, and our lives so untethered to any particular place.

The second, meanwhile, is a tendency to parse between different types of mobile people and ways of being in the world. Ulf Hannerz, for instance, has distinguished in a much-quoted essay between 'cosmopolitans and locals in world culture'. The latter merely assimilate 'items of some distinct provenance into a fundamentally local culture', whose 'structures of meaning' are hardly altered by these convenient new additions. Cosmopolitanism, meanwhile, demands a 'greater involvement with a plurality of contrasting cultures', an 'intellectual and aesthetic openness toward divergent cultural experiences, a search for contrasts rather than uniformity'.[4] In a similar vein, Pnina Werbner draws a line between cosmopolitan subjects, those 'gorgeous butterflies in the greenhouse of global culture', flitting from one source of sustenance to another, and 'transnational bees and ants who build new hives and nests in foreign lands', remaining 'anchored in translocal social networks and cultural diasporas rather than the global ecumene'.[5] Arguing that they rest on a 'teleology of progress', in which 'speed', 'ease of mobility and omniscience' count for everything, Engseng Ho has taken these 'hypermodern' accounts to task for losing sight of the slow and difficult ways in which diasporas form over time.[6] One might go further still, and make the case that these texts are frankly infatuated with a particular kind of movement; haunted by the spectres of modernisation theory, with its idealisation of mobility, they all too easily draw a barrier between those who seek to live in the world and those who merely wish to reproduce home.[7]

Things, I would argue, were not so simple. Whether in their quotidian lives or in their political thoughts and sentiments, Lebanese migrants to West Africa collapsed the distinction between the home and the world. On the one hand, they were at home in the world, seeking to live comfortable existences far from the places of their birth, even as they came to terms with movement and its discombobulating effects. On the other hand, the world was their home. For not only did they maintain relations with friends, relatives and commercial partners in far afield locales; they also adopted discursive repertoires and practices which operated at a global scale, striving for a universality that might erase the inconvenient traces of their particular circumstances. While it would be wrong to assume blithely that all was best in the best of all possible worlds, and to occlude the many tales of unhappiness, failure and strife that have marked Lebanese migration to AOF, the lives of these men and women in the colonial period were marked not so much by dislocation as by constant tactical accommodation to their surroundings.

Moreover, this particular story can allow us to trace the resilient afterlives of colonial discourses. For this is a tale not just of the movement of men and women through the world, but also of the circulation of ideas through the French empire, and of the capacity of discursive constructions to shape the ways in which historical actors have understood their lives. French settlers, commercial workers, administrators and propagandists, I have argued, regarded Eastern Mediterranean migrants to AOF as interlopers of empire—an awkward intermediary term, breaking up the seemingly clear binaries of the colonial order of things. Furthermore, they drew upon metropolitan registers of racial thought—with all its deep-rooted suspicion of movement and sniffy condescension for commerce—to craft exclusionary discourses that depicted these migrants as errant beings, who lived always beyond the pale; unproductive parasites leaching upon the labour of others, their sharp practices and very presence, in such accounts, deprived honest and honourable members of the body politic of their livelihoods. I have sought, on one level, to untangle the world from these webs of language, suggesting that the colonial situation cannot be understood through the stark dichotomies of colonial administrators and anti-colonial polemicists alike, with their vision of a world cut in two. (The same, indeed, might be said of my efforts to come to terms with diasporic discourse, with its continuing distinction between the comforts of home and the disconsolate existence of the exile.) But, on another level, I have sought to show the ways such language was taken on by French settlers, African producers and politicians, and Lebanese traders and dignitaries alike: even as some attempted to refute the charges of shiftlessness and malfeasance regularly levelled at the Lebanese, most accepted the status of this community as intermediaries, figures caught between black and white, whose status flickers uncertainly between acceptance and denunciation. Such representations live on in the post-colony.

The time of decolonisation

For this tale has not yet ended. Much of my account has concentrated on the decades between the late nineteenth century and the Second World War. This seems, in some senses, a natural breaking point. The 1940s and 1950s brought, alongside continuity, a great deal of change to the lives of Lebanese migrants to AOF. To be sure, those who had arrived in the 1920s and 1930s, and whose businesses had survived the vagaries of the war, began to call upon their relatives, wives and children as they acquired a measure of prosperity, and found that their presence in West Africa was rather more permanent than they had initially envisaged. This was the case, for instance, of the Zrariyya-born Jamil Qujuq, who had arrived in Dakar in 1940 to take over the business of his brother, Sharif, who had lived in Senegal since 1934 and had decided to return to the Eastern Mediterranean upon the outbreak of war. Between 1949 and 1953, Jamil put in a series of visa requests, not just for Sharif— who had decided to return to AOF, in a reminder of the continuing circularity of Lebanese migration to the region—but also for his sons Ahmad, Khudr and Tarraf, his daughter Maria, and his nephew Muhammad.[8] Such familiar patterns of family reconstitution served to swell further the ranks of Lebanese migrant society, at a time when it was rapidly expanding. The Directorat des Libanais d'Outre-Mer thus estimated in the late 1950s that AOF was home to some 18,300 Lebanese citizens—a threefold increase upon the mid-1930s. Another 6,200 lived in Nigeria, and a further 3,000 in Sierra Leone.[9]

And, just as they had long done, migrants continued to move about through AOF; following the fluctuations of the colonial economy, they flocked to those localities or territories that promised the richest pickings. But this, in itself, led to a significant, and long-lasting, change in the demographic distribution of the Lebanese communities of West Africa. As we have seen, Côte d'Ivoire was already in the interwar years an attractive posting for those who had newly arrived from the Eastern Mediterranean, or for the children of successful migrants who wished to get out from under their fathers' shadows. However, its popularity grew formidably with the commodity boom of the early 1950s. Coffee production increased from 44,800 tonnes in 1950 to 86,900 tonnes in 1955; cocoa production, meanwhile, increased from 55,000 tonnes to 61,900 tonnes in the same period. Though Lebanese migrants later remembered that the hard work of drying and sorting coffee and cocoa beans was still performed by hand in this period, which made it difficult to guarantee the quality of the product, the growth in commodity production undoubtedly proved a boon to these traders. They served, as they had long done, not just as brokers, but also as suppliers of much-prized consumer goods to plantation workers with disposable income, to whom they sold 'pipe tobacco, cigarettes, milk, soap, sardines, and tinned tomatoes'. And, increasingly, they came to import such goods themselves, securing bills of commission and letters of credit from the French firms and banks of Grand-Bassam and Dakar.[10] The opportunities of this period set in train the reorientation of Lebanese migrant life away from Senegal and—especially—Dakar, long its centre of gravity, and towards Côte d'Ivoire. This change was a slow one. By 1960, Senegal was still home to 10,000 Lebanese citizens, and Côte d'Ivoire to a mere 2,000.[11] But by the late 1980s, anywhere between 85,000 and 100,000 Lebanese migrants could be found in Côte d'Ivoire, home to around half of all those who lived in West Africa.[12]

In the political realm, too, the late 1940s and 1950s brought change. The period, to be sure, brought repeated attacks upon Lebanese migrants, which directly echoed the earlier campaigns of French commercial workers and propagandists like Jean Paillard. From 1947 until 1956, a journalist named Maurice Voisin sought to rouse the populations of AOF against the *Libano-Syriens*. Voisin, who had arrived in Guinea in December 1945,[13] leaving behind him a wife, a mistress[14] and a doubtful wartime past, 'had, like so many others, settled in the colony in the hope of getting rich quick, and rapidly understood that a systematic exploitation of scandals, both great and small … should enable him to attain his goal'.[15] He painted, in relentlessly reiterative terms, a stock image of the vulgar migrant who 'splashes his cash, acts like the boss, pushes and shoves, shouts … and eyes up his neighbour's woman'—a coarse, corrupt, covetous, lascivious 'Stranger', involved in endless murky 'trafficking', and always ready to resort to bribes and violence when cornered.[16] However, his publications did not exclusively target Eastern Mediterranean migrants. Rather, Voisin, who adopted the sobriquet 'Petit Jules' in an attempt to convey his demotic credentials, welded his xenophobia to a crude populism. He and his acolytes attacked with alacrity the 'BIG FRENCH COMPANIES', as he put it in strident capitals, which failed to 'support the SMALL FRENCHMEN', the Section Française de l'Internationale Ouvrière (SFIO), which 'gave its protection … to foreigners', and the Government-General of AOF—asserting in one issue that 'our anti-Lebanese campaign' would, 'until an energetic man heads the Federation', target instead an administration which had utterly failed in its duties.[17] It is a telling sign of both the outlook of Voisin, a dedicated 'denigrator of the … Fourth Republic',[18] and of his forever thwarted ambitions, that he should have sought in 1956 to establish a branch of Pierre Poujade's Union de Défense du Commerce et de l'Artisanat (UDCA) in AOF, only to have his overtures rebuffed by the hero of the shopkeepers.[19]

Voisin's articles, and the responses they elicited from African and Lebanese readers alike, cannot be understood in isolation from the debates unfolding in the period on the changing political configuration of the French empire-state. For while Voisin indulged in dark mutterings on the fate of France's North African possessions, foreseeing the descent of a once glorious empire into bloody inter-racial carnage, his opponents accused him of inciting such conflicts. In 1947, *L'AOF*, the SFIO newspaper edited by the Socialist deputy and mayor of Dakar, Lamine Guèye, published a stinging rebuttal of Voisin's 'virulent campaign'. 'The black market', it declared, 'is by no means the sole preserve of the *Libano-Syriens*. The large firms indulged in it on a large scale. … The exploitation of the black man! That has been going on for a long time. And, in this domain, the French and foreign trusts have beaten all records.' No matter the truth of the claims levelled against Eastern Mediterranean migrants, they could not be deemed to be the sole culprits. Moreover, such attacks were, the article's authors insisted, an 'undertaking' driven by 'HATE and DIVISION'. The only response, they argued, was to create a Committee of Republican Vigilance, to 'fight … resolutely, bitterly, so that ALL MEN living on the territories of the FRENCH UNION should know the SAME EQUAL JUSTICE FOR ALL, benefit from the same FREEDOMS, and belong to the same FRATERNITY OF PEOPLES'.[20]

On the one hand, this language showed the ways in which French African intellectuals drew in the post-war years upon the lineages of republican thought to justify a vision of confederate life for all French territories shorn of privilege and prejudice, and founded on universalist tolerance. On the other, it hints at the increasingly solid linkages Lebanese migrants forged with African leaders like Guèye, Léopold Sédar Senghor, Ahmed Sékou Touré and Félix Houphouët-Boigny. Senghor's Bloc Démocratique Sénégalais, for instance, held its first rally in 1950 in the Star Cinéma, which its owner, the Lebanese businessman 'Abd al-Karim Burji, had lent out for the occasion.[21] Others lent their support to the electoral campaigns of the Rassemblement Démocratique Africain in Côte d'Ivoire and Guinea, discreetly bankrolling Touré's attempts to hold on to the post of mayor of Conakry, and helped to sustain striking railway workers. One figure, Nadim Khuri, was arrested for illegally transporting political correspondence on behalf of Houphouët; the latter, then a deputy, weighed in personally to secure his release.[22]

But even as they provided material support to these leaders, the political status of Lebanese migrants had itself changed. While they continued in one sense to live imperial lives, moving through the territories of AOF and participating—even if in discreet, seemingly tangential ways—in debates on the political future of the French Union, on another level they negotiated the new realities of national independence. For the Lebanese state, which had finally secured its independence from France in 1943, was busily attempting to strengthen its ties to its migrants. Henri Pharaon, the Lebanese minister of foreign affairs, had already complained in 1945 to the French plenipotentiary in Beirut of the 'strong hostility currently developing towards his compatriots' in AOF, at a time when tensions were still riding high between France and Lebanon and Syria, whose decision to break the ties of Mandatory rule had angered the former.[23] Tellingly, this document made no mention of the amicable relations between Lebanon and France, or of the principle of reciprocity. If the Lebanese were to be ensured good treatment, Pharaon intimated, it would be on their own terms, not as France's friends. In 1946, Lebanon appointed its first consul to AOF, Muhammad Sabra—a Shi'a member of the Nida al-Qawmi party founded by the country's prime minister, Riyad al-Sulh.[24] These administrative moves marked a bilateral shift: Lebanon was no longer an ambiguous part of the French empire, an annex to this vast construct, but a fully sovereign state, and its citizens were to be treated as such. The situation of Lebanese migrants to AOF in these years is a reminder, then, of the incongruent chronologies and inconsistent course of decolonisation. These men and women lived at once within the confines of empire, and beyond its suffocating embrace. But the administrative innovations of the late 1940s also signalled a change in the relation of Lebanon to its diaspora. On the one hand, the territorial nation attempted to hold these men and women in its embrace. On the other, it increasingly came to treat them as an awkward appendage, not fully integrated into a state which remained largely founded upon a conventional understanding of the relations between the polity and the land upon which it lay.

Lebanese lives in the African post-colony

The effects of this shift are still to be felt, just as the traces and trails of Lebanese migrants to West Africa are there to be found in airport queues and on street corners, in seemingly withdrawn villages in the Lebanese mountain, bustling African capitals and plush Parisian neighbourhoods. The presence of these migrants—at once striving for inconspicuousness, and ostentatious in its striving drive towards prosperity—manifests itself in different ways in the various places at which they alighted. While Lebanese traders continue to operate many of the restaurants, electronic goods stores, and textile and clothes shops of Dakar, Bamako or Abidjan, selling mobile phones and laptop computers, children's outfits, flyswats and the like, more affluent members of these communities have long since diversified. Commercial dynasties like the Fakhry (Fakhri), Wehbe (Wihbi), Noujaïm (Nujaim) or Dagher (Daghir) have built upon the trend towards engaging in industrial production and wholesale import-export activities already apparent in the late colonial period. Taking advantage of their longstanding dispersion, many of these families have built veritable transnational commercial empires, conglomerates whose interests are spread through West Africa and beyond. While the 'Umais of Côte d'Ivoire own the country's first plastic factory, SOTICI, founded in 1972, their Senegalese relatives own a large food concern, Patisen. Sa'id Fakhri, the patriarch of the Senegalese branch of this family, runs the Savonnerie Africaine Fakhry, whose products hold a significant share of the market. In Côte d'Ivoire, meanwhile, the family's interests include the franchise for

Wrangler jeans, the wholesale distributors Trade Center, a hotel holding company, Ivotel, and a controlling stake in a hospital. As the head of the family, 'Abdul Fakhri, puts it: 'our priority is diversification'.[25]

These big men sit atop long vertical networks of production and distribution whose different branches are arranged according to the unsteady ties of kin and locality. Thus, while migrants from Qana retain control of textile production in Côte d'Ivoire, those from Zrariyya dominate the plastics business, producing 'all types and colours of plastic commodities from polyethylene bags to plastic plates and cups' and their speciality, 'injection-moulded plastic shoes, slippers or sandals'. While magnates like the 'Umais who dominate the upper rungs of this industry operate large, sophisticated plants, smaller concerns can sometimes consist of a workshop with just one machine, operated by the husband, and a small outlet, managed by his wife or child. So marked is the preponderance of migrants from Zrariyya in the shoe trade that the inhabitants of Abidjan know the thoroughfare on which their stores are found as Rue Zrariyye. More telling still, the Adjamé market, in which so many of the city's Lebanese retailers cluster together, is known as Little Beirut.[26] And the forms this presence takes provide telling indication of their relationship to particular locales, and their place in the world.

Thus, while such monikers remind us of the enduring presence of migrants from the Eastern Mediterranean in West Africa, the ways in which the Lebanese inhabit Dakar and move through its spaces reveal their enduringly ambiguous position in the societies of the region. For they are at once everywhere and nowhere, at once absent and present. Their longstanding installation has received official recognition, leaving its mark on the city's map: one of the arteries crossing the quarter around Avenue Pompidou—still referred to by many locals by its old colonial name of Avenue Ponty—is named after 'Abd al-Karim Burji, Senghor's long-time ally; a little further, nearer the throbbing Sandaga market, lies the Rue du Liban. These names tell us something of the manner in which the Lebanese have secured their position in independent Senegal, while also hinting at the ways in which the postcolonial leaders of this country have come to think about its place in the world. For they run into, or alongside, streets and avenues named not just after Senegalese politicians like Lamine Guèye or Galandou Diouf—like Guèye a deputy in the French National Assembly in the mid-twentieth century—but also French luminaries like Jules Ferry or Félix Faure, colonial figures like Albert Sarraut—governor-general of Indochina and minister of colonies before he was prime minister—and the Moroccan rulers Hassan II and Muhammad V. This panoply of names, of course, serves to situate Senegal in the postcolonial Francophone world of which it remains such a central part.

But it is also patterned on the demography of the Plateau, which remains—at least in its commercial life—the 'mixed' neighbourhood of colonial times, with its Moroccan stores crammed with miscellany, its French restaurants and bars catering to a clientele of affluent businessmen and legionnaires on leave, and Lebanese *shawarma* joints and hotels. Of course, many wealthier Lebanese have long since moved out of the densely crowded streets of downtown Dakar, heavy with traffic and noise and car fumes, to grand whitewashed villas in Fann or Point E, the chic seaside neighbour-hoods of the Senegalese capital, where they live, secluded behind their iron grilles, alongside foreign diplomats and members of the country's political and mercantile elite. Others have left the country altogether, settling in Marseille, Paris or Beirut. The Nujaim family, for instance, while maintaining significant business interests in West Africa—not least its Dakar sweet factory—no longer regards Senegal as a per-manent place of residence, and most of its members share their time between the affluent Parisian suburb of Neuilly and a comfortable pied-à-terre in the Beirut quarter of Ashrafiyyeh, visiting the country only for a brief holiday or hunting trip. As Souha Tarraf-Najib—herself born in Dakar to Lebanese migrant parents—has noted, the sense of the Plateau as a 'Lebanese neighbourhood' is 'being diluted', as it loses its 'particular rhythm and demographic density'.[27]

Nevertheless, one still sees many Lebanese as one walks through its gridded streets: young mothers in sober headscarves hanging out laundry and beating carpets on their balconies, as their children run between their legs; managers of restaurants like the popular sandwich place Ali Baba, who alternate between Arabic, Wolof and French as they take orders, shout out commands at the waiters scurrying past, and converse; teenagers weaving through the traffic on their mopeds; older men ensconced in the air-conditioned seclusion of their 4x4s, their fingers impatiently drumming on the steering wheel or scrolling at mobile phones; and families lounging about at hotel beaches and seafood restaurants, the men chatting away about business and the women sunning themselves in coral-coloured bikinis while the children are tended to by Senegalese nurses. And yet, despite such constant reminders of their immersion in Senegalese life, there is no 'Lebanese ethnic territory' in Dakar. Succes-sive generations of migrants have avoided signalling their 'ethnic visibility' by 'mark-ing public space'. On the contrary, they have long sought 'to dwell in the city, in the quarter, in the street (one's own street) without showing it', and drawing undue attention to their difference.[28]

This same discretion is apparent in their political lives. Lebanese migrants have consistently shirked political office; exceptions like Monie Captan (Qabtan), Liberian minister of foreign affairs from 1996 to 2003, are few and far between. To be sure, this is at least in part a consequence of the stringent restrictions on political participa-tion implemented in states like Sierra Leone. There, the political career of the Lebanese-born John Akar ('Akar), the first director of the Sierra Leone Broadcasting Society and composer of the country's national anthem, was brutally curtailed by Milton Margai, in the wake of the victory of the latter's Sierra Leone People's Party (SLPP) in the 1962 elections. Margai, fearing a challenge from Akar in his home district of Moyamba, modified the constitution he had himself helped to frame a year earlier to restrict citizenship, previously founded on the principle of *jus soli*, to those of 'negro African descent'.[29] While preferring to avoid such open manipulation of legislative regimes and repeatedly deploying a language of understanding and coop-eration quite different from the exclusionary tropes of Sierra Leone's postcolonial leaders, Houphouët-Boigny cannily warned Lebanese migrants against participation in both Ivorian and Lebanese politics. These men and women, he insisted, should not become so acculturated as to take open positions on domestic affairs; but nor should they make Abidjan into a 'Beirut on the lagoon', treating it as the terrain of a trans-regional conflict.[30]

Lebanese migrants have themselves tended to shy away from overt participation in political life. Men like Kazem Sharara, adviser to the former Senegalese president Abdou Diouf, Hassan Hejeij (Hajaij), an intimate of Omar Bongo, the ruler of Gabon from 1967 until his death in 2009, or the prominent Côte d'Ivoire business-man Roland Daghir prefer to serve as *éminences grises*; holding the keys to the palace, they can always slip away when need be.[31] Indeed, Daghir is notable for having continued to support Félix Houphouët-Boigny's heir apparent, Henri Konan Bédié, after the latter's fall from grace.[32] More in keeping with the general order of things was his decision to return to the fold, accepting Laurent Gbagbo's offer of a position on the country's Social and Economic Council, alongside his compatriot, Fouad Omaïs (Fu'ad 'Umais). For on the whole, Lebanese migrants have been notably legitimist in their political alignments, a position which has largely served them well, earning them toleration and praise from long-serving rulers like Houphouët-Boigny and Senghor, whose early electoral campaigns they so assiduously supported. If the postcolonial African state is, as Jean-François Bayart has argued, a rhizomic struc-ture—a hierarchical set of networks of 'information, requests, gifts and symbolic celebrations' reaching through society and characterised by the 'extreme personalisa-tion of power relations'—then Lebanese migrants have been adept at manipulating, and working their way into, such circuits.[33] Typical of this pattern was the Afro-Lebanese diamond dealer Neil Leighton met in Sierra Leone in the 1970s. The most important 'intermediary' in this fantastically lucrative sector with a repertory of some 7,000 'customers', he had in his indenture hundreds of miners to whom he leased matériel and sold food. Keeping at all times a fleet of six to eight Mercedes Benz cars, to be distributed as 'bonuses' or favours in the course of his commercial dealings, he was popularly known as the 'Prime Minister of Kono' for his close association with Sir Albert Margai, whose SLPP he was rumoured to bankroll.[34] Lebanese migrants may only rarely play prominent roles in the ceremonials, simulacra and factional scrambling of public life—what Senghor called *la politique politique*, or 'political politics'. However, they are central participants in the political culture of postcolonial West Africa, with its enduring stress upon presidential prerogative and personal linkages.[35] And, like African leaders and their agents, they lay claim to working in invisibility while remaining in plain sight.

These men and women, then, are quite clearly not inconspicuous. Far from it—they are there for all who care to notice. But theirs is a particular kind of presence—always visible, and yet fleeting, moving, withdrawn. This odd, seemingly contradic-tory admixture of ostentation and discretion, of deep immersion and constant introspection, is one that has long been remarked upon. Already apparent, as I have argued, in the colonial period, when migrants tussled with the twin urges to show off their success and to dissimulate and dissemble, the better to preserve their pros-

CODA

perity, it has remained an awkward trait of Lebanese life under the postcolonial state. Thus, a 1976 article in the Abidjan magazine *Voix d'Afrique* noted at once the strains caused by the showiness and effrontery of the Lebanese youth of Dakar—a 'new "wild bunch"', as the Senegalese newspaper *Le Soleil* described them, with their 'tight t-shirts', their 'mechanical purebreds (Honda, Yamaha, etc.)' and fondness for karate, who behaved like 'vandals'—and the yearning of their elders for discretion. 'The Lebanese [migrant] is discreet', its author remarked; 'he does not like to talk about himself, and he doesn't much like others to talk about him, as he knows from experience that discretion is one of the conditions on which rests the tolerance he enjoys.'[36]

This half-hidden, inconsistent form of life—a scattered, distinctly diasporic presence—is born, one might argue, of the lasting liminality of Lebanese migrants in the African post-colony. They have, to be sure, enjoyed rather more cordial relations, and comfortable positions, in Senegal, Côte d'Ivoire and Mali than elsewhere in the region. Nevertheless, they have come under repeated attack from politicians and ordinary citizens alike in language that reprises the tropes deployed in the colonial period by French settlers and commercial workers. Thus, *Voix d'Afrique* noted that the Lebanese migrants were still often tasked with being 'invasive'—'non-productive parasites, whose purely commercial occupations could no longer have any social or economic justification, they grew rich at the expense of [African] nationals by depriving them of work, or by using unfair means in trade'. They were widely seen, then, as 'an obstacle' standing in the way of 'the promotion of nationals, [and] blocking their access to numerous commercial positions'. To make matters worse, they were regarded as haughty and harbouring 'racial prejudices'; 'holding on to a racial division of society', they 'suffered from a superiority complex'.[37]

These claims are wont to resurface at regular intervals in the post-colony, stirred up by disputes over commercial stakes and urban space, like that which erupted in 2011 between the powerful Lebanese businessman Fu'ad 'Umais and the inhabitants of the Cité RAN in the Marcory district of Abidjan. Brandishing property deeds to a part of the land on which this housing development stands, 'Umais obtained a court order requesting the 'departure' of its inhabitants and the 'demolition' of their dwellings. He rested his claim on the contention that the contested plot, which had been in the hands of the Société de Gestion du Patrimoine Ferroviaire, had lapsed to the Ivorian state, from which he had in turn purchased it. However, the local spokesman Richard Kassi disputed this. Speaking to a reporter over shouts of 'Omaïs voleur! Omaïs voleur!' from his neighbours, he insisted that 'Umais' claim was invalid. For not only had the housing project been 'built in 1953 for our parents who were railway … workers'. Furthermore, 'Umais had received his deeds from the 'illegal government of Laurent Gbagbo', 'coming to an arrangement with a judge' to obtain a favourable ruling.[38] On the one hand, this was a legacy of late colonial developmentalism, a boon on which its inhabitants deserve to hold customary rights because of their parents' service to the state. On the other, 'Umais was discredited in the eyes of the denizens of RAN because of his association with Gbagbo, and the venality and illegitimacy of his regime. This, one might argue, was not merely a dispute over

235

property. Nor was it simply a confrontation between autochthonous and interloper, which we might understand through the prism of the politics of indigeneity. Rather, it serves as an illustration both of the tangled legacies of late colonialism, and the ways in which contemporary actors deploy this past to make sense of their present, and of the rhetorical and juridical means by which ordinary citizens seek to dispute and resist the imperious measures of Lebanese and African 'big men' alike.[39] For, significantly, Kassi regarded 'Umais not just as corrupt in and of himself, but also as inexorably tainted by his links to Gbagbo. It is clear that in cases like this, Lebanese migrants are caught up in broader debates on the atrophying maladies of the postcolonial state—on corruption, the instability of law and the flimsiness of legitimacy.

However, I do not wish to suggest that the Lebanese are merely convenient scapegoats, standing in for something else entirely. A quick glance at readers' comments on this news story reveals a deep streak of animus towards these figures. One more considered post opined, 'fed up with these Lebanese'—*y'en a vraiment marre de ces libanais*—'Abidjan isn't Beirut'. Others followed in the same vein: 'under Gbagbo', one read, 'those bastards … were untouchable, and impunity always covered up corruption. We're tired of them, let them go make up their laws in Lebanon.' Another commentator wrote, 'Enough is enough with these bloody Lebboes'—*trop c'est trop avec ces liboules à la con*—'they … take themselves for the masters on the land of Côte d'Ivoire, for fuck's sake they've had too much freedom and privilege and all because of our ex-leaders'.[40] While these online posts still followed the tenor of the article in drawing explicit connections between the transgressions of the Lebanese and the failings of the country's rulers, a thread following a further report on the dispute between 'Umais and the inhabitants of RAN focused, in more virulent detail, on the Lebanese themselves: 'these bastards kill steal cheat do what they want with our sisters they think they can do what they want lol bullshit', one reader wrote, before adding 'I hate those demons'.[41]

But, for all its violence, this language cannot merely be seen as the discursive product of an unchanging animus existing outside of time, and born of the refusal of the autochthonous inhabitants of West Africa to accept these interlopers in their midst. To be sure, the tropes of venality, brutality, theft and lasciviousness recur time and again in such declarations. However, these pronouncements are not just rhetorical constructs, detached from the world. They are rooted in the palpable circumstances of everyday life, with its uncertainties and discord, its malfeasance and intrigue. As I have argued throughout this work, the word and the world are profoundly entangled; we cannot parse practices from pronouncements, for they remain bound together in a mutually constitutive relationship. Indeed, it is not to diminish the undoubted force of feeling they manifest to suggest that their deployment remains contingent upon changing political and economic circumstances. The ire of these commentators—for all its palpable, bilious, corporeality—is, on one level, a tactical response to the disorder of the post-colony. In this respect, it is by no means exceptional to Côte d'Ivoire. One Nigerian reader thus recently commented on an online report of the death of a young Lebanese man, 'Adil Bijjani, in Lagos that while some migrants have lived in Africa 'without problem', one 'striking characteristic of most Lebanese residing in Africa is that they are generally criminals, economic sabo-teurs, slave drivers, mindless profiteers and drug pushers'.[42]

Nevertheless, such responses are also conditioned by the particularities of Ivorian life. Thus, they draw some of their force from the rancorous discourses of indigeneity that have emerged in Côte d'Ivoire since the late 1980s, with their stress upon ties to the land, and the connections of kith and kin tying 'real' Ivoiriens together. They can be situated, then, in the context of what John Lonsdale has called 'political tribal-ism'—the use of ethnic categories as a means of claiming a 'share in public resources'.[43] But, interestingly, these political and juridical contests between Africans and Lebanese are also quite explicitly moral reckonings. We cannot, it might be argued, draw hard-and-fast distinctions between a 'moral ethnicity' 'internal' to the collective, and subordinating its members to 'certain moral imperatives', and an 'external dimension', founded upon the 'competitive confrontation of "ethnic con-tenders"' for the material resources' to which control of the commanding heights of the state might open access.[44] The assertion of rights against others is also founded on certain ethical prescriptions of just conduct and moral propriety; to breach these is to renounce one's claim to the spoils of the post-colony. In a sense, this is to return to Lonsdale's initial contention: just as the 'tribe' is like the 'nation', an imagined community of moral argument, so the 'nation' is like the 'tribe'. Its contests are not simply a Hobbesian war of all against all, as some are too fond of suggesting about Africa, but are draped in claims of civility.

Many Lebanese migrants have, to be sure, sought to refute the claims made against them, and to stake their place in African society. Some have resorted, in their efforts to deflect accusations that they are little more than parasites, feeding upon the pro-ductive force of Africans, to discourses of political solidarity and economic utility. In a 1969 meeting with the Ivorian president Félix Houphouët-Boigny, a delegation of Lebanese dignitaries underlined that 'many Lebanese who have lived for more than forty years in Côte d'Ivoire shared the pains and miseries of the Ivorian people under colonial rule, and they now, like the latter, breathe the air of freedom and indepen-dence'.[45] In this account, a shared memory of past pains and a shared expectation of future potential justified the presence of the Lebanese within Ivorian society, in an almost Renan-like narrative of remembrance and anticipation.

The Lebanese lawyer Joseph Ashqar went further still in the same period, devoting an entire book to making a case for the continuing presence of his compatriots. For all that the latter maintained a 'sympathy for the French cause' because of their 'assimilation to French culture and the longstanding ties binding them to France', they 'had never in any shape or form constituted an obstacle to the liberation of West Africa; on the contrary, they had always helped dominated people to free themselves from the colonial yoke'. Moreover, the task these migrants had accomplished was a 'grandiose and remarkable one'. They had contributed not just to the commercial evolution of West Africa, but also to the 'development of urbanism' across the region, as their buildings 'sprouted like mushrooms' in all the 'great towns of West Africa', from Dakar and Kaolack to Kayes, Bamako and Mopti, Bobo-Dioulasso, Daloa and Abidjan. The 'epic tale of the Lebanese', then, would come to be seen by later generations as a singular 'contribution' to Africa's 'exploration and development'; they had served as 'the precious auxiliaries of French colonial expansion, carrying because of their culture and love for France the benefits of France's effulgent influence in the world'. But, Ashqar noted, 'national construction … require[s] a change in methods and a new orientation, which are the indispensable conditions of a significant contribution to … economic growth'. Thus, the Lebanese were to 'move away from the commercial sector, towards activities on a larger scale, most notably in industry'. After all, it was 'normal for Africans to take the place of the Lebanese' in trade, and for the latter to 'devote themselves to other … activities which require important capital, … in harmony with the general imperatives of production and development'. So long as the 'hospitality and liberalism' of African states would allow 'each and every one' of their inhabitants 'to live and to work freely in the most varied of domains', the 'Lebanese presence in Africa would result in sure advantages' to the continent.[46]

The 'future of Lebanese migration in Africa', then, seemed assured. While some leaders had adopted intransigent nationalist positions, which cast doubt on the presence of foreigners in their states, such instances had thankfully remained 'isolated'. On the whole, 'Africans are partisans of a policy of openness to the outside world, and are proud to welcome other ethnicities in their national society, so that their civilisation might be enriched by the contribution of other civilisations, and so that they may in turn contribute to the development of the universal civilisation, which some of the most distinguished and well-known of African leaders promulgate with conviction.' With this rhetorical move, Ashqar signalled a shift from the national to the international. 'In today's world', he argued, 'national independence is relative. No country, no matter how powerful, can pretend to live in a vacuum and break ties with the world. We need each other politically, but also economically … All the States of the world are interdependent.' And, he maintained, this 'policy of openness and dialogue' was dependent upon 'international understanding and solidarity between peoples'. One could claim, then, that 'our existence in Africa is considered favourable to the rapprochement between states, and the preservation of a common Negro-Berber and Afro-Arab civilisation'.[47]

This was an argument that owed much to the discourses of those colonial functionaries and migrants who had sought in earlier decades to depict the latter as valuable auxiliaries, who participated wholeheartedly in the vast undertaking of *mise en valeur*. But it was also unmistakably a postcolonial case. More than simply harping upon the role of the Lebanese as intermediaries, as earlier accounts had done, it also stressed their capacity to move into new sectors of the economy, their willingness to compromise and continuing utility to African economies in dire need of industrial capacity.[48] No one, Ashqar suggested, could quibble with the Africanisation of trade, but the Lebanese still had an important role to play as burgeoning industrialists and urban developers; only they had the capital and know-how to conduct such undertakings so essential to African modernity. It would not only be unjust, but also rash, to expel them or shut them out of particular sectors in which they might still have a useful function. Moreover, this was a distinctively African—and Senegalese—argument. After all, we should not forget that Ashqar practised law in Kaolack. This particular feature was perhaps most noticeable in his encomium to non-alignment, and in the less than subtle tribute he paid to Senghor's universalist humanism and commitment to African civilisation.[49] Lebanese migrants, he suggested, could be a factor in a civilisational comity that reached far beyond the borders of the postcolonial state. But even his stress on the need for commercial openness and international economic cooperation, and on the immersion of the Lebanese in French culture, accorded well with Senghor's anxious economic extraversion and sense of an enduring *Francophonie* surviving the dissolution of the French Union. Regardless of their rhetorical efficacy, the very deployment of these tropes testified to the ways in which life in Africa had inflected the arguments of Lebanese migrants, and shaped the manner in which they conceived of their place in the postcolonial state—and the world. While not quite African, they were—in their own eyes—but one of the several ethnicities that made up the composite societies of contemporary Africa.

Others, meanwhile, have founded their claims in the rich loam of quotidian experience. This is especially true of those born and raised over the course of the decades in Côte d'Ivoire, Senegal or Mali, and for whom these countries were the terrain of their earliest, fondest experiences. Thus, Tamir Fakhri, brought up in Côte d'Ivoire, regarded himself as a 'child of Africa'. The continent, he told the historian Salma Kojok, was 'always there in his thoughts' and 'childhood memories'; this was a 'link to Africa', a 'real link, a lived link' that 'no-one could take away' from him.[50] The Dakar-born Yusuf, meanwhile, remarked in a conversation with the sociologist Souha Tarraf-Najib that 'we are slowly becoming Senegalese, it takes time, perhaps another generation; we won't be able to speak to our children of the "village in Lebanon", as our parents do. Even our Arabic is going....' Indeed, this was more than mere rhetoric. Another of Tarraf-Najib's respondents, Charlie, could not muster the name of the village his family hailed from in Lebanon; his embarrassed mother and sister had to whisper it to him as they sat around their formica kitchen table in their modest apartment in a 'small and rather decrepit building' in the Médina, the 'African' quarter of Dakar. Lebanon, Tarraf-Najib noted, was 'inexistent' for him; he was only preoccupied with the boisterous competition between Lebanese youth living in the various neighbourhoods of Dakar. Even his mother had 'never known Lebanon, nor anything but the country of her birth'. Born in Rufisque, she had never left Senegal, and spoke a 'strong pidgin', made up of French and Wolof, with a few words of broken Arabic. And while she recalled that her own parents originated in the Biqaʻ village of Qabb Elias, she knew only that she was Catholic, her inability—or lack of desire—to go further a telling sign that she had given up on that most Lebanese marker of the self, confession.[51] These are signs, I would argue, not just of the drift over time of some away from Lebanon, their growing detachment from an increasingly distant 'homeland', but also of the deep disparities of wealth and opportunity among the Lebanese of West Africa. These, it would seem, only grew deeper in the 1990s with the growing success of *baol-baol*, or hawkers and petty traders belonging to the Murid Sufi brotherhood, in selling groceries, white goods and the like, previously the preserve of the Lebanese. Thus, Dalal Darwish, director of the Dakar-based women's association al-Huda—'the guidance'—stressed in 2009 that 'without exaggeration, we can say that about 60 per cent [of Lebanese migrants in Senegal] are poor or have experienced economic difficulties. Their lifestyles have considerably deteriorated in the last twenty years.'[52] Indeed, if Charlie and his family have never travelled to Lebanon, and know little of the country, it is not just because of the lack of any pressing need to maintain such ties, but also because of the considerable cost of doing so.

But by no means do all Lebanese men and women regard an irrevocable 'assimilation' into African society, a rupture with Lebanon, as the sole path open to them as they navigate their way through the world. Some—especially, perhaps, those with the means to do so—have come to look upon themselves as composites made up of the disparate cultural elements of postcolonial life. One migrant resident in Côte d'Ivoire, Faris 'Attiya, thus described himself as a 'hybrid being, a third French, a third Lebanese, a third African'.[53] This sense of a multiple self, at once divided between different cultures and drawing benefit from their cumulative effects, was echoed by Salwa, an articulate young PhD student the anthropologist Anja Peleikis met on her fieldwork in the southern Lebanese village of Zrariyya and Abidjan in the mid-1990s. On the one hand, Salwa spoke of her 'struggle for [her] cultural identity': 'an immigrant child … living in different worlds', she felt a seemingly insoluble 'conflict between the different cultural elements inside of me'; 'sandwiched' between the values she had imbibed at home, and those she learned at school, she 'had the impression that there were walls dividing these different cultures'. On the other, she was also able to recall with fondness the various elements of her education, the 'Arabic culture' she received from her father, the 'French culture' her mother and school passed on to her and the 'elements of African culture' she 'personally adapted … as a result of my daily life there'. Indeed, she told Peleikis, 'I love Africa very, very much and I can't bear to see it suffer, it makes me suffer, too'. Gradually, over time, she had come to see this plurality as a 'chance to feel at home in both Côte d'Ivoire and Lebanon'. For, Salwa insisted, her personal disquiet was no consequence of her immediate surroundings—she had 'never felt strange in Côte d'Ivoire'. And, though she only 'visited Lebanon for the first time when I was 20 years old, … I didn't feel like a stranger there either'. By the time of her encounter with Peleikis, Salwa had come to conceive of herself as a skein of many strands, whose ends she could pick up and tug upon, depending upon her context and inclination.[54]

However, even as she sought to hold them all together, she had invested more meaning in one particular part of herself; 'returning' to Lebanon, she completed her doctoral studies, took up a teaching position in history at the Jesuit Université Saint-Joseph and threw herself into civil society, her father's staunch secularism informing her commitment to the campaign for optional civil marriage—until very recently a legal impossibility in Lebanon, where personal statute remains the domain of the country's various religious confessions. Salwa's tale, then, spoke both of the ways in which Lebanese migrants have taken on the language of cultural conflict and pluralism, and sought to make sense of their lives through its appealing tropes, and of their tendency to foreground this or that particular aspect of themselves. But if they privilege one identity or another, it is not simply for tactical reasons, but also because of personal inclination, and the ways in which material constraints and possibilities have shaped the range of options available to them.[55]

Salwa's repeated moves back and forth between Abidjan, Zrariyya and Beirut may seem typical of a particular form of transnational life. Its moving contours are more apparent still in another of Peleikis' subjects, Laila. In her mid-forties at the time of Peleikis' fieldwork, she lived in, and between, Abijdan, Zrariyya and Beirut. She would travel regularly from Abidjan to Beirut, where she would tend to her children, at university in the Lebanese capital, during the week and drive down to Jabal 'Amil on the weekend to visit her parents and parents-in-law. All the while, she spoke regularly on her mobile phone not just with her husband in Abidjan, but also with her sister, who lived in the densely Shi'a Lebanese community of Dearborn, Michigan, and her brother, who 'commute[d] regularly' between Côte d'Ivoire, France and Lebanon. As Peleikis noted, such constantly mobile lives remain the preserve of those who can afford them. But, as is clear even from Laila's case, such contacts are not necessarily contingent upon direct, face-to-face contact. People draw upon a constantly changing repertoire of technologies to sustain such communication: just as migrants in the colonial period would descend to the docks to greet new arrivals who would bring with them letters, greetings and anecdotes, or transmit news through the mail packets and telegraph wires that connected together the far-flung parts of the world's colonial empires, their successors in the 1980s and 1990s would ask travelling friends or relatives to convey letters, cassettes and videotapes. These brought news not just of joyous events like weddings and births, but also reports of rather more sombre events like wakes. Indeed, some began to film confrontations with the Israeli forces then occupying much of southern Lebanon, and the funerals of those who died, 'martyrs to the resistance'—a reminder of the ways in which political life could impinge upon, and embed itself in, such transregional networks, and latch onto existing modes of communication.[56]

But even those with the necessary wherewithal do not always engage with territorial Lebanon in such sustained fashion. Though he considered himself Lebanese, spoke fluent colloquial Arabic, frequented other Lebanese and served Lebanese dishes in his restaurant, the owner of the hotel in which I stayed during my time in Dakar confided in me that he simply had no desire to return to Lebanon; having gone there once, he told me, he came back to Senegal distinctly unimpressed. His, then, was a distinctly diasporic sense of Lebanese belonging. It was dependent neither on residence in the Eastern Mediterranean, nor upon regular return trips to the region. Rather, it was built upon certain inherited attributes of Lebanese life. In a similar vein, Souha Tarraf-Najib has argued that 'Senegalese Lebanese' structure their lives around distinctively local referents, distinguishing between the Dakar neighbourhoods in which they dwell—the *quartiers d'en haut*, in the Médina, and the *quartiers d'en bas*, of the Plateau and Ponty, with their clear evocation of socio-economic difference—but also between the 'Lebanese of Dakar, and the others', the Lebanese of 'the bush'. Mocking the latter's accents, Dakarois migrants portray them as rural bumpkins, even when they hail from cities like Saint-Louis, Kaolack or Ziguinchor.

Also important for many—though not, as we have seen, for all—are local attachments of another type, to the home village in Lebanon. Until the early 1980s, noted Tarraf-Najib, who herself grew up in Dakar, football matches between youth whose parents hailed from Shaqra, Zrariyya, 'Abbasiyya or Khiyam became occasions for the playing out of local rivalries, often descending into fistfights before the final whistle blew. It is not for nothing that I call these local, rather than 'translocal' or 'transnational'. For they did not so much transcend locality as transfer it, mapping the village—that dense, tender, conflict-ridden web of relations and affective commitments—onto the terrain of the city. As one migrant told Anja Peleikis, 'Abidjan is like Zrariye and seems much closer to Zrariye than Beirut.'[57] The Lebanese national state simply dropped out of view in such moments, holding no meaning as a territorial referent. To be Lebanese, for many migrants resident in West Africa, is not necessarily to belong to territorial Lebanon.

That is not to say, though, that Lebanese migrants feel entirely comfortable about their place in West Africa. For a deep-rooted sense of creeping insecurity continues to define the worlds of many. Yusuf told Souha Tarraf-Najib that he felt confident that 'the Lebanese will remain in Senegal—unless there is a decision from on high, from the government, against us'. And yet, he confided, he could only with difficulty conceive of his future in the country, because 'the Senegalese have a tendency to regard us as responsible for all their problems. We're becoming like North Africans in France, we're considered like the Jews of Africa.'[58] This was a telling choice of comparisons, one that framed the situation of the Lebanese both in the ahistorical terms of diasporic discourse, with its stress upon estrangement from one's surroundings and the perpetual dangers of dependence upon the fickle hospitality of others, and in startlingly contemporary, postcolonial terms. But this fearfulness is no mere rhetorical effect. Lebanese migrants, for all the economic heft of their communities, remain all too aware of the precariousness of their collective and individual fates. Just as resilient memories of the 1919 Freetown riots resonated through the talk of migrants in the colonial period, news of kidnappings, robberies and murders now rapidly moves along networks of communication, fuelling a sense of immanent danger. The comments of Lebanese readers on the recent death of 'Adil Bijjani, a 29-year-old Lebanese hotel manager working in Lagos, killed by intruders he surprised in his home, reveal in stark, arresting fashion the anxiety and contempt that Africa still provokes. Thus, one commentator—his name shielded by an avatar, but his political affiliations clear from the image of the deceased Christian militia leader Bashir Jummayil which adorns his pronouncements—wrote:

For those who may not know, Nigeria has long been known for its terrible crime rate. For example, if you live in Lagos and its suburbs, if you are invited for diner [*sic*], then this is the drill: you leave early well before darkness sets in, better still in a convoy, take your pajamas with what you need for the night and the stay the night over at your hosts'. Nobody leaves in the night, that is suicidal. Please everyone, when a job offer comes to you for Nigeria, do your research well, ask questions, double check if not quadruple check, but make sure that you make a [*sic*] informed decision.[59]

Like the indictments levelled by Africans at Lebanese migrants, such an account refracts the discourses and practices of everyday life—the fear of criminality and the nagging sense of being particularly visible and open to threats, and the concomitant desire for security—through familiar tropes of Africa as a disordered, dangerous place. Nigeria may play an exceptional role in such tales of migrant life as a perilous adventure; all too often portrayed as a place of incomparable criminality and corruption, it retains a dubious status as a synecdoche for the ills of postcolonial Africa. But there is no denying the sense of individual risk that continues to undergird Lebanese accounts of Africa, with their admixture of rancorous racism and genuine apprehension.

Moreover, migrants have remained all too aware of the instability of their own situations. On the one hand, they regard themselves, not without reason, as figures standing on shifting sands, whose commercial undertakings—and presence—remain contingent upon the tolerance of changing regimes. This assessment is informed by memories of the expulsions and departures that followed legislative measures taken by the governments of Sékou Touré in Guinea or K.A. Busia and Jerry Rawlings in Ghana. On the other hand, the Lebanese have been pushed about this way and that, like many other inhabitants of the region, by the violent conflagrations that consumed Sierra Leone and Liberia for much of the 1990s, and by the more recent conflict in Côte d'Ivoire. Bouts of violence in the latter country in the early 2000s and again in late 2010 and early 2011 cost those migrants whose businesses were looted, or simply paralysed, dear, and led many to retreat towards Dakar and Senegal, whose Lebanese community grew to levels it had not seen since the 1960s, and others to leave for new destinations in Africa, like Angola and the DRC, and further afield, in the Gulf and North America. 'I left Lebanon thirty years ago because of the civil war, and here I am again fleeing another civil war,' bitterly commented one migrant, the Sur-born Yusuf Safi al-Din, during the wave of violence that erupted following the contested presidential elections of November 2010, in which the incumbent, Laurent Gbagbo, refused to cede power to the man widely recognised by the international community as the victor, Alassane Ouattara. While hundreds were reported as fleeing, fearing a recurrence of the civil strife that had shaken the country in the early 2000s, others took a more hard-bitten, pragmatic line. 'Abbas Dakhlallah, though he had left Abidjan for Qana, noted wryly that 'the Lebanese are accustomed to civil war, they have lived it'; Muhammad Fraim echoed this sentiment—'we Lebanese', he told a journalist, 'are used to violence, and I'll return to Abidjan next week, come what may'.

Ironically, their own attempts to protect and preserve their positions have sometimes contributed only to worsening their plight. Thus, the legitimism that has typified Lebanese political stances in postcolonial Africa had, in the eyes of some, served in this instance not so much to protect them as to put them in harm's way. While Lebanon's ambassador to Côte d'Ivoire defended the decision of the country's minister of foreign affairs, 'Ali Shami, to dispatch him to the investiture ceremony of Laurent Gbagbo, arguing that '90 per cent of our community lives in zones controlled' by the incumbent, many expressed anger at Shami's 'behaviour'; regarding it as a 'mistake', they expressed fears that such overt support for Gbagbo's contested claim had 'put the security of the Lebanese community at risk'.[60] Nevertheless, this represents one of the ways in which these men and women have sought at once to shield their interests against instability, and to draw profit from the particular workings of postcolonial African states.

Migrants have attempted to hedge their bets in other ways, spreading their investments and concerns—as their forebears had long done—throughout the region, or moving beyond its confines. Thus, partial withdrawal to Britain and France is not untypical, even for the many migrants who cannot match families like the Nujaim in wealth and social capital: my local dry cleaner in London is run by a Lebanese woman who grew up in the Sierra Leone town of Magburaka before moving to Britain as a young adult. These moves are born not just of the enduring attraction of Europe, with its commodities, modern ways and comforts, but also of the stolid stability migrants see in France or Britain. These countries serve, in their eyes, as convenient refuge from the disorder of African life. The constant concern with movement these men and women exhibit in their lives, then, is not just a product of the growing decentralisation of commercial and financial activity in the contemporary world, and the 'novel articulations between the regime of the family, the state and capital' born of 'late capitalism', as Aihwa Ong has argued. It is not, in other words, simply a question of 'flexible accumulation'.[61] Rather, their desire to divide up their time and interests, to hold multiple passports, to maintain contact with relatives and partners in scattered locales, and to preserve a foothold in safe havens is also a product of fear, of the need to play it safe and have something to fall back on should the need arise. The Lebanese migrants of West Africa are aware, to be sure, of the profits to be drawn from mobility; they, and their forerunners, have long since led networked existences. But they are also aware of the perils of such a life, and of the enduring precariousness of their liminal position across the region.

Lebanon and its meanings

While maintaining a base in Europe offers one solution to this quandary, many others continue to divide their time between West Africa and the Eastern Mediterranean, or to operate along the triangular networks linking up these regions to France and Britain. Indeed, the effects of migration to Africa can be felt across Lebanon—though often in ways that testify to the enduring liminality of the men and women who have undertaken the journey to Dakar and Freetown, Lagos and Abidjan. I still remember that morning in August 2005, a few days after I had returned to Lebanon for the first time in fifteen years. Stepping out barefoot onto the balcony of my aunt's apartment, high up in the Kisrwan, with a cup of steaming, sugary tea in my hands, I looked out down at the dense, shimmering haze of pollution and rising heat covering Beirut, down below on the coast, then up to the next ridge of mountains. There, amidst the pine forests, lies a blush of red roofs, broken by seven spires. Calling inside to my aunt, busy getting herself ready for the day, I ask her the name of that village, with its pretty Provençal tiles: 'that's Bait Shabab', comes the reply, 'where they make the church bells'. Only later, as I went about my own travels, wading through archives in Dakar and Paris, did I learn that many of these homes were built not with the money its inhabitants earned casting bells for the mountain's Christian churches, but in large part with the unsteady contributions of sericulture, then with the sums generations of villagers had accumulated in Africa, during their sojourns in colonial Guinea, Senegal and French Soudan. Though absent from the locality, its men and women asserted their enduring presence through these imposing sandstone dwellings, which exuded solidity, permanence and prosperity. These were the houses that migration built—hard to miss, even when they lay unoccupied, their owners away in the *mahjar*, they signalled at their desire to be noticed, to be counted and considered as members of the fold, even when they strayed beyond its confines.

This dual presence, at once multiple and divided, still endures: spending a lazy day in August 2008 watching the *pétanque* tournament played each year in the *manshiyyeh*, or public park, of the handsome Shuf town of Dair al-Qamar, I hear voices conversing in African-accented French behind me, an unusual occurrence in a part of the world where the heavy mountain accent is *de rigueur*. Turning around, I see the Bait Shabab team getting ready for their next game: rotund men with flush, hale faces and neat moustaches, they all wear Côte d'Ivoire football shirts stretched over their generous bellies, the distinctive green, gold and red identifying them as *Ifriqiyin*, 'Africans' rendered distinct from other Lebanese by long years in West Africa. This is an experience repeated elsewhere, at other points in Lebanon, where an incongruous African accent, a stray reminiscence or a sudden burst of prosperity remind one of the scattered ways of this diaspora and its enduring presence in Lebanon. It is there, for instance, in the northern town of Miziara, where an aeroplane-shaped social club stands as a bold reminder of the migration of its inhabitants to Nigeria.

And it can be found, too, in the ruins of the Crusader fortress of Beaufort in southern Lebanon, a construct that retains some of its old air of impregnability, despite the damage done by a series of confrontations between the Israeli army and Hizballah and AMAL. Walking along the ruined old ramparts high up above the Litani valley with a group of friends one hot August afternoon, we suddenly hear voices calling up greetings in African-accented French from the courtyard below; looking down, we wave in answer to a small party picnicking on an outlaid rug, boys and veiled girls barely out of their teens, visiting Lebanon for the summer from Senegal or Côte d'Ivoire. As we continue our drive through Jabal 'Amil, down to Bint

Jubail and then back to Sur and Beirut, those villages that have experienced migration to Africa can easily be parsed from those whose inhabitants have remained rather more immobile: suddenly, among the tobacco fields, corrugated iron and rough, unfinished concrete, rise up plush, garish villas standing behind gold-plated gates, their owners' Mercedes parked in the drive. With their 'pagoda-like roofs, children's bedrooms in the shape of yachts or boats, … and external lifts', the mansions of migrants make a village such as Juwayya into a 'capital of rural kitsch', in the words of one reporter.[62] 'African' *nouveaux riches* like Abu Muhammad, who migrated in the 1960s to Côte d'Ivoire, where he made a fortune in the manufacture of plastic goods before leaving his businesses in the care of his sons and returning to Lebanon, have made a point of building 'extravagant palaces' for themselves and their families, which have utterly transformed the appearance of the villages of their birth.

Migration to West Africa, however, has not just imposed often garish cosmetic changes on 'African' towns like Miziara, Bait Shabab or Juwayya, Zrariyya, Burj Rahhal and 'Abbasiyya in Jabal 'Amil. More than this, it has radically altered social relations. Migrants—some retired, others only visiting for a few short weeks or months in summer—shop in stores like Yussuf's Coffee Shop; run by a man who spent several years in Abidjan, it caters to their affluent tastes, selling Bahlsen biscuits, Kinder eggs and Langnese honey—imported goods capable of satisfying their urge to be seen as global subjects. In doing so, some complain, they have contributed to the infatuation of the *jil al-naylun*—or 'nylon generation'—with ostentatious consumption and glossy lives of leisure, sustained by the labours of Sri Lankan domestic workers.[63] But, far from simply spending their money on cosmopolitan commodities to demonstrate their globalist credentials, migrants have been careful to invest their earnings in these localities, to distribute resources through their families and to contribute in ostentatious ways to the life of the community. Sur's seaside promenade—tellingly renamed the Avenue du Sénégal—is lined with branches of the Banque du Liban et de l'Outremer, Byblos Bank, Fransabank and other financial establishments catering to—and in some cases, like the Jammal Trust Bank, founded by—migrants and their relatives. Indeed, migrants to Africa—and the Gulf—have proven far more active investors in the Lebanese banking sector than those who have chosen to settle in North America. Others have chosen to plough their wealth into commercial or industrial undertakings. Thus, a 1982 survey found that around two-thirds of those who returned to Bait Shabab from West Africa established businesses in Lebanon—of these, some 45 per cent opened textile stores or supermarkets, 30 per cent put their money into manufacturing and 10 per cent chose to invest in services.[64] While the names of the shopping centres that line the dusty roads of Jabal 'Amil—Ghana Center, Ivoire Shopping and the like—bear witness to the investment strategies of these men and women, mosques, hospitals and other conspicuous symbols of charity serve as reminders of their benevolence.[65] Zrariyya alone had no fewer than six mosques in the late 1990s, all but one of them built by migrants. In the words of one of Peleikis' interlocutors, a wizened old agriculturalist called Abu 'Ali, for whom migration had never held much appeal: 'every wealthy migrant builds a mosque with money made in Africa'.[66] The town's artesian well, meanwhile, was also the gift of an 'African' migrant, Husain Ta'n.[67] Migration, then, has helped to sustain certain practices of ostentatious giving. But it has also created inequalities and patterns of dependency between those who move and those who stay behind. And, in doing so, it has helped to sustain a particular form of economic extraversion, which leads generation after generation to take the paths of the *mahjar*.

Of course, migrants to West Africa are not alone in building homes or establishing businesses and charitable institutions in Lebanon. However, it might be argued that they have shown a propensity to return matched only by those who began to move to Saudi Arabia, Kuwait, and the United Arab Emirates from the 1960s onwards. Thus, 24 per cent of migrants to West Africa and 27 per cent of migrants to the Gulf have expressed a desire to wish to return to Lebanon after a spell. By contrast, only 11.4 per cent of those living in Australia, and 12.8 per cent of those who had settled in North America, shared this desire; the overwhelming majority—67.4 per cent in the case of Australia, and 61.5 per cent in that of North America—declared that they had no intention of returning to the Eastern Mediterranean, and were quite happy to stay put.[68] One might distinguish, then, between two streams of contemporary migration from Lebanon. While Europe, North America, and Australia are widely regarded as definitive destinations, to which one moves to settle, migration to West Africa and the Gulf is still seen as an essentially circular process; one only sojourns in these countries, before coming back to the Eastern Mediterranean. Such circulation may play itself out, in the case of West Africa, over the span of lifetimes and generations—individuals born in Senegal or Côte d'Ivoire returning to Lebanon for their education, before heading back out to West Africa to run their families' businesses and, eventually, leaving their interests to their children and returning to their 'home' village. But the expectation is still that those who can afford to do so will maintain their ties to the localities of their forebears. It is certainly true that places such as Bait Shabab or Zrariyya have come to be like 'ships'.[69] Far from enclosed settlements occupying a fixed point on the map, they 'move around within networks of agents, human and non-human',[70] becoming embodied in proliferating webs of 'translocal kinship relations' as much as in physical markers such as homes, streets or orchards.[71] Nevertheless, many migrants to West Africa have retained an intense tie to the localities of their birth.

Furthermore, those who return to Lebanon have not just invested their earnings or made show of their affective commitments. They have also striven to insert themselves into Lebanese political networks, helping in the process to shape the country's particular political culture. Alongside members of the 'new Shia intelligentsia—lawyers, civil servants, physicians', the 'new men with new money' of West Africa played a significant part in the *harakat al-mahrumin*, or 'movement of the deprived', founded by the deeply charismatic Iranian-born cleric Musa al-Sadr in 1974. 'Frenzied and pushy individuals' eager to make their mark, they found their access to politics closed off by the *zu'ama*, or big men, of Jabal 'Amil, like the omnipotent Kamil Bek al-As'ad. The latter, though 'uncomfortable' with the way the world was changing all around him, continued to regard the rich men who returned from Nigeria, Côte d'Ivoire or Senegal to buy up land and request a place in parliament as so many 'peasants' unworthy of his consideration. Flattered by Sadr's attentions, these men joined the movement he had established to break the hold of quasi-feudal families like the As'ad, and to draw the Shi'a away from secular organisations, whether leftist like the Lebanese Communist Party or the Druze leader Kamal Jumblat's Socialist Progressive Party, or rightist, like the Syrian Social Nationalist Party or Kamil Sham'un's National Liberal Party.[72] Indeed, 'Africans' continue to play a significant role in AMAL—as the organisation Sadr founded is now known. These include men like Yasin Jabir. Born in 1951 in Lagos, Jabir completed his schooling at the International College in Beirut in 1970, before studying for a degree in business administration at the American University of Beirut. A wealthy businessman with investments in Nigeria and London as well as Lebanon, he has been deputy for the district of Nabatiyya since 1992. But perhaps most prominent of all is the movement's leader, Nabih Berri. Born in 1938 in the Sierra Leone town of Bo, he too returned to Lebanon for his education, attending schools in Jabal 'Amil and Beirut before obtaining a law degree from the Lebanese University in 1963. He has served as speaker of the Lebanese parliament since 1992, his eviction of his longstanding predecessor, Husain al-Husaini, signalling a changing of the guard from the old Shi'a elites of post-independence Lebanon to the new men, flush with their African wealth, who first came to the fore in the 1960s. It is little surprise, given such entanglements, that both AMAL and Hizballah should enjoy strong support among Shi'a migrants to West Africa. For not only do these men and women stem from localities which have fallen under the sway of these organisations; they have also found their way back into Lebanese political life through them.

This is a reminder of the ways in which migrants to West Africa are, in some senses, conventionally Lebanese in their political attachments and practices. This is evident, too, in the conversations at a poolside party, on another summer day in Lebanon. Young men of my age stand lazily about in their board shorts and flip-flops, drinking beer and chatting. Casually moving from Arabic to English, and back, they seem no different to other Lebanese. In other ways, too, they are difficult to tell apart from their peers. They all hold degrees in engineering or business administration from the American University of Beirut or the Lebanese American University, and all have now embarked on migratory journeys of their own, finding careers in the United Arab Emirates, Saudi Arabia or, in the case of one particularly garrulous, portly fellow, Shanghai. But all are 'Africans', who spent much of their early life in Nigeria or Sierra Leone before 'returning' to Lebanon to complete their studies. Reminiscing about childhoods spent conversing in Pidgin and Krio and eating groundnut stew, they show off on their smart phones photos of their latest hunting party, blurry snapshots of figures in camouflage gear, hunting rifle in one hand, standing cockily next to African assistants holding up bedraggled ducks. For all their memories, they speak proudly of their Lebanese home towns, of Miziara or the Greek Orthodox villages of the Kura, finding in these an enduring source of distinction that imbues their African lives with distinctively Eastern Mediterranean overtones: as they explain to me, 'in Sierra Leone, there was us, and then there were the Shi'a, and in Nigeria, there were Miziara people, and the Shi'a'. These moments remind one of the ways in which the lives of Lebanese migrants to West Africa resemble those of their compatriots who have stayed behind in the Eastern Mediterranean, or who have migrated elsewhere, but also of the apparent differences which mark them apart, those often small distinctions barely perceptible to the outsider, but which take on such great importance in the eyes of the Lebanese themselves. For migrants to West Africa are, without any doubt, seen as different both to *al-muqimin*—'residents', as those who remain in Lebanon are known in official parlance—and to those who have chosen other destinations elsewhere in the *buldan al-ightirab*—the 'countries of migration'. And perceptions of these men and women are made up of a web of contradictions.

On the one hand, migrants to Côte d'Ivoire, Senegal, Sierra Leone or Nigeria are regarded as somehow more 'civilised' than those who have stayed behind, despite the deeply entrenched racial prejudices of many Lebanese towards Africa and its autochthonous inhabitants: *ils sont plus civilisés*, I am told when asked the subject of my research—*'andun hadara*, 'they have civilisation'. 'Africans', then, stand in stark contrast to the apparent decrepitude of Lebanon itself, whose cramped roads, failing electricity system, rampant construction, lack of civility, atrophied bureaucracy and political corruption its denizens bemoan. In part, this is perhaps simply a product of their absence from Lebanon—living away from it, they can better elude the ills that envelope, and take over, those who remain. This is a sentiment voiced both by *al-muqimin*, those who reside permanently in Lebanon, anticipating the summer season and the 'descent' of migrants upon the country, and those who live for most of the years in West Africa. As Yusuf told Souha Tarraf-Najib, 'people in Lebanon have a special mentality, a way of thinking … I can't get along with them. I socialised in France with Lebanese from Lebanon: they're too politicised, all they talk about is confessions, and all that….'[73] The casts of mind of those who remain in Lebanon, in such an account, are so particular, so introverted, as to be unpalatable to those who live elsewhere and are able to free themselves from the country's all-consuming factionalism and sectarianism.

There is also, for those wealthier migrants who flit between West Africa, Europe and the Eastern Mediterranean, an element of mockery for the lack of linguistic—and cultural—fluency of resident Lebanese. This is palpable even in the smallest of everyday interactions. In one instance, I watched the scion of a wealthy Senegalese business family order a coffee in a chic Lebanese beach-club: *baddi es-B-resso*, he called out to the waiter in his broken Arabic, 'I want an espresso', taking particular care to put heavy stress on that plosive B sound, the better to underline the clumsy way in which ordinary Lebanese handle—and mangle—European words, those markers of sophistication and civility. Caring little for his own uncertain grasp of the Arabic language, he sought to contrast his own cosmopolitan, well-travelled manners with the isolation and stasis of those who remain in Lebanon, stuck in their ways. At such moments, one sees something like the celebration of flexibility Aihwa Ong noted among elite members of the Chinese diaspora of South-East Asia.[74] Like the apostles of modernisation theory, migrants are wont to see mobility as a sign of modernity and stillness as one of backwardness—a reminder of the ways in which the language of the social sciences percolates beyond the academy, shaping the way in which we view and inhabit the world.[75]

On the other hand, the Lebanese can look upon those who have left for Africa in rather harsher terms. The wealth of some can, to be sure, elicit envy and admiration. But it can also prompt disgusted responses from some, like Karen, an affluent inhabitant of the largely Christian Beirut neighbourhood of Ashrafiyyeh, who heaps scorn upon these 'nouveaux riches': hailing from 'humble backgrounds, and with little culture, they come back to spend their money in an ostentatious fashion to show off their success'.[76] Such talk—like that of migrants themselves, who look down upon the waiters who serve them and their unsophisticated ways—is inextricably tied up in issues of class, and uneven access to cultural and economic capital. But it also reminds us of the enduring cleavage between those who remain and those who return.

This sense of estrangement from Lebanese society, and the increasingly dysfunctional state that claims to preside over it, was apparent in the weeks after the crash of Ethiopian Airlines ET409. For this not only prompted an outpouring of grief among the Lebanese of West Africa, but also revealed their continuing anger and frustration at their treatment at the hands of the national state. It shed all too stark a light on their predicament, liminal beings living on the margins both of the African states in which they spend much of their time, and of Lebanon—that 'homeland' to which they maintain resilient, ambivalent, ties. With mourning came inevitable recrimination. Some demanded to know why the Lebanese national carrier, Middle East Airlines, did not offer direct flights to the African cities in which so many of the country's citizens had long lived. The Nabatiyya-born Husain Ja'far thus angrily told of the circuitous route he was forced to take between Lebanon and his base in Libreville, the capital of Gabon. This flight, he noted, takes only five hours and twenty minutes. But, he explained:

Middle East Airlines does not fly to Africa, except for one flight each week to Abidjan. From Abidjan to Libreville, it is another four hours' flight, and you have to spend one or two nights in the Ivorian capital. Over the years, we've taken Air Congo, Air Algérie, and now Ethiopian Airlines. A Beirut-Libreville flight, via this company, takes ten hours. Air France does fly to Africa, but it is expensive, and we're badly treated in French airports, and searched thoroughly, as though we were terrorists. Last [time], they even searched my medicine box… MEA is one of the best airlines in the world, but it only flies to Europe and the Gulf. Is it too much to ask that we expect it to fly two or three times a week to the African destinations in which many Lebanese work?[77]

This apparent neglect on the part of Lebanon's state-owned national carrier, then, was a sign for many not just of the failings of the Lebanese state, but also of its lack of concern for its—migrant—citizens. For some, it was also confirmation of the contempt with which the political and commercial elites of Beirut continued to look upon Jabal 'Amil and its Shi'a inhabitants, long seen by the petty bourgeois and patrician grandees of the Lebanese capital as synonymous with everything that was retrograde and reprehensible.

For others, it was a reminder of the enduring travails of postcolonial Lebanon. Some thus asked themselves why the Lebanese still had to go abroad in search of a better life, more than a century after men and women from the villages and market towns of the Eastern Mediterranean seaboard first took the paths of migration. One of the deceased, Yasir Isma'il, a 36-year-old father of two, had left his home town in Jabal 'Amil soon after completing his studies, unable to find a job in Lebanon; after five years working in a Lebanese restaurant in London, he moved to Sudan to work as a computer engineer, then to Angola, where he was finally able to set up his own business. His was a tale in which old and new, change and continuity, mixed together. On the one hand, it showed the ways in which new destinations in Europe and Africa have opened up for Lebanese migrants in recent decades; on the other, it showed the continuing integration of Africa into wider circuits of circulation and the enduring appeal of migration as a strategy for social mobility, in the face of unappealing prospects at home. Yasir was, in the words of his uncle, Riyad Isma'il, 'like all young guys in Lebanon. His motives were to build a better future and to provide for his family. He was far away from his family and always wanted to return home. He came home to give them money and then died. It is a tragedy.' A desire to make something of oneself, to come good, but also to do so in as short a time as possible, before returning home a richer man—these are still common longings for many Lebanese. But into this desire for social betterment is mixed a deep streak of political disaffection. As Riyad Ismai'l put it: '[w]hen we find answers to who is responsible for this crash we have to ask another question: why does the young generation of Lebanese have to live in exile?'[78] Such questions were raised again after the death of 'Adil Bijjani, the young Lebanese hotel manager killed by intruders he surprised in his Lagos home. When one comment asked, 'Why do we allow our citizens to live in that hole Nigeria?', another responded 'Because Lebanon has nothing to offer? Because they choose to live in nigeria rather than lebanon [sic]? Because most lebanese have chosen since 100 years ago that it is better to live in africa, south america, the arab world and the west.'[79] Migration, as much as a secular social strategy, has become for many another symptom of the profound malaise blighting contemporary Lebanon. It is not for nothing that some wags have suggested that the cedar that stands so proud in the centre of the Lebanese flag should be replaced with a suitcase. Lebanon, more than ever, is a country of migrants—to the dismay of ordinary people, religious figures and politicians alike, who look upon this outflow as a drain upon its vital force.

Indeed, a fresh crop of Lebanese migrants has flowed into West Africa in recent years. Some are merely taking over their families' businesses after spending their early years in the Eastern Mediterranean, where they were raised by their mother or grandparents. But others have no previous connection to Africa; university graduates with degrees in engineering, business administration, hospitality or computer science, they have eagerly taken up the entreaties of Lebanese-owned firms in the absence of any opportunities in Lebanon itself. I can still recall the excitement with which the Maronite priest of Notre-Dame du Liban in Dakar pointed to a group of young men in their mid-twenties coming out of Mass one Sunday morning, with their shiny suits and rugged stubble. Recently arrived from Lebanon, they were the first new members of the congregation in over a decade. Having grown dissatisfied with the prospects on offer in Dubai and London, an acquaintance of mine who had spent his childhood travelling back and forth between Lebanon and Sierra Leone with his Lebanese father chose to take up an offer to work in a Cape Verde resort owned by the wealthy Shaghury family, whose interests are spread between West Africa and Lebanon. Another group I know of decided to set up a telecom business in the DRC, Angola and Mozambique, having tired of life in the Gulf.

Furthermore, the crash of flight ET409 also served to underline the asymmetrical relations between the Lebanese state, and those of its citizens who remain resident within its borders, and the country's large diaspora. Contemporary Lebanon is, in several senses, a nation of migrants. By one measure, some 45 per cent of Lebanese households can count at least one member who had 'travelled'—as many Lebanese now call migration, their preference for this casual term betraying their continuing understanding of displacement as a temporary condition, but also their unease at its pervasive presence all around them—abroad between 1992 and 2007.[80] By another, some 18 per cent of Lebanon's citizens are migrants, who reside beyond the confines of the territorial state. And this propensity for movement shows no sign of abating: 350,000 men and women migrated between 1997 and 2007.[81]

But migration is not just demographically significant, it is also economically vital. Long of crucial importance to many Lebanese localities and regions, remittances have only grown in amplitude in the last decade. Despite—or perhaps because of—global economic woe, the amount of money transferred electronically to Lebanon has gone from $4,743 million in 2003 to $5,759 million in 2007 and $8,177 million in 2010. The causes of this increase remain uncertain. Some have argued that Lebanese migrants regard their country's large banking sector, relatively insulated by draconian regulation from the ravages of the subprime crisis, as a safe haven. Others have insisted that it has been driven by continuing political and economic uncertainty in Lebanon, which has shrunk already precarious livelihoods and pushed many to rely ever more on relatives abroad.[82] But, whatever the case, it is clear that remittances remain a principal source of income for many. In 2009, they represented no less than 21.7 per cent of Lebanon's GDP, a quite staggering figure.[83] The effects of this assistance are clearer still at the local level. In a study conducted in 1995 among Shi'a inhabitants of Beirut's southern suburbs, the sociologist Mounzer Jaber found that around 64 per cent of his respondents received regular assistance from relatives established abroad. The 2,500 remaining inhabitants of the Biqa' village of Lala, meanwhile, depend on its 7,000 or so *mughtaribin*, or migrants, for 70 per cent of their income.[84] Migration, it is clear, has led those who stay behind to become increasingly reliant on those who leave, and has helped to sustain a particular form of economic extraversion, which leads generation after generation to go abroad in search of prosperity.

And yet, migrants receive little in the way of official recognition for their continuing contributions to Lebanon's economy. On the contrary, officials have tended to think of the diaspora as little more than a vast 'cash cow' to be milked for all it is worth. As Laurie Brand has pointed out, there is general agreement among former ambassadors that 'successive governments have been concerned with maintaining or rebuilding ties between the expatriates (and their descendents) and Lebanon, especially with the goals of encouraging tourism and investment, and of lobbying for Lebanon on critical occasions with their host countries'.[85] Indeed, official pronouncements by the likes of Haitham Jum'ah, the longstanding head of the General Directorate for Migrants, have tended to make demands of migrants, while offering little in return. Taking up the famous words of Pope John Paul II, Jum'ah asserted in one speech that Lebanon, 'more than just a country, is a message'; the members of the country's diaspora, meanwhile, were to be its 'purveyors', tasked with 'establishing' an image of their homeland as a place for the 'meeting of civilisations and the spread of love in the world'.[86] This instrumental approach to the diaspora as financial provider and diplomatic facilitator was apparent in the recent visit of the Lebanese president, Michel Sleiman (Sulaiman), to West Africa. While the tour, which resulted in a number of reciprocal trade agreements, was hailed by some as 'boosting ties' with Senegal, Côte d'Ivoire, Ghana and Nigeria,[87] the advertising executive Talal Makdisi (Muqaddasi), who accompanied Sleiman, stressed that the visit was 'absolutely necessary to link those expats that are supporting our economy' and 'contributing hugely to the reconstruction' of Lebanon, to the country. While he presented this as a beneficent move to bring these migrants back into the fold of the nation, Makdisi also mentioned that the official delegation had 'already been in contact with Lebanese business communities', in the hope of laying the 'groundwork for future partnerships'.[88] Sleiman, for his part, urged migrants to 'stay in touch with their native country'.[89] There is no denying that migrants may derive benefits, both economic and political, from the strengthening of relations between Lebanon and West African states. Nevertheless, one cannot help but sense that they are being asked to do the lion's share of the work in cementing these ties.

The fulfilment of such duties has rarely been accompanied by significant concessions on the part of the Lebanese state, which has lagged behind others in implementing out-of-country voting, citing both a lack of personnel and a dearth of interest on the part of the diaspora. A telling sign of this disregard is the decision to house the General Directorate of Migrants within the Ministry of Foreign Affairs. There is, perhaps, nothing untoward in this, for it naturally falls upon Lebanon's diplomatic delegations to attempt as best they can to maintain contact with migrants. Nevertheless, this bureaucratic division of labour does resonate with a broader tendency to cast diasporic citizens as situated *barrat Lubnan*—or 'outside Lebanon'—

both physically and, far more significantly, in political and social terms. For all that the high-flown rhetoric representing Lebanon as a bird with two wings—one 'resident', the other 'migrant'—appears, on the face of it, to insist upon the intrinsic ties between Lebanon and its diaspora, two inseparable parts of a broader whole, it is also a bifurcated vision, maintaining them at a safe distance from one another.

Despite the country's heavy dependence on migrants, their return visits, real estate investments and remittances, its resident inhabitants and functionaries do not, for the most part, regard it as a diasporic polity loosened from territorial ties. Some—in particular Maronite clerics and politicians who dream of reclaiming for the country, and its Christian confessions, men and women lost to diaspora—remain, it is true, wedded to the language of *intishar*, or diffusion, a discourse of circulation which pays less heed to territorial markers and confines. Most, however, remain intensely committed to an essentially conventional vision of the nation as a landed estate, neatly fenced off from its neighbours. This is apparent from the slogans and claims of many parties—whether the attachment of the Christian Phalangist and Lebanese Forces to an integral Lebanon of 10,452 square kilometres, a figure that has become something of a mantra for the members of these parties, or the insistence of AMAL and Hizballah that their resistance to Israel cannot stop until every last parcel of contested land in Ghajar and the Shib'a farms is liberated. Far from spilling over and transcending its borders, Lebanon continues to be defined by them. Migrants can hold but a bit part in such a story.

Conclusion: the newness of diaspora

It is difficult to speak of diasporic experience in the singular. Travelling existences take a multiplicity of different forms, as men and women go—and are led—down different routes through life. Nevertheless, it seems true to say that Lebanese migrants to postcolonial West Africa are 'not quite African, but no longer Lebanese'.[90] Liminal figures, they stand at the cusp of the regions and states they live in, putting one foot over the threshold and keeping one outside. However, it has not always been thus. Rather, one might argue that while the independence, first of Lebanon, then of the various states of what is now Francophone West Africa—their transformation into sovereign units, each one an island unto itself—did not put an end to movement between these regions, it did create new casts of minds. In the time of the nation-state, travelling lives—and notions of belonging founded in webs of human community, rather than rooted in the soil of the territorial polity—became harder to countenance. It would be wrong, then, to regard diasporas as 'indifferent to the idiosyncracies of nation-states', as social formations whose quicksilver mobility serves as a stark contrast to the staid presence of the territorial polity, and which demonstrate its 'inherent fragility'. To be sure, the 'relationship between people and place' is negotiable, as it were—endlessly mutable and open to revision.[91] However, I would argue that late modern understandings of the territorial nation-state and of its diasporas are not so much diametrically opposed as dialectically bound together. The

middle decades of the twentieth century—the time of self-determination, decolonisation and national independence—brought, to be sure, an immense sense of relief and
optimism to many across the world. This was a moment pregnant with potential, in
which new possibilities opened up and new political forms could be essayed which,
many hoped, would bring liberty and happiness to people who had previously lived
under colonial rule. But this, it might be argued, was also a moment of closure. For
the formidable 'contagion of sovereignty' which coursed through the world in these
decades made of the nation-state—the underpinning of what some still call the
Westphalian system—the political norm throughout the world.[92] As Sunil Amrith
has recently argued, the triumph of territorial nationalism closed off certain routes
for circulation, and curtailed certain patterns of movement and ways of thinking
about the world.[93] For many, horizons at once expanded in some ways, and narrowed
in others. The pervasive sense of liminality that seems to stalk Lebanese migrants to
West Africa as they move through the world, then, is no testament to the transhistorical commonalities of diasporic experience. Rather, like everything else, it is a
product of history.

NOTES

INTRODUCTION: MOVING PEOPLES, ENTANGLED HISTORIES

1. Aspe-Fleurimont, Lucien, *La Guinée Française: Conakry et Rivières du Sud. Étude Économique et Commerciale*, Paris: Augustin Challavel, 1900, p. 217.
2. *BCAF* 14, 12 (December 1904), p. 374.
3. Rouget, Fernand, *La Guinée. Notice du Gouvernement-Général de l'Afrique Occidentale Française à l'Occasion de l'Exposition Coloniale de Marseille*, Paris: Émile Larose, 1906, p. 403.
4. Aspe-Fleurimont, *La Guinée*, p. 29.
5. The Federation of Afrique Occidentale Française was created in 1895 as a union of Senegal, Soudan, Guinea and Côte d'Ivoire. In 1902, its separate territorial administrations were subordinated to a Government-General, whose seat lay first in Saint-Louis, then from 1904 in Dakar. It was also in 1904 that Dahomey was included in this group of colonies. Mauritania and Niger remained *territoires militaires*, administered by military men answering to the Ministry of Defence, until—respectively—the 1920s and the 1940s, while the colony of Haute-Volta (present-day Burkina Faso) was created only in 1919. For accounts of the shifting make-up of AOF, see Coquery-Vidrovitch, Catherine, and Odile Goerg, eds, *L'Afrique Occidentale au Temps des Français: Colonisateurs et Colonisés, c. 1860–1960*, Paris: Éditions La Découverte, 1992; and Conklin, Alice, *A Mission to Civilize: The Republican Empire in France and West Africa, 1895–1930*, Stanford, CA: Stanford University Press, 1997.
6. Cruise O'Brien, Rita, 'Lebanese entrepreneurs in Senegal', *Cahiers d'Études Africaines*, 15, 1 (1975), p. 98.
7. Winder, R. Bayly, 'The Lebanese in West Africa', *Comparative Studies in Society and History*, 4, 3 (1962), p. 300.
8. Hushaimah, 'Abdallah, *Fi Bilad al-Zunuj, aw Thamaniyyat Ashhur fi Ifriqiya al-Gharbiyya*, Beirut: Matabi' Quzma, n.d. 1931, p. 332.
9. van der Laan, H. Laurens, *The Lebanese Traders of Sierra Leone*, The Hague: Mouton, 1975, p. 1.
10. Chakrabarty, Dipesh, *Provincializing Europe: Postcolonial Thought and Historical Difference*, Princeton, NJ: Princeton University Press, 2000, pp. 18, 31.
11. Ginzburg, Carlo, 'De près de loin', *Vacarme*, 18 (2002), http://www.vacarme.org/article235.html, last accessed 12 Aug. 2009; Thompson, E.P., *The Making of the English Working Class*, London: Penguin, 1991 [1963], p. 12.
12. Levi, Giovanni, 'On microhistory', in Burke, Peter, ed., *New Perspectives on Historical Writing*, Cambridge: Polity, 1997, pp. 94, 96.
13. Hill, Polly, 'A plea for indigenous economics: the West African example', in *Studies in Rural Capitalism in West Africa*, Cambridge: Cambridge University Press, 1990, p. 3; Hart, Keith, 'Kinship, contract, and trust: the economic organisation of migrants in an African City slum', in Gambetta, Diego, ed., *Trust: Making and Breaking Collaborative Relationships*, Oxford: Blackwell, 1988, p. 177.
14. There is a growing, if diffuse and uneven, body of scholarship on Eastern Mediterranean migration to these various locations. For a general survey, see the essays in Hourani, Albert H. and Nadim Shehadi, eds, *The Lebanese in the World: A Hundred Years of Emigration*, London: I.B. Tauris, 1992. On migration to the United States, see in particular Gualtieri, Sarah, *Between Arab and White: Race and Ethnicity in the Early Syrian American Diaspora*, Berkeley, CA: University of California Press, 2009; Khater, Akram, *Inventing Home: Emigration, Gender and the*

Middle Class in Lebanon, 1870–1920, Berkeley, CA: University of California Press, 2001; and Naff, Alixa, *Becoming American: The Early Arab Immigrant Experience*, Carbondale, IL: Southern Illinois University Press, 1985. On Canada, see Abu-Laban, Baha, *An Olive Branch on the Family Tree: The Arabs in Canada*, Toronto: McClelland and Stewart, 1980. On Australia, see Andrew and Trevor Batrouney, *The Lebanese in Australia*, Melbourne: AE Press, 1985; and Burnley, I.H., 'Lebanese migration and settlement in Sydney, Australia', *International Migration Review*, 16, 57 (1982), pp. 102–32. On Latin America, see Klich, Ignacio and Jeff Lesser, eds, *Arab and Jewish Immigrants in Latin America: Images and Realities*, London: Frank Cass, 1998. On Brazil, see Karam, John Tofik, *Another Arabesque: Syrian-Lebanese Ethnicity in Neo-Liberal Brazil*, Philadelphia, PA: Temple University Press, 2007; and Truzzi, Oswaldo, *Sírios e Libaneses: narrativas de história e cultura*, São Paulo: Companhia Editoria Nacional, 2005. On Argentina, see in particular Bertoni, Liliana Ana, 'De Turquia a Buenos Aires. Una colectividad nueva a fines del siglo XIX', *Estudios Migratorios Latinoamericanos*, 9, 26 (1994), pp. 67–94; Bestene, Jorge, 'La inmigración Sirio-Libanesa en la Argentina: una aproximación', *Estudios Migratorios Latinoamericanos*, 9 (1988), pp. 239–68; and Tasso, Alberto, 'Migracion y identidad social. Una comunidad de inmigrantes en Santiago del estero', *Estudios Migratorios Latinoamericanos*, 8 (1987), pp. 321–36. On the Caribbean, see Lafleur, Gérard, *Les Libanais et Syriens de Guadeloupe*, Paris: Karthala, 1999; and Nicholls, David, 'No hawkers and pedlars: Arabs of the Antilles', in *Haiti in Caribbean Context: Ethnicity, Economy and Revolt*, Basingstoke: Macmillan, 1985, pp. 135–64. For a recent account of Eastern Mediterranean migration to South-East Asia, see Clarence-Smith, William Gervase, 'Middle Eastern migrants in the Philippines: entrepreneurs and cultural brokers', *Asian Journal of Social Sciences*, 32, 3 (2004), pp. 425–57.

15. Boumedouha, Saïd, 'The Lebanese in Senegal: A history of the relationship between an immigrant community and its French and African Rulers', Ph.D. thesis, Centre for West African Studies, University of Birmingham, 1987; van der Laan, *Lebanese Traders*.

16. Bauer, P.T., *West African Trade: A Study of Competition, Oligopoly and Monopoly in a Changing Economy*, Cambridge: Cambridge University Press, 1954, p. 164; Leighton, Neil, 'Lebanese emigration: its effect on the political economy of Sierra Leone', in Hourani and Shehadi, eds, *Hundred Years*, p. 598. See also Leighton, Neil, 'The political economy of a stranger population: the Lebanese of Sierra Leone', in Shack, William A. and Elliott P. Skinner, eds, *Strangers in African History*, Berkeley, CA: University of California Press, 1979, pp. 85–104.

17. Amin, Samir, 'La politique coloniale française à l'égard de la bourgeoisie commerçante sénégalaise', in Meillassoux, Claude, ed., *The Development of Indigenous Trade and Markets in West Africa*, London: Oxford University Press, 1971, espec. pp. 366–8; Kaniki, Martin, 'The psychology of early Lebanese immigrants in West Africa', in *International Seminar: Asian Trading Minorities in Tropical Africa, Afrika Studiencentrum, Leiden, 15–19 December 1975*, Leiden: n.p., 1976, pp. 3–14; and Suret-Canale, Jean, *French Colonialism in Tropical Africa, 1900–1945*, transl. Gottheimer, Till, London: Heinemann, 1971, pp. 67–8. For broader statements of such views see, in particular, Amin, Samir, *Impérialisme et Sous-Développement en Afrique*, Paris: Anthropos, 1976; Rodney, Walter, *How Europe Underdeveloped Africa*, London: Bogle L'Ouverture, 1972; and Frank, André Gunder, *Capitalism and Underdevelopment in Latin America: Historical Studies of Chile and Brazil*, New York: Monthly Review Press, 1967. For helpful overviews of the *dependentista* school, see in particular Kay, Cristóbal, *Latin American Theories of Development and Underdevelopment*, London: Routledge, 1989; and O'Brien, Philip J., 'Dependency revisited', in Abel, Christopher and Colin Lewis, eds, *Latin America, Economic Imperialism and the State*, London: Institute of Latin American Studies, 1985, pp. 40–69. Timothy Mitchell has recently argued that Amin's arguments first took shape in the early 1950s, quite independently from the work of *dependentistas* like Gunder Frank and Raúl Prebisch; see Mitchell, Timothy, 'The Middle East in the past and future of Middle Eastern studies', in Szenton, David, ed., *The Politics of Knowledge: Area Studies and the Disciplines*, Berkeley, CA: University of California Press, 2004, pp. 74–118.

18. Ong, Aihwa, *Flexible Citizenship: The Cultural Logics of Transnationality*, Durham, NC: Duke University Press, 1999.

19. 'Tenacity and risk—the Lebanese in West Africa', http://news.bbc.co.uk/1/hi/world/africa/8479134.stm, last accessed 6 Jun. 2012.

20. 'Afrique: la longue marche des Libanais', *JA* (13/10/2009).

21. On these figures see, 'Sénégal-Liban: quelques épopées', *JA* (13/10/2009); 'Côte d'Ivoire-Liban: Daghir, un homme d'Influence', *JA* (13/10/2009); and Smith, Stephen W., 'Nodding and winking', *London Review of Books*, 32, 3 (11/02/2010), pp. 10–2.

22. 'Syrians as shopkeepers in Sierra Leone: minority activities in village trading', *The Times British Colonies Review*,

25 (1st quarter, 1957), p. 15. For treatments of Eastern Mediterranean migration to particular colonial territories, see Bierwirth, Chris, 'Like fish in the sea: the Lebanese diaspora in Côte d'Ivoire, 1925–1990', Ph.D dissertation, University of Michigan, 1994; Bierwirth, 'The initial establishment of the Lebanese community in Côte d'Ivoire, ca. 1925–45', *International Journal of African Historical Studies*, 30, 2 (1997), pp. 325–48; Boumedouha, 'The Lebanese in Senegal'; Cruise O'Brien, 'Lebanese entrepreneurs'; Kojok, Salma. 'Les Libanais en Côte d'Ivoire de 1920 à 1960', unpublished Ph.D dissertation, Université de Nantes, 2002, 2 vols.; van der Laan, *Lebanese Traders*. For a more general, if outdated, treatment, see Winder, 'The Lebanese'.

23. CARAN AOF NS 21 G 142 [200 Mi 3071], 'RENSEIGNEMENTS', Dakar, 25/04/1940.

24. Winder, 'Lebanese', p. 297; Bierwirth, Chris, 'The Lebanese communities of Côte d'Ivoire', *African Affairs*, 99 (1998), p. 79. See also Crowder, Michael, *West Africa under Colonial Rule*, Evanston, IL: Northwestern University Press, 1968, pp. 293–7.

25. Shack, William A., 'Introduction', in Shack and Skinner, eds, *Strangers*, p. 4. See Simmel, Georg, 'The stranger', in Wolff, Kurt H., transl. and ed. *The Sociology of Georg Simmel*, London: Macmillan, 1964, pp. 402–8.

26. Fanon, Frantz, *Les Damnés de la Terre*, Paris: Gallimard, 1991 [1961], pp. 68–71.

27. Cooper, Frederick, 'Conflict and connection: rethinking colonial African history', *American Historical Review*, 99, 5 (1994), p. 1544. On late colonial developmental discourse, see Cooper, Frederick, *Decolonisation and African Society: The Labour Question in French and British Africa*, Cambridge: Cambridge University Press, 1996; and Shipway, Martin, *Decolonisation and its Impact: A Comparative Approach to the End of the Colonial Empires*, Oxford: Blackwell, 2008, pp. 114–35.

28. Memmi, Albert, *Portrait du Colonisé Précédé du Portrait du Colonisateur*, Montréal: L'Etincelle, 1972, p. 12.

29. Vaughan, Megan, 'Liminal', *London Review of Books*, 28, 6 (23/03/2006), p. 16.

30. Memmi, *Portrait*, p. 16.

31. Ibid., p. 36.

32. For an account of the Mediterranean journeys of migrants, see Mallah, 'Abdallah, *al-Hijra min Mutasarrifiyyat Jabal Lubnan*, Beirut: n.p., 2003.

33. CARAN AOF NS 21 G 142 [200 Mi 3072], 'RÉSUMÉ RELATIF A LA QUESTION DE L'IMMIGRATION LIBANO-SYRIENNE EN A.O.F.', Dakar, 17/11/1937.

34. 'Ayyad, Mustafa, 'Bayna Suriyya wa Ifriqiya ma' bakhirat al-Shambullion', *al-'Irfan* 21, 4–5 (1931), pp. 511–4.

35. Filfili, Nadra, *Ma Vie: Cinquante Ans de Vie au Sénégal*, dictated to and translated by Karim Filfili, Dakar: n.p, 1973, p. 68.

36. Desbordes, *L'Immigration*, p. 15.

37. ANS AOF NS 10 F 14, Governor-General of AOF to Commissioner for the Colonies, 'Colonisation Libano-Syrienne', n.d. 1943.

38. I draw here upon the argument made by Latour, Bruno, 'Technology is society made durable', in Law, John, ed., *A Sociology of Monsters: Essays on Power, Technology and Domination*, London: Routledge, 1991, p. 118; and upon Marcus, George E., 'Ethnography in/of the World System: the emergence of multi-sited ethnography', *Annual Review of Anthropology*, 24 (1995), pp. 95–117. For a recent example of such an approach, see MacGaffey, Janet and Rémy Bazenguissa-Ganga, *Congo-Paris: Transnational Traders on the Margins of the Law*, Oxford: James Currey, 2000.

39. Rouse, Roger, 'Mexican migration and the social space of postmodernity', *Diaspora*, 1, 1 (1991), p. 14. For attempts to understand the complexities of such multi-sited communities, see Nabti, Patricia, 'Emigration from a Lebanese village: a case study of Bishmizzine', in Hourani and Shehadi, eds, *The Lebanese*, pp. 41–63; Peleikis, Anja, 'The emergence of a translocal community: the case of a South Lebanese village and its migrant connections to Ivory Coast', *Cahiers d'Études sur la Méditerranée Orientale et le Monde Turco-Iranien*, 30 (2000), pp. 297–317. For a contrary view, see Safran, William, 'Diasporas in modern societies: myths of homeland and return', *Diaspora*, 1, 1 (1991), pp. 83–99.

40. Clifford, James, 'Prologue: in media res', in *Routes: Travel and Translation in the Late Twentieth Century*, Cambridge, MA: Harvard University Press, 1997, p. 2.

41. McKeown, Adam, 'Global migration, 1846–1940', *Journal of World History*, 15, 2 (2004), pp. 155–89. On the late nineteenth century as a global age, and the limits of such a conception, see Bayly, C.A., *The Birth of the Modern World, 1780–1914: Global Connections and Comparisons*, Oxford: Blackwell, 2004; Cooper, Frederick, 'Globalization', in *Colonialism in Question: Theory, Knowledge, History*. Berkeley, CA: University of California

Press, 2005, pp. 91–112; and the essays in Hopkins, A.G., ed., *Globalization in World History*, London: Pimlico, 2002.

42. McKeown, Adam, *Melancholy Order: Asian Migration and the Globalization of Borders*, New York: Columbia University Press, 2008; Torpey, John, *The Invention of the Passport: Surveillance, Citizenship, and the State*, Cambridge: Cambridge University Press, 2000.

43. Gabaccia, Donna, *Italy's Many Diasporas*, Seattle, WA: University of Washington Press, 2000.

44. See Amrith, Sunil, *Migration and Diaspora in Modern Asia*, Cambridge: Cambridge University Press, 2011; Bose, Sugata, *A Hundred Horizons: the Indian Ocean in the Age of Global Empire*, Cambridge, MA: Harvard University Press, 2006; Metcalf, Thomas, *Imperial Connections: India in the Indian Ocean Arena, 1860–1920*, Berkeley, CA: University of California Press, 2007.

45. McKeown, Adam, *Chinese Migrant Networks and Cultural Change: Peru, Chicago, Hawaii, 1900–1936*, Chicago, IL: University of Chicago Press, 2001; Reid, Anthony, ed., *Sojourners and Settlers: Histories of Southeast Asia and the Chinese*, London: Allen & Unwin, 1996; Tagliacozzo, Eric and Wen-Chin Chang, eds, *Chinese Circulations: Capital, Commodities, and Networks in Southeast Asia*, Durham, NC: Duke University Press, 2011.

46. Tölölyan, Khachig, 'The nation state and its others: in lieu of a preface', *Diaspora*, 1, 1 (1991), p. 4.

47. Said, Edward, 'Zionism from the standpoint of its victims', *Social Text*, 1 (1979), p. 18. Said refers in this passage to George Eliot's portrayal of her protagonists in *Daniel Deronda* as 'wandering and alienated beings', forever in search of a home. See also Said, Edward, *Out of Place: A Memoir*, London: Granta, 1999.

48. Hall, Stuart, 'Thinking the diaspora: home-thoughts from abroad', *Small Axe*, 6 (1999), p. 9.

49. Clifford, James, quoted in Chambers, Iain, *Migrancy, Culture, Identity*, London: Routledge, 1993, p. 1. See, for particularly relevant interventions, Clifford, James, 'Diasporas', *Cultural Anthropology*, 9, 3 (1994), pp. 302–38; Gupta, Akhil and James Ferguson, 'Beyond "Culture": space, identity, and the politics of difference', *Cultural Anthropology*, 7, 1 (1992), pp. 6–23; Malkki, Liisa, 'National Geographic: the rooting of peoples and the territorialization of national identity among scholars and refugees', *Cultural Anthropology*, 7, 1, (1992), pp. 24–44; McKeown, Adam, 'Conceptualising Chinese diasporas, 1842 to 1949', *Journal of Asian Studies*, 58, 2 (1999), pp. 306–37; Tölölian, 'The nation state', pp. 3–7.

50. Bhabha, Homi, *The Location of Culture*, London: Routledge, 1994, p. 9.

51. al-Muruwwah, 'Ali 'Abdallah, 'Kalimat muhajir 'an Ifriqiya', *Al-'Irfan* 22, 4 (1931), p. 531.

52. Safa, Elie, *L'Émigration Libanaise*, Beirut: Université Saint-Joseph, 1961, p. 132.

53. ANS AOF NS 10 F 14, Governor of Guinea to Governor-General of AOF, 'a/s situation des Libano-Syriens', Conakry, 12/03/1945.

54. Hall, Stuart, 'Cultural identity and diaspora', in Braziel, Jana Evans and Anita Mannur, eds, *Theorizing Diaspora: A Reader*, Oxford: Blackwell, 2003, p. 236.

55. Tilly, Charles, 'Transplanted networks', in Yans-McLaughlin, Virginia, ed., *Immigration Reconsidered: History, Society, Politics*, Oxford: Oxford University Press, 1990, p. 83.

56. Ibid., p. 84.

57. Appadurai, Arjun, 'Global ethnoscapes: notes and queries for a transnational history', in Fox, Richard G., ed., *Recapturing Anthropology*, Santa Fe, NM: School of American Research Press, 1991, p. 193.

58. Breckenridge, Carol and Arjun Appadurai, 'Editors' comment: on moving targets', *Public Culture*, 2, 1 (1989), p. iii.

59. Lévi-Strauss, Claude, *La Pensée Sauvage*, Paris: Plon, 1962; de Certeau, Michel, *L'Invention du Quotidien*, vol. 1, Arts de Faire, Paris: Gallimard, 1990.

60. Ho, Engseng, *The Graves of Tarim: Genealogy and Mobility across the Indian Ocean*, Berkeley, CA: University of California Press, 2005, p. 18.

61. This is the sense in which my use of the dialectic of absence and presence most closely resembles its application in Freudian psychoanalytic theory. See Ogden, T. H., 'The dialectically constituted/decentred subject of psychoanalysis. 1. The Freudian subject', *International Journal of Psychoanalysis*, 73 (1992), p. 520. For Freud's own discussion of this idea, which centres upon psychic repression, see Freud, Sigmund, 'Negation', in Strachey, J., transl. and ed., *The Ego and the Id and Other Works, Standard Edition of the Complete Psychological Works of Sigmund Freud*, vol. XIX (1923–25), Harmondsworth: Penguin, 1962, pp. 233–40.

62. For richly suggestive accounts of material life in Beirut and its surrounds in the late nineteenth century and early twentieth centuries, see Abou-Hodeib, Toufoul, 'Authentic modern: domesticity and the emergence of a middle class culture in late Ottoman Beirut', Ph.D dissertation, University of Chicago, 2010; Abou-Hodeib, 'Taste

and class in late Ottoman Beirut', *International Journal of Middle East Studies*, 43, 3 (2011), pp. 475–92; Kassir, Samir, *Histoire de Beyrouth*, Paris: Fayard, 2003; and Sehnaoui, Nada, *L'Occidentalisation de la Vie Quotidienne à Beyrouth 1860–1914*, Beirut: Editions Dar an-Nahar, 2002.

63. On the fundamental importance of discourses of gender in interwar Lebanon and Syria, and the ways in which these underwent revision, see Thompson, Elizabeth, *Colonial Citizens: Republican Rights, Paternal Privilege and Gender in French Syria and Lebanon*, New York: Columbia University Press, 2000. On shifting, contested notions of femininity in the years before 1914, see inter alia Baron, Beth, *The Women's Awakening in Egypt*, New Haven, CT: Yale University Press, 1994; Booth, Marilyn, *May Her Likes Be Multiplied: Biography and Gender Politics in Egypt*, Berkeley, CA: University of California Press, 2001; and Khater, *Inventing Home*.

64. For recent exceptions, see Dakhli, Leyla, *Une Génération d'Intellectuels Arabes Syrie et Liban (1908–1940)*, Paris: Karthala, 2009; Gualtieri, *Between Arab and White*; Khuri-Makdisi, Ilham, *The Eastern Mediterranean and the Making of Global Radicalism, 1860–1914*, Berkeley, CA: University of California Press, 2010; and del Mar Logroño Narbona, Maria, 'The development of nationalist identities in French Syria and Lebanon: a transnational dialogue with Arab immigrants to Argentina and Brazil, 1915–1929', Ph.D. dissertation, University of California at Santa Barbara, 2007.

65. See, inter alia, Eppel, Michael, 'The elite, the effendiyya, and the growth of nationalism and Pan-Arabism in Hashemite Iraq, 1921–1958', *International Journal of Middle East Studies*, 30, 2 (1998), pp. 227–50; and Khoury, Philip S., *Syria and the French Mandate: the Politics of Arab Nationalism, 1920–1945*, Princeton, NJ: Princeton University Press, 1987. For individual studies, see Cleveland, William, *Making of an Arab Nationalist: Ottomanism and Arabism in the Life and Thought of Sati' al-Husri*, Princeton, NJ: Princeton University Press, 1972; and Provence, Michael, 'Ottoman modernity, colonialism, and insurgency in the interwar Middle East', *International Journal of Middle East Studies*, 43, 2 (2011), pp. 205–25.

66. Gershoni, Israel and James Jankowski, eds, *Rethinking Nationalism in the Middle East*, New York: Columbia University Press, 1997.

67. See Matthews, Weldon C., *Confronting an Empire, Constructing a Nation: Arab Nationalists and Popular Politics in Mandate Palestine*, London: I.B. Tauris, 2006; and Provence, Michael, *The Great Syrian Revolt and the Rise of Arab Nationalism*, Austin, TX: University of Texas Press, 2005.

68. Gupta and Ferguson, 'Beyond "Culture"', p. 7. Shohat, Ella, 'Area studies', in Essed, Philomena, David Theo Golberg and Audrey Koyabashi, eds, *A Companion to Gender Studies*, Oxford: Blackwell, 2004, Blackwell Reference Online, http://www.blackwellreference.com/subscriber/tocnode?id=g9780631221098_chunk_g97806312 210983, last accessed 18 Nov. 2010. For a discussion of the regionalism of Eastern Mediterranean history, see Bayly, C.A. and Leila Tarazi Fawaz, 'Introduction: the connected world of empires', in Fawaz, Leila Tarazi and C.A. Bayly with Robert Ilbert, eds, *Modernity and Culture From the Mediterranean to the Indian Ocean*, New York: Columbia University Press, 1999, pp. 1–27; for important discussions of 'area studies', see Rafael, Vicente, 'The culture of area studies in the United States', Social Text (1994), pp. 91–111; and Rafael, V.L. 'Regionalism, area studies, and the accidents of agency', *American Historical Review*, 104, 4 (1999), pp. 1208–20; and for an early statement of such concerns, see Wolf, Eric, *Europe and the People without History*, Berkeley, CA: University of California Press, 1982. For notable exceptions, see Gualtieri, *Between Arab and White*; and Khater, *Inventing Home*.

69. Duara, Prasenjit, *Rescuing History from the Nation: Questioning Narratives of Modern China*, Chicago, IL: University of Chicago Press, 1995, p. 27. See Gelvin, James, *Divided Loyalties: Nationalism and Mass Politics in Syria at the Close of Empire*, Berkeley, CA: University of California Press, 1998; Watenpaugh, Keith, *Being Modern in the Middle East: Revolution, Nationalism, Colonialism and the Arab Middle Class*, Princeton, NJ: Princeton University Press, 2006. For a work with similar ambitions focusing on the Maghrib, see McDougall, James, *History and the Culture of Nationalism in Algeria*, Cambridge: Cambridge University Press, 2006.

70. Abu-Lughod, Lila, 'Introduction: feminist longings and postcolonial positions', in Abu-Lughod, Lila, ed., *Remaking Women: Feminism and Modernity in the Middle East*, Princeton, NJ: Princeton University Press, 1998, pp. 3–31; Mitchell, Timothy, Colonising Egypt, Berkeley, CA: University of California Press, 1991; Najmabadi, Afsaneh, *Women with Mustaches and Men without Beards: Gender and Sexual Anxieties of Iranian Modernity*, Berkeley, CA: University of California Press, 2005.

71. Said, Edward, *Orientalism*, London: Penguin, 2003 [1978], p. 6.

72. Davis, Natalie Zemon, *Fiction in the Archives: Pardon Tales and their Tellers in Sixteenth-Century France*, Stanford, CA: Stanford University Press, 1987, p. 3.

73. Gilman, Sander, *The Jew's Body*, London: Routledge, 1991, p. 4.

74. David Prochaska's work remains probably the best evocation of French colonial life in one particular setting. Prochaska, David, *Making Algeria French: Colonialism in Bône, 1870–1920*, Cambridge: Cambridge University Press, 1990.

75. Girault, Arthur, *Principes de Colonisation et de Législation Coloniale*, Paris: Librairie de la Société du Recueil Sirey, 1921, 4th ed., p. 136.

76. Delavignette, Robert, *Les Vrais Chefs de l'Empire*, Paris: Gallimard, 1939, p. 30.

77. MAE T SL NS 115, Minister of Colonies to Minister of Foreign Affairs, Paris, 17/02/1911.

78. Cooper, Frederick and Ann Laura Stoler, 'Introduction', in Cooper, Frederick and Ann Laura Stoler, eds, *Tensions of Empire*, Berkeley, CA: University of California Press, 1997, p. 3. For attempts to examine the intertwined webs of empire, see the programmatic essay by Conklin, Alice L. and Julia Clancy-Smith, 'Introduction: writing colonial histories', *French Historical Studies*, 27, 3 (2004), pp. 497–505; and Mann, Gregory, 'Locating colonial histories: between France and West Africa', *American Historical Review*, 110, 2 (2005), pp. 409–34. For a recent synthetic history of French colonialism, see Thomas, Martin, *The French Empire Between the Wars: Imperialism, Politics and Society*, Manchester: Manchester University Press, 2005.

79. See Burton, Antoinette, *At the Heart of the Empire: Indians and the Colonial Encounter in Late-Victorian Britain*, Berkeley, CA: University of California Press, 1998; Colley, Linda, *Captives: Britain, Empire and the World*, 1600–1850, London: Pimlico, 2002; Hall, Catherine, *Civilising Subjects: Metropole and Colony in the English Imagination 1830–1867*, Cambridge: Polity, 2002; Wilson, Kathleen, ed., *A New Imperial History: Culture, Identity and Modernity in Britain and the Empire, 1660–1840*, Cambridge: Cambridge University Press, 2004.

80. Rabinow, Paul, *French Modern: Norms and Forms of the Social Environment*, Cambridge, MA: MIT Press, 1989; Wright, Gwendolyn, *The Politics of Design in French Colonial Urbanism*, Chicago, IL: University of Chicago Press, 1991.

81. Wilder, Gary, 'Unthinking French history: colonial studies beyond national identity', in Burton, Antoinette, ed., *After the Imperial Turn: Thinking With and Through the Nation*, Durham, NC: Duke University Press, 2003, pp. 126, 130. For an attempt by French scholars to reflect on the legacy of colonialism, see the essays in Blanchard, Pascal, Nicolas Bancel and Sandrine Lemaire, eds, *La Fracture Coloniale: La Société Française au Prisme de l'Héritage Colonial*, Paris: La Découverte, 2005. For a similar attempt to puncture the complexities and contradictions of the notion of Francophonie in French literary studies, see Forsdick, Charles and David Murphy, 'Introduction: the case for Francophone postcolonial studies', in Forsdick, Charles and David Murphy, eds, *Francophone Postcolonial Studies: An Introduction*, London: Arnold, 2003, pp. 1–14. On discourses of citizenship in France, see Silverman, Maxim, *Deconstructing the Nation: Immigration, Racism and Citizenship in Modern France*, London: Routledge, 1992; Brubaker, Rogers, *Citizenship and Nationhood in France and Germany*, Cambridge, MA: Harvard University Press, 1992.

82. See Wilder, Gary, *The French Imperial Nation-State: Negritude and Colonial Humanism between the Two World Wars*, Chicago, IL: Chicago University Press, 2005; and Cooper, Frederick, 'Provincializing France', in Stoler, Ann Laura, Carole McGranahan, and Peter C. Perdue, eds, *Imperial Formations*, Oxford: James Currey, 2007, pp. 341–78.

83. Peabody, Sue and Tyler Stovall, 'Introduction: race, France, histories', in Peabody, Sue and Tyler Stovall, eds, *The Color of Liberty: Histories of Race in France*, Durham, NC: Duke University Press, 2003, p. 4.

84. I distinguish here between the traffic in exclusionary racial discourses and the circulation of notions of social organisation. Christopher Harrison and Alice Conklin have long since pointed to the ways in which Republican disdain for feudalism and clericalism informed the attitudes of administrators towards African societies in the early twentieth century. See Harrison, Christopher, *France and Islam in West Africa, 1860–1960*, Cambridge: Cambridge University Press, 1988, p. 42; Conklin, Alice, *A Mission*, p. 3.

85. Foucault, Michel, *The Order of Things: An Archaeology of the Human Sciences*, London: Tavistock, 1970, p. 387.

86. For evocative explorations of the historian's endeavours—sometimes febrile, at others tedious—in the archives, see Dening, Greg, *History's Anthropology: The Death of William Gooch*, London: University Press of North America, 1988, espec. pp. 27–9; Farge, Arlette, *Le Goût de l'Archive*, Paris: Seuil, 1989; and Steedman, Carolyn, *Dust*, Manchester: Manchester University Press, 2001, pp. 17–19.

87. Rabinow, *French Modern*, p. 13. The notion of 'grids of intelligibility' is drawn from Foucault's idea of grilles et cases.

88. Barthes, Roland, *Camera Lucida: Reflections on Photography*, trans. Howard, Richard, London: Vintage, 1993, p. 26.
89. Rabinow, *French Modern*, p. 9.
90. Stoler, Ann Laura, 'Colonial archives and the arts of governance: on the content in the form', in Hamilton, Carolyn, Verne Harris, Jane Taylor, Michele Rickover, Graeme Reid and Rezia Saleh, eds, *Refiguring the Archive*, Dordrecht: Kluwer, 2001, p. 92.
91. On the role of such 'epistemic anxieties', see Bayly, C.A., *Empire and Information: Intelligence Gathering and Social Information in India, 1780–1870*, Cambridge: Cambridge University Press, 1996, p. 6; Stoler, Ann Laura, *Along the Archival Grain: Epistemic Anxieties and Colonial Commonsense*, Princeton, NJ: Princeton University Press, 2009.
92. See Cohen, William, *Rulers of Empire: the French Colonial Service in Africa*, Stanford, CA: Hoover Institute Press, 1971; Wilder, *Imperial Nation-State*.
93. Guha, Ranajit, *Elementary Aspects of Peasant Insurgency in Colonial India*, Durham, NC: Duke University Press, 1999 [1983], pp. 15–17. See also Guha, Ranajit, 'The prose of counter-insurgency', in Guha, Ranajit and Gayatri Chakravorty Spivak, eds, *Selected Subaltern Studies*, Oxford: Oxford University Press, 1988, espec. pp. 47–53.
94. I borrow this term from Ho, Engseng, 'Empire through diasporic eyes: a view from the other boat', *Comparative Studies in Society and History* (2004), pp. 210–46.
95. Ballantyne, Tony, *Orientalism and Race: Aryanism in the British Empire*, Basingstoke: Macmillan, 2002, p. 15.

1. A TALE OF TWO MOUNTAINS

1. Desbordes, Jean-Gabriel, *L'Immigration Libano-Syrienne en Afrique Occidentale Française*, Poitiers: Renault & Cie, 1938, pp. 28–32.
2. Knowlton, Clark S., 'The social and spatial mobility of the Syrian and Lebanese community in Sao Paulo, Brazil', in Hourani, Albert and Nadim Shehadi, eds, *The Lebanese in the World: A Hundred Years of Emigration*, London: I.B. Tauris, 1992, p. 286.
3. Issawi, Charles, 'The historical background of Lebanese emigration, 1830–1914', in Hourani and Shehadi, eds, *Lebanese*, p. 31.
4. See Hanioğlu, Şükrü, 'The Young Turks and the Arabs before the revolution of 1908', in Khalidi, Rashid, Lisa Anderson, Muhammad Muslih, and Reeva S. Simon, eds, *The Origins of Arab Nationalism*, New York: Columbia University Press, 1991, pp. 31–49; and Kayalı, Hasan, *Arabs and Young Turks: Ottomanism, Arabism, and Islamism in the Ottoman Empire, 1908–1918*, Berkeley, CA: University of California Press, 1997.
5. Ganem, Halil, *Études d'Histoire Orientale: Les Sultans Ottomans*, vol. 1, Paris: n.p., 1901, p. ix.
6. Ibid., pp. i–ii.
7. Comité Libanais de Paris, *Mémoire sur la Question du Liban*, Paris: n.p., 1912, pp. 5–6.
8. Desbordes, *L'Immigration Libano-Syrienne*, p. 10.
9. Shediack, George, 'The Shediack migration: a saga sustained by faith and love', *Journal of Maronite Studies*, (January 1998), http://maroniteinstitute.org/MARI/JMS/january98/The_Shediack_Migration.htm, last accessed 10 Mar. 2013.
10. Saadi, Edward T., 'Our Lady of Deliverance: immigration of the Saadi, Abraham, Elum, and Hayik families', *Journal of Maronite Studies*, (July 1998) http://maroniteinstitute.org/MARI/JMS/july98/Our_Lady_of_Deliverance.htm, last accessed 10 Mar. 2013.
11. al-'Usairan, Nur al-Din Muhyi al-Din, 'Al-Hijra', *al-'Irfan*, 21, 4–5 (1931), p. 524.
12. Kojok, Salma, 'Les Libanais en Côte d'Ivoire de 1920 à 1960', unpublished Ph.D dissertation, Université de Nantes, 2002, 2 vols., vol. 1, pp. 52–3.
13. Akarlı, Engin, *The Long Peace: Ottoman Lebanon, 1861–1920*, London: I.B. Tauris, 1993.
14. Khater, Akram, *Inventing Home: Emigration, Gender and the Middle Class in Lebanon, 1870–1920*, Berkeley, CA: University of California Press, 2001, pp. 49–52.
15. Ibid., p. 54.
16. Ibid., p. 53.
17. There is a large body of literature on the events of 1860. See in particular Chevallier, Dominique, *La Société du Mont Liban à l'Epoque de la Révolution Industrielle*, Paris: Geuthner, 1971; Fawaz, Leila Tarazi, *An Occasion for*

War: Civil Conflict in Beirut and Damascus in 1860, Berkeley, CA: University of California Press, 1994; and Makdisi, Ussama, *The Culture of Sectarianism: Community, History, and Violence in Nineteenth Century Ottoman Lebanon*, Berkeley, CA: University of California Press, 2001.

18. On earlier unrest in the Christian area of Kisrwan, see Buheiry, Marwan, 'The Peasant Revolution of 1858 in Mount Lebanon: rising expectations, economic malaise and the incentive to arm', in Khalidi, Tarif, ed., *Land Tenure and Social Transformation in the Middle East*, Beirut: American University of Beirut, 1984, pp. 291–301; Chevallier, Dominique, 'Aux origines des troubles agraires libanais', *Annales ESC*, 14 (1959), pp. 35–64; and Porath, Yehoshua, 'The Peasant Revolt of 1858–61 in Kisrawan', *Asian and African Studies*, 2 (1966), pp. 77–157.

19. Makdisi, Ussama and Joel Silverstein, 'Introduction', in Makdisi, Ussama and Joel Silverstein, eds, *Memory and Violence in the Modern Middle East*, Bloomington, IN: University of Indiana Press, 2006, pp. 1, 7–8.

20. Fawaz, Leila Tarazi, *Merchants and Migrants in Nineteenth Century Beirut*, Cambridge, MA: Harvard University Press, 1983, p. 113.

21. Akarlı, Engin, 'Ottoman attitudes towards Lebanese emigration, 1885–1910', in Hourani and Shehadi, eds, *Lebanese*, p. 111.

22. Montiel, Luz Maria Martinez, 'The Lebanese community in Mexico: its meaning, importance and the history of its communities', in Hourani and Shehadi, eds, *Lebanese*, p. 382.

23. Makdisi, *Culture*, pp. 171–2.

24. Fawaz, *Merchants*, pp. 50, 53.

25. Harik, Iliya, *Politics and Change in a Traditional Society, Lebanon 1711–1845*, Princeton, NJ: Princeton University Press, 1968, chs. 4, 5.

26. Labaki, Boutros, *Introduction à l'Histoire Economique du Liban: Soie et Commerce Extérieur en Fin de Période Ottomane*, Beirut: Presses de l'Université Libanaise, 1984, pp. 79–86.

27. Owen, Roger, *The Middle East in the World Economy, 1800–1914*, London: I.B. Tauris, 1993, p. 157.

28. Chevallier, *La Société*, p. 220. Labaki, *Introduction*, p. 86.

29. Chevallier, *La Société*, pp. 30, 230. An *oka* is roughly equivalent to 1.28 kilograms.

30. Owen, *Middle East*, p. 165.

31. Ibid., p. 157.

32. Khater, Akram, 'House to goddess of the house: gender, class, and silk in nineteenth century Mount Lebanon', *International Journal of Middle East Studies*, 28, 3 (1996), p. 327.

33. Labaki, *Introduction*, p. 110.

34. Ibid., p. 111.

35. Ibid., p. 122.

36. Ibid., pp. 394–7.

37. Firro, Kais, 'Silk and socio-economic change in Lebanon, 1860–1919', in Kedourie, Elie and Sylvia Haim, eds, *Essays on the Economic History of the Middle East*, London: Frank Cass, 1988, Table 2, p. 23.

38. Much the same argument holds for the Greek Orthodox village of Bishmizzine in the Kura. See Nabti, Patricia, 'Emigration from a Lebanese village: a case study of Bishmizzine', in Hourani and Shehadi, eds, *Lebanese*, pp. 41–63; and Tannous, Afif, 'Social change in an Arab village', *American Sociological Review*, 6, 5 (1941), pp. 650–62; and Tannous, 'Emigration: a force of social change in an Arab village', *Rural Sociology*, 7 (1942), pp. 62–74.

39. Khater, 'House', p. 327.

40. Labaki, *Introduction*, p. 155.

41. Khater, *Inventing Home*, p. 57.

42. Labaki, *Introduction*, pp. 52–3.

43. Owen, *Middle East*, p. 249.

44. Issawi, Charles, *An Economic History of the Middle East and North Africa*, London: Methuen, 1982, p. 86.

45. Feghali, Michel, *Proverbes et Dictons Syro-Libanais: Texte Arabe, Transcription, Traduction, Commentaire et Index Analytique*, Paris: Institut d'Ethnologie, 1935, p. 14.

46. Furayha, Anis, *Modern Lebanese Proverbs Collected at Ras al-Matn: Collated, Annotated and Translated into English*, Beirut: American University of Beirut, 1953, p. 23.

47. Khater, *Inventing Home*, p. 44.

48. Ibid., p. 43.

49. Khater, 'House', p. 329.

50. Chevallier, *La Société*, pp. 286–7.

51. Firro, 'Socio-economic change', Table 3, p. 23.

52. Ibid., Table 4, p. 25.

53. Saba, Paul, 'The creation of the Lebanese economy: economic growth in the nineteenth and twentieth centuries', in Owen, Roger, ed., *Essays on the Crisis in Lebanon*, London: Ithaca, 1976, pp. 20–21.

54. Khater, 'House', p. 328.

55. Khater, *Inventing Home*, p. 59.

56. Owen, *Middle East*, p. 251.

57. Khater, *Inventing Home*, p. 328.

58. Chevallier, *La Société*, pp. 233–7.

59. Khater, 'House', p. 326.

60. Owen, *Middle East*, p. 249.

61. Khater, 'House', p. 329.

62. Khater, *Inventing Home*, p. 58.

63. Owen, *Middle East*, p. 166.

64. Khater, *Inventing Home*, p. 56.

65. Labaki, *Introduction*, p. 130.

66. Firro, 'Socio-economic change', p. 40.

67. Klich, Ignacio, '*Criollos* and Arabic speakers in Argentina: an uneasy *Pas de Deux*, 1888–1914', in Hourani and Shehadi, eds, *Lebanese*, p. 267.

68. Desbordes, *L'Immigration*, p. 17.

69. Labaki, *Introduction*, p. 395.

70. Tamimi, Muhammad Rafiq and Muhammad Bahjat, *Wilayat Bayrut*, vol. 2, *Al-Qism al-Shimali*, Beirut: Matba'at al-Wilaya, 1917, p. 269.

71. MAE NS T SL 107, De Sercey to Delcassé, Beirut, 26/02/1903.

72. Labaki, *Introduction*, p. 122.

73. Khater, *Inventing Home*, p. 59.

74. Ibid., p. 60.

75. MAE NS T SL 107, De Sercey to Delcassé, Beirut, 26/02/1903.

76. Sa'id, 'Abdallah, *Ashkal al-Milkiyya wa Anwa' al-Aradi fi Mutasarrifiyyat Jabal Lubnan wa Sahl al-Biqa', 1861–1914: Dirasa Muqarana fi al-Tarikh al-Rifi, Istinadan ila Watha'iq Asliyya*, Beirut: Maktaba Baisan, 1995, pp. 196–9. A *dunum* is roughly equivalent to an acre.

77. Sa'id, 'Abdallah, *Tatawwur al-Milkiyya al-'Aqariyya fi Jabal Lubnan fi 'Ahd al-Mutasarrifiyya Istinadan ila Watha'iq Asliyya: Namudhaj al-Matn al-A'la*, Beirut: Dar al-Mada, 1986, pp. 124–9. Khater, 'House', p. 327.

78. Khater, *Inventing Home*, p. 60.

79. Ibid.

80. Khater, 'House', p. 331.

81. Naff, Alixa, *Becoming American: The Early Arab Immigrant Experience*, Carbondale, IL: Southern Illinois University Press, 1985, p. 60.

82. Khater, *Inventing Home*, p. 62.

83. Naff, Alixa, 'Lebanese immigration into the United States: 1880s to the present', in Hourani and Shehadi, eds, *Lebanese*, p. 144.

84. Khater, *Inventing Home*, p. 62.

85. Naff, *Becoming American*, p. 94.

86. Akarlı, 'Ottoman attitudes', p. 112.

87. Knowlton, 'Spatial mobility', p. 288.

88. Ruppin, Arthur, 'Syrien als Wirtschaftsgebiet', in Issawi, Charles, ed., *The Economic History of the Middle East 1800–1914: A Book of Readings*, Chicago, IL: University of Chicago Press, 1966, p. 271.

89. Khater, *Inventing Home*, p. 111.

90. Ruppin, 'Syrien', p. 271; MAE NS T SL 107, De Sercey to Delcassé, Beirut, 26/02/1903.

91. Zeine, Zeine N., *Arab-Turkish Relations and the Emergence of Arab Nationalism*, Beirut: Khayat's, 1958, pp. 41–2.

92. MAE NS T SL 107, De Sercey to Delcassé, Beirut, 26/02/1903.

93. Ruppin, 'Syrien', p. 272. A *fiddan* is equivalent to 2,812.5 square metres.

94. Firro, 'Socio-economic Change', p. 40.
95. Owen, *Middle East*, p. 251.
96. Ruppin, 'Syrien', p. 270.
97. Schilcher, Linda Schatkowski, 'The famine of 1915–1918 in Greater Syria', in Spagnolo, John, ed., *Problems of the Modern Middle East in Historical Perspective: Essays in Honour of Albert Hourani*, London: Ithaca, 1992, pp. 235–8.
98. Thompson, Elizabeth, *Colonial Citizens: Republican Rights, Paternal Privilege and Gender in French Syria and Lebanon*, New York: Columbia University Press, 2000, p. 20.
99. Schilcher, 'Famine', p. 231.
100. Thompson, *Colonial Citizens*, p. 20.
101. Schilcher, 'Famine', pp. 229; fn. 7, 230.
102. Thompson, *Colonial Citizens*, p. 25.
103. Ibid., p. 31. On the similar trajectories of two women themselves pushed to migration by their husbands' absences, see Gualtieri, Sarah, 'Gendering the Chain Migration Thesis: women and Syrian transatlantic migration, 1878–1924', *Comparative Studies of South Asia, Africa and the Middle East*, 24, 1 (2004), pp. 67–78; and Akram and Antoine Khater, 'Assaf: a peasant of Mount Lebanon', in Burke III, Edmund, ed., *Struggle and Survival in the Modern Middle East*, Berkeley, CA: University of California Press, 1993, pp. 31–43.
104. Filfili, Nadra, *Ma Vie: Cinquante Ans de Vie au Sénégal*, dictated to and translated by Filfili, Karim, Dakar: n.p 1973, pp. 60–3.
105. Ibid., pp. 59, 61.
106. Owen, Roger and Şevket Pamuk, *A History of Middle Eastern Economies in the Twentieth Century*, London: I.B. Tauris, 1998, p. 6.
107. Firro, 'Socio-economic change', p. 44.
108. Owen and Pamuk, *Middle Eastern Economies*.
109. Firro, 'Socio-economic change', p. 46.
110. Cited in Owen and Pamuk, *Middle Eastern Economies*, fn. 7, 16.
111. Nasser, Liliane, 'Marseille et l'émigration libanaise', unpublished DEA thesis, Université de Provence, 1986, p. 13.
112. Owen and Pamuk, *Middle Eastern Economies*.
113. CARAN AOF NS 21 G 142 [200 Mi 3071], 'RESUME RELATIF A LA QUESTION DE L'IMMIGRATION LIBANO-SYRIENNE EN AOF', Dakar, 17/11/1937.
114. *CO* 372 (December 1928), p. 254.
115. Widmer, Robert, 'Population', in Himadeh, Said B., ed., *Economic Organization of Syria*, Beirut: American University Press, 1936, p. 15.
116. Filfili, *Ma Vie*, p. 60.
117. Widmer, 'Population', p. 15.
118. Himadeh, ed., *Economic Organization*, Appendix I-C 2, pp. 410–1.
119. MAE NS T SL 107, De Sercey to Delcassé, Beirut, 26/02/1903.
120. Desbordes, *L'Immigration*, p. 29.
121. See Dahir, Mas'ud, 'Al-Hijra ila Misr', in *Watha'iq Mu'tamar Tarikh Sur al-Awwal*, Sur: Muntada Sur al-Thaqafi; and Bazzi, Mustafa, *Al-Hijra wa al-Nuzuh min Lubnan khilal al-Qarn al-'Ashrin (1900–2006) (Namudhaj Janub Lubnan)*, Beirut: Dar al-Mahajja al-Bayda, 2008, pp. 303–8. On movement between the Syrian lands and Egypt more generally, see Dahir, Mas'ud, *Al-Hijra al-Lubnaniyya ila Misr: Hijrat al-Shawwam*, Beirut: Lebanese University, 1986; and Philipp, Thomas, *The Syrians in Egypt, 1725–1975*, Stuttgart: Steiner, 1985.
122. al-Khuri, Michel Thabit, *Tarikh Abrashiyat Sur 1800–1914*, Beirut: Dar al-Mawasim, 2003, pp. 65, 73.
123. Tamimi and Bahjat, *Wilayat Bayrut*, p. 294.
124. Cuinet, Vital, *Syrie Liban et Palestine Géographie. Administrative Statistique Descriptive et Raisonnée*, Paris: Ernest Leroux, 1896, p. 84.
125. Bazzi, Mustafa, *Bint Jubail: Hadirat Jabal 'Amil*, Beirut: Dar al-Amir li-l-Thaqafa wa al-'Ulum, 1998, pp. 338–9. Baydoun, Ahmad, 'Bint-Jbeil, Michigan, suivi de (ou poursuivi par) Bint-Jbeil, Liban', *Maghreb-Machrek*, 125 (1989), p. 77.
126. Tarraf-Najib, Souha, *Zrariyyé, Village Chiite du Liban-Sud*, Beirut: CERMOC, 1992, p. 34.

127. al-Amin, Muhsin, *Khitat Jabal 'Amil*, vol. 1, Beirut: Matba'at al-Insaf, 1961, pp. 141–2.

128. al-Zahir, Sulaiman, *Mu'jam Qura Jabal 'Amil*, vol. 2, Beirut: Mu'asasa al-Imam al-Sadiq li-l-Buhuth fi Turath 'Ulama' Jabal 'Amil, 2006 [1928], pp. 326–7.

129. Al-Amin, *Khitat*, pp. 141–2.

130. Tarraf-Najib, *Zrariyyé*, p. 27.

131. Zahir, *Mu'jam*, pp. 327, 331.

132. Gualtieri, Sarah, *Between Arab and White: Race and Ethnicity in the Early Syrian American Diaspora*, Berkeley, CA: University of California Press, 2009.

133. Kojok, 'Les Libanais', pp. 53–4.

134. Salih, Farhan, *Janub Lubnan: Waqi'hu wa Qadayahu*, Beirut: Dar al-Tal'iyya, 1973; and Donon, Jean, cited in Halawi, Majed, *A Lebanon Defied: Musa al-Sadr and the Shi'a Community*, Boulder, CO: Westview, 1992, p. 38.

135. Tarraf-Najib, *Zrariyyé*, pp. 36–7.

136. On the 'learned families', as he calls them, see Peters, Emrys, 'Aspects of rank and status among Muslims in a Lebanese village', in Pitt-Rivers, Julian, ed., *Mediterranean Countrymen: Essays in the Social Anthropology of the Mediterranean*, Paris: Mouton, 1963, pp. 159–200; and Peters, 'Shifts in power in a Lebanese village', in Antoun, Richard and Iliya Harik, eds, *Rural Politics and Social Change in the Middle East*, Bloomington, IN: Indiana University Press, 1972, pp. 165–97.

2. ROOTS AND ROUTES: THE PATHS OF LEBANESE MIGRATION

1. Handlin, Oscar, *The Uprooted: The Epic Story of the Great Migrations that Made the American People*, Boston, MA: Little, Brown, 1952. See also de Crèvecoeur, Jean Hector St John, *Letters from an American Farmer*, Manning, Susan, ed., Oxford: Oxford University Press, 1997.

2. See Baily, Samuel, *Immigrants in the Lands of Promise: Italians in Buenos Aires and New York, 1870–1914*, Cornell, NY: Cornell University Press, 1999; Gabaccia, Donna, 'Kinship, culture and migration: a Sicilian example', *Journal of American Ethnic History*, 3 1984, pp. 43–7; John and Leatrice McDonald, 'Chain migration, ethnic neighbourhood formation and social networks', *Milbank Memorial Fund Quarterly*, 42 (1964), pp. 82–97; Tilly, Charles and C. Harold Brown, 'On uprooting, kinship and the auspices of migration', *International Journal of Comparative Sociology*, 8 (1968), pp. 139–64; Vecoli, Rudolph, '*Contadini* in Chicago: a critique of *The Uprooted*', *Journal of American History*, 51, 3 (1964), pp. 404–17; Vecoli, 'The formation of Chicago's "Little Italies"', *Journal of American Ethnic History*, 2 (1983), pp. 5–20.

3. Khater, Akram, *Inventing Home: Emigration, Gender and the Middle Class in Lebanon, 1870–1920*, Berkeley, CA: University of California Press, 2001; Naff, Alixa, *Becoming American: The Early Arab Immigrant Experience*, Carbondale, IL: Southern Illinois University Press, 1985.

4. Fuller, Anne, *Buarij: Portrait of a Lebanese Muslim Village*, Cambridge, MA: Harvard University Press, 1961, p. 6.

5. Sahlins, Marshall, *Islands of History*, London: Tavistock, 1985, p. 27. For the perspective of a historian who takes after Sahlins, stressing the constant interplay between structure and *praxis*, see Sewell Jr., William, 'The concept(s) of culture', in Hunt, Lynn and Victoria Bonnell, eds, *Beyond the Cultural Turn: New Directions in the Study of Society and Culture*, Berkeley, CA: University of California Press, 1999, pp. 35–61.

6. Khater, *Inventing Home*, p. 10.

7. Winder, R. Bayly, 'The Lebanese in West Africa', *Comparative Studies in Society and History*, 4, 3 (1962), p. 300.

8. Muruwwah, Kamil, *Nahnu fi Ifriqiya: al-Hijra al-Lubnaniyya al-Suriyya ila Ifriqiya al-Gharbiyya, Madiha, Hadiriha, Mustaqbaliha*, Beirut: Al-Makshuf, 1938, p. 190.

9. Hushaimah, 'Abdallah, *Fi Bilad-al-Zunuj, aw Thamaniyat Ashhur fi Ifriqiya al-Gharbiyya*, Beirut: Matabi' Quzma, n.d., [1931], pp. 79–80.

10. Desbordes, Jean-Gabriel, *L'Immigration Libano-Syrienne en Afrique Occidentale Française*, Poitiers: Renault & Co., 1938, pp. 17–8.

11. *JOGF* 99 (15/11/1905), p. 577.

12. On the role of Dakar as a coaling station, and its slow growth as a town, see Seck, Assane, *Dakar*, Dakar: Faculté des Lettres et Sciences Humaines de Dakar, n.d.; Pasquier, Roger, 'Villes du Sénégal au XIXe siècle', *Revue Française d'Histoire d'Outre-Mer*, 47 (1960) pp. 387–426.

13. Muruwwah, *Nahnu fi Ifriqiya*, p. 196.

14. Conversation with Nabil Milan, Dakar, June 2007.

15. Hushaimah, *Fi Bilad al-Zunuj*, p. 187.

16. Desbordes, *L'Immigration*, p. 14.

17. Naff, *Becoming American*, p. 97.

18. Muruwwah, *Nahnu fi Ifriqiya*, p. 191.

19. Kojok, Salma, 'Les Libanais en Côte d'Ivoire de 1920 à 1960', unpublished Ph.D dissertation, Université de Nantes, 2002, 2 vols., vol. 1, p. 52.

20. Muruwwah, *Nahnu fi Ifriqiya*, p. 192.

21. Ibid., p. 208.

22. Goerg, Odile, *Commerce et Colonisation en Guinée 1850–1913*, Paris: L'Harmattan, 1986, pp. 338–9.

23. Copans, Jean, 'From Senegambia to Senegal: the evolution of peasantries', in Klein, Martin, ed., *Peasants in Africa: Historical and Contemporary Perspectives*, London: Sage, 1980, p. 90.

24. Searing, James, *'God Alone is King': Islam and Emancipation in Senegal. The Wolof Kingdoms of Kajoor and Baol, 1859–1914*, Oxford: James Currey, 2002, p. 199.

25. David, Philippe, *Les Navétanes: Histoire des Migrants Saisonniers de l'Arachide en Sénégambie des Origines à nos Jours*, Dakar: Les Nouvelles Editions Africaines, 1980, p. 54.

26. al-Rihani, Ameen [Amin], *The Book of Khalid*, Beirut: Rihani House, 1973 [1911], pp. 48–9.

27. ADBR 4 M 2172, Ministère de l'Intérieur, Commissariat Spécial des Chemins de Fer, des Ports, et de l'Emigration, 'Affaire Sursock', Marseille, 23/04/1891.

28. CCIMP ML 42731/01 'Passage à Marseille de l'émigration syrienne vers les Amériques [mémoire du Dr Bollama]'. See also Nasser, Liliane, 'Marseille et l'émigration libanaise', unpublished DEA thesis, Université de Provence, 1986. For a general account of Marseille's role as both a node of transatlantic migration, and a destination in its own right, see Lopez, Renée and Émile Témime, *L'Expansion Marseillaise et "l'Invasion Italienne" (1830–1918)*, Paris: Jeanne Lafitte, 2007 [1990], espec. pp. 22–7.

29. CCIMP ML 4274/01, Commissariat Spécial de Marseille, 'Création à Marseille d'un Hôtel d'Emigrants', Marseille, 11/07/1902.

30. Naaman, Abdallah, *Histoire des Orientaux de France du Ier au XXe Siècle*, Paris: Eclipse, 2004, p. 108.

31. 'Abduh, Najib, *Al-Safr al-Mufid fi al-'Alam al-Jadid, wa al-Dalil al-Tijari li-Abna al-Lugha al-'Arabiyya fi al-'Alam Ajma'* [Useful Travels in the New World, and a Commercial Directory of the Arabic-Speakers of the World], New York: Meraat ul-Gharb Publishing House, 1907, p. 428. Naaman, *Histoire*, p. 108.

32. Naaman, *Histoire*, p. 108.

33. CCIMP 2274/01, 'MEMOIRE sur l'affaire Fares-Abouarab contre les sieurs Lignon et Eskaf'.

34. Rihani, *The Book of Khalid*, p. 49.

35. CCIMP 2274/01, 'MEMOIRE sur l'affaire Fares-Abouarab contre les sieurs Lignon et Eskaf'.

36. CCIMP 2273/01, 'Passage à Marseille de l'émigration Syrienne vers les Amériques [mémoire du Dr Bollama]'.

37. ADBR 4 M 2152, 'Procès-verbal', 19/09/1899.

38. Londres, Albert, *Marseille: Porte du Sud*, Marseille: Jean Lafitte, 1980 [1927], p. 78.

39. See, for an account of such rhetoric, Fletcher, Yaël Simpson, '"Capital of the Colonies": real and imagined boundaries between metropole and empire in 1920s Marseille', in Driver, Felix and Martin Gilbert, eds, *Imperial Cities: Landscape, Display and Identity*, Manchester: Manchester University Press, 1999 pp. 136–151. For examinations of the very real economic connections which underpinned such representations, see in particular Daumalin, Xavier. *Marseille et l'Ouest Africain. L'Outre-Mer des Industriels (1841–1956)*, Marseille: Chambre de Commerce et d'Industrie Marseille-Provence, 1992; and Courdurié, Marcel and Guy Durand, eds, *Entrepreneurs d'Afrique*, Marseille: Chambre de Commerce et d'Industrie Marseille-Provence, 1998.

40. Naaman, *Histoire*, p. 108.

41. Nasser, *Marseille*, pp. 28, 29.

42. MAE T SL NS 115, Couget to Cruppi, Beirut, 13/04/1911.

43. CARAN AOF AS 21 G 33 [200 Mi 1099–1100], 'Copie de lettre non envoyée', n.d. [1918].

44. Saliba, Najib, 'Emigration from Syria', in Abraham, Sameer and Nabeel Abraham, eds, *Arabs in the New World: Studies on Arab-American Communities*, Detroit, MI: Wayne State University, 1983, p. 39. Saliba transliterates this phrase as Bait al-Ijaza—the holiday home—but translates it as the 'home of the aged'. Whatever the meaning, this wordplay underlines the ways migration redrew social relations in a place like Bait Shabab.

45. ANS AOF 11 D 3/37, 'ÉTAT DE L'IMMIGRATION SYRIENNE DANS LE CERCLE DE THIÈS—ANNÉE 1924'.

46. The census of foreign residents conducted by the government of Guinea in late 1918 provides valuable information on migration to the colony in the years before 1914: CARAN AS 21 G 38 [200 Mi 1100–1101], 'Recensement des Étrangers Résidant en Guinée Française Indiquant: a) Leur pays d'origine b) La date de leur arrivée dans la colonie c) Leur situation dans les maisons qui les emploient d) Renseignements généraux sur leur manière d'être', Conakry, 28/10/1918.

47. van der Laan, H. Laurens, *The Lebanese Traders of Sierra Leone*, The Hague: Mouton, 1975, pp. 235–6; Aswad, Barbara, 'The Lebanese community in Dearborn, Michigan', in Hourani, Albert and Nadim Shehadi, eds, *The Lebanese in the World: A Hundred Years of Emigration*, London: I.B. Tauris, 1992, p. 170.

48. Aswad, 'Dearborn', p. 170.

49. See Choldin, Harvey, 'Kinship networks in the migration process', *International Migration Review*, 7, 2 (1973), pp. 166–7.

50. CARAN AOF AS 21 G 38 [200 Mi 1100–1101], 'Recensement des Étrangers Résidant en Guinée Française Indiquant: a) Leur pays d'origine b) La date de leur arrivée dans la colonie c) Leur situation dans les maisons qui les emploient d) Renseignements généraux sur leur manière d'être', Conakry, 28/10/1918.

51. CARAN AOF AS 21 G 44 [200 Mi 1103], Abdoulay Hamit ['Abdallah Hamid] to Délégué of the Governor of Senegal, Dakar, 05/10/1917.

52. CARAN AOF AS 21 G 43 [200 Mi 1102], Ganamet to Governor-General of AOF, Dakar, 15/10/1916.

53. Khuri, Fuad, 'Kinship, emigration, and trade partnership among the Lebanese of West Africa', *Africa*, 35, 4 (1965), p. 389.

54. ANS AOF 11 D 3/37, 'État nominatif des Syriens installés dans le cercle du CAYOR', n.d. [1924].

55. ANS AOF 11 D 3/37, 'ÉTAT DE L'IMMIGRATION SYRIENNE DANS LE CERCLE DE THIÈS—ANNÉE 1924'.

56. CARAN AOF AS 21 G 32 [200 Mi 1099], 'État de santé des Syriens actuellement à Rufisque', 07/07/1900.

57. CARAN AOF AS 21 G 32 [200 Mi 1099], 'État nominatif des Syriens présents à Saint-Louis à la date du 30 Août 1900'.

58. Harney, Robert, 'Men without women: Italian migrants in Canada, 1885–1930', in Boyd, Betty, Robert Harney and Lydio Tomasi, eds, *The Italian Immigrant Woman in North America*, Toronto: The Multicultural History Society of Toronto, 1978, pp. 79–103.

59. See Brettell, Carole, *The Men Who Migrate and the Women Who Wait: Population and History in a Portuguese Parish*, Cambridge: Cambridge University Press, 1986. See Akram and Antoine Khater, 'Assaf: a peasant of Mount Lebanon', in Burke III, Edmund, ed., *Struggle and Survival in the Modern Middle East*, Berkeley, CA: University of California Press, 1993, pp. 31–43, for an attempt to tell both sides of migration in a Lebanese context.

60. Gualtieri, Sarah, 'Gendering the chain migration thesis: women and Syrian transatlantic migration, 1878–1924', *Comparative Studies of South Asia, Africa and the Middle East*, 24, 1 (2004), p. 67.

61. CARAN AS 21 G 38 [200 Mi 1100–1101], 'EXECUTION DES PRESCRIPTIONS DE LA CIRCULAIRE CONFIDENTIELLE Nº 44 du 12 JUIN 1918—TABLEAU DES ETRANGERS RESIDANT AU HAUT SENEGAL-NIGER—CERCLE DE KAYES'.

62. Desbordes, *L'Immigration*, p. 17.

63. Gualtieri, 'Gendering', p. 67.

64. Desbordes, *L'Immigration*, p. 17.

65. Hushaimah, *Fi Bilad-al-Zunuj*, p. 128.

66. Kojok, 'Les Libanais', vol. 1, p. 319.

67. Desbordes, *L'Immigration*, p. 34.

68. On this, see the rich series of visa requests from these years, organised by claimant, in ANS AOF 21 G 227.

69. See in particular Gualtieri, 'Gendering'; Naff, *Becoming American*; Khater, *Inventing Home*; and Shakir, Evelyn, *Bint Arab: Arab and Arab American Women in the United States*, Westport, CT: Praeger, 1997. For programmatic attempts to integrate an understanding of women's movements into our understanding of migration, see Gabaccia, Donna, 'Women of the mass migrations', in Moch, Leslie and Dirk Hoerder, eds, *European Migrants: Global and Local Perspectives*, Boston, MA: Northeastern University Press, 1996, pp. 90–111; Morokvasic, Mirjana, 'Birds of passage are also women…', *International Migration Review*, (1984), pp. 886–907; and the essays in Phizacklea, Annie, ed., *One Way Ticket: Migration and Female Labour*, London: RKP, 1983.

70. Desbordes, *L'Immigration*, p. 18.
71. CARAN AOF NS 21 G 23 [200 Mi 3023–24], 'NOTE sur Cheikh Sleiman Daher, et la bibliothèque de "Djabal Amel" à Nabatié'; CARAN AOF NS 21 G 23 [200 Mi 3023–24], Commissaire de Police of Kaolack to Commandant de Cercle of Sine-Saloum, Kaolack, 22/09/1930.
72. CAOM MC FM AP 1432/1, Governor-General of AOF to Secretary of State for the Colonies, Dakar, 18/10/1941.
73. CARAN AOF AS 21 G 43 [200 Mi 1102], Lieutenant-Governor of Guinea to Governor-General of AOF, Conakry, 20/04/1918 and 26/04/1918.
74. Desbordes, *L'Immigration*, p. 32.
75. Anthony, Farid Raymond, *Sawpit Boy*, Freetown: n.p., 1980.
76. CAOM MC FM AP 1432/1, Governor-General High-Commissioner of French Africa to Secretary of State for the Colonies, Dakar, 06/01/1942.
77. CAOM FM AP 1432/1, Governor-General High-Commissioner of French Africa to Secretary of State for the Colonies, Dakar, 23/01/1942.
78. CAOM FM AP 1432/1, Governor-General High-Commissioner of French Africa to Secretary of State for the Colonies, Dakar, 23/01/1942, enclosures.
79. CAOM FM AP 1432/1, 'MESSAGES EMANANT DE LIBANO-SYRIENS, DESTINES A ETRE DIFFUSES PAR LE POSTE "LA VOIX DE FRANCE"', enclosure, Governor-General to Secretary of State for the Colonies, Dakar, 30/01/1942.
80. CARAN AOF AS 21 G 33 [200 Mi 1099–1100], Joseph Constantin to Governor-General of AOF, Mopti, 28/01/1919.
81. CARAN AOF AS 21 G 33 [1099–1100], Antoine Abdo to Governor-General of AOF, Dakar, 01/02/1919.
82. CARAN AOF AS 21 G 44 [200 Mi 1103], Ebraham Zougaïb [Ibrahim Zughaib] to Governor-General of AOF, Dakar, 16/03/1917.
83. CARAN AOF AS 21 G 44 [200 Mi 1103], Marie Gastoune [Qastun] to Governor-General of AOF, Dakar, 04/08/1917.
84. CARAN AOF AS 21 G 44 [200 Mi 1103], Commissioner of Police to Administrateur de Cercle, Thiès, 10/03/1917.
85. CAOM MC FM AP 2303/1, Governor-General of AOF to Commissioner for the Colonies, 'a/s Commerçant libanais Ahmed El Haj Hassan', Dakar, 24/07/1944.
86. CARAN AOF AS 21 G 38 [200 Mi 1100–1101], 'Recensement des Étrangers Résidant en Guinée Française Indiquant: a) Leur pays d'origine b) La date de leur arrivée dans la colonie c) Leur situation dans les maisons qui les emploient d) Renseignements généraux sur leur manière d'être', Conakry, 28/10/1918.
87. These men and women gave, as was common practice in Jabal Lubnan, the names of their fathers and grandfathers, and the monikers which distinguished their particular branch of a larger patronymic group. Mansur, for instance, was the name of the father of Joseph and Hanna Mukarzil; Naja and Ma'ushi, which came in time to become surnames themselves, were the names of the smaller family units Faris Harb Naja Mukarzil and Qais Na'man Ma'ushi Mukarzil belonged to. Such naming practices allow us to untangle the messy threads of kin which bound them to each other. On naming practices in Arabic-speaking cultures, see Eickelman, Dale, *The Middle East: An Anthropological Approach*, Englewood Cliffs, NJ: Prentice Hall, 1989, 2nd ed., pp. 181–7.
88. AN AS 21 G 38 [200 Mi 1100–1101], 'Recensement des Étrangers Résidant en Guinée Française Indiquant: a) Leur pays d'origine b) La date de leur arrivée dans la colonie c) Leur situation dans les maisons qui les emploient d) Renseignements généraux sur leur manière d'être', Conakry, 28/10/1918.
89. On the complexity of kinship ties in two Lebanese villages, one Shi'a and the other Maronite, see Peters, Emrys, 'Aspects of rank and status among Muslims in a Lebanese village', in Pitt-Rivers, Julian, ed., *Mediterranean Countrymen: Essays in the Social Anthropology of the Mediterranean*, Paris: Mouton, 1963, espec. pp. 181–94; and Touma, Toufic, *Un Village de Montagne au Liban (Hadeth el-Jobbé)*, Paris: Mouton, 1958, p. 118. For a programmatic call to pay attention to the complex and constantly shifting arrangements of kin which characterised Eastern Mediterranean societies, see Doumani, Beshara, 'Introduction', in Doumani, Beshara, ed., *Family History in the Middle East: Household, Property and Gender*, Albany, NY: State University of New York Press, 2003, pp. 1–19. See also Doumani, Beshara, 'Endowing family: *waqf*, property devolution, and gender in Greater Syria, 1800 to 1860', *Comparative Studies in Society and History*, 40, 1 (1998), pp. 3–41; Duben, Alan and Cem Behar, *Istanbul Households: Marriage, Family, and Fertility, 1880–1940*, Cambridge: Cambridge University Press,

1991; and Meriwether, Margaret, *The Kin who Count: Family and Society in Ottoman Aleppo, 1770–1840*, Austin, TX: University of Texas Press, 1999.

90. Chevallier, Dominique, *La Société du Mont Liban à l'Époque de la Révolution Industrielle*, Paris: Geuthner, 1971, p. 134.

91. Desbordes, *L'Immigration*, p. 18.

92. AOF AS 21 G 44 [200 Mi 1103], Ministry of Colonies to Governor-General of AOF, Paris, 24/07/1917.

93. CARAN AOF AS 21 G 38 [200 Mi 1100–1101], 'COLONIE DE LA CÔTE D'IVOIRE—CONTROLE DES ÉTRANGERS', 1918.

94. CARAN AOF AS 21 G 44 [200 Mi 1103], Abu Hatab to Délégué du Gouvernement du Sénégal, Dakar, 08/11/1917.

95. CARAN AOF AS 21 G 44 [200 Mi 1103], Ministry of Colonies to Governor-General of AOF, Paris, 24/07/1917.

96. CARAN AOF AS 21 G 44 [200 Mi 1103], Abu Hatab to Délégué du Gouvernement du Sénégal, Dakar, 08/11/1917.

97. CARAN AOF AS 21 G 33 [200 Mi 1099–1100], 'Copie de lettre non envoyée', Angoulvant, n.d. [1918].

98. ANS AOF NS 10 F 14, 'RENSEIGNEMENTS concernant les LIBANO-SYRIENS en résidence au SOUDAN', Bamako, November 1944.

99. ANS AOF NS 10 F 14, 'NOTE RELATIVE A L'IMMIGRATION LIBANO-SYRIENNE au cours de l'année 1935'.

100. CARAN AOF NS 21 G 23 [200 Mi 3023–24], Commissaire de Police of Kaolack to Commandant de Cercle of Sine Saloum, Kaolack, 22/10/1930.

101. CARAN AOF NS 21 G 23 [200 Mi 3023–24], 'Exposé de l'Affaire pour Monsieur le Gouverneur Général', Dakar, 29/10/1930.

102. ANS AOF NS 10 F 14, Governor-General of AOF to Commissioner for Colonies, Dakar, n.d. [1943].

103. Desbordes, *L'Immigration*, p. 14–5.

104. CARAN AOF 21 G 61 [200 Mi 3039], Governor-General of AOF to Minister of Colonies, Dakar, 26/01/1938.

105. The quote is from CARAN AOF NS 21 G 142 [200 Mi 3072], 'Interview de Monsieur le Gouverneur Général de l'AOF', 13/05/1938.

106. Nasser, 'Marseille', p. 19.

107. Kojok, 'Les Libanais', vol. 2, pp. 228, 230.

108. CARAN AOF NS 21 G 142 [200 Mi 3072], 'RESUME RELATIF A LA QUESTION DE L'IMMIGRATION LIBANO-SYRIENNE EN A.O.F.', Dakar, 17/11/1937.

109. David, Philippe, *Les Navétanes*, pp. 464–5, Tables 1-B, 1-C, 1-D.

110. Khuri, 'Kinship', pp. 389, 393.

111. CARAN AOF NS 21 G 61 [200 Mi 3039], Governor-General to Minister of Colonies, 'A/S Immigration Libano-Syrienne', Dakar, 26/01/1938.

112. Muruwwah, *Nahnu fi Ifriqiya*, p. 189.

113. ANS AOF 11 D 3/37, 'Cercle du Sine Saloum—Subdivision de Foundiougne—État immigration syrienne', n.d. (1924).

114. ANS AOF 11 D 3/37, 'État nominatif des étrangers résidant dans le cercle', Louga, 21/03/1928,.

115. ANS AOF 11 D 3/37, 'Recensement de la population étrangère de la ville de Rufisque en décembre 1927'.

116. Filfili, Nadra, *Ma Vie: Cinquante Ans de Vie au Sénégal*, dictated to and translated by Filfili, Karim, Dakar: n.p 1973, *Ma Vie*, p. 65.

117. Issawi, Charles, 'The historical background of Lebanese emigration, 1830–1914', in Hourani and Shehadi, eds, *The Lebanese*, p. 30.

118. Andrew and Trevor Batrouney, *The Lebanese in Australia*, Melbourne: AE Press, 1985, p. 21.

119. Muruwwah, *Nahnu fi Ifriqiya*, p. 192.

120. Hoerder, Dirk, 'From dreams to possibilities: the secularization of hope and the quest for independence', in Hoerder, Dirk and Horst Rössler, eds, *Distant Magnets: Expectations and Realities in the Immigrant Experience, 1840–1930*, New York: Holmes & Meier, 1993, p. 11.

121. Filfili, *Ma Vie*, p. 63.

122. al-Muruwwah, 'Ali 'Abdallah, 'Kalimat muhajir 'an Ifriqiya', *Al-'Irfan*, 22, 4 (1931), p. 531.

123. Appadurai, Arjun, *Modernity at Large: Cultural Dimensions of Globalisation*, Minneapolis, MN: Minnesota University Press, 1996, p. 7.

124. Filfili, *Ma Vie*, p. 65.

125. On American missionary activity in the Eastern Mediterranean in the nineteenth century, see Makdisi, Ussama, *Artillery of Heaven: American Missionaries and the Failed Conversion of the Middle East*, Princeton, NJ: Princeton University Press, 2008; and the older, but still valuable Tibawi, A.L., *American Interests in Syria 1800–1901: A Study of Economic, Literary and Religious Work*, Oxford: Clarendon Press, 1966.

126. Hitti, Philip, *The Syrians in America*, New York: George H. Doran Company, 1924, p. 55.

127. Rihbany, Abraham Mitrie, *A Far Journey*, Boston, MA: Houghton Mifflin, 1914, pp. 143–5.

128. ANS AOF NS 10 F 14, 'RENSEIGNEMENTS concernant les LIBANO-SYRIENS en résidence au SOUDAN', Bamako, November 1944.

129. ANS AOF 10 F 14, Lebanese colony of Thiès to Commandant de Cercle, Thiès, 13/09/1933.

130. ANS AOF 10 F 14, enclosure, n.d. (1933).

131. ANS AOF 10 F 14, Commandant de Cercle of Séguéla to Governor of Côte d'Ivoire, Séguéla, 16/03/1945.

132. CAOM MC FM AP 1432/1, 'NOTICE DE RENSEIGNEMENTS concernant HUSSEIN ALI WEHBE'.

133. Thistlethwaite, Frank, 'Migration from Europe overseas in the nineteenth and twentieth centuries', in Vecoli, Rudolph and Suzanne Sinke, eds, *A Century of European Migrations 1830–1930*, Urbana, IL: University of Illinois Press, 1991, p. 28. For a recent attempt to distinguish scrupulously between different streams of migration from a single region in South Asia, pointing to their different geographical dispersion and commercial activities, see Markovits, Claude, *The Global World of Indian Merchants, 1750–1947*, Cambridge: Cambridge University Press, 2000, pp. 1–9.

134. Desbordes, *L'Immigration*, p. 34.

135. ANS AOF 11 D 3/37, 'État nominatif des Syriens installés dans le cercle du CAYOR', n.d. [1924].

136. ANS AOF 11 D 3/37, 'Immigration Syrienne en Casamance', n.d. [1924].

137. ANS AOF 11 D 3/37, 'Subdivision de Foundiougne. État Immigration Syrienne', n.d. [1924].

138. Muruwwah, *Nahnu fi Ifriqiya*, p. 245.

139. ANS AOF 11 D 3/37, 'COLONIE DU SENEGAL—Population Syrienne et Libanaise', n.d. [1931].

140. ANS AOF 10 F 14, 'RENSEIGNEMENTS concernant les SYRO-LIBANAIS en résidence au SOUDAN', Bamako, November 1944.

141. CAOM MC FM AP 2303/5, 'RAPPORT sur la situation des Libano-Syriens en Afrique Occidentale Française et au Togo', Dakar, 30/05/1945.

142. Makdisi, Ussama, *The Culture of Sectarianism: Community, History, and Violence in Nineteenth Century Ottoman Lebanon*, Berkeley, CA: University of California Press, 2001, p. 7.

143. Hourani, Albert, 'Ideologies of the Mountain and the city', in Owen, Roger, ed., *Essays on the Crisis in Lebanon*, London: Ithaca, 1976, p. 36.

144. Bierwirth, Chris, 'The initial establishment of the Lebanese community in Côte d'Ivoire, ca. 1925–45', *International Journal of African Historical Studies*, 30, 2 (1997), fn. 18, p. 330.

145. Martin, Vincent, *Recensement Démographique de la Ville de Dakar (1955). Résultats Définitifs*, vol. 2, *Étude Socio-Démographique de la Ville de Dakar*, Dakar: Ministère du Plan, Service de la Statistique, 1962, Table A.11, Appendix p. 7.

146. ANS AOF 11 D 3/37, 'ÉTAT DE L'IMMIGRATION SYRIENNE DANS LE CERCLE DE THIÈS—ANNÉE 1924'.

147. Muruwwah, *Nahnu fi Ifriqiya*, pp. 212–3.

148. ANS AOF 11 D 3/37, 'Subdivision de Foundiougne. État Immigration Syrienne', n.d. [1924]; 'Subdivision de Kaolack. Immigration Syrienne', n.d. [1924].

149. CARAN AOF AS 21 G 38 [200 Mi 1100–1101[, 'État des des Étrangers résidant dans la Colonie du Sénégal', Dakar, n.d. [1918].

150. Kojok, 'Les Libanais', vol. 1, pp. 192–3.

151. Tamimi, Muhammad Rafiq and Muhammad Bahjat, *Wilayat Bairut*, vol. 1, *Al-Qism al-Janubi* [Beirut Province, vol. 1, the Southern Part], Beirut: Matba'at al-Iqbal, 1917, p. 292.

152. Mervin, Sabrina, *Un Réformisme Chiite. Ulémas et lettrés du Ǧabal Āmil (Actuel Liban-Sud) de la Fin de l'Empire Ottoman à l'Indépendance du Liban*, Paris: Karthala, 2000, p. 40.

153. Tamimi and Bahjat, *Wilayat Bairut*, p. 293.

154. Qubaisi, Hasan, *Tatawwur Madinat Sur, 1900–1950*, Beirut: Dar al-Qadmus, 1982, p. 58.

155. Peleikis, Anja, 'Shifting identities, reconstructing boundaries. The case of a multi-confessional locality in post-war Lebanon', *Die Welts des Islams*, 41, 3 (2001), p. 409.

156. Makdisi, *The Culture of Sectarianism*, pp. 110–11; Mervin, *Réformisme*, pp. 360–2.

157. al-Zahir, Sulaiman, *Jabal 'Amil fi al-Harb al-Kawniyya*, Beirut: Dar al-Matbu'at al-Sharqiyya, 1986, pp. 22–4.

158. See Chapter 5.

159. Sahlins, *Islands*, p. 27.

160. Desbordes, *L'Immigration Libano-Syrienne*, pp. 17–18.

161. Muruwwah, *Nahnu fi Ifriqiya*, p. 195.

162. Seck, Assane, *Dakar*, Dakar: Faculté des Lettres et Sciences Humaines de Dakar, n.d., p. 9.

163. *BCAF*, 46, 7 (July 1936), pp. 378–9.

164. Camara, Camille, *Saint-Louis-du-Sénégal: Évolution d'une Ville en Milieu Africain*, Dakar: InstitutFondamental d'Afrique Noire, 1968, p. 78.

165. *Afrique Occidentale Française Togo*, Les Guides Bleus, Paris: Hachette, 1958, p. 315.

166. Ibid., p. 60.

167. Seck, *Dakar*, p. 11.

168. ANS AOF 11 D 3/37, 'Cercle du Sine Saloum—Subdivision de Foundiougne—État immigration syrienne', n.d. [1924]; 'Subdivision de Kaolack Immigration Syrienne', n.d. [1924]; 'Subdivision de Fatick—Etat Immigration Syrienne', n.d. [1924].

169. ANS AOF 11 D 3/37, 'Liste des Syriens établis dans le CERCLE du BAOL', n.d. [1924].

170. ANS AOF 11 D 3/37, 'Etat nominatif des Syriens installés dans le cercle du CAYOR', n.d. [1924].

171. ANS AOF 11 D 3/37, 'Immigration syrienne en Casamance', n.d. [1924]; 'Etat de l'immigration syrienne à Saint-Louis', Saint-Louis, 21/03/1924.

172. ANS AOF 11 D 3/37, 'ETAT nominatif des Etrangers habitant la subdivision de KAOLACK', Kaolack, 31/08/1927; 'ETAT nominatif des étrangers résidant dans la Commune-Mixte de Kaolack', n.d. [1927].

173. Guggisberg, Decima Moore and F.G. Guggisberg, *We Two in West Africa*, London: Heinemann, 1909, pp. 39–40.

174. CARAN AOF AS 21 G 38 [200 Mi 1100–1101], 'Recensement des Étrangers Résidant en Guinée Française Indiquant: a) Leur pays d'origine b) La date de leur arrivée dans la colonie c) Leur situation dans les maisons qui les emploient d) Renseignements généraux sur leur manière d'être', Conakry, 28/10/1918.

175. Goerg, Odile, *Commerce et Colonisation en Guinée 1850–1913*, Paris: L'Harmattan, 1986, fn. 67, p. 396.

176. ANS AOF 2 G 11/43, 'Cercle du Sine-Saloum—Rapport Mensuel—Juillet 1911', Kaolack, 31/07/1911.

177. On Mamou, see CARAN AOF AS 21 G 33 [200 Mi 1099–1100], 'Copie de lettre non envoyée', n.d. [1918]; Goerg, *Commerce*, pp. 282–3; *BCAF*, 22, 8 (August 1912), pp. 297–309.

178. AN AS 21 G 38 [200 Mi 1100–1101], 'Recensement des Étrangers Résidant en Guinée Française Indiquant: a) Leur pays d'origine b) La date de leur arrivée dans la colonie c) Leur situation dans les maisons qui les emploient d) Renseignements généraux sur leur manière d'être', Conakry, 28/10/1918.

179. CARAN AOF AS 21 G 37 [200 Mi 1100], Administrateur du Cercle de Dagana to Lieutenant-Governor of Senegal, Dagana, 24/03/1911.

180. CARAN AOF AS 21 G 37 [200 Mi 1100], Administrateur du Cercle de Dagana to Lieutenant-Governor of Senegal, Dagana, 24/02/1911.

181. CARAN AOF AS 21 G 37 [200 Mi 1100], Lieutenant-Governor of Senegal to Governor-General of AOF, Dakar, 31/03/1911.

3. FEARS OF A 'SYRIAN GUINEA': COMMERCE, CONTAGION AND RACE IN FRENCH WEST AFRICA, 1898–1914

1. 'Pétition du Commerce de Conakry au Sujet des Marchands Syriens', in Aspe-Fleurimont, Lucien, *La Guinée Française: Conakry et Rivières du Sud. Etude Economique et Commerciale*, Paris: Augustin Challavel, 1900, pp. 320–1.

2. On the measures demanded in 1902 see 'Les revendeurs Syriens et la hausse du caoutchouc', *QC*, XI, 128 (25 April 1902), p. 245; and Goerg, Odile, *Commerce et Colonisation en Guinée 1850–1913*, Paris: L'Harmattan, 1986, pp. 400, 402. On the 1904 boycott see 'Protection contre les Syriens', *QC*, XIV, 177 (10 May 1904), p. 305; and 'La question des Syriens', *BCAF*, 14, 12 (December 1904), p. 374. Finally, on the failure of the 1898 boycott, see Goerg, *Commerce*, p. 401.

3. CAOM MC/FM/SG XIII 11, 'Plaintes d'un groupe de petits commerçants', Boke, 21/02/1907; and Goerg, *Commerce*, p. 400.

4. I take this helpful image from Ware, Vron, *Beyond the Pale: White Women, Racism and History*, London: Verso, 1992.

5. See, in particular, Stoler, Ann Laura, *Carnal Knowledge and Imperial Power: Race and the Intimate in Colonial Rule*, Berkeley, CA: California University Press, 2002. See also Ballantyne, Tony and Antoinette Burton, 'Introduction: bodies, empires, and world histories', in Ballantyne and Burton, eds, *Bodies in Contact: Rethinking Colonial Encounters in World History*, Durham, NC: Duke University Press, 2005, pp. 1–15; Burton, Antoinette, 'Introduction', in Burton, Antoinette, ed., *Gender, Sexuality and Colonial Modernities*, London: Routledge, 1997, pp. 1–16; Gouda, Frances and Julia Clancy-Smith, 'Introduction', in Gouda and Clancy-Smith, eds, *Domesticating the Empire: Race, Gender and Family Life in French and Dutch Colonialism*, Charlottesville, VA: University Press of Virginia, 1998, pp. 1–20; Levine, Philippa, 'Modernity, medicine and colonialism: the contagious diseases ordinance in Hong Kong and the Straits Settlements', in Burton, ed., *Gender*, pp. 35–48; Shah, Nayan, 'Cleansing motherhood: hygiene and the culture of domesticity in San Francisco's Chinatown, 1875–1900' in Burton, ed., *Gender*, pp. 19–34;.

6. Stoler, Ann Laura, 'Genealogies of the intimate: movements in colonial studies', in *Carnal Knowledge*, p. 6.

7. Arnold, David, 'European orphans and vagrants in India in the nineteenth century', *Journal of Imperial and Commonwealth History*, 7, 2 (1979), pp. 104–27; White, Owen, 'The decivilizing mission: Auguste Dupuis-Yakouba and French Timbuktu', *French Historical Studies*, 27, 3 (Summer 2004), pp. 541–68.

8. Stoler, Ann Laura, 'Sexual affronts and racial frontiers: European colonies and the cultural politics of exclusion in colonial South-East Asia', in Cooper, Frederick and Ann Laura Stoler, eds, *Tensions of Empire: Colonial Cultures in a Bourgeois World*, Berkeley, CA: University of California Press, 1997, pp. 198–237; White, Owen, *Children of the French Empire: Miscegenation and Colonial Society in French West Africa, 1895–1960*, Oxford: Clarendon Press, 1999.

9. Stoler, Ann Laura, *Race and the Education of Desire: Foucault's 'History of Sexuality' and the Colonial Order of Things*, Durham, NC: Duke University Press, 1996.

10. Nye, Robert A., *Masculinity and Male Codes of Honour in Modern France*, Oxford: Oxford University Press, 1993, p. 41. William Reddy has called for greater attention to the commercial conventions which complemented notions of public honour. Reddy, *The Invisible Code: Honor and Sentiment in Postrevolutionary France, 1814–1848*, Berkeley, CA: University of California Press, 1997, p. xii.

11. Schneider, William H., *An Empire for the Masses: The French Popular Image of Africa, 1870–1900*, London: Greenwood Press, 1982, pp. 154, 158. See also Conklin, Alice, *A Mission to Civilize: The Republican Empire in France and West Africa, 1895–1930*, Stanford, CA: Stanford University Press, 1997.

12. Nye, *Masculinity*, p. 13. Vigarello, Georges, *Le Propre et le Sale: l'Hygiène du Corps depuis le Moyen-Age*, Paris: Seuil, 1985, p. 229.

13. Goerg, *Commerce*, p. 269.

14. On efforts to legislate the movements of 'Dioula', see Goerg, *Commerce*, pp. 375–81, and CARAN AOF AS 21 G 31 [200 Mi 1099], Governor-General of AOF to Lieutenant-Governors, 'Institution d'une carte d'identité pour les déplacements des indigènes', Dakar, 27/03/1918.

15. Aspe-Fleurimont, *La Guinée*, pp. 29–30.

16. Rouget, Fernand, *La Guinée*, Paris: Émile Larose, 1906, pp. 403–4.

17. *BCAF*, 14, 12 (December 1904), p. 374.

18. Aspe-Fleurimont, *La Guinée*, p. 203. See also Goerg, *Commerce*, pp. 362–3.

19. Aspe-Fleurimont, *La Guinée*, p. 31.

20. Ibid., pp. 215–7.

21. Ibid., pp. 237–8, 196–8

22. 'Pétition', p. 323.

23. CAOM MC FM SG Guinée XIII Dossier 11, 'Plaintes d'un groupe de petits commerçants', AOF answer to telegram, Dakar, 13/03/1907.

24. Goerg, *Commerce*, p. 399.

25. Arcin, André, *La Guinée Française: Races, Religions, Coutumes, Production, Commerce*, Paris: Augustin Challavel, 1907, pp. vi, 93, 100.

26. Goerg, *Commerce*, fn. 74, p. 401.

27. *QC*, XI, 128 (25 April 1902), p. 245.

28. *BCAF*, 14, 12 (December 1904), p. 375.

29. Ibid.

30. Daumalin, Xavier, 'Frédéric Bohn: l'Africain, 1852–1923', in Courdurie, Marcel and Guy Durand, eds, *Entreprises d'Afrique*, Marseille: CCIM-Provence, 1998, espec. pp. 212–3.

31. Bonin, Hubert, *CFAO: Cent Ans de Compétition*, Paris: Economica, 1987, p. 79.

32. Tombs, Robert, introduction to part I, 'Sentiment and ideology', in Tombs, ed., *Nationhood and Nationalism in France from Boulangism to the Great War, 1889–1918*, London: HarperCollins, 1991, p. 5.

33. 'Pétition', p. 322.

34. Ibid., p. 323.

35. Ibid., pp. 320, 321.

36. Ibid., pp. 320–2.

37. Aspe-Fleurimont, *La Guinée*, pp. 29, 30, 31, 216, 218.

38. On celebrations by the French bourgeoisie of the 'honourability of work and its own honour', as a '"new aristocracy" of work, competence, and wealth', see Nye, *Masculinity*, p. 41.

39. Aspe-Fleurimont, *La Guinée*, p. 31.

40. ANS 2 G 1/40, Rapport d'Ensemble for French Guinea, 1899.

41. Aspe-Fleurimont, *La Guinée*, p. 30.

42. Goerg, *Commerce*, p. 354, fn. 77, p. 403.

43. Arcin, *La Guinée*, p. 95.

44. AN AOF 1 G 267, 'Rapport de M. Boulland de l'Escale Syndic de la Presse Coloniale Française, sur sa Mission Économique et de Vulgarisation en Afrique Occidentale', p. 116.

45. Goerg, *Commerce*, pp. 339, 403.

46. Rouget, *La Guinée*, p. 403.

47. Arcin, *La Guinée*, pp. 93, 100.

48. *BCAF*, 14, 12 (December 1904), p. 374.

49. Vigarello, *Le Propre et le Sale*, pp. 207, 215.

50. *BCAF*, 21, 6 (June 1911), p. 202.

51. Arcin, *La Guinée*, p. 93.

52. 'Pétition', p. 320.

53. Nordman, Daniel, 'Sauf-conduits et passeports en France à la Renaissance', in Léard, Jean and Jean-Claude Margolin, eds, *Voyager à la Renaissance: Actes du Colloque de Tours 30 Juin–13 Juillet 1983*, Paris: Maisonneuve et Larose, 1987, p. 152.

54. Wilson, Stephen, *Ideology and Experience: Antisemitism in France at the Time of the Dreyfus Affair*, London: Associated University Presses, 1982, p. 299.

55. AN AOF AS 21 G 36 [200 Mi 1100], Governor-General to Lieutenant-Governors, 'a/s de l'arrêté du 1ᵉʳ mai 1911, règlementant l'immigration étrangère en AOF', Dakar, 24/05/1911.

56. Aspe-Fleurimont, *La Guinée*, p. 218. 'Pétition', p. 322.

57. AN AOF AS 21 G 36 [200 Mi 1100], Governor-General to Lieutenant-Governors, 'a/s de l'arrêté du 1ᵉʳ mai 1911, règlementant l'immigration étrangère en AOF', Dakar, 24/05/1911.

58. *L'AOF* 128, 19/11/1910.

59. Leroy-Beaulieu, Paul, *De la Colonisation chez les Peuples Modernes*, Paris: Guillaumin et Cie, 1891 [1874], 4th ed., p. xv.

60. Aspe-Fleurimont, *La Guinée*, p. 31.

61. 'Pétition', p. 321. Conklin, *Mission to Civilize*, p. 52.

62. 'La Guinée Française est une colonie ruinée', *L'AOF* 234, 30/07/1913.

63. Arcin, *La Guinée*, pp. 93, 99.

64. 'Les "Undesirable" de l'Afrique Occidentale', *BCAF*, 21, 6 (June 1911), p. 202.

65. Arcin, *La Guinée*, p. 99.

66. 'La question des Syriens en Guinée', *BCAF*, 21, 6 (June 1911), p. 202.

67. On bacteriology, the work of reference remains Latour, Bruno, *The Pasteurization of France*, transl. Sheridan, John and John Law, Cambridge, MA: Harvard University Press, 1988. For recent interventions in the scholarship on climatic theory and tropical medicine, see *inter alia* Anderson, Warwick, 'Immunities of empire: race,

disease, and the new tropical medicine', *Bulletin of the History of Medicine*, 70, 1 (1996), pp. 94–118; Harrison, Mark, '"The Tender Frame of Man": disease, climate, and racial difference in India and the West Indies', *Bulletin of the History of Medicine*, 70, 1 (1996), pp. 68–93; Jennings, Eric, *Curing the Colonizers: Hydrotherapy, Climatology and French Colonial Spas*, Durham, NC: Duke University Press, 2006; Livingstone, David N., 'Race, space and moral climatology: notes towards a genealogy', *Journal of Historical Geography*, 28, 2 (2002), pp. 159–80; Osborne, Michael, *Nature, the Exotic and the Science of French Colonialism*, Bloomington, IN: Indiana University Press, 1994.

68. CAOM MC/FM/SG Guinée XI 6, Governor Guinée Française to Minister of Colonies, 'a/s mesures sanitaires pour l'arrivée des Syriens', Conakry, 27/02/1901.

69. Latour, *Pasteurization*, p. 19.

70. CAOM MC/FM/SG Sénégal XI 50, 'Mission Sanitaire au Sénégal (M.M. Grall, Marchoux et Jacquerez). 1901. Motif: Causes de l'épidémie de fièvre jaune et moyens d'en éviter le retour'.

71. This argument draws upon Douglas, Mary, *Purity and Danger: an Analysis of Concepts of Pollution and Taboo*, London: Routledge, 1978 [1966], pp. 29–32, 35. Kraut, Alan M., *Silent Travellers: Germs, Genes and the Immigrant Menace*, Baltimore: Johns Hopkins University Press, 1994, pp. 2–3. On instances of such associations between disease and particular immigrant, or 'foreign', groups in metropolitan France, see MacMaster, Neil, *Colonial Migrants and Racism: Algerians in France, 1900–1962*, Basingstoke: Macmillan, 1997, especially pp. 138–9; Rosenberg, Clifford, 'The colonial politics of health care provision in interwar Paris', *French Historical Studies*, 27, 3 (2004), pp. 637–8; and Surkis, Judith, 'The enemy within: venereal disease and the defence of French masculinity in between the wars', in Forth, Christopher E. and Bertrand Taithe, eds, *French Masculinities: History, Culture and Politics*, Basingstoke: Palgrave, 2007, pp. 103–22.

72. Arcin, *La Guinée*, p. 93.

73. *QC*, XV, 177 (10 May1904), p. 305.

74. Barot, M., with Desbordes, Meynier, Chalot, Pierre, Gimet-Fontalirant, *Guide Pratique de l'Européen dans l'Afrique Occidentale à l'Usage des Militaires, Fonctionnaires, Commerçants, Colons et Touristes*, Paris: Flammarion, n.d. [1902], pp. 94, 98.

75. Jennings, *Curing the Colonizers*, p. 29.

76. AN AOF AS 21 G 36 [200 Mi 1100], Governor-General to Lieutenant-Governors, 'a/s de l'arrêté du 1er mai 1911, règlementant l'immigration étrangère en AOF', Dakar, 24/05/1911.

77. *BCAF*, 21, 6 (June 1911), p. 202.

78. Sorlin, Pierre, 'Words and images of nationhood', in Tombs, ed., *Nationhood*, p. 84.

79. Schneider, William H., *Quality and Quantity: the Quest for Biological Regeneration in Twentieth Century France*, Cambridge: Cambridge University Press, 1990.

80. Ministère des Affaires Etrangères, Paris, Turquie/Syrie-Liban/Nouvelle Série 115, Minister of Colonies to Minister of Foreign Affairs, 'a/s Mission en Syrie de M. Poulet, Secrétaire Général de la Guinée Française', Paris, 17/02/1911.

81. Drumont, Édouard, *La France Juive: Edition Populaire*, Paris: Librairie Victor Palmé, 1888, pp. 2, 6. This was an abridged, single-volume, version of the first, two-volume, edition of 1886, *La France Juive: Essai d'Histoire Contemporaine*, Dijon: Imprimerie Darantière, 1886. All quotes, unless indicated, are from the *Edition Populaire*. McMillan, James F., *Twentieth Century France: Society and Politics 1898–1991*, London: Arnold, 2003 [1992], p. 11.

82. On the events of 1898, see Wilson, Stephen, 'The antisemitic riots of 1898 in France', *Historical Journal*, 26, 4 (1973), pp. 789–806; and Birnbaum, Pierre, *Le Moment Antisémite: Un Tour de la France en 1898*, Paris: Fayard, 1998.

83. Wilson, *Ideology and Experience*, p. 279.

84. Ibid.

85. Wilson, 'Antisemitic riots', p. 798.

86. Winock, Michel, *Nationalisme, Antisémitisme et Fascisme en France*, Paris: Seuil, 1990, p. 118; and Winock, *La France et les Juifs de 1789 à nos Jours*, Paris: Seuil, 2004, p. 87.

87. 'L'Invasion', *L'AOF* 127 (12/11/1910).

88. Forth, Christopher E., *The Dreyfus Affair and the Crisis of French Manhood*, Baltimore, MD: Johns Hopkins University Press, 2004, pp. 113–4.

89. *L'AOF* 127 (12/11/1910).

90. Reddy, *The Invisible Code*, pp. xiii, 12.

91. Shapiro, Anne-Louise, 'Disordered bodies, disorderly acts: medical discourse and the female criminal', *Breaking the Codes: Female Criminality in Fin-de-Siècle Paris*, Stanford, CA: Stanford University Press, 1996, pp. 94–135.

92. 'Mamou. Comme en Syrie Musulmans et Catholiques se fusillent', *L'AOF*, 116 (23/07/1910). See also 'Mamou. Les coups de Browning et de matraque continuent à pleuvoir dur entre Orientaux', *L'AOF* 125 (22/10/1910).

93. *L'AOF* 127 (12/11/1910).

94. Winock, *Nationalisme*, p. 49.

95. Rouget, *La Guinée*, p. 403.

96. Wilson, *Ideology and Experience*, p. 262.

97. Drumont, *La France Juive*, p. 11.

98. Wilson, *Ideology and Experience*, p. 262.

99. Arcin, *La Guinée*, p. 93.

100. Wilson, *Ideology and Experience*, p. 262.

101. Drumont, quoted in Forth, *The Dreyfus Affair*, p. 48.

102. Drumont, *La France Juive*, p. 10.

103. Wilson, *Ideology and Experience*, p. 262.

104. Birnbaum, Pierre, *Un Mythe Politique: La 'République Juive' de Léon Blum à Mendès France*, Paris: Gallimard, 1995 [1988], 2nd ed., p. 134.

105. Wilson, *Ideology and Experience*, p. 267.

106. *BCAF*, 14, 12 (December 1904), p. 374. On Moroccan migration to Senegambia in the colonial period, see el Fareh, Yahia Abou, Abdelouahed Akmir and Abdelmalek Beni Azza, *La Présence Marocaine en Afrique de l'Ouest: Cas du Sénégal, du Mali et de la Côte d'Ivoire*, Rabat: Publications de l'Institut des Etudes Africaines, 1997, pp. 21–86.

107. Cohn, Bernard, *Colonialism and its Forms of Knowledge: the British in India*, Princeton, NJ: Princeton University Press, 1996; Scott, James, *Seeing Like A State: How Certain Schemes to Improve the Human Condition Have Failed*, New Haven, CT: Yale University Press, 1998.

108. Arcin, *La Guinée*, pp. 92–3.

109. *BCAF*, 14, 12 (December 1904), p. 374.

110. Birnbaum, *Le Moment Antisémite*, p. 233.

111. Drumont, *France Juive*, p. 316.

112. Rouget, *La Guinée*, p. 403.

113. Wilson, *Ideology and Experience*, p. 298.

114. On this point, see Matard-Bonucci, Marie-Anne, 'Introduction: l'imagination et la représentation des Juifs entre culture et politique (1848–1939)', in Matard-Bonucci, Marie-Anne, ed., *Antisémythes: L'Image des Juifs entre Culture et Politique*, Paris: Nouveau Monde, 2004, pp. 13–40.

115. Wilson, *Ideology and Experience*, pp. 456, 462.

116. *BCAF*, 21, 2 (February 1911), p. 69.

117. Arcin, *La Guinée*, pp. 92–3; the italics are my own.

118. Guébhard, Paul, *Au Fouta-Dialon—Elevage—Agriculture—Commerce—Régime Foncier—Religion*, Paris: Augustin Challamel, 1910, pp. 76–7.

119. The comparison is striking on another level for the equation it sets up between the Fula society of Futa Jalon and medieval European feudalism. On attitudes towards the Fula in French writing of the period, see Harrison, Christopher, *France and Islam in West Africa, 1860–1960*, Cambridge: Cambridge University Press, 1988, ch. 5, and especially pp. 71–2.

120. 'Les Dioulas. Leurs méthodes commerciales. Les Syriens', p. 86 and following.

121. Arcin, *La Guinée*, p. 93.

122. Ibid., pp. 91–2.

123. Rouget, *La Guinée*, p. 398.

124. Aspe-Fleurimont, *La Guinée*, p. 29.

125. Rouget, *La Guinée*, p. 403.

126. 'Pétition', p. 320.

127. Anderson, Warwick, *The Cultivation of Whiteness: Science, Health and Racial Destiny in Australia*, New York: Basic Books, 2003, pp. 1, 2.

4. FAILING TO STEM THE TIDE: LEBANESE MIGRATION AND THE COMPETING PREROGATIVES OF THE IMPERIAL STATE

1. For broad surveys of these changes, see McKeown, Adam, *Melancholy Order: Asian Migration and the Globalisation of Borders*, New York: Columbia University Press, 2008; and Torpey, John, *The Invention of the Passport: Surveillance, Citizenship and the State*, Cambridge: Cambridge University Press, 2000, especially chs. 4–5.

2. See, on the United States, McKeown, Adam, 'Ritualization of regulation: the enforcement of Chinese Exclusion in the United States and China', *American Historical Review*, 108, 2 (2003), pp. 377–403; and Zolberg, Aristide, 'The great wall against China: responses to the first immigration crisis, 1885–1925', in Jan and Leo Lucassen, eds, *Migration, Migration History, History: Old Paradigms and New Perspectives*, New York: Peter Lang, 1997, pp. 291–315. For a comparative approach, see MacDonald, Andrew, 'Colonial trespassers in the making of South Africa's international borders 1900 to c.1950', Ph.D dissertation, University of Cambridge, 2012; Martens, Jeremy, 'A transnational history of immigration restriction: Natal and New South Wales, 1896–97', *Journal of Imperial and Commonwealth History*, 34, 3 (2006), pp. 323–44; and Weil, Patrick, 'Races at the gate: racial distinctions in immigration policy: a comparison between France and the United States', in Fahrmeir, Andreas, Olivier Faro, and Patrick Weil, eds, *Migration Control in the North Atlantic World: the Evolution of State Practices in Europe and the United States from the French Revolution to the Interwar Period*, Oxford: Berghahn, 2003, pp. 271–97. On efforts to check the movements of itinerant peoples in metropolitan France, see Delclitte, Christophe, 'La catégorie juridique "Nomade" dans la Loi de 1912', *Hommes et Migrations*, 1188–9 (1995), pp. 23–30.

3. Caestecker, Franck, 'The transformation of nineteenth century expulsion policy, 1880–1914', in Fahrmeir et al., eds, *Migration Control*, pp. 120–37.

4. For details of these measures, see Hutchinson, Edward P., *Legislative History of American Immigration Policy, 1798–1965*, Philadelphia, PA: University of Pennsylvania Press, 1981; and Zolberg, Aristide, *A Nation by Design: Immigration Policy in the Fashioning of America*, Cambridge, MA: Harvard University Press, 2006.

5. Zolberg, Aristide, 'Matters of state: theorizing immigration policy', in Hirschman, Charles, Philip Kasinitz and Josh DeWind, eds, *The Handbook of International Migration: the American Experience*, New York: Russell Sage Foundation 1999, pp. 75–6; Zolberg, 'The archaeology of remote control', in Fahrmeir et al., eds, *Migration Control*, pp. 195–222.

6. Fahrmeir, Andreas, Olivier Faron and Patrick Weil, 'Introduction', in Fahrmeir et al., eds, *Migration Control*, p. 7.

7. McKeown, *Melancholy Order*, pp. 2–3.

8. Zolberg, 'Matters', p. 71.

9. See Ballantyne, Tony and Antoinette Burton, 'Introduction: bodies, empires, and world histories', in Ballantyne, Tony, and Antoinette Burton, eds, *Bodies in Contact: Rethinking Colonial Encounters in World History*, Durham, NC: Duke University Press, 2005, pp. 1–15.

10. Thomas, Martin, *The French Empire Between the Wars: Imperialism, Politics and Society*, Manchester: Manchester University Press, 2005, p. 1. See also Cooper, Frederick, 'States, empires, and political imagination', in *Colonialism in Question: Theory, Knowledge, History*, Berkeley, CA: University of California Press, 2005, pp. 153–203; Wilder, Gary, *The French Imperial Nation-State: Negritude and Colonial Humanism Between the Two World Wars*, Chicago, IL: University of Chicago Press, 2005, in particular pp. 27, 36; Wilder, 'Unthinking French history: colonial studies beyond national identity', in Burton, Antoinette, ed., *After the Imperial Turn: Thinking With and Through the Nation*, Durham, NC: Duke University Press, 2003, pp. 125–43.

11. There has been a revival of interest in the Mandate states in recent years. See, in particular, Thompson, Elizabeth, *Colonial Citizens: Republican Rights, Paternal Privilege and Gender in French Syria and Lebanon*, New York: Columbia University Press, 2000. For two helpful collections of essays concerned with teasing out the particularities of French rule over Lebanon and Syria, see Méouchy, Nadine and Peter Sluglett, eds, *The British and French Mandates in Comparative Perspective*, Leiden: Brill, 2004; Méouchy, Nadine, ed., *France, Syrie et Liban 1918–1946 Les Ambiguïtés et les Dynamiques de la Relation Mandataire*, Damascus: IFEAD, 2002. On the high political life of Lebanon and Syria, see Zamir, Meir, *Lebanon's Quest: The Road to Statehood 1926–1939*, London: I.B. Tauris, 1997; Firro, Kais, *Inventing Lebanon: Nationalism and the State under the Mandate*, London: I.B. Tauris, 2003; and Khoury, Philip S., *Syria and the French Mandate: the Politics of Arab Nationalism, 1920–1945*, Princeton, NJ: Princeton University Press, 1987.

12. Dodge, Toby, *Inventing Iraq: The Failure of Nation-Building and a History Denied*, London: Hurst & Company, 2003, p. 1. The notion of a colonial citizenry is borrowed, of course, from Elizabeth Thompson.

13. See Lafleur, Gérard, *Les Libanais et les Syriens de Guadeloupe*, Paris: Karthala, 1999, p. 69.

14. Rosenberg, Clifford, *Policing Paris: The Origins of Modern Immigration Control between the Wars*, Ithaca, NY: Cornell University Press, 2006, pp. 124–5.

15. Lewis, Mary Dewhurst, *The Boundaries of the Republic: Migrants Rights and the Limits of Universalism in France, 1918–1940*, Stanford, CA: University of California Press, 2007, pp. 19–21. See also Rosenberg, *Policing Paris*, p. 10.

16. Samson, Jane, *Imperial Benevolence: Making British Authority in the Pacific Islands*, Honolulu, HI: University of Hawai'i Press, 1998.

17. Matsuda, Matt, *Empire of Love: Histories of France and the Pacific*, Oxford: Oxford University Press, 2005, pp. 3–4, 15.

18. Stoler, Ann Laura, 'Affective states', in Nugent, David and Joan Vincent, eds, *A Companion to the Anthropology of Politics*, Oxford: Blackwell, 2004, pp. 6–7; Stoler, Ann Laura, *Along the Archival Grain: Epistemic Anxieties and Colonial Commonsense*, Princeton, NJ: Princeton University Press, 2009, pp. 40–1, 63.

19. Thompson, *Colonial Citizens*, pp. 1, 6–7, 12.

20. Ibid, p. 1.

21. This is a paraphrase upon Lauren Benton's highly useful notion of 'jurisdictional politics'. See Benton, Lauren, 'Colonial law and cultural difference: jurisdictional politics and the formation of the colonial state', *Comparative Studies in Society and History*, 41, 3 (1999), pp. 563–88. For further uses of the term, see Lewis, Mary Dewhurst, 'Geographies of power: the Tunisian civic order, jurisdictional politics, and imperial rivalry in the Mediterranean, 1881–1935', *Journal of Modern History*, 80 (2008), espec. p. 797; and McDougall, James, 'The secular state's Islamic empire: Muslim spaces and subjects of jurisdiction in Paris and Algiers, 1905–1957', *Comparative Studies in Society and History*, 52, 3 (2010), pp. 553–80. See also Cooper, Frederick, *Decolonisation and African Society: The Labour Question in French and British Africa*, Cambridge: Cambridge University Press, 1996.

22. Weber, Max, 'Bureaucracy', in Gerth, H.H., and C. Wright Mills, transl., eds, *From Max Weber: Essays in Society*, London: Routledge, 1991, p. 196.

23. Noiriel, Gérard, *La Tyrannie du National: Le Droit d'Asile en Europe 1793–1993*, Paris: Calmann-Lévy, 1991, pp. 60–1, 260–3.

24. For a statement of this view, see Young, Crawford, *The African Colonial State in Comparative Perspective*, New Haven, CT: Yale University Press, 1994. For discussions of distinctly colonial forms of rationality, see Comaroff, John, 'Governmentality, materiality, legality, modernity. On the colonial state in Africa', in Deutsch, Jan-Georg, Peter Probst and Heike Schmidt, eds, *African Modernities: Entangled Meanings in Current Debates*, Oxford: James Currey, 2002; Scott, David, 'Colonial governmentality', *Social Text*, 43 (1995), pp. 191–220.

25. Herbst, Jeffrey, *States and Power in Africa: Comparative Lessons in Authority and Control*, Princeton, NJ: Princeton University Press, 2000, p. 1.

26. Zinoman, Peter, *The Colonial Bastille: A History of Imprisonment in Vietnam, 1862–1940*, Berkeley, CA: University of California Press, 2001, p. 70.

27. Cooper, Frederick, 'Conflict and connection: rethinking African colonial history', *American Historical Review*, 99, 5 (December 1994), p. 1533.

28. For an examination of the hopes and ambitions of one such administrator, Lyautey, and his endeavours to 'escape' Third Republic politicking and create a new social order in Morocco, see Rabinow, Paul, *French Modern: Norms and Forms of the Social Environment*, Cambridge, MA: MIT Press, 1989, especially pp. 289–91.

29. This quote is from Nadine Gordimer's magnificently uneasy short story 'Train From Rhodesia', in which the locomotive stands as a synecdoche for a rather defective, strained version of colonial modernity. Gordimer, *Selected Stories*, Harmondsworth: Penguin, 1983, p. 50.

30. Torpey, *Invention*, p. 3.

31. Cohen, William, *Rulers of Empire: the French Colonial Service in Africa*, Stanford, CA: Hoover Institute Press, 1971, p. 57.

32. Durand, Bernard, 'Les pouvoirs du Gouverneur Général de l'AOF', in Becker, Charles, Saliou M'Baye and Ibrahima Thioub, eds, *AOF: Réalités et Héritages. Sociétés Ouest-africaines et Ordre Colonial, 1895–1960*, Dakar, Direction des Archives du Sénégal, 1997, pp. 50, 56–7.

33. Andrew, Christopher and A.S. Kanya-Forstner, *France Overseas: the Great War and the Climax of French Imperial Expansion*, London: Thames & Hudson, 1981, pp. 19, 21.

34. Torpey, *Invention*, pp. 4–5.

35. Andrew and Kanya-Forstner, *France Overseas*, p. 42. See also Burrows, Mathew, '"Mission civilisatrice": French cultural policy in the Middle East, 1860–1914', *Historical Journal*, 29 (1986), pp. 103–35; Chevallier, Dominique, 'Aux bases d'une intervention: Lyon et la Syrie en 1919', in *Villes et Travail en Syrie du XIXe au XXe Siècles*, Paris: Maisonneuve & Larose, 1982, pp. 41–86; Shorrock, William, *French Imperialism in the Middle East: the Failure of Policy in Lebanon and Syria 1900–1914*, Madison, WI: University of Wisconsin Press, 1976; Spagnolo, John P., *France and Ottoman Lebanon: 1861–1914*, London: Ithaca Press, 1977.

36. Comité de Défense des Intérêts Français en Orient, *Rapport sur un Voyage en Egypte et en Turquie d'Asie (Janvier-Août 1912), par Maurice Pernot*, Paris: n.p., 1913, p. 224.

37. Spagnolo, John P., *France and Ottoman Lebanon: 1861–1914*, p. 1.

38. Shorrock, *French Imperialism*, pp. 138–9. On French economic activity in the Ottoman Empire, see also Jacques Thobie's immense, scrupulously detailed *Intérêts et Impérialisme Français dans l'Empire Ottoman (1895–1914)*, Paris: Imprimerie Nationale, 1977.

39. Hanotaux, Gabriel and Alfred Martineau, *Histoire des Colonies Françaises et de l'Expansion de la France dans le Monde*, vol. I, Paris: Plon, 1929, pp. xvi-xvii.

40. Ristelhueber, René, *Les Traditions Françaises au Liban*, Paris: Librairie Félix Alcan, 1925, p. 5.

41. Barrès, Maurice, *Une Enquête aux Pays du Levant*, Paris: Plon, 1923, vol. 1, p. 70.

42. Hanotaux, Gabriel, 'Préface', in Ristelhueber, *Traditions Françaises*, p. vi. Italics in the original.

43. Quoted in Flandin, Etienne, *Groupe Sénatorial pour la Défense des Intérêts Français à l'Etranger, Rapport sur la Syrie et la Palestine Présenté par M. Etienne Flandin, Sénateur*, Paris: Société Anonyme de Publications Périodiques, 1915, p. 6.

44. Cambon, Jules, *Le Diplomate*, Paris: Hachette, 1926 p. 76. My italics.

45. Barrès, *Enquête*, vol. 1, p. 5; vol. 2, pp. 183–4.

46. Stoler, 'Affective states', p. 5.

47. Andrew and Kanya-Forstner, *France Overseas*, pp. 27–8.

48. Khoury, Gérard, 'Robert de Caix et Louis Massignon: deux visions de la politique Française au Levant en 1920', in Méouchy and Sluglett, eds, *Mandates*, p. 170.

49. Andrew and Kanya-Forstner, *France Overseas*, p. 28.

50. Noiriel, Gérard, *Le Creuset Français: Histoire de l'Immigration XIXe-XXe Siècles*, Paris: Seuil, 1988, pp. 84–5.

51. CARAN AOF AS 21 G 33, Governor-General to Ministry of Colonies, Dakar, no date (1918).

52. Desbordes, *L'Immigration*, pp. 53–4.

53. MAE T/SL/NS 115, Couget to Minister of Foreign Affairs, 'a/s de l'Emigration Syrienne vers la Guinée et de la mission de M. Poulet', Damascus, 18/04/1911.

54. MAE T/SL/NS 108, Delcassé, Paris, 29/01/1902.

55. MAE NS/Haïti/10, 'Note pour la Direction des Affaires Politiques. Mesures prises contre les Syriens par le Gouvernement Haïtien', Paris, 12/09/1903. On the Eastern Mediterranean communities of Haiti, see Nicholls, David, 'No hawkers and pedlars: Levantines in the Caribbean', *Ethnic and Racial Studies*, 4, 4 (1981), pp. 415–31; and Plummer, Brenda Gayle, 'Race, nationality and trade in the Caribbean: the Syrians in Haiti, 1903–1934', *International History Review*, 3 (1981), pp. 517–39.

56. MAE T/SL/NS 108, 'Extrait d'un rapport adressé par M. Paul Desprez, Ministre de France en Haïti, à M. Delcassé, Ministre des Affaires Etrangères', Port-au-Prince, 07/03/1902. Delcassé had explicitly circumscribed the keeping of registers, as such a measure effectively recognised the right to official protection of Ottoman subjects, and had stressed that while the granting of passports was legally permissible, it should be 'scrupulously avoided' beyond the direct confines of the territory where it was issued (MAE T/SL/NS 108, Delcassé, Paris, 29/01/1902).

57. MAE T/SL/NS 108, Boulard-Ponqueville to MFA, Bogotá, 25/03/1902.

58. On France's cultural policies in Latin America in this period, see Daughton, J.P., 'When Argentina was "French": rethinking cultural politics and European imperialism in Belle-Epoque Buenos Aires', *Journal of Modern History*, 80 (2008), pp. 831–64.

59. JOGF 15/11/1905, Arrêtés passed on 09/11/1905. These measures were repealed by an Arrêté on 18/01/1906, recorded in the *JOGF* on 30/01/1906.

60. CARAN AOF AS 21 G 36, GOVERNOR-GENERAL to Lieutenant-Governor (LIEUTENANT-GOVER-NOR) of Guinea, 'a/s d'arrêtés relatifs à l'embarquement et au séjour des étrangers en Guinée', Dakar, 14/01/1906.

61. Desbordes, *L'Immigration*, fn. 3, p. 55.

62. Ibid., p. 58. *BCAF*, 21, 6 (June 1911), p. 202.
63. CARAN AOF AS 21 G 33, Angoulvant to MINISTRY OF COLONIES, Dakar, no date [1918].
64. Guy, Camille, *L'Afrique Occidentale Française*, Paris: Emile Larose, 1929, p. 74.
65. *JOGF*, 15/12/1910, Arrêté of 07/12/1910, and *JOGF*, 01/05/1911.
66. Desbordes, *L'Immigration*, p. 59.
67. CARAN AOF AS 21 G 36, Governor-General to Lieutenant-Governors, 'a/s de l'arrêté du 1ᵉʳ mai 1911, règlementant l'immigration étrangère en AOF', Dakar, 24/05/1911.
68. CARAN AOF AS 21 G 34, Governor-General to Lieutenant-Governor of Guinea, Dakar, 24/05/1918 and Governor-General to Lieutenant-Governors, Dakar, 24/05/1918.
69. CARAN AOF AS 21 G 33, Governor-General to Minister of Colonies, 'a/s des Syriens', Dakar, 09/11/1918.
70. CARAN AOF AS 21 G 33, Governor-General to Lieutenant-Governors, Dakar, 13/06/1918, and Lieutenant-Governor of Senegal to Governor-General, 'a/s des étrangers', Dakar, 11/11/1918.
71. CARAN AOF AS 21 G 33, Governor-General to Minister of Colonies, 'a/s de la prochaine campagne d'arachides', Dakar, 01/08/1918.
72. CARAN AOF AS 21 G 33, Governor-General to Minister of Colonies, Dakar, 15/08/1918.
73. CARAN AOF AS 21 G 33, Governor-General to Minister of Colonies, Dakar, 02/03/1918.
74. Stoler, *Archival Grain*, p. 40.
75. CARAN AOF AS 21 G 33, Ministry of Colonies to Governor-General, Paris, 13/11/1918.
76. CARAN AOF AS 21 G 39, Ministry of Colonies to Governor-General, Paris, 25/05/1917.
77. CARAN AOF AS 21 G 34, Direction des Affaires Politiques et Commerciales, Ministry of Foreign Affairs, Paris, no date (November 1918).
78. CARAN AOF AS 21 G 34, Ministry of Colonies to Governor-General, Paris, 23/11/1918.
79. 'French Mandate for Syria and the Lebanon', *The American Journal of International Law*, 17, 3 (1923), p. 178.
80. Rosenberg, *Policing Paris*, pp. 124, 144–5.
81. Thomas, Martin, *Empires of Intelligence: Security Services and Colonial Disorder after 1914*, Berkeley, CA: University of California Press, 2008, p. 214.
82. Rosenberg, *Policing Paris*, pp. 130–1.
83. Ibid., p. 144; Thomas, *Empires*, p. 213.
84. Lewis, *Boundaries*, pp. 21–2.
85. MAE NS/E/SL 129, High Commissioner to Minister of Foreign Affairs, 'a/s Protection consulaire des Syriens et Libanais en Guinée Portugaise', Beirut, 22/06/1929.
86. Jackson, Simon, 'Mandatory development: the political economy of the French Mandate in Syria and Lebanon, 1915–1939', Ph.D dissertation, New York University, 2009, pp. 394–5, 397.
87. MAE NS/E/SL 413, answer attached to Peytaud, Monrovia, 26/03/1928, Paris, n.d.
88. 'French Mandate', p. 179.
89. MAE NS/E/SL 413, answer attached to Peytaud, Monrovia, 26/03/1928, Paris, n.d.
90. Desbordes, *L'Immigration*, pp. 63, 65. *JOAOF*, (1921), pp. 676–8; *JOAOF*, (1923), pp. 458–9.
91. Desbordes, *L'Immigration*, pp. 66–80. *JOAOF*, (1925), pp. 219–20; *JOAOF*, (1927), pp. 300–1; *JOAOF*, (1932), pp. 297–302.
92. *JOAOF*, (1925), p. 634; *JOAOF*, (1926), p. 773.
93. By Article 3 of the decree of 5 March 1927, which stipulated that the caution could be replaced by a document attesting that the government of the country of origin of an indigent migrant was prepared to provide the costs of repatriation; *JOAOF*, 1177 (09/04/1927), p. 301.
94. *JOAOF*, (1925), p. 634.
95. CARAN AOF NS 21 G 61, Governor-General to Minister of Colonies, 'a/s immigration libano-syrienne', Dakar, 02/12/1936.
96. CARAN AOF NS 21 G 142, 'Résumé relatif à la question de l'immigration libano-syrienne en AOF', Dakar, 17/11/1937.
97. Ibid.
98. CARAN AOF NS 21 G 61, Direction des Affaires Politiques et Administratives, 'a/s immigration libano-syrienne', Dakar, 13/10/1936.
99. CARAN AOF NS 21 G 61, 'Compte-rendu de la réunion du 25 novembre 1937 au sujet de la question de l'immigration libano-syrienne en AOF'.

100. 'Modus Vivendi relatif à l'établissement des Libanais en France', http://www.doc.diplomatie.gouv.fr/BASIS/pacte/webext/bilat/DDD/19340025.pdf, last accessed 25 Jan. 2008.

101. CARAN AOF NS 21 G 61 [200 Mi 3039], 'Compte-rendu de la réunion du 25 novembre 1937 au sujet de la question de l'immigration libano-syrienne en AOF'.

102. These were, as in metropolitan law, distinct offences—the one punished by expulsion, the other by *refoulement*. See Gordon, Daniel, 'The back-door of the nation-state: expulsion of foreigners and continuity in twentieth-century France', *Past & Present*, 186 (2005), pp. 201–32.

103. MAE T/SL/NS 114, Bompard to Minister of Foreign Affairs, Therapia, 20/06/1910; Minister of Colonies to Minister of Foreign Affairs, Paris, 19/10/1910; Bompard to Minister of Foreign Affairs, Paris, 31/12/1910.

104. Jackson, 'Mandatory development', pp. 398, 402. See Saada, Emmanuelle, 'The empire of law: dignity, prestige and domination in the "Situation coloniale"', *French Politics, Culture and Society*, 20, 2 (2002), pp. 98–120.

105. CAOM MC FM AP 1432/1, Fighali to Minister of Colonies, Paris, 31/12/1936.

106. CAOM MC FM AP 1432/1, Fighali to Governor-General, Paris, 03/06/1936.

107. CAOM MC FM AP 1432/1, Fighali to Governor-General, Paris, 29/06/1936.

108. CAOM MC FM AP 1432/1, Governor-General to Fighali, Dakar, 13/07/1936.

5. MERCHANTS AND MAGPIES: THE TRADING LIVES OF EASTERN MEDITERRANEAN MIGRANTS

1. For attempts to deal with this history of extraversion, and to understand the limits of such an approach, see Bayart, Jean-François, 'Africa in the world: a history of extraversion', transl. Ellis, Stephen, *African Affairs*, 99 (2000), pp. 217–67; Cooper, Frederick, 'Africa and the world economy', *African Studies Review*, 24, 2/3 (1981), pp. 1–86; Vaughan, Megan, 'Africa and the Birth of the Modern World', *Transactions of the Royal Historical Society*, 16 (2006), pp. 143–62.

2. Crowder, Michael, *West Africa under Colonial Rule*, Evanston, IL: Northwestern University Press, 1968, pp. 293–7.

3. Leighton, Neil, 'Lebanese emigration: its effect on the political economy of Sierra Leone', in Hourani, Albert and Nadim Shehadi, eds, *The Lebanese in the World: A Hundred Years of Emigration*, London: I.B. Tauris, 1992, p. 598. See also Leighton, Neil, 'The political economy of a stranger population: the Lebanese of Sierra Leone', in Shack, William A. and Elliott P. Skinner, eds, *Strangers in African History*, Berkeley, CA: University of California Press, 1979.

4. Bauer, P.T., *West African Trade: A Study of Competition, Oligopoly and Monopoly in a Changing Economy*, Cambridge: Cambridge University Press, 1954, p. 164.

5. Kaniki, Martin, 'The psychology of early Lebanese immigrants in West Africa', in *International Seminar: Asian Trading Minorities in Tropical Africa, Afrika Studiencentrum, Leiden, 15–19 December 1975*, Leiden: n.p., 1976, p. 12.

6. Amin, Samir, 'La politique coloniale française à l'égard de la bourgeoisie commerçante sénégalaise', in Meillassoux, Claude, ed., *The Development of Indigenous Trade and Markets in West Africa*, London: Oxford University Press, 1971, pp. 366–8.

7. Suret-Canale, Jean, *French Colonialism in Tropical Africa, 1900–1945*, transl. Gottheimer, Till, London: Heinemann, 1971, pp. 67–8.

8. See, on the history of the Chinese in South-East Asia, Reid, Anthony, ed., *Sojourners and Settlers: Histories of South-East Asia and the Chinese*, London: Allen & Unwin, 1996. On South Asians in East Africa, see Delf, George, *Asians in East Africa*, London: Oxford University Press, 1963; Gregory, Robert S., *South Asians in East Africa: An Economic and Social History 1890–1980*, Boulder, CO: Westview, 1993; Mangat, J.S., *A History of the Asians in East Africa since c. 1886 to 1945*, Oxford: Clarendon, 1969.

9. Boumedouha, Saïd, 'The Lebanese in Senegal: a history of the relationship between an immigrant community and its French and African Rulers', Ph.D thesis, Centre for West African Studies, University of Birmingham, 1987, pp. i, 25.

10. van der Laan, H. Laurens, *The Lebanese Traders of Sierra Leone*, The Hague: Mouton, 1975, pp. 15, 233.

11. Crowder, *West Africa*, p. 295.

12. Shack, William A., 'Introduction', in Shack and Skinner, eds, *Strangers in African Societies*, p. 4.

13. van der Laan, *Lebanese Traders in Sierra Leone*, p. 222.

14. Crowder, *West Africa*, p. 294.

282

15. van der Laan, *Lebanese Traders*, p. 234.

16. Crowder, *West Africa*, p. 295; Mars, J., 'Extra-territorial enterprises', in Perham, Margery, ed., *Mining, Commerce and Finance in Nigeria*, London: Faber & Faber, 1948, p. 96.

17. Boeke, J.H., *Economics and Economic Policy of Dual Societies as Exemplified by Indonesia*, Haarlem: HD Tjeenk Willink & Zoon, 1953.

18. van Leur, J.C., *Asian Trade and Society: Essays in Asian Social and Economic History*, The Hague: van Hoeve, 1955.

19. Geertz, Clifford, *Peddlers and Princes: Social Change and Economic Organisation in Two Indonesian Towns*, Chicago, IL: Chicago University Press, 1963; Geertz, 'Suq: the bazaar economy in Sefrou', in Geertz, Clifford, Hildred Geertz and Lawrence Rosen, *Meaning and Order in Moroccan Society: Three Essays in Cultural Analysis*, Cambridge: Cambridge University Press, 1979, pp. 123–263.

20. For a synthetic statement of this view, see Harding, Leonhard, 'Les grands commerçants africains en Afrique de l'Ouest: le cas du Sénégal et de la Côte d'Ivoire: essai de synthèse', in Harding, Leonhard and Boubacar Barry, eds, *Le Sénégal*, Commerce et Commerçants en Afrique de l'Ouest, vol. 1, Paris: L'Harmattan, 1992, pp. 5–27. For more specific statements, on Guinea, see Goerg, Odile, *Commerce et Colonisation en Guinée 1850–1913*, Paris: L'Harmattan, 1986; on Senegal, see Barry, Boubacar, 'Introduction: commerce et commerçants sénégalais dans la longue durée. Etude d'une formation economique dépendante', in Harding and Barry, eds, *Le Sénégal*, pp. 35–58; Marfaing, Laurence, *L'Evolution du Commerce au Sénégal 1820–1930*, Paris: L'Harmattan, 1991; Marfaing, Laurence and Mariam Sow, *Les Opérateurs Economiques au Sénégal: Entre le Formel et l'Informel (1930– 1996)*, Paris: Karthala, 1999.

21. Harding, 'Grands commerçants', p. 18.

22. Amselle, Jean-Loup, 'Préface', in Grégoire, Emmanuel and Pascal Labazée, eds, *Grands Commerçants d'Afrique de l'Ouest: Logiques et Pratiques d'un Groupe d'Hommes d'Affaires Contemporains*, Paris: Karthala, 1993, p. 7. See also Labazée, Pascal, 'Un terrain anthropologique à explorer: l'entreprise africaine', *Cahiers d'Études Africaines*, 31, 124 (1991), pp. 533–52. For a more general attempt to state the similarities between Western and non-Western modes of exchange and commodity value, see Appadurai, Arjun, 'Introduction: commodities and the politics of value', in Appadurai, Arjun, ed., *The Social Life of Things: Commodities in Cultural Perspective*, Cambridge: Cambridge University Press, 1988, pp. 3–63.

23. Ray, Rajat Kanta, 'Asian capital in the age of European domination: the rise of the bazaar, 1800–1914', *Modern Asian Studies*, 29, 3 (1995), p. 449.

24. McCabe, Ina Baghdiantz, Gelina Harlaftis and Ioanna Pepelasis Minoglou, 'Introduction', in McCabe, Ina Baghdiantz, Gelina Harlaftis and Ioanna Pepelasis Minoglou, eds, *Diaspora Entrepreneurial Networks: Four Centuries of History*, Oxford: Berg, 2005, p. xxii. The term is that of Cohen, Abner, 'Cultural strategies in the organization of trading diasporas', in Meillassoux, Claude, ed, *The Development of Indigenous Trade and Markets in West Africa*, London: Oxford University Press, 1971, pp. 266–281. For a synthetic treatment, see Curtin, P.D., *Cross-Cultural Trade in World History*, Cambridge: Cambridge University Press, 1984. On African trading networks, see Amselle, Jean-Loup, *Les Négociants de la Savane: Histoire et Organisation Sociale des Kooroko (Mali)*, Paris: Anthropos, 1977; Cohen, Abner, *Custom and Politics in Urban Africa: A Study of Hausa Migrants in Yoruba Towns*, London: Routledge, 1969; and Lovejoy, P.E., *Caravans of Kola: The Hausa Kola Trade, 1700–1900*, Zaria: Ahmadu Bello University Press, 1980.

25. ANS AOF 5 M 344, 'LIQUIDATION JUDICIAIRE SALIM SALKA—RAPPORT DU LIQUIDATEUR SUR L'ETAT APPARENT DE LA LIQUIDATION', Dakar, 30/06/1930.

26. ANS AOF 11 D 3/37, 'Rapport', n.d. [1923/4].

27. Muruwwah, Kamil, *Nahnu fi Ifriqiya: al-Hijra al-Lubnaniyya al-Suriyya ila Ifriqiya al-Gharbiyya, Madiha, Hadiriha, Mustaqbaliha*, Beirut: Al-Makshuf, 1938, pp. 245–6.

28. CARAN AOF NS 21 G 142 [200 Mi 3071], 'RENSEIGNEMENTS', Dakar, 20/10/1937. See also Muruwwah, *Nahnu fi Ifriqiya*, p. 246.

29. ANS AOF NS 21 G 118, Administrateur de la Circonscription de Dakar et Dépendances to Governor-General of AOF, 'Situation des Libano-Syriens de l'AOF', Dakar, 14/03/1945.

30. Muruwwah, *Nahnu fi Ifriqiya*, p. 246.

31. Khuri, Fuad, 'Kinship, emigration, and trade partnership among the Lebanese of West Africa', *Africa* 35, 4 (1965), pp. 393–4.

32. I draw here on the insights of Lorenz, Edward H., 'Neither friends nor strangers: informal networks of subcontracting in French industry', in Gambetta, Diego, ed., *Trust: Making and Breaking Cooperative Relations*, Oxford:

Blackwell, 1991, pp. 194–210. See also Jarillo, J. Carlos, 'On strategic networks', *Strategic Management Journal*, 9 (1988), pp. 31–41; and Powell, Walter J., 'Neither market nor hierarchy: network forms of organisation', *Organizational Behaviour*, 12 (1990), pp. 295–336.

33. Muruwwah, *Nahnu fi Ifriqiya*, p. 251.

34. Grégoire, Emmanuel and Pascal Labazée, 'Introduction: approche comparative des réseaux ouest-africains contemporains', in Grégoire and Labazée, eds, *Grands Commerçants d'Afrique*, p. 19.

35. Muruwwah, *Nahnu fi Ifriqiya*, pp. 250–2.

36. Grégoire and Labazée, 'Introduction', p. 19.

37. Muruwwah, *Nahnu fi Ifriqiya*, p. 249.

38. Cruise O'Brien, Rita, 'Lebanese entrepreneurs in Senegal', *Cahiers d'Études Africaines*, 15, 1 (1975), p. 96.

39. Bonin, Hubert, *CFAO: Cent Ans de Compétition*, Paris: Economica, 1987, p. 135. On the relations between Senegalese and *Soudanais* traders and the CFAO in Côte d'Ivoire, see Gonnin, Gilbert and Julien Zonon, 'Le commerce de la zone forestière ouest ivoirienne depuis le XIXe siècle: une activité à prédominance etrangère', in Harding, Leonhard and Pierre Kipré, eds, *La Côte d'Ivoire*, Commerce et Commerçants en Afrique de l'Ouest, vol. 2, Paris: L'Harmattan, 1992, pp. 149–87; and Zie, Gnato and Vrih Gbazah, 'Les commerçants Sénégalais en Côte d'Ivoire de 1880 à 1970', in Harding and Kipré, eds, *La Côte d'Ivoire*, pp. 235–71.

40. As one of its managers put it in 1895. Quoted in Fall, Babacar and Abdoul Sow, 'Les traitants Saint-Louisiens dans les villes-escales du Sénégal 1850–1930', in Harding and Barry, eds, *Le Sénégal*, p. 171.

41. On these practices, see Marfaing, Laurence, *L'Evolution du Commerce au Sénégal 1820–1930*, Paris: L'Harmattan, 1991, pp. 184–90.

42. CARAN AOF NS 21 G 141 [200 Mi 3070], 'RENSEIGNEMENTS', Dakar, 23/12/1937.

43. ANS AOF NS 10 F 14, Administrateur de la Circonscription de Dakar to Governor-General of AOF, Dakar, 14/10/1935.

44. Muruwwah, *Nahnu fi Ifriqiya*, p. 250.

45. ANS AOF 5 M 344, 'FAILLITE JAMIL HADDAD'.

46. ANS AOF 5 M 344, 'FAILLITE FARID GAFHARI'.

47. ANS AOF 5 M 344, 'LIQUIDATION JUDICIAIRE MICHEL ABDALLAH'.

48. ANS AOF 5 M 344, 'LIQUIDATION JUDICIAIRE ABBAS ABBOUD'.

49. ANS AOF 5 M 344, 'LIQUIDATION JUDICIAIRE RICHA FRERES'.

50. ANS AOF 5 M 344, 'LIQUIDATION JUDICIAIRE MICHEL ABDALLAH'.

51. ANS AOF 5 M 344, 'LIQUIDATION JUDICIAIRE ABBAS ABBOUD'.

52. ANS AOF 5 M 344, 'MEMOIRE SUR L'ETAT APPARENT DE LA LIQUIDATION JUDICIAIRE AHMAD ZAIAT'.

53. ANS AOF NS 21 G 118, Administrateur de la Circonscription de Dakar et Dépendances to Governor-General of AOF, 'Situation des Libano-Syriens de l'AOF', Dakar, 14/03/1945.

54. ANS AOF NS 10 F 14, 'SITUATION DES LIBANO-SYRIENS—RESIDENCE: CONAKRY—NOM: BOTROS RESZK'.

55. ANS AOF NS 10 F 14, 'RENSEIGNEMENTS concernant les LIBANO-SYRIENS en résidence au SOUDAN', Bamako, November 1944.

56. Muruwwah, *Nahnu fi Ifriqiya*, p. 260.

57. ANS AOF NS 10 F 14, 'RENSEIGNEMENTS concernant les LIBANO-SYRIENS en résidence au SOUDAN', Bamako, November 1944.

58. ANS AOF NS 21 G 118, Administrateur de la Circonscription de Dakar et Dépendances to Governor-General of AOF, 'Situation des Libano-Syriens de l'AOF', Dakar, 14/03/1945.

59. ANS AOF NS 10 F 14, 'RENSEIGNEMENTS concernant les LIBANO-SYRIENS en résidence au SOUDAN', Bamako, November 1944.

60. ANS AOF NS 10 F 14, 'SITUATION DES LIBANO-SYRIENS—RESIDENCE: CONAKRY—NOM: NAJA frères'.

61. ANS AOF NS 10 F 14, 'SITUATION DES LIBANO-SYRIENS—RESIDENCE: CONAKRY—NOM: JAFFAL ABDALLAH'; 'SITUATION DES LIBANO-SYRIENS—RESIDENCE: CONAKRY—NOM: FAKOURY'.

62. ANS AOF NS 10 F 14, 'ORDRE D'IMPORTANCE DES FORTUNES PRESUMEES DES LIBANO-SYRIENS DE LA COTE D'IVOIRE'; Administrateur to Governor of Côte d'Ivoire, Grand Bassam, 28/02/1945.

63. Muruwwah, *Nahnu fi Ifriqiya*, p. 198.

64. ANS AOF 5 M 344, 'LIQUIDATION JUDICIAIRE ABBAS ABBOUD'.

65. Muruwwah, *Nahnu fi Ifriqiya*, pp. 195–6, 264.

66. ANS AOF 5 M 344, 'LIQUIDATION JUDICIAIRE RICHA FRERES', Dakar, 31/08/1931.

67. De La Rue, Sidney, *The Land of the Pepper Bird: Liberia*, London: G.P. Putnam, 1930, p. 296.

68. ANS AOF 10 F 14, Administrateur du Cercle de Seguela to Governor of Côte d'Ivoire, Seguela, 16/03/1945.

69. ANS AOF 5 M 344, 'LIQUIDATION JUDICIAIRE BASHIR SOUNIEZ', Dakar, 22/02/1931.

70. ANS AOF 5 M 344, 'RAPPORT à Monsieur le Directeur de la Police et de la Sûreté Générale', Dakar, n.d. [1931].

71. ANS AOF NS 10 F 14, 'ORDRE D'IMPORTANCE DES FORTUNES PRESUMEES DES LIBANO-SYRIENS DE LA COTE D'IVOIRE'; Administrateur to Governor of Côte d'Ivoire, Grand Bassam, 28/02/1945.

72. ANS AOF NS 10 F 14, Administrateur du Cercle de Grand-Bassam to Governor of Côte d'Ivoire, Grand-Bassam, 28/02/1945.

73. Muruwwah, *Nahnu fi Ifriqiya*, pp. 198, 212.

74. ANS AOF NS 10 F 14, 'RENSEIGNEMENTS concernant les LIBANO-SYRIENS en résidence au SOUDAN', Bamako, November 1944.

75. ANS AOF NS 21 G 118, Administrateur de la Circonscription de Dakar et Dépendances to Governor-General of AOF, 'Situation des Libano-Syriens de l'AOF', Dakar, 14/03/1945.

76. Filfili, *Ma Vie*, p. 69.

77. ANS AOF 10 F 14, Administrateur de la Circonscription de Dakar to Governor-General of AOF, Dakar, 14/10/1935.

78. Muruwwah, *Nahnu fi Ifriqiya*, p. 251.

79. *BCAF*, 22, 8 (August 1912), p. 318.

80. Ibid.

81. ANS AOF 5 M 346, 'ASSEMBLEE CONCARDATAIRE (MICHEL ABDALLAH)—RAPPORT DU LIQUIDATEUR', Dakar, 24/10/1931.

82. ANS AOF 5 M 346, 'INVENTAIRE—Boutique FATICK', Dakar, 05/06/1934.

83. For a sense of such seasonal migrations, see ANS AOF 2 G 17/24 (3), 'Rapport d'Ensemble—Dakar'.

84. ANS AOF 2 G 32/83, 'Cercle du Sine-Saloum (Kaolack)—Rapport Annuel d'Ensemble 1932'.

85. ANS AOF 2 G 33/81, 'SENEGAL—Cercle de Kaolack—Rapport sur la traite 1932–1933'.

86. ANS AOF 2 G 35/71, 'Louga—Rapport sur la traite 1935'.

87. Marfaing and Sow, *Opérateurs*, pp. 87–8.

88. ANS AOF NS 17 G 127, La Population Indigène du Sine-Saloum to Monsieur le Général de GAULLE, Chef de la France Libre, Président du Comité Français de la Libération Nationale, de Passage à Kaolack.

89. Muruwwah, *Nahnu fi Ifriqiya*, p. 252.

90. Fouquet, Joseph, *La Traite des Arachides dans le Pays de Kaolack, et ses Conséquences Économiques, Sociales et Juridiques*, Saint-Louis: Centre de l'Institut Français d'Afrique Noire, 1958, p. 44.

91. Savonnet, G., *La Ville de Thiès: Étude de Géographie Humaine*, Études Sénégalaises 6, Saint-Louis: Centre de l'Institut Français d'Afrique Noire, p. 119.

92. ANS AOF NS 10 F 14, Administrateur de la Circonscription de Dakar to Governor-General of AOF, Dakar, 14/10/1935.

93. ANS AOF 5 M 358, 'Livre Compte de Nicolas Issa', Dakar, 07/07/1938.

94. Savonnet, *Thiès*, p. 118. On the uses and arrangements of credit in one West African setting, see Falola, Toyin, 'Money and informal credit institutions in colonial Western Nigeria', in Guyer, Jane, ed., *Money Matters: Instability, Values, and Social Payments in the Modern History of West African Communities*, London: James Currey, 1995, pp. 162–87. For more general introductions, see Austin, Gareth, 'Indigenous credit institutions in West Africa, 1750–1960', in Austin, Gareth and Kaoru Sugihara, eds, *Local Suppliers of Credit in the Third World*, Basingstoke: Macmillan, 1993, pp. 93–159; and Stiansen, André and Jane Guyer, 'Introduction', in Guyer, Jane, ed., *Credit, Currencies and Culture: African Financial Institutions in Historical Perspective*, Stockholm: Nordiska Afrikainstitutet, 1999, pp. 1–14.

95. ANS AOF NS 10 F 14, Administrateur de la Circonscription de Dakar to Governor-General of AOF, Dakar, 14/10/1935.

96. *L'AOF*, 02/09/1948.

97. Searing, James, *'God Alone is King': Islam and Emancipation in Senegal. The Wolof Kingdoms of Kajoor and Baol, 1859–1914*, Oxford: James Currey, 2002, fn. 80, p. 229.
98. Ibid., p. 202.
99. Iliffe, John, *The Emergence of African Capitalism*, Basingstoke: Macmillan, 1981, p. 55.
100. Searing, *'God Alone'*, pp. 195, 202, 217, 223.
101. See Berry, Sara, 'Stable prices, unstable values: some thoughts on monetization and the meaning of transactions in West African economies' in Guyer, Jane I., ed., *Credit, Currencies and Culture: African Financial Institutions in Historical Perspective*, Stockholm: Nordiska Afrikainstitutet, 1999, pp. 299–313.
102. Geertz, Clifford, 'The bazaar economy: information and search in peasant marketing', *Supplement to the American Economic Review*, 68 (1978), pp. 28–32.
103. Savonnet, *Thiès*, p. 118.
104. Khuri, Fuad, 'The etiquette of bargaining in the Middle East', *American Anthropologist*, 70, 4 (1968), p. 702.
105. ANS AOF 10 F 14, 'SITUATION DES LIBANO-SYRIENS—RESIDENCE: KOUROUSSA—NOM: AID DAHER'; 'SITUATION DES LIBANO-SYRIENS—RESIDENCE: KOUROUSSA—Vve MOUSSI ET ASSAD GANTOUS'.
106. van der Laan, *Lebanese Traders*, p. 45.
107. Fouquet, *Kaolack*, p. 45.
108. Savonnet, *Thiès*, p. 94.
109. CARAN AOF AS 21 G 37 [200 Mi 1100], Officier du Ministère Public to Administrateur Supérieur de la Casamance, Ziguinchor, 05/10/1910.
110. ANS AOF 5 M 344, 'FAILLITE AHMET AIDARA', Dakar, 20/01/1931.
111. On networks of smugglers, and the manner in which they profited from the production of colonial space, see Nugent, Paul, 'The art of dissimulation: smugglers, informers and the preventive service along the Ghana–Togo frontier, 1920–1939', in Dubois, Colette, Marc Michel and Pierre Soumille, eds, *Frontières Plurielles, Frontières Conflictuelles en Afrique Subsaharienne*, Paris: L'Harmattan, 2000, pp. 209–231; and Nugent, Paul, *Smugglers, Secessionists and Loyal Citizens on the Ghana-Togo Frontier: the Lie of the Borderlands since 1914*, Oxford: James Currey, 2002.
112. ANS AOF NS 10 F 14, Administrateur de la Circonscription de Dakar to Governor-General of AOF, Dakar, 14/10/1935.
113. For a fine study of traders operating on 'the margins of the law', see MacGaffey, Janet and Rémy Bazenguissa-Ganga, *Congo-Paris: Transnational Traders on the Margins of the Law*, Oxford: James Currey, 2000,
114. Sar, Moustapha, 'Louga: sa ville et sa région: essai d'intégration des rapports ville-campagne dans la problématique du développement', Thèse de Troisième Cycle de Géographie Appliquée, Université Cheikh Anta Diop, Dakar, 1970.
115. Muruwwah, *Nahnu fi Ifriqiya*, p. 246.
116. CARAN AOF 1 G 267, 'Rapport de M. Boulland de l'Escale, Syndic de la Presse Coloniale Française, sur sa Mission Economique et de Vulgarisation en Afrique Occidentale'.
117. *BCAF*, 14, 12 (December 1904), p. 374.
118. Filfili, Nadra, *Ma Vie: Cinquante Ans de Vie au Sénégal*, dictated to and translated by Filfili, Karim, n.p., 1973, p. 72.
119. Alfaro-Velcamp, Theresa, *So Far from Allah, So Close to Mexico: Middle Eastern Immigrants in Modern Mexico*, Austin, TX: University of Texas Press, 2007, Table 8, p. 173.
120. For an attempt at comparison, see Truzzi, Oswaldo, 'The right place at the right time: Syrians and Lebanese in Brazil and the United States, a comparative approach', *Journal of American Ethnic History*, 16, 2 (1997), pp. 3–34.
121. Labaki, Boutros, *Introduction à l'Histoire Economique du Liban: Soie et Commerce Extérieur en Fin de Période Ottomane*, Beirut: Presses de l'Université Libanaise, 1984, pp. 40–1.
122. Chevallier, Dominique, *La Société du Mont Liban à l'Epoque de la Révolution Industrielle*, Paris: Geuthner, 1971, pp. 131–4.
123. Harper, T.N., 'Empire, diaspora and the languages of globalism, 1850–1914', in Hopkins, A.G., ed., *Globalisation and World History*, London: Pimlico, 2002.
124. Searing, *'God Alone'*, p. 214.
125. Savonnet, *Thiès*, p. 95.

126. ANS AOF NS 10 F 14, Administrateur de la Circonscription de Dakar to Governor-General of AOF, Dakar, 14/10/1935.
127. ANS 2 G 35/71, Commandant de Cercle of Louga to Governor of Senegal, 'a/s compte-rendu de la traite', Louga, 07/01/1935.
128. CARAN AOF 1 G 267, 'Rapport de M. Boulland de l'Escale, Syndic de la Presse Coloniale Française, sur sa Mission Économique et de Vulgarisation en Afrique Occidentale', 1908.
129. Fouquet, *La Traite*, p. 97.
130. Savonnet, *Thiès*, p. 108.
131. Cruise O'Brien, Rita, *White Society in Black Africa: The French in Senegal*, London: Faber, 1972, p. 56.
132. Fouquet, *La Traite*, p. 44.
133. Geertz, *Peddlers*, p. 28; Geertz, 'Suq', p. 214.
134. I have borrowed the term from Guyer, Jane, 'Wealth in people—wealth in things: Introduction', *Journal of African History*, 36 (1995), p. 87.
135. Hart, Keith, 'Informal income opportunities and urban employment in Ghana', *Journal of Modern African Studies*, 11, 1 (1973), p. 68.
136. Jarillo, 'Networks', p. 35.
137. ANS AOF NS 21 G 118, Administrateur de la Circonscription de Dakar et Dépendances to Governor-General of AOF, 'Situation des Libano-Syriens de l'AOF', Dakar, 14/03/1945.
138. Muruwwah, *Nahnu fi Ifriqiya*, p. 250.
139. ANS AOF NS 21 G 118, Administrateur de la Circonscription de Dakar et Dépendances to Governor-General of AOF, 'Situation des Libano-Syriens de l'AOF', Dakar, 14/03/1945.
140. ANS AOF NS 10 F 14, 'RENSEIGNEMENTS concernant les LIBANO-SYRIENS en résidence au SOUDAN', Bamako, November 1944';
141. *BCAF*, 22, 8 (August 1912), p. 318.
142. Arcin, André, *La Guinée Française: Races, Religions, Coutumes, Production, Commerce*, Paris: Augustin Challavel, 1907, fn. 3, p. 93.
143. Muruwwah, *Nahnu fi Ifriqiya*, p. 209.
144. CARAN AOF AS 21 G 33 [200 Mi 1099–1100], 'Copie de lettre non envoyée', n.d. [1918].
145. Fawcett, Louise L'Estrange, 'Lebanese, Palestinians and Syrians in Colombia', in Hourani, Albert and Nadim Shehadi, eds, *The Lebanese in the World: A Hundred Years of Emigration*, London: I.B. Tauris, 1992, p. 370.
146. Touma, Toufic, *Un Village de Montagne au Liban (Hadeth el-Jobbé)*, Paris: Mouton, 1958, p. 90.
147. CCIMP ML 42731/01, 'Passage à Marseille de l'émigration Syrienne vers les Amériques [mémoire du Dr Bollama]', 15/07/1901.
148. 'Abduh, Najib, *Al-Safr al-Mufid fi al-'Alam al-Jadid, wa al-Dalil al-Tijari li-Abna al-Lugha al-'Arabiyya fi al-'Alm Ajma'*, New York: Meraat ul-Gharb Publishing House, 1907, p. 428. See also Gonzalez, Nancie L., *Dollar, Dove, and Eagle: One Hundred Years of Palestinian Migration to Honduras*, Ann Arbor, MI: University of Michigan Press, 1992.
149. 'Abduh, *Al-Safr al-Mufid*, p. 428.
150. Fawcett, 'Lebanese emigration', fn. 37, p. 370.
151. 'Abduh, *Al-Safr al-Mufid*, p. 428. See also Ma'luf, 'Isa Iskandar, *Tarikh al-Usar al-Sharqiyya*, Trabulsi, Fawwaz, ed., Beirut: Riad al-Rayyes, 2008 [1924], vol. 4, pp. 36–8.
152. 'Wufud al-Mu'tamar', in Al-Lajna al-'Aliyya li-l-Hizb al-Lamarkaziyya al-Idariyya al-'Uthmani, *Al-Mu'tamar al-'Arabi al-Awwal*, Cairo: Matba'at al-Busfur, 1913, p. 15.
153. CARAN AOF AS 21 G 44 [200 Mi 1103], Minister of Colonies to Governor-General of AOF, Paris, 14/11/1917.
154. CARAN AOF AS 21 G 44 [200 Mi 1103], Minister of Colonies to Governor-General of AOF, Paris, 11/11/1916.
155. CARAN AOF AS 21 G 44 [200 Mi 1103], César Abdo ['Abduh] to Governor of Senegal, Dakar, 06/02/1917.
156. Rambert, Gaston, *Marseille. La Formation d'une Grande Cité Moderne. Etude de Géographie Urbaine*, Marseille: Société Anonyme du Sémaphore de Marseille, 1934.
157. CARAN AOF AS 21 43 [200 Mi 1102], Lieutenant-Governor of Guinea to Governor-General of AOF, Conakry, 21/08/1916.
158. CARAN AOF AS 21 43 [200 Mi 1102], Najib Jabre [Jabir] to Governor-General of AOF, Dakar, 18/06/1918.
159. ANS AOF NS 10 F 14, 'SITUATION DES LIBANO-SYRIENS—RESIDENCE: KANKAN—NOM: JABRE Najib'.

287

160. CARAN AOF AS 21 G 34 [200 Mi 1100], Lieutenant-Governor of Dahomey to Governor-General, Porto-Novo, 08/03/1919.

161. CAOM MC FM AP 2303/5, 'RAPPORT sur la situation des Libano-Syriens en Afrique Occidentale Française et au Togo'.

162. CARAN AOF AS 21 G 44 [200 Mi 1103], Joseph Ganamet to Lieutenant-Governor of Senegal, 11/01/1916.

163. CARAN AOF AS 21 G 44 [200 Mi 1103], Joseph Ganamet to Governor-General of AOF, 15/09/1917.

164. ANS AOF 11 D 3/37, 'Immigration Syrienne en Casamance', n.d. [1924].

165. Trincaz, Pierre Xavier, *Colonisation et Régionalisme: Ziguinchor en Casamance*, Paris: ORSTOM, 1984, pp. 102–3.

166. CARAN AOF AS 21 G 35 [200 Mi 1100], Governor of Soudan to Governor-General of AOF, Koulouba, 12/11/1918.

167. CARAN AOF AS 21 G 43 [200 Mi 1102], Governor of Guinea to Governor-General of AOF, Conakry, 22/08/1916.

168. CARAN AOF AS 21 G 44 [200 Mi 1103], Governor of Guinea to Governor-General of AOF, Conakry, 04/02/1918.

169. ANS AOF 10 F 14, Administrateur of Bassam to Governor of Côte d'Ivoire, Grand-Bassam, 28/02/1945.

170. Bierwirth, 'Initial establishment', p. 337.

171. ANS AOF NS 10 F 14, Governor of Guinea to Governor-General of AOF, Conakry, 12/03/1945.

172. Macmillan, Allister, *The Red Book of British West Africa. Historical and Descriptive Commercial and Industrial Facts, Figures and Resources, Compiled and Edited by Allister Macmillan FRGS*, London: W.H. & L. Collingridge, 1920, p. 103.

173. Muruwwah, *Nahnu fi Ifriqiya*, p. 258.

174. Kojok, Salma, 'Les Libanais en Côte d'Ivoire de 1920 à 1960', unpublished Ph.D dissertation, Université de Nantes, 2002, 2 vols., vol. 1, p. 160.

175. CARAN AOF AS 21 G 44 [200 Mi 1103], Georges Salomon [Sleiman] to Governor-General of AOF, Dakar.

176. CARAN AOF AS 21 G 43 [200 Mi 1102], Governor of Guinea to Governor-General of AOF, Conakry, 23/04/1917.

177. CARAN AOF AS 21 G 43 [200 Mi 1102], Joseph Ganamet to Governor-General of AOF, Dakar, 07/01/1918.

178. CARAN AOF AS 21 G 43 [200 Mi 1102], S.A. Charaf [Sharaf] to Governor-General of AOF, Dakar, 22/08/1918.

179. For some of these telegrams, see CARAN AOF AS 21 G 33 [200 Mi 1099–1100].

180. Macmillan, *Red Book*, p. 263.

181. CARAN AOF AS 21 G 38 [200 Mi 1100–1101], 'Etat des Etrangers résidant dans la Colonie du Sénégal', 1918.

182. Kojok, 'Les Libanais', p. 159.

183. Muruwwah, *Nahnu fi Ifriqiya*, p. 258.

184. Kojok, 'Les Libanais', pp. 77, 159, 162.

185. ANS AOF 10 F 14, 'RAPPORT à Monsieur le Gouverneur sur la situation des Libano-Syriens', Daloa, 28/03/1945.

186. Bierwirth, 'Initial establishment', p. 337.

187. Amselle, *Négociants*, pp. 189, 218; ANS AOF 11 D 3/37, 'ETAT Nominatif des étrangers résidant dans la Commune-Mixte de Kaolack'.

188. ANS AOF NS 10 F 14, Governor of French Soudan to Governor-General of AOF, 'Situation des Libano-Syriens en AOF', Bamako, 16/03/1945.

189. Bierwirth, 'Initial establishment', fn. 6, p. 327.

190. Amselle, *Négociants*, pp. 189–91; Cohen, *Custom and Politics*, pp. 18–9; Lovejoy, *Caravans*, p. 6.

191. Lovejoy, *Caravans*, pp. 93–4.

192. Macmillan, *Red Book*, p. 263.

193. *BCAF*, 46, 5 (1936), pp. 290–1.

194. Zie and Gbazah, 'Commerçants Sénégalais', p. 239.

195. ANS AOF 10 F 14, Administrateur Commandant le Cercle de Bouaké to Governor of Côte d'Ivoire, Bouaké, 13/03/1945.

196. Boumedouha, 'Lebanese', fn. 60, p. 99.

197. ANS AOF 10 F 14, Administrateur Commandant le Cercle de Bouaké to Governor of Côte d'Ivoire, Bouaké, 13/03/1945.

198. Amselle, Jean-Loup, *Les Négociants de la Savane: Histoire et Organisation Sociale des Kooroko*, Paris: Anthropos, 1977, fn. 1, p. 218.

6. HERE, THERE AND EVERYWHERE: THE LIVES OF LEBANESE MIGRANTS IN AOF

1. Khater, Akram, *Inventing Home: Emigration, Gender, and the Middle Class in Lebanon 1870–1920*, Berkeley: University of California Press, 2001, p. 2.

2. Filfili, Nadra, *Ma Vie: Cinquante Ans de Vie au Sénégal*, dictated to and translated by Filfili, Karim, Dakar: n.p 1973, pp. 80, 88; Muruwwah, Kamil, *Nahnu fi Ifriqiya: al-Hijra al-Lubnaniyya al-Suriyya ila Ifriqiya al-Gharbiyya, Madiha, Hadiriha, Mustaqbaliha*, Beirut: Al-Makshuf, 1938, p. 283; CARAN AOF NS 21 G 142 [200 Mi 3071], 'OPINION D'UN COMMERCANT LIBANAIS SUR LA QUESTION DU RECENSEMENT DE SES COMPATRIOTES', Dakar, 03/05/1940; Muruwwah, 'Ali 'AbdAllah, 'Kalimat muhajir 'an Ifriqiya', *Al-'Irfan*, 22, 4 (1931), p. 530.

3. CARAN AOF NS 21 G 142 [200 Mi 3071], 'Séance du Jeudi 25 Novembre 1937 Relative à l'Immigration Libano-Syrienne', Dakar.

4. Tarraf-Najib, Souha, 'Immigration ancienne et territorialisation inaccomplie. Les familles libanaises du Sénégal', *Cahiers d'Études sur la Méditerranée et le Monde Turco-Iranien*, 30 (2000), p. 273.

5. CARAN AOF NS 21 G 142 [200 Mi 3071], 'RENSEIGNEMENTS', Dakar, 25/04/1940.

6. Winder, R. Bayly, 'The Lebanese in West Africa', *Comparative Studies in Society and History*, 4, 3 (1962), p. 297.

7. Muruwwah, *Nahnu fi Ifriqiya*, p. 249.

8. Achcar [Ashqar], Joseph, *Les Libanais en Afrique Occidentale Française et dans le Monde*, Beirut: Dar al-Kitab al-Lubnani, n.d., p. 10.

9. Winder, R. Bayly, 'The Lebanese in West Africa', *Comparative Studies in Society and History*, 4, 3 (1962), p. 297.

10. Bhabha, Homi, *The Location of Culture*, London: Routledge, 1994, p. 2.

11. Memmi, Albert, *Portrait du Colonisé Précédé du Portrait du Colonisateur*, Correa: Buchet/Chastel, 1957, pp. 22, 23.

12. Bhabha, *Location*, pp. 85–6.

13. Watenpaugh, Keith, *Being Modern in the Middle East: Revolution, Nationalism, Colonialism, and the Arab Middle Class*, Princeton, NJ: Princeton University Press, 2006, p. 293.

14. López, A. Ricardo with Barbara Weinstein, 'Introduction—we shall be all: towards a transnational history of the middle class', in López and Weinstein, eds, *The Making of the Middle Class: Towards a Transnational History*, Durham, NC: Duke University Press, 2012, p. 4.

15. Ibid., p. 11.

16. See Baron, Beth, *The Women's Awakening in Egypt: Culture, Society, and the Press*, New Haven, CT: Yale University Press, 1994; Booth, Marilyn, *May Her Likes Be Multiplied: Biography and Gender Politics in Egypt*, Berkeley, CA: University of California Press, 2001; Khater, *Inventing Home*.

17. See Harootunian, Harry, *History's Disquiet: Modernity, Cultural Practice, and the Question of Everyday Life*, New York: Columbia University Press, 2000.

18. Chakrabarty, Dipesh, 'Adda, Calcutta: dwelling in modernity', *Public Culture*, 11, 1 (1999), pp. 109–45; and Chakrabarty, *Habitations of Modernity: Essays in the Wake of Subaltern Studies*, Chicago, IL: University of Chicago Press, 2002.

19. Berman, Marshall, *All That is Solid Melts into Air: The Experience of Modernity*, London: Verso, 2010 [1982]; Cooper, Frederick, *Colonialism in Question: Theory, Knowledge, History*, Berkeley, CA: University of California Press, 2005, pp. 113–49.

20. Ross, Kristin, *Fast Cars, Clean Bodies: Decolonisation and the Reordering of French Culture*, Cambridge, MA: MIT Press, 1999, p. 11. See also Owensby, Brian, *Intimate Ironies: Modernity and the Making of Middle-Class Lives in Brazil*, Stanford, CA: Stanford University Press, 1999.

21. Joshi, Sanjay, *Fractured Modernity: Making of a Middle Class in Colonial North India*, Delhi: Oxford University Press, 2001; Watenpaugh, *Being Modern*.

22. ANS AOF 10 F 14, 'RAPPORT à Monsieur le Gouverneur sur la situation des Libano-Syriens', Daloa, 28/03/1945.

23. For an early, and prescient, synthetic examination of such 'stranger' communities in the historical *longue durée*,

and their changing conditions of life in postcolonial states, see Skinner, Elliott P., 'Strangers in West African societies', *Africa*, 33, 4 (1963), pp. 307–20.

24. Curtin, Philip D., *Economic Change in Precolonial Africa: Senegambia in the Era of the Slave Trade*, Madison: University of Wisconsin Press, 1975, p. 97.

25. Diouf, Mamadou, *Le Kajoor au XIXe Siècle: Pouvoir Ceddo et Conquête Coloniale*, Paris: Karthala, 1990, p. 30.

26. Ibid., p. 28.

27. For relatively succinct accounts of this stratification, see Barry, Boubacar, *Senegambia and the Atlantic Slave Trade*, transl. Armah, Ayi Kwei, Cambridge: Cambridge University Press, 1998, pp. 27–9; Diouf, *Le Kajoor*, p. 28; and Gamble, David, *The Wolof of Senegambia, Together with Notes on the Lebu and the Serer*, London: International Anthropological Institute, 1957, pp. 44–5. For a historical sociology which, despite its title, presents an essentially static picture of such arrangements, see Diop, Abdoulaye-Bara, *La Société Wolof: Tradition et Changement. Les Systèmes d'Inégalité et de Domination*, Paris: Karthala, 1981.

28. Barry, *Senegambia*, p. 29.

29. Ibid., p. 33. On the *juula* and *jakhanke* in particular, see Curtin, *Economic Change*, pp. 66–91.

30. For a sweeping overview of these 'trading diasporas' see ibid., pp. 92–152; on the *signères*, see Brooks, George E., *Eurafricans in Western Africa: Commerce, Social Status, Gender and Religious Observance from the Sixteenth to the Eighteenth Centuries*, Athens, OH: University of Ohio Press, 2003; for a closer examination of the economic ties of Saint-Louis with the Wolof states in the eighteenth and early nineteenth century, see Searing, James, *West African Slavery and Atlantic Commerce: the Senegal River Valley, 1700–1860*, Cambridge: Cambridge University Press, 1993; on the Wolof traders of the town in the later nineteenth century, see Robinson, David, *Paths of Accommodation: Muslim Societies and French Colonial Authorities in Senegal and Mauritania, 1880–1920*, Oxford: James Currey, 2000.

31. The role of 'stranger-traders' has, of course, attracted a great deal of interest among Anglophone scholars who have focused largely on the trading diasporas operating in the central and southern regions of present-day Ghana and Nigeria. The foundational texts in anthropology are Cohen, Abner, *Custom and Politics in Urban Africa: A Study of Hausa Migrants in Yoruba Towns*, London: Routledge, 1969; Cohen, Abner, 'Cultural strategies in the organization of trading diasporas', in Meillassoux, Claude, ed., *The Development of Indigenous Trade and Markets in West Africa*, London: Oxford University Press, 1971, pp. 266–81; and Hill, Polly, 'Landlords and brokers: a West African trading system (with a note on Kumasi butchers)', *Cahiers d'Études Africaines*, 6, 23 (1966), pp. 349–66. For two historical explorations, see Arhin, Kwame, *West African Traders in Ghana in the Nineteenth and Twentieth Centuries*, London: Longman, 1979; Eades, Jeremy, *Strangers and Traders: Yoruba Migrants, Markets and the State in Northern Ghana*, Edinburgh: Edinburgh University Press, 1993.

32. Amselle, Jean-Loup, *Logiques Métisses: Anthropologie de l'Identité en Afrique et Ailleurs*, Paris: Payot, 1990, pp. 71, 75.

33. Person, Yves, *Samori. Une Révolution Dyula*, vol. 1, Dakar: Institut Fondamental d'Afrique Noire, 1968, p. 97. On the *juula* of Côte d'Ivoire, see also Launay, Robert, 'Transactional spheres and inter-societal exchange in Ivory Coast', *Cahiers d'Études Africaines*, 18, 72 (1978), pp. 561–73; and Launay, 'Landlords, hosts and strangers among the Dyula', *Ethnology*, 19, 1 (1979), pp. 71–83.

34. Ouattara, Nagnin, 'Commerçants dioulas en Côte d'Ivoire: permanence et ruptures dans un milieu socioprofessionel', in Harding, Leonhard and Pierre Kipré, eds, *La Côte d'Ivoire*, Commerce et Commerçants en Afrique de l'Ouest, vol. 2, Paris: L'Harmattan, 1992, p. 78.

35. Khuri, Fuad, *An Invitation to Laughter: An Anthropologist in the Arab World*, Chicago, IL: University of Chicago Press, 2007, p. 35.

36. Searing, James, *'God Alone is King': Islam and Emancipation in Senegal. The Wolof Kingdoms of Kajoor and Bawol, 1859–1914*, Oxford: James Currey, 2002, p. 223. Mbodj, Mohammed, cited in Tarraf-Najib, 'Immigration ancienne', p. 275.

37. Camara, Camille, *Saint-Louis-du-Sénégal*, Dakar: Institut Fondamental d'Afrique Noire, 1968, p. 78.

38. On this, see Searing, *'God Alone'*, p. 212.

39. David, Philippe, *Les Navétanes: Histoire des Migrants Saisonniers de l'Arachide en Sénégambie des Origines à nos Jours*, Dakar: Les Nouvelles Editions Africaines, 1980, pp. 34–5, 61, 87, 88. On one particular such stream, see Manchuelle, François, *Willing Migrants: Soninke Labor Diasporas, 1848–1960*, Oxford: James Currey, 1997.

40. David, *Les Navétanes*, p. 60.

41. Pélissier, Paul, *Les Paysans du Sénégal. Les Civilisations Agraires du Cayor à la Casamance*, Saint-Yrieix: n.p., 1966, p. 305.

42. ANS AOF 2 G 11/43, 'Cercle du Sine-Saloum—Rapport Mensuel—Juillet 1911', Kaolack, 31/07/1911.

43. Marty, Paulm, quoted in Cruise O'Brien, Donal, *The Mourides of Senegal: The Political and Economic Organization of an Islamic Brotherhood*, Oxford: Clarendon Press, 1971, p. 193.

44. Pélissier, *Les Paysans*, pp. 345–6.

45. Filfili, Nadra, *Ma Vie: Cinquante Ans de Vie au Sénégal*, dictated to and translated by Filfili, Karim, Dakar: n.p, 1973, pp. 84–6, 88–9.

46. Ferguson, James, *Expectations of Modernity: Myths and Meanings of Life on the Zambian Copperbelt*, Berkeley, CA: University of California Press, 1999, p. 208.

47. Kojok, Salma, 'Les Libanais en Côte d'Ivoire de 1920 à 1960', unpublished Ph.D dissertation, Université de Nantes, 2002, 2 vols., vol. 2, p. 204.

48. Muruwwah, 'Ali, 'Shay' 'an Shatt al-'Aj', *Al-'Irfan*, 23, 1 (1932), pp. 109–14.

49. al-Zayma, Muhammad Adib, 'Kayfa Tahhawala al-Insan al-Shabih bi-l-Qurd ila Insan? Tabi' Bahth Asl al-Insan Jara bayn al-Duktur William Gregory wa al-Mister Michel Mook', *Al-'Irfan*, 23, 1 (1932), pp. 102–8.

50. Muruwwah, 'Shay 'an Shatt al-'Aj', p. 113.

51. Weiss, Max, 'Don't throw yourself away to the Dark Continent: Shi'i migration to West Africa and the hierarchies of exclusion in Lebanese culture', *Studies in Ethnicity and Nationalism*, 7, 1 (2007), pp. 51, 53.

52. CAOM MC FM AP 2303/1, Délégué-Général au Levant to Commissioner for Colonies, Beirut, 06/04/1944.

53. Hayik, Michel, *Fi Majahil Ifriqiya*, Beirut: Matba'at al-'Alam, n.p.; Hushaimah, 'Abdallah, *Fi Bilad al Zunuj, aw Thamaniyat Ashhur fi Ifriqiya al-Gharbiyya*, Beirut: Matabi' Quzma, n.d. [1931]; Muruwwah, *Nahnu fi Ifriqiya*.

54. ANS AOF 10 F 14, 'RAPPORT à Monsieur le Gouverneur sur la situation des Libano-Syriens', Daloa, 28/03/1945.

55. CARAN AOF AS 21 G 38, [200 Mi 1100–1101], Lieutenant-Colonel Lefebvre to Governor-General of AOF, Zinder, 11/08/1918.

56. Khuri, Fuad, 'The African-Lebanese mulattoes of West Africa: a racial frontier', *Anthropological Quarterly*, 12 (1968), p. 91.

57. ANS AOF 10 F 14, Commandant de Cercle of Seguela to Governor of Côte d'Ivoire, Seguela, 16/03/1945.

58. Khuri, 'African-Lebanese mulattoes', p. 97.

59. Muruwwah, *Nahnu fi Ifriqiya*, p. 290.

60. Kojok, 'Les Libanais', vol. 2, p. 216.

61. Muruwwah, *Nahnu fi Ifriqiya*, p. 247.

62. ANS AOF NS 10 F 14, 'RAPPORT à Monsieur le Gouverneur sur la situation des Libano-Syriens', Daloa, 28/03/1945.

63. ANS AOF 10 F 14, Administrateur of Bassam to Governor of Côte d'Ivoire, Grand-Bassam, 28/02/1945.

64. ANS AOF 10 F 14, Governor of Guinea to Governor-General of AOF, Dakar, 12/03/1945.

65. ANS AOF 10 F 14, Governor-General of AOF to Commissioner for Colonies, Dakar, n.d. [1943]

66. Muruwwah, *Nahnu fi Ifriqiya*, p. 288.

67. Kojok, 'Les Libanais', vol. 2, p. 316.

68. Stoler, Ann Laura, *Carnal Knowledge and Imperial Power: Race and the Intimate in Colonial Rule*, Berkeley, CA: University of California Press, 2002, pp. 112–39.

69. Muruwwah, *Nahnu fi Ifriqiya*, p. 290.

70. Fanon, Frantz, *Les Damnés de la Terre*, Paris: Gallimard, 1991 [1961], p. 68.

71. Seck, Assane, *Dakar*, Dakar: Faculté des Lettres et Sciences Humaines de Dakar, n.d., p. 16.

72. Cruise O'Brien, Rita, 'Lebanese entrepreneurs in Senegal', *Cahiers d'Études Africaines*, 15, 1 (1975), p. 55.

73. Tarraf-Najib, 'Immigration', p. 273.

74. Dresch, Jean, cited in Tarraf-Najib, 'Immigration', p. 274.

75. As Charles Morazé wrote in 1936, presumptuously using the past tense. Quoted in Seck, *Dakar*, p. 16.

76. On Diagne, see Johnson, G. Wesley, *The Emergence of Black Politics in Senegal: The Struggle for Power in the Four Communes, 1900–1920*, Stanford, CA: Stanford University Press, 1971.

77. Betts, Raymond, 'The establishment of the Medina in Dakar, Senegal, 1914', *Africa*, 41, 2 (1971), p. 149.

78. Ibid., p. 148. For this residential distribution, see Martin, Vincent, *Recensement Démographique de la Ville de*

Dakar (1955). Résultats Définitifs, vol. 2, *Étude Socio-Démographique de la Ville de Dakar*, Dakar: Ministère du Plan, Service de la Statistique, 1962, p. 18.

79.　Angrand, Armand, *Les Lébous de la Presqu'île du Cap Vert. Essai sur leur Histoire et leurs Coutumes*, Dakar: E. Gensul, 1946, p. 127.

80.　See ANS AOF 2 G 18/20(3), 'Dakar-Gorée-Rufisque et Banlieue de Dakar', 1918.

81.　Sinou, Alain, *Comptoirs et Villes Coloniales du Sénégal. Saint Louis, Gorée, Dakar*, Paris: Karthala, 1993, pp. 304–5.

82.　ANS AOF NS 21 G 227, 'Vol d'une caisse renfermant des flacons de brillantine "CADORICH"', Dakar, 22/07/1942; 'AUDITION DU SIEUR KAOUK AHMED, TÉMOIN', Dakar, 20/01/1943.

83.　ANS AOF NS 21 G 227, Inspecteur Principal de Police, 3rd district, to Commissaire Central, Dakar, 23/06/1950.

84.　Anthony, Farid Raymond, *Sawpit Boy*, n.p., 1980, pp. 26, 99, 128–31.

85.　CARAN AOF NS 21 G 142 [200 Mi 3071], Governor-General of AOF to Minister of Colonies, 'a/s Recensement des Libano-Syriens (décret du 11 mars 1940), Dakar, 15/04/1940.

86.　CARAN AOF NS 21 G 142 [200 Mi 3071], 'RENSEIGNEMENTS', Dakar, 25/04/1940.

87.　Khalaf, Samir, 'The background and causes of Lebanese/Syrian immigration to the United States before World War One', in Hooglund, Eric, ed., *Crossing the Waters: Arabic-Speaking Immigrants to the United States before 1940*, Washington, DC: Smithsonian Institute Press, 1987, p. 29.

88.　CARAN AOF AS 21 G 37 [200 Mi 1100], Governor-General of AOF to Lieutenant-Governor of Senegal, Dakar, 07/08/1910.

89.　CARAN AOF NS 21 G 142 [200 Mi 3071], 'RENSEIGNEMENTS', Kaolack, 19/04/1940.

90.　Kaniki, Martin, 'Attitudes and reactions towards the Lebanese in Sierra Leone during the colonial period', *Canadian Journal of African Studies*, 7, 1 (1973), p. 102.

91.　CARAN AOF AS 21 G 33 [200 Mi 1099–1100].

92.　CARAN AOF NS 21 G 23 [200 Mi 3023–24], Madame Antoine Char to Maronite Patriarch, Dakar, 13/03/1943.

93.　CARAN AOF NS 21 G 142 [200 Mi 3071], 'OPINION D'UN COMMERCANT LIBANAIS SUR LA QUESTION DU RECENSEMENT DE SES COMPATRIOTES', Dakar, 03/05/1940.

94.　CARAN AOF NS 21 G 142 [200 Mi 3071], 'OPINION D'UN COMMERCANT LIBANAIS SUR LA QUESTION DU RECENSEMENT DE SES COMPATRIOTES', Dakar, 03/05/1940.

95.　CARAN AOF NS 21 G 142 [200 Mi 3071], 'RENSEIGNEMENTS', Kaolack, 19/04/1940.

96.　CARAN AOF NS 21 G 142 [200 Mi 3071], 'OPINION D'UN COMMERCANT LIBANAIS SUR LA QUESTION DU RECENSEMENT DE SES COMPATRIOTES', Dakar, 03/05/1940.

97.　I borrow the compelling notion of broadcasting from Herbst, Jeffrey, *States and Power in Africa: Comparative Lessons in Authority and Control*, Princeton, NJ: Princeton University Press, 2000, p. 1.

98.　CARAN AOF NS 21 G 142 [200 Mi 3071], 'OPINION D'UN COMMERCANT LIBANAIS SUR LA QUESTION DU RECENSEMENT DE SES COMPATRIOTES', Dakar, 03/05/1940.

99.　CARAN AOF NS 21 G 142 [200 Mi 3071], 'RENSEIGNEMENTS', Dakar, 24/04/1940.

100.　'AU LECTEUR', *FAN*, 1 (August 1935), pp. 1–2.

101.　ANS AOF NS 10 F 14, 'Renseignements', Dakar, 30/05/1935.

102.　Dioudonnat, Pierre-Marie, *Les 700 Rédacteurs de 'JSP' 1930–1944*, Paris: DEDOPOLS, 1993, p. 70.

103.　Dioudonnat, Pierre-Marie, *Je Suis Partout 1930–1944 Les Maurrassiens devant la Tentation Fasciste*, Paris: La Table Ronde, 1973, fn. 144, p. 174.

104.　This was later expanded into a book: Paillard, Jean, *Faut-il Faire de l'Algérie un Dominion?* Paris: F. Sorlot, 1939.

105.　Weber, Eugen, *Action Française: Royalism and Reaction in Twentieth-Century France*, Stanford, CA: Stanford University Press, 1962, pp. 351, 369; Blanchard, Pascal, 'Discours, politique et propagande. L'AOF et les Africains au temps de la révolution nationale (1940–1944)', tekrur-ucad.refer.sn/IMG/pdf/P4BLANCH.pdf, p. 321.

106.　Le Crom, Jean-Pierre, *Syndicats, Nous Voilà!: Vichy et le Corporatisme*, Paris: Editions de l'Atelier, 1995, p. 127.

107.　Blanchard, Pascal, 'Discours,', p. 321.

108.　A pathological scribbler, Paillard also wrote accounts of his travels. See Paillard, *Périple Noir: Sénégal—Soudan—Niger—Haute Volta—Nigeria—Hoggar*, Paris: Les Oeuvres Françaises, 1935; and *Ghâna: Ville Perdue, Epopée Nigérienne*, Paris: Les Oeuvres Françaises, 1938.

109.　'Une Conférence de M. Jean Paillard', *PA*, 298 (1 June1935).

110. *FAN*, 15 (October 1936), inside cover.

111. Paillard, Jean, *La Fin des Français en Afrique Noire*, Paris: Les Oeuvres Françaises, 1935, p. 187. For the broader circulation of such ideas among the French right, see Girardet, Raoul, *L'Idée Coloniale en France de 1871 à 1962*, Paris: La Table Ronde, 1972, espec. pp. 119–26.

112. 'Danger politique de l'invasion Libano-Syrienne en AOF', *FAN*, 2 (September 1935), p. 26.

113. 'Compte rendu de l'Assemblée Générale du SCES', *FAN*, 1 (August 1935), p. 7. 'Un état dans l'état', *FAN*, 14 (September 1936), p. 7.

114. Paillard, *Périple*, p. 45.

115. 'La Haute Administration Coloniale de l'AOF au service du communisme et de l'étranger', *FAN*, 32 (April 1938), p. 1; 'Français et Indigènes de l'AOF c'est volontairement que le gouvernement vous sacrifie aux Libano-Syriens, Levantins et métèques', *FAN*, 15 (October 1936), p. 7. On the policies of the Popular Front in AOF, see Bernard-Duquenet, Nicole, *Le Sénégal et le Front Populaire*, Paris: L'Harmattan, 1986; Chafer, Tony and Amanda Sackur, 'Introduction', in Chafer and Sackur, eds, *The French Colonial Empire and the Popular Front*, Basingstoke: Palgrave Macmillan, 1999, pp. 1–29; Cohen, William B., 'The colonial policy of the Popular Front', *French Historical Studies*, 7 (1971–2), pp. 368–75; Coquery-Vidrovitch, Catherine, 'The Popular Front and the colonial question. French West Africa: an example of reformist colonialism', in Chafer and Sackur, eds, *French Colonial Empire*, pp. 155–69; Wilder, Gary, 'The politics of failure: historicising Popular Front colonial policy in French West Africa', in Chafer and Sackur, eds, *French Colonial Empire*, pp. 33–55.

116. Kaplan, Alice Yaeger, *Reproductions of Banality: Fascism, Literature, and French Intellectual Life*, Minneapolis, MN: University of Minneapolis Press, 1986, p. 45.

117. Mersadier, Yves, 'La crise de l'arachide sénégalaise au début des années trente', *Bulletin de l'Institut Fondamental de l'Afrique Noire*, 28B (1986), p. 828.

118. Fouquet, Joseph, *La Traite des Arachides dans le Pays de Kaolack, et ses Conséquences Économiques, Sociales et Juridiques*, Saint-Louis: Centre de l'IFAN, 1958, p. 76.

119. Boumedouha, Said, 'The Lebanese in Senegal: the history of the relationship between an immigrant community and its French and African rulers', unpublished Ph.D. thesis, University of Birmingham, 1989, p. 83.

120. Savonnet, G., *La Ville de Thiès: Étude de Géographie Urbaine*, Saint-Louis: Centre de l'IFAN, 1955, p. 101.

121. 'Compte-Rendu de l'Assemblée Générale du SCES', *FAN*, 1 (August 1935), p. 16.

122. *PA*, 77, 12 December 1931.

123. *BMCCD*, 124 (August 1935), p. 277.

124. ANS AOF NS 10 F 14, President of the Dakar Chamber of Commerce to Lieutenant-Governor of Senegal, Dakar, 20/08/1935.

125. CARAN AOF NS 21 G 8 [200 Mi 3021], Agboville, 08/06/1945.

126. CARAN AOF NS 21 G 8 [200 Mi 3021], Abidjan, 14/06/1945.

127. ANS AOF NS 21 G 118, 'RENSEIGNEMENTS', Dakar, 30/05/1945.

128. CARAN AOF NS 21 G 142 [200 Mi 3071], 'RENSEIGNEMENTS', Dakar, 17/04/1940.

129. CARAN AOF NS 21 G 142 [200 Mi 3071], Governor-General of AOF to Minister of Colonies, 'a/s Recensement des Libano-Syriens (décret du 11 mars 1940), Dakar, 15/04/1940.

130. CARAN AOF NS 21 G 23 [200 Mi 3023–24], 'RENSEIGNEMENTS', Dakar, 17/04/1943.

131. CARAN AOF NS 21 G 142 [200 Mi 3071], undated intelligence note [1942].

132. Muruwwah, *Nahnu fi Ifriqiya*, image facing p. 280.

133. ANS AOF NS O 33, Directeur Général des Travaux Publics to Governor-General of AOF, Dakar, n.d. [1947].

134. ANS AOF NS O 33, Directeur Général des Affaires Politiques, Sociales et Administratives to Directeur du Cabinet, Dakar, 17/04/1947.

135. Muruwwah, *Nahnu fi Ifriqiya*, pp. 275–6.

136. Kojok, 'Les Libanais', vol. 2, p. 208.

137. 'TRIBUNE LIBRE—la question libano-syrienne', *PA*, 315 (28 September 1935).

138. 'Toujours la question Syrienne', *PA*, 316 (5 October 1935).

139. 'Su'ud al-fustuq', *IT*, (29 February 1932).

140. 'Kullu Bidaya liha Nihaya', *IT*, (20 July 1931).

141. 'Al-Tijara 'ind al-'Arab fi al-Tarikh', *IT*, (7 December 1931).

142. 'Kaifa Nutajir', *IT*, (29 February 1932).

143. 'Al-Qard al-Zira'i', *IT*, (12 July 1931).

293

144. Hushaimah, *Fi Bilad al-Zunuj*, p. 56.

145. CARAN AOF NS 21 G 142 [200 Mi 3071], 'Statuts du Comité Libanais Saint-Louis'.

146. CARAN AOF NS 21 G 142 [200 Mi 3071], President of the Comité Coopératif Libanais to Governor-General of AOF, Dakar, 22/07/1939.

147. CARAN AOF NS 21 G 142 [200 Mi 3071], Comité d'Adhésion et de Bienfaisance to Governor-General of AOF, 22/07/1939.

148. CARAN AOF NS 21 G 142 [200 Mi 3071], 'STATUTS DU CLUB LIBANAIS DE KANKAN' [1939].

149. 'Toujours la question Syrienne', *PA*, 316 (5 October 1935).

150. CARAN AOF NS 21 G 142 [200 Mi 3071], Comité d'Adhésion et de Bienfaisance to Governor-General of AOF, 22/07/1939.

151. Hushaimah, *Fi Bilad al-Zunuj*, p. 57.

152. Muruwwah, *Nahnu fi Ifriqiya*, pp. 283, 285.

153. Hushaimah, *Fi Bilad al-Zunuj*, p. 67.

154. ANS AOF 10 F 14, 'RAPPORT à Monsieur le Gouverneur sur la situation des Libano-Syriens', Daloa, 28/03/1945.

155. Muruwwah, *Nahnu fi Ifriqiya*, pp. 253–4.

156. Kojok, 'Les Libanais', vol. 2, p. 325.

157. Blell, John Michael, 'Health, hygiene, and medical care of the Lebano-Syrian community in Sierra Leone (Recollections and Comments of a Lebanese Medical Doctor)', in *International Seminar: Asian Trading Minorities in Tropical Africa, Afrika Studiencentrum, Leiden, 15–19 December 1975*, Leiden: n.p., 1976, p. 3.

158. Muruwwah, *Nahnu fi Ifriqiya*, p. 264.

159. Blell, 'Health', p. 18.

160. de Certeau, Michel, Luce Giard and Pierre Mayol, *L'Invention du Quotidien*, vol. 2, *Habiter, Cuisiner*, Paris: Gallimard, 1994, pp. 240, 253.

161. el Fareh, Yahia Abou, Abdelouahed Akmir and Abdelmalek Beni Azza, *La Présence Marocaine en Afrique de l'Ouest: Cas du Sénégal, du Mali et de la Côte d'Ivoire*, Rabat: Publications de l'Institut des Etudes Africaines, 1997, p. 135.

162. CARAN AOF AS 21 G 32 [200 Mi 1099], Commissaire de Police-Adjoint, Saint-Louis, 20/08/1900.

163. Anthony, *Sawpit Boy*, p. 16; Muruwwah, *Nahnu fi Ifriqiya*, p. 247.

164. Chevallier, Dominique, *La Société du Mont Liban à l'Epoque de la Révolution Industrielle*, Paris: Geuthner, 1971, pp. 151–2.

165. Kojok, 'Les Libanais', vol. 1, p. 44.

166. Muruwwah, *Nahnu fi Ifriqiya*, p. 287.

167. Ibid.

168. Anthony, *Sawpit Boy*, p. 16.

169. Muruwwah, *Nahnu fi Ifriqiya*, p. 287.

170. Anthony, *Sawpit Boy*, p. 16.

171. Hushaimah, *Fi Bilad al-Zunuj*, p. 102.

172. Blell, 'Health', p. 5.

173. Kojok, 'Les Libanais', vol. 1, p. 192.

174. CARAN AOF NS 21 G 23 [200 Mi 3023–24], Directeur-Adjoint de la Police et de la Sûreté Générale to Administrateur de la Circonscription de Dakar et Dépendances, Dakar, 28/06/1930; Brigade de la Sûreté Générale, 'Rapport', Dakar, 29/10/1930.

175. Boumedouha, 'The Lebanese', p. 259.

176. Tamimi, Muhammad Rafiq and Muhammad Bahjat, *Wilayat Bayrut*, vol. 1, *Al-Qism al-Janubi*, Beirut: Matba'at al-Iqbal, 1917, p. 293.

177. Mervin, Sabrina, *Un Réformisme Chiite. Ulémas et lettrés du Ǧabal ʿĀmil (Actuel Liban-Sud) de la Fin de l'Empire Ottoman à l'Indépendance du Liban*, Paris: Karthala, 2000, pp. 54–6.

178. Tamimi and Bahjat, *Wilayat Bayrut*, p. 293.

179. Mervin, *Réformisme*, pp. 54–6.

180. Anthony, *Sawpit Boy*, p. 26.

181. Hushaimah, *Fi Bilad al-Zunuj*, p. 67.

182. CARAN AOF AS 21 G 37 [200 Mi 1100], Lieutenant-Governor of Guinea to Governor-General of AOF, Conakry, 14/08/1907.
183. Anthony, *Sawpit Boy*, p. 26.
184. Hushaimah, *Fi Bilad al-Zunuj*, p. 111.
185. Kojok, 'Les Libanais', vol. 1, pp. 44, 61.
186. Blell, 'Health', p. 5.
187. Muruwwah, *Nahnu fi Ifriqiya*, pp. 288–9.
188. 'Mubarrat al-Utfal', *IT*, (13 July 1931).
189. Kojok, 'Les Libanais', vol. 2, p. 325.
190. Khater, Akram, 'House to goddess of the house: gender, class, and silk in nineteenth century Mount Lebanon', *International Journal of Middle East Studies*, 28, 3 (1996), pp. 325–48.
191. Abisaab, Malek, *Militant Women of a Fragile Nation*, Syracuse, NY: Syracuse University Press, 2010.
192. Kojok, 'Les Libanais', vol. 1, p. 168.
193. Watenpaugh, *Being Modern*, p. 293. On the schooling of children, see chapter 3.
194. ANS AOF 11 D 3/37, 'Recensement de la population étrangère de la ville de Rufisque en Décembre 1927'.
195. Anthony, *Sawpit Boy*, p. 82.
196. Muruwwah, *Nahnu fi Ifriqiya*, p. 199.
197. *IT*, (23 November 1931).
198. *IT*, (20 July 1931).
199. Muruwwah, *Nahnu fi Ifriqiya*, p. 279.
200. CAOM MC FM AP 2303/5, 'RAPPORT sur la situation des Libano-Syriens en Afrique Occidentale Française et au Togo', Dakar, 30/05/1945.
201. CARAN AOF AS 21 G 33 [200 Mi 1099–1100], 'Copie de lettre non envoyée', n.d. [1918].
202. *IT*, (23 November 1931).
203. ANS AOF 10 F 14, Governor of Guinea to Governor-General of AOF, Dakar, 12/03/1945.
204. Ross, *Fast Cars*, p. 10.
205. Hushaimah, *Fi Bilad al-Zunuj*, pp. 101–2.
206. Savonnet, *Thiès*, p. 135.

7. THE TIES THAT BIND: DIASPORIC POLITICAL CULTURE IN AOF

1. Duara, Prasenjit, *Rescuing History from the Nation: Questioning Narratives of Modern China*, Chicago, IL: University of Chicago Press, 1995.
2. Albert Hourani's magisterial *Arabic Thought in the Liberal Age, 1798–1939*. Cambridge: Cambridge University Press, 1992 [1962], remains, in many ways, the seminal statement on these exchanges. See also Reid, Donald M., 'Arabic thought in the liberal age twenty years after', *International Journal of Middle East Studies*, 14, 4 (1982), pp. 541–57.
3. For some recent exceptions, see Arsan, Andrew, 'This age is the age of associations: committees, petitions, and the roots of interwar Middle Eastern internationalism', *Journal of Global History*, 7 (2012), pp. 166–88; Dakhli, Leyla, *Une Génération d'Intellectuels Arabes: Syrie et Liban, 1908–1940*, Paris: Karthala, 2008; Gualtieri, Sarah, *Between Arab and White: Race and Ethnicity in the Early Syrian American Diaspora*, Berkeley, CA: University of California Press, 2008; and Khuri-Makdisi, Ilham, *The Eastern Mediterranean and the Making of Global Radicalism, 1860–1914*, Berkeley, CA: University of California Press, 2010.
4. Guha, Ranajit, 'Chandra's death', in Guha, Ranajit, ed., *Subaltern Studies V: Writings on South Asian History and Society*, Delhi: Oxford University Press, 1987, p. 138.
5. Cooper, Frederick and Ann Laura Stoler, 'Between metropole and colony: rethinking a research agenda', in Cooper, Frederick and Ann Laura Stoler, eds, *Tensions of Empire: Colonial Cultures in a Bourgeois World*, Berkeley, CA: University of California Press, 1997, p. 21.
6. Bayly, C.A., *Empire and Information: Intelligence Gathering and Social Communication in India, 1780–1870*, Cambridge: Cambridge University Press, 1996, p. 6.
7. CARAN AOF NS 21 G 23 [200 Mi 3023–24], Chef de Bureau de l'Administration Générale to Brigade de Sûreté du Sénégal, Dakar, 29/10/1930.
8. Ginzburg, Carlo and Carlo Proni, 'The name of the game: unequal exchange and the historiographical market-

place', transl. Branch, Eren, in Muir, Ed and Guido Ruggieri, eds, *Microhistory and the Lost Peoples of Europe*, Baltimore, MD: Johns Hopkins University Press, 1991, p. 6.

9. Ginzburg, Carlo, 'Preface', in *Myths, Emblems, Clues*, transl. John and Anne C. Tedeschi, London: Hutchinson Rodius, 1990, p. viii. See also, for a discussion of this 'conjectural paradigm', as he calls it, Ginzburg, Carlo, 'Clues: roots of an evidential paradigm', in *Myths*, pp. 96–125.

10. Baker, Keith, *Inventing the French Revolution: Essays on French Political Culture in the Eighteenth Century*, Cambridge: Cambridge University Press, 1990, p. 4. See also Hunt, Lynn, *The Family Romance of the French Revolution*, London: Routledge, 1992.

11. On sectarianism as a political practice and way of living in the world, see Makdisi, Ussama, *The Culture of Sectarianism: Community, History, and Violence in Nineteenth-Century Lebanon*, Berkeley, CA: University of California Press, 2001; and Weiss, Max, *In the Shadow of Sectarianism: Law, Shi'ism and the Making of Modern Lebanon*, Cambridge, MA: Harvard University Press, 2010.

12. See Khalidi, Rashid, *Palestinian Identity: the Construction of a Modern National Consciousness*, New York: Columbia University Press, 1997.

13. For a survey of this crowded field, see Gershoni, Israel, 'Rethinking the formation of Arab nationalism in the Middle East, 1920–1945: old and new narratives', in Gershoni and James Jankowski, eds, *Rethinking Nationalism in the Arab Middle East*, New York: Columbia University Press, 1997, pp. 3–25.

14. Firro, Kais, *Inventing Lebanon: Nationalism and the State under the Mandate*, London: I.B. Tauris, 2003; Hakim, Carol, *The Origins of the Lebanese National Idea, 1840–1920*, Berkeley, CA: University of California Press, 2013; Kaufman, Asher, *Reviving Phoenicia: The Search for Identity in Lebanon*, London: I.B. Tauris, 2004; al-Solh, Raghid, *Lebanon and Arabism: National Identity and Social Formation*, London: I.B. Tauris, 1996.

15. See Beydoun, Ahmad, *Identité Confessionelle et Temps Social chez les Historiens Libanais Contemporains*, Beirut: Université Libanaise, 1984; and Salibi, Kamal, *A House of Many Mansions: the History of Lebanon Reconsidered*, Berkeley: University of California Press, 1988.

16. al-Safa, Muhammad Jabir, *Tarikh Jabal 'Amil*, Beirut: Dar al-Nahar, 1981, 2nd ed., pp. 208, 230. On the writings of Safa and his acolytes, see in particular Mervin, Sabrina, *Un Réformisme Chiite. Ulémas et lettrés du Ǧabal Āmil (Actuel Liban-Sud) de la Fin de l'Empire Ottoman à l'Indépendance du Liban*, Paris: Karthala, 2000.

17. Bazzi, Mustafa, *Jabal 'Amil fi Muhitahu al-'Arabi, 1864–1948*, Beirut: Markaz al-Dirasat wa al-Tawthiq wa al-Nashr, 1993. See also Halawi, Majed, *A Lebanon Defied: Musa al-Sadr and the Shi'a Community*, Boulder, CO: Westview, 1992.

18. Chalabi, Tamara, *The Shi'is of Jabal 'Amil and the New Lebanon: Community and Nation-State, 1918–1943*, Basingstoke: Macmillan, 2006; and Weiss, *In the Shadow of Sectarianism*. See also Shu'ayyib, 'Ali, *Matalib Jabal 'Amil: al-Wuhda, al-Musawa fi Lubnan al-Kabir 1900–1936*, Beirut: Mu'asasa al-Jam'iyya, 1987.

19. For recent attempts to move away from notions of the nation, see Bashkin, Orit, *The Other Iraq: Pluralism, Intellectuals and Culture in Hashemite Iraq, 1921–1958*, Stanford, CA: Stanford University Press, 2009; Elshakry, Marwa, 'Darwin's legacy in the Arab East: science, religion and politics, 1870–1914', unpublished Ph.D. dissertation, Princeton University, 2003; El Shakry, Omnia, *The Great Social Laboratory: Subjects of Knowledge in Colonial and Postcolonial Egypt*, Stanford, CA: Stanford University Press, 2007; Khuri-Makdisi, *The Eastern Mediterranean*; Schumann, Christoph, ed., *Liberal Thought in the Eastern Mediterranean: Late Nineteenth Century until the 1960s*, Leiden: Brill, 2008.

20. Cronin, Stephanie, ed., *Subalterns and Social Protest: History from Below in the Middle East and North Africa*, London: Routledge, 2007; Matthews, Weldon, *Confronting an Empire, Constructing a Nation: Arab Nationalists and Popular Politics in Mandate Palestine*, Austin, TX: University of Texas Press, 2006; Provence, Michael, *The Great Syrian Revolt and the Rise of Arab Nationalism*, Austin, TX: University of Texas Press, 2005; Khalidi, *Palestinian Identity*, ch. 5.

21. Gershoni, Israel and Ursula Wocöck, 'Doing history: modern Middle Eastern studies today', in Gershoni, Israel and Ursula Wocöck with Hakan Erdem, eds, *Histories of the Modern Middle East*, Boulder, CO: Lynne Rienner, 2002, p. 13. For a thoughtful examination of such approaches, see Khoury, Philip S., 'The paradoxical in Arab nationalism: interwar Syria revisited', in Gershoni, Israel and James Jankowski, eds, *Rethinking Nationalism*, pp. 273–87.

22. Provence, *Syrian Revolt*, p. 22.

23. Watenpaugh, Keith, *Being Modern in the Middle East: Revolution, Nationalism, Colonialism and the Arab Middle Class*, Princeton, NJ: Princeton University Press, 2006, p. 182.

24. Khalidi, *Palestinian Identity*, p. 114.
25. Provence, *Syrian Revolt*, p. 21.
26. Watenpaugh, *Being Modern*, p. 182.
27. See Watenpaugh, Keith, 'Towards a new category of colonial theory: colonial cooperation and the survivors' bargain—the case of the post-genocide Armenian community of Syria under French Mandate', in Sluglett, Peter and Nadine Méouchy with Gérard Khoury and Geoffrey Schad, eds, *The British and French Mandates in Comparative Perspective*, Leiden: Brill, 2004, pp. 597–622.
28. Gibb, H.A.R., *Modern Trends in Islam*, Chicago, IL: Chicago University Press, 1947. For an astute reading, see Gershoni, Israel, 'The theory of crisis and the crisis in a theory: intellectual history in twentieth century Middle Eastern studies', in Gershoni, Israel, Amy Singer and Hakan Erdem, eds, *Middle Eastern Historiographies: Narrating the Twentieth Century*, Seattle, WA: University of Washington Press, 2006, pp. 131–82.
29. See, in particular, the encyclopaedic tome of Batatu, Hanna, *The Old Social Classes and the Revolutionary Movements of Iraq: A Study of Iraq's Old Landed and Commercial Classes and of its Communists, Ba'thists and Free Officers*, Princeton, NJ: Princeton University Press, 1978; Gelvin, James, *Divided Loyalties: Nationalism and Mass Politics in Syria at the Close of Empire*, Berkeley, CA: University of California Press, 1998; Khoury, Philip S., *Urban Notables and Arab Nationalism: The Politics of Damascus, 1860–1920*, Cambridge: Cambridge University Press, 1982; and Khoury, *Syria and the French Mandate: the Politics of Arab Nationalism, 1920–1945*, Princeton, NJ: Princeton University Press, 1987.
30. Dawn, Ernest, 'The rise of Arabism in Syria', in *From Ottomanism to Arabism: Essays on the Origins of Arab Nationalism*, Urbana, IL: University of Illinois Press, 1973; Eppel, Michael, 'The elite, the effendiyya, and the growth of Arab nationalism and pan-Arabism in Hashemite Iraq, 1921–1958', *International Journal of Middle East Studies*, 30, 2 (1998), pp. 227–50; and, in its most dyspectic register, Kedourie, Elie, *The Chatham House Version: and Other Middle Eastern Studies*, London: Weidenfeld and Nicolson, 1970.
31. Butler, Judith, *Precarious Life: the Powers of Mourning and Violence*, London: Verso, 2006, p. 22.
32. See also Wien, Peter, 'The long and intricate funeral of Yasin al-Hashimi: pan-Arabism, civil religion, and popular nationalism in Damascus, 1937', *International Journal of Middle East Studies*, 43 (2011), pp. 271–92.
33. Anderson, Benedict, 'Long-distance nationalism', in *The Spectre of Comparisons: Nationalism, South-East Asia, and the World*, London: Verso, 1998, pp. 58–74.
34. Skrbiš, Zlatko, *Long-Distance Nationalism: Diasporas, Homelands, and Identities*, Aldershot: Aldgate, 1999, p. xiii.
35. Schiller, Nina Glick and Georges Eugene Fouron, *Georges Woke Up Laughing: Long-Distance Nationalism and the Search for Home*, Durham, NC: Duke University Press, 2001, pp. 19–20.
36. Butler, Judith, *Parting Ways: Jewishness and the Critique of Zionism*, New York: Columbia University Press, 2012, p. 118.
37. Sivasundaram, Sujit, 'Sciences and the global: on methods, questions, and theory', *Isis*, 101, 10 (2010), p. 158.
38. Chambers, David Wade and Richard Gillespie, 'Locality in the history of science: colonial science, technoscience, and indigenous knowledge', *Osiris*, 2nd series, 15 (2000), p. 223.
39. Cole, Juan, 'Printing and urban Islam in the Mediterranean world, 1890–1920', in Fawaz, Leila Tarazi and C.A. Bayly, eds, *Modernity and Culture: From the Mediterranean to the Indian Ocean*, New York: Columbia University Press, 2002, p. 346.
40. Muruwwah, Kamil, *Nahnu fi Ifriqiya: al-Hijra al-Lubnaniyya al-Suriyya ila Ifriqiya al-Gharbiyya, Madiha, Hadiriha, Mustaqbaliha*, Beirut: Al-Makshuf, 1938, p. 201.
41. Hayik, Michel, *Batl Lubnan Yusuf Bek Karam*, Beirut: Jaridat al-Ijtihad, 1922, p. 3, in CARAN AOF NS, 19 G 24 [200 Mi 2842], enclosure dated 04/10/1922.
42. Hayik, Michel, *Fi Majahil Ifriqiya*, Beirut: Matba't al-'Alam, n.d., p. 5.
43. CARAN AOF NS 19 G 24 [200 Mi 2842], Governor-General to Lieutenant-Governors, 'Journaux Arabes', 05/11/1922.
44. CARAN AOF NS 19 G 24 [200 Mi 2842], Governor-General to Lieutenant-Governors, 'Journaux Arabes', 05/11/1922; CARAN AOF NS 21 G 46 [200 Mi 3035], Direction des Affaires Politiques et Administratives, 'Traduction. Extrait de Deir el-Kamar (Liban) journal politique et littéraire arabe (numéro du 7 août 1931)'; Direction des Affaires Politiques et Administratives to Directeur de la Sûreté Générale, 'a/s traduction d'un article tendancieux de "AL WADI" journal libanais', Dakar, 13/03/1931. For more details of these local newspapers, see Daghir, Yusuf Sa'd, *Qamus al-Sahafa al-Lubnaniyya 1858–1974*, Beirut: Université Libanaise, 1978.

297

45. Khoury, Gérard, *La France et l'Orient Arabe: La Naissance du Liban Moderne, 1914–1922*, Paris: Armand Colin, 1993.

46. Comité Central Syrien, *L'Opinion Syrienne à l'Etranger Pendant la Guerre: Documents*, Paris: n.p., 1918, p. 19.

47. *CO*, 202 (25 November 1918), p. 282.

48. *CO*, 199 (10 October 1918), p. 185.

49. *CO*, 208 (28 February 1919), p. 169. On these measures, and their abrogation, see chapter 3.

50. See Benton, Lauren, 'Colonial law and cultural difference: jurisdictional politics and the formation of the colonial state', *Comparative Studies in Society and History*, 41, 3 (1999), pp. 563–88; Lewis, Mary Dewhurst, 'Geographies of power: the Tunisian civic order, jurisdictional politics, and imperial rivalry in the Mediterranean, 1881–1935', *Journal of Modern History*, 80 (2008), pp. 791–830. On claim-making, see Cooper, Frederick, *Decolonization and African Society: The Labour Question in French and British Africa*, Cambridge: Cambridge University Press, 1996.

51. *CO*, 206 (30 January 1919), p. 82.

52. Comité de l'Orient, *La Question Syrienne: Exposé—Solution. Statut Politique. Rapport du Dr Georges Samné*, Paris: n.p., 1918, pp. 6, 21.

53. Comité Central Syrien, *La Question Syrienne Exposée par les Syriens—à L.L. Excellences les Plénipotentiaires Alliés et Associés à la Conférence de Paix*, Paris: n.p., 1919, p. 43.

54. For an extended treatment of this argument, see Arsan, '"This age"'.

55. CARAN AOF NS 19 G 24 [200 Mi 2842], inserts.

56. 'Akhbar 'Alamiyya—Mahaliyya'; 'Barqiyyat 'Umumiyya', *IT*, (20 July 1931).

57. 'Akhbar Lubnan was Suriya bil-Barid al-Jawwi'; 'Risalat Lubnan'; Risalat Falastin', *IT*, (14 September 1935).

58. Anderson, Benedict, *Imagined Communities: Reflections on the Origins and Spread of Nationalism*, London: Verso, 2006.

59. 'Arjahiya mahajir', *IT*, (23 November 1931).

60. 'Ihsa al-Lubnaniyyin fi kulli makan', *IT*, (28 March 1932).

61. 'Arjahiya mahajir', *IT*, (23 November 1931).

62. ''Anba' al-watan', *IT*, (12 July 1931).

63. Muruwwah, *Nahnu fi Ifriqiya*, title page, p. 187.

64. 'Salah al-mujtama'', *IT*, (16 November 1931).

65. 'Min al-qalb ila al-qalb', *IT*, (8 February 1932).

66. 'Kalimat', *IT*, (23 November 1932).

67. Foucault, Michel, 'Omnes et singulatim: towards a criticism of political reason', in McMurrin, Sterling, ed., *The Tanner Lectures on Human Values*, vol. 2, Salt Lake City, UT: University of Utah Press, 1981, pp. 223–54.

68. This argument relies in part on Gupta, Akhil and James Ferguson, 'Beyond "Culture": space, identity, and the politics of difference', *Cultural Anthropology*, 7, 1 (1992), pp. 6–23.

69. See Cruise O'Brien, Donal, 'Towards an "Islamic Policy" in French West Africa, 1858–1914', *Journal of African History*, 8, 2 (1967), pp. 303–16; Mann, Gregory, 'Fetishizing religion: Allah Koura and French "Islamic Policy" in late colonial French Soudan (Mali)', *Journal of African History*, 44, 2 (2003), pp. 263–82; and Robinson, David, 'French "Islamic" policy and practice in late nineteenth-century Senegal', *Journal of African History*, 29, 3 (1988), pp. 415–35. For two overviews, see Harrison, Christopher, *France and Islam in West Africa, 1860–1960*, Cambridge: Cambridge University Press, 1988; and Robinson, David, *Paths of Accommodation: Muslim Societies and French Colonial Authorities in Senegal and Mauritania, 1880–1920*, Oxford: James Currey, 2000.

70. Harrison, *France and Islam*, pp. 147–9.

71. For an examination of such fears which focuses on France and Britain's imperial possessions in North Africa and the Middle East, see Thomas, Martin, *Empires of Intelligence: Security Services and Colonial Disorder after 1914*, Berkeley, CA: University of California Press, 2008.

72. CARAN AOF NS 21 G 23 [200 Mi 3023–3024], Governor-General of AOF to Lieutenant-Governors, 'a/s Mouvement Nationaliste en SYRIE', Dakar, 09/07/1922.

73. CARAN AOF NS 21 G 53 [200 Mi 3037], Governor-General to Administrateur de la Circonscription de Dakar et Dépendances, Dakar, 21/11/1933.

74. CAOM MC FM AP 1432/1, Governor-General to Lieutenant-Governors, 'Panarabisme et panislamisme. Propagande extrémiste', Dakar, 14/04/1934.

75. CARAN AOF NS 21 G 23 [200 Mi 3023–24], Directeur-Adjoint de la Police et de la Sûreté Générale to Administrateur de la Circonscription de Dakar et Dépendances, Dakar, 28/06/1930.
76. Muruwwah, *Nahnu fi Ifriqiya*, p. 285.
77. On the meanings of *'irfan*, see Corbin, Henry, *Face de Dieu, Face de l'Homme: Herméneutique et Soufisme*, Paris: Flammarion, 1983.
78. Khalidi, Tarif, 'Shaykh Ahmad 'Arif al-Zain and *al-'Irfan*', in Buheiry, Marwan, ed., *Intellectual Life in the Arab East 1890–1939*, Beirut: American University of Beirut, 1981, p. 110; Chalabi, *Shi'is*, p. 169.
79. Chalabi, *Shi'is*, p. 171.
80. For differing accounts of this, see Rida, Ahmad, *Mudhakkirat li-Tarikh Hawadith Jabal 'Amil, 1914–1922*, Jabir, Munzir, ed., Beirut: Dar al-Nahar and IFPO, 2009, pp. 110–14; and the responses of Sayyid Ja'far Sharaf al-Din and Shaikh Muhammad Jawwad al-Mughniyya, ibid., pp. 235–8 and 240–2.
81. Shu'ayyib, *Matalib*, pp. 104–9.
82. See Rida, Ahmad, *Mu'jam Matn al-Lugha*, Beirut: Dar Maktabat al-Hayat, 1958–60; Rida, *Mudhakkirat*; al-Zahir, Sulaiman, *Safahat min Tarikh Jabal 'Amil*, Beirut: Dar al-Islamiyya, 2002; and Zahir, *Mu'jam Qura Jabal 'Amil*, Beirut: Mu'asasat al-Imam al-Sadiq li-l-Buhuth fi Turath 'Ulama' Jabal 'Amil, 2006 [1928].
83. Chalabi, *Shi'is*, pp. 33, 37, 171.
84. CARAN AOF NS 21 G 23 [200 Mi 3023–24], Directeur-Adjoint de la Police et de la Sûreté Générale to Administrateur de la Circonscription de Dakar et Dépendances, Dakar, 28/06/1930.
85. Bazzi, Mustafa, *Tatawwur al-Ta'lim wa al-Thaqafa fi Jabal 'Amil mundhu Nihayat al-Qarn al-Tasi' 'Ashar hatta Muntasaf al-Qarn al-'Ashrin*, Beirut: Hi'yat Inma' al-Mintaqa al-Hududiyya, 1995, p. 346.
86. CARAN AOF NS 21 G 23 [200 Mi 3023–24], 'NOTE sur Cheikh Sleiman Daher, et la bibliothèque de "Djabal Amel" à Nabatié'.
87. CARAN AOF NS 21 G 23 [200 Mi 3023–24], High Commissioner to Minister of Foreign Affairs, Beirut, 08/10/1930.
88. Bazzi, *Tatawwur al-Ta'lim*, p. 347.
89. Mervin, *Réformisme*, p. 367.
90. CARAN AOF NS 21 G 23 [200 Mi 3023–24], 'Rapport', 29/10/1930.
91. Ayalon, Ami, *Reading Palestine: Printing and Literacy, 1900–1948*, Austin, TX: University of Texas Press, 2004, pp. 47, 84–5.
92. Bazzi, *Tatawwur al-Ta'lim*, p. 346.
93. CARAN AOF NS 21 G 23 [200 Mi 3023–24], Direction de la Sûreté Générale to Directeur des Affaires Politiques, 'Propagande Libano-Syrienne Suspecte', Dakar, 05/03/1931.
94. CARAN AOF NS 21 G 23 [200 Mi 3023–24], Direction de la Sûreté Générale to Directeur des Affaires Politiques, 'Propagande Libano-Syrienne Suspecte', Dakar, 05/03/1931, enclosure.
95. CARAN AOF NS 21 G 23 [200 Mi 3023–24], Direction de la Sûreté Générale to Directeur des Affaires Politiques, 'Propagande Libano-Syrienne Suspecte', Dakar, 05/03/1931, enclosure.
96. Chelkowski, Peter J., ed., *Eternal Performance: Ta'ziehs and Other Shiite Rituals (Enactments)*, Chicago, IL: Chicago University Press, 2010; Mervin, Sabrina, 'Les larmes et le sang des Chiites: corps et pratiques rituelles lors des célébrations de 'Ashûrâ' (Liban, Syrie)', *REMMM*, 113–114 (2006), pp. 153–66.
97. CARAN AOF NS 21 G 23 [200 Mi 3023–24], Commissaire de Police of Kaolack to Commandant de Cercle of Sine-Saloum, Kaolack, 22/09/1930.
98. On Humani, see al-Makki, Muhammad Kazim, *Al-Haraka al-Fikriyya wa al-Adabiyya fi Jabal 'Amil*, Beirut: Dar al-Andalus, 1963, p. 209; and Chalabi, *Shi'is*, pp. 40, 173.
99. Chalabi, *Shi'is*, p. 109.
100. Khalidi, 'Shaykh Ahmad', p. 116; Chalabi, *Shi'is*, p. 108.
101. CARAN AOF NS 21 G 46 [200 Mi 3035], 'Traduction de la Lettre-Circulaire', 24/04/1931.
102. CARAN AOF NS 21 G 23 [200 Mi 3023–24], Governor-General of AOF to Minister of Colonies, 'a/s activité libano-syrienne en AOF', 18/04/1936, Dakar.
103. CAOM MC FM AP 1432/1, Governor-General of AOF to Minister of Colonies, 'a/s el HOUMANI et Mohamed HILAL', Dakar, 02/05/1936.
104. CARAN AOF NS 21 G 28 [200 Mi 3025–26], Toumadou Kamara, Interprète des Affaires Musulmanes, 'Renseignements', Dakar, 27/03/1936. CARAN AOF NS 21 G 23 [200 Mi 3023–24], Governor-General of AOF to Minister of Colonies, 'a/s activité libano-syrienne en AOF', 18/04/1936, Dakar.

105. Chalabi, *Shi'is*, pp. 149–50.

106. CARAN AOF NS 21 G 28 [200 Mi 3025–26], Toumadou Kamara, Interprète des Affaires Musulmanes, 'Renseignements', Dakar, 27/03/1936. Chalabi, *Shi'is*, p. 150.

107. Muruwwah, *Nahnu fi Ifriqiya*, p. 11.

108. CAOM MC FP 2258/4, Haut Commissaire de la République to Ministre de la France d'Outremer, Dakar, 24/05/1948.

109. CAOM MC FP 2258/4, Haut Commissaire de la République to Ministre de la France d'Outremer, Dakar, 28/07/1948.

110. CARAN AOF NS 21 G 28 [200 Mi 3025–26], Toumadou Kamara, Interprète des Affaires Musulmanes, 'Renseignements', Dakar, 27/03/1936.

111. CARAN AOF NS 21 G 23 [200 Mi 3023–24], Governor-General of AOF to Minister of Colonies, 'a/s activité libano-syrienne en AOF', Dakar, 18/04/1936. CARAN AOF NS 21 G 28 [200 Mi 3025–26], Direction de la Sûreté Générale, 'Mohamed El Houmani', Dakar, 29/02/1936.

112. CARAN AOF NS 21 G 23 [200 Mi 3023–24], Governor-General of AOF to Minister of Colonies, 'a/s activité libano-syrienne en AOF', Dakar, 18/04/1936.

113. CARAN AOF NS 21 G 142 [200 Mi 3071], 'Note au sujet du Comité d'Adhésion et de Bienfaisance', Dakar, 22/08/1939. The Committee of Support and Benevolence was known simply in Arabic as the Jam'iyya al-Lubnaniyya al-Suriyya, or Lebanese Syrian Association.

114. CARAN AOF NS 21 G 28 [200 Mi 3025–26], Toumadou Kamara, Interprète des Affaires Musulmanes, 'Renseignements', Dakar, 27/03/1936.

115. CARAN AOF NS 21 G 53 [200 Mi 3037], Administrateur de la Circonscription de Dakar to Governor-General of AOF, Dakar, 31/10/1933.

116. Mervin, *Réformisme*, p. 368.

117. CARAN AOF NS 21 G 53 [200 Mi 3037], 'OUVERTURE DE LA REUNION, par l'élégie du regretté Fayçal.—Par Houssein ASSIRAN'.

118. CARAN AOF NS 21 G 53 [200 Mi 3037], No 3.—AHMAD JAWAD TAGGEDDINE'.

119. CARAN AOF NS 21 G 53 [200 Mi 3037], 'No 13.—HASSAN ARAB'.

120. CARAN AOF NS 21 G 53 [200 Mi 3037], 'OUVERTURE DE LA REUNION, par l'élégie du regretté Fayçal.—Par Houssein ASSIRAN'.

121. I draw here upon the insights of contextualist intellectual history. See, for two retrospective statements of intent, Pocock, J.G.A., *Political Thought and History: Essays on Theory and Method*, Cambridge: Cambridge University Press, 2010; Skinner, Quentin, *Visions of Politics*, vol. 1, *Regarding Method*, Cambridge: Cambridge University Press, 2002.

122. CARAN AOF NS 21 G 53 [200 Mi 3037], 'No 5.—ABDULLAH RIDA JABER'.

123. CARAN AOF NS 21 G 53 [200 Mi 3037], 'No 8/SID LAHBIB BEN AMOUR'.

124. CARAN AOF NS 21 G 23 [200 Mi 3023–24], Directeur-Adjoint de la Police et de la Sûreté Générale to Directeur des Affaires Politiques et Administratives, Dakar, 25/07/1930.

125. Chalabi, *Shi'is*, p. 24.

126. CARAN AOF NS 21 G 23 [200 Mi 3023–24], Directeur-Adjoint de la Police et de la Sûreté Générale to Directeur des Affaires Politiques et Administratives, Dakar, 25/07/1930.

127. Chalabi, *Shi'is*, pp. 59, 64. FAOM MC/FM/AP 1432/1, Governor-General of AOF to Minister of Colonies, Dakar, 18/04/1936.

128. CAOM MC FM AP 1432/1, 'NOTICE DE RENSEIGNEMENTS concernant HUSSEIN ALI WEHBE'.

129. CARAN AOF NS 21 G 142 [200 Mi 3071], 'HILAL, Mohamed—Vice-Président de l'ASSOCIATION D'ADHESION ET DE BIENFAISANCE' and 'TSHAM, Ibrahim—Imprimeur et Libraire—Secrétaire Général de l'ASSOCIATION D'ADHESION ET DE BIENFAISANCE'. Chalabi, *Shi'is*, p. 59.

130. CARAN AOF NS 21 G 53 [200 Mi 3037], 'No 14.—MOHAMED HILAL'.

131. CAOM MC FM AP 1432/1, Governor-General of AOF to Minister of Colonies, Dakar, 18/04/1936. On the Jerusalem convention, see Landau, Jacob, *The Politics of Pan-Islam: Ideology and Organisation*, Oxford: Clarendon, 1990, p. 241.

132. CARAN AOF NS 21 G 142 [200 Mi 3071], 'HILAL, Mohamed—Vice-Président de l'ASSOCIATION D'ADHESION ET DE BIENFAISANCE'.

133. Chalabi, *Shi'is*, pp. 37–8.

134. Mervin, *Réformisme*, pp. 367–8.
135. Nafi, Basheer M., *Arabism, Islamism, and the Palestine Question 1908–1941: A Political History*, Reading: Ithaca, 1998, p. 211.
136. CARAN AOF NS 21 G 142 [200 Mi 3071], 'TSHAM, Ibrahim—Imprimeur et Libraire—Secrétaire Général de l'ASSOCIATION D'ADHESION ET DE BIENFAISANCE'.
137. Darnton, Robert, *The Kiss of Lamourette: Reflections in Cultural History*, London: Faber & Faber, 1990, p. 130.
138. Simon, Jacques, *L'Etoile Nord-Africaine, 1926–1937*, Paris: L'Harmattan, 2003; Stora, Benjamin, *Messali Hadj: Pionnier du Nationalisme Algérien (1898–1974)*, Paris: L'Harmattan, 1986.
139. al-Din al-Afghani, Jamal and Muhammad 'Abduh, *al-'Urwa al-Wuthqa*, Beirut: al-Maktaba al-Ahliyya, 1933.
140. Lévi-Strauss, Claude, *La Pensée Sauvage*, Paris: Plon, 1962, pp. 26–7.
141. Eisenstein, Elizabeth, *The Printing Revolution in Early Modern Europe*, Cambridge: Cambridge University Press, 1983, p. 46.
142. CARAN AOF NS 21 G 142, 'NOTE AU SUJET DU COMITE D'ADHESION ET DE BIENFAISANCE', 22/08/1939.
143. ANS NS 5 G 50, Administrateur de Daloa to Chef du Bureau Politique, Bingerville, Daloa, 27/12/1933.
144. Baydoun, Ahmad, 'Bint-Jbeil, Michigan, suivi de (ou poursuivi par) Bint-Jbeil, Liban', *Maghreb-Machrek*, 125 (1989), pp. 76–7.
145. Nafi, *Arabism*, p. 191.
146. Jankowski, James, 'Egyptian responses to the Palestinian problem in the interwar period', *International Journal of Middle East Studies*, 12, 1 (August 1980), pp. 2, 4, 6, 20–1.
147. CARAN AOF NS 21 G 41 [200 Mi 3032], Governor-General of AOF to Minister of Colonies, Dakar, 09/12/1935.
148. Yamak, Labib Zuwiyya, *The Syrian Social Nationalist Party: an Ideological Analysis*, Cambridge: Harvard University Press and Harvard Centre for Middle Eastern Studies, 1966, pp. 55–6. See also Sa'ada, Antun, *al-Athar al-Kamila*, Beirut: 'Umdat al-Thaqafa fi al-Hizb al-Suri al-Qawmi al-Ijtima'i, 1975.
149. Yamak, *Syrian Social Nationalist Party*, p. 84.
150. CARAN AOF NS 21 G 41 [200 Mi 3032], 'SAOUT UL-AHRAR No 656 du 18 Novembre 1935'.
151. Maatouk, Mohamad, 'A critical study of Antun Sa'ada and his impact on politics, the history of ideas and literature in the Middle East', unpublished doctoral dissertation, University of London, 1992, p. 167.
152. Yamak, *Syrian Social Nationalist Party*, p. 78.
153. Ibid., p. 79.
154. Maatouk, 'Critical study', p. 169.
155. Yamak, *Syrian Social Nationalist Party*, p. 79.
156. Maatouk, 'Critical study', p. 169.
157. Yamak, *Syrian Social Nationalist Party*, pp. 82, 86.
158. Méouchy, Nadine, 'Etat et espaces communitaires dans le Liban sous Mandat Français', *Maghreb Machrek*, 123 (1989), p. 91.
159. Mervin, *Réformisme*, p. 380.
160. Maatouk, 'Critical study', pp. 21–2, 25–7, 155. Yamak, *Syrian Social Nationalist Party*, pp. 54, 59.
161. CARAN AOF NS 21 G 23 [200 Mi 3023–24], Governor-General of AOF to Minister of Colonies, 'a/s activité libano-syrienne en AOF', Dakar, 18/04/1936.
162. CARAN AOF NS 21 G 142 [200 Mi 3071], 'Note au sujet du Comité d'Adhésion et de Bienfaisance', Dakar, 22/08/1939.

8. CODA: THE MAKING OF POSTCOLONIAL SELVES

1. Hatoum, Milton, *Tale of a Certain Orient*, transl. Gledson, John, London: Bloomsbury 2007, p. 57.
2. http://news.bbc.co.uk/1/hi/world/middle_east/8502741.stm, last accessed 6 Apr. 2013.
3. Aciman, André, *False Papers: Essays on Exile and Memory*, New York: Picador, 2000, p. 39.
4. Hannerz, Ulf, *Transnational Connections: Culture, People, Places*, London: Routledge, 1996, p. 103.
5. Werbner, Pnina, 'Introduction: the dialectics of cultural hybridity', in Werbner, Pnina and Tariq Modood, eds, *Debating Cultural Hybridity: Multicultural Identities and the Politics of Anti-Racism*, London: Zed, 1997, p. 12.

6. Ho, Engseng, *The Graves of Tarim: Genealogy and Mobility Across the Indian Ocean*, Berkeley, CA: University of California Press, 2006, pp. 4, 10.

7. Lerner, Daniel, *The Passing of Traditional Society: Modernizing the Middle East*, New York: Free Press of Glencoe, 1958.

8. ANS AOF NS 21 G 227, 'Kojok, Jamil'.

9. Safa, Elie, *L'Emigration Libanaise*, Beirut: Université Saint-Joseph, 1960, pp. 119–20.

10. Kojok, Salma, 'Les Libanais en Côte d'Ivoire de 1920 à 1960', unpublished Ph.D dissertation, Université de Nantes, 2002, 2 vols., vol. 2, pp. 342–6.

11. Safa, *L'Emigration*, pp. 119–20.

12. Bigo, Didier, 'The Lebanese community in the Ivory Coast: a non-native network at the heart of power', in Hourani, Albert and Nadim Shehadi, eds, *The Lebanese in the World: A Hundred Years of Emigration*, London: I.B. Tauris, 1992, p. 516.

13. 'Problème Libano-Syrien—DIX pour CENT', *EA*, 8 (26 April 1947).

14. ANS AOF NS 17 G 530, Ministère de l'Intérieur, Direction Générale de la Sûreté Nationale, Direction des Renseignements Généraux, 'a/s du nommé VOISIN Maurice', Paris, 03/11/1949.

15. ANS AOF NS 17 G 530/1949, 'Renseignements a/s Maurice Voisin', Dakar, 27/12/1949.

16. 'Problème Libano-Syrien—DIX pour CENT', *EA*, 8 (26 April 1947); 'ALERTE AUX PETITS COMMERCANTS EUROPEENS ET AFRICAINS—Trusts et Libano-Syriens vont-ils réussir à couler le petit commerce français?—une enquête de Jean Paris', *EA*, 26 (30 August 1947).

17. 'Problème Libano-Syrien—DIX pour CENT', *EA*, 8 (26 April 1947); 'Notre position: ANTI-SURPLUS LIBANAIS' n'a pas varié d'un millimètre *et nous ne varierons jamais…*', *EAN*, 45 (24 February 1951).

18. ANS AOF 17 G 590/1951, 'LES ACTIVITES DE M. M VOISIN D'AOUT 1950 à AVRIL 1951'.

19. ANS AOF 17 G 590/1956, 'A/S des ACTIVITES de MAURICE VOISIN dans le cadre de l'U.D.C.A.', Dakar, 15/05/1956.

20. 'Autour du problème Libano-Syrien—Manifeste du Comité Antiraciste de Vigilance Républicaine', *L'AOF* (1 August 1947).

21. Boumedouha, Saïd, 'The Lebanese in Senegal: a history of the relationship between an immigrant community and its French and African rulers', Ph.D thesis, Centre for West African Studies, University of Birmingham, 1987, p. 187.

22. Kojok, 'Les Libanais', pp. 368–74.

23. CAOM MC FM AP 2303/6, Pharaon to Reynet, Beirut, 24/07/1945.

24. CAOM MC FM AP 3411/5, Chargé d'Affaires to Ministre des Affaires Etrangères, Beirut, 12/12/1946.

25. 'Omaïs et Fakhry: deux familles qui ont réussi', *JA* (13 October 2009); 'Sénégal-Liban: quelques épopées', *JA* (13 October 2009).

26. Peleikis, Anja, 'The emergence of a translocal community: the case of a south Lebanese village and its migrant connections to Ivory Coast', *Cahiers d'Études sur la Méditerranée Orientale et le Monde Turco-Iranien*, 30 (2000), p. 305.

27. Tarraf-Najib, Souha, 'Immigration ancienne et territorialisation inaccomplie. les familles libanaises au Sénégal', *Cahiers d'Études sur la Méditerranée et le Monde Turco-Iranien*, 30 (2000), p. 287.

28. Ibid., p. 287.

29. Beydoun, Lina, 'The complexities of citizenship among Lebanese immigrants in Sierra Leone', unpublished paper in the possession of the author, pp. 17–8.

30. Bigo, 'The Lebanese community', p. 522.

31. 'Afrique: la longue marche des Libanais', *JA* (13 October 2009).

32. 'Côte d'Ivoire-Liban: Daghir, un homme d'influence', *JA* (13 October 2009).

33. Bayart, Jean-François, *L'Etat en Afrique: La Politique du Ventre*, Paris: Fayard, 1989, pp. 270–2. See also Berman, Bruce, 'Ethnicity, patronage and the African state: the politics of uncivil nationalism', *African Affairs*, 97 (1998), pp. 305–41.

34. Leighton, Neil, 'Lebanese emigration: its effects on the political economy of Sierra Leone', in Hourani, Albert and Nadim Shehadi, eds, *The Lebanese in the World: A Hundred Years of Emigration*, London: I.B. Tauris, 1992, p. 596.

35. van de Walle, Nicolas, 'Presidentialism and clientelism in Africa's emerging party systems', *Journal of Modern African Studies*, 41, 2 (2003), pp. 297–321.

36. *Le Soleil* (20 July 1976); 'Les Libanais en Afrique: parasites ou agents de développement?', *Voix d'Afrique* (4–17 October 1976), p. 14.

37. *Voix d'Afrique* (4–17 October 1976), pp. 13–4.

38. 'Menacées de déguerpissement, les populations de la Cité RAN de Marcory Crient à l'injustice', http://news.abidjan.net/h/408776.html, last accessed 26 Aug. 2011.

39. Mamdani, Mahmoud, *Citizen and Subject: Contemporary Africa and the Legacy of Late Colonialism*, Princeton, NJ: Princeton University Press, 2006; Mann, Gregory, *Native Sons: West African Veterans and France in the Twentieth Century*, Durham, NC: Duke University Press, 2006.

40. 'Menacées de déguerpissement, les populations de la Cité RAN de Marcory crient à l'Injustice', http://news.abidjan.net/h/408776.html, last accessed 26 Aug. 2011.

41. 'Bras de fer autour de la Cité Ran, Zone 4c/Fouad Omaïs vide les occupants: ils refusent de partir', http://news.abidjan.net/h/408871.html, last accessed 29 Aug. 2011.

42. 'Lebanese man found dead at his home in Nigeria after robbery operation', http://www.naharnet.com/stories/en/81127, last accessed 27 Apr. 2013.

43. Lonsdale, John, 'Moral and political argument in Kenya', in Berman, Bruce, Dickson Eyoh and Will Kymlicka, eds, *Ethnicity and Democracy in Africa*, Oxford: James Currey, 2004, p. 76. See also Berman, Bruce, '"A Palimpsest of Contradictions": ethnicity, class, and politics in Africa', *International Journal of African Historical Studies*, 37, 1 (2004), pp. 13–31; Lonsdale, John, 'The moral economy of Mau Mau: wealth, poverty, and virtue in Kikuyu political thought', in Berman, Bruce and John Lonsdale, *Unhappy Valley: Conflict in Kenya and Africa*, London: James Currey, 1990, pp. 315–505; and Lonsdale, John, 'Moral ethnicity and political tribalism', in Kaarsholm, Preben and Jan Hultin, eds, *Inventions and Boundaries: Historical and Anthropological Approaches to the Study of Ethnicity and Nationalism*, Roskilde: University of Roskilde, 1994, pp. 131–50.

44. Berman, Bruce, Dickson Eyoh and Will Kymlicka, 'Introduction: ethnicity and the politics of democratic nation-building in Africa', in Berman et al., eds, *Ethnicity and Democracy*, p. 4.

45. Ibid., p. 14.

46. Achcar [Ashqar], Joseph, *Les Libanais en Afrique Occidentale Française et dans le Monde*, Beirut: Dar al-Kitab al-Lubnani, n.d., pp. 5, 43, 46, 48, 62, 141–2.

47. Ibid., pp. 201–4.

48. On a comparable shift in policy and discourse, see Malki, Isaac Xerxes, 'Productive aliens: economic planning and the Lebanese in Ghana, c.1930–1972', *Mashriq & Mahjar: A Journal of Middle East Migration Studies*, 1, 1 (2013), pp. 85–114.

49. See Markovitz, Irving Leonard, *Léopold Sédar Senghor and the Politics of Negritude*, London: Heinemann, 1969, and Vaillant, Janet, *Black, French, and African: A Life of Léopold Sédar Senghor*, Cambridge, MA: Harvard University Press, 1990.

50. Kojok, 'Les Libanais', p. 317.

51. Tarraf-Najib, 'Immigration ancienne', pp. 288–9. 293.

52. 'Sénégal-Liban: la face cachée de l'intégration', *JA* (13 October 2009).

53. Kojok, 'Les Libanais', vol. 2, p. 317.

54. Peleikis, Anja, *Lebanese in Motion: Gender and the Making of a Translocal Village*, Piscataway, NJ: Transaction, 2003, pp. 167–9.

55. Ibid., p. 174.

56. Peleikis, 'The emergence', pp. 303, 308–9.

57. Peleikis, *Lebanese in Motion*, p. 84.

58. Tarraf-Najib, 'Immigration ancienne', p. 293.

59. 'Lebanese man found dead at his home in Nigeria after robbery operation', http://www.naharnet.com/stories/en/81127. last accessed 27 Apr. 2013.

60. 'Par centaines, des Libanais fuient la Côte d'Ivoire pour revenir au pays', *OLJ* (3 January 2011).

61. Ong, Aihwa, *Flexible Citizenship: The Cultural Logics of Transnationality*, Durham, NC: Duke University Press, 1999.

62. 'Liban: "Nos très chers compatriotes"', *JA* (13 October 2009).

63. Peleikis, *Lebanese in Motion*, pp. 64–6, 95–6.

64. Labaki, Boutros, 'The role of transnational communities in fostering development in countries of origin', Beirut: United Nations Department of Social and Economic Affairs, 2006, p. 6.

65. 'Liban: "Nos très chers compatriotes"', *JA* (13 October 2009).

66. Peleikis, *Lebanese in Motion*, pp. 64.

67. Labaki, 'The role of transnational communities', p. 8.

68. Kasparian, Choghig, *L'Entrée des Jeunes Libanais dans la Vie Active et l'Emigration: Enquête Réalisée par l'Université Saint-Joseph*, Beirut: Université Saint-Joseph, 2003, pp. 25–7.

69. Hetherington, Kevin, 'Place of geometry: the materiality of place', in Hetherington, Kevin and Rolland Munro, eds, *Ideas of Difference: Social Spaces and the Labour of Division*, Oxford: Blackwell, 1997, p. 185.

70. Urry, John, *Sociology beyond Societies: Mobilities for the Twenty-First Century*, London: Routledge, 2000, p. 134.

71. Peleikis, 'The emergence', p. 299.

72. Ajami, Fouad, *The Vanished Imam: Musa al-Sadr and the Shia of Lebanon*, Ithaca, NY: Cornell University Press, 1986, pp. 57–8, 69, 97–9.

73. Tarraf-Najib, 'Immigration ancienne', p. 293.

74. Ong, *Flexible Citizenship*, p. 19.

75. Lerner, *The Passing*.

76. 'Liban: "Nos très chers compatriotes"', *JA* (13 October 2009).

77. 'La ville de Nabatiyeh porte le deuil de quatre de ses fils', *OLJ* (29 January 2010).

78. http://www.guardian.co.uk/world/2010/jan/25/ethiopian-airlines-crash-lebanon, last accessed 6 Apr. 2013.

79. 'Lebanese man found dead at his home in Nigeria after robbery operation', http://www.naharnet.com/stories/en/81127, (27 Apr. 2013).

80. Kasparian, Choghig, *L'Emigration des Jeunes Libanais et leurs Projets d'Avenir*, vol. 2, *Les Jeunes Libanais dans la Vague d'Emigration de 1992 à 2007*, Beirut: Presses de l'Université Saint-Joseph, 2009, p. 6.

81. Abi Samra, Marwan, *L'Emigration Libanaise et son Impact sur l'Economie et le Développement*, Geneva: International Labour Organization, 2010, pp. 8, 27.

82. See Byblos Bank, 'The global crisis and expatriates' remittances to Lebanon: trends and elements of resilience', Beirut: Byblos Bank, 2011.

83. Ratha, Dilip, Sanket Mohapatra and Ani Silwal, *The Migration Remittances Factbook 2011*, Washington, DC: World Bank, 2011.

84. Abi Samra, 'L'emigration Libanaise', p. 79.

85. Brand, Laurie, *Citizens Abroad: Emigration and the State in the Middle East and North Africa*, Cambridge: Cambridge University Press, 2006, p. 144.

86. al-Jumhuriyya al-Lubnaniyya (Lebanese Republic), Wizarat al-Kharijiyya wa-l-Mughtaribin and al-Mudiriyya al-'Amma li-l-Mughtaribin, 'Kalimat Mudir 'Amm li-l-Mughtaribin al-Ustadh Haitham Jum'ah fi al-Yum al-'Alami li-l-Mughtarib al-Lubnani fi 09/03/2008'.

87. 'Sleiman's Africa trip produces 10 agreements', *The Daily Star* (20 March 2013).

88. 'Sleiman visits Africa under shadow of hostage crisis', *The Daily Star* (12 March 2013).

89. 'Sleiman's Africa trip produces 10 agreements', *The Daily Star* (20 March 2013).

90. 'Afrique: la longue marche des Libanais', *JA* (13 October 2009).

91. Breckenridge, Carol and Arjun Appadurai, 'Editors' comments: on moving targets', *Public Culture*, 2, 1 (1989), p. i.

92. For different accounts of this process, see Armitage, David, *The Declaration of Independence: A Global History*, Cambridge, MA: Harvard University Press, 2007; Cooper, Frederick, *Colonialism in Question: Theory, Knowledge, History*, Berkeley, CA: University of California Press, 2005; Dodge, Toby, *Inventing Iraq: The Failure of Nation-Building and a History Denied*, London: Hurst & Company, 2003; and Manela, Erez, *The Wilsonian Moment: Self-Determination and the International Origins of Anticolonial Nationalism*, Oxford: Oxford University Press, 2007. See also Krasner, Stephen. 'Compromising Westphalia', *International Security*, 20, 3 (1995–6), pp. 115–51; and Osiander, Andreas. 'Sovereignty, international relations, and the Westphalian myth', *International Organization*, 55, 2 (2001), pp. 251–87.

93. Amrith, Sunil, *Crossing the Bay of Bengal: The Furies of Nature and the Fortunes of Migrants*, Cambridge, MA: Harvard University Press, 2013.

BIBLIOGRAPHY

Archival sources

Archives Départementales des Bouches-du-Rhône, Marseille

4 M 2152
4 M 2172

Chambre de Commerce et d'Industrie de Marseille-Provence

2273/01
2274/01

Archives du Ministère des Affaires Étrangères, Paris

Nouvelle Série/Turquie/Syrie-Liban

108
109
114
115

Centre d'Accueil et de Recherche des Archives Nationales, Paris

Fonds AOF (AS: Ancienne Série [pre-1920]; NS: Nouvelle Série [post-1920])

Série 1 G—Études générales, monographies, thèses

1 G 267

Série 19 G—Affaires Musulmanes

NS 19 G 24, 'Presse arabe contrôle de la propagande musulmane—1920–24'
NS 19 G 25, 'Contrôle des livres en arabe'

Série 21 G—Police et Sûreté

AS 21 G 30
AS 21 G 31, 'Cartes d'identité pour les ambulants'
AS 21 G 32, 'Syriens 1900'
AS 21 G 33
AS 21 G 34
AS 21 G 35
AS 21 G 36
AS 21 G 37
AS 21 G 38

BIBLIOGRAPHY

AS 21 G 39
AS 21 G 43
AS 21 G 44
NS 21 G 23, 'Libano-Syriens'
NS 21 G 28, 'Dossiers individuels de personnes suspectes en AOF, 1925–40'
NS 21 G 41, 'Associations et comités suspects'
NS 21 G 46, 'Presse'
NS 21 G 53, 'Associations et propagande'
NS 21 G 61, 'Libano-Syriens'
NS 21 G 73, 'Associations étrangères'
NS 21 G 106, 'Sociétés d'inspiration étrangère en AOF'
NS 21 G 132, 'Propagande anti-française 1921'
NS 21 G 133, 'Renseignements et correspondances 1921–33'
NS 21 G 139, 'Contrôle de la presse arabe, 1931'
NS 21 G 141, 'Renseignements journaliers, 1936–37'
NS 21 G 142, 'Associations'

Centre des Archives d'Outre-Mer, Aix-en-Provence

Fonds Ministériel

Affaires Politiques

AP 1432/1, 'Libano-Syriens en AOF 1923–24, 1931–32'
AP 2303/1, 'Situation des Libano-Syriens de la France d'Outremer Correspondance et Dossiers Personnels 1940–44'
AP 2303/5, 'Instructions au sujet des Libano-Syriens de la France d'Outremer 1944–47'
AP 3411/5

Série Géographique Guinée XIII

Dossier 11, 'Agriculture, commerce et industrie 1902–1910'

Série Géographique Sénégal XI

Dossier 50, 'Police, hygiène et assistance 1895–1904'

Archives Nationales du Sénégal, Dakar

Série D—Sénégal—Affaires Politiques et Administratives

11 D 3/37, 'État des Libano-Syriens résidant dans les cercles du Sénégal 1916–31'
11 D 3/59, 'Correspondance relative aux incidents de Kaolack, 1927'

Série 10 F—Affaires Étrangères

NS 10 F 5, 'Consulats G à P—Liban 1946–53'
NS 10 F 14, 'Libano-Syriens—Syrie'

Série 2 G—Rapports Périodiques

2 G 1/40, 'Rapport d'Ensemble Guinée Française', 1899.
2 G 10/6, 'Dakar Rapport d'Ensemble 3ème Trimestre 1910'
2 G 11/43, 'Kaolack, rapports d'ensemble'
2 G 12/45, 'Dakar—3ème trimestre 1912'
2 G 13/46, 'Dakar-Gorée-Rufisque-Casamance—4ème trimestre 1913'
2 G 15/28(3), 'Dakar—2ème trimestre 1915'
2 G 17/24(3), 'Rapport d'Ensemble—Dakar'

BIBLIOGRAPHY

2 G 18/20(3), 'Dakar-Gorée-Rufisque et Banlieue de Dakar'

2 G 25/11, 'Dakar et Dépendances—Rapport Annuel d'Ensemble'

2 G 26/9, 'Dakar et Dépendances—Rapport Annuel d'Ensemble'

2 G 27/19, 'Dakar et Dépendances—Rapport Annuel d'Ensemble'

2 G 29/7, 'Dakar et Dépendances—Rapport Annuel d'Ensemble'

2 G 31/32, 'Dakar et Dépendances—Rapport Annuel d'Ensemble'

2 G 32/83, 'Cercle du Sine Saloum (Kaolack)—Rapport Annuel d'Ensemble 1932'

2 G 33/62, 'Cercle de Kaolack—Rapport d'Ensemble 1933'

2 G 33/81, 'Cercle de Kaolack—Sine-Saloum—Rapport sur la Traite 1932–33'

2 G 35/26, 'Dakar et Dépendances—Rapport Annuel d'Ensemble'

2 G 35/71, 'Sénégal, affaires économiques, rapports mensuels des cercles sur la traite 1934–35 (Diourbel et Louga)'

2 G 36/2, 'Dakar et Dépendances—Rapport Annuel d'Ensemble'

2 G 37/3, 'Dakar et Dépendances—Rapport Annuel d'Ensemble'

2 G 38/25, 'Dakar et Dépendances—Rapport Annuel d'Ensemble'

Série 17 G—Affaires Politiques, AOF, Généralités

NS 17 G 109, 'Note sur les considérations d'immigration 1937'

NS 17 G 127, 'Pétition au Général de Gaulle 1943–44'

NS 17 G 413, 'Conduite à suivre auprès des Libano-Syriens 1944'

NS 17 G 530

NS 17 G 590

Série 21 G—Police et Sûreté

NS G 77, 'Immigrations'

NS 21 G 118, 'Situation des Libano-Syriens de Dakar, 1945'

NS 21 G 151, 'Moral des populations 1940'

NS 21 G 227, 'Dossiers individuels'

Série 5 M—Justice—Tribunaux Judiciaires 1819–1956

5 M 344, 'Affaires commerciales, faillites et liquidations judiciaires 1929–31'

5 M 346, 'Affaires commerciales, faillites et liquidations judiciaires 1931–36'

5 M 358, 'Livre-compte de Nicolas Issa'

Série O—Enseignement—Sciences et Arts

NS O 33

Published primary sources

'Abduh, Najib, *Al-Safr al-Mufid fi al-'Alam al-Jadid, wa al-Dalil al-Tijari li-Abna al-Lugha al-'Arabiyya fi al-'Alm Ajma'*, New York: Meraat ul-Gharb Publishing House, 1907.

Achcar [Ashqar], Joseph, *Les Libanais en Afrique Occidentale Française et dans le Monde*, Beirut: Dar al-Kitab al-Lubnani, n.d.

al-Afghani, Jamal al-Din and Muhammad 'Abduh, *al-'Urwa al-Wuthqa*, Beirut: al-Maktaba al-Ahliyya, 1933.

Afrique Occidentale Française Togo, Les Guides Bleus, Paris: Hachette, 1958.

al-Amin, Muhsin, *Khitat Jabal 'Amil*, Beirut: Matba'at al-Insaf, 1961, vol. 1.

Angrand, Armand, *Les Lébous de la Presqu'île du Cap Vert. Essai sur leur Histoire et leurs Coutumes*, Dakar: E. Gensul, 1946.

Anthony, Farid Raymond, *Sawpit Boy*, n.p., 1980.

Arcin, André, *La Guinée Française: Races, Religions, Coutumes, Production, Commerce*, Paris: Augustin Challavel, 1907.

———, *Histoire de la Guinée Française*, Paris: Augustin Challavel, 1911.

BIBLIOGRAPHY

Aspe-Fleurimont, Lucien, *La Guinée Française: Conakry et Rivières du Sud. Etude Economique et Commerçiale*, Paris: Augustin Challavel, 1900.

Barot, M., with Desbordes, Meynier, Chalot, Pierre, Gimet-Fontalirant, *Guide Pratique de l'Européen dans l'Afrique Occidentale à l'Usage des Militaires, Fonctionnaires, Commerçants, Colons et Touristes*, Paris: Flammarion, n.d. [1902].

Barrès, Maurice, *Une Enquête aux Pays du Levant*, 2 vols., Paris: Plon, 1923.

Blell, John Michael, 'Health, hygiene, and medical care of the Lebano-Syrian community in Sierra Leone (Recollections and comments of a Lebanese medical doctor)', mimeographed text in *International Seminar: Asian Trading Minorities in Tropical Africa, Afrika Studiencentrum, Leiden, 15–19 December 1975*, Leiden: n.p., 1976.

Cambon, Jules, *Le Diplomate*, Paris: Hachette, 1926.

Comité Central Syrien, *L'Opinion Syrienne à l'Etranger Pendant la Guerre: Documents*, Paris: n.p., 1918.

———, *La Question Syrienne Exposée par les Syriens—à L.L. Excellences les Plénipotentiaires Alliés et Associés à la Conférence de la Paix*, Paris: n.p., 1919.

Comité de Défense des Intérêts Français en Orient, *Rapport sur un Voyage en Egypte et en Turquie d'Asie (Janvier–Août 1912), par Maurice Pernot*, Paris: n.p., 1913.

Comité Libanais de Paris, *Mémoire sur la Question du Liban*, Paris: n.p., 1912.

Cuinet, Vital, *Syrie Liban et Palestine Géographie Administrative Statistique Descriptive et Raisonnée*, Paris: Ernest Leroux, 1896.

De La Rue, Sydney, *The Land of the Pepper Bird: Liberia*, New York: G.P. Putnam, 1930.

Desbordes, Jean-Gabriel, *L'Immigration Libano-Syrienne en Afrique Occidentale Française*, Poitiers: Renault & Co., 1938.

Delavignette, Robert, *Les Vrais Chefs de l'Empire*, Paris: Gallimard, 1939.

Drumont, Édouard, *La France Juive: Edition Populaire*, Paris: Librairie Victor Palmé, 1888.

Filfili, Nadra, *Ma Vie: Cinquante Ans de Vie au Sénégal*, dictated to and translated by Filfili Karim, n.p., 1973.

Flandin, Etienne, *Groupe Sénatorial pour la Défense des Intérêts Français à l'Etranger, Rapport sur la Syrie et la Palestine Présenté par M. Etienne Flandin, Sénateur*, Paris: Société Anonyme de Publications Périodiques, 1915.

'French Mandate for Syria and the Lebanon', *The American Journal of International Law*, 17, 3 Supplement: Official Documents, July 1923.

Ganem, Halil, *Etudes d'Histoire Orientale: Les Sultans Ottomans*, vol. 1 Paris: n.p., 1901.

Girault, Arthur, *Principes de Colonisation et de Législation Coloniale*, Paris: Librairie de la Société du Recueil Sirey, 1921, 4th ed.

Guébhard, Paul, *Au Fouta-Dialon—Elevage—Agriculture—Commerce—Régime Foncier—Religion*, Paris: Augustin Challamel, 1910.

Guggisberg, Decima Moore, and F.G. Guggisberg, *We Two in West Africa*, London: Heinemann, 1909.

Guy, Camille, *L'Afrique Occidentale Française*, Paris: Emile Larose, 1929.

Hanotaux, Gabriel and Alfred Martineau, *Histoire des Colonies Françaises et de l'Expansion de la France dans le Monde*, vol. 1 Paris: Plon, 1929.

Hayik, Michel, *Batl Lubnan Yusuf Bek Karam*, Beirut: Jaridat al-Ijtihad, 1922.

———, *Fi Majahil Ifriqiya*, Beirut: Matba'at al-'Alam, n.p.

Hitti, Philip, *The Syrians in America*, New York: George H. Doran Company, 1924.

Hushaimah, 'Abdallah, *Fi Bilad al Zunuj, aw Thamaniyyat Ashhur fi Ifriqiya al-Gharbiyya*, Beirut: Matabi' Quzma, n.d. [1931].

al-Lubnaniyya, Al-Jumhuriyya, Wizarat al-Kharijiyya wa-l-Mughtaribin and al-Mudiriyya al-'Amma li-l-Mughtaribin, 'Kalimat Mudir 'Amm li-l-Mughtaribin al-Ustadh Haitham Jum'ah fi al-Yum al-'Alami li-l-Mughtarib al-Lubnani fi 09/03/2008'.

Kuczynski, Richard, *Demographic Survey of the British Colonial Empire*, vol. 1, *West Africa*, London: Oxford University Press, 1948.

Al-Lajna al-'Aliyya li-l-Hizb al-Lamarkaziyya al-Idariyya al-'Uthmani, *Al-Mu'tamar al-'Arabi al-Awwal*, Cairo: Matba'at al-Busfur, 1913.

Leroy-Beaulieu, Paul, *De la Colonisation chez les Peuples Modernes*, Paris: Guillaumin et Cie, 1891 [1874], 4th ed.

Lewis, Roy, *Sierra Leone: A Modern Portrait*, London: HMSO, 1954.

Londres, Albert, *Marseille: Porte du Sud*, Marseille: Jean Lafitte, 1980 [1927].

BIBLIOGRAPHY

Macmillan, Allister, *The Red Book of British West Africa. Historical and Descriptive Commercial and Industrial Facts, Figures and Resources, Compiled and Edited by Allister Macmillan FRGS*, London: W.H. & L. Collingridge, 1920.

Ma'luf, 'Isa Iskandar, *Tarikh al-Usar al-Sharqiyya*, Trabulsi, Fawwaz, ed., 7 vols., Beirut: Riad al-Rayyes, 2008 [1924].

Martin, Vincent, *Recensement Démographique de la Ville de Dakar (1955). Résultats Définitifs*, vol. 2, *Etude Socio-Démographique de la Ville de Dakar*, Dakar: Ministère du Plan, Service de la Statistique, 1962.

Maurras, Charles, *Mes Idées Politiques*, Paris: Albatros, 1987 [1937].

Muruwwah, Kamil, *Nahnu fi Ifriqiya: al-Hijra al-Lubnaniyya al-Suriyya ila Ifriqiya al-Gharbiyya, Madiha, Hadiriha, Mustaqbaliha*, Beirut: Al-Makshuf, 1938.

Paillard, Jean, *La Fin des Français en Afrique Noire*, Paris: Les Oeuvres Françaises, 1935.

———, *Périple Noir: Sénégal—Soudan—Niger—Haute Volta—Nigeria—Hoggar*, Paris: Les Oeuvres Françaises, 1935.

———, *Faut-il Faire de l'Algérie un Dominion?*, Paris: Fernand Sorlot, 1939.

———, *L'ABC du Corporatisme*, Paris: Jean Lesfauries for Institut d'Études Corporatives et Sociales, 1943.

'Pétition du commerce de Conakry au sujet des marchands Syriens', in Aspe-Fleurimont, Lucien, *La Guinée Française: Conakry et Rivières du Sud. Etude Economique et Commerciale*, Paris: Augustin Challavel, 1900, pp. 320–1.

Rambert, Gaston, *Marseille. La Formation d'une Grande Cité Moderne. Etude de Géographie Urbaine*, Marseille: Société Anonyme du Sémaphore de Marseille, 1934.

Ratha, Dilip, Sanket Mohapatra and Ani Silwal, *The Migration Remittances Factbook 2011*, Washington, DC: World Bank, 2011.

Rida, Ahmad, *Mu'jam Matn al-Lugha*, Beirut: Dar Maktabat al-Hayat, 1958–60.

———, *Mudhakkirat li-Tarikh Hawadith Jabal 'Amil, 1914–1922*, edited by Munzir Jabir, Beirut: Dar al-Nahar and IFPO, 2009.

Rihbany, Abraham Mitrie, *A Far Journey*, Boston, MA: Houghton Mifflin, 1914.

al-Rihani, Ameen [Amin], *The Book of Khalid*, Beirut: Rihani House, 1973 [1911].

Ristelhueber, René, *Les Traditions Françaises au Liban*, Paris: Librairie Félix Alcan, 1925 [1917].

Rouget, Fernand, *La Guinée. Notice du Gouvernement-Général de l'Afrique Occidentale Française à l'Occasion de l'Exposition Coloniale de Marseille*, Paris: Émile Larose, 1906.

Ruppin, Arthur, 'Syrien als Wirtschaftsgebiet', in Issawi, Charles, ed., *The Economic History of the Middle East 1800–1914: A Book of Readings*, Chicago, IL: University of Chicago Press, 1966, pp. 269–73.

Sa'ada, Antun, *al-Athar al-Kamila*, Beirut: 'Umdat al-Thaqafa fi al-Hizb al-Suri al-Qawmi al-Ijtima'i, 1975–1989.

Saadi, Edward T., 'Our Lady of Deliverance: immigration of the Saadi, Abraham, Elum, and Hayik families', *Journal of Maronite Studies*, (July 1998) http://maroniteinstitute.org/MARI/JMS/july98/Our_Lady_of_Deliverance.htm

al-Safa, Muhammad Jabir, *Tarikh Jabal 'Amil*, Beirut: Dar al-Nahar, 1981, 2nd ed.

Samné, Georges, *La Syrie*, Paris: Bossard, 1920.

Shediack, George, 'The Shediack migration: a saga sustained by faith and love', *Journal of Maronite Studies*, (January 1998) http://maroniteinstitute.org/MARI/JMS/january98/The_Shediack_Migration.htm

Tamimi, Muhammad Rafiq and Muhammad Bahjat, *Wilayat Bayrut*, Beirut: Matba'at al-Iqbal, 1917, 2 vols.

Widmer, Robert, 'Population', in Himadeh, Said B., ed., *Economic Organization of Syria*, Beirut: American University Press, 1936, pp. 3–26.

al-Zahir, Sulayman, *Jabal 'Amil fi al-Harb al-Kawniyya*, Beirut: Dar al-Matbu'at al-Sharqiyya, 1986.

———, *Safahat min Tarikh Jabal 'Amil*, Beirut: Dar al-Islamiyya, 2002.

———, *Mu'jam Qura Jabal 'Amil*, Beirut: Mu'asasat al-Imam al-Sadiq li-l-Buhuth fi Turath 'Ulama' Jabal 'Amil, 2006 [1928], 2 vols.

Official publications

Journal Officiel de l'Afrique Occidentale Française (1921, 1923, 1925–1936)
Journal Officiel de la Guinée Française (1905, 1911, 1912)

Periodicals (years consulted between brackets)

A Travers le Monde (1905), Paris
L'AOF (1935–39, 1948), Dakar

BIBLIOGRAPHY

L' AOF—Echo de la Côte Occidentale d'Afrique (1910–39), Conakry 1910–17

L'A.O.F. Echo de la Côte Occidentale d'Afrique—Organe de la Fédération Socialiste SFIO de l'A.O.F. (1947)

Les Annales Coloniales, newspaper edition (1934–37), Paris

Bulletin du Comité de l'Afrique Française (1900–39), Paris

Bulletin du Comité de l'Asie Française (1911, 1935–6), Paris

Bulletin Mensuel de la Chambre de Commerce de Dakar (1928–38), Dakar

Correspondance d'Orient (1908–39), Paris

The Daily Star (2013), Beirut

Les Echos Africains—Satiriques—Humoristiques—Documentaires Libres (1947)

Les Echos d'Afrique Noire: Le Grand Hebdomadaire Colonial de Défense Française (1951)

France Afrique Noire—Organe de Défense des Intérêts Français en Afrique Noire (1935–39), Paris

Al-'Irfan (1930–31), Saida

Jeune Afrique (2009), Paris

Ifriqiya al-Tijariyya (1931–35), Dakar

L'Orient-Le Jour (2009–10), Beirut

Périscope Africain (Le)—Journal Indépendant Défendant les Intérêts de l'AOF et de l'AEF (1931–35), Dakar

La Quinzaine Coloniale (1898–1911), Paris

Le Soleil (1976), Dakar

Times British Colonies Review (1957), London

Voix d'Afrique (1976), Abidjan

Websites

www.naharnet.com

http://news.abidjan.net

http://news.bbc.co.uk

Secondary sources

Abisaab, Malek, *Militant Women of a Fragile Nation*, Syracuse, NY: Syracuse University Press, 2010.

Abi Samra, Marwan, *L'Emigration Libanaise et son Impact sur l'Economie et le Développement*, Geneva: International Labour Organization, 2010.

Abou el Fareh, Yahia, Abdelouahed Akmir and Abdelmalek Beni Azza, *La Présence Marocaine en Afrique de l'Ouest: Cas du Sénégal, du Mali et de la Côte d'Ivoire*, Rabat: Publications de l'Institut des Etudes Africaines, 1997.

Abou-Hodeib, Toufoul, 'Authentic modern: domesticity and the emergence of a middle class culture in late Ottoman Beirut', Ph.D dissertation, University of Chicago, 2010.

———, 'Taste and class in late Ottoman Beirut', *International Journal of Middle East Studies*, 43, 3 (2011), pp. 475–92

Abu-Laban, Baha, *An Olive Branch on the Family Tree: The Arabs in Canada*, Toronto: McClelland and Stewart, 1980.

Abu-Lughod, Lila, 'Introduction: feminist longings and postcolonial positions', in Abu-Lughod, Lila, ed., *Remaking Women: Feminism and Modernity in the Middle East*, Princeton: Princeton University Press, 1998, pp. 3–31.

Aciman, André, *False Papers: Essays on Exile and Memory*, New York: Picador, 2000.

Ajami, Fouad, *The Vanished Imam: Musa al-Sadr and the Shia of Lebanon*, Ithaca, NY: Cornell University Press, 1986.

Akarlı, Engin, 'Ottoman Attitudes Towards Lebanese Emigration, 1885–1910', in Hourani, Albert and Nadim Shehadi, eds, *The Lebanese in the World: A Hundred Years of Emigration*, London: I.B. Tauris, 1992, pp. 109–38.

———, *The Long Peace: Ottoman Lebanon, 1861–1920*, London: I.B. Tauris, 1993.

Alfaro-Velcamp, Theresa, *So Far from Allah, So Close to Mexico: Middle Eastern Immigrants in Modern Mexico*, Austin, TX: University of Texas Press, 2007.

Amin, Samir, 'La politique coloniale Française à l'égard de la bourgeoisie commerçante Sénégalaise', in Meillassoux, Claude, ed., *The Development of Indigenous Trade and Markets in West Africa*, London: Oxford University Press, 1971.

———, *Impérialisme et Sous-Développement en Afrique*, Paris: Anthropos, 1976.

Amrith, Sunil, 'Tamil diasporas across the Bay of Bengal', *American Historical Review*, 114, 2 (2009), pp. 547–72.

———, *Migration and Diaspora in Modern Asia*, Cambridge: Cambridge University Press, 2011.

BIBLIOGRAPHY

———, *Crossing the Bay of Bengal: The Furies of Nature and the Fortunes of Migrants*, Cambridge, MA: Harvard University Press, 2013.

Amselle, Jean-Loup, *Les Négociants de la Savane: Histoire et Organisation Sociale des Kooroko (Mali)*, Paris: Anthropos, 1977.

———, *Logiques Métisses: Anthropologie de l'Identité en Afrique et Ailleurs*. Paris: Payot, 1990.

———, 'Préface', in Grégoire, Emmanuel and Pascal Labazée, eds, *Grands Commerçants d'Afrique de l'Ouest: Logiques et Pratiques d'un Groupe d'Hommes d'Affaires Contemporains*, Paris: Karthala, 1993.

Anderson, Benedict, 'Long-distance nationalism', in Anderson, Benedict, *The Spectre of Comparisons: Nationalism, South-East Asia, and the World*, London: Verso, 1998.

———, *Imagined Communities: Reflections on the Origins and Spread of Nationalism*, London: Verso, 1996.

Anderson, Warwick, 'Immunities of empire: race, disease, and the new tropical medicine', *Bulletin of the History of Medicine*, 70, 1 (1996), pp. 94–118.

———, *The Cultivation of Whiteness: Science, Health and Racial Destiny in Australia*, New York: Basic Books, 2003.

Andrew, Christopher and Sydney Kanya-Forstner, *France Overseas: The Great War and the Climax of French Imperial Expansion*, London: Thames & Hudson, 1981.

Appadurai, Arjun, 'Introduction: commodities and the politics of value', in Appadurai, Arjun, ed., *The Social Life of Things: Commodities in Cultural Perspective*, Cambridge: Cambridge University Press, 1988, pp. 3–63.

———, 'Global ethnoscapes: notes and queries for a transnational history', in Fox, Richard G., ed., *Recapturing Anthropology*, Santa Fe, NM: School of American Research Press, 1991.

———, *Modernity at Large: Cultural Dimensions of Globalization*, Minneapolis, MN: Minnesota University Press, 1996.

Arhin, Kwame, *West African Traders in Ghana in the Nineteenth and Twentieth Centuries*, London: Longman, 1979.

Armitage, David, *The Declaration of Independence: A Global History*, Cambridge, MA: Harvard University Press, 2007.

Arnold, David, 'European orphans and vagrants in India in the nineteenth century', *Journal of Imperial and Commonwealth History*, 7, 2 (1979), pp. 104–27.

Arsan, Andrew, 'This age is the age of associations: committees, petitions, and the roots of interwar Middle Eastern internationalism', *Journal of Global History*, 7 (2012), pp. 166–88.

Aswad, Barbara, 'The Lebanese community in Dearborn, Michigan', in Hourani, Albert and Nadim Shehadi, eds, *The Lebanese in the World: A Hundred Years of Emigration*, London: I.B. Tauris, 1992, pp. 167–87.

Austin, Gareth, 'Indigenous credit institutions in West Africa, 1750–1960', in Austin, Gareth and Kaoru Sugihara, eds, *Local Suppliers of Credit in the Third World*, Basingstoke: Macmillan, 1993, pp. 93–159.

Ayalon, Ami, *Reading Palestine: Printing and Literacy, 1900–1948*, Austin, TX: University of Texas Press, 2004.

Baghdiantz McCabe, Ina, Gelina Harlaftis and Ioanna Pepelasis Minoglou, 'Introduction', in Baghdiantz McCabe, Ina, Gelina Harlaftis and Ioanna Pepelasis Minoglou, eds, *Diaspora Entrepreneurial Networks: Four Centuries of History*, Oxford: Berg, 2005.

Baily, Samuel, *Immigrants in the Lands of Promise: Italians in Buenos Aires and New York, 1870–1914*, Ithaca, NY: Cornell University Press, 1999.

Baker, Keith, *Inventing the French Revolution: Essays on French Political Culture in the Eighteenth Century*, Cambridge: Cambridge University Press, 1990.

Ballantyne, Tony, *Orientalism and Race: Aryanism in the British Empire*, Basingstoke: Macmillan, 2002.

Ballantyne, Tony and Antoinette Burton, 'Introduction: bodies, empires, and world histories', in Ballantyne, Tony and Antoinette Burton, eds, *Bodies in Contact: Rethinking Colonial Encounters in World History*, Durham, NC: Duke University Press, 2005, pp. 1–15.

Baron, Beth, *The Women's Awakening in Egypt: Culture, Society, and the Press*, New Haven, CT: Yale University Press, 1994.

Barry, Boubacar, 'Introduction: commerce et commerçants sénégalais dans la longue durée. Étude d'une formation économique dépendante', in Harding, Leonhard and Boubacar Barry, eds, *Commerce et Commerçants en Afrique de l'Ouest*, vol. 1, Paris: L'Harmattan, 1992 pp. 35–58.

———, *Senegambia and the Atlantic Slave Trade*, transl. Armah Ayi Kwei, Cambridge: Cambridge University Press, 1998.

Barthes, Roland, *Camera Lucida: Reflections on Photography*, trans. Howard, Richard, London: Vintage, 1993.

BIBLIOGRAPHY

Barton, H. Arnold, ed., *Letters from the Promised Land: Swedes in America 1840–1914*, Minneapolis, University of Minnesota Press, 1975.

Bashkin, Orit, *The Other Iraq: Pluralism, Intellectuals and Culture in Hashemite Iraq, 1921–1958*, Stanford, CA: Stanford University Press, 2009.

Batatu, Hanna, *The Old Social Classes and the Revolutionary Movements of Iraq: A Study of Iraq's Old Landed and Commercial Classes and of its Communists, Ba'thists and Free Officers*, Princeton, NJ: Princeton University Press, 1978.

Batrouney, Andrew and Trevor, *The Lebanese in Australia*, Melbourne: AE Press, 1985.

Bauer, P.T., *West African Trade: A Study of Competition, Oligopoly and Monopoly in a Changing Economy*, Cambridge: Cambridge University Press, 1954.

Bayart, Jean-François, *L'Etat en Afrique: La Politique du Ventre*, Paris: Fayard, 1989.

———, 'Africa in the world: a history of extraversion', transl. Ellis, Stephen, *African Affairs*, 99 (2000), pp. 217–67.

Baydoun, Ahmad, *Identité Confessionelle et Temps Social chez les Historiens Libanais Contemporains*, Beirut: Université Libanaise, 1984.

———, 'Bint-Jbeil, Michigan, suivi de (ou poursuivi par) Bint-Jbeil, Liban', *Maghreb-Machrek*, 125 (1989), pp. 69–81.

Bayly, C.A., *Empire and Information: Intelligence Gathering and Social Information in India, 1780–1870*, Cambridge: Cambridge University Press, 1996.

———, *The Birth of the Modern World, 1780–1914: Global Connections and Comparisons*, Oxford: Blackwell, 2004.

Bayly, C.A. and Leila Tarazi Fawaz, 'Introduction: the connected world of empires', in Fawaz, Leila Tarazi and C.A. Bayly with Robert Ilbert, eds, *Modernity and Culture From the Mediterranean to the Indian Ocean*, New York: Columbia University Press, 1999, pp. 1–27.

Bayly, Susan, *Asian Voices in a Postcolonial Age: Vietnam, India and Beyond*, Cambridge: Cambridge University Press, 2007.

Bazzi, Mustafa, *Jabal 'Amil fi Muhitahu al-'Arabi, 1864–1948*, Beirut: Markaz al-Dirasat wa al-Tawthiq wa al-Nashr, 1993.

———, *Tatawwur al-Ta'lim wa al-Thaqafa fi Jabal 'Amil mundhu Nihayat al-Qarn al-Tasi' 'Ashar hatta Muntasaf al-Qarn al-'Ashrin*, Beirut: Hi'yat Inma' al-Mintaqa al-Hududiyya, 1995.

———, *Bint Jubail: Hadirat Jabal 'Amil*, Beirut: Dar al-Amir li-l-Thaqafa wa al-'Ulum, 1998.

———, *Al-Hijra wa al-Nuzuh min Lubnan khilal al-Qarn al-'Ashrin (1900–2006) (Namudhaj Janub Lubnan)*, Beirut: Dar al-Mahajja al-Bayda, 2008.

Benton, Lauren, 'Colonial law and cultural difference: jurisdictional politics and the formation of the colonial state', *Comparative Studies in Society and History*, 41, 3 (1999), pp. 563–88.

Berman, Bruce, 'Ethnicity, patronage and the African state: the politics of uncivil nationalism', *African Affairs*, 97 (1998), pp. 305–41.

———, '"A palimpsest of contradictions": ethnicity, class, and politics in Africa', *International Journal of African Historical Studies*, 37, 1 (2004), pp. 13–31.

Berman, Bruce, Dickson Eyoh and Will Kymlicka, 'Introduction: ethnicity and the politics of democratic nation-building in Africa', in Berman, Bruce, Dickson Eyoh and Will Kymlicka, eds, *Ethnicity and Democracy in Africa*, Oxford: James Currey, 2004, pp. 1–21.

Berman, Marshall, *All That is Solid Melts into Air: The Experience of Modernity*, London: Verso, 2010 [1982].

Bernard-Duquenet, Nicole, *Le Sénégal et le Front Populaire*, Paris: Éditions de Demain, 1986.

Berry, Sara, 'Stable prices, unstable values: some thoughts on monetization and the meaning of transactions in West African economies' in Guyer, Jane I., ed., *Credit, Currencies and Culture: African Financial Institutions in Historical Perspective*, Stockholm: Nordiska Afrikainstitutet, 1999, pp. 299–313.

Bertoni, Liliana Ana, 'De Turquia a Buenos Aires. Una colectividad nueva a fines del siglo XIX', *Estudios Migratorios Latinoamericanos*, 9, 26 (1994), pp. 67–94.

Bestene, Jorge, 'Inmigración sirio-libanesa en la Argentina: Una aproximación,' *Estudios Migratorios Latinoamericanos*, 9 (August 1988), pp. 239–68.

Betts, Raymond, 'The establishment of the Medina in Dakar, Senegal, 1914', *Africa* 41, 2 (1971).

Beydoun, Lina, 'The complexities of citizenship among Lebanese immigrants in Sierra Leone', unpublished paper in the possession of the author.

BIBLIOGRAPHY

Bhabha, Homi, *The Location of Culture*, London: Routledge, 1994.

Bierwirth, Chris, 'Like fish in the sea: the Lebanese diaspora in Côte d'Ivoire, 1925–1990', Ph.D dissertation, University of Michigan, 1994.

———, 'The initial establishment of the Lebanese community in Côte d'Ivoire, ca. 1925–45', *International Journal of African Historical Studies*, 30, 2 (1997).

———, 'The Lebanese communities of Côte d'Ivoire', *African Affairs*, 99 (1998).

Bigo, Didier, 'The Lebanese community in the Ivory Coast: a non-native network at the heart of power', in Hourani, Albert and Nadim Shehadi, eds, *The Lebanese in the World: A Hundred Years of Emigration*, London: I.B. Tauris, 1992, pp. 509–30.

Birnbaum, Pierre, *Un Mythe Politique: La 'République Juive' de Léon Blum à Mendès France*, Paris: Gallimard, 1995 [1988].

———, *Le Moment Antisémite: Un Tour de la France en 1898*, Paris: Fayard, 1998.

Blanchard, Pascal, 'Mentalité coloniale, images de l'Afrique noire et de l'Africain à travers la presse d'Action Française (1899–1939)', Mémoire de Maîtrise, Université Paris-I 1988.

———, 'Nationalisme et colonies. Idéologie coloniale, discours sur l'Afrique et les Africains de la droite nationaliste Française des années 30 à la Révolution Nationale', Thèse de Doctorat, Université Paris-I, 1994.

———, 'Discours, politique et propagande. L'AOF et les Africains au temps de la Révolution Nationale (1940–1944)', http://tekrur-ucad.refer.sn/IMG/pdf/P4BLANCH.pdf

Blanchard, Pascal, Nicolas Bancel and Sandrine Lemaire, eds, *La Fracture Coloniale: La Société Française au Prisme de l'Héritage Colonial*, Paris: La Découverte, 2005.

Boeke, J.H., *Economics and Economic Policy of Dual Societies as Exemplified by Indonesia*, Haarlem: HD Tjeenk Willink & Zoon, 1953.

Bonin, Hubert, *CFAO: Cent Ans de Compétition*, Paris: Economica, 1987.

Booth, Marilyn, *May Her Likes Be Multiplied: Biography and Gender Politics in Egypt*, Berkeley, CA: University of California Press, 2001.

Boumedouha, Saïd, 'The Lebanese in Senegal: a history of the relationship between an immigrant community and its French and African rulers', Ph.D. thesis, Centre for West African Studies, University of Birmingham, 1987.

Bose, Sugata, *A Hundred Horizons: the Indian Ocean in the Age of Global Empire*, Cambridge, MA: Harvard University Press, 2006.

Brand, Laurie, *Citizens Abroad: Emigration and the State in the Middle East and North Africa*, Cambridge: Cambridge University Press, 2006.

Breckenridge, Carol and Arjun Appadurai, 'Editors' comment: on moving targets', *Public Culture*, 2, 1 (1989).

Brettell, Carole, *The Men Who Migrate and the Women Who Wait: Population and History in a Portuguese Parish*, Cambridge: Cambridge University Press, 1986.

Brooks, George E., *Eurafricans in Western Africa: Commerce, Social Status, Gender and Religious Observance from the Sixteenth to the Eighteenth Centuries*, Athens, OH: University of Ohio Press, 2003.

Brubaker, Rogers, *Citizenship and Nationhood in France and Germany*, Cambridge, MA: Harvard University Press, 1992.

Buheiry, Marwan, 'The Peasant Revolution of 1858 in Mount Lebanon: rising expectations, economic malaise and the incentive to arm', in Khalidi, Tarif, ed., *Land Tenure and Social Transformation in the Middle East*, Beirut: American University of Beirut, 1984, pp. 291–301.

Burnley, I.H., 'Lebanese migration and settlement in Sydney, Australia', *International Migration Review*, 16, 57 (1982), pp. 102–32.

Burrows, Colin, '"Mission Civilisatrice": French cultural policy in the Middle East, 1860–1914', *Historical Journal*, 29 (1986), pp. 103–35.

Burton, Antoinette, 'Introduction', in Burton, Antoinette, ed., *Gender, Sexuality and Colonial Modernities*, London: Routledge, 1997, pp. 1–16.

———, *At the Heart of the Empire: Indians and the Colonial Encounter in Late-Victorian Britain*, Berkeley, CA: University of California Press, 1998.

Butler, Judith, *Precarious Life: the Powers of Mourning and Violence*, London: Verso, 2006.

———, *Parting Ways: Jewishness and the Critique of Zionism*, New York: Columbia University Press, 2012.

Byblos Bank, 'The global crisis and expatriates' remittances to Lebanon: trends and elements of resilience', Beirut: Byblos Bank, 2011.

BIBLIOGRAPHY

Caestecker, Franck, 'The transformation of nineteenth century expulsion policy, 1880–1914', in Fahrmeir, Andreas, Olivier Faron and Patrick Weil, eds, *Migration Control in the North Atlantic World: the Evolution of State Practices in Europe and the United States from the French Revolution to the Interwar Period*, Oxford: Berghahn, 2003, pp. 120–37.

Camara, Camille, *Saint-Louis-du-Sénégal: Évolution d'une Ville en Milieu Africain*, Dakar: Institut Fondamental d'Afrique Noire, 1968.

Capitan Peter, Colette, *Charles Maurras et l'Idéologie d'Action Française: Étude Sociologique d'une Pensée de Droite*, Paris: Seuil, 1972.

de Certeau, Michel, *L'Invention du Quotidien*, vol. 1, *Arts de Faire*, Paris: Gallimard, 1990.

de Certeau, Michel, Luce Giard and Pierre Mayol, *L'Invention du Quotidien*, vol. 2, *Habiter, Cuisiner*, Paris: Gallimard, 1994.

Chafer, Tony and Amanda Sackur, 'Introduction', in Chafer, Tony and Amanda Sackur, eds, *The French Colonial Empire and the Popular Front*, Basingstoke: Macmillan, 1999, pp. 1–29.

Chakrabarty, Dipesh, '*Adda*, Calcutta: dwelling in modernity', *Public Culture*, 11, 1 (1999), pp. 109–45.

———, *Provincializing Europe: Postcolonial Thought and Historical Difference*, Princeton, NJ: Princeton University Press, 2000.

———, *Habitations of Modernity: Essays in the Wake of Subaltern Studies*, Chicago, IL: University of Chicago Press, 2002.

Chalabi, Tamara, *The Shi'is of Jabal 'Amil and the New Lebanon: Community and Nation-State, 1918–1943*, Basingstoke: Macmillan, 2006.

Chambers, Iain, *Migrancy, Culture, Identity*, London: Routledge, 1993.

Chambers, David Wade and Richard Gillespie, 'Locality in the history of science: colonial science, technoscience, and indigenous knowledge', *Osiris*, 2nd series, 15 (2000), pp. 221–40.

Chebel d'Appollonia, Ariane, *L'Extrême Droite en France. De Maurras à Le Pen*, Paris: Editions Complexe, 1996.

Chelkowski, Peter J., ed., *Eternal Performance: Ta'ziehs and Other Shiite Rituals (Enactments)*, Chicago, IL: Chicago University Press, 2010.

Chevallier, Dominique, 'Aux origines des troubles agraires Libanais', *Annales ESC*, 14 (1959), pp. 35–64.

———, *La Société du Mont Liban à l'Epoque de la Révolution Industrielle*, Paris: Geuthner, 1971.

———, 'Aux bases d'une intervention: Lyon et la Syrie en 1919', in Chevallier, Dominique, *Villes et Travail en Syrie du XIXe au XXe Siècles*, Paris: Maisonneuve & Larose, 1982, pp. 41–86.

Choldin, Harvey, 'Kinship networks in the migration process', *International Migration Review*, 7, 2 (1973), pp. 163–75.

Choueiri, Youssef M., *Arab Nationalism: A History*, Oxford: Blackwell, 2000.

Clarence-Smith, William Gervase, 'Middle Eastern migrants in the Philippines: entrepreneurs and cultural brokers', *Asian Journal of Social Sciences*, 32, 3 (2004), pp. 425–57.

Cleveland, William, *Making of an Arab Nationalist: Ottomanism and Arabism in the Life and Thought of Sati' al-Husri*, Princeton, NJ: Princeton University Press, 1972.

Clifford, James, 'Diasporas', *Cultural Anthropology*, 9, 3 (1994), pp. 302–38.

———, *Routes: Travel and Translation in the Late Twentieth Century*, Cambridge, MA: Harvard University Press, 1997.

Cohen, Abner, *Custom and Politics in Urban Africa: A Study of Hausa Migrants in Yoruba Towns*, London: Routledge, 1969.

———, 'Cultural strategies in the organization of trading diasporas', in Meillassoux, Claude, ed., *The Development of Indigenous Trade and Markets in West Africa*, London: Oxford University Press, 1971, pp. 266–81.

Cohen, William B., 'The colonial policy of the Popular Front', *French Historical Studies*, 7 (1971–2), pp. 368–75.

———, *Rulers of Empire: the French Colonial Service in Africa*, Stanford, CA: Hoover Institute Press, 1971.

Cohn, Bernard, *Colonialism and its Forms of Knowledge: the British in India*, Princeton, NJ: Princeton University Press, 1996.

Cole, Juan R.I., 'Printing and urban Islam in the Mediterranean world, 1890–1920', in Fawaz, Leila Tarazi and Christopher Bayly with Robert Ilbert, eds, *Modernity and Culture: From the Mediterranean to the Indian Ocean*, New York: Columbia University Press, 2002, pp. 344–64.

Colley, Linda, *Captives: Britain, Empire and the World, 1600–1850*, London: Pimlico, 2002.

Comaroff, John, 'Governmentality, materiality, legality, modernity. On the colonial state in Africa', in Deutsch,

BIBLIOGRAPHY

Jan-Georg, Peter Probst and Heike Schmidt, eds, *African Modernities: Entangled Meanings in Current Debates*, Oxford: James Currey, 2002.

Conklin, Alice, *A Mission to Civilize: The Republican Empire in France and West Africa, 1895–1930*, Stanford, CA: Stanford University Press, 1997.

Conklin, Alice and Julia Clancy-Smith, 'Introduction: writing colonial histories', *French Historical Studies*, 27, 3 (2004) pp. 497–505.

Cooper, Frederick, 'Africa and the world economy', *African Studies Review*, 24, 2/3 (1981), pp. 1–86.

——, 'Conflict and connection: rethinking colonial African history', *American Historical Review*, 99, 5 (1994), pp. 1516–45.

——, *Decolonisation and African Society: The Labour Question in French and British Africa*, Cambridge: Cambridge University Press, 1996.

——, 'Globalization', in *Colonialism in Question: Theory, Knowledge, History*, Berkeley, CA: University of California Press, 2005, pp. 91–112.

——, 'Provincializing France', in Stoler, Ann Laura, Carole McGranahan and Peter C. Perdue, eds, *Imperial Formations*, Oxford: James Currey, 2007, pp. 341–78.

Cooper, Frederick and Ann Laura Stoler, 'Between metropole and colony: rethinking a research agenda', in Cooper and Stoler, eds, *Tensions of Empire: Colonial Cultures in a Bourgeois World*, Berkeley, CA: University of California Press, 1997, pp. 1–36.

Copans, Jean, 'From Senegambia to Senegal: the evolution of peasantries', in Klein, Martin, ed., *Peasants in Africa: Historical and Contemporary Perspectives*, London: Sage, 1980.

Coquery-Vidrovitch, Catherine, 'The Popular Front and the colonial question. French West Africa: an example of reformist colonialism', in Chafer, Tony and Amanda Sackur, eds, *The French Colonial Empire and the Popular Front*, Basingstoke: Macmillan, 1999, pp. 155–69.

Coquery-Vidrovitch, Catherine and Odile Goerg, eds, *L'Afrique Occidentale au Temps des Français: Colonisateurs et Colonisés, c. 1860–1960*, Paris: Editions La Découverte, 1992.

Corbin, Henry, *Face de Dieu, Face de l'Homme: Herméneutique et Soufisme*, Paris: Flammarion, 1983.

Cormick, Martyn, 'Maurras, Charles Marie Photius (1868–1952)', in Bell, David S., Douglas Johnson and Peter Morris, eds, *Biographical Dictionary of French Political Leaders Since 1870*, London: Harvester Wheatsheaf, 1990, pp. 275–8.

Courdurié, Marcel and Guy Durand, eds, *Entrepreneurs d'Afrique*, Marseille: Chambre de Commerce et d'Industrie Marseille-Provence, 1998.

Cronin, Stephanie, ed., *Subalterns and Social Protest: History from Below in the Middle East and North Africa*, London: Routledge, 2007.

Crowder, Michael, *West Africa under Colonial Rule*, Evanston, IL: Northwestern University Press, 1968.

Cruise O'Brien, Donal, 'Towards an "Islamic Policy" in French West Africa, 1858–1914', *Journal of African History*, 8, 2 (1967), pp. 303–16.

——, *The Mourides of Senegal: The Political and Economic Organization of an Islamic Brotherhood*, Oxford: Clarendon Press, 1971.

Cruise O'Brien, Rita, *White Society in Black Africa: The French in Senegal*, London: Faber, 1972.

——, 'Lebanese entrepreneurs in Senegal', *Cahiers d'Études Africaines*, 15, 1 (1975), pp. 95–115.

Curtin, Philip D., *Economic Change in Precolonial Africa: Senegambia in the Era of the Slave Trade*, Madison, WI: University of Wisconsin Press, 1975.

——, *Cross-Cultural Trade in World History*, Cambridge: Cambridge University Press, 1984.

Daghir, Yusuf Sa'd, *Qamus al-Sahafa al-Lubnaniyya 1858–1974*, Beirut: Université Libanaise, 1974.

Dahir, Mas'ud, *Al-Hijra al-Lubnaniyya ila Misr: Hijrat al-Shawwam*, Beirut: Lebanese University, 1986.

——, 'Al-Hijra ila Misr', in Muntada Sur al-Thaqafi, *Watha'iq Mu'tamar Tarikh Sur al-Awwal*, Sur: Muntada Sur al-Thaqafi.

Dakhli, Leyla, *Une génération d'intellectuels arabes. Syrie et Liban, 1908–1940*, Paris: Karthala, 2009.

Darnton, Robert, *The Kiss of Lamourette: Reflections in Cultural History*, London: Faber & Faber, 1990.

Daughton, J.P., 'When Argentina was "French": rethinking cultural politics and European imperialism in Belle-Epoque Buenos Aires', *Journal of Modern History*, 80 (2008), pp. 831–64.

Daumalin, Xavier, *Marseille et l'Ouest Africain. L'Outre-Mer des Industriels (1841–1956)*, Marseille: Chambre de Commerce et d'Industrie Marseille-Provence, 1992.

BIBLIOGRAPHY

———, 'Frédéric Bohn: l'Africain, 1852–1923', in Courdurié, Marcel and Guy Durand, eds, *Entreprises d'Afrique*, Marseille: Chambre de Commerce et d'Industrie Marseille-Provence, 1998, pp. 198–267.

David, Philippe, *Les Navétanes: Histoire des Migrants Saisonniers de l'Arachide en Sénégambie des Origines à nos Jours*, Dakar: Les Nouvelles Éditions Africaines, 1980.

Dawn, Ernest, 'The rise of Arabism in Syria', in Dawn, Ernest, *From Ottomanism to Arabism: Essays on the Origins of Arab Nationalism*, Urbana, IL: University of Illinois Press, 1973.

Delclitte, Christophe, 'La catégorie juridique "Nomade" dans la Loi de 1912', *Hommes et Migrations*, 1188–1189 (1995), pp. 23–30.

Delf, George, *Asians in East Africa*, London: Oxford University Press, 1963.

Dening, Greg, *History's Anthropology: The Death of William Gooch*, London: University Press of North America, 1988.

Diop, Abdoulaye-Bara, *La Société Wolof: Tradition et Changement. Les Systèmes d'Inégalité et de Domination*, Paris: Karthala, 1981.

Dioudonnat, Pierre-Marie, *Je Suis Partout 1930–1944. Les Maurrassiens devant la Tentation Fasciste*, Paris: La Table Ronde, 1973.

———, *Les 700 Rédacteurs de 'JSP' 1930–1944*, Paris: DEDOPOLS, 1993.

Diouf, Mamadou, *Le Kajoor au XIXe Siècle: Pouvoir Ceddo et Conquête Coloniale*, Paris: Karthala, 1990.

Dodge, Toby, *Inventing Iraq: The Failure of Nation-Building and a History Denied*, London: Hurst & Company, 2003.

Douglas, Mary, *Purity and Danger: an Analysis of Concepts of Pollution and Taboo*, London: Routledge, 1978 [1966].

Doumani, Beshara, 'Introduction', in Doumani, Beshara, ed., *Family History in the Middle East: Household, Property and Gender*, Albany, NY: State University of New York Press, 2003, pp. 1–19.

———, 'Endowing family: *Waqf*, property devolution, and gender in Greater Syria, 1800 to 1860', *Comparative Studies in Society and History*, 40, 1 (1998), pp. 3–41.

Duara, Prasenjit, *Rescuing History from the Nation: Questioning Narratives of Modern China*, Chicago, IL: University of Chicago Press, 1995.

Duben, Alan and Cem Behar, *Istanbul Households: Marriage, Family, and Fertility, 1880–1940*, Cambridge: Cambridge University Press, 1991.

Durand, Bernard, 'Les pouvoirs du Gouverneur Général de l'AOF', in Becker, Charles, Saliou M'Baye and Ibrahima Thioub, eds, *AOF: Réalités et Héritages. Sociétés Ouest-africaines et Ordre Colonial, 1895–1960*, Dakar: Direction des Archives du Sénégal, 1997.

Eades, Jeremy, *Strangers and Traders: Yoruba Migrants, Markets and the State in Northern Ghana*, Edinburgh: Edinburgh University Press, 1993.

Eddé, Carla, 'La mobilisation populaire à Beyrouth à l'époque du mandat, le cas des boycotts des trams et de l'électricité', in Méouchy, Nadine, ed., *France, Syrie et Liban 1918–1946 Les Ambiguïtés et les Dynamiques de la Relation Mandataire*, Damascus: IFEAD, 2002, pp. 349–75.

Eickelman, Dale, *The Middle East: An Anthropological Approach*, Englewood Cliffs: Prentice Hall, 1989, 2nd ed.

Eisenstein, Elizabeth, *The Printing Revolution in Early Modern Europe*, Cambridge: Cambridge University Press, 1983.

Elshakry, Marwa, 'Darwin's legacy in the Arab East: science, religion and politics, 1870–1914', Ph.D dissertation, Princeton University. 2003.

El Shakry, Omnia, *The Great Social Laboratory: Subjects of Knowledge in Colonial and Postcolonial Egypt*, Stanford, CA: Stanford University Press, 2007.

Eppel, Michael, 'The elite, the effendiyya, and the growth of nationalism and Pan-Arabism in Hashemite Iraq, 1921–1958', *International Journal of Middle East Studies*, 30, 2 (1998), pp. 227–50.

Fall, Babacar and Abdoul Sow, 'Les traitants saint-louisiens dans les villes-escales du Sénégal 1850–1930', in Harding, Leonhard and Boubacar Barry, eds, *Le Sénégal, Commerce et Commerçants en Afrique de l'Ouest*, vol. 1, Paris: L'Harmattan, 1992.

Falola, Toyin, 'Money and informal credit institutions in colonial Western Nigeria', in Guyer, Jane, ed., *Money Matters: Instability, Values, and Social Payments in the Modern History of West African Communities*, London: James Currey, 1995, pp. 162–87.

Fahrmeir, Andreas, Olivier Faron and Patrick Weil, 'Introduction', in Fahrmeir, Andreas, Olivier Faron and Patrick Weil, eds, *Migration Control in the North Atlantic World: the Evolution of State Practices in Europe and the United States from the French Revolution to the Interwar Period*, Oxford: Berghahn, 2003, pp. 1–7.

Fanon, Frantz, *Les Damnés de la Terre*, Paris: Gallimard, 1991 [1961].

BIBLIOGRAPHY

Farge, Arlette, *Le Goût de l'Archive*, Paris: Seuil, 1989.

Fawaz, Leila Tarazi, *Merchants and Migrants in Nineteenth Century Beirut*, Cambridge, MA: Harvard University Press, 1983.

———, *An Occasion for War: Civil Conflict in Beirut and Damascus in 1860*, Berkeley, MA: University of California Press, 1994.

Fawcett, Louise L'Estrange, 'Lebanese, Palestinians and Syrians in Colombia', in Hourani, Albert and Nadim Shehadi, eds, *The Lebanese in the World: A Hundred Years of Emigration*, London: I.B. Tauris, 1992, pp. 361–77.

Feghali, Michel, *Proverbes et Dictons Syro-Libanais: Texte Arabe, Transcription, Traduction, Commentaire et Index Analytique*, Paris: Institut d'Ethnologie, 1935.

Ferguson, James, *Expectations of Modernity: Myths and Meanings of Life on the Zambian Copperbelt*, Berkeley, CA: University of California Press, 1999.

Firro, Kais, 'Silk and socio-economic change in Lebanon, 1860–1919', in Kedourie, Elie and Sylvia Haim, eds, *Essays on the Economic History of the Middle East*, London: Frank Cass, 1988.

———, *Inventing Lebanon: Nationalism and the State under the Mandate*, London: I.B. Tauris, 2003.

Fletcher, Yaël Simpson, '"Capital of the Colonies": real and imagined boundaries between metropole and empire in 1920s Marseille', in Driver, Felix and Martin Gilbert, eds, *Imperial Cities: Landscape, Display and Identity*, Manchester: Manchester University Press, 1999, pp. 136–51.

Forsdick, Charles and David Murphy, 'Introduction: the case for Francophone postcolonial studies', in Forsdick, Charles and David Murphy, eds, *Francophone Postcolonial Studies: An Introduction*, London: Arnold, 2003, pp. 1–14.

Forth, Christopher E., *The Dreyfus Affair and the Crisis of French Manhood*, Baltimore, MD: Johns Hopkins University Press, 2004.

Foucault, Michel, *The Order of Things: An Archaeology of the Human Sciences*, London: Tavistock, 1970.

———, 'Omnes et singulatim: towards a criticism of political reason', in McMurrin, Sterling, ed., *The Tanner Lectures on Human Values*, vol. 2, Salt Lake City, UT: University of Utah Press, 1981, pp. 223–54.

Fouquet, Joseph, *La Traite des Arachides dans le Pays de Kaolack, et ses Conséquences Économiques, Sociales et Juridiques*, Saint Louis: Centre de l'Institut Français d'Afrique Noire, 1958.

Freud, Sigmund, 'Negation' in Strachey, J., transl. and ed., *The Ego and the Id and Other Works*, Standard Edition of the Complete Psychological Works of Sigmund Freud, vol. XIX (1923–25), Harmondsworth: Penguin, 1962, pp. 233–40.

Fuller, Anne, *Buarij: Portrait of a Lebanese Muslim Village*, Cambridge: Harvard University Press, 1961.

Furayha, Anis, *Modern Lebanese Proverbs Collected at Ras al-Matn: Collated, Annotated and Translated into English*, Beirut: American University of Beirut, 1953.

Gabaccia, Donna, 'Kinship, culture and migration: a Sicilian example', *Journal of American Ethnic History*, 3 (1984), pp. 43–7.

———, 'Women of the mass migrations', Moch, Leslie and Dirk Hoerder, eds, in Hoerder, Dirk, and Leslie Page Moch, *European Migrants: Global and Local Perspectives*, Boston: Northeastern University Press, 1996, pp. 90–111.

———, *Italy's Many Diasporas*, Seattle, WA: University of Washington Press, 2000.

Gamble, David, *The Wolof of Senegambia, Together with Notes on the Lebu and the Serer*, London: International Anthropological Institute, 1957.

Geertz, Clifford, *Peddlers and Princes: Social Change and Economic Organisation in Two Indonesian Towns*, Chicago, IL: Chicago University Press, 1963.

———, 'The bazaar economy: information and search in peasant marketing', *Supplement to the American Economic Review*, 68 (1978), pp. 28–32.

———, 'Suq: the bazaar economy in Sefrou', in Geertz, Clifford, Hildred Geertz and Lawrence Rosen, *Meaning and Order in Moroccan Society: Three Essays in Cultural Analysis*, Cambridge: Cambridge University Press, 1979, pp. 123–263.

Gelvin, James, *Divided Loyalties: Nationalism and Mass Politics in Syria at the Close of Empire*, Berkeley, CA: University of California Press, 1998.

Gershoni, Israel, 'Rethinking the formation of Arab nationalism in the Middle East, 1920–1945: old and new narratives', in Gershoni, Israel and James Jankowski, eds, *Rethinking Nationalism in the Arab Middle East*, New York: Columbia University Press, 1997, pp. 3–25.

BIBLIOGRAPHY

———, 'The theory of crisis and the crisis in a theory: intellectual history in twentieth century Middle Eastern studies', in Gershoni, Israel, Amy Singer and Hakan Erdem, eds, *Middle Eastern Historiographies: Narrating the Twentieth Century*, Seattle, WA: University of Washington Press, 2006, pp. 131–82.

Gershoni, Israel and James Jankowski, eds, *Rethinking Nationalism in the Arab Middle East*, New York: Columbia University Press, 1997.

Gershoni, Israel and Ursula Wocöck, 'Doing history: modern Middle Eastern studies today', in Gershoni, Israel and Ursula Wocöck with Hakan Erdem, eds, *Histories of the Modern Middle East*, Boulder, CO: Lynne Riener, 2002.

Gibb, H.A.R., *Modern Trends in Islam*, Chicago, IL: Chicago University Press, 1947.

Gilman, Sander, *The Jew's Body*, London: Routledge, 1991.

Ginzburg, Carlo, *Myths, Emblems, Clues*, transl. John and Anne C. Tedeschi, London: Hutchinson Rodius, 1990.

———, 'De près de Loin', *Vacarme*, 18 (2002), http://www.vacarme.org/article235.html

Ginzburg, Carlo and Carlo Proni, 'The name of the game: unequal exchange and the historiographical marketplace', transl. Branch, Eren, in Muir, Ed and Guido Ruggieri, eds, *Microhistory and the Lost Peoples of Europe*, Baltimore, MD: Johns Hopkins University Press, 1991.

Girardet, Raoul, *L'Idée Coloniale en France de 1871 à 1962*, Paris: La Table Ronde, 1972.

Goerg, Odile, *Commerce et Colonisation en Guinée 1850–1913*, Paris: L'Harmattan, 1986.

Gonnin, Gilbert and Julien Zonon, 'Le commerce de la zone forestière ouest ivoirienne depuis le XIXe siècle: une activité à prédominance étrangère', in Harding, Leonhard and Pierre Kipré, eds, *La Côte d'Ivoire*, Paris: L'Harmattan, 1992, pp. 149–87.

Gonzalez, Nancie L., *Dollar, Dove, and Eagle: One Hundred Years of Palestinian Migration to Honduras*, Ann Arbor, MI: University of Michigan Press, 1992.

Gordimer, Nadine, *Selected Stories*, Harmondsworth: Penguin, 1983.

Gordon, Daniel, 'The back-door of the nation-state: expulsion of foreigners and continuity in twentieth-century France', *Past & Present*, 186 (2005), pp. 201–32.

Gouda, Frances and Julia Clancy-Smith, 'Introduction', in Gouda, Frances and Julia Clancy-Smith, eds, *Domesticating the Empire: Race, Gender and Family Life in French and Dutch Colonialism*, Charlottesville, VA: University Press of Virginia, 1998, pp. 1–20.

Grégoire, Emmanuel and Pascal Labazée, 'Introduction: approche comparative des réseaux ouest-africains contemporains', in Grégoire, Emmanuel and Pascal Labazée, eds, *Grands Commerçants d'Afrique de l'Ouest: Logiques et Pratiques d'un Groupe d'Hommes d'Affaires Contemporains*, Paris: Karthala, 1993.

Gregory, Robert S., *South Asians in East Africa: An Economic and Social History 1890–1980*, Boulder, CO: Westview, 1993.

Gualtieri, Sarah, 'Gendering the chain migration thesis: women and Syrian transatlantic migration, 1878–1924', *Comparative Studies of South Asia, Africa and the Middle East*, 24, 1 (2004), pp. 67–78.

———, *Between Arab and White: Race and Ethnicity in the Early Syrian American Diaspora*, Berkeley, CA: University of California Press, 2009.

Guha, Ranajit, 'Chandra's death', in Guha, Ranajit, ed., *Subaltern Studies V: Writings on South Asian History and Society*, Delhi: Oxford University Press, 1987.

———, 'The prose of counter-insurgency', in Guha, Ranajit and Gayatri Chakravorty Spivak, eds, *Selected Subaltern Studies*, Oxford: Oxford University Press, 1988.

———, *Elementary Aspects of Peasant Insurgency in Colonial India*, Durham, NC: Duke University Press, 1999 [1983].

Frank, André Gunder, *Capitalism and Underdevelopment in Latin America: Historical Studies of Chile and Brazil*, New York: Monthly Review Press, 1967.

Gupta, Akhil and James Ferguson, 'Beyond "Culture": space, identity, and the politics of difference', *Cultural Anthropology*, 7, 1 (1992), pp. 6–23.

Guyer, Jane, 'Wealth in people—wealth in things: introduction', *Journal of African History*, 36 (1995), pp. 83–90.

Hakim, Carol, *The Origins of the Lebanese National Idea, 1840–1920*, Berkeley, CA: University of California Press, 2013.

Halawi, Majed, *A Lebanon Defied: Musa al-Sadr and the Shi'a Community*, Boulder, CO: Westview, 1992.

Hall, Catherine, *Civilising Subjects: Metropole and Colony in the English Imagination 1830–1867*, Cambridge: Polity, 2002.

Hall, Stuart, 'Thinking the diaspora: home-thoughts from abroad', *Small Axe*, 6 (1999), p. 1.

BIBLIOGRAPHY

———, 'Cultural identity and diaspora', in Braziel, Jana Evans and Anna Mannur, eds, *Theorizing Diaspora: A Reader*, Oxford: Blackwell, 2003,

Handlin, Oscar, *The Uprooted: The Epic Story of the Great Migrations that Made the American People*, Boston: Little, Brown, 1952.

Hanioğlu, Şükrü, 'The Young Turks and the Arabs before the Revolution of 1908', in Khalidi, Rashid, Lisa Anderson, Muhammad Muslih and Reeva S. Simon, eds, *The Origins of Arab Nationalism*, New York: Columbia University Press, 1991, pp. 31–49.

Hannerz, Ulf, *Transnational Connections: Culture, People, Places*, London: Routledge, 1996.

Harding, Leonhard, 'Les grands commerçants africains en Afrique de l'ouest: le cas du Sénégal et de la Côte d'Ivoire: essai de synthèse', in Harding, Leonhard and Boubacar Barry, eds, *Le Sénégal*, Paris: L'Harmattan, 1992, pp. 5–27.

Harik, Iliya, *Politics and Change in a Traditional Society, Lebanon 1711–1845*, Princeton, NJ: Princeton University Press, 1968.

Harney, Robert, 'Men without women: Italian migrants in Canada, 1885–1930', in Boyd, Betty, Robert Harney and Lydio Tomasi, eds, *The Italian Immigrant Woman in North America*, Toronto: The Multicultural History Society of Toronto, 1978, pp. 79–103.

Harootunian, Harry, *History's Disquiet: Modernity, Cultural Practice, and the Question of Everyday Life*, New York: Columbia University Press, 2000.

Harper, T.N., 'Empire, diaspora and the languages of globalism, 1850–1914', in Hopkins, A.G., ed., *Globalisation and World History*, London: Pimlico, 2002, pp. 141–66.

Harrison, Christopher, *France and Islam in West Africa, 1860–1960*, Cambridge: Cambridge University Press, 1988.

Harrison, Mark, '"The Tender Frame of Man": disease, climate, and racial difference in India and the West Indies', *Bulletin of the History of Medicine*, 70, 1 (1996), pp. 68–93.

Hart, Keith, 'Informal income opportunities and urban employment in Ghana', *Journal of Modern African Studies*, 11, 1 (1973), pp. 61–89.

———, 'Kinship, contract, and trust: the economic organisation of migrants in an African city slum', in Gambetta, Diego, ed., *Trust: Making and Breaking Collaborative Relationships*, Oxford: Blackwell, 1988, pp. 176–93.

Hatoum, Milton, *Tale of a Certain Orient*, transl. Gledson, John, London: Bloomsbury 2007.

Herbst, Jeffrey, *States and Power in Africa: Comparative Lessons in Authority and Control*, Princeton, NJ: Princeton University Press, 2000.

Hetherington, Kevin, 'Place of geometry: the materiality of place', in Hetherington, Kevin and Rolland Munro, eds, *Ideas of Difference: Social Spaces and the Labour of Division*, Oxford: Blackwell, 1997, pp. 183–99.

Hill, Polly, 'Landlords and brokers: a West African trading system (with a note on Kumasi butchers)', *Cahiers d'Études Africaines*, 6, 23 (1966), pp. 349–66.

———, *Studies in Rural Capitalism in West Africa*, Cambridge: Cambridge University Press, 1990.

Ho, Engseng, 'Empire through diasporic eyes: a view from the other boat', *Comparative Studies in Society and History*, 46, 2 (2004), pp. 210–46.

———, *The Graves of Tarim: Genealogy and Mobility across the Indian Ocean*, Berkeley, CA: University of California Press, 2006.

Hopkins, A.G., ed., *Globalization in World History*, London: Pimlico, 2002.

Hoerder, Dirk, 'From dreams to possibilities: the secularization of hope and the quest for independence', in Hoerder, Dirk and Horst Rössler, eds, *Distant Magnets: Expectations and Realities in the Immigrant Experience, 1840–1930*, New York: Holmes & Meier, 1993.

Hourani, Albert, *Lebanon and Syria: A Political Essay*, London: Oxford University Press, 1946.

———, 'Ideologies of the mountain and the city', in Owen, Roger, ed., *Essays on the Crisis in Lebanon*, London: Ithaca, 1976, pp. 33–41.

———, *Arabic Thought in the Liberal Age, 1798–1939*, Cambridge: Cambridge University Press, 1992 [1962].

Hourani, Albert and Nadim Shehadi, eds, *The Lebanese in the World: A Hundred Years of Emigration*, London: I.B. Tauris, 1992.

Hunt, Lynn, *The Family Romance of the French Revolution*, London: Routledge, 1992.

Hutchinson, Edward P., *Legislative History of American Immigration Policy, 1798–1965*, Philadelphia, PA: University of Pennsylvania Press, 1981.

Iliffe, John, *The Emergence of African Capitalism*, Basingstoke: Macmillan, 1981.

Issawi, Charles, *An Economic History of the Middle East and North Africa*, London: Methuen, 1982.

BIBLIOGRAPHY

———, 'The historical background of Lebanese emigration, 1830–1914', in Hourani, Albert and Nadim Shehadi, eds, *The Lebanese in the World: A Hundred Years of Emigration*, London: I.B. Tauris, 1992, pp. 13–31.

Jackson, Simon, 'Mandatory development: the political economy of the French Mandate in Syria and Lebanon, 1915–1939', Ph.D dissertation, New York University, 2009.

Jankowski, James, 'Egyptian responses to the Palestinian problem in the interwar period', *International Journal of Middle East Studies*, 12, 1 (August 1980).

Jarillo, J. Carlos, 'On strategic networks', *Strategic Management Journal*, 9 (1988), pp. 31–41.

Jennings, Eric, *Curing the Colonizers: Hydrotherapy, Climatology and French Colonial Spas*, Durham, NC: Duke University Press, 2006.

Johnson, G. Wesley, *The Emergence of Black Politics in Senegal: The Struggle for Power in the Four Communes, 1900–1920*, Stanford: Stanford University Press, 1971.

Joshi, Sanjay, *Fractured Modernity: Making of a Middle Class in Colonial North India*, Delhi: Oxford University Press, 2001.

Kamphoefner, Walter D., Wolfgang Helbich and Ülrike Somner, eds, *News from the Land of Freedom. German Immigrants Write Home*, Ithaca and London: Cornell University Press, 1991.

Kaniki, Martin, 'Attitudes and reactions towards the Lebanese in Sierra Leone during the colonial period', *Canadian Journal of African Studies*, 7, 1 (1973).

———, 'The psychology of early Lebanese immigrants in West Africa', in *International Seminar: Asian Trading Minorities in Tropical Africa, Afrika Studiencentrum, Leiden, 15–19 December 1975*, Leiden: n.p., 1976.

Kaplan, Alice Yaeger, *Reproductions of Banality: Fascism, Literature, and French Intellectual Life*, Minneapolis, MN: University of Minneapolis Press, 1986.

Karam, John Tofik, *Another Arabesque: Syrian-Lebanese Ethnicity in Neo-Liberal Brazil*, Philadelphia, PA: Temple University Press, 2007.

Kasparian, Choghig, *L'Entrée des Jeunes Libanais dans la Vie Active et l'Emigration: Enquête Réalisée par l'Université Saint-Joseph*, Beirut: Université Saint-Joseph, 2003.

———, *L'Emigration des Jeunes Libanais et leurs Projets d'Avenir*, vol. 2, *Les Jeunes Libanais dans la Vague d'Emigration de 1992 à 2007*, Beirut: Presses de l'Université Saint-Joseph, 2009.

Kassir, Samir, *Histoire de Beyrouth*, Paris: Fayard, 2003.

Kaufman, Asher, *Reviving Phoenicia: The Search for Identity in Lebanon*, London: I.B. Tauris, 2004.

Kay, Cristóbal, *Latin American Theories of Development and Underdevelopment*, London: Routledge, 1989.

Kayalı, Hasan, *Arabs and Young Turks: Ottomanism, Arabism, and Islamism in the Ottoman Empire, 1908–1918*, Berkeley, CA: University of California Press, 1997.

Karpat, Kemal, 'The Ottoman Emigration to America, 1860–1914', *International Journal of Middle East Studies*, 17, 2 (1985).

Kedourie, Elie, *The Chatham House Version and Other Middle East Studies*, London: Weidenfeld and Nicolson, 1970.

Khalaf, Samir, 'The background and causes of Lebanese/Syrian immigration to the United States before World War One', in Hooglund, Eric J., ed., *Crossing the Waters: Arabic-Speaking Immigrants in the United States before 1940*, Washington, DC: Smithsonian Institution Press, 1987, pp. 17–35.

Khalidi, Rashid, *Palestinian Identity: the Construction of a Modern National Consciousness*, New York: Columbia University Press, 1997.

Khalidi, Tarif, 'Shaikh Ahmad 'Arif al-Zain and *al-'Irfan*', in Buheiry, Marwan, ed., *Intellectual Life in the Arab East 1890–1939*, Beirut: American University of Beirut, 1981.

Khater, Akram, 'House to goddess of the house: gender, class, and silk in nineteenth century Mount Lebanon', *International Journal of Middle East Studies*, 28, 3 (1996), pp. 325–48.

———, *Inventing Home: Emigration, Gender and the Middle Class in Lebanon, 1870–1920*, Berkeley, CA: University of California Press, 2001.

Akram and Antoine Khater, 'Assaf: a peasant of Mount Lebanon', in Burke III, Edmund, ed., *Struggle and Survival in the Modern Middle East*, Berkeley, CA: University of California Press, 1993, pp. 31–43.

Khoury, Gérard, *La France et l'Orient Arabe: La Naissance du Liban Moderne, 1914–1922*, Paris, 1993.

———, 'Robert de Caix et Louis Massignon: deux visions de la politique française au Levant en 1920', in Méouchy, Nadine and Peter Sluglett with Gérard Khoury and Geoffrey Schad, eds, *The British and French Mandates in Comparative Perspective/Les Mandats Français et Anglais dans une Perspective Comparative*, Leiden: Brill, 2004.

BIBLIOGRAPHY

Khoury, Philip S., *Urban Notables and Arab Nationalism: The Politics of Damascus, 1860–1920*, Cambridge: Cambridge University Press, 1982.

———, *Syria and the French Mandate*, Princeton, NJ: Princeton University Press, 1987.

———, 'The paradoxical in Arab nationalism: interwar Syria revisited', in Gershoni, Israel and James Jankowski, eds, *Rethinking Nationalism in the Arab Middle East*, New York: Columbia University Press, 1997, pp. 273–87.

Khuri, Fuad, 'Kinship, emigration, and trade partnership among the Lebanese of West Africa', *Africa*, 35, 4 (1965), pp. 385–95.

———, 'The African-Lebanese mulattoes of West Africa: a racial frontier', *Anthropological Quarterly*, 12 (1968), pp. 90–101.

———, 'The etiquette of bargaining in the Middle East', *American Anthropologist*, 70, 4 (1968).

———, *From Village to Suburb: Order and Change in Greater Beirut*, Chicago and London: University of Chicago Press, 1975.

———, *An Invitation to Laughter: An Anthropologist in the Arab World*, Chicago: University of Chicago Press, 2007.

Khuri-Makdisi, Ilham, *The Eastern Mediterranean and the Making of Global Radicalism, 1860–1914*, Berkeley, BA: University of California Press, 2010.

Klich, Ignacio, '*Criollos* and Arabic speakers in Argentina: an uneasy *Pas de Deux*, 1888–1914', in Hourani, Albert and Nadim Shehadi, eds, *The Lebanese in the World: A Hundred Years of Emigration*, London: I.B. Tauris, 1992, pp. 243–84.

Klich, Ignacio and Jeff Lesser, eds, *Arab and Jewish Immigrants in Latin America: Images and Realities*, London: Frank Cass, 1998.

Knowlton, Clark S., 'The social and spatial mobility of the Syrian and Lebanese community in São Paulo, Brazil', in Hourani, Albert and Nadim Shehadi, eds, *The Lebanese in the World: A Hundred Years of Emigration*, London: I.B. Tauris, 1992, pp. 285–311.

Kojok, Salma, 'Les Libanais en Côte d'Ivoire', Ph.D thesis, Université de Nantes, 2002, 2 vols.

Krasner, Stephen, 'Compromising Westphalia', *International Security*, 20, 3 (1995–6), pp. 115–51.

Kraut, Alan M., *Silent Travellers: Germs, Genes and the Immigrant Menace*, Baltimore, MD: Johns Hopkins University Press, 1994.

Labaki, Boutros, *Introduction à l'Histoire Economique du Liban: Soie et Commerce Extérieur en Fin de Période Ottomane*, Beirut: Presses de l'Université Libanaise, 1984.

———, 'The role of transnational communities in fostering development in countries of origin', Beirut: United Nations Department of Social and Economic Affairs, 2006.

Labazée, Pascal, 'Un terrain anthropologique à explorer: l'entreprise africaine', *Cahiers d'Études Africaines*, 31, 124 (1991), pp. 533–52.

Lafleur, Gérard, *Les Libanais et Syriens de Guadeloupe*, Paris: Karthala, 1999.

Landau, Jacob, *The Politics of Pan-Islam: Ideology and Organisation*, Oxford: Clarendon, 1990.

Latour, Bruno, *The Pasteurization of France*, transl. Sheridan, John and John Law, Cambridge: Harvard University Press, 1988.

———, 'Technology is society made durable', in Law, John, ed., *A Sociology of Monsters: Essays on Power, Technology and Domination*, London: Routledge, 1991.

Launay, Robert, 'Transactional spheres and inter-societal exchange in Ivory Coast', *Cahiers d'Études Africaines*, 18, 72 (1978), pp. 561–73.

———, 'Landlords, hosts and strangers among the Dyula', *Ethnology*, 19, 1 (1979), pp. 71–83.

Le Crom, Jean-Pierre, *Syndicats, Nous Voilà!: Vichy et le Corporatisme*, Paris: Editions de l'Atelier, 1995.

Leighton, Neil, 'The political economy of a stranger population: the Lebanese of Sierra Leone', in Shack, William A. and Elliott P. Skinner, eds, *Strangers in African History*, Berkeley, CA: University of California Press, 1979, pp. 85–104.

———, 'Lebanese emigration: its effect on the political economy of Sierra Leone', in Hourani, Albert and Nadim Shehadi, eds, *The Lebanese in the World: A Hundred Years of Emigration*, London: I.B. Tauris, 1992, pp. 579–601.

Lerner, Daniel, *The Passing of Traditional Society: Modernizing the Middle East*, New York: Free Press of Glencoe, 1958.

Levi, Giovanni, 'On microhistory', in Burke, Peter, ed., *New Perspectives on Historical Writing*, Cambridge: Polity, 1997.

BIBLIOGRAPHY

Lévi-Strauss, Claude, *La Pensée Sauvage*, Paris: Plon, 1962.

Levine, Philippa, 'Modernity, medicine and colonialism: the contagious diseases ordinance in Hong Kong and the Straits Settlements', in Burton, Antoinette, ed., *Gender, Sexuality and Colonial Modernities*, London: Routledge, 1997, pp. 35–48.

Lewis, Mary Dewhurst. *The Boundaries of the Republic: Migrants Rights and the Limits of Universalism in France, 1918–1940*, Stanford, CA: University of California Press, 2007.

———, 'Geographies of power: the Tunisian civic order, jurisdictional politics, and imperial rivalry in the Mediterranean, 1881–1935', *Journal of Modern History*, 80 (2008), pp. 791–830.

Livingstone, David N., 'Race, space and moral climatology: notes towards a genealogy', *Journal of Historical Geography*, 28, 2 (2002), pp. 159–180.

Longrigg, Stephen, *Syria and Lebanon under French Mandate*, London: Oxford University Press, 1958.

Lonsdale, John, 'The moral economy of Mau Mau: wealth, poverty, and virtue in Kikuyu political thought', in Berman, Bruce and John Lonsdale, *Unhappy Valley: Conflict in Kenya and Africa*, London: James Currey, 1990, pp. 315–505.

———, 'Moral ethnicity and political tribalism', in Kaarsholm, Preben and Jan Hultin, eds, *Inventions and Boundaries: Historical and Anthropological Approaches to the Study of Ethnicity and Nationalism*, Roskilde: University of Roskilde, 1994, pp. 131–50.

———, 'Moral and political argument in Kenya', in Berman, Bruce, Dickson Eyoh and Will Kymlicka, eds, *Ethnicity and Democracy in Africa*, Oxford: James Currey, 2004, pp. 73–95.

Lopez, Renée and Emile Témime, *L'Expansion Marseillaise et 'l'Invasion Italienne' (1830–1918)*, Paris: Jeanne Lafitte, 2007 [1990].

López, A. Ricardo with Barbara Weinstein, 'Introduction—we shall be all: towards a transnational history of the middle class', in López, Ricardo and Barbara Weinstein, eds, *The Making of the Middle Class: Towards a Transnational History*, Durham, NC: Duke University Press, 2012.

Lorenz, Edward H., 'Neither friends nor strangers: informal networks of subcontracting in French industry', in Gambetta, Diego, ed., *Trust: Making and Breaking Cooperative Relations*, Oxford: Blackwell, 1991, pp. 194–210.

Lovejoy, P.E., *Caravans of Kola: The Hausa Kola Trade, 1700–1900*, Zaria: Ahmadu Bello University Press, 1980.

Maatouk, Mohamad, 'A critical study of Antun Sa'ada and his impact on politics, the history of ideas and literature in the Middle East', Ph.D dissertation, University of London, 1992.

MacDonald, Andrew, 'Colonial trespassers in the making of South Africa's international borders 1900 to c.1950', Ph.D dissertation, University of Cambridge, 2012.

MacGaffey, Janet and Rémy Bazenguissa-Ganga, *Congo-Paris: Transnational Traders on the Margins of the Law*, Oxford: James Currey, 2000.

MacMaster, Neil, *Colonial Migrants and Racism: Algerians in France, 1900–1962*, Basingstoke: Macmillan, 1997.

Makdisi, Ussama, *The Culture of Sectarianism: Community, History, and Violence in Nineteenth Century Ottoman Lebanon*, Berkeley, CA: University of California Press, 2001.

———, *Artillery of Heaven: American Missionaries and the Failed Conversion of the Middle East*, Princeton, NJ: Princeton University Press, 2008.

Makdisi, Ussama and Joel Silverstein, 'Introduction', *Memory and Violence in the Modern Middle East*, Makdisi, Ussama and Joel Silverstein, eds, Bloomington, IN: University of Indiana Press, 2006.

al-Makki, Muhammad Kazim, *Al-Haraka al-Fikriyya wa al-Adabiyya fi Jabal 'Amil*, Beirut: Dar al-Andalus, 1963.

Malki, Isaac Xerxes, 'Productive aliens: economic planning and the Lebanese in Ghana, c.1930–1972', *Mashriq & Mahjar: A Journal of Middle East Migration Studies*, 1,1 (2013), pp. 85–114.

Malkki, Liisa, 'National geographic: the rooting of peoples and the territorialization of national identity among scholars and refugees', *Cultural Anthropology*, 7, 1 (February 1992), pp. 24–44.

Mallah, 'Abdallah, *Al Baladiyyat fi Mutasarifiyyat Jabal Lubnan*, Beirut: n.p., 1998.

———, *Al Majlis al-Idari al-awwal fi Mutasarrifiyyat Jabal Lubnan*, Beirut: Matba'a Bulusiyya, 2001.

———, *Al-Hijra min Mutasarrifiyyat Jabal Lubnan*, Beirut: n.p., 2003.

Manchuelle, François, *Willing Migrants: Soninke Labor Diasporas, 1848–1960*, Oxford: James Currey, 1997.

Manela, Erez, *The Wilsonian Moment: Self-Determination and the International Origins of Anticolonial Nationalism*, Oxford: Oxford University Press, 2007.

Mangat, J.S., *A History of the Asians in East Africa since c. 1886 to 1945*, Oxford: Clarendon, 1969.

BIBLIOGRAPHY

Mann, Gregory, 'Fetishizing religion: Allah Koura and French "Islamic Policy" in late colonial French Soudan (Mali)', *Journal of African History*, 44, 2 (2003), pp. 263–82.

———, 'Locating colonial histories: between France and West Africa', *American Historical Review*, 110, 2 (2005), pp. 409–34.

———, *Native Sons: West African Veterans and France in the Twentieth Century*, Durham, NC: Duke University Press, 2006.

Narbona, Maria del Mar Logroño, 'The development of nationalist identities in French Syria and Lebanon: a transnational dialogue with Arab immigrants to Argentina and Brazil, 1915–1929', Ph.D dissertation, University of California at Santa Barbara, 2007.

Marcus, George E., 'Ethnography in/of the world system: the emergence of multi-sited ethnography', *Annual Review of Anthropology*, 24 (1995), pp. 95–117.

Marfaing, Laurence, *L'Evolution du Commerce au Sénégal 1820–1930*, Paris: L'Harmattan, 1991.

Marfaing, Laurence and Mariam Sow, *Les Opérateurs Economiques au Sénégal: Entre le Formel et l'Informel (1930–1996)*, Paris: Karthala, 1999.

Markovits, Claude, *The Global World of Indian Merchants, 1750–1947*, Cambridge: Cambridge University Press, 2000.

Markovitz, Irving Leonard, *Léopold Sédar Senghor and the Politics of Negritude*, London: Heinemann, 1969.

Mars, J., 'Extra-territorial enterprises', in Perham, Margery, ed., *Mining, Commerce, and Finance in Nigeria*, London: Faber & Faber, 1954.

Martens, Jeremy, 'A transnational history of immigration restriction: Natal and New South Wales, 1896–97', *Journal of Imperial and Commonwealth History*, 34, 3 (2006), pp. 323–44.

Martinez Montiel, Luz Maria, 'The Lebanese community in Mexico: its meaning, importance and the history of its communities', in Hourani, Albert and Nadim Shehadi, eds, *The Lebanese in the World: A Hundred Years of Emigration*, London: I.B. Tauris, 1992, pp. 379–92.

Matard-Bonucci, Marie-Anne, 'Introduction: l'imagination et la représentation des Juifs entre culture et politique (1848–1939)', in Matard-Bonucci, Marie-Anne, ed., *Antisémythes: L'Image des Juifs entre Culture et Politique*, Paris: Nouveau Monde, 2004, pp. 13–40.

Matsuda, Matt, *Empire of Love: Histories of France and the Pacific*, Oxford: Oxford University Press, 2005.

Matthews, Weldon C., *Confronting an Empire, Constructing a Nation: Arab Nationalists and Popular Politics in Mandate Palestine*, London: I.B. Tauris, 2006.

McDonald, John and Leatrice, 'Chain migration, ethnic neighbourhood formation and social networks', *Milbank Memorial Fund Quarterly*, 42 (1964), pp. 82–97.

McDougall, James, *History and the Culture of Nationalism in Algeria*, Cambridge: Cambridge University Press, 2006.

———, 'The secular state's Islamic empire: Muslim spaces and subjects of jurisdiction in Paris and Algiers, 1905–1957', *Comparative Studies in Society and History*, 52, 3 (2010), pp. 553–80.

McKeown, Adam, 'Conceptualizing Chinese diasporas, 1842 to 1949', *Journal of Asian Studies*, 58, 2 (1999), pp. 306–37.

———, *Chinese Migrant Networks and Cultural Change: Peru, Chicago, Hawaii, 1900–1936*, Chicago, IL: University of Chicago Press, 2001.

———, 'Ritualization of regulation: the enforcement of Chinese exclusion in the United States and China', *American Historical Review*, 108, 2 (2003), pp. 377–403.

———, 'Global migration, 1846–1940', *Journal of World History*, 15, 2 (2004), pp. 155–89.

———, *Melancholy Order: Asian Migration and the Globalization of Borders*, New York: Columbia University Press, 2008.

McMillan, James F., *Twentieth Century France: Society and Politics 1898–1991*, London: Arnold, 2003 [1992].

Memmi, Albert, *Portrait du Colonisé Précédé du Portrait du Colonisateur*, Montréal: L'Etincelle, 1972.

Méouchy, Nadine, 'Etat et espaces communitaires dans le Liban sous Mandat Français', *Maghreb Machrek*, 123 (1989), pp. 88–95.

———, ed., *France, Syrie et Liban 1918–1946 Les Ambiguités et les Dynamiques de la Relation Mandataire*, Damascus: IFEAD, 2002.

Méouchy, Nadine and Peter Sluglett with Gérard Khoury and Geoffrey Schad, eds, *The British and French Mandates in Comparative Perspective/Les Mandats Français et Anglais dans une Perspective Comparative*, Leiden: Brill, 2004.

BIBLIOGRAPHY

Meriwether, Margaret, *The Kin who Count: Family and Society in Ottoman Aleppo, 1770–1840*, Austin, TX: University of Texas Press, 1999.

Mersadier, Yves, 'La crise de l'arachide sénégalaise au début des années trente', *Bulletin de l'Institut Fondamental de l'Afrique Noire*, 28B (1986), pp. 826–77.

Mervin, Sabrina, *Un Réformisme Chiite: Ulémas et Lettrés du Ǧabal Āmil (Actuel Liban-Sud) de la Fin de l'Empire Ottoman à l'Indépendance du Liban*, Paris: Karthala, 2000.

———, 'Les larmes et le sang des chiites: corps et pratiques rituelles lors des célébrations de 'Ashûrâ' (Liban, Syrie)', *REMMM*, 113–114 (2006).

Metcalf, Thomas, *Imperial Connections: India in the Indian Ocean Arena, 1860–1920*, Berkeley, CA: University of California Press, 2007.

Michel, Marc, 'La colonisation', in Sirinelli, Jean-François, ed., *Histoire des Droites en France*, vol. 3, *Sensibilités*, Paris: Gallimard, 1992, pp. 49–69.

Mitchell, Timothy, *Colonising Egypt*, Berkeley, CA: University of California Press, 1991.

———, 'The Middle East in the past and future of Middle Eastern studies', in Szenton, David, ed., *The Politics of Knowledge: Area Studies and the Disciplines*, Berkeley, CA: University of California Press, 2004, pp. 74–118.

Morokvasic, Mirjana, 'Birds of passage are also women…', *International Migration Review*, (1984), pp. 886–907.

Naaman, Abdallah, *Histoire des Orientaux de France du Ier au XXe Siècle*, Paris: Eclipse, 2004.

Nabti, Patricia, 'Emigration from a Lebanese village: a case study of Bishmizzine', in Hourani, Albert and Nadim Shehadi, eds, *The Lebanese in the World: A Hundred Years of Emigration*, London: I.B. Tauris, 1992, pp. 41–63.

Naff, Alixa, *Becoming American: The Early Arab Immigrant Experience*, Carbondale, IL: Southern Illinois University Press, 1985.

———, 'Lebanese immigration into the United States: 1880s to the present', in Hourani, Albert and Nadim Shehadi, eds, *The Lebanese in the World: A Hundred Years of Emigration*, London: I.B. Tauris, 1992.

Nafi, Basheer M., *Arabism, Islamism, and the Palestine Question 1908–1941: A Political History*, Reading: Ithaca, 1998.

Najmabadi, Afsaneh, *Women with Mustaches and Men without Beards: Gender and Sexual Anxieties of Iranian Modernity*, Cambridge, MA: Harvard University Press, 2005.

Nasser, Liliane, 'Marseille et l'émigration libanaise', DEA thesis, Université de Provence, 1986.

Nicholls, David, 'No hawkers and pedlars: Levantines in the Caribbean', *Ethnic and Racial Studies*, 4, 4 (1981), pp. 415–31.

———, 'No hawkers and pedlars: Arabs of the Antilles', in Nicholls, David, *Haiti in Caribbean Context: Ethnicity, Economy and Revolt*, Basingstoke: Macmillan, 1985, pp. 135–64.

Noiriel, Gérard, *Le Creuset Français: Histoire de l'Immigration XIXe-XXe Siècles*, Paris: Seuil, 1988.

———, *La Tyrannie du National: Le Droit d'Asile en Europe 1793–1993*, Paris: Calmann-Lévy, 1991.

Nordman, Daniel, 'Sauf-conduits et passeports en France à la Renaissance', in Léard, Jean and Jean-Claude Margolin, eds, *Voyager à la Renaissance: Actes du Colloque de Tours 30 Juin–13 Juillet 1983*, Paris: Maisonneuve et Larose, 1987.

Nugent, Paul, 'The art of dissimulation: smugglers, informers and the preventive service along the Ghana-Togo frontier, 1920–1939', in Dubois, Colette, Marc Michel and Pierre Soumille, eds, *Frontières Plurielles, Frontières Conflictuelles en Afrique Subsaharienne*, Paris: L'Harmattan, 2000), pp. 209–31.

———, *Smugglers, Secessionists and Loyal Citizens on the Ghana-Togo Frontier: the Lie of the Borderlands since 1914*, Oxford: James Currey, 2002.

Nye, Robert A., *Masculinity and Male Codes of Honour in Modern France*, Oxford: Oxford University Press, 1993.

O'Brien, Philip J., 'Dependency revisited', in Abel, Christopher and Colin Lewis, eds, *Latin America, Economic Imperialism and the State*, London: Institute of Latin American Studies, 1985, pp. 40–69.

Ogden, T.H., 'The dialectically constituted/decentred subject of psychoanalysis. 1. The Freudian subject', *International Journal of Psychoanalysis*, 73 (1992), pp. 613–26.

Ong, Aihwa, *Flexible Citizenship: The Cultural Logics of Transnationality*, Durham, NC: Duke University Press, 1999.

Osborne, Michael, *Nature, the Exotic and the Science of French Colonialism*, Bloomington, IN: Indiana University Press, 1994.

Osiander, Andreas, 'Sovereignty, international relations, and the Westphalian myth', *International Organization*, 55, 2 (2001), pp. 251–87.

BIBLIOGRAPHY

Ouattara, Nagnin, 'Commerçants dioulas en Côte d'Ivoire: permanence et ruptures dans un milieu socioprofessionel', in Harding, Leonhard and Pierre Kipré, eds, *La Côte d'Ivoire*, Paris: L'Harmattan, 1992.

Owen, Roger, *The Middle East in the World Economy, 1800–1914*, London: I.B. Tauris, 1993.

Owen, Roger and Şevket Pamuk, *A History of Middle Eastern Economies in the Twentieth Century*, London: I.B. Tauris, 1998.

Owensby, Brian, *Intimate Ironies: Modernity and the Making of Middle-Class Lives in Brazil*, Stanford, CA: Stanford University Press, 1999.

Pasquier, Roger, 'Villes du Sénégal au XIXe siècle', *Revue Française d'Histoire d'Outre-Mer*, 47 (1960), pp. 387–426.

Paxton, Robert O., *Vichy France: Old Guard and New Order 1940–1944*, New York: Columbia University Press, 2001 [1972].

Peabody, Sue and Tyler Stovall, 'Introduction: race, France, histories', in Peabody, Sue and Tyler Stovall, eds, *The Color of Liberty: Histories of Race in France*, Durham, NC: Duke University Press, 2003, pp. 1–7.

Peleikis, Anja, 'The emergence of a translocal community: the case of a south Lebanese village and its migrant connections to Ivory Coast', *Cahiers d'Études sur la Méditerranée Orientale et le Monde Turco-Iranien*, 30 (2000), pp. 297–317.

———, 'Shifting identities, reconstructing boundaries. The case of a multi-confessional locality in post-war Lebanon', *Die Welts des Islam*, 41, 3 (2001).

———, *Lebanese in Motion: Gender and the Making of a Translocal Village*, Piscataway, NJ: Transcript, 2003.

Pélissier, Paul, *Les Paysans du Sénégal. Les Civilisations Agraires du Cayor à la Casamance*, Saint-Yrieix: n.p., 1966.

Person, Yves, *Samori. Une Révolution Dyula*, vol. 1, Dakar: Institut Fondamental d'Afrique Noire, 1968.

Peters, Emrys, 'Aspects of rank and status among Muslims in a Lebanese village', in Pitt-Rivers, Julian, ed., *Mediterranean Countrymen: Essays in the Social Anthropology of the Mediterranean*, Paris: Mouton, 1963, pp. 159–200.

———, 'Shifts in power in a Lebanese village', in Antoun, Richard and Iliya Harik, eds, *Rural Politics and Social Change in the Middle East*, Bloomington, IN: Indiana University Press, 1972, pp. 165–97.

Philipp, Thomas, *The Syrians in Egypt, 1725–1975*, Stuttgart: Steiner, 1985.

Phizacklea, Annie, ed., *One Way Ticket: Migration and Female Labour*, London: RKP, 1983.

Plummer, Brenda Gayle, 'Race, nationality and trade in the Caribbean: the Syrians in Haiti, 1903–1934', *International History Review*, 3 (1981), pp. 517–39.

Pocock, J.G.A., *Political Thought and History: Essays on Theory and Method*, Cambridge: Cambridge University Press, 2010.

Porath, Yehoshua, 'The Peasant Revolt of 1858–61 in Kisrawan', *Asian and African Studies*, 2 (1966), pp. 77–157.

Powell, Walter J., 'Neither market nor hierarchy: network forms of organisation', *Organizational Behaviour*, 12 (1990), pp. 295–336.

Prochaska, David, *Making Algeria French: Colonialism in Bône, 1870–1920*, Cambridge: Cambridge University Press, 1990.

Provence, Michael, *The Great Syrian Revolt and the Rise of Arab Nationalism*, Austin: University of Texas Press, 2005.

———, 'Ottoman modernity, colonialism, and insurgency in the interwar Middle East', *International Journal of Middle East Studies*, 43, 2 (2011), pp. 205–25.

Qubaisi, Hasan, *Tatawwur Madinat Sur, 1900–1950*, Beirut: Dar al-Qadmus, 1982.

Rabinow, Paul, *French Modern: Norms and Forms of the Social Environment*, Cambridge, MA: MIT Press, 1989.

Rafael, Vicente, 'The culture of area studies in the United States', *Social Text* (1994), pp. 91–111.

———, 'Regionalism, area studies, and the accidents of agency', *American Historical Review*, 104, 4 (1999), pp. 1208–20.

Ray, Rajat Kanta, 'Asian capital in the age of European domination: the rise of the bazaar, 1800–1914', *Modern Asian Studies*, 29, 3 (1995), pp. 449–554.

Reddy, William, *The Invisible Code: Honor and Sentiment in Postrevolutionary France, 1814–1848*, Berkeley, CA: University of California Press, 1997.

Reid, Anthony, ed., *Sojourners and Settlers: Histories of South-East Asia and the Chinese*, London: Allen & Unwin, 1996.

Reid, Donald M., 'Arabic thought in the liberal age twenty years after', *International Journal of Middle East Studies*, 14, 4 (1982), pp. 541–57.

BIBLIOGRAPHY

Robinson, David, 'French "Islamic" policy and practice in late nineteenth-century Senegal', *Journal of African History*, 29, 3 (1988), pp. 415–35.

———, *Paths of Accommodation: Muslim Societies and French Colonial Authorities in Senegal and Mauritania, 1880–1920*, Oxford: James Currey, 2000.

Rodney, Walter, *How Europe Underdeveloped Africa*, London: Bogle L'Ouverture, 1972.

Rosenberg, Clifford, 'The colonial politics of health care provision in interwar Paris', *French Historical Studies*, 27, 3 (2004), pp. 637–68.

———, *Policing Paris: The Origins of Modern Immigration Control between the Wars*, Ithaca, NY: Cornell University Press, 2006.

Ross, Kristin, *Fast Cars, Clean Bodies: Decolonisation and the Reordering of French Culture*, Cambridge, MA: MIT Press, 1999.

Rouse, Roger, 'Mexican migration and the social space of postmodernity', *Diaspora*, 1, 1 (1991), pp. 8–23.

Saada, Emmanuelle, 'The empire of law: dignity, prestige and domination in the "colonial situation"', *French Politics, Culture and Society*, 20, 2 (2002), pp. 98–120.

Saba, Paul, 'The creation of the Lebanese economy: economic growth in the nineteenth and twentieth centuries', in Owen, Roger, ed., *Essays on the Crisis in Lebanon*, London: Ithaca, 1976.

Safa, Elie, *L'Émigration Libanaise*, Beirut: Université Saint-Joseph, 1961.

Safran, William, 'Diasporas in modern societies: myths of homeland and return', *Diaspora*, 1,1 (1991) pp. 83–99.

Sahlins, Marshall, *Islands of History*, London: Tavistock, 1985.

Sa'id, 'Abdallah, *Tatawwur al-Milkiyya al-'Aqariyya fi Jabal Lubnan fi 'Ahd al-Mutasarrifiyya Istinadan ila Watha'iq Asliyya: Namuzaj al-Matn al-A'la*, Beirut: Dar al-Mada, 1986.

———, *Ashkal al-Milkiyya wa Anwa' al-Aradi fi Mutasarrafiyyat Jabal Lubnan wa Sahl al-Biqa', 1861–1914: Dirasa Muqarana fi al-Tarikh al-Rifi, Istinadan ila Watha'iq Asliya*, Beirut: Maktaba Baisan, 1995.

Said, Edward, 'Zionism from the standpoint of its victims', *Social Text*, 1 (1979).

———, *Out of Place: A Memoir*, London: Granta, 1999.

———, *Orientalism*, London: Penguin, 2003 [1978].

Saliba, Najib, 'Emigration from Syria', in Abraham, Sameer and Nabeel Abraham, eds, *Arabs in the New World: Studies on Arab-American Communities*, Detroit, MI: Wayne State University, 1983.

Salibi, Kamal, *A House of Many Mansions: The History of Lebanon Reconsidered*, Berkeley: University of California Press, 1988.

Salih, Farhan, *Janub Lubnan: Waqi'hu wa Qadayahu*, Beirut: Dar al-Tal'iyya, 1973.

Samson, Jane, *Imperial Benevolence: Making British Authority in the Pacific Islands*, Honolulu, HI: University of Hawai'i Press, 1998.

Sar, Moustapha, 'Louga: sa ville et sa région: essai d'intégration des rapports ville-campagne dans la problématique du développement', Thèse de Troisième Cycle de Géographie Appliquée, Université Cheikh Anta Diop, Dakar, 1970.

Savonnet, G., *La Ville de Thiès: Etude de Géographie Humaine*, Etudes Sénégalaises 6, Saint-Louis: Centre de l'Institut Français d'Afrique Noire.

Schatkowski Schilcher, Linda, 'The famine of 1915–1918 in Greater Syria', in Spagnolo, John, ed., *Problems of the Modern Middle East in Historical Perspective: Essays in Honour of Albert Hourani*, London: Ithaca, 1992, pp. 229–58.

Schiller, Nina Glick and Georges Eugene Fouron, *Georges Woke Up Laughing: Long-Distance Nationalism and the Search for Home*, Durham, NC: Duke University Press, 2001.

Schneider, William H., *An Empire for the Masses: The French Popular Image of Africa, 1870–1900*, London: Greenwood Press, 1982.

———, *Quality and Quantity: the Quest for Biological Regeneration in Twentieth Century France*, Cambridge: Cambridge University Press, 1990.

Schumann, Christoph, ed., *Liberal Thought in the Eastern Mediterranean: Late Nineteenth Century until the 1960s*, Leiden: Brill, 2008.

Scott, David, 'Colonial governmentality', *Social Text*, 43 (1995), pp. 191–220.

Scott, James, *Seeing Like A State: How Certain Schemes to Improve the Human Condition Have Failed*, New Haven, CT: Yale University Press, 1998.

BIBLIOGRAPHY

Searing, James, *West African Slavery and Atlantic Commerce: the Senegal River Valley, 1700–1860*, Cambridge: Cambridge University Press, 1993.

———, *'God Alone is King': Islam and Emancipation in Senegal. The Wolof Kingdoms of Kajoor and Baol, 1859–1914*, Oxford: James Currey, 2002.

Seck, Assane, *Dakar*, Dakar: Faculté des Lettres et Sciences Humaines de Dakar, n.d..

Sehnaoui, Nada, *L'Occidentalisation de la Vie Quotidienne à Beyrouth 1860–1914*, Beirut: Editions Dar an-Nahar, 2002.

Sewell Jr., William, 'The concept(s) of culture', in Hunt, Lynn and Victoria Bonnell, eds, *Beyond the Cultural Turn: New Directions in the Study of Society and Culture*, Berkeley, CA: University of California Press, 1999, pp. 35–61.

Shack, William A., 'Introduction', in Shack, W.A. and Elliott Skinner, eds, *Strangers in African Societies*, Berkeley, CA: University of California Press, 1979.

Shah, Nayan, 'Cleansing motherhood: hygiene and the culture of domesticity in San Francisco's Chinatown, 1875–1900', in Burton, Antoinette, ed., *Gender, Sexuality and Colonial Modernities*, London: Routledge, 1997, pp. 19–34.

Shakir, Evelyn, *Bint Arab: Arab and Arab American Women in the United States*, Westport: Praeger, 1997.

Shapiro, Anne-Louise, 'Disordered bodies, disorderly acts: medical discourse and the female criminal', in *Breaking the Codes: Female Criminality in Fin-de-Siècle Paris*, Stanford, CA: Stanford University Press, 1996, pp. 94–135.

Shipway, Martin, *Decolonisation and its Impact: A Comparative Approach to the End of the Colonial Empires*, Oxford: Blackwell, 2008.

Shohat, Ella, 'Area studies', in Essed, Philomena, David Theo Golberg and Audrey Koyabashi, eds, *A Companion to Gender Studies*, Oxford: Blackwell, 2004, Blackwell Reference Online, http://www.blackwellreference.com/subscriber/tocnode?id=g9780631221098_chunk_g97806312210983

Shorrock, William, *French Imperialism in the Middle East: the Failure of Policy in Lebanon and Syria 1900–1914*, Madison, WI: University of Wisconsin Press, 1976.

Shu'ayyib, 'Ali, *Matalib Jabal 'Amil: al-Wuhda, al-Musawa fi Lubnan al-Kabir 1900–1936*, Beirut: Mu'asasa al-Jam'iyya, 1987.

Silverman, Maxim, *Deconstructing the Nation: Immigration, Racism and Citizenship in Modern France*, London: Routledge, 1992.

Simmel, Georg, 'The stranger', in Wolff, Kurt H., transl. and ed., *The Sociology of Georg Simmel*, London: Macmillan, 1964, pp. 402–8.

Simon, Jacques, *L'Etoile Nord-Africaine, 1926–1937*, Paris: L'Harmattan, 2003.

Sinou, Alain, *Comptoirs et Villes Coloniales du Sénégal. Saint Louis, Gorée, Dakar*, Paris: Karthala, 1993.

Sivasundaram, Sujit, 'Sciences and the global: on methods, questions, and theory', *Isis*, 101, 10 (2010), pp. 146–58.

Skinner, Elliott P., 'Strangers in West African societies', *Africa*, 33, 4 (1963), pp. 307–20.

Skinner, Quentin, *Visions of Politics*, vol. 1, *Regarding Method*, Cambridge: Cambridge University Press, 2002.

Skrbiš, Zlatko, *Long-Distance Nationalism: Diasporas, Homelands, and Identities*, Aldershot: Aldgate, 1999.

Smith, Stephen W., 'Nodding and winking', *London Review of Books*, 32, 3 (11 February 2010), pp. 10–12.

al-Solh, Raghid, *Lebanon and Arabism: National Identity and Social Formation*, London: I.B. Tauris, 1996.

Sorlin, Pierre, 'Words and images of nationhood', in Tombs, Robert, ed. *Nationhood and Nationalism in France from Boulangism to the Great War, 1889–1918*, London: HarperCollins, 1991, pp. 74–88.

Spagnolo, John P., *France and Ottoman Lebanon: 1861–1914*, London: Ithaca Press, 1977.

Steedman, Carolyn, *Dust*, Manchester: Manchester University Press, 2001.

Stiansen, André and Jane Guyer, 'Introduction', in Guyer, Jane, ed., *Credit, Currencies and Culture: African Financial Institutions in Historical Perspective*, Stockholm: Nordiska Afrikainstitutet, 1999, pp. 1–14.

Stoler, Ann Laura, *Race and the Education of Desire: Foucault's 'History of Sexuality' and the Colonial Order of Things*, Durham, NC: Duke University Press, 1996.

———, 'Sexual affronts and racial frontiers: European colonies and the cultural politics of exclusion in colonial South-East Asia', in Cooper, Frederick and Ann Laura Stoler, eds, *Tensions of Empire: Colonial Cultures in a Bourgeois World*, Berkeley, CA: University of California Press, 1997, pp. 198–237.

———, *Carnal Knowledge and Imperial Power: Race and the Intimate in Colonial Rule*, Berkeley, CA: California University Press, 2002.

———, 'Colonial archives and the arts of governance: on the content in the form', in Hamilton, Carolyn, Verne

BIBLIOGRAPHY

Harris, Jane Taylor, Michele Rickover, Graeme Reid and Rezia Saleh, eds, *Refiguring the Archive*, Dordrecht: Kluwer, 2002.

———, 'Affective states', in Nugent, David and Joan Vincent, eds, *A Companion to the Anthropology of Politics*, Oxford: Blackwell, 2004, pp. 4–20.

———, *Along the Archival Grain: Epistemic Anxieties and Colonial Commonsense*, Princeton, NJ: Princeton University Press, 2009.

Stora, Benjamin, *Messali Hadj: Pionnier du Nationalisme Algérien (1898–1974)*, Paris: L'Harmattan, 1986.

Suret-Canale, Jean, *French Colonialism in Tropical Africa, 1900–1945*, Gottheimer, Till, transl., London: Heinemann, 1971.

Surkis, Judith, 'The enemy within: venereal disease and the defence of French masculinity in between the wars', in Forth, Christopher E. and Bertrand Taithe, eds, *French Masculinities: History, Culture and Politics*, Basingstoke: Palgrave, 2007, pp. 103–22.

Tagliacozzo, Eric and Wen-Chin Chang, eds, *Chinese Circulations: Capital, Commodities, and Networks in Southeast Asia*, Durham, NC: Duke University Press, 2011.

Tannenbaum, Edward, *The Action Française: Die-Hard Reactionaries in Twentieth Century France*, London: John Wiley & Sons, 1962.

Tannous, Afif, 'Social change in an Arab village', *American Sociological Review*, 6, 5 (1941), pp. 650–62.

———, 'Emigration: a force of social change in an Arab village', *Rural Sociology*, 7 (1942), pp. 62–74.

Tarraf-Najib, Souha, *Zrariyyé, Village Chiite du Liban-Sud*, Beirut: CERMOC, 1992.

———, 'Immigration ancienne et territorialisation inaccomplie. Les familles libanaises du Sénégal', *Cahiers d'Études sur la Méditerranée et le Monde Turco-Iranien*, 30 (2000), pp. 273–95.

Tasso, Alberto, 'Migración y identidad social. Una comunidad de inmigrantes en Santiago del estero', *Estudios Migratorios Latinoamericanos*, (1987), pp. 321–36.

Thabit al-Khuri, Michel, *Tarikh Abrashiyat Sur 1800–1914*, Beirut: Dar al-Mawasim, 2003.

Thistlethwaite, Frank, 'Migration from Europe overseas in the nineteenth and twentieth centuries', in Vecoli, Rudolph and Suzanne Sinke, eds, *A Century of European Migrations 1830–1930*, Urbana, IL: University of Illinois Press, 1991.

Thobie, Jacques, *Intérêts et Impérialisme Français dans l'Empire Ottoman (1895–1914)*, Paris: Imprimerie Nationale, 1977.

Thomas, Martin, *The French Empire Between the Wars: Imperialism, Politics and Society*, Manchester: Manchester University Press, 2005.

———, *Empires of Intelligence: Security Services and Colonial Disorder after 1914*, Berkeley, CA: University of California Press, 2008.

Thompson, Elizabeth, *Colonial Citizens: Republican Rights, Paternal Privilege and Gender in French Syria and Lebanon*, New York: Columbia University Press, 2000.

Thompson, E.P., *The Making of the English Working Class*, London: Penguin, 1991 [1963].

Tibawi, A.L., *American Interests in Syria 1800–1901: A Study of Economic, Literary and Religious Work*, Oxford: Clarendon Press, 1966.

Tilly, Charles, 'Transplanted networks', in Yans-McLaughlin, Virginia, ed., *Immigration Reconsidered: History, Society, Politics*, Oxford: Oxford University Press, 1990.

Tilly, Charles and C. Harold Brown, 'On uprooting, kinship and the auspices of migration', *International Journal of Comparative Sociology*, 8 (1968), pp. 139–64.

Tölölian, Khachig, 'The nation state and its others: In lieu of a preface', *Diaspora* 1, 1 (1991), pp. 3–7.

Tombs, Robert, introduction to part I, 'Sentiment and ideology', in Tombs, Robert, ed., *Nationhood and Nationalism in France from Boulangism to the Great War, 1889–1918*, London: Harper Collins, 1991, pp. 3–7.

Torpey, John, *The Invention of the Passport: Surveillance, Citizenship, and the State*, Cambridge: Cambridge University Press, 2000.

Touma, Toufic, *Un Village de Montagne au Liban (Hadeth el-Jobbé)*, Paris: Mouton, 1958.

Trincaz, Pierre Xavier, *Colonisation et Régionalisme: Ziguinchor en Casamance*, Paris: ORSTOM, 1984.

Truzzi, Oswaldo, 'The right place at the right time: Syrians and the United States, a comparative approach', *Journal of American Ethnic History*, 16, 2 (1997), pp. 3–34.

———, *Sírios e Libaneses: narrativas de história e cultura*, São Paulo: Companhia Editoria Nacional, 2005.

Urry, John, *Sociology beyond Societies: Mobilities for the Twenty-First Century*, London: Routledge, 2000.

BIBLIOGRAPHY

Vaillant, Janet, *Black, French, and African: A Life of Léopold Sédar Senghor*, Cambridge, MA: Harvard University Press, 1990.

van de Walle, Nicolas, 'Presidentialism and clientelism in Africa's emerging party systems', *Journal of Modern African Studies*, 41, 2 (2003), pp. 297–321.

van der Laan, H. Laurens, *The Lebanese Traders of Sierra Leone*, The Hague: Mouton, 1975.

van Leur, J.C., *Asian Trade and Society: Essays in Asian Social and Economic History*, The Hague: van Hoeve, 1955.

Vaughan, Megan, 'Africa and the birth of the modern world', *Transactions of the Royal Historical Society*, 16 (2006), pp. 143–62.

———, 'Liminal', *London Review of Books*, 28, 6 (23 March 2006).

Vecoli, Rudolph, '*Contadini* in Chicago: a critique of *The Uprooted*', *Journal of American History*, 51, 3 (1964), pp. 404–17.

———, 'The formation of Chicago's "Little Italies"', *Journal of American Ethnic History*, 2 (1983), pp. 5–20.

Vigarello, Georges, *Le Propre et le Sale: l'Hygiène du Corps depuis le Moyen-Age*, Paris: Seuil, 1985.

Wardaugh, Jessica, *In Pursuit of the People: Political Culture in France, 1934–39*, Basingstoke: Palgrave, 2009.

Ware, Vron, *Beyond the Pale: White Women, Racism and History*, London: Verso, 1992.

Watenpaugh, Keith, 'Towards a new category of colonial theory: colonial cooperation and the survivors' bargain—the case of the post-genocide Armenian community of Syria under French Mandate', in Sluglett, Peter and Nadine Méouchy with Gérard Khoury and Geoffrey Schad, eds, *The British and French Mandates in Comparative Perspective*, Leiden: Brill, 2004, pp. 597–622.

———, *Being Modern in the Middle East: Revolution, Nationalism, Colonialism and the Arab Middle Class*, Princeton, NJ: Princeton University Press, 2006.

Weber, Eugen, *Action Française: Royalism and Reaction in Twentieth-Century France*, Stanford: Stanford University Press, 1962.

Weber, Max, 'Bureaucracy', in Gerth, H.H. and C. Wright Mills, transl., eds, *From Max Weber: Essays in Society*, London: Routledge, 1991.

Weil, Patrick, 'Races at the gate: racial distinctions in immigration policy: a comparison between France and the United States', in Fahrmeir, Andreas, Olivier Faron and Patrick Weil, eds, *Migration Control in the North Atlantic World: the Evolution of State Practices in Europe and the United States from the French Revolution to the Interwar Period*, Oxford: Berghahn, 2003, pp. 271–97.

Weiss, Max, 'Don't throw yourself away to the Dark Continent: Shi'i migration to West Africa and the hierarchies of exclusion in Lebanese culture', *Studies in Ethnicity and Nationalism*, 7, 1 (2007), pp. 46–63.

———, *In the Shadow of Sectarianism: Law, Shi'ism and the Making of Modern Lebanon*, Cambridge, MA: Harvard University Press, 2010.

Werbner, Pnina, 'Introduction: the dialectics of cultural hybridity', in Werbner, Pnina and Tariq Modood, eds, *Debating Cultural Hybridity: Multicultural Identities and the Politics of Anti-Racism*, London: Zed, 1997, pp. 1–26.

White, Owen, *Children of the French Empire: Miscegenation and Colonial Society in French West Africa, 1895–1960*, Oxford: Clarendon Press, 1999.

———, 'The decivilizing mission: Auguste Dupuis-Yakouba and French Timbuktu', *French Historical Studies*, 27, 3 (Summer 2004), pp. 541–68.

Wien, Peter, 'The long and intricate funeral of Yasin al-Hashimi: pan-Arabism, civil religion, and popular nationalism in Damascus, 1937', *International Journal of Middle East Studies*, 43 (2011), pp. 271–92.

Wilder, Gary, 'The politics of failure: historicising Popular Front colonial policy in French West Africa', in Chafer, Tony and Amanda Sackur, eds, *The French Colonial Empire and the Popular Front*, Basingstoke: Macmillan, 1999, pp. 33–55.

———, 'Unthinking French history: colonial studies beyond national identity', in Burton, Antoinette, ed., *After the Imperial Turn: Thinking With and Through the Nation*, Durham, NC: Duke University Press, 2003.

———, *The French Imperial Nation-State: Négritude and Colonial Humanism Between the Two World Wars*, Chicago, IL: University of Chicago Press, 2005.

Wilson, Kathleen, ed., *A New Imperial History: Culture, Identity and Modernity in Britain and the Empire, 1660–1840*, Cambridge: Cambridge University Press, 2004.

Wilson, Stephen, 'The 'Action Française' in French intellectual life', *Historical Journal*, 12, 2 (1969), pp. 328–50.

———, 'The antisemitic riots of 1898 in France', *Historical Journal*, 26, 4 (1973), pp. 789–806.

BIBLIOGRAPHY

———, *Ideology and Experience: Antisemitism in France at the Time of the Dreyfus Affair*, London: Associated University Presses, 1982.

Winder, R. Bayly, 'The Lebanese in West Africa', *Comparative Studies in Society and History*, 4, 3 (1962), pp. 296–333.

Winock, Michel, *Nationalisme, Antisémitisme et Fascisme en France*, Paris: Seuil, 1990.

———, *La France et les Juifs de 1789 à nos Jours*, Paris: Seuil, 2004.

Wolf, Eric, *Europe and the People without History*, Berkeley, CA: University of California Press, 1982.

Wright, Gwendolyn, *The Politics of Design in French Colonial Urbanism*, Chicago: University of Chicago Press, 1991.

Yamak, Labib Zuwiyya, *The Syrian Social Nationalist Party: an Ideological Analysis*, Cambridge, MA: Harvard University Press and Harvard Centre for Middle Eastern Studies, 1966.

Young, Crawford, *The African Colonial State in Comparative Perspective*, New Haven, CT: Yale University Press, 1994.

Zamir, Meir, *The Formation of Modern Lebanon*, London: Croon Helm, 1985.

———, *Lebanon's Quest: The Road to Statehood 1926–1939*, London: I.B. Tauris, 1997.

Zeine, Zeine N., *Arabic-Turkish Relations and the Emergence of Arab Nationalism*, Beirut: Khayat's, 1958.

Zemon Davis, Natalie, *Fiction in the Archives: Pardon Tales and their Tellers in Sixteenth-Century France*, Stanford, CA: Stanford University Press, 1987.

Zie, Gnato and Vrih Gbazah, 'Les commerçants sénégalais en Côte d'Ivoire de 1880 à 1970', in Harding, Leonhard and Pierre Kipré, eds, *La Côte d'Ivoire*, Commerce et Commerçants en Afrique de l'Ouest, vol. 2, Paris: L'Harmattan, 1992, pp. 235–71.

Zinoman, Peter, *The Colonial Bastille: A History of Imprisonment in Vietnam, 1862–1940*, Berkeley, CA: University of California Press, 2001.

Zolberg, Aristide, 'The great wall against China: responses to the first immigration crisis, 1885–1925', in Lucassen, Jan and Leo Lucassen, eds, *Migration, Migration History, History: Old Paradigms and New Perspectives*, New York: Peter Lang, 1997, pp. 291–315.

———, 'Matters of state: theorizing immigration policy', in Hirschman, Charles, Philip Kasinitz and Josh DeWind, eds, *The Handbook of International Migration: the American Experience*, New York: Russell Sage Foundation, 1999, pp. 75–6.

———, 'The archaeology of remote control', in Fahrmeir, Andreas, Olivier Faron and Patrick Weil, eds, *Migration Control in the North Atlantic World: the Evolution of State Practices in Europe and the United States from the French Revolution to the Interwar Period*, Oxford: Berghahn, 2003, pp. 195–222.

———, *A Nation by Design: Immigration Policy in the Fashioning of America*, Cambridge, MA: Harvard University Press, 2006.

INDEX

331

INDEX